ISLAMIC TERRORISM
Myth or Reality

ISLAMIC TERRORISM

MYTH OR REALITY

(In Two Volumes)

(Volume 1)

Editor

M.H. Syed

PUBLICATIONS

KALPAZ PUBLICATIONS

DELHI - 110052

ISLAMIC TERRORISM: Myth or Reality
[*Terrorism*]

Rs. 1800 (Set)
Rs. 900 each volume

ISBN: 81-7835-117-X (Set)
ISBN: 81-7835-139-0 (Vol. 1)

Published in 2002 in India by
Kalpaz Publications
C-30, Satyawati Nagar
Delhi-110052
e-mail: kalpaz@hotmail.com

Laser Typeset at: Alphabet, Delhi
Printed at: Chawla Offset Press, Delhi

Contents

Preface

Islam is not only a faith or religion. It is the philosophy, discipline and way of life. But, in spite of being a purely scientific and progressive religion, Islam is perhaps, the most misunderstood religion in the world. People talk of Islam but never make an attempt to know, what real Islam is. They simply do not bother to study *the religion, at all,* but always prefer to criticise. Indeed it has become a common practice. It appears that the whole West seems to be at war against Islam.

Recently, Islam has been attached to violence, coercion and terrorism, as incidentally or otherwise, many of the groups, engaged in struggle against various regimes, all over the world, are followers of Islam. But that does not necessarily mean, that all their acts are in accordance with the true spirit of Islam. And that's the prime difference, between the two things.

One should realise that Islam and Muslims are two different entities. Islam is what was preached by Prophet Mohammad (PBUH), Islam is not what is depicted by the action and behaviour of its followers—known as Muslims. Frankly speaking all the followers are not 'true followers' of the faith. Hence, there must be no confusion. If one desires to know the real Islam, then he or she should flip through the pages of Holy Quran, the Traditions and other scriptures and apply their mind to ascertain what the truth is. Only then, one may be able to know Islam—the real one.

Similarly, *Jehad* or holy war may be Islamic, but, the battles being fought in different parts of the world are not *Jehad*. This is really very dangerous to confuse some warring groups with Islamic *Jehadis* and their militant struggles with real *Jehad*.

This study, though a modest attempt, is a step in the direction of understanding Islam and eradicating the confusion and misunderstanding spread about Islam, as a faith.

Hopefully this humble endeavour should succeed in creating an awareness about the subject and erase the doubts resulted from half-baked publications in the west in particular and elsewhere in general. If this much happens, then the undersigned would feel honoured and rewarded in the academic world.

Editor

Preface

Introduction

Ironically, many a scholar in the West seem to view the end of the last century as the era of the "Islamic threat". The emergence of Islam into the political scenario is often perceived as an anachronism. Is it possible, in the 21st century, to return to the Middle Ages? One witnesses bearded clerics everywhere, surging forth from mosques and reminaries to attack the modern-day Babylons, seeking to create a reactionary, irrational, and violent world. What history has taught us is that barbarity is inherent in orthodoxy and has never signalled a return to what came before. It is not that the Middle Ages are descending upon our modern world, but rather that modernity itself produces its own forms of protest.

In our existing outlook we remain prisoners of the old schema of the enlightenment whereby there is only one form of progress: as we see it, political modernity, manifested in parliamentary democracy, goes hand in hand with economic development, the relaxation of moral codes, and secularization. In this respect our memory is short and selective. How many revolutions have been essentially puritanical, even profoundly religious ones, from Cromwell to Robespierre? How much industrial modernization has taken place under dictatorships, from Napoleon III to Mussolini? How many dictatorships have been secular, or even anti-religious, from faraway Mexico to the Soviet Union?

Islamism as a Third World Movement

The Islamist sphere of influence encompasses the entire spectrum of activist groups who, in the second half of the twentieth century, see their actions as the broadening of the concepts elaborated by the founder of the Muslim Brotherhood in Egypt,

Hasan al-Banna (1906-1949), and by Abul-Ala Maududi (1903-1978), the creator of the Jamaat-i-Islami in the Indian subcontinent. Revolutionary Shiite political thoughts share many elements with the Muslim Brotherhood but remain different (both more leftist and more clerical): it has drawn inspiration from Ayatollah Khomeini, Baqir al-Sadr, and Taliqani, as well as from a secular Ali Shariati.

From the outset, then, we find Islam divided into three prominent geographic and cultural tendencies: the Sunni Arab Middle East, the Sunni Indian subcontinent, and Irano-Arab Shiism; Turkey, detached from the Arab world, has however its own organizations. These groups are as distinct politically as they are geographically, which is why it is more appropriate to speak of an Islamist sphere of influence than that of an international union. The largest organizations are those of the Arab world's Muslim Brotherhood (MB), imprecisely dependent on their Egyptian leadership but in reality organized on a national basis; several discordant and minority groups, generally influenced by the most radical ideas of the MB's Sayyid Qutb (1906-1966), have diverted from this common base (Hizb al-Tahrir in 1952, the Islamic Jihad in the 1970s, and so on). Next we find organizations belonging to the Indian subcontinent (the various Jamaat-i Islamis of Pakistan, India, and Bangladesh), the Afghan *mujahidin* (Hizb-i Islami, Jammat-i Islami), and, more recently, the North African Islamists (the Algerian FIS, or Islamic Salvation Front; the Tunisian Nahda party) and the Islamic Renaissance Party in the former Soviet Union. This alliance has recently tended to merge with older, apolitical fundamentalist movements (the Saudi Wahhabis, the Pakistani Ahl-i Hadith), thus somewhat losing definition. As for the revolutionary Shiite movement, it is the only one to have taken power by way of a genuine Islamic revolution; it has, therefore, become identified with the Iranian state, which used it as a tool in its strategy for emerging as a regional power, even though the multiplicity of Shiite groups reflects local particularities (in Lebanon, Afghanistan, or Iraq) as much as it does the factional struggles of Tehran.

Colonel Qaddafi's Libya, despite its vigorous activism (which in fact was more economy based than ideological), has been outside the Islamist sphere ever since Qaddafi outlawed the Libyan Muslim Brotherhood in 1973 and affected the disappearance of the powerful head of the Lebanese Shiite, Musa al-Sadr, in 1978.

The Islamist movement has developed over half a century, beginning around 1940. Concepts have evolved, historical circumstances have changed, and splits and differences have brought diversity. Nevertheless, there are conceptual conditions and a sociological base common to all the groups.

Indeed, as much from a sociological as from an intellectual point of view, these movements are upshots of the modern world. The militants are rarely mullahs; they are young products of the modern educational system, and those who are university educated try to be more scientific than literary; they come from recently-urbanized families or from the impoverished middle classes. Islamists consider Islam to be as much a religion as an "ideology", a neologism which they introduced and which remains a curse to the ulema (the clerical). They received their political education not in religious schools but on college and university campuses, where they came across militant Marxists, whose concepts they often borrowed (in particular the idea of revolution) and infused with Quranic terminology (*da'wa*, designating preaching/propaganda). Emphasis is given to the organization, a framework reminiscent both of Leninist-type parties (in which the Amir replaces the president and the *shura*-the advisory council — the central committee) and of Sufi brotherhoods. For them, taking total control of the state will allow for the spread of Islam in a society corrupted by Western values and for a simultaneous appropriation of science and technology. They do not endorse a return to what existed before, as do fundamentalists in the true sense of the word, but a reappropriation of society and modern technology based on politics.

The masses who follow the Islamists are not "traditional" or "traditionalists" either: they live with the values of the modern urban life — consumerism and upward social mobility; they left behind the old forms of conviviality, respect for elders and for consensus, when they left their villages. These followers, enchanted by the values of consumerism imparted by the shop windows of the large metropolises, live in a world of movie theatres, cafes, jeans, video, and sports, but they live hazardously on menial jobs or remain unemployed in immigrant ghettos, with the frustration inherent in an unattainable consumerist world.

The Islamist adaptation to the modern, urban setting is noticeable — from the use of modern weapons and communications technology to the organization of large demonstrations. Their militant actions exist in symbiosis with their urban environment: except Kurdistan and till recently in Afghanistan, the guerrillas of the contemporary Muslim world belong to urban areas.

Thus, far from being a sudden entry of an irrational, archaic phenomenon, the Islamist movement is in keeping with two preexisting tendencies. One, of course, is the call to fundamentalism, centred on the *sharia*: this call is as old as Islam itself and yet new because it has never been fulfilled. It is a tendency that is always setting the reformer, the censor, and the tribunal against the corruption of the times and of sovereigns, against foreign influence, political opportunism, moral slackness, and the forgetting of sacred texts. The other tendency, more recent and therefore more difficult to see, is that of anti-colonialism, of anti-imperialism, which has today become anti-Westernism—from Cairo to Tehran, the crowds that in the 1950s demonstrated under the red or a national flag now march beneath the green banner. The targets have remained the same: foreign banks, night clubs, local governments accused of complacency towards the West. The continuity is evident not only in these targets but also in the participants: the same individuals who followed Nasser or Marx in the 1960s have become Islamists today. There is an abundance of connections between Marxist groups and the Islamist sphere (the secular Palestinian Ahmad Jibril, for instance, has close ties with the Lebanese Hizbullah). Without doubt the Shiites have provided the best bridge between the two Third World movements: Ali Shariati, an ideologist of the contestant Shiite movement, was a great reader of Frantz Fanon. Finally, it is the Islamic revolution in Iran that has best reflected the Third World continuity of the Islamist movement by expressing the North-South opposition in religious terms.

The secular, Marxist, and nationalist revolutionary movements of the Third World were caught off-guard by their victories, and their ideals were corrupted by the lust for power. Islam has taken up the firebrand of the Third World, but with slogans that can no longer be shared by Western leftists or by other Third World movements: religious universalism has killed universalism plain and simple.

The parallels between the Muslim and Christian worlds are undoubtedly striking with regard to recent history, no doubt because the two intelligentsias shared common political references. The 1950s and 1960s were decades of communion: the Algerian guerrilla fighter and the Palestinian activist seemed to be the brother of dynamic Western militants. Their violence made sense. The separation occurred in the 1970s: one could no more understand the new militants of political Islam. Yet in their social origins, their relationship to knowledge, and even in the values that replaced their Marxist-leaning universalism, they are still the cousins of the Western "militants" of the 1970s: they have in common the craze of the return to the past, of authenticity and purity; the concern with dress, food, and cheerfulness, the rebuilding of a "traditional" way of life in a context and by methods that presuppose that the tradition is obsolete; the shift into terrorism for the most radical fringe. For the most sectarian, *hijra*, hegira, in the caves of Egypt is quite related a return to the countryside. There are resemblances between the Italian Red Brigade and the new extremist Muslim intelligentsia: its members, "micro-intellectuals" whose social integration falls short of their expectations, drag themselves into political violence based on the self-taught Marxist (or elsewhere Islamist) dogma. The distinctive logorrhea of the communiques of the French "Action directe" movement is a good example of this relationship.

The connection between the two Third World tendencies is much stronger than it appears. Previously, in the Marxist-leaning sphere of influence, we found the same synthesis between revolution and Christian theology (liberation theology), the same voluntarist activism, and the same quest for an "authenticity" that would disintegrate with Western, including Soviet, models. The Marxist-leaning revolutionary currents of the 1970s—Hafizullah Amin in Afghanistan, Pol Pot in Cambodia, the Shining Path in Peru—all sought, beneath a dictatorial Marxist line, to invent a new "national" model built around a "lumpenintelligentsia," particularly the "indigenous" or traditional sectors of the population (tribes, peasants, Indians). Strangely, whereas the Marxist guerrillas were peasants, the Islamists were urban, and thus *sociologically* more modern. The parallel between Islamism and Third World movements extends to their breakdown and the shift of their most far-reaching sectors into terrorism, which is a product of the 1970s and not an Islamic invention. But we have lost the common frame of reference, the Third World Marxist vulgate that allowed a few to "understand" the Baader-Meinhof Gang or the Red Brigades, even the Palestinian hijackers, but not the Hizbullah hostage-takers.

Not that we have heard the last of the Third World. The collapse of the Soviet Union as well as of communism makes it likely that Islam will no long be the dominant force in the mobilization of the Muslim world's masses at crucial junctures, and the Third World is still in crisis. But unlike Marxism, Islam cannot reach beyond its cultural domain: the age of converting entire peoples is past. Religious universalism spreads only through individual conversion and defines a community separate from others: it thus draws its own limits and produces a "culture war" effect that makes it tough to see the relationship between the Third World contestation and Islamist self-assertion. The present day Islamist activists are obsessed with conversion: rumours that Western celebrities or entire groups are converting are hailed enthusiastically by the core militants. Indeed, even as a political ideology Islamism cannot escape the issue of individual belief, whereas Marxism allowed one to explain and thus to influence a social movement on the basis of group determinisms. Religion needs individual conversion, transforming the dynamic of conversion to Islam among Christians into a matter of simple arithmetic rather than a mass sociopolitical phenomenon: you go on adding until the number of converts shifts the balance of the society. But here is where the hardship lies: anyone in a Christian environment who converts to Islam is psychologically choosing a sect structure, which generally indicates a marginalized person, an extremist, or a true mystic—in other words, a loner, which thus precludes desire for a mass movement.

From where does Political Modernity Originate?

The said: comparisons don't prove anything. To show the modernity, and thus the deep historical aspect, of Islamist movements is interesting in terms of political sociology, but is against the Islamists' own arguments. For them, there is only one Islam, that of the age of the Prophet, which has since lost its way, for modernity. But this vision of Islam as possessing only one essence is not unique to the Islamists, since we find in among traditionalist ulemas and also among many Western Orientalists, who are in turn adopting Max Weber's reading of Islam: a culture, a civilization, a closed system. Islamist and Orientalist thinkers are, of course, as to what constitutes the essence of Islam, but all speak in terms of a global, timeless system—a mirror effect that no doubt explains both the violence and the abortiveness of the polemics. The pages that follow will seem at times to accept this presupposition, by the simple fact that we take at their word the arguments of the actors: to which conceptual arrangements are referring when they conceive of Islam as a political system? To what extent does this configuration function in their political action?

The "Orientalist" belief consists, among Western specialists or essayists, in defining a timeless "Islamic culture", a conceptual framework that structures both political life and urban architecture, the thought of the ulema and of their slanderers, and whose consequence would be the non-emergence of capitalism (M. Weber) and the absence of both an autonomous space for politics and institutions (B. Badie). A timeless civilization in which everything is interrelated and reflects a same structure, from the stucco arabesque to the legal treatise, but a civilization brutally faced with the challenge of a modernity arisen from outside. According to this view, ("Islamic culture") is the major stumbling-block prohibiting access to political modernity.

What is this presupposition of political modernity? We find today under the bylines of many authors, after the Third World movement during which the West masochistically beat its breast, the Weberian idea according to which a single civilization—to say, Europe—invented a true universalist culture. In the political domain, the invention of modernity lies in the rise of an autonomous political space, separate from both the religious and private spheres and embodied in the modern, law-based state. Secularity and politics are born of a closing-in of Christian thought onto itself. This is not to deny that there has been some remarkable historical and political research addressing the birth of politics and the modern state. But the result of this work has been to suggest that there is no salvation (no modernity) outside the Western political model. The "popularized" argument that is put forth, based on these works and aimed at Muslim intellectuals, is two-fold: (1) parliamentary democracy, the ideology of human rights, and the law-based state are ethically desirable and economically more efficient; (2) historically, this arrangement comes out of Christian Europe. In post-colonial settings this argument is very badly received, and not only in Islamist or traditionalist circles. The Gulf War revealed that even among secular, Westernized, and "democratic" Muslim intellectuals there was a mindful choice, whether tortured or enthusiastic, in favour of Saddam Husain, who all agreed was a dictator ... a bad Muslim. This emotional reaction implies an admission of failure: the absence of an alternative aside from a miracle, a sign from God.

The problem is about comparativism. Comparativism tends to take one of the elements of the comparison as the norm for the other, discovering that there is either a resemblance or a lack of one, but never questioning the original configuration. Comparativism thus risks isolating the two entities, ignoring not only their individual dynamics, but particularly the truthfulness of the relationship between one and the other: this dialectic tends both to fix in the imagination differences that are more symbolic than real and to obscure their factual specificity. While there is definitely an Islamic political collection, from the traditionalist ulemas to the Islamists, it is difficult if not downright specious to assume a simple equivalency between a civilization and a history on the one hand and this collection on the other.

In comparativism, one is constantly moving between the Islamic collection (the texts produced by scholars and intellectuals) and the genuine sociological reality: the "lack" of modernity in Muslim countries is explained at times by the effects of the absence of a conceptual category that is very much present in Western thought (for example, since the concept of a state based on territory is absent from the corpus of Islamic politics, it is impossible to achieve a modern state, which is by definition territorialized); at times by the existence of a sociological category not reflected in the collection (the patrimonial state, the segmentation into "solidarity groups," *asabiyya*). The first approach confirms the impossibility of the rise of an autonomous political authority within the framework of "Islamic culture"; the second, in contrast, highlights the autonomy of the political authority although a premodern political authority (a patrimonial state)—with respect of Islamic thought.

But far from being originally marked by a lack, Islamic political thought is inscribed within a different configuration of the relationship between power and the law. That this arrangement is in turn a source of difficulties is not in doubt, but one must measure it in comparison to its original meaning, not in relation to the Western state. What is original is the place of the *sharia*, Muslim law, with respect to power. The *sharia* has two characteristics: its autonomy and its incompletion. It does not depend on any state, on any actual, positive law, on any political decision and thereby creates a space that is parallel to the political space, to power, which, can circumvent the *sharia* or manipulate it (hence the strong theme of the corruption of the judge), but which cannot make it into something other than what it is: an autonomous, infinite commentary. For the *sharia* is not dependent on any official body, church or clergy; the *fatwa*, formal legal opinions that decide matters not mentioned in the text, are always pronounced in the here and now and can be declared invalid by a subsequent authority. The *sharia* is never closed, for it is based not on a core of concepts, but rather on a collection of precepts which is at times general, at times precise, and which expands to include the totality of human acts through induction, analogy, extension, commentary, and interpretation. While the basic precepts, as they are broadly formulated, cannot be called into question, their extension is a matter of casuistics. The job of the judge is not to apply a principle or a concept, but to bring the case before him back into the realm of what is already known.

These two "shortcomings" in the *sharia* (no institutional closure, no conceptual closure) also make totalitarianism, understood as the absorption of the totality of the social realm into the political realm, foreign to Islamic culture: its warning symptoms appear only when this culture in a shambles (Iraq). At the same time, no one can lay claim to Islam and simultaneously contest the sharia: secularity can result only from violence (Ataturk's Turkey) or from escheat, through a change in lifestyles and customs.

The excess of state, which is inherent in the place the state occupies in the West, is totalitarianism. It is not surprising that Western contemporary thought on the formation of the state would also be a reflection on and against totalitarianism. In Islam, it is because there is a weakness in the political sphere that totalitarianism does not occur, which naturally does not mean that there is no state or arbitrary violence, which, when it occurs, is considered to be "unjust tyranny," in the Islamic political imagination, is not liberty, but justice. Ethics, is the watchword of protest, paving the way for every kind of populism. This is how one must interpret the limitation of democratic demand in a Muslim country. It is not that there is an acceptance in dictatorship, but that a different demand is made: first of all, the respect for privacy, for the family space, the home, honor (*namus*); next, the demand for justice (the repetition of the theme of the good sovereign). Liberty is demanded in the sphere of the family, in the private sphere, and not in the political sphere where the value expected is justice.

These brief reflections aim to show that there are different arrangements and problematics in the relationships between the state and society in Islamic and Western cultures. To investigate the first culture on the basis of the concepts of the second, raised to the level of universality, can only bring to light an absence, that is the lack of a modern state — without making it clear that what prevents the emergence of this state (the *sharia* and the horizontal bonds of solidarity groups) is also what makes Islamic totalitarianism impossible. This doesn't suggest that I am equating the *sharia* with Western democracy: simply that comparativism must be viewed as a conclusion and not as a premise. It is a question of methodology.

The Muslim responses to the "Orientalist" discourse are mostly stereotypical and can be classified into three categories:

(1) the nostalgia argument ("it was Islam that brought civilization to the West"); (2) rejection of the hypothesis ("in what way are Western values superior?"), combined with a denunciation of Western double speak which applies its strict requirements only to others; (3) the apologia for Islam ("everything is in the Quran and the Sunna, and Islam is the best religion"). The first two are defensive: they escape the question while accepting as fact that there is a modernity that produces its own values. The third constitutes the topic of this book.

In fact both Islamism and the traditional fundamentalism of the ulemas have difficulty posing the genuine question: why does Western Orientalism study Islam *sub specie aeternitatis*, while approaching Western civilization as a "socio-historical configuration"? The reason is that the Islamic political imagination accepts and even demands the belief according to which Islam exists *sub specie aeternitatis*. The dominant corpus in Sunni Islamic culture, that of the ulemas, as well as those of the Salafist reformists and contemporary Islamists, conceive of Islam as eternal, a historical, and beyond criticism. We must, therefore, understand the reasons for the hegemony of the assertion for "oneness" among Muslim scholars and intellectuals, a hegemony that entails the marginalization of other points of view; it is interesting to see that it is "Western" researchers who detect the atypical thinkers of the Muslim world (such as Ibn Khaldun), whose thought then becomes suspect to many Muslim intellectuals. But is it genuine, considering the nonhistoricity that Islamic thought attributes to itself, to infer that Muslim societies are incapable of achieving political modernity?

Islamic Political Imagination

We decline to allow ourselves to establish a relationship of causality between, on the one hand, the manner in which the Islamic tradition treats politics and, on the other, the reality of the regimes and institutions in Muslim countries, or even to consider that one is a direct expression of the other. There exists certainly what one might call an "Islamic political imagination" (in the sense of a horizon of thought), which recurs in the corpus of the ulemas and is evident in the texts of the Salafists (nineteenth-century reformers) and the Islamists. This "imagination" is not "Islamic culture", for we must be watchful of unruly generalizations. There is another classical corpus (philosophy); there are other thoughts, other practices; there are intellectuals who think beyond this horizon. But one need only scan the literature of the ulemas or the Islamists, or listen to the lectures in the mosques, to admit that there is an Islamic political imagination dominated by a single paradigm: that of the first community of believers contemporary to the Prophet and of the first four caliphs.

Independently of its historical reality, this model offers the militants of political Islam an ideal for Muslim society. Islam emerged as a sect and as a society, a political and religious community where existed neither institutions nor clergy nor specialized functions, and in which the Prophet Muhammad was the sole narrator and interpreter of a divine and transcendent law that governed all human activities. An egalitarian, undifferentiated society, placed under the auspices of a man who didn't authorise, but who stated the revelation: this oneness (*tawhid*), extends to the individual, whose practices are considered in the entirety and not classified according to the area in which they are implemented (the social, private, devotional, political, or economic sphere). This paradigm would obviously mark the relationships between Islam and politics even if the original community, nostalgia for which haunts Islamic political reflection, was never to be rebuilt. This pattern of the original community, which rejects any internal rift (ethnicities, tribes) and derives its unity from a powerful leader, would even be reinterpreted in secular fashion and included in Arab nationalist ideology.

From this paradigm result a certain number of recurring themes in Islamic political thought. The nonseparation of the religious, legal, and political spheres is stated. The *sharia* should be the sole source of law as well as the norm for individual behaviour, both for the sovereign and for the simple believer. The definition of an autonomous political sphere, with its own rules, its positive laws, and its own values, is prohibited. Finally, the state is never considered in terms of a territorialized nation-state: the criterion is to have a power that would rule over the entirety of the *umma*, the community of the faithful, while proper power is exercised over a segment of the *umma* whose borders are contingent, provisional, and incomplete.

It is thus customary to say that in the Islamic political imagination, no distinction is made between the religious and the political orders. This idea is one of the deep beliefs of the political actors in contemporary Islam: on the basis of this fact alone, independently of any theological analysis of its validity, it should be given a serious thought. We, therefore, should study the effect it produces on thought and political practice, and not consider it a needful fact in the history and the actual political practice of Islam, which would mean an absence of a specifically political authority.

Debate on the State of Muslim Society

According to the Orientalist perspective, the intellectual configuration described above has been a hindrance to the appearance of a political space and to the emergence of a modern state. This is not the place to revisit a historical debate. But there are two problems we cannot overcome: the appearance of a political space in the practice of power in classical Islam, and the condition of contemporary states in Muslim countries.

In reality, since the time of the original community there has always been a *de facto* autonomous political presence in the Muslim world: what has been lacking is a political thought regarding the autonomy of this space, which has, therefore, been perceived by the traditionalists as group and by the Islamists as deviant. As early as the end of the first century of the hegira, a *de facto* separation between political power (sultans, amirs) and religious power (the caliph) was created and institutionalized. But this relevance always resulted from a division that was different from the one that developed in the West. No positive law originates from the centre of power: the sovereign reigns in the empirical, the contingent. Any intervention into the private sphere is perceived as arbitrary, precisely because social relationship, administered by the *sharia*, is not supposed to be subject to arbitrariness and violence. It is because Islam occupies the sphere of law and of social regulation that the power of the sovereign, even of a fair sovereign, cannot help but seem contingent and arbitrary, for he can mediate only in what is outside the domain of the *sharia*, and thus only in nonessential matters. There is, in Islam, a civil society unconcerned to the state. There is no "oriental despotism."

Yet, according to the tradition, the sovereign has a "religious" function: to defend Islam and the *sharia*. The state, too, has an objective to enable Muslims to live as good Muslims. The state is an instrument and not an end in itself. Thus writings on Muslim law contain a section devoted to the exercise of power. The good sovereign is one who fulfills this function; the bad, one who exercises an "unjust tyranny". "Justice" is at the centre of this ethic of the good prince. The sultan (power in fact) is not the caliph (a successor to Muhammad), and yet the Muslims must obey the sultan if he initiates the *sharia* and defends the Islamic community against its enemies. The sultan is a sword (*sayfal-din*, the "sword of religion," an often conferred title), not an ethical model, but his virtue is essentially important. Similarly, his genuineness is indirectly religious, in that he ensures the public good (*maslaha*), enabling the believer to observe his religion: this legitimacy is symbolised by the right to coin money and to have the Friday prayer (*khutba*) said in his name.

This configuration is meaningful for the "classical" period. There is no doubt that it marks the imagination and beliefs of traditionalist mullahs. But if we look at recent history and at the nature of present Muslim states, "Islamic culture" as applied to politics tends to lose a good deal of its relevance: there are genuine historical developments in Muslim societies and the rise of modern state tendencies in the early nineteenth century.

In the post-Weberian analyses of the state in Muslim countries, we find two analyses explaining its precariousness, its lack of legitimacy, and its seizure by solidarity groups (*asabiyya*). The one (Badie), as we saw earlier, views this as a result of "Islamic culture": the absence of an autonomous political sphere and the confusion between public and private spaces give rise to a kind of neopatrimonial state. The Mother (M. Seurat) explains it by the imported and recent nature of the modern state in the Middle East. "The modern state in the Middle East ... is a successful *asabiyya*," which is to say that a solidarity group, generally a clan or a minority, seizes control of the state structure and turns it into an instrument for the economic exploitation of the society; such a state is predatory and lives off unearned income (oil proceeds, money extorted from rich countries by threat of harm, proceeds from influence peddling and speculation). Seurat's analysis applies aptly to Syria and Iraq: a minority group (the Alawis in Syria, the Sunni Takritis in Iraq) first infiltrates the army, then takes over the state, which it turns against its very own society (dictatorship and massacres); this state in fact lives from external exploitative practices (direct in the case of Lebanon, and, for a few months, of Iraq in Kuwait; indirect as in the case of Syria, which cashes in on its power as a potential menace to obtain Saudi subsidies), from oil dividends (Iraq), and from taxes on foreign trade (sale of export licenses, "farming out" sources of private revenue to dignitaries: drugs, customs, technical ministries). But in the words of Seurat, Syria and Iraq are secular states, engaged in bloody battle with the Islamists. M. Seurat's work, which refers constantly to Ibn Khaldun and not to the collection of the ulemas, shows that the position of the state in the political configuration of the Middle East is not necessarily a consequence of "Islamic culture," but rather a "Third World" type of phenomenon, resulting from the inhuman importation of the European model into a divided and unstructured society. In fact, the state, employed as a source of revenue by a group or family, is a phenomenon that exists in every culture, from the Marcoses' Philippines to Mobutu's Zaire.

The contemporary Muslim world is no more alike the medieval Muslim world than the European state, according to Machiavelli, was that of Thomas Aquinas. There is an authentic history of the state in the Middle East, but this history is inseparable from the conflict with the West, which figures into the political make-up of the current Islamic world for better or for worse, just as it figures into Islamist thought and the consumer values of present-day societies.

There is a historical process to the construction of states, dating from pre-colonial era (Morocco, Egypt, Iran, and even Afghanistan). In the nineteenth century, the latter three countries and the Ottoman Empire began a transformation of the state from the top down, based on the model of enlightened autocracy and beginning with an army and the construction of a modern state sector (schools, universities, and so on). It is true that Europe constantly severed the wings of these states, which were poorly implanted in any case. Military operations (Egypt in 1840, Iran in 1907, the coup d'etat against Musaddiq in 1953), growing indebtedness, the random erection of borders (in 1918 and at other times) have always shattered the impulse toward the construction of self-sufficient states. The most recent war, the Gulf War, was not the result of an effort to restructure the political landscape: the same actors and the same regimes were used to re-enact the same play according to a different strategic power relationship. In brief, from Disraeli to Bush, by way of Clemenceau and Kissinger, the West has never been concerned with encouraging political modernisation in the Middle East.

Nevertheless, as cynical as this policy is and as acerbic as the writings of Arab intellectuals have been regarding the role of the West, one fact is undeniable: the nation-states currently existing in the Middle East have held up, with or without genuineness. After each crisis, they again become the keys to negotiations; the longer they last, the more reality they acquire. These states have confronted all the "pan ... ism" crises: pan-Arabism and pan-Islamism. Arab nationalists have secularised the notion of the *umma* and in theory rejected the territorialised state: Egypt (whose official name from 1958 to 1972 was the "United Arab Republic"), Syria, and Iraq consider themselves to be parties, "regions", in a future Arab nation. And yet all the designs to unite (the most serious of which was the Syrian-Egyptian union of 1958) have failed: each time there is a return to the preexisting states.

Similarly, the exaltation of the Arab combat against Israel cannot hide the fact that each state pursues its own interests, to the harm of the Palestinians if need be. The same is true of pan-Islamism: the Iraqi masses, who as Shiites are victimized by their own state, did not join the Iranian revolutionaries during the first Gulf unrest. The latest Gulf crises saw the same states, the same leaders, the same borders re-emerge, now legitimised by the peace proceedings.

Since the Iranian revolution, the countries of the Middle East have experienced great stability in their regimes and leaders. For even if these states hold together by the great personalisation of their leaders, by the absence or weakness of a proper democratic space, by the disdain for rules of law, even if they have often been taken over by factions, by an *asabiyya*, and are based on an over-abundant and equally corrupt bureaucracy, they exist. There are state mechanisms, sectors of the economy tied to the existence of the state, strata of the population (in particular the new intelligentsia) that live solitarily from the state, modern armies. The last Gulf War, for example, showed the power of the Iraqi state apparatus, which survived a military defeat, to remain in place. Even if these states maintain themselves mostly because of the vulnerabilities of the opposition, the lack of democratic "demand," or the diversities of the civil society, their persistence indicates that there is a "state fact" more resistant to analysis and to events than was formerly believed. Regimes can change, but the states remain.

The existence of these states is also fixed by the globalisation of politics: the great powers and the United Nations guarantee the world map, thus the borders, thus the territories, and thus, ultimately, the states that incarnate them. Territorialisation, characteristic of the modern state, may not be inherent in the thought either to the "Islamic imagination" or of Arabism, but it is essential of the balance of international forces. The Kuwaiti identity might have been weak before the Gulf War; now it is very real, especially since Kuwait is certain to endure under the American umbrella. Today's political globalisation operates in favour of the consolidation of the existing states. Inclusion in a world order gives these states a socio-political consistency as well, no doubt, as a psychological reality in the minds of their "nationals".

Yet, these states are not revolutionary. Their politics cannot be explained, as Seurat aptly demonstrates, without reference to the concept of the *asabiyya*, to division and esprit de corps, which is to say to the establishment of clientele networks more inclined towards their own prosperity than with that of the state. But these networks do not represent the eternity of a tradition behind a mere facade of modernity. The structures of the traditional *asabiyya* were demolished by urbanization, by the shuffling of society, by ideologization: they reconstructed themselves along different lines (political patronage and economic mafias), but they may also disappear. The modern *asabiyya* are recompositions of the esprit de corps based on the fact of the state and the globalisation of economic and financial networks; they are translations of a traditional relationship of solidarity into the modern domain. It is still important to know who is from which village, who married whom, but also who is of what rank at the military academy or who studied with which theology professor. The modern *asabiyya* are not simply the permanence of tribalism or religious fanaticism: they may be reconstituted on the basis of modern sociological elements (the new intelligentsia versus the old families), but they function as predators and commemorated themselves through matrimonial alliances. Their space is no longer the grandfather's village but the modern city. The militia of Beirut may function as old urban *asabiyya*—the *futuwwa*, brotherhoods of bad boys who safeguard order and "protection" in the areas poorly patrolled by the palace—while political parties may function as patronage networks around important notables, but these militia and these parties are still something other than the mère continuation of an old tradition: the stakes they represent, the type of activities they engage in with regard to international conflicts, the insertion of the bazaar into a globalised economy — all this makes them into something other than surviving remains, the residue of tradition in modern times. Even in a traditional society such as Afghanistan, the network that develops around a small-time local commander, himself promoted into an "international" network for the circulation of goods (arms and sometimes drugs), is no longer the clan that existed before, but a recomposition of the traditional partition around a new political elite and the globalized flow of wealth.

Challenging the Orientalist vision of the state in Muslim countries are critics from three milieus in the Muslim society: the "Westernized" intellectuals (those who accept the values of the modern state), the ulemas, and the Islamists.

The first accuses not the Western model of the state, but the double talk by which the West does everything in its power to prevent the universal model it proposes from becoming a reality. This argument, which is often well-founded, nonetheless carries with it an intellectual risk: that of blaming the foreigner for all one's problems. Segmentation is seen as a Western strategy (Berberism, Kurds ...) and charismatic dictators as the best response to Western duplicity. The worse legacy of the West was no doubt to offer the Muslim populace a ready-to-wear devil: conspiracy theory is currently paralysing Muslim political thought. For to say that every failure is the devil's work is the same as asking God, or the devil himself (which is to say, these days, the Americans), to solve one's problems. Between the wonder that doesn't happen and the pact in which one loses one's soul, there is plenty of room for discontent.

Among the ulemas, mullahs, and their followers, the historical evolution of the Muslim society has had little effect on the political imagination derived from the paradigm of the "Islamic society," a paradigm that also reappears in Islamist movements. The "Islamic political imagination" has endeavoured to ignore or disqualify anything new. Not that the ulemas have always fought innovation: on the contrary, by allowing sovereigns to render *fatwa* they acknowledged the establishment of a new state order (for which they would later be reproached by the Islamists); however, aside from a division of Shiite clergy, they simply neither developed a new form of thought nor integrated the new facts into their discourse. The eternity of the mullahs' and ulemas' discourse is striking to this day. History is something that must be endured; whatever is new is company and merits only a *fatwa* from time to time. Modernization exists side by side with the old discourse.

As for Islamist thought, it sees itself as a response to the problematics of the imported state and of segmentation: it has something to say about the Muslim world's backwardness in comparison with Europe, about industrialisation, about the Islamic economy, and so on. It notes, rightly, that secularity and nationalism are not *ipso facto* modernisation. The seizing of power by *asabiyya* in the secular and nationalist states of Syria and Iraq, the role of tribalism and patronage, and the formation of social strata born of and parasite to the state are continual themes of Islamist propaganda. Islamist protest occurs in the name of the universality of the social body (conceived of as the religious community) against the particularism of the state, against split, against both the new state-managed and the old tribal societies. Islam is seen as the introduction of a universal outlook and the common good against particularism and communalism.

The modernity of Islamist thought is in this pursuit for a universal state. The Islamists' reference to the original society and their rejection of history are not enough in and of themselves to mark their thought as outmoded. Another fundamentalist mode of thought, the Protestant Reformation, was, as we know, one of the best forces for access to economic and political modernity. Referring to the Tradition (with a capital T) of the Prophet allows one to evade the tradition issued from history and thus to integrate a modernity which is no more a purely external phenomenon, as it is for the Salafists, but which is a fact of Muslim society.

But does Islamist thought fulfill its programme? This is the subject of our inquiry. In my view, it has failed because Islamist thought, at the end of an intellectual trajectory that attempts to integrate modernity, at last meets up with the "Islamic political imagination" of the tradition and its essential premise: politics can be founded only on individual virtue.

The Internalised West

With respect to the effect of Western domination, it is imperative to examine not only the economic and political structures of the contemporary Muslim society (political backwardness would thus be an effect of neocolonialism, evoking emotional identification with the *umma* even at the price of secular dictators such as Saddam Husain) but also the thought of this world, the conceptual framework of Islamist intellectuals. One thing is indeed significant: most Islamists were educated in a "Westernised" environment, yet they hold to the corpus of the ulemas (whom they accuse of passing of having poorly managed this corpus). All their literature insists on the rationality of religious prescriptions; this militant sensibility is a sign that modernity has worked its way into the very heart of Islamist discourse, which is so rationalist that it ends up denying its own religious practices.

But does Islamist discourse truly dominate the Muslim world? In addressing this question we need not consider either the number of books published or the opinions of professors or journalists, but the networks through which these works are distributed, and the places and languages in which they are written—in other words, the public that is impressed by them. The publication and distribution networks are financed today by conservative, often Saudi milieus. The Islamists have their own public which cannot or does not want to read Westernized intellectuals. Apart from some ephemeral Marxist writings, and at least with respect to the Arab world, it is as if the only audience for Westernized Muslim intellectuals writing within the fabric of the modern social sciences were in fact within the periphery of Western world. On the Indian subcontinent, "modern" Muslim intellectuals write in English, leaving the writings for the masses, whether Islamist or neofundamentalist, in Urdu. One does not witness the same phenomenon in Central Asia, where Russian will long remain the language of the social sciences. The Maghreb is graded into three languages (French, literary Arabic, and Arabic dialect): in choosing a language, one chooses an audience. Only Turkey, Iran, and Egypt produce social science texts in the vernacular form. In France, and especially in the United States, we are witnessing an astounding "brain drain" of non-Islamist intellectuals, particularly in the social sciences. With the elite gone, the world of thought has been inhabited by "new intellectuals." And as we shall see, these new intellectuals have a "religious" association to their own knowledge. They will not be the ones to open up the ulemas' corpus. The modernity they brought to the reading of Islam exhausted itself in stereotyped uncritical and undemonstrative defence of Islam, which for them has answers to all the problems of the modern world.

But Islamism's ultimate failure in its attempt to concentrate on modernity doesn't prevent modernity from turning into sociological facts and movements. Modernity creeps into Muslim countries regardless of Islam, and the Islamists themselves play a part in this secularisation of the religion. They are a stage toward the "disenchantment of the world." By rejecting Westernization that is already in place, they express the myth of authenticity in a borrowed, ingenuine language. For they borrow from this modernity the refusal to return to the real tradition in the name of an imaginary Tradition: they condemn popular religious practice, the village, Sufism, philosophy. They themselves deny and undermine what is and was Muslim civilisation and ensure the triumph of fast food (*halal*, of course — religiously correct), of jeans, Coke, and English. The urban lifestyle (in the ethnological sense) of the Islamists strikingly resembles that of any modern Western suburb. And the reinvention of a vestiary tradition that never existed (raincoats, gloves and scarves for women, beards and parkas for men) will not bring about a new authenticity.

Modernisation occurred, but outside any conceptual framework: it happened through rural exodus, emigration, consumption, the gradual change in family pattern (a lower birthrate), but also through the cinema, music, clothing, satellite antennas, that is, through the globalisation of culture. It also occurred through the establishment of states that, fragile, corrupt, and clientele oriented though they may be, are nonetheless seriously new in their method of legitimation, their social base, and their division into territories frozen by international agreements. Dissent against the West, which includes contesting the existing states, is on the same order as Western ecology or anti-immigrant arguments: they are arguments one propounds when it is too late. Just as France is never going to return to a preindustrial society, and its immigrants are there to stay, so Muslim cities will never return to the harmony of the bazaar and of guilds. It is a composite world, a world of nostalgia. Only when it is too late do we dream of the past, and then our dreams encompass everything we want to deny. The tradition of which the nostalgic dream, like the tradition condemned by modernists, never existed.

The Failure of Islamism

In retrospect, it seems that the political action of the Islamists, far from leading to the establishment of states or of Islamic societies, falls in either with the logic of the state (Iran), or with traditional, if reconfigured, division (Afghanistan). No matter what the actors say, any political action amounts to the automatic creation of a secular space or a return to traditional segmentation. Herein lies the limit of the politicisation of a religion, of any religion. Our problem, then, is not to survey to what extent Islam allows for a secular space in its texts and age-old practice (this would pose considerable problems of methodology and amounts to returning to the conceptual categories of those whom one is critiquing), but to study a coherent group, limited in time and space, of texts, practices, and political organisations that deeply marked the political life of Muslim countries and their relationships with the countries of the North, while tending to alter the Muslims' perception of Islam in a sterner moral direction.

The thought of the movements we are studying traverses between two poles: a revolutionary pole, for whom the Islamisation of the society occurs through state power; and a reformist pole, for whom social and political action aims primarily to re-Islamise the society from the bottom up, bringing about, *ipso facto*, the advent of an Islamic state. The split lies not on the issue of the necessity of an Islamic state, but on the means by which to arrive at one and on the attitude to adopt with respect to the powers in place: destruction, opposition, collaboration, unconcernness. The entire spectrum of attitudes is possible: the Jordanian MB participated in parliamentary elections, the Jamaat-i Islami of Pakistan and the Sudanese MB supported military putsches, the Egyptian Islamic Jihad initiated a campaign of assassinations of government personalities. Can the two poles be placed on a chronological scale that would move from Islamisation from the top down (Islamism) to Islamisation from the bottom up (neofundamentalism)? Yes and no. On the one hand, there is no systematic correspondence between intellectual radicalism and political extremism: the Jamaat-i Islami of Pakistan, which is utterly vocal in its demand for a fully Islamic society, has always remained within a legal framework, even when its results in elections were laughable; in Afghanistan, it is often tough to comprehend the ideological differences between the Hizb-i Islami and the Jamaat-i Islami, although the first has carried out separatist and quite violent actions, and the second has always proved to be a party of openness. What is more, the Islamist movements themselves constantly rotate between political activism and neofundamentalism, that is, between primacy accorded the political struggle and that given to the Islamisation of the society. Al-Banna, for one, has at times advocated the rejection of settlement, at times called for collaboration. Certain things have remained unchanged, of course, over the last fifty years: Ayatollah Khomeini has always advocated a radical break (but in language that is sometimes traditionalist, at times revolutionary); the Arab Muslim Brotherhoods involved in armed confrontation only when forced into it by external repression (Syria); the Jamaat-i Islami of Pakistan has continued to act legally; the revolutionary movements — the Iranian sphere of influence, the Afghan Islamists, and fanatic Arab groups (Jihad, Takfir wal-Hijra)—emerged only later, after the 1967 Arab-Israeli war.

The revolutionary path was a failure: the Iranian revolution got bogged down in internal struggles and the economic slowdown, the activism of the MB opposing groups never managed to achieve a change in regime in an Arab country. The Sunni extremist groups marginalised themselves, the Shiites, on the contrary, became pawns in state strategies (the manipulation of terrorism by Syria and Iran). But Islamism has largely marked the political goings-on and contemporary Muslim society.

Towards the end of the 1980s, the failure of the Islamist revolutionary idea brought about the course of a revolutionary, political, Third World type of Islamism, incarnated in the Iranian revolution, toward a puritanical, preaching, populist, conservative neofundamentalism, wealthy until recently by Saudi Arabia but violently anti-Western, particularly since the end of the East-West confrontation has ceased to cast communism as a foil. The Algerian FIS (Islamic Salvation Front) is the model for this sort of group: a conjunction of the political heritage of Islamism, Saudi money (until 1990), and the influence of a more pious that political return to Islam. Yet the difference that we are exploring here between Islamism and neofundamentalism has no chronological cut off point; it is a difference in emphasis. Islamist militants did not suddenly become neofundamentalists starting in 1984 or 1985. On the other hand, the diminishing possibilities for political revolution, the growing influence of Saudi money, the inability of Islamist thought to go beyond the founding texts, the appearance of a new generation of militants less politically conscious and more concerned with the *sharia* and respecting rituals than with an Islamic revolution, all this set a different tone for the Islamist movement and confused, without erasing, what distinguished it from traditional fundamentalism. This is why it is important, on a given point, to note the differences between Islamism and neofundamentalism (the inversely proportional place accorded the *sharia* and women, the concept of revolution) and, on other points, to note the resemblances (the relationship to knowledge, the critique of the official ulemas, the definition of the economy).

Islamist ideas have spread throughout broad sectors of Muslim societies, losing part of their political force in this popularisation. An obvious re-Islamisation is occurring in high places and on the street. Since the end of the 1970s, the states have reintroduced principles from the *sharia* into their constitutions and laws; secularity is declining in the legal domain (family statute in Algeria in 1984). From below, one may note the increased visibility of fundamentalist Islam (in attire: the wearing of beards by men, and the veils of scarves by city women) and a larger externality of practice, with the growth of neighbourhood mosques uncontrolled by the state.

Yet basically, the influence of Islamism is more superficial than it appears. The *sharia* has been put only partially into practice in the most conservative states (Saudi Arabia, Pakistan, Sudan). The existing regimes have proved stable in the face of Islamist contestation; the leaders have experienced great political sustenance: in the 1980s, from Morocco to Pakistan (with the exception of Lebanon, Sudan, and Afghanistan), the only heads of state who disappeared did so due to illness or death (Bourguiba, Khomeini, Zia ul-Haqq); all the others (Hasan II, Chadli Benjedid, Mubarak, Husayn of Jordan, Asad of Syria, Fahd of Saudi Arabia, Saddam Husain, Jabir al-Sabah of Kuwait, Qabus of Oman, Abdallah Salih of North Yemen) remained in place the whole decade.

Re-Islamisation has in no way changed the rules of the political or economic game. The geostrategy of the Middle East is connected to the existing states, not to the popular or international Islamist uprisings. The victory of Islamist movements such as the FIS in Algeria will not give rise to a new pan-Islamism, but on the contrary to "Islamo-nationalisms". Everywhere, even within the Islamist sphere of influence, the exploited is resurfacing: ethnic and tribal segmentation, political manoeuvring, personal rivalries, but also evil ... corruption, speculation. These mechanisms are not thought out. The essential premise of the Islamist movement is that the political model it proposes assumes the virtue of individuals, but that this virtue can be acquired only if the society is truly Islamic. All the rest is plot, sin or illusion.

The changes that marked the minds of so many during the 1980s have ultimately had nominal influence on the facts and history: in the end we find the countries, states, regimes and borders that existed ten years earlier. After the second war in the Gulf, the dependence of Muslim countries on the North has never been greater.

Nonetheless, the socioeconomic happenings that sustained the Islamist wave are still here and are not going to change: poverty, uprootedness, crises in values and identities, the decline in educational systems, the North-South opposition, the problem of immigrant integration into the host societies. The Islamic revolution, the Islamic state, the Islamic economy are considered as myths, but we have not heard the last of Islamist protestation. The coming to power of movements such as the FIS will only make more apparent the hollowness of the phantasm of the "Islamic state".

One

Terrorism and its Definitions

Twentieth-century terrorism has come of age. In Britain, children of this age of terrorism are old enough to exercise their franchise. In the USA, the first-born of the age of terrorism can now legally taste alcohol. It was in the mid 1960s that the word itself began to gain (or, very retrospectively, to regain) international headline currency: around 1964, when the Palestine Liberation Organisation came into being, as an umbrella organisation for the previously disparate radical Palestinian groupings.

Though the precise make-up of the PLO was of minimal relevance, what the world saw in its actions, and those of many other factions who began at about the same time, was the emergence of modern terrorism, a phenomenon so specifically dependent on the communications, technologies and political organisation of the times as to differentiate it from any earlier form. It seemed almost impossible, close to twenty years later, to reconstruct the sense of strangeness that most observers felt about these incidents. Almost invariably the terrorism concerned a 'quarrel in a faraway country between people of whom we know nothing', to borrow Chamberlain's 1938 critical remark on a far more visible and concrete form of conflict. Here were groups and individuals from unexpected corners of the world, representing causes and minorities of which the established post-war order of NATO, SEATO and all the rest took no notice, demanding a place on the agenda of international policy.

There was something distinguishing of the decade in the first flush of terrorism. The terrorists were evidently men and women of their time, who like their non-combatant contemporaries were rejecting aspects of the old order. Many modern terrorists began their careers in fundamentalism-instilled student politics in

1968 — the year of 'student revolution' across Europe. Women's liberation would not have been more explicitly portrayed than by Leila Khaled, the Palestinian woman who hijacked a jet plane to London and was promptly released. Such dramatic non-conformism and rebelliousness was apparently the basis of much uncritical support from politically native students, excited more by the superficial appeal of agitprop slogans and images than the elements of their functioning. But instead of taking drugs, these rebels were taking lives; instead of holding sit-ins, they were holding hostages.

Western European fundamentalists, for the first time, identified — and romanticised — Palestinians as displaced Arab nationalists who had established a novel publicity tactic: that of commandeering international aircrafts and forcing them to fly to new destinations in the vast Arab world — though sometimes they boldly flew into startled Western capitals. Sometimes they blew the planes up — but international aircrafts were a rather faceless and quite acceptable target for the political generation of 1968.

After twenty years of modern terrorism, and — equally important — of the unsuccessful efforts of every kind of government to eliminate it, there can no longer be any question but that terrorism has emerged, and will remain, a permanent fixture in the linked worlds of politics and conflict. The practice of terrorism is immersed in the functions of modern international relations, and there is no conclusive evidence to support the great weight of wishful rhetoric, that terrorism or the terrorists can be eradicated. It has been observed that terrorism is not a uniquely isolated form of political activity, but part of a continuum that runs from conventional war at one end, through guerilla warfare, insurgency, sabotage, espionage, intelligence warfare, state despotism and persecution, and torture. In this context, the chief distinguishing feature of terrorism is that its practitioners lack official legitimacy: even if terrorists do act on behalf of bonafide states, the legitimation of state sanction is always denied in public. It is due to this reason that terrorism works more disturbingly and provokes greater outrage than any other example of the political use of force and power. A movement which has nothing at its disposal but terrorist tactics will fail; but with a political programme, a sense of diplomacy and relative mass support, it may thrive. The most effective terrorists are those who make the effort to combine their 'military' abilities — the willingness to act violently with 'political' sophistication turning violence into persuasion, rather than mere brutal protest.

Until the mid-1960s the Palestinians were known by veterans of the Palestine protectorate and UN peacekeeping forces as one of the world's most cursed refugee people. What has distinguished Palestinian nationalism since then has been its combination of terrorism with a dynamic political programme, which has for some years lent the PLO quasi-national status. In effect, Palestinian nationalist organisations occupy several different positions on the political continuum simultaneously. The PLO has acted at numerous levels first, by raising massive financial support from the Gulf; then by using terrorism to exert political pressure on the West; by galvanising support among Palestinians wherever they may be; and by attempting cross-border warfare and internal strife and unrest against Israel.

Agenda of Terrorism

The agenda of terrorism in the present-day world is set not only by terrorist groups and their actions, but also by the requirements of state policy, campaign trail rhetoric and strategic interests. The political dimension is in no way insignificant in sustaining the clamour of terrorism than the availability of weapons and explosives. Thus, the political agenda of terrorism consists simply in states failing to condemn the terrorism, inevitably, either of their allies or of special interest bodies close to their strategic political ideologies; and in denouncing the terrorism of their enemies.

It, thus, remains to be seen what are the criteria which provide the basis for an objective definition of terrorism? For the lay observer, there are two contradictory problems: firstly, every intelligent or regular reader of the newspapers knows precisely what terrorism is, to his or her own satisfaction; secondly, for political reasons, no definition will achieve universal agreement. The hardships are illustrated by a case in September 1985, when three Palestinian terrorists boarded an Israeli sail-cruiser hitched overnight in the marina at Larnaca, in Southern Cyprus. Three Israeli tourists on board became hostages at gunpoint. This was undoubtedly a classic terrorist act. The threat of violence was amplified by the first actual violence the one woman on board was fatally shot at. But even as terrorism experts and journalists began to discuss the new security risks represented by the incident, it developed in quite unexpected ways.

It raised question whether the incident then was really terrorism, or did it merely have that appearance while in fact being part of an intelligence war. The problem for observers is that everyone knows what terrorism is until they seek to define it. Nevertheless there are objective standards by which one can define terrorism whatever claims the terrorists make for themselves as 'freedom-fighters' or 'commandos for justice'. If an act has specific features and fallouts, terrorism it is. Even if a terrorist act is carried out by a diplomat or soldier of a legitimate state, the agent can objectively and impartially be called a terrorist.

— Terrorist acts or campaigns have two levels of objectives. Tactically, the objective is publicity, and recognition of a problem or claim. For the terrorist with a cause to promote, the advertisers' apocryphal saying holds true: all publicity is justified, and bad publicity is better than none. Terrorism without publicity is a weapon firing only blanks. At the strategic level, the objective is absolute change — freedom, independence or revolution.

— Terrorism always involves a criminal act; the use of the threat of violence against the person in crimes of murder, kidnap or hostage-taking; the perpetration of violence against property and assets in vandalism, arson and bombings.

— Terrorism presents the unprecedented danger of a readiness to kill at random, not in anger or hatred, but deliberately to demonstrate a political shockwave with the intention of bringing forward change.

— Terrorism is not war, subject to conventions which define the immunity of many classes of persons. Many terrorists claim a fake legitimacy by asserting that they are in a 'state of war' with a government. However, they ignore those rules of war which define neutral territory and non-combatants and forbid the taking of hostages and atrocities mrted out to prisoners. Indeed terrorism may specifically attack the soft, civilian, undefended targets because of their normally accepted immunity.

— Terrorism involves surprise and therefore required to be planned an structured in advance, though individual targets may be selected more for reasons of opportunity than anything else.

— Terrorism plays no-part in riots - impulsive public disorders which may share some political origins with terrorist actions. Though the violence or anger involve may have similar effect to terrorism on the public audience, riots lack any calculating element of political blackmail.

— The terrorist is almost never a lone individual — clearly the actions of deranged individuals should be excepted, even though they may have some strange sounding political fantasy directing their actions.

— The left has no monopoly on terrorism, though leftists often condemn studies of terrorism for ignoring its right-wing exponents. Terrorism perpetrated by the left consists of far more incidents, damage and victims than that of the right, but the right acts in a far less systematic, more random and more deliberately shocking manner. There is no doubt that the occasional major neo-fascist attacks, for instance in Italy, with as many as eighty dead in a single incident, have helped create an atmosphere of public abhorrence which has in turn been directed more determinedly and certainly more successfully — against the somewhat less murderous, though still dangerous terrorists of the left. Neo-fascist terrorists are less in number, more militaristically secretive and inaccessible, and occasionally subject to the protection of the co-conspiratorial state.

— Terrorists are never likely to fail to claim responsibility for their violence. Without political motivation, mere criminal violence would have no impact or repercussions.

— Terrorism is broadly considered to be the antithesis of assassination in the spectrum of political violence. Assassination dictates the selective killing of an individual enemy in the hope that his policies will one day perish with him.

— The physical target of a terrorist act, the individual victim, may be less significant, even random, in itself; the most important 'target' is the larger audience. Terrorism is designed to produce a psychological effect far wider than the concrete results of a particular unruly incident. The murder of one police officer, or the bombing of one military factory, implies and intends an enduring threat to all such officers and factories and to the society in which they operate.

Campaign of Terrorism

Almost every campaign of terrorism will develop according to a predictable pattern of incidents and stages. The first event will in all likelihood be a bombing, causing damage but no casualties, followed by a telephone call, usually to an international news agency, either directly claiming responsibility for the dastardly attack or giving instructions on where to find a 'communique' which does so:

If the terrorists manage to survive the security response to their use of random violence, they will begin to enjoy a magnificent sense of their power, believing themselves to be the enemies and equals of the state. The faction, organised probably in a cell-structure with a central command and individual cells which do not contact each other, will be compelled to live amidst increasing secrecy. Clandestine life ironically requires all the more support from those sympathisers who sustain the outlaw terrorists while not involving themselves in 'active service'. As its victory fails to arrive, the terrorist outfit will often divert its attention from the obvious primary targets to secondary targets, sometimes in a zeal almost of petulance. The Armenian terrorist organisation, ASALA, for instance, moved on from assassinating Turkish diplomats (and sometimes their close relatives) to attacking the airlines and tourist offices of other countries which are involved in trade and exchange air travel with Turkey. ASALA also attacked the French government because it had not supported the Armenian cause despite the considerable Armenian population in France.

This pattern of events, though by no means infallible, holds true for most terrorist outfits, even those few cases whose struggles have already lasted many years. Terrorists are not politically ignorant, and they certainly see that the prospects of genuine success via terrorism are dim indeed. What they also see and the sheer volume of states' security apparatus, rhetoric and reaction confirms it is that terrorist tactics guarantee and audience. And that too guarantees the future of terrorism, for anyone with a grievance has first to get a hearing; and when peaceful representation fails to provide one, violence — as the Palestinians and Armenians have shown achieves it promptly, intensely and urgently.

Terrorism, therefore, is a subversive activity which, while close to simple, violent 'common' crime, belongs particularly to the invisible, dispossessed, powerless and unelectable fragments of political opinion in otherwise orderly states. Seizure and exercise of power by the disorderly power of life and death over hostages, power of negotiation with police and armed forces, power of press attention and power of fear over large sections of the population inevitably scandalises, outrages and undermines those who lead and rule their states by consent and through electoral process. Terrorists kill one man to threaten a thousand, or to intimidate an industry; to breed public insecurity; and to compel governments into reconsidering the policies which generate these violently negative consequences in otherwise orderly states. For the purposes of definition it is particularly important to distinguish it from two close relatives of distasteful political stand on the one hand, state terror, and on the other, guerilla warfare.

Some even argue that terrorism and state terror are two sides of the same coin, and that to distinguish them is to discriminate against the already-oppressed political minorities in favour of an unexamined *status quo*. But the concept of state terror is a separate subject: the actual number of incidents and victims infinitely outweighs the toll of terrorism, and is in many ways far more significant and deserving of increasing international concern. When the state terrorizes its own masses, it commits an offence more intolerable even than the terrorism perpetrated by a particular group which is essentially powerless.

State terror is the abuse of legitimate power, of the methods of control generally available to a state for more or less legitimate purposes of national defence, domestic order and state security. The concept of a political state is meaningless unless its government has the right to exercise such powers in specific and reasonable circumstances.

State terror can often be the breeding-ground for terrorism—or of its military cousin, guerrilla warfare: though they in turn are not at all the same thing. For quite some time the words 'terrorists' and 'guerrilla' were used interchangeably, but inaccurately. The phrase 'guerrilla war' gives the right military emphasis, and it is more properly interchangeable with 'insurgency', a form of warfare that military men easily recognise what domestic police and security forces fail to do. While terrorism is the outgrowth of conventional political protest, guerrilla activity is the preamble to civil war.

— Guerrilla outfits usually operate in semi-developed states or in the less urban areas of the state, while terrorism almost always has an urban setting.

Guerrillas almost unfailingly hold territory within the state which they wish to oust, or have a secure cross-border base; they usually have the direct support of a state hostile, and probably adjacent, to the one they are opposing.

Guerrillas generally launch on the state's infrastructure: its transport, communications and energy arteries (railway lines, power stations, telephone exchanges, factories); while terrorist mostly fix their targets on the political figureheads and symbols.

Guerrillas often abduct or coerce civilians to join them and fight against the existing government, while terrorists are extremely careful in screening their recruits.

Guerrillas operate relatively openly and have a form of military command structure, engaged as they are in semi-conventional warfare; while governments normally respond to terrorist campaigns with enhanced police activity and legislation, guerilla warfare brings a military response.

It is of considerable interest in this context to review the remarks of two men whose names are frequently invoked in reflections on terrorism and guerrilla warfare. Fidel Castro, who led a significantly successful and popular peasant revolution to overthrow the Cuban ruler Battista, had once argued that the place of the guerrilla is the countryside and that the city 'is the graveyard of the revolutionary freedom-fighter'. Che Guevara, who fought with Castro and later died in combat, wrote a substantial handbook called *Guerrilla Warfare*.

Political Criminality

Having attempted to define the objective criteria by which an individual act of political criminality can be categorised as terrorism, we should embark on the 'political agenda' of the phenomenon. In the simplest possible terms, states take sides in almost all international political arguments, border disputes, historical grievances and revolutionary unrests. In taking sides, national self-interest too often overrides the observance of objective criteria — thus much of the agenda of terrorism in the present-day world is set in the context of states' understandable, but real, biases.

Identifying terrorism is not a matter of mere opinion, nor of fashion. Yet the single most widely accepted observation about terrorism is also the most misleading — the statement that 'one man's terrorist is another man's freedom fighter'. This should not, of course, be convincing. If terrorism can be objectively defined the definition should be applied where appropriate but it is an indication of the political leverage the word enjoys that while some commentators have dismissed the cliche as confusing, they have simultaneously demonstrated the partiality which has given it currency.

In a gesture which was equally guilty of political bias, President Reagan had twice issued official declarations listing 'Terrorists States' from the White House. No one could have been surprised that the lists named only states which were already deeply hostile to Washington's global influence and interests. By the same evidence, the terrorist action of an ally can be overlooked entirely. The French Secret Service sabotage of the Greenpeace vessel *Rainbow Warrior* in Auckland Harbour baldly labelled 'terrorism' by the incensed the then New Zealand Prime Minister David Lange - has not provoked Washington's condemnation. The attack was certainly masterminded to intimidate Greenpeace and its surviving activists from their course of physical observation of French nuclear testing in the South Pacific; but France did not appear on any of President Reagan's lists of terrorist states, reserved as they are for purposes of political abuse rather than objective judgements. In the present age of terrorism, the need of the hour is to define it in official publications and speeches, and not unexpectedly the definitions differ according to individual political factors.

In France, where a revolutionary constitution presents distressing problems in separating terrorists from political refugees, a Senate report of 17 May 1984 began its analysis of the problem of terrorism with five pages devoted to 'The Quest for a Definition'.

The report's 'Analyse Descriptive' can be summarised as follows:—

1. Motivation ... the first element to be taken into consideration...
2. Terrorism is a mediated phenomenon, and in a double sense. The victim of a terrorist act is the messenger as much as the target. The victim carries the message to the real addresses who are the most numerous and widespread witnesses possible. ...In a second sense the terrorist act brings into play an active pedagogy: the important thing is not the act in itself but the hold on conscience or the revelation that it involves from the spectator or the participant of the necessity and the possibility of important changes in the organisation of society.
3. Terrorism is a communications phenomenon.
4. Terrorism attempts to win hearts and minds.

The Senate report concluded in these terms:

Finally, and since one knows that any definition is practically guaranteed to fail, let us restrict ourselves to remembering that the terrorist act is an act of violence which tries in a legitimate state to impose a broadly minority. For that purpose it makes use of the effects of surprise and mobilises reactions of fear among a public that is not very prepared for this shock treatment.

It is perhaps in the nature of the French approach to terrorism that their definition should be wide-ranging and explanatory. In the official publications of United States agencies, on the other hand, terrorism is defined in a cold and explicit manner. The State Department's Office for Combating Terrorism a division with an impressive brief in itself - carries the following definitions inside the front cover of its periodic statistical reports:

Terrorism: The threat or use of violence for political purposes by individuals or groups, whether acting for or in opposition to established governmental authority, when such actions are intended to shock, stun, or intimidate a target group wider than the immediate victims.

International Terrorism: Terrorism conducted with the support of a foreign government or organisation and/or directed against foreign nationals, institutions, or governments. International terrorism has involved groups seeking to overthrow specific regimes, to rectify national or group grievances, or to undermine international order as an end in itself.

Although the first definition offers considerable clarity, the second is a description of almost any kind of international hostility short of a large-scale war, and lends itself to the prejudiced employment of the term against political enemies. In September 1984, the State Department's annual survey 'Patterns of Global Terrorism: 1983' carried two simplified definitions, with a disclaimer.

There are a wide variety of definitions used by experts to describe the phenomenon of terrorism, but no single one has gained universal acceptance. For purposes of recording and coding data on terrorist incidents, we have adhered to definitions that represent a middle ground within the broad range of expert opinion, both foreign and domestic.

Terrorism is premeditated, politically motivated violence perpetrated against noncombatant targets by sub-national groups or clandestine state agents.

International Terrorism is terrorism involving citizens or territory of more than one country.

But these were not the only US official definitions. Alongside the State Department's there is an FBI definition, which predictably focussed on the criminal aspect of terrorism: 'Terrorism is the unlawful use of force or violence against persons or property to intimidate or pressurise a government, the civilian population, or any segment thereof, in furtherance of political or social objectives.

Clearly the most important definition for any state which has the rule of law as its basis, is the legal definition. Until recently, a number of terrorist acts were not properly defined under American Federal law, and terrorists could largely be prosecuted under State law for the common crime aspects of their actions. The increasingly high-profile political role of Central Government in responding to terrorism was only reflected legislatively in 1984, when the United States Congress passed into law the Comprehensive Crime Control Act.

The reaction and rhetoric employed by political leaders following the terrorist attacks is probably essential yet almost certainly futile. Legal definitions of terrorism can improve the management of the problem for police and security agencies to a minimum extent, and give a public impression that the phenomenon has a high priority: but they rarely diminish its incidence. It is considered, nothing can be more useful to terrorists than that after their attack, which will have generated its own publicity, the pot should be kept boiling by politicians' or police and security authorities' condemnations. Given that they have made the fearful decision to proceed with violence, one should assume that they are immune to the criticism as such what they regard as a benefit, simply, is the widening publicity for the cause.

Terrorism both the event and the response to it does offer a platform, it does deliver an audience, and it does communicate a message that is most likely heard by no other means. That is exactly why terrorism has such a profoundly unnerving effect upon the 'governing classes'. Studies of terrorism, and political initiatives to deal with terrorist outfits, have approached the problem as a mere question of mechanics, and have been distinguished by the absence of real insight into the thinking, motivation and strategies of terrorists. Academics have studied the case histories of terrorist activities, causes and individuals as a branch of historical studies. Experts in international defence and strategic studies examine terrorism in the context of the dynamics of power-alliance. Military men present terrorism as another form of military campaign - as insurgency or irregular warfare to which military tactics can be applied.

Psychiatrists and psychologists debate the family history or the technical sanity of the individual terrorist. All these approaches have some interest, but none of them has much value without the essential recognition that in some (and increasingly abundant) circumstances, terrorism makes sense and offers hope to groups of people who see no other route to achievement. This proposition

— apparently revolutionary in all government, political and security circles — is actually self-evident. But to admit that one can identify intellectually, if not emotionally - with the terrorist subverts the received wisdom that he is beyond the pale, a kind of pathological leper. To call someone a terrorist dismisses his claim upon human sympathy.

However, unpleasant the political illness may be, to determine it accurately must be the first step in reducing the symptoms and ultimately controlling, if not curing, the disease. The case for terrorism, for the small and die-hard factions, is that it is the only weapon (but a potent one) available to those for whom the political process is discredited, or too slow to deliver. Governments prefer to explain terrorism backwards — taking the massacre and destruction as evidence of psychopathic tendencies. Instead they should regard terrorist acts as a logical step, if one that inspires revulsion, towards substantial political gains, derived from recognisable political objectives and frustrations.

Only when governments replaces rhetoric with an acceptance that, for some, terrorism makes sense, will they step closer to containing or reducing it. Terrorism can work for ill-motivated states and even the powerful nations, because its low-tech methods are cheap, mobile, deniable and less drastic than the commitment of conventional military force; and simply more effective than diplomacy.

A world in which some states denounce terrorism while others employ it is not susceptible to simplistic formulas. Though some government reactions are a propaganda effort to marginalise the support or likely support for terrorist groupings, a propaganda war rarely ends in victory for either side. It is simply not possible for any government to protect everything and everyone, everywhere and constantly. The terrorist can strike at anyone, anywhere, at any time.

Two

Small Weapons of Terror—Guns

The weapons of terror have become industrialised since the Old Man of the Mountains sent his Assassins armed with their long knives to convince his enemies of the justness of his cause and Jael, one of the first of the 'freedom fighters', carried out the political assassination of Sisera by hammering a tent peg through his skull. But the three prime requirements of such weapons remain the same: availability, simplicity and efficiency. Other requirements have been added over the years. It is necessary for terrorists to be able to kill a number of people from a distance, so fire-power has become significant. This entails the use of automatic weapons but not those with too rapid a rate of fire, for the limited amount of ammunition that can normally be carried on a mission of terror precludes its waste. To conduct urban terrorism, weapons need to be concealed, so miniaturisation is also essential. When these features are added to easy access to guns, the bullets to fit them and the simplicity which precludes weapons jamming at the very moment, the perfect weapon of terror emerges.

The following weapons possess these requirements to a greater or lesser extent; some are more efficient than others but they all carry the same guarantee of usage. These are the chosen weapons of terrorism.

Kalashnikov or AK 47

This Russian assault rifle is the perfect weapon of revolution. The brilliant invention of a Siberian peasant boy who became a soldier and designed weapons while he was recovering after being wounded in the tank battle for Bryansk in the Second World War, hundreds of thousands of various models of this rifle have been made in the Communist countries and supplied to Russia's clients and revolutionary movements around the world. It is the standard weapon of the Iron Curtain nations, the Arab armies, the Palestinian movements, Cuba and the armies of black Africa. It functioned in Vietnam under conditions which jammed the American M16. Solid and dependable, it was the weapon for ill-educated peasant armies. There had been reports that the IRA also had a small number. Two hundred and fifty of them were seized when the IRA arms ship *Claudia* was nabbed in 1973.

Assessment: This excellent weapon is reliable and, despite its short barrel, not noticeably less accurate than Western rifles. It has excellent stopping power. Captured Kalashnikovs were preferred by American troops in Vietnam and by Israeli soldiers to their own weapons.

VZ 58 V Assault Rifle

This Czech designed and made weapon was used by the three Japanese Red Army terrorists when they conducted the massacre at Lod Airport in 1972, using buttless VZ 58s and grenades which they had hidden in their luggage. Following this, a unit of the Japanese Red Army gave itself the name: VZ 58.

Assessment: This effective weapon resembles the AK 47 but differs in design and manufacture. It is not as foolproof as the AK 47 in that it can be assembled and fired without the locking piece thus creating an explosion in the breech.

Skorpion VZ 61

This cozy, Czech-made machine pistol is one of the most desired weapons of terrorism. It was used by the Red Brigades to kill Signor Aldo Moro, and ballistics showed that it was the same gun which had been used earlier to kill Signor Francesco Coco, the chief prosecutor of Genoa. It has also been supplied to a number of African countries and forms a significant part of the arsenal of urban guerrillas in Southern Africa. It has been used particularly by assassination gangs in Johannesburg. It also figured in the cache of weapons left behind by Carlos in one of his Paris hideouts, and it was also used in the attempted assassination of Princess Ashraf of Iran in Juan les Pins, September 1977. It is a standard weapon of the Czech security forces.

Assessment: This has all the qualities for a weapon of terrorism. It has an effective rate of fire and is deadly at close range. It can also be fitted with a highly efficient silencer. The silencer lessens the effective range to about a hundred yards but as terrorist operations are rarely carried out at a range of more than ten yards this is of no result. The silencer, apart from deadening the sound of shooting, has the additional quality of spreading the shot around, giving the weapon something of a shotgun feature making a hit more probable. It is no longer being made; existing stocks are being sold off by Omnipol.

Heckler and Koch MP 5

This sub-machine-gun was developed from the G3 rifle which has been a standard arm of Germany and thirty-four other countries for quite a long time. Made at the Heckler and Koch factory outside Stuttgart from designs being developed by the German Army towards the end of the Second World War, the G 3 is also manufactured in Britain and France. The sub-machine-gun version has become almost as widely used by terrorists. It is particularly favoured by the Baader-Meinhof gang's successors and was used in the abduction of Herr Hans-Martin Schleyer in Cologne in September 1977. The MP 5 has been issued to the various police forces of Germany and has also been bought by the security forces of many other nations. Those used in the Schleyer kidnapping, in which three bodyguards and a driver had been killed, were among a batch stolen in Switzerland. A drawing of the MP 5 set against the background of a five-pointed star forms the insignia of the Red Army Faction which carried out the abduction.

Assessment: This conforms to the highest standards of German automatic weapon production. It fulfils all the requirements and is particularly suitable for German terrorists because it can be stolen from police armouries, and the ammunition is also available in quantity.

Armalite AR - 18

This American designed rifle is the weapon of the IRA terrorists who lay up in ruined buildings or seize flats with a commanding view and then pump a burst of small, high-velocity rounds into an army vehicle or patrol. Originally made as the successor to the AR-16, America's standard infantry weapon in Vietnam, it was not adopted by the US Army because so many AR-16s had been produced. It has however been manufactured commercially in Japan, California and, under licence, by the Sterling Armament Co. in England. The IRA has acquired some of these weapons from Japan but most of them come from the gunshops of New York state where they are bought legitimately and then smuggled. Some of these AR-180s have been modified by IRA gunsmiths to fire bursts but most remain single-shot guns and are only issued to expert shots who are able to get off three or four aimed rounds very fast. It is the weapon which has killed more British soldiers than any other in Ulster.

Assessment: This weapon's accuracy and the penetrating power of its small bullet make it a fierce weapon. The bullet can penetrate body armour, medium steel plate and steel helmets at 500 yards and inflict a devastating wound. The impact of even a minor wound inflicted by these high velocity rounds can kill. It is, however, too large a weapon to be used in a normal terrorist operation.

Thompson Sub-machine-gun

This weapon, which achieved such notoriety as the gangsters' 'Chicago Piano', was originally designed by General John Thompson as a means of breaking the impasse on the Western Front in the First World War by giving Allied troops portable fire power for their attacks on the well-defended German trenches. Its prototype, was called the 'Trench Broom' but it had not been accepted by the authorities by the time the war ended. Then, despite its gangster phase, it languished until the outbreak of the Second World War when it was put into mass production and used in quantity by the Allies. By then, however, it had become the favourite weapon of the Irish Republican Army gunmen in the trench coat and Tommy Gun era. The IRA has retained its affection for the gun and although it has been replaced by more modern sophisticated weapons there are still a number of well-oiled Thompsons hidden in rabbit holes and barns throughout Ireland — and some of them are occasionally taken out and used. It is estimated that nearly a million and a half of various types of these guns had been made. Also used in London by the Angry Brigade England's native terrorist movement of the Baader-Meinhof type. It collapsed in 1972, when most of its members had been arrested and sent to prison for long terms the following year.

Assessment: A first-class Second World War field weapon which proved extremely effective for house-clearing, it is too big and cumbersome to impress to modern terrorists. The old-fashioned drum magazines which held either 50 or 100 rounds are still available but these gangster models tended to jam under field conditions and were substituted by straight boxes in the military version.

Sten Sub-machine-gun

Mass-manufactured for the British Army and the European resistance movements during the Second World War, over two million Sten guns were made and its development, the Sterling, is still in service with the British Army. With this great number of weapons spread around the world — thousands were parachuted into occupied Europe — many drifted into the hands of terrorist outfits. They were, however, too large for most urban terrorist work and have largely been replaced by smaller, more effective automatic weapons in the European and Middle Eastern terrorist groups. One of them was found among the armoury of the Balcombe Street gang and, like the Tommy Gun, it was brought out of its caches during times of trouble in Ireland.

Assessment: This excellent mass-produced weapon provides automatic fire at close range but, because it was mass-produced, has several quirks which are still dangerous to its users even today. It tends to jam so that it will not fire or, even more disconcerting, jams on full automatic. This was principally because the lips of the stamped metal magazine could easily be damaged. The fault was largely corrected on later models.

M1 Carbine

This Second World War weapon, like the Tommy Gun and the Sten gun, has virtually disappeared from the armouries of terrorism. Two of them were among the weapons captured from the Balcombe Street raiders who were the most successful of the Provisional IRA's Active Service Units operating in England. It was developed by the Winchester Arms Company, the design being accepted in October 1941 only one year after the United States Ordnance Department had issued a specification for a light rifle. Production began almost immediately and the huge total of 3,527,827 of various marks of this carbine were produced by nine companies.

Assessment: This carbine was chiefly suited to jungle warfare, being light and handy, and for that reason is also suitable for street fighting. Reliable and safe with no vices, it was once a useful weapon for training recruits and is used in that role by the IRA.

Beretta Model 12 Sub-machine-gun

This compact, accurate weapon is one among the Beretta series of sub-machine-guns and is issued to commando units of the Italian Army. It has also been sold to countries in Africa, South America and the Middle East. Two of these were among the equipment used by the Carlos group to mount the raid on OPEC headquarters in Vienna.

Assessment: This weapon ranks with the Czech Skorpion as one of the most efficient automatic weapons. It is sleek, elegant, having two safety systems. With its metal stock unfolded it can also be used effectively at longer ranges.

Astra .357 Magnum

This is the Big Bertha of assassination weapons. The size of its bullet and its tremendous power makes death almost an inevitability if it is used at close range. The Balcombe Street group used it to kill the right-wing propagandist Ross Mc-Whirter in 1975 — because he had offered a reward of £50,000 for the capture of the 'Active Service Unit' which was then terrorising London. This particular gun was found in the Balcombe Street arsenal and was matched by ballistics experts. A similar gun was used to kill businessman Alan Quartermaine while he was being driven home in Chelsea in 1974. Ballistics tests showed that the gun that killed Quartermaine was used to cover the retreat of an IRA squad after a bomb attack on the Naval and Military Club in Piccadilly in December 1974.

Assessment: This highly efficient weapon's only drawback is its size. It is one of the most powerful handgun in the terrorist armoury.

M52 Pistol

Another well-made, reliable weapon designed and made by the Czechs who had appeared determined to remain independent of the Soviet's armouries. Has been phased out of front-line service in Czech Republic and passed on to various 'liberation groups'. Carlos had a large quantity of these weapons in his various caches in London and Paris. He used one of them to kill Michel Moukharbel, the friend he thought had betrayed him, and two French police personnel, and seriously wounded Commissaire Jean Herranz in the shooting in the Rue Toullier after he was being arrested.

Assessment: At the close ranges at which terrorists are taught to use pistols, any reliable weapon is just as powerful as another when it comes to killing. Where the M52 differs, however, is in its extremely powerful cartridge which gives it a muzzle velocity of more than twice that of an old-fashioned British service revolver. It is definitely an assassin's weapon.

Browning High Power Pistol

This is probably one of the best known of all the automatic pistols. Designed in 1925 by the gun genius John Moses Browning it was used throughout the Second World War by the Western Allies and was also made in Belgium for the special use of the SS. Many thousands have been produced and it has drifted into general use all across the world. It was a gun of this type which Carlos had fired at Teddy Sieff, President of Marks & Spencer, in December 1973. If Carlos had used the M52 its even higher powered cartridge would probably have taken the Zionist leader's head off. Ballistic tests revealed that the Browning found in Carlos's London cache was the gun which had been used in the Sieff operation. Gudrun Ensslin of Baader-Meinhof was carrying one of these guns when she was nabbed in a boutique in Hamburg.

Assessment: This reliable, effective weapon for close-range work is easily available and there is no difficulty in acquiring suitable ammunition. One of its benefits is the large capacity of its magazine which holds thirteen rounds.

Makarov Pistol

This is the Communist equivalent of the Browning pistol and is in general service with the Russian-supplied armies of Eastern Europe and Soviet client countries. It is also made by China. Like the Browning, many thousands have been made and it is now in general use throughout the world. It has come into terrorist hands chiefly through the Arab terrorist organisations which have been supplied from the Soviet armoury. The most spectacular operation in which it has been used was the Carlos-led assault on OPEC headquarters in Vienna on 21 December 1975. Each of the six-strong kidnap team carried a Makarov as a personal weapon along with a mixed bag of sub-machine-guns, grenades and other explosives. Gabrielle Krocher-Tiedemann, one of the German Baader-Meinhof gang who was involved in this operation, carried two. With them she murdered two men, an Austrian policeman and the bodyguard of the Iraqi oil minister. Carlos used his Makarov to murder senior member of the Libyan delegation who grappled with him and almost succeeded in wresting his sub-machine-gun from him. Gabrielle was arrested gun in hand by Swiss police along the French frontier in 1977.

Assessment: This has been a solid reliable piece of work. Simple to use, it proved its worth as a close-range weapon of terrorism in Vienna.

Tokarev (TT-33)

This Soviet pistol was replaced by the Makarov in the Eastern European countries but is still effective and is used by many Asian Communist countries with numerous instances filtering through to Arab terror groups. One variant, the 9 mm Parabellum Tokagypt, has a curious history. It was made in Hungary and supplied in large quantities to President Nasser when he was seeking the arms rejected him by Secretary of State Dulles. The Egyptians were, however, not too keen on it and deliveries were halted. It was these pistols on which Ulrike Meinhof and Andreas Baader were instructed to shoot at an Arab training camp in Jordan and which eventually became the standard weapon in the Baader-Meinhof armoury. A number of Firebirds were bought by gang member Rolf Pohle from German gunshops. He used counterfeited papers and licences but was eventually caught when an arms dealer in Ulm became suspicious of his papers.

Assessment: This is an old-fashioned pistol in the classical style, but despite its military obsolescence it is still an effective weapon of terrorism — as the Baader-Meinhof faction has proved.

Walther P38

This pistol is so popular with the Italian Red Brigade faction of terrorists that they have become known as the 'P Thirty eighters'. In 1975 they started a clandestine journal entitled *Mai piu Senza Fusile* ('Never without a gun') and the P38 was that gun. It has been used in abductions and particularly in the crippling shootings in which the Red Brigade specialises in which victims — right-wing journalists, lawyers, policemen, etc. — were ambushed.

Assessment: This is a modern weapon, in service with the German armed forces, and is available in a commercial model. It is easy to operate and works effectively under most operational conditions. It is a good all-round weapon.

Smith and Wesson Revolver

Nearly a million of these revolvers were produced from 1940 to 1945 and they became a standard weapon of the British Forces. It was also issued to police forces in England and Ireland. A huge quantities of these had come into the possession of the IRA and they have been used in many assassinations. Two of these were found among the armoury of the Balcombe Street gang.

Assessment: It used to be said by cynical weapons instructors in the British Army that the best way of bring down an enemy with one of these revolvers was to hurl it at him. Certainly it takes an expert shot to hit a man at anything over ten yards. Nevertheless, at short range this was a reliable and effective weapon and there have been many funerals in Ireland to prove it.

RGD - 5 Anti-personnel Hand Grenade

This modern Russian grenade was used by the FLOSY terrorists in Aden in their attacks on the British Army and the sight of one of these bombs rolling towards a patrol along an alley in the Crater was always unpleasant. It was used by the Viet Cong and also by Carlos and his gang during the raid on the OPEC headquarters in Vienna. Hans-Joachim Klein lobbed one of them at the policemen on guard at OPEC. Those used in Aden were made in China and were supplied to FLOSY by Peking.

Assessment: Light, this grenade can be hurled for some 35 to 40 yards and with its killing radius of 18 to 22 yards is an effective weapon. Its oval-shaped steel body has a serrated liner which bursts into a pattern of killing fragments.

SAM 7 Strela (Arrow)

The SAM 7, translated, is the seventh type of surface-to-air missile produced by the erstwhile Soviet Union. It is also known by the NATO code-name of Grail but achieved its fame as SAM 7 along with the SAM 2 and SAM 6 in bombing down Israeli aircraft during the Yom Kippur War in October 1973. Its use by terrorists was first disclosed earlier that year when Italian police raided a flat at Ostia just three miles along the main flight path from Rome's airport and there found two SAM 7s hidden in a wardrobe.

Assessment: This hand-held anti-aircraft weapon is similar to Western missiles such as the American Redeye and the British Blowpipe and like them was amplified for battlefield use by individual soldiers to protect units against low-level strafing. Its infra-red guidance control automatically homes in on the heat given off by the targeting aircraft's engine. It can be confused by electronic counter-measures and evasive action by high-speed fighters but would be dangerous against big jet liners approaching slowly along a flight path. Its drawback is that its high explosive warhead is not particularly powerful and a well-built aircraft could, if not hit in the key area, survive its explosion. Its advantage as a terrorist anti-aircraft weapon is that it can be carried around in the back seat of a car and fired whenever a target comes within its range.

M26 Grenade

This is a standard American Army weapon, known as a fragmentation grenade because of its coiled inner liner which is indented to fragment when the grenade explodes and so cause the maximum number of casualties. This has given rise to its own language; American troops in Vietnam who thought that their officers were becoming too interested in their search for a fight with the Viet Cong were apt to throw an M26 into the officer's fox hole. This became known as 'fragging'. This grenade later became notorious as a terrorist weapon after a large number were stolen by the Baader-Meinhof gang in 1971 from the US Army base at Miesau in Germany. They were used by the Japanese Red Army in their occupation of the French embassy in the Hague in September 1974; by Carlos when he had killed two and wounded thirty-four uninvolved customers in his attack on Le Drugstore in Paris designed to coincide with the Japanese occupation of the embassy; and were carried by his group during the OPEC raid in December 1975. The use of this stolen batch of grenades, traceable by their serial numbers, enabled the security forces of Europe to connect links between terrorist outfits as the grenades were passed on from one to another.

Assessment: The notched inner lining of this grenade, coiled under tension, makes it a deadly anti-personnel weapon, ideal for terrorist use in crowded areas where the maximum number of casualties can be inflicted and the maximum amount of terror caused.

RPG-7 Portable Rocket-launcher

This Russian weapon is the artillery of terrorism. It was used extensively by the Viet Cong and had started to be feared by the American Army both in its role as an anti-personnel fragmentation weapon and as an anti-tank rocket which could blow the turret off a modern tank. It has been supplied to the then Rhodesian rebel organisations and to the various Palestinian groups. In purely terrorist terms it was used twice by Carlos' gang in Paris when they attempted to destroy Israeli passenger jets on the runway at Orly. It seems possible that this was the weapon which a mixed German and Palestinian 'commando' attempted to use against an El Al plane at Nairobi Airport in 1976, another raid which was thwarted by an Israeli secret service tip-off. They have also been used against British Army posts in Ulster by the Provisional IRA, a small batch being supplied by Colonel Gaddafi. A much larger consignment was captured when the arms ship *Claudia* was captured off the Irish coast on the last stage of its run from Libya.

Assessment: This is not a particularly accurate weapon, especially at long distance and in high winds. Nevertheless it can do a considerable amount of damage. It is simple to make - Al Fatah has its own RPG factory — and easy to fire, but care must be taken to make sure no one is standing behind the weapon when it is fired, as the burning gases from the rocket motor can cause almost as much damage as the grenade itself. It gives an individual the ability to deliver an explosive charge the equivalent of a medium gun shell and then pick up the launcher and another half a dozen projectiles slung in a bandolier across his shoulders. In urban guerrilla parlance it gives the terrorist an artillery capacity denied the security forces in the early stages of confrontation.

M60 General Purpose Machine-gun

A great furore was made early in 1978 when the IRA paraded one of its newly-acquired M60s, standard equipment in the American Army. Between three and six of these machine-guns were believed to have been smuggled into Ulster from the Middle East via Cyprus and Antwerp concealed aboard a tanker. They were exhibited during a parade marking the sixth anniversary of 'Bloody Sunday' (when the British Army opened fire during a riot in Londonderry and killed thirteen).

Assessment: This is an excellent infantry weapon but it has serious limitations as a weapon of terror. Most terrorist weapons are used in ambush and in urban surroundings. The M60 has too fast a rate of fire, is too heavy and too long to be a profitable weapon of urban warfare. An essential of this type of warfare is that a weapon should be light, simple and not require more than one man to handle it. One is left with the feeling that anything an

M60 can do in their role, an Armalite can do better. It is in fact a weapon of propaganda rather than terror.

The Japanese security forces, clarifying after the student attempts to block the opening of the new Tokyo airport, had discovered several examples of a new weapon of terror, a sophisticated 'cattle prod', a two-pronged electrical staff about three feet long connected a current-producing belt pack. This weapon could deliver a charge of some 500 volts and was capable of knocking a man out and, in some cases, of killing.

Three

Big Weapons of Terror—Bombs

The modern terrorist's bomb still fulfils the same function as the crude device of 'the Professor': it is used to carry out killings; or threaten to kill, and thereby destroy the economic and social fabric of a country, to instil fear; in fact, to terrorise. But the bombs themselves, their mechanisms and their explosives have become far more efficient. They are easier to manufacture, safer to handle, can be made much smaller, and can be triggered by a variety of ingenious methods, thus enabling them to be used in situations which were out of reach of nineteenth-century terrorists. Terrorists of that period could derail a train but they did not have at their mercy Jumbo Jets carrying nearly 400 people at 600 miles an hour 35,000 feet above the ground. The derailing of a train could kill a number of people but when an airliner is blown out of the sky everybody dies. So not only are today's bombs are more effective, they are also capable, because of the development of mass air travel, of causing far greater losses in human and material terms and of instilling fear. It is this potential which makes the aerial hijacker's slab of plastic explosive such a powerful weapon.

In this chapter, we propose to show how the modern bombers carry out their business. If the information is not as detailed as some of our readers might wish it is because we have set out to report how things are done and not to provide a textbook on how to prepare bombs. Almost every schoolboy knows how to mix gunpowder and pack it into a cardboard tube to make a firework, quite a number know how to make explosive out of fertiliser. There is a great deal of expert knowledge freely available. We do not wish to make it any easier for people to make bombs but intend to demonstrate how the bombers use their explosive expertise to attack society.

Role of Security Forces

One of the tough tasks of the security forces is to cut the terrorists' supply of explosives. When the terrorists are supported by countries with diplomatic representation this becomes virtually impossible, because those countries which actively encourage terrorism have no compunction about using the diplomatic bag to smuggle weapons and explosives to their surrogate warriors. Libya has been particularly to blame in this regard. Colonel Gaddafi has often used his diplomatic missions abroad to supply Soviet-made arms and explosive to 'anti-imperialist' terror groups in many different countries.

The advantage of such a supply route is that once the supporting country has decided to send arms, the terrorists do not need to go through any risky step to obtain them, the lines of communication are secured by diplomatic usage. The explosives supplied are of a military type, usually plastic, which is stable and can be moulded to any required shape.

Palestinian terrorist outfits are also heavily involved in the supply of arms and explosives to groups which support their cause. The favourite explosive is again military plastic. The stability of this explosive makes it easy for it to be smuggled — sometimes moulded into simple, cozy shapes like children's putty — by boat, car, even the rucksacks of travelling students.

The second main source of supply is the theft of commercial explosives from mines and quarries. It is a simple matter to raid the magazines of deserted workings and such raids, often with the connivance of sympathisers on the workforce, have provided much of the explosive used by the IRA and the South American uprisings. The Angry Brigade used French commercial explosives in their bombs. These explosives, Nitrotex, Nitromite and Gomme L, were handed over to women couriers by French sympathisers and smuggled into Britain on the cross-Channel ferries.

Another way of obtaining explosives is by raiding military establishments. But any terrorist who does this must be prepared for a pitched battle if things go against his plans. It is a tactic pursued more in South America than anywhere else. An even more desperate method, usually only attempted by guerrilla movements in the earlier stages of development, is to remove the filling from unexploded shells and bombs. This is a very risky method and those who practise it are more likely to meet a sticky end than their enemies.

Having obtained the explosive, the terrorists need to build it into an 'infernal device' and provide the fuse to set it off. Fuses come under four vital headings: flame; chemical; electric; and mechanical.

Flame fuses are probably the least used because their comparatively fast burning time allows the bomber little time to get clear of the explosion and because the burning fuse provides visible proof that something nasty is going on. Military or commercial fuse of various types provides a fixed burning rate per foot, so that the time between ignition and explosion can be judged by cutting the fuse to a specific length. It is fitted into a detonator, normally a metal tube about two inches long filled with a sensitive explosive, usually fulminate of mercury. Such detonators can also be exploded by firing a cap similar to that used in the base of a bullet cartridge, or by passing an electric current from a battery through a fuse wire or a wire filament similar to what is used in a light bulb.

Chemical Weapons

Chemical fuses are basically similar to the fuse used by 'the Professor', but modern methods require a phial of acid to be crushed inside something which provides a time lag. The most popular is a rubber contraceptive. The acid gradually burns through the rubber before it comes in contact with the chemical and produces the spark which set off the explosive. Metal containers can also be used. And if the contraceptive is faulty, the result could be even more embarrassing than if it were used for its proper purpose. In their previous bombs the Angry Brigade used a combined chemical-mechanical fuse in which sulphuric acid dropped slowly on to a retaining tape.

Electric devices are the most common form of time fuse. They involve the use of clocks and watches wired so that when the hands reach a particular position on the clock face they touch terminals connected to a battery which then, with the circuit completed, sends a charge of electricity through the detonator and helps in explosion of the bomb. Baader-Meinhof used clockwork egg-timers to provide the spark for some of their bombs, and in Belfast the IRA bought up a supply of the clockwork buzzers which tell you when your time is up at the parking meter.

Another method is that familiar to moviegoers of wires strung from an explosive charge and connected to a plunger which when depressed produces a current and sets off the bomb. This version is commonly used to set off heavy charges placed under roads, in culverts and hedges or in buildings. A plunger is not always necessary. The charge can be exploded by completing the circuit on a battery. But a disadvantage of this system is that it needs wires to be trailed through a building or across fields and they can be detected by security patrols.

A more remote and therefore safer form of electric fuse is the radio fuse. By using the same system as that used for controlling model planes and boats, the bomber can send a signal which will explode his bomb immediately.

Mechanical fuses at their simplest are aroused by pulling out a safety pin which releases a spring which in turn either causes a firing pin to strike a detonator as in a hand grenade, or closes an electrical circuit or, by friction, produces a spark. These fuses can also be set off by opening a door, lifting the lid of a box of chocolates, or opening a car boot, an action in fact which involves the movement of some component.

Pressure fuses are another simple type of mechanical detonation. A bomb may be set under a car seat or a floor board or a mattress so that the pressure of the victim's body will release a plunger and so explode the bomb. A more sophisticated pressure bomb than this is that used in aircraft.

At its simplest, the modern bomb is still crude. The IRA uses several sticks of gelignite or dynamite bound together and set off by a short length of combustible fuse. These bombs are mostly wrapped with six inch nails or coach bolts which form a lethal burst of shrapnel when the bombs explode. Other simple bombs are constructed of lengths of pipe filled with pieces of metal junk, which with a specific grim humour the IRA calls 'shipyard confetti'.

The problem for terrorists in making these crude devices is that they are so simple that every raw recruit thinks he is a professional, and before they learn the faults of their ways it is too late, they have 'scored an own goal' and blown themselves to pieces.

Commercial Explosive

The use of commercial explosive which has started to degrade, to sweat, is one cause of accidents. And so, amazingly enough, is the practice of smoking while making bombs. One theory is that it was a carelessly handled cigarette which causes the Weathermen to blow themselves out of existence when they were manufacturing bombs in their Greenwich Village headquarters in 1970.

In their campaign designed to wreck the economy of Ulster the IRA have learnt that fire is their best ally. With explosives, and especially detonators, becoming more difficult to obtain, they have turned away from big, destructive bombs to easily concealed small ones which they cover with tins of petrol. One of their favourite devices is an incendiary bomb made out of a tape recorder cassette.

A common form of car bomb is the device concealed inside a car designed to kill the driver. There are a number of types, the simplest being the 'Mafia' type which is a bundle of explosive wired to the starting system so that when the ignition is switched on car and driver are destroyed. This was used so frequently that most people at risk prudently inspected their engines before switching on. This precaution was circumvented by attaching plastic to exhaust pipes which exploded when the pipes grew immensely hot, or, as in the case of Mohammed Boudia, who was PFLP's chief operative in Europe, putting a pressure bomb under his seat. He was killed by an Israeli hit squad and his death had the unforeseen result of bringing Carlos on to the terrorist scene, for Carlos, 'sleeping' in London, was called upon to replace Boudia.

Professor Gordon Hamilton-Fairley, the cancer specialist, was killed in October, 1975 when he bent down to examine a doubtful package under his neighbour's car. It was designed not for him, but to kill his neighbour, Tory MP Hugh Fraser, a forthright opponent of the IRA, when he drove off.

Another manner of killing a man in a car is the 'big bang', designed to destroy a vehicle as it passes a certain spot. The British Army has become only too familiar with mines buried in the roadside.

The IRA had a special liking for culvert bombs, packing explosives into the drains which ran under so many Irish roads. The army had become very suspicious of these culverts and always checked them before driving across. The Israelis used to do exactly the same in the early 1970s when Palestinians would cross the border and lay culvert mines. But the Israelis had a special tool for doing it — a girder sticking out of the front of an armoured car with a steel plated seat welded to the girder's end. The crew members of the armoured car would then take it in turns to perch out there and examine the road surface for mines and wires. It was truly a hot seat.

It was a matter of shame and stupidity that similar expertise was not used to guard Christopher Ewart-Biggs, the British Ambassador to Dublin who was killed by a culvert bomb 180 yards frcm his official residence in July, 1976. There is no doubt that a routine inspection before he left the house would have found the mine, which consisted of at least 100 lb of explosives and was detonated by wire from a wooded hill some 300 yards from the road.

Another man assassinated by a version of the culvert bomb was the Premier of Spain, Admiral Carrero Blanco in December 1973. He had made the mistake of travelling by the same route every day.

The Israelis are considered to be experts in the use of letter and parcel bombs. Bassam Abu Sherif, spokesman for PFLP, is hideously scarred — the result of opening a similar box of chocolates — and a number of other Palestinian officials have been murdered and wounded by letter bombs.

A most unusual form of letter bomb came to light in October, 1972 when a Dutchman of Jewish origin received a letter posted in Karlsruhe, the then West Germany. He was suspicious and passed the letter to the police, who found it was not letter bomb but a poison gas bomb. It contained 40 grams of cyanide in powder form.

Another terrifying development in bomb-making was perfected by the International Spanish Communist Party, a Maoist faction, who in January 1976 taped a bomb to the chest of Dr Joaquin Viola Sauret, a former mayor of Barcelona. The bomb was boobytrapped so that it could only be safely removed when instructions were sent by the terrorists. These instructions were not to be given until specific demands had been met. But the bomb went off prematurely, killing Dr Sauret and his wife and injuring one of the terrorists.

Barometric Bomb

Perhaps the most cynical form of terror device is the barometric bomb. This appalling weapon is designed to demonish an aircraft in flight and therefore everybody on board, innocent men, women and children, even sympathisers to the terrorists' cause, all die.

In August 1972, two Palestinians in Rome, Adnam Ali Hashan and Ahmed Zaid, picked up two English girls on holiday. The girls fell for the handsome Palestinians who suggested they should all go to Israel. The girls consented and the Arabs bought them tickets to Lod Airport and gave them a tape recorder. At the last moment the two men, who were posing as Iranians, said they had to fly to Tehran to collect money. They had made plans to meet in Jerusalem. The girls, fortunately, did not carry the tape recorder on to the plane as hand luggage but had it put in the hold with their other luggage. It was filled with explosive and its barometric firing device was set to explode when the plane reached a certain height. It exploded perfectly as it was designed to do, but the force of the explosion was contained by the armoured hold, built into all El Al planes following tests with explosions in mid-air over the desert. The wearisome, crushed plane landed safely, and when the two girls told their story, Hashan and Zaid were arrested in Italy.

Radio-fired bombs were of another form to come from the bombers' bag of tricks, and at first sight they seem to have the advantage over all other bombs of being absolutely under the control of the bomber. There is no need for him to set light to a fuse or to start a mechanism which will inexorably fire at a fixed time — unless it is stopped manually — or even to trust the uncertain effect of acid on a contraceptive. He can decide when the explosion is going to occur. He can make adjustments for unforeseen circumstances. He can advance or retard the timing of the explosion.

And he can do all this from safety with nothing seemingly connecting him with the bomb. He might even be out with his son, playing with his radio controlled aircraft. All he has to do is to send a certain signal and the bomb blows up. There is a limitation, however, for if the security forces are sufficiently adept at signals intelligence, there are ways and means for them to send signals which would certify that the terrorists were blown up with their own bomb.

And that brings us to booby traps. Almost anything can be boobytrapped. A man's pipe can be boobytrapped so that it blows his head off the moment he lights it. A dead soldier can have his backside stuffed with explosive so that he blows up the men sent to carry him in. With a sufficiently wild imagination allied to a sober expertise, anything can be boobytrapped. And dealing with the traps involves wearisome, dangerous battle of wits between the bomber and the bomb disposal squads. Occasionally the two sides get to know each other's work very well, even to appreciate the finer aspects of a good technical piece of work carried out by the opposition.

Another anti-handling device is a photo-electric cell which explodes the bomb when it is exposed to light, either by the opening of a suitcase bomb. Then there are 'trembler' devices which are activated after a bomb has been carried to the place where it is to explode. When it has been set any movement will cause a steel ball to roll or a pendulum to swing, either action completing an electrical circuit and so exploding the bomb. The simplest-looking bomb of a type which the bomb disposal expert defuse can be adjusted to contain one or other of these devices. It was in this fashion that the Balcombe Street gang killed bomb disposal expert Captain Roger Goad in August 1975.

One other type of bomb remains to be discussed, the ultimate: the nuclear bomb. In essence the terrorists' tasks in constructing a nuclear weapon is almost the same as that in making a conventional bomb. First he has to acquire the material and then he has to build the bomb.

The Royal Commission on Environmental Pollution, headed by Sir Brian Flowers, put the technical aspect of building a 'nuke' into perspective in a report in September 1976 when it said: "The equipment required would not be significantly more elaborate than that already used by criminal groups engaged in the illicit manufacture of heroin." In fact the technical know-how is well within the range of one of the IRA's bomb experts, a point made by the French magazine *L'Express* (27 January - 2 February 1975), which presented a summary of a group of terrorists stealing containers of nitrate of potassium from a factory. 'It is not necessary', the magazine said, 'to be a Noble prize-winner to extract plutonium from this solution'.

Report of Royal Commission

In 1976 a report by the Royal Commission on Environmental Pollution stated that could make a crude but effective nuclear weapon using plutonium and argued that the government had not appreciated the full implications of this possibility. It also stated that members of the commission who visited nuclear installations in Britain got the impression that not enough attention was given to some aspects of security. We understand that their criticisms concentrated largely on the lack of security on shipments of radio-active material. As in America, security arrangements have now been strengthened and the Ministry of Defence is playing a large part in guarding shipments.

Ralph Lapp, the American nuclear scientist, estimated that a worker taking out twenty pellets of atomic fuel a day for 160 days would accumulate enough plutonium to make a bomb equivalent in power to the one that had destroyed Nagasaki.

The blackmail potential of such a weapon is enormous. A leaflet, *Towards a People's Bomb*, which was published in London in 1972 by a London group called Undercurrents, told its readers how to extract plutonium and even published a diagram of a crude bomb. It might have functioned, but the implications of its threat were that if it was detonated in the left luggage office in Charing Cross station, it would demolish among other things 'Buckingham Palace, the Houses of Parliament, Scotland Yard and the Elephant and Castle — not to state vaporising a fair chunk of the River Thames'. What government could resist the demands of a terrorist group if evidence was given that a nuclear weapon had been placed in just such a spot? The whole world could be held to ransom.

There are other ways in which countries can be held to ransom or even dealt crippling blows by terrorists and individual fanatics. Water supplies could be poisoned, the theft of nerve gases — one minuscule drop of which can kill a man — could create panic, and as was seen at the beginning of 1978, agricultural terrorism could be employed to wreck a country's economy. The discovery of a few Jaffa oranges injected with mercury had a serious effect on Israel's citrus fruit sales. An organisation called Arab Revolutionary Army claimed that it was 'poisoning thousands of export-selected oranges before plucking' and 'poisoning thousands of oranges during export preparation'. 'Our aim', it asserted, 'is not indiscriminately to kill your population, but to sabotage the Israeli economy.'

The fact remains that the people who jabbed the oranges with mercury-filled syringes were able to induce fear. And that is what terrorism is all about. That sense of fear would be multiplied a million times if all the dangers of a nuclear explosion — explosive destruction, fire, radioactive poisoning, the genetic impact on future generations — were used in the cause of terrorism. The 'Big Nuke' is the ultimate weapon of terror.

Four

Terrorists: Behind the Mask

'George Washington was a terrorist. To describe a man as a terrorist is a term of honour'. So spoke one of the Baader-Meinhof defendants following his arrest in Germany. The thinking behind this statement is that acts of violence are not criminal when carried out in opposition to the force used by a state which is itself supposed to be criminal by the terrorists concerned. The German Red Army Faction believed that the American war in Vietnam was an 'unfair' one, and that in this respect it might be compared to the eighteenth-century English war against the American revolutionaries.

One man's terrorist can well be another man's freedom fighter. While that may be true with respect to historical movements opposing national tyranny when no other means were available, it is more formidable to sustain it considering terrorist movements in the last decade which have cut across recognised national and ideological parameters. In the cases we have already considered, Ireland and Palestine, there are obvious, though confused, territorial targets for the violent movements involved. But many of the outfits now most active kidnap and kill to achieve objectives which are international, doctrinal and revolutionary for revolution's sake. Their campaigns involve guerrilla and terrorist leaders who, unlike the guerrilla squads of the Irish and the Palestinians, have received better than average education and often come from prosperous families.

In the case histories so far considered only the leaders are persons of superior education. Dominant terrorists and the theorists who enthuse them have the conviction that they can impose their beliefs on others. But for every one who goes on to become leader of a powerful politico-terror movement, for every one who ultimately becomes head of state or prime minister, there are thousands of common soldiers of terrorism. They can expect only death, imprisonment or disillusion.

Little is recorded of their personalities, or even their fate. Yet only by examining flesh and blood instances is it possible to discover what makes such a terrorist, and to decide why young men and women forsake their studies and abandon their careers with a view to take to the political maquis. Fortunately, those terror groups which operate in Europe and in Japan are now better known, and their personnel can be examined in more detail. The best documented are Baader-Meinhof, the Japanese Red Army, the Red Brigades of Italy and unimportant groups of the same sort in Britain and the United States — the Angry Brigade and the Weathermen. All share almost the same emotive political convictions. 'One of our tasks is to lay bare and liberate the type of man who wants revolution, who must have revolution because otherwise he would fall apart,' opined Herbert Marcuse in one of his lectures (in *Five Lectures*). In another context that is our task too, and it is certainly true that some have indeed fallen apart.

The case of Hans-Joachim Klein in this context is equally significant. Born in 1947 he became involved with the Red Army Faction in Germany by way of friends with whom he lived in a Frankfurt commune. This settlement was connected with a revolutionary publishing enterprise called Red Star. There, he met Klaus Croissant, who sympathised with the Baader-Meinhof outfit and became one of their defending lawyers. Croissant later fled to France to escape charges of helping the terrorists plan operations even while they were incarcerated.

In Frankfurt Klein met Carlos, and it was as one of Carlos' men that he took part in the raid on the OPEC conference in Vienna. He was shot during the raid, and although he was badly wounded the gang took him to Libya where he received treatment from a German doctor before disappearing into the terrorist underworld.

Early in 1977 he sent a remarkable letter together with a set of his fingerprints to prove the letter's genuineness and a Czech-made pistol and ammunition to the then West German magazine *Der Spiegel*. Klein declared that thinking about the Vienna affair during the two months it took him to recover from his wound had brought him to the decision to abandon terrorism. His letter told of his disillusion:

> What I heard in a month about the way in which revolutionary violence would bring about a fairer and more humane world made me sick. This was a cause for which I would have gone into the streets. Both my own experiences and the plans I heard about at that time gave me food for thought. That was the most important thing that happened to me ... I haven't changed from Saul to Paul, but from Saul I have changed back to a person with sensible political thinking and behaviour ... For this I had to pay a hell of a price

In Germany

In Germany although some have turned aside in horror from the movement they once backed, and although the leaders, Ulrike Meinhof, Andreas Baader and Gudrun Ensslin, have taken their own lives in despair in prison, the movement they launched still exists and kills.

In the beginning it was hope and humanity which inspired the young recruits to the Red Army Faction, for they were inculcated with the enthusiasms of the New Left for reforms of the universities and of society in general. But the movement went on after the universities had carried out the reforms for which the students had fought. It was still intellectual and its members were almost all middle class. Indeed, except for one euphoric moment in the course of the Paris revolution when the masses seemed to be following, the workers had never shared the revolutionary zeal of their betters. In Germany most of the early supporters were to be found in the ranks of clergymen, doctors, professors and journalists.

The protest finally turned to violence, for it was not enough simply to march and shout slogans. The first stages of violence in Germany had to do with the Third World and in particular the war in Vietnam. They had to buy the weapons, at first from Palestinians who were well supplied. In order to pay the Palestinians they robbed banks. And to rob banks they needed more weapons and getaway vehicles and so it went on. Even those who became involved for high-minded reasons found themselves gun in hand, launching assaults at the forces of law and order, for had not the police killed Benno Ohnesorg in Berlin without any real reason? They began to feel that they were acting in self-defence.

As had already happened in other parts of the world when terrorist outfits turned to bank robbing, they soon attracted recruits drawn more by the idea of easy money than by idealism. A case in point was Karl-Heinz Ruhland, a motor mechanic, and therefore so far as the Baader crowd were concerned, a bonafide member of the working class. He needed money to pay off his debts and when they asked him to doctor stolen cars for the gang, he agreed — provided that he was suitably rewarded. He had not, he said, ever heard of this Marighella that they mentioned but promised to read a pamphlet and help to make the revolution. Immediately he was asked to take part in bank robbery. They gave him a sub-machine-gun and off they went to rob the bank. Nervously, Ruhland was hopeful that no one would give the alarm - 'All they had to do was to stay nicely away from their desks so that the police were not called too soon and I would not have to start shooting.'

The German groups provide numerous instances of the many different paths by which people get caught up in political violence. Some of the most die-hard members joined Baader-Meinhof through the influence of Dr. Wolfgang Huber, a Heidelberg psychiatrist, who taught his group therapy patients that only a major revolutionary change could cure the sick capitalist society of the then West Germany which, he said, produced nothing but sick people. The Socialist Patients' Collective (SPK) which he founded had a 'Working Circle (Explosives)' led by Frau Huber, where the patients learned how to make bombs. Among those who attended was Siegfried Hausner who took up bombing on behalf of the Red Army Faction in order to heal his own mental disorders through therapeutic attacks on the 'sick' society. He helped to plant bombs at the Hamburg offices of Springer Publications and he subsequently died after blowing himself up with his own bomb during the raid on the then West German embassy in Stockholm in 1975.

Some joined for money, some for therapy, some for excitement. When the Bonnie and Clyde image of Baader-Meinhof had spread, others joined the movement attracted by the combination of excitement and the possibility of sexual pleasure. Others considered terrorism as a kind of student happening 'with arms'. Yet the original members remained to the end self-righteous, arrogantly of their own moral and intellectual superiority.

Ulrike Meinhof, the most intriguing study among the Germans, had more complicated motives for changing her life-style and becoming a terrorist. As the star columnist of *Konkret*, a popular mixture of soft porn and radical politics, she had a wide following and she placed an overwhelming seal of respectability on the Baader-Ensslin arson attack in Frankfurt by praising it as a daring act of criminality.

She had been brought up by a gentle but firm foster mother only a little older than herself, Dr Renate Riemeck, a Christian pacifist. As a student Ulrike became a nuclear disarmer and then moved on to condemn the comfortable and prosperous society of the Federal Republic. This rather attractive woman, by then married to the playboy publisher and editor of *Konkret*, was successful and well-to-do. She appeared a thoroughly unlikely candidate for service as a terrorist leader.

Her marriage to Klaus Rainer Rohl was not a happy one and after the Frankfurt episode she left her home in Hamburg taking her twin children with her and set up for a while in an upper-class commune in a smart section of the erstwhile West Berlin. Plunging into the subculture world, and the world of student politics at the Free University, she came into closer contact with Gudrun Ensslin, a daughter of the manse, brought up as a devout Protestant, who, through pacifism, had moved on into the anti-authoritarian protest movement. Gudrun and her lover Andreas Baader had already taken to political violence. When Baader had been arrested and imprisoned she joined with Gudrun in plotting and then executing the raid which freed him. She literally hurried into the new life through the window of the library where Baader had been allowed to work. She had broken the law and was committed to a new life as a terrorist.

Jillian Becker in her excellent book *Hitler's Children* brought her own novelist's insight to bear on the real reason for Ulrike Meinhof becoming a terrorist. Writing of Baader and Meinhof making off together she had this to say:

> An illusory sense of power and a certainty of victory would make them feel their own capabilities to be great. Each could seek personal relief through acts of violence and blood and terror, and always with a grandiose moral justification. They could call a lust for revenge 'a thirst for justice', and terrorism a righteous fury that 'society' had called down upon itself. In Ulrike's case 'society' was an euphemism (which she could not recognise, her insight into her own motives not having matured with her years) for her own feelings, and for Klaus Rainer Rohl. And her committing of herself to a life outside the law was a venture to overcome not governments, nor systems, but private despair.

Certainty of Victory

Andreas Baader too became a terrorist because he was dark, handsome, attractive and braggadocio. He was more interested in getting girls to bed than in getting the world put to rights, for till then as he was concerned politics was all meaningless. Only by accident had he come to read Marcuse and the other philosophers of terror, and the accident was named Gudrun Ensslin, already a devotee of political action. They found each other highly compatible sexually and she prepared with him and took him off to live in Frankfurt. It was there that they celebrated their initiation into terrorism by setting fire to the department store.

Although Andreas Baader learned to parrot the correct slogans, there is little to show that he had any genuine political convictions. He took naturally to the rather comfortable life of the West German terrorists. There had always been enough well-heeled sympathisers who could permit themselves the luxury of lending flats and providing money for those who had wanted to overthrow the society in which they flourish. In Germany, students, teachers and professional people had all given help to the terrorists. 'Sheltering a Red Army man on the run is almost as good as setting up your own operation,' remarked one student. Providing refuge for fugitive terrorists has been described as both a patriotic duty and a protest against the system. On several occasions Baader-Meinhof members, even those who were known to have had murdered and maimed people, had been given protection by German clergymen and priests.

And even more remarkable fact of the situation in Germany was the number of women, most of them young and attractive, who took part in terrorist operations. The fact that no less than half of the twenty-eight most wanted urban guerrillas on the police list in the then West Germany were girls shows that they are much more than just terrorists' molls and providers of safe houses.

Attention was again drawn to women terrorists during the Red Army Faction's onslaught in the summer of 1977. When they raided the opulent home of Juergen Ponto, one of the country's most influential bankers, and killed him, it was his 26-year-old god-daughter who got the killers admitted to his well-protected house. 'It's me, Susanne,' cried the girl, Susanne Albrecht, and she carried with her a bunch of roses to give to her godfather. There was a struggle — possibly the intention was to kidnap him — and he was shot dead. Susanne, had been a student at Hamburg University before dropping out to join squatters' groups, graduating to terrorism and becoming instrumental in bringing about the murder of the man who cared her like a daughter.

A Hard Core Woman Terrorist

Another notorious woman terrorist, who led a desperate prison break-out, is Inge Viet, who, like Susanne, had hailed from Hamburg. Two other girl terrorists were in the group which broke out and escaped: Gabriele Rollnik, a sociologist from Dortmund, and Juliane Plambeck, a student of philology from Munich who was on the list of fifteen people suspected of complicity in the murder of Hans-Martin Schleyer. Miss Plambeck's other claim to fame was that she was known among her male comrades as the 'trophy for the erotic challenge cup'.

Yet another group of female terrorists was that known as the Croissant Group, because, according to the authorities, they were mainly recruited through the lawyers' office in Stuttgart run by

Klaus Croissant. Before he escaped to France, he ran a 'lawyers' collective' and devoted most of his energy to looking after their interests. Susanne Albrecht was one of those who worked in his office. Two other girls were known members of the same faction and thought to be connected with the Ponto affair — Angelika Speitel, and Silke Maier-Witt, intelligence office for the group. Just how these young women, most of them hailing from decent families, came to involve themselves with terrorism remained a puzzle to the West German authorities for a long time.

One of the theories put forward by psychiatrists and criminologists to explain why so many German women were involved in urban guerrilla movements is that it had provided them with a form of liberation. Armand Mergen of Mainz University perceived that the girls need to emancipate themselves through violence. Because they were from good homes and had been well educated, they considered themselves superior to men and had wanted to display that superiority in action. This was probably the true reason why women terrorists had aimed to be more brutal than their male colleagues.

A contrary theory is that the girls had become sexually dependent on their male comrades. There is no doubt that sex is powerfully connected with political violence in the elitist groups we are examining. Certainly so far as the European factions are concerned there is ample evidence that many who took to the gun and the bomb had started out by living in communes where partners were easily swapped and where experimental sex had been part of the everyday life. Many of the most active terrorists were marijuana smokers and some had taken to heavier drugs. Excitement, sensual pleasure and comfortable living outside normal routines while still enjoying widespread approval for the high-minded ideology preached, had been all incitements to young people to involve themselves.

There was another factor to be considered when dealing with the German groups is that the post-war generation of students seemed obsessed by killing and death. How far such feelings were prompted by memories of the Hitler period and the horrors of the Nazi system of which their parents were a part had been a question which needs much more detailed investigation than is possible in this book. Even so it is worth observing that there had been something unnatural about the pleasure taken in German universities at news of the murders and kidnappings of 1977. After the kidnapping of Dr Schleyer, wall writings at Heidelberg proclaimed, 'It is impossible to hide our joy.' The delight expressed in university pamphlets issued by some groups on the fringe of left-wing politics gave the impression that these faction had a hatred of the very concept of parliamentary democracy as well as its 'bourgeois' representatives and institutions.

Views of a Journalist

Kurt Reumann, a well-known German journalist after analysing such pamphlets in *Encounter* (October 1977) pointed out that following the murder of Herr Buback, the Federal public prosecutor, the publications placed the moral guilt for his killing not on the terrorists but 'on that sociological catch-all, namely social conditions'. So many of the outfits were approving murder and asking 'Who will sentence to death Herr so-and-so? that he felt compelled to ask: 'Is the spirit of death abroad in the land?' It is undoubtedly true that in the decade of West German terrorism the feelings of compassion and humanity which stirred an entire generation into political action were soon corrupted into an avenging use of brutality in which those amiable qualities were lost. Despite the confusions in personality and upbringing of the leaders of the Red Army Faction, they had founded a movement which remained among the most feared and powerful in the world of international terror. Those early members who survived and the new recruits who had joined them seemed not only more brutal, but also more effective and more skilled with their weapons than those who launched the movement.

As the German outfits became more violent after the end of the Stuttgart trial in 1977 at which the original leaders were sentenced to long-terms of imprisonment, a similar movement on the other side of the world had moved into action. The Japanese Red Army, which had been dormant for two years, carried out a successful hijack in September 1977. By seizing a Japanese DC8 airliner in Bombay and threatening to blow it up and kill the passengers of many nationalities they compelled the Tokyo government to pay a ransom of $6 million and to release six of their members imprisoned after earlier raids. It was a dramatic reactivation of the movement.

The Japanese Red Army shares many features with the German Red Army Faction. Its members, though more mystical, proclaimed the same general philosophy and the leader had been a woman, Fusako Shigenobu. The hijack to Bangladesh marked the thirty-second birthday of this fanatic who had been called to 'Red Queen of Terror'.

Fusako Shigenobu was born into the new Japanese society of the economic miracle following the Second World War and like her political sisters in Europe she had passed into the university ferment of the 1960s. Vietnam again was the cause, though in the case of the Japanese they also protested over American occupation of Okinawa. The first act of her fanatical career was when she had smuggled oak staves hidden in golf bags to demonstrators besieged in Tokyo University.

The Red Army, composed of a small group of students, intellectuals and other middle-class supporters, failed to farewell in Japan. It was because of its failure on home ground that Miss Shigenobu and her supporters shifted towards the Popular Front for the Liberation of Palestine. Eventually a number of Red Army people went to the Middle East for guerrilla training in the refugee camps. It was in Israel at Lod Airport that the Japanese carried out their most gruesome action, slaughtering twenty-six people with grenades and machine-gun fire. Significantly, it was from the Middle East in 1977 that Fusako Shigenobu plotted the Bombay hijack which restored her Japanese Red Army as a fighting force, and it was Leila Khaled who collected the ransom amount for the Japanese Red Army and the PFLP.

In a letter to the PFLP newspaper, *Al Hadaf*, Shigenobu spelled out the main theme of her terrorist philosophy following an earlier hijack.

> These two operations were staged to consolidate the international revolutionary alliance against the imperialists of the world. We in the Red Army declare anew our preparedness to fight hand in hand with Palestinians and wage joint onslaughts at any time to defeat the Israeli

> enemy. We should not be bound by international laws or by resistance within the framework of these laws ... because only revolutionary violence would enable us to defeat imperialists throughout the world ...

Other leaders of the Red Army followed the same themes, adding more detail. They masterminded acts of terror which they hope would spark the peoples' revolution, a revolution which would destroy capitalism and imperialism. Emperor Hirohito was one of their prime targets. They believed he had borne responsibility for the death of millions in the Second World War. But despite these grandiose aims the Red Army has spent most of its effort in trying to free its own members imprisoned in their earlier actions. And they were bound to the PFLP because they could not survive without the sanctuary and financial and logistic assistance provided by the Palestinians.

At his trial in Israel, Kozo Okamoto, the one survivor of the Lod raid, gave a frightening insight into the mentality of the Japanese terrorists. He was, in his own words, a soldier preparing for the Third World War — 'We believe slaughtering of human bodies is inevitable. We know it will become more severe than battles between nations.' Such blood-curdling thoughts give enough indication of the feelings of the Japanese Red Army and the fanaticism of the men and women in its ranks. Even though the group is not large enough in terms of manpower it has the capacity to create yet more bloodshed in the world.

The Red Brigades which terrorised Italy for several years had strong affiliations with the other 'Red' revolutionary bands elsewhere in the world but the historic leaders of the movement were young people of extravagant personality. The life of Renato Curcio, best known of the founders, is the stuff of which grand opera is made. Although the background from which he came was comparable with that of the erstwhile West German comrades there had been extra touches which can only be described as Italian.

His father, a member of the Zampa family and brother of a famous film producer, Luigi Zampa, had a respectable position in Roman society. Married to an elderly American heiress he busily conducted other affairs, even within his own household. Like all great men in history before him he had been imprisoned for what he believes.' According to her, Renato had a perfectly normal upbringing and she could recall no traumatic events in his early life which might have impelled him to become a revolutionary.

After the death of Renato Zampa's wife he offered to marry Yolande. She refused though she did accept money which provided her son with an excellent education at good schools in Italy. Finally he went to Trento University in Northern Italy, a place which specialises in sociology and — as had been expected — was a hotbed of revolutionary activity.

One of the key witnesses for the prosecution at the prolonged trial of Renato Curcio and his friends was Silvano Girotto, a 39 year-old Franciscan suspended from his religious duties. Known as the 'Machine-gun Friar', he all of a sudden appeared in Turin dressed in jeans, anorak and gym shoes 'to denounce these criminals'. But this strange personality had himself played significant role in the Red Brigades, which he joined in 1974 at the suggestion of a Carabinieri, Captain Pignero, to spy on their activities. He was already known as the 'Machine-gun Friar' because he had developed a reputation as a guerrilla fighter in Bolivia and in Chile. Whether or not this was justified is not known for the Friar was a fantasist who also claimed that he had once joined the French Foreign Legion. Be that as it may, he was accepted by the comrades of the Red Brigades and was soon on friendly terms with Renato Curcio and acquainted with their organisation. Finally he denounced them to the Carabinieri and this made possible the arrest of Curcio. At the trial he declared: 'I was convinced of the absurdity of their methods from the start'.

Renato Curcio's first steps into terrorism were taken in 1972 when he and his friends seized 'enemies of the people' such as Etteri Amarilo, a Siemens official who had been personnel manager at Fiat. They also seized a man called Bruno, described as a Fascist trade union leader. In each case after a mock trial before a 'People's Court' they thrashed those men and released them. After some members of the gang had been arrested they kidnapped a state prosecutor to try to secure their release.

In 1970 Curcio met and had married a 25-year-old fellow student at Trento named Margarita Cagol. This thoughtful and gentle girl, the daughter of a rich Catholic and conservative family was, until she took up sociology, mostly interested in music and dancing. There can be little doubt that it was the revolutionary atmosphere of Trento University which drew her into the world of terrorisms.

For her doctorate Margarita wrote a thesis on German workers' movements. Soon she was at work with her husband and his friends trying to convince Italian workers to occupy their premises and begin the great revolution. In this they failed to convince the workers. Many of them were die-hard Communist Party members and had no wish to involve themselves with and take orders from a bunch of sociology students.

Role of Revolutionaries

In despair Renato and his friends decided like many other such revolutionaries with a mission, even if the others stubbornly refused to follow. They heaped scorn upon the workers for their bourgeois attitudes and attacked the Communist Party for its divisive attitudes towards the softer brand of Eurocommunism. More and more strongly Curcio identified himself with an uncle called Armando who had died fighting the Germans with an Italian separatist unit.

With support from southern groups known as Armed Proletarian Cells, Curcio and his wife began raiding in the Baader-Meinhof manner. They collected ransoms, kidnapped and murdered those they considered their enemies. In 1974 Renato was taken by the police but only a few months later Margarita led an armed attack on the prison at Castal Montferrato and rescued him.

That same summer of 1975 the Red Brigades kidnapped one of the Gancias, the Italian wine and aperitif family, and held him in a 'People's Prison' — a secluded farmhouse in Piedmont. There the security forces discovered them and besieged the farm for several days before making the final assault.

Renato survived as a terrorist leader for almost a year before he too was wounded and arrested. Threats and fresh terrorist acts continually postponed his trial and that of other squad leaders arrested with him. When the trial did finally start at Turin early in

1978 terrorists still at large shot dead one of the supremos of the anti-terrorist group and then kidnapped and murdered Aldo Moro, one of Italy's most respected politicians.

Thus, only a few months after the autumn of terror launched by the Germans and the Japanese it was the new model Red Brigades which marched to the centre of the world terrorist stage. Although the Moro kidnapping and the murder of high officials was seemingly planned to secure the release of the old leaders from prison, events showed that the new men of the movement were tougher and better organised than the original 'Robin Hoods'. For weeks on end they were successful in throwing the state into disarray.

Compared to the West Germans, the Japanese and the Italians, the Anglo-Saxon groups, who to some extent believed in the same causes, had appeared extremely mild. Nevertheless, there were those in Britain and America who set out on the same road, and similar groups soon revived under a harder leadership to bring the same methods of terror to bear in London and Washington.

The best known of the white, as opposed to black, terror movements in the United States was the small outfit called the Weathermen. It came into being as a result of squabbles at a conference in June 1969 of the SDS. Many supporters visited Cuba and Vietnam and, fired with enthusiasm for those places, they began learning to make Molotov cocktails ready for the attack on American society. They declared that unlike their models in the Third World they would make anti-national revolution, for otherwise they might fall into the trap of imperialist, national chauvinism. The student revolutionaries tried in vain to merge with the Black Panthers. They made arson raids, and it is claimed that the Weathermen had taken part in some 500 incidents of bombing and raiding in 1969. They planted a bomb at the University of Wisconsin and demanded that the Officers' Training Corps there be demobilised, and that Black Panther leaders under arrest should be released.

The Weathermen were really the creation of Mark Rudd from Columbia University who proclaimed himself a Marxist devoted to the destruction of a 'corrupt imperialist pig society'. His aim, similar to that of the European comrades, was to provoke the authorities into repressive action and to make it appear that brave resistance forces were fighting against the forces of repression. But most of their actions were more like student happenings than genuine guerrilla operations. They were designed to shock the bourgeoisie and its morality by, for instance, killing and eating an alley cat and expressing admiration for the murderous orgies of the Manson 'family'. On one occasion, however, they stole material from a biological warfare store and even threatened to infect city water supplies.

It is doubtful if the Weathermen ever had more than a thousand supporters of whom very few were activists and it all came to an end suddenly when their store of explosives in a Greenwich Village house blew up. Most of the leaders were killed by this accident and the movement, already out of mode faded away. Mark Rudd, the surviving leader, had gone underground in 1970 and was not heard of again until he surrendered at the age of thirty to the New York police seven years later.

For a while at the height of public unrest about the war in Vietnam the Weathermen had looked dangerous but this highly personalised band of urban guerrillas was neither tough enough, nor devoted enough, to exist. The truth was that too many of its supporters were in its for kicks. They were 'guns and grass' revolutionaries who enjoyed the excitement for a while, appreciated the life-style more than the politics and took pleasure that they could 'epater la bourgeoisie'. When they spoke of the people, it was obvious that they had never really been in contact with them and that they were simply working off their hang-ups.

Another offshoot of the Students for a Democratic Society was the Revolutionary Union, a Maoist faction with more serious political appeal and a rather more mature following. One of the founders was Professor Franklin of Stanford University. Besides there were Robert Avakian, a student expelled from Berkely in 1966, and Steve Hamilton. Financed from China by way of a Hong Kong Communist-infiltrated union, the Revolutionary Union indeed produced a manifesto though it created less stir than the Weathermen. From it developed yet another Maoist group called the Venceremos Organisation which had close acquaintances with Cuba to which a 'Brigade' was despatched in the early 1970s.

An even more extreme group, the Symbionese Liberation Army (SLA), attracted rather greater attention by its violent activities in the United States. It claimed to be a 'loving' group devoted to drawing together oppressed minorities in the 'Fascist' United States. It had a number of apostate aims and was remarkable for the number of women it drew to the cause. Because they attracted so few militants, not more than two score, the Symbionese Army turned to dramatic activity to attract attention and publicity.

The SLA is best known for its kidnap of the heiress, Patricia Hearst, and her partial indoctrination. She was arrested along with two others trying to keep the organisation alive after Donald De Freeze, the organisation's black leader, and five others had been killed in a raid by FBI agents and the Los Angeles police at Compton, one of that city's all black districts.

The end of the war in Vietnam dispossessed the small American terrorist movements of their mainspring. None of them was able to follow the lead of the international terror groups, though there is still a danger that racism may still provide new organisations with the necessary impetus for renewed action.

In Britain too, groups tempted by terrorism have made a flimsy showing apart from the Irish 'territorial' ones already discussed. But for a time the angry Brigade, similar in some respects to the Weathermen, did cause some panic. Between 1968 and 1971 the Angry Brigade planted twenty-seven bombs and were involved in machine-gunning public buildings in Britain.

This curious English group had many things in common with the Baader-Meinhof gang and with other international terror outfits. Anna Mendelson an erstwhile English Graduate of Essex University, and a number of her friends were found guilty, and she was sentenced to ten years imprisonment, though she was released in 1977 after serving only four years. Most of the other members of the Angry Brigade were students and graduates from British universities who shared with their continental opposite numbers disappointment with the failure of the 1968 revolution in Paris. Both Anna Mendelson and John Barker, also sentenced to ten years, were veterans of the days of exultation at the Sorbonne, and they returned to London determined to further the causes behind whose banners they had marched.

The people concerned attacked the consumer society which had so concerned the French students a few years before. Then, under the influence of a Spanish terrorist outfit called the 'First of May Group', they began to use bombs to make their point, meanwhile living in communes and financing themselves by means of stolen cheques and credit card forgeries in the classical terrorist manner. When police had moved in to arrest members of the group they were beginning to imitate the Red Army Faction with raids on post offices and banks.

In passing sentence Mr Justice James, who had cautiously kept the trial as apolitical as possible, told those found guilty: 'I am sorry to see such educated people in your situation. Undoubtedly a warped understanding of sociology has brought you to the state in which you are.'

Whether as Miss Mendelson foretold those in prison had not changed it is impossible to know. But since the trial there had been no further manifestations of the Angry Brigade, or any successor organisation. So far as Great Britain is concerned at the moment the terrorist world is a monopoly of the Provisional Irish Republican Army.

In the summer of 1978 there were modest signs of activity from right-wing terror outfits in Britain. Letter bombs were sent to the Communist newspaper *Morning Star* and to a left-wing bookshop. But these were negligible incidents.

However, terrorism still flourishes in other parts of the world. The same category of people are still kidnapping, murdering, bombing and hijacking. The Palestinians had gone into action to express their disapproval of President Sadat's historic pilgrimage to Jerusalem and the Basque ETA group produced a more radical faction just as the Spanish government moved towards satisfying some of their demands. And so it continues even today. So long as the young extremists of 'left fascism' believe that violence is the sole way in which they can achieve their political aims, so terrorism will continue on a greater or lesser level according to the success of the security forces.

Five

Money: The Budget of Death

Money is the fuel of terrorism. The notion that the use of terror is the poor man's method of waging war is no longer valid. The Palestinian, South American and German groups that seek to annihilate the bourgeois way of life are among the richest sections of the affluent society.

One or two impoverished groups remain, notably the South Moluccans who pursue their hopeless campaign in Holland and who have minimal resources. Their cause is such an impossible and unpopular one that no major power, no well-established terrorist group, can see any great advantage in back them and, so far, they have not learnt to hold up banks and to kidnap for ransom. Elsewhere, the picture of the ragged revolutionary living off the country, stealing his weaponry and supplies from 'the forces of repression', is as outmoded as red-coated soldiers. Modern terrorists need to be rich and the transnational outfits need to be very rich indeed — first class airline tickets are expensive.

Ever more complicated arms have to be paid for, so do safe houses, radio sets, cars and hotel suites. The terrorists themselves have to be paid and need expenses so that they can merge into the societies in which they operate. If, for instance, an observation team of three were to keep watch over a businessman in order to mount a kidnap operation, they would need to be dressed in a fashion which would not excite comment in plushy restaurants.

Harry Duggan, the leader of the Balcombe Street gang, was described as 'looking like a junior hotel manager'. Michel Moukharbel, Carlos' administrator in Paris, was also the assassin's book-keeper and he kept detailed records of the money that he and Carlos spent on their different enterprises. Because of these details — hotel bills, train fares, car hire accounts — the authorities were able not only to trace Carlos' movements but also to build up a financial impression of the infrastructure of terror. This infrastructure closely follows the normal financial pattern of big business, even down to pension schemes for the disabled and the widows and families of men slained on 'company business'.

Gaddafi's Strategy

When Colonel Gaddafi set up his own multinational militant organisation, he set up a fund to provide this kind of social insurance. One of his men, who surrendered after hijacking a plane to Kuwait, told his interrogators that the Libyan President had promised his team before they left that he would pay compensation of £250,000 to the families of any of them killed in the enterprise. Hans-Joachim Klein, who was injured during the OPEC operation, had his pain assuaged by an insurance payment of £100,000 from Gaddafi.

And so the expenses increase. Cars cannot always be stolen— the theft could attract too much attention — and so they have to be hired. Wireless equipment has to be bought, and, if the faction is mixing its own explosives, the ingredients have to be purchased. The well placed 'sleepers' whose services are only called upon at crucial junctures have to be funded. Officials have to be bribed and yet more money is eaten up in the mundane business of running offices. People, even the most dedicated of terrorists, have to eat and drink and be attired. The air fares for a five-strong hijack team could easily amount to £3000 in addition to the money spent on the reconnaissance team which had prospected the route.

Where does the money come from? The answer to that question depends on the type of organisation involved and on the countries likely to support it. The IRA, for instance, has always relied on funds collected by sympathisers in Ireland and especially upon money donated by sentimental Irish-Americans across the Atlantic, who are accessible for the men with the collecting boxes who claim that they need the money to relieve the hardship brought about by what they term the atrocities of the British Army. Some of them of course actively support the bombers and the murderers, but most turn a blind eye to the inevitable destination of their money. Even the people who operate the Northern Ireland Aid

Committee in New York seem genuinely to believe that the money they collect will be used for humanitarian purposes.

However, after a campaign by the British government and the government of Southern Ireland to explain the true state of Provisional IRA activities to the Irish-Americans, there was evidence by 1977 that this emotional money was drying up. The raffles and the dances and the monthly commitments raised $600,000 in 1972 but five years hence this sum had fallen to $150,000. The Provos were forced to return to the classic form of terrorist fund raising — the robbing of banks. They enjoyed great success. It was estimated that they stole £2 million in 215 attacks on banks in a single year.

In one of the classic paradoxes of terrorism, it is the Palestinians, who hail from the poverty of the refugee camp shacks, who are the richest terrorists. They never needed to mount bank raids — except during the Lebanese civil war, when they were able to walk into deserted banks and load the entire contents of strong rooms on to lorries. This absurdity stems from the fact that their movement mobilised support from the Arab world at precisely the moment when the oil states of the Middle East were beginning to savour their immense, newly acquired wealth. Because even conventional and anti-revolutionary Arabs could not resist the emotional appeals to help free Palestine of the Israelis and to recover the holy places of Islam lost to the Jews, money spend into the coffers of the Palestinian organisations. This flow of money also entitled recognition by the Arab states that none of them was strong enough to withstand Israel on the field of battle and that the only way harm could be inflicted on the Israelis was by means of terrorism but obviously that was before the Arabs realised that in control of the supply of oil they had a weapon far more powerful than even the nuclear bomb.

The fact that gives this situation a touch of Alice in Wonderland is that the oil states know the fact that they themselves are next on the terrorists' list after the Israelis and yet, by the weird logic of Arab politics, they are forced to provide the money to keep the terrorists in being. They make an endeavour at rationalisation by giving their donations not directly to the terrorists but to the Palestine Liberation Organisation, but as the terrorist outfits are an integral part of the PLO, the money inevitably filters through to them and from them it is passed on to the transnational groups, thus uniting with oil money, German nihilists, Japanese revolutionaries, Latin American romantics and Turkish nationalists.

Role of Al Fatah

It was estimated in 1975 that Al Fatah, the largest of the groups which made up the PLO, had an income of almost $200 million; according to the Israelis, the Popular Front for the Liberation of Palestine, the most radical of the Arab organisations, had a similar sum at its disposal. In July 1977 *Time* magazine reported that when Yasser Arafat flew to Saudi Arabia to ask King Khalid to convince the Syrians not to attack the Palestinians in the Lebanon the Saudi government refused. But as a kind of consolation prize Crown Prince Fahd wrote Arafat a cheque for $5 million. The gift was in further the annual subvention from Saudi Arabia to the PLO of $25 million.

Saudi Arabia is just one of the sources of revenue. The Kuwaitis and the Gulf Emirates also provide substantial contributions as a type of *danegeld* to ensure that guerrillas are not tempted to get too active in their territories. In brief, the whole Arab world backs the liberation movements with money. One of the most generous supporters is Colonel Gaddafi who spares no financial effort to keep the Palestine movements in action.

In addition to his regular contributions to the funds of Palestine liberation outfits, Gaddafi also offered large bonuses for successful operations against Israel. To express his appreciation to Black September for their action at the Munich Olympic Games he gave them a cash reward of £5 million. And following the seizure of the OPEC oil ministers in Vienna, Carlos received a gift of one million pounds. In addition, ransom money for the lives of the Saudi and Iranian ministers abducted on that occasion brought some $25 million into the Palestinian coffers. Terrorism in these circumstances can be a profitable business.

In addition there are the contributions from Palestinians who live and work in the Gulf oil states and who had a 5 per cent tax 'to sustain the cause' imposed on their incomes. Colonel Gaddafi is harsher. He imposed an 8 per cent tax on Palestinians employed in his country. In addition to these sources of revenue the Palestinians receive large sums as gifts from rich individuals anxious to prove their keenness for the cause — and there is no shortage of Arab millionaires.

With such a huge income the Palestine Liberation Organisation has come to echo a multinational business corporation, with an amalgam of terrorism and diplomacy as its end product. None of its resources are considered to be used to improve conditions in the refugee camps of the Middle East where Arabs live in disgustingly squalid conditions. There is reason in this ostensible inconsistency, for the camps provide the endless flow of recruits for terrorist duties. To improve conditions there, which is perfectly possible, would remove the causes of bitterness which keep good and decent Arabs ever ready to fight and destroy Israel. Even the improverished in the camps are themselves forced to contribute their mite.

Most of the money is spent on military training and on terrorist operations. But a good deal also goes on funding the huge bureaucracy which now controls the movements. They have modern offices with executives, PR men, secretaries in petty dresses and the whole belongings of a modern business corporation — although the young men in the offices spoil the cut of their trousers with pistols stuck into their waistbands.

In addition to its headquarters in Beirut, the PLO also operates its own diplomatic service with offices which have near diplomatic status in no less than 100 nations and maintains an 'observer' delegation at the United Nations. The heads of these missions in the more important countries of Western Europe and the United States are paid up to $1,500 a month. Such amounts are in stark contrast to the pay of a guerrilla fighting man who gets only $70 plus family allowances.

During the Beirut fighting one establishment remained untouched, for it was strongly protected throughout by regular Palestinian force. No harm came to the Arab Bank Ltd., a strong financial establishment based in Amman, Jordan, and presided over by a Jerusalem born Arab. In the Middle East this bank, which has assets exceeding $4 billion, is often called the 'PLO Bank', for it is generally believed that it controls the investments made by the organisation in European and American stock exchanges. In Beirut it owns hotels and has bought land on the West Bank of the Jordan — in Israeli-held territory. Such investments give a yardstick of independence from the financial pressures of Arab governments.

Other Palestinian Organisations

In recent years the Palestinian organisations have increased their revenue by commercial endeavours such as poultry farms, night clubs and the setting up of factories and workshops for the production of handicrafts, clothes and furniture. But not all their business establishments are so respectable. Palestinian leaders have let it be known that they have made big money from the illegal sale of drugs in Israel.

In the summer of 1977 the trial and conviction in London of a British drug smuggler had revealed a profitable trade in cannabis designed to bring large sums of money to the Palestinian organisations. The cannabis, grown in northern Lebanon, was accommodated in lorries through Turkey and Bulgaria to Yugoslavia, where the hidden cargoes were split up and smuggled across Europe to Britain in secret compartments built into private cars. The supply from Lebanon declined during the worst period of the civil war but the Palestinians became active again as the fighting died down. Had the network not been unravelled by international anti-drug squads it is believed that the next consignment would have netted half a million pounds. And their traffic was a two-way affair. The transports which delivered the cannabis through Turkey were to have returned loaded with weapons made in Eastern Europe, paid for with the drug profits.

Terrorist funds, like all kinds of big money, attract corruption and criminals. Several PLO officials with notions above their terrorist station were thrown into prison for gambling away a £250,000 chunk of organisation money in Cairo's casinos. And even the more reasonable funds of the Provisional IRA have proved too great a temptation for sticky-fingered comrades. One Provo who acquired £100,000 for the cause by a specifically successful bank raid had transferred it to his own account in the United States.

Even terrorists who proclaim the purity of their motives are susceptible to the rustle of banknotes. It is one of the ironies of the modern world that the West, with its dependence on Arab oil, provides some of the wealth which is passed on to men dedicated to destroying the structure of Western society.

In other parts of the world terrorists have to work harder to make their money. A good example of self-funding is provided by the ERP, the Ejército Revolucionario del Pueblo or People's Revolutionary Army of Argentina who, although formed as the armed wing of a Trotskyist revolutionary group, might well be described as the capitalists of terror. Formed in 1970, it concentrated the activity of its military cells on fund-raising by 'expropriation' or, less politely, bank robbery and abduction for ransom. Estimated to be 5000 strong by 1974, their ranks were increased by Tupanaros escaping from Uruguay and Mirista radicals who fled from the military *coup* in Chile which ousted the Marxist Allende government.

Their initial capital came from a bank raid in Cordoba but they rapidly increased this by kidnapping a business executive whose ransom was paid at a million dollars. Not unnaturally, this success pointed the way to a profitable line of business and they switched their activities almost entirely to kidnapping the executives of top-notch companies, especially of the multinationals who had set up business in Argentina and had filled many of their senior posts with their own countrymen. The abductions, therefore, fulfilled three functions. They brought in a great deal of money; they enabled the ERP to maintain a correct radical approach; and they pleased xenophobic Argentinians by launching attacks on foreign concerns and foreign officials.

In 1972 after the completion of negotiations for the million dollars ransom of Oberdan Sallustro, a Fiat executive, the police discovered and subsequently attacked the hideout where he was being held. Four of the terrorists were captured. But Sallustro had to pay a greater price than the ransom was worth. He was murdered when the police stormed the 'people's prison'.

The following year, after a partially successful attempt to seize a Ford Motor Company executive in Buenos Aires in the course of which he received injuries, it was reported that the company had handed over a million dollars for 'protection' against any new attempt. It is not uncommon for big firms to pay up in this way in order to avoid trouble — in the same manner that some airlines make regular payments to ensure that their aircraft are not hijacked. This was one of the ERP's Robin Hood' actions. In accordance with their directives the ransom was paid in the form of medical supplies and other help for the poor.

In the early 1970s the amount of money demanded by ERP continually enhanced — two million dollars for Charles Lockwood, a British executive of Acrow Steel, three million for John R. Thompson, the American president of Firestone Tyres Argentinian subsidiary — until ultimately it reached the then record of $14,200,000 for Victor Samuelson, an EXXON executive.

Argentinian Terrorist Group

In June 1975 the Montoneros, the other main Argentinian terrorist group, who followed a leftist-Peronist philosophy, had announced that they had pulled off the most lucrative kidnapping so far. Jorge Born was held for nine months while the negotiations were conducted, but his brother Juan was so affected by his imprisonment in a 'people's prison' that the Montoneros feared for his mental condition and his life and rather than jeopardise the deal, they made a realistic business decision and released him before the ransom had been paid.

The authorities had, however, pursued another enquiry with utmost diligence. In August 1976, an executive jet with two pilots and a lone passenger crashed in the mountains south of Mexico City. The plane had been hired in the name of one David Graiver, the 35-year-old scion of the Graiver family of Polish Jews who had settled in Argentina in the 1930s and had become powerful bankers in the prevalent but unpopular Jewish community in Buenos Aires. Graiver was a financial whizkid, a flamboyant wheeler-dealer who juggled with enormous sums of money. It appeared that he had run out of luck.

When Graiver crashed, so did his empire. Banks in America, Belgium and the Argentina investigated his dealings and when the sums were done it appeared that some $50 million of other people's money had been unaccounted for. It had all the hallmarks of a massive international fraud.

Then, eight months later, the affair assumed on a new proportion when *La Nueva Provincia,* a right-wing newspaper connected with General Iberico Saint-Jean, a hardline rightist who had been head of the secret police, arraigned Graiver of being the investment banker of the Montoneros. The newspaper alleged that Graiver had channelled at least $17 million of the Montoneros' money through his Banco Commercial de la Plata into investments in Argentina and abroad. This took place at a time when the Montoneros' profits from their kidnappings were far in excess of their immediate requirements and so they did what any major business concern would do.

The newspaper investigation of Graiver provided detailed information about the business cover of the terrorists. Every month two well-dressed gentle-looking men known as Dr Paz and Dr Penaloza took the high speed lift to the twenty-ninth floor of the Graivèr bank in the centre of Buenos Aires. Because it was equipped with so many sophisticated devices this office was known as 'The Bunker'. The Junta led by General Jorge Videla was by then conducting a repressive but successful campaign against the terrorists, and followed up the newspaper accusation by claiming it could prove that Graiver was enthusiastically handling Montoneros funds and had in fact become so enmeshed that his banking empire depended on the inflow of terrorist money. General Videla announced: 'This so-called Graiver group worked for the subversives. They received millions of dollars in deposits to be invested here and abroad for the benefit of subversion, and they knew where the money had come from.' Evidence against Graiver began to accumulate and the police had unexpectedly succeeded when they raided a Montoneros 'safe house' and found documents linking him with the organisation's finances.

In December 1977 a court martial compose of military officers sitting in secret sentenced David Graiver's father, Juan, his widow, Lidia, and his brother, Isidoro, to fifteen years' imprisonment, the maximum, for conspiring with terrorist groups. The military communique announcing the sentences did not give any details of the trial but military sources said that the substance of the charge of investing illegal funds abroad had been obtained by interrogating Jorge Rubenstein, a financial adviser to the Graiver banking establishments.

There were many questions still to be answered, however. What happened to all the money? How much was the case against the Graivers part of the current wave of antisemitism in the Argentina? And, the most tantalising of all, is David Graiver still alive? In April 1978 Robert Morgenthau, the Manhattan District Attorney, declared 'There is a basis to believe he is still alive,' and other sources reported in the *Wall Street Journal* had stated it seemed likely that Graiver was behind the Iron Curtain. The District Attorney announced that his detectives had been searching for Graiver and that they would seek the help of Interpol. This news began fresh speculation in Argentina where it was generally believed that Graiver became involved with the terrorists after the kidnapping of his brother Isidoro by the Montoneros early in the 1970s. After he was freed it was generally believed that the family had paid a ransom, but later there had been speculation that David Graiver made a deal agreeing to manage their money in return for his family being left alone. What appeared certain is that the Montoneros lost a sizeable chunk of their unwisely invested gains. It proved in fact that capitalism does not always pay.

The Baader-Meinhof faction and its successors in Germany had, of course, set out to prove this point from the other direction. From the beginning of their existence they had geared their organisation to theft on the precepts of Carlos Marighella, the Brazilian outlaw who taught that bank robbery was the just way of financing revolution. The fact that he was killed in pursuance of his own teaching did not deter the Germans. They mounted six banks robberies within a span of two months in 1972 and walked away with $185,000.

Ulrike Meinhof set out her justification for robbing banks in her pamphlet *Urban Guerrillas and Class Conflict*. She wrote:

> No one claims that bank robbery of itself changes anything... for the revolutionary organisation it means first of all a solution of financial problems. It is logistically correct, since otherwise the financial problem could not be solved at all. It is tactically correct because it is a proletarian action. It is strategically correct because it serves the financing of the guerrilla.

But the German terrorists also had financial assistance, as

did the Japanese Red Army, from Arab funds made available to help them in return for services rendered, such as attacks on Israeli offices and factories working for the Israelis. The Red Army Faction did not need such huge funds on its own account as some terrorist movements, for a great deal of its support was provided by well-to-do German sympathisers. There was never any shortage of hideouts; and cars and equipments were easy to acquire in an affluent Western country. Even though Andreas Baader liked his comforts and Ulrike Meinhof complained when she had to live in an unhygienic condition, money was never a problem for these middle-class terrorists. Miss Meinhof had money of her own, and many of the girl terrorists were able to get it from their financially affluent parents.

Klaus Rohl, husband of Ulrike, revealed in his biography that both of them had been secret members of the Communist Party from 1956 until 1961. He further said that his magazine *Konkret* had been subsidised from Soviet funds. On concealed visits to East Europe he and Ulrike had collected upwards of a million marks by way of Prague.

Whenever the Baader-Meinhof crowd did run short of money they organised more bank raids. Even in 1977 that same process was still continuing. So common was it for the then West German banks to be held up at gun point that they became known as 'terrorist treasuries'.

The early bank raids did not always produce as much as the Baader-Meinhof gang would have liked. In one case Baader managed to rob off only DM 8000 having failed to notice a carton of notes worth more than ten times as much. The comrades mocked him for his failure, saying: 'You could earn that much doing dirty work for *Konkret* magazine.' After he had collected the money he flew back to Europe and cashed the original travellers' cheques. A cheap little trick but then, all things are permissible as long as they serve the cause.

Perhaps the most telling words on the financial philosophy of terrorism may be taken from Horst Mahler, who, on entering a bank, had declared. 'This is a stick-up! Hands up and keep quiet and nothing will happen to you. After all, it's not your money.'

But while bank raids and small-time chicanery kept the

money flowing, the really big profits came from hijacking and abductions. As a result of the kidnapping of the politician Peter Lorenz in West Berlin, five imprisoned terrorists were released and flown to South Yemen with DM'20,000 apiece as pocket money.

Hadad, incidentally, smarted for years over this hijack because the South Yemenis had charged him a million dollars as a 'landing fee' and also, his hit team failed to discover that one of the passengers was Joseph P. Kennedy III, the son of the late Robert Kennedy and apparently worth more in ransom money than all the other passengers put together.

In Italy the Red Brigades took a leaf out of the Mafia's book and began conducting their terrorist network as a money-making organisation. When anti-terror investigators made a breakthrough in the mid 1970s and succeeded in arresting the original leadership and also breaking their networks they had discovered detailed accounts. By that time ransom money and protection payments had come in such quantities that the Red Brigades had a budget of a milliard Lira. The terrorists' finance managers had sensibly invested large sums. It was estimated that 300 million Lira had been placed in property and real estate and the income from this was used to purchase weapons, cars and equipment. Some of the property bought by Red Brigades was even used to provide safe houses and 'people's prisons', but usually their real estate was used simply to provide a solid income. Like the Palestinians the accountants of the Red Brigades ignored large sums to pay their terrorists operators and they also operated a social security system to look after the dependants of those killed or imprisoned in the course of their terrorist onslaughts. Despite the healthy income enjoyed by the Red Brigades they still had money worries. While in prison awaiting trial, Renato Curcio had complained about the high and increasing cost of keeping underground units operational.

Japanese Red Army

The Japanese Red Army has always had the reputation of being as much a mercenary force as an ideological one. Because the Japanese police clamped down on them after their first small operations at home, this group was forced to flee and re-form abroad with no noticeable means of support. They went to work for the Palestinians in return for subsidies to help their movement exist but also turned to hijacking to maintain a semblance of independence. However, they were not particularly successful and so the Red Army's woman leader, Fusako Shigenobu, masterminded a series of kidnappings of Japanese businessmen in Europe to restore the financial situation. In order to do this the entire Red Army treasury — $10,000 — was sent by courier from the Middle East to Paris to fund the operations. But the courier was arrested at Orly airport and when the dollars were examined they were found to be poor forgeries.

The Red Army had to switch over to the PFLP to bail them out. It was not until the summer of 1977 that the Red Army made a startling comeback by seizing a Japanese Airlines plane minutes after it had taken off from Bombay and forcing it to fly to Bangladesh and then to Algiers. The Japanese government abjectly surrendered to their demands and agreed to release a mixed bag of six confined terrorists and criminals. They thus provided the Red Army with a renewed fighting force.

We said at the beginning of this chapter that money is the fuel of terrorism - without it nothing runs. But at the same time it is probably the easiest of essentials for terrorists to obtain. For, once they had relinquished normal morality and convinced themselves that anything was justified in pursuance of their cause, then bank robbery, kidnapping and hijackings became not only justified but actual acts of virtue. When this philosophy is joined with the sophisticated investment of its rewards and is supported by the flow of Arab petrodollars to organisations judged to be of assistance to the Palestinian cause, there are fortunes to be made.

Six

Terrorism: The Factors Behind

What really makes a terrorist? Some come to it by chance, some by design, for 'wide is the gate and broad is the way' that leads to this particular category of destruction. The ranks of the urban guerrilla armies include many types, idealists as well as criminals and psychopaths. And yet, despite their difference, they have a common factor: they have all come under the influence of those political thinkers who preach that violence is essential to make the world a better place 'for the masses'.

Anti-Colonialist Wars

As the anti-colonialist wars in several parts of the world came to an end in the 1950s and 1960s the concept of a Third World composed of the poor and impoverished countries came into being and acted as a magnet for the interest and compassion of young people in the Western world and in Japan, the only perfectly industrialised nation in the entire East, who identified with its struggles and with the poverty of less fortunate people in their own countries.

Meanwhile, a feeling grew among young intellectuals that rich countries should do more for the poor, and that in the West we should feel a sense of guilt for our past colonial exploitation and pay for that guilt through massive programmes of aid — the paradox being, of course, that many of the newly-liberated countries have falled into tribal discord, corruption and inefficiency and are far worse off than they were under colonialism.

It was in this atmosphere of repugnance against the luxuries of life that capitalism has brought to the middle classes of the developed world, that the philosophers of terror started writing their volumes of theory — and in some cases of practice — about the effectiveness and morality of guerrilla and urban guerrilla warfare. The inspiration was Latin American, for Castro's triumph in Cuba had far-reaching implications; he had shown how a small band of guerrillas could overthrow the regular army of a dictator and he and his companions became instant heroes in the universities. Before long the students of Europe and America began devouring the new literature of subversion.

Among the earliest and most influential of the new upsurge philosophers was Frantz Fanon, a black doctor born in Martinique who took over as head of the Psychiatric Department of Blida Hospital in Algeria. He became a supporter of the National Liberation Front but did not live to see it achieve independence. Though not a violent man himself, Fanon was consumed with hatred for colonialism and racial oppression, and he made a charisma out of violence. 'Violence alone, violence committed by the people and educated by its leaders, makes it possible for the masses to understand social realities and gives the key to them,' he wrote in a book entitled *The Wretched of the Earth*.

Not only was violence a means of ending colonial oppression, he argued, but was also an improving element in itself, 'a cleansing force'. 'It frees the native from his inferiority complex and from his tribulation and inaction; it makes him fearless and restores his self-respect.'

Fanon justified such beliefs by the premise that European affluence was in itself scandalous because it emanated from robbery of the very soil of the Third World and from slavery. A Marxist in theory, Fanon observed nothing but scorn for the working class in the West, for it had simply accepted the benefits of latter-day colonialism. During the Algerian war he even castigated Jean-Paul Sartre, whom he had otherwise admired. Simone de Beauvoir reported: 'He could not forget that Sartre was French and he blamed him for not having expiated that crime sufficiently.'

The violent preachings of Fanon are significant because they began to set a pattern of thought among leftward-looking intellectuals in the Western world. This helps to narrate the process by which students turned to terrorism. His books instilled that sense of guilt, that feeling that the Third World of the ex-colonies had right on its side, which had provided so much support for global terrorists. The Germans of the Baader-Meinhof groups and before them the French students, whose revolt in Paris in 1968 coincided with a culmination of anti-Americanism over the war in Vietnam, drew inspiration from Fanon's impassioned pleading on behalf of the colonially exploited and oppressed. He helped set the stage for international terrorism by justifying resort to it as a legitimate way of attacking injustice.

If the inspiration of latter-day terrorism came from Fanon and his Algerian experiences, the tactics of the present style were made in Latin America. The founding father of this school of violence was Carlos Marighella, who practised what he advocated, running a revolutionary group in Brazil. In his chapter "Handbook of Urban Guerrilla Warfare" in *For the Liberation of Brazil* he wrote:

Bank Raids

> Bank raids are the most popular form of action. In Brazil they are very common. In this particular activity, revolutionaries have two types of competitors — bandits and right-wing counter-revolutionaries. This to some extent confuses ordinary people, and therefore the guerrilla will try to make clear the purpose of his action, in two ways: he will refuse to behave like a bandit, either by misguided violence, or by taking money or personal possessions from customers who may be in the bank; and he will back up his expropriation by some form of propaganda — writing slogans attacking the ruling classes and imperialism on the walls, handing out pamphlets, or giving people leaflets explaining the political purpose of what he is doing.

The above passage gives an account of the naïve and extraordinary advice handed out by the master. Yet it was taken seriously not only in Latin America but also by the European bands. Baader-Meinhof terrorists, who on a number of occasions left copies of the Marighella handbook in their abandoned cars, specialised in bank robberies. Moreover, on one occasion in Berlin they had attempted to carry out the helpful advice to placate the customers of banks under attack by offering them chocolate-covered cakes known as 'Negro Kisses'. It is not surprising that

Andreas Baader had once remarked that he found the gathering of money stolen from banks 'a particularly pleasing experience'. The petrified customers at the Berlin bank made no comment on their feelings.

In Britain, the Angry Brigade, a much less effective group which shared many concepts in common with Baader-Meinhof, and by no means unacquainted with the works of Marighella, amassed assets more modestly by stealing cheque books and credit cards. But shortly before the ringleaders were arrested they began planning raids on post offices and banks, justifying themselves with a feeling that respect for the law should never be more than a tactical consideration.

Marighella's Suggestion

In Brazil, Marighella's suggestion was carried through by his followers more mercilessly, and in less than a year they lifted the best part of half a million pounds from banks in Rio and Sao Paulo. The government gave in to their demands in order to avoid bloodshed and diplomatic embarrassment. Encouraged by this thumping victory the terrorists went on to other acts, gradually escalating their demands for the release of more prisoners. Five were handed over for the life of the kidnapped Japanese consul, forty more for the erstwhile West German ambassador and finally seventy for the Swiss ambassador. Finally, the lesson was learned by the government of Brazil that it did not pay to give in to terrorist blackmail. But the successes of the hostage-takers also showed that from their point of view the advice of Carlos Marighella was substantial.

That the tactical precepts of Marighella were taken seriously by followers all over the world is proved by a glance at the subsequent activities of the international groups. The Palestinians turned to hostage taking, and the murder of diplomats and celebrated foreigners; Baader-Meinhof and the Moluccans in Holland took hostages and demanded either the release of prisoners, or the publication of political communiques in return for their lives. 'Carlos' went so far as to hold hostage the entire ministerial strength of OPEC, the worldwide oil body and possibly the most powerful group of men in the world. In every case, the terrorists accepted the dictum of Marighella that the task of a revolutionary is to make the revolution. They were no doubt flattered by his outline of the personal qualities of an urban guerrilla— courage and initiative, good strategies and a good aim with a gun, the use of skill and cunning. They amount to what used to be called in the British Army 'OLQ' - Officer-like Qualities.

Although Marighella was assassinated in 1969 in the wave of repression which the actions of his supporters had provoked, he is still very much amidst us in the form of his teachings. His book became the standard work for ambitious terrorist leaders, and when it was translated into French in 1970 the French government prohibited its distribution and sale.

His military theories are neither sensational nor very unique but his book did help to popularise the term 'urban guerrilla'. He declared that urban guerrilla warfare started in Brazil in 1968. But the theories are largely derivative from Chairman Mao's instructions to the Communists on how to take over China from the Nationalists.

Tactics of the Guevara

When such tactics were exercised in Latin America by people like Che Guevara they met with far less success. Conditions in the assorted republics of that continent were different from those existing in the Far East. Because Mao had formulated the principle that Communist guerrillas could inhibit the cities from the countryside and had, moreover, proved it in battle, the 'encirclement of the city by the countryside' became holy writ. But in Western industrialised societies, and in many other parts of Latin America, the great majority of people stay in cities. In such places it is hardly possible for the country minority to 'strangle' the city majority.

Even at the time that Marighella was first in action, counter-insurgency forces with new techniques and good training were in the process of annihilating rural guerrillas in Latin America. Guevara, who planned to provoke American military intervention in Bolivia and so create a prolonged war like that in Vietnam, had over-reached himself. Rural guerrillas had also failed in Brazil.

The rural *foco* - or focus - advocated by Guevara was a

guerrilla-occupied foundation for activity in the countryside into which recruits theoretically poured to form a miniature revolutionary state. In Latin America the rural guerrillas failed to win the support which theorists believed would be forthcoming from farmers and peasants. What Marighella had done was to adapt the *foco* principle to urban activities, and so the terrorists came to town. It was in the towns that enthusiastic converts such as students and intellectuals were most at home and there they stood a much better chance of survival.

In Latin America the turning point in the terrorist campaigns came with the death of Che Guevara in Bolivia in 1967. In the early 1960s insurgent movements had mushroomed in Guatemala, Brazil, Peru and other countries in the hemisphere. Their inspiration came from Cuba, where Fidel Castro set about using his Island base to encourage revolutionary movements on the continent. Tyranny and capitalist imperialism symbolised by the United States were the enemy. "I was born in Argentina, I fought in Cuba, and I began to be a revolutionary in Guatemala," was how Che Guevara summarised his autobiography. It was this Spanish-Irishman who became not only the theorist but also the wandering missionary of revolution in Latin America. Cuba was his only successful campaign in the field. Despite his meticulous writing on the subject his advice was plagiarised and in action he made mistake after mistake.

As the Guevara cult expanded, he exerted greater influence on more capable guerrilla leaders and on the terrorists as well, although he himself favoured guerrilla war as opposed to terror strikes. He once warned against the dangers of terrorism which hindered 'contact with the masses and makes impossible unification for actions that will be necessary at the critical moment'. He visualised the need to win the support of local populations in order to get recruits, and there was about him a knightly aura of the social reformer in arms who fought only with the support of the oppressed masses.

The Guevara cult and the ideas of the man were spread to Western Europe by his admirer Regis Debray, the French intellectual and philosopher. What was fascinating for Europeans in the Guevara theory was the adapted doctrine of proletarian internationalism. Parties and political programmes appeared less important to the revolutionary than the fighting itself, far from the armed clash political beliefs would eventually emanate.

When Guevara went off questing for more action once Cuba had been liberated, it was already too late for him in Latin America. The guerrillas were outfought and outmanoeuvred by counter-insurgency operations who had themselves learned the Cuban lesson. An enthusiastic though blundering commander, he fought his forlorn battles in Bolivia until 1967 when the Bolivian Eighth Division, some of its troops disguised as peasants, surrounded Guevara and his band in the Santa Cruz district. Guevara, himself wounded, was ultimately captured.

His death in such romantic circumstances generated a whole new mythology and it was not long before 'Che Guevara lives' became the encouraging call for leftist rebels throughout the world. His name still lived in 1976 when the ill-fated Entebbe raiders proclaimed that they were called the 'Che Guevara - Gaza Group', taking the name at one remove from a Palestinian terrorist who styled himself the Che Guevara of Gaza.

Dashing posters of Che in full guerrilla regalia appeared everywhere and it almost seemed as though everybody under the age of twenty-five aspired to be a guerrilla. What was less obvious at the time was that already such irregular forces, trounced in Latin America, were transforming themselves into urban guerrillas, that is to say town terrorists. It was not long before like-minded groups in different parts of the world and in Europe specifically turned from national to international targets. It was the US Army and the CIA who had helped to train the counter-insurgency forces which dented revolutionary hopes.

Radicals in American and European Universities

The new radicals in American and European universities approved of the action for they found it easy enough to identify with the man in the round cap who died for a cause in the Bolivian mountains. Emotionally at least, students who captured buildings in London or Berlin, who fought the Chicago police at the Democratic Convention there, were the spiritual followers of Che. In one way or another they were determined on using different degrees of violence to change the established order.

A new nihilism based on rash though high-minded principles was emerging. Regis Debray, the French follower of Che Guevara who made him more famous after his death than he had been in life, was sentenced in Bolivia for assisting the guerrillas, and his lengthy defence of his own actions and of guerrilla war were widely read. He served only three years of a thirty-year sentence.

Inspiration of Herbert Marcuse

The other philosopher who inspired similar thoughts in the universities was Herbert Marcuse, a theoretician and sociologist who had become Professor of Political Thought at the University of California. He belonged to the Frankfurt school of philosophy whose supporters had already established the connection between Western prosperity and Third World misery. On the one hand, they said, there was material plenty and 'choice' which gave a misconception of freedom; on the other was the war in Vietnam, black ghettos in the United States, and the sufferings of peasants in Bolivia and Uruguay.

The Frankfurt philosophers busied themselves confirming and justifying feelings abroad in the rioting 1960s. In addition, the Marcusian argument that Western power elites had provided a surfeit of material needs by creating artificial demand for a superfluity of goods appealed most to the radical chic factions (known in Germany as the *Schili*) as well as to students. Most of them were middle and upper-class people had a feeling of remorse because they in particular were so well provided with worldly goods. And nowhere did this take hold so firmly as in erstwhile West Germany where the economic miracle had brought a cornucopia to people.

Marcuse also preached that the scientific and technological revolution had changed the set-up of the working class, thus altering classic Marxist assumptions. A new technologically-based society had emerged in the West bringing an affinity between big business and the working class, which was no longer revolutionary or intent on ousting the established order. 'The people, previously the ferment of social change have moved up to become the ferment of social cohesion...' The development created a situation in which only what he called the 'outsiders' were the proper revolutionaries.

These outsiders were those forced from the system because they were unemployable in it; those maltreated for their colour; the exploited masses of the Third World; and the students disgusted by comfortable consumerism in the West.

Marcuse had observed that in the 1960s several young people were already in revolt against their elders and their ways. He encouraged them in what he called the 'great refusal' to take part in the rat race. He arranged laws and rules and offered an explanation for their discontent and made a flattering suggestion that they were the vanguard, 'the most advanced consciousness of humanity'. Their goal was to lead the powerless and ignorant substratum of society in revolutionary uprising. They were urged not to commit themselves to a society whose interests needed the peaceful continuance of its ways; and when legal methods failed, to resort to illegal ones.

The German philosopher from California provided a complete though devious justification for student agitation by telling them that they were no more free than those who lived in totalitarian states east of the Berlin Wall. They rather enjoyed only an illusion of freedom because the consumer society foisted upon them comfort and luxury.

In the United States, where Marcuse had as massive a following as he latter won in Europe, the same ideas were prevalent. But there the student movement concentrated on the Vietnam war and its sonsequences. Students and radicals molested against its cruelties, though more against American than against Vietnamese brutalities. They also attacked the universities themselves because they were used both for military research and for recruitment to the forces. The big monopolies were also a target in their attacks on ostentatious wealth and exploitation.

Student Uprising

The same themes were obvious as student uprising spread to Europe. The proximity of the erstwhile East Berlin and its Communist oppressions originally drove East Germans to seek freedom in the West to demonstrate against their red masters, but when the enthusiasm dried up after the building of the Berlin Wall the students, lacking the experience of the refugees, moved leftwards.

The German universities were still fairly uninteresting, crowded and old-fashioned places. Though the Free University, established after the Second World War, was the most modern of them, this failed to prevent it from becoming a focus for trouble. It was the place for sit-in demonstrations, talk-ins and all the other 'happenings' which became so familiar in the 1960s. All these events became permanently stamped upon the personalities of those who later took to terrorism in Germany.

One event in particular had a long-lasting effect. In 1967 the Shah of Persia made a state visit to West Germany and undertook the ritual pilgrimage to West Berlin, its besieged outpost. The students seized upon him as a natural enemy, the representative of oppression in the Third World. In the course of the demonstration the police opened fire on the crowd and killed a mild demonstrator named Benno Ohnesorg, a 26-year-old Protestant student from Hanover. This killing horrified the demonstrators and left a remarkable mark on the whole student movement.

A similar incident took place in 1970 in the United States when National Guardsmen opened fire without warning on students rioting at Kent State University in Ohio as a mark of protest against President Nixon's invasion of Cambodia. Although Nixon dismissed the incident as an inevitable consequence of 'the resort to violence' — violence of the young that is — it provided for young people throughout the Western world a glaring example of violence by the State.

Both the Berlin episode and the Kent State University slaughter convinced student radicals that the state and the authorities were the violent oppressors and that they were justified in replying state violence with revolutionary violence.

Coincidentally it was while Marcuse was visiting the Free University on 13 May 1968 that a large-scale protest movement similar to the German one was at its climax in Paris. There thousands of students were marching behind the red flags of Communism and the black flags of lawlessness. The revolution had begun in the form of protest against the over-crowded and archaic universities of France. But as the barricades went up on the boulevards and clashes with riot police developed, it became evident that French students were determined to follow through the idea that they should give a lead to the sluggish workers by advancing to overthrow capitalism.

For a short while the ecstasy and the excitement of that revolution did spread to the workers, who although they resented the students and their methods, did go on strike and did in many cases occupy their workplaces. It began to look as though General de Gaulle's Fifth Republic would be destroyed. Then, mostly through his extraordinary energy and the counter-magic of his personality, the Republic was saved. The terrified bourgeoisie regrouped to his cause, troop reinforcements were brought back from Germany and significantly the workers gave up their occupations of factory and office in return for more money and better conditions.

May 1968 was the high period of student revolt. The Red Bases which had been set up in the Sorbonne and at Nanterre, the new branch of the University of Paris, failed to carry out a successful revolution, but they had created a new mythology. It had briefly united the new radical themes: violence advocated by Fanon; the *foco* theory of Guevara and Debray tried out in the streets rather than the jungles; and the student vanguard of Marcuse's outsiders. The predictions of Marcuse had come to pass. After ritual strikes and noises of revolution the workers returned to the pleasures of 'terror consumption'. Perhaps they were invincibly ignorant in the matter of revolution and really were in league with the capitalists. After the impulsive excitement of the barricades the young revolutionaries savoured bitterness and disappointment. There was no further point in advocating the classic Communist Parties, far less the old-fashioned socialists. They needed something more extreme and this was their justification for turning to terrorism.

This then was the progress which made young students into terrorists. However, it would be wrong to think that all terrorists are intellectuals fighting for idealistic purposes.

Role of Harry Duggan

Harry Duggan, a baby-faced IRA gunman captured in London after being confined in the Balcombe Street flat with three other terrorists in possession of an arsenal of weapons, took his first steps on the road to murder six years before, when he started going to Provisional Sinn Fein meetings. He came from a village called Feakle, and had become an apprentice in a chipboard factory where his father worked as a carpenter. He was rated by the Provisional Army Council as 'a very useful man', and at a time when his mother in Ireland was saying that he had always been a good boy at school, he was already selected to go on a terror mission to London. The group he belonged to killed Ross McWhirter, editor of the *Guinness Book of Records*, besides blowing up an eminent cancer specialist in a London street.

Duggan started his career at Irish political meetings where loquacious Provos denounced the British and their evil means, and soon he was out on the banks of the river Shannon practising with .22 rifles and specially adapted Webley .38 revolvers. But he was still described by friends as a modest boy who, at the age of twenty-three looked as if he should be singing in the local church choir.

Operations of IRA

Although some of the cliches of international terrorism have entered the limited idiom of the IRA and there has been some operational contact between the international factions and the IRA, that organisation remains an insular movement, content with its own myths. One of the oldest of the terrorist movements, it has a reasonable reputation for strict discipline. In the first eight months of 1977 its kangaroo courts carried out no less than eighty-two 'kneecappings' in which atrocity is inflicted by shooting in the back of the knee.

But apart from its brutalities, the movement depends on the kind of patriotic fervour which inspires some of its hit men. Many are those who have moved into the terror business for sentimental purposes. And probably as many Irishmen have gone off gun in hand through the influence of whiskey and black porter, hymned on by the catchy traditional revolutionary songs, as through any intolerant political conviction or true revolutionary philosophy.

Between the start of the terror campaigns in Ulster in 1969 and the end of 1978 the IRA killed 490 members of the security forces and 1400 civilians. It executed all this with the active support of only a small percentage of the population, and without achieving any real political objective.

It is not without interest that when intellectuals and middle-class revolutionaries from outside have tried to assist the cause of the IRA they have been treated with suspicion and contempt. To Irish hit men, the kind of terrorists who would be welcomed by, for instance, the German Red Army Faction are simply an embarrassment.

In this respect the IRA was by no means typical of present-day terrorist movements, most of which have international support and strong transnational contacts. The IRA was a much more earthy group, more suspicious of outsiders and unwelcoming to the student revolutionaries to be found in most similar movements.

The only acceptable outsiders giving support to the IRA are Irish-Americans. Here again the link is sentimental and signified by all those Irish of Boston and New York who take part in St. Patrick's day parades and dig into their pockets to support those on 'the ould sod', fighting against the British.

Over the last few years, and broadly because the Southern Irish government has gone out of its way to inform leaders of Irish-American opinion about the true image of Irish terrorism, the number of dollars flowing into IRA funds had fallen.

Because it fought a traditional cause of some antiquity the Irish Republican Army had attracted a higher proportion of mature terrorists to its colours than almost any other. For similar historical reasons Irish terrorists tend to be more working class and less intellectual than is the case with other 'liberation' movements.

The original IRA was formed with a view to fight in a patriotic cause against an occupying army. Thus, it had much in common with the Spanish guerrillas who fought against Napoleon, and with the Algerian National Liberation Front struggling against the French who governed their country.

It is often accepted as fact that the terrorist activities of the old IRA won the establishment of the Republic of Southern Ireland. The claim is renounced by many Irishmen in the south, including Conor Cruise O'Brien, a former minister in a Dublin government.

Even when the democrats had negotiated the formation of the new stage with Lloyd George in 1921, they then had to defend it against the staunch Republicans and the continuing gunmen. Michael Collins, who had successfully negotiated with the British, was assassinated the next year by the IRA because he had agreed to compromise over the six largely Protestant countries in the north which remained part of the United Kingdom. From 1922 onwards the IRA was involved in fighting against the government of the Republic of Ireland, and against the Irish Catholics who elected it.

In the 1960s the IRA had started to acquire a political flavour of Marxism; that was largely through the influence of one man, David O'Connell, on its leadership. But within a few years it became evident that most members, including those active in terrorism, were not interested in political ideology so much as in the basic nationalism of their cause. The Provisional IRA which took over venture in the north was simpler in its philosophy.

What attracts apprentice killers to its cause was the very simplicity of the movement's basic objectives, which may be summed up as 'get the army and the British out of Northern Ireland'. Their ostensible aim was to allow the Irish government in the south to rule over the whole. What they really wanted was to destroy the democratic government of Dublin as well, and to sever connections with Europe of the Common Market, as well as with England. The Provisional IRA had in its mind a rather woolly concept of creating a *new* Ireland. Dr Conor Cruise O'Brien once remarked in his Oxford lecture, "The achievement of that *new* Ireland would I think require two rather basic changes for the island of Ireland: a new geographical location and a new population. These may prove difficult either to negotiate or to extort by political force".

The fundamental aim of the IRA was separatist and nationalist. Here we have an important divide in the aspirations of terrorist movements in the modern world, for it is important to differentiate between those movements in Europe, America and Japan who use their form of warfare to make international revolution and overthrow the present system; and those who, like the Irish, are distressed with establishing power in their homeland. In this respect the Irish have something in common with the Israelis who succeeded in setting up their own state through using of the terror as a weapon: indeed the Israeli Prime Minister, Menachem Begin, was once leader of the 700-strong force of terrorists known as Irgun Zvi Leumi.

The two outstanding instances of what may be called 'territorial' terrorists are the IRA and the various branches of Palestine Liberation forces. But the Palestinians, unlike the Irish, are much more willing to accept the assist and support of outsiders and conduct their campaigns worldwide. In fact after Munich, when every Arab in Europe was marked down as a potential terrorist, they came to trust international groups to carry out their missions. In addition they provided training, weapons and money for these groups of ideological terrorists had little reason to be involved in the underground war between Arabs and Jews. Into this category also fell members of Baader-Meinhof, the Japanese Red Army and the notorious 'Carlos' network.

For all that, the various Palestinian organisations, which are the best publicised of all guerrilla and terrorist outfits, remain fundamentally interested in territorial aims. To them Palestine means the whole of Palestine, and they wanted to recover that land from Israeli possession and to control it ally by themselves. However their campaign has been a long one, and in the course of it various brands of revolutionary Marxism have impressed themselves upon individual leaders.

Arab Oil Power

It may well be that if the Arab oil powers, and the 'confrontation' states sponsored by them, namely Egypt and Syria, finally accept an international political settlement of the Palestine problem, the fundamentalist Palestinian movements will turn their attacks on those countries with the aim of producing revolutionary governments in them. Already there have been terrorist attacks, against the Egyptian government. The leadership of this trend which takes Palestinian terrorism out of its purely territorial role and involves it in worldwide revolution rests with men like Dr George Habash and Wadi Hadad, who until his death in April 1978 was his chief of operations. They ran the most active and ruthless outfit, the Popular Front for the Liberation of Palestine (PFLP).

PFLP was believed to be fiercely committed not only to the destruction of Israel but also to creating a Marxist-Leninist revolution throughout the Arab world. And after it had disposed of the 'feudal' Arab states, then it intended to terrorise in the cause of world revolution. That is why Dr. Habash's men are so ready to provide foundations and training for international movements working in the same cause and to make use of their members. Habash's philosophy is that there is no point in classic military struggle against Israel, only terror can be effective.

There can be little doubt that the effectiveness of PFLP operations led to the birth of Black September, established originally to take revenge for the annihilation of the guerrilla movement in Jordan by King Hussein, but expanded after its success in killing Wasfi Tell, the erstwhile Jordanian Prime Minister, into an international organisation which proved its savagery by carrying out the carnage at the Munich Olympics.

Another Arab terror group is a breakaway from PFLP. Known as the Popular Democratic Front for the Liberation of Palestine, it was led by a revolutionary named Naif Hawatmeh. Like several other splinter groups it was under the umbrella of the Palestine Liberation Organisation led by Yasser Arafat, who is recognised at the United Nations as the respectable statesman of the Palestine cause. But he also led the politico-military organisation known as Al Fatah ('The Struggle') which itself controlled Black September. Arafat, seeing that he was making more headway through the Council Chamber than by terrorism, had ordered Black September to cease operations. He is an excellent example of a leader in transition from terrorism to political leadership.

Many of these leaders have been influenced by the international theorists of terrorism, its aims and methods, whose doctrines we shall outline. If Marighella and Che Guevara are renowned as the philosophers and writers of revolution by subversive warfare, they are the terrorist warlords. Through their influence and petrodollar resource they were in a position to get the most modern weapons for their own followers. They also supplied supporters in the groups of brother terrorists. From the great arsenal of Soviet weapons bought by Colonel Gaddafi, supplies of advanced and sophisticated weapons trickle through the hands of Palestine groups to other terrorists in the West willing to use them in the cause.

In this process yet another of the warlords of terror, code-named Carlos, still played a large part. He was an interesting case history for in his own career he had brought together a number of the threads which weave into the fabric of international terrorism.

Carlos worked on behalf of the Palestinians in Europe and elsewhere. He was organisationally in touch with Baader-Meinhof factions in Frankfurt and in Hamburg but he first came to wide public attention when, in order to escape arrest in Paris, he killed his own fellow terrorist Michel Moukharbel and two officers of the French DST.

Carlos was acting out the role of a grand spokesman, a diplomat of terror. But he could not resist using melodramatic language - "you will have heard of me already; I am Carlos. You can tell that to the others," he proclaimed, according to Sheikh Yamani over Saudi radio and in conversation with Payne. When his German girl accomplice told him she had just killed two people, he smiled and said, "Quite right, I killed one myself." To Sheikh Yamani he spoke happily of putting pressure on the Austrian government, he boasted of his power and of his sexual exploits, but the political content of his speech rang false to Yamani. Carlos claimed mockingly to be a democrat who consulted his fellow terrorists before making any decision. But Yamani observed that Carlos is not a committed Communist... does not believe in the Palestinian cause or in Arab nationalism but ... [considers] them as factors which might be exploited to help spread the international revolutionary movement".

That is the picture of a successful terrorist warlord who achieved a measure of fame and fortune by the skill with which he carries out his raids. Such men are ready to use even the most devastating weapons for self-glorification in the supposed cause of imposing their ill-thought-out philosophies.

Seven

Training: Indoctrination and Skills

Although terrorist outfits rate political indoctrination of high importance in the formation of their recruits, Carlos Marighella, the inspirer of all urban guerrillas, was under no illusion about the significance of practical military knowledge. "No one can become a guerrilla without undergoing a period of technical preparation", he declared in his *Handbook of Urban Guerrilla Warfare*. 'You can only become a good fighter by learning the art of fighting.'

For the Latin American guru of terrorism this entailed everything from physical training to the learning of many kinds of jobs, especially those covering manual skills. Writing in a fashion which would please a drill sergeant in any army, he exhorted that physical training was the basis of the physical resistance which every good fighter needs. After that, he wrote, the urban guerrilla should learn to fight in different ways, some entailing attack and others self-defence, just like a professional soldier.

Advice of Marighella

Marighella urged his pupils to go in for what might be described as boy scout activities. They were to hike, camp, spend long periods of time in rough country and do trekking, swimming, canoeing, fishing and hunting for food. Quite how many of the young ladies of Baader-Meinhof would have these accomplishments had never been discovered, but the military value of such training was undisputed.

An accomplished terrorist should know something of the mechanics of radio, telephones and electronics; he should be able to prepare maps and plans, measure distance and locate his position on the ground by use of the compass. To survive in a society he is out to destroy he should also acquire a knowledge of chemistry, and also the ability to make rubber stamps and imitate other people's handwriting in order to forge documents convincingly. Marighella's section on technical training concluded:

> The most important element in technical training, however, remains that of handling such weapons as sub-machine-guns, revolvers, automatics, mortars, bazookas, FAL guns and other types of carbine — as well as knowledge of the various kinds of ammunition and explosives. Dynamite is one instance; it is vital to know how to use it, just as it is vital to know how to use incendiary bombs, smoke bombs, and so on. The guerrilla must also learn to make and repair weapons, to make Molotov cocktails, bombs and mines, and how to destroy bridges, dislodge or destroy railway lines and sleepers.
>
> The urban guerrilla will complete his training in a specially organised technical centre, but only after being tested in action, having actually fought the enemy.

This has been a constant theme of terrorist training, that the recruit should prove himself in action before being given complete training, and certainly there are many instances among the Germans, Palestinians and Latin Americans of this process in action. Indeed in some movements in Latin America the raw terrorist is needed, as an act of good faith, to kill a policeman or soldier before he is fully accepted into the band.

The Montoneros in Argentina produced extensive training manuals for their militants — 15,000 of them according to claims by the leadership. The cover of the most ambitious task, which showed a strong hand clutching an automatic weapon, bears the title *Regulations for Organising Political Military Activity*. Another, the *Military Instruction Manual* and instructions were given to members in guerrilla warfare as well as urban terrorism. The manuals also deal with more technical advice on manufacturing of bombs and how to endure torture and interrogation.

In the matter of training guerrillas for offensive stance against German troops during the Second World War, a manual composed by the British Secret Operations Executive adopted a much brisker and more practical method than Marighella. Hundreds of thousands of copies of the booklet were parachuted into occupied

Europe, and it was written in five languages as well as English. The text began:

> The easiest way for small parties of offensively minded men to attack the enemy is by the use of explosives. Immense damage can be caused with a small quantity of supplies.
>
> If the instructions given in this Booklet are followed carefully, even a person with no previous knowledge of explosives will be able to hit the enemy where it will do him most damage.

The most effective instructors in the strictly martial arts of terrorism have been without doubt the Arabs and Palestinians. Numerous training camps in the Middle East set up to prepare young men and women for active service against Israel at first turned out guerrillas. The duty of *fedayeen* soldiers was to fight a classic guerrilla war against an occupying army. But after sometime, the same camps switched their attention to instructing hijackers and kidnappers to carry on the war by less conventional means. This was necessary because the commandos had failed to make any more noticeable impact on Israel than the Arab armies.

Late in 1971 the Popular Front for the Liberation of Palestine through its many international links had begun bringing in revolutionary-minded foreigners ready to help in their campaigns. Among them was Kozo Okamoto, student from Kyoto University who already had been a member of the Japanese Red Army.

Early in 1972 he arrived in Beirut, Lebanon, by way of New York. In March PFLP instructors took him three companions to the terrorist training camp at Baalbek, the classical site of antiquity in the mountains above Beirut. The training began as it would have done in any military establishment with a course of physical training to get the volunteers into shape. The Arab instructors gave lesson other subjects, starting with explosives drill and how to handle detonators and how to make bombs. Finally they took lessons about grenades. Okamoto and his friends were then given special training for the job they were to do — to make an attack on Lod Airport in Tel Aviv. At this point intelligence officers briefed them about airport procedures and the design of the arrival hall there.

A couple of days later the group flew off to Rome, where they were armed, and caught a French airliner to carry out the ghastly massacre at the Israeli airport. Okamoto himself survived and under interrogation described his recruitment and training to Israeli security men.

It appears from this example of a Japanese Red Army man who learned his deadly trade in Baalbek, one among several dozen Arab training camps in Lebanon at the time, that the training was neither long nor entirely thorough. It is typical of the kind of course offered in the Middle East.

Red Army Faction members from erstwhile West Germany taking a similar crash course made a less favourable impression on their instructors. They were as keen on smoking pot and making love as on learning how to massacre effectively. Andreas Baader, the arrogant founder member of the gang, was called a coward because he had refused to crawl beneath barbed wire while live bullets were fired over his head. Baader complained about this, saying that assault courses were not the appropriate kind of training for urban guerrillas.

In this he was not totally wrong, though the reasoning behind his argument was snobbish rather than militarily realistic. A terrorist certainly needs discipline and has to be taught the virtue of following orders, but after that the need is more for a grounding in intelligence work than in strictly commando-type operations. Above all what he needs is small-arms instruction, enough range practice and a thorough knowledge of explosives and detonators. It is clear from the study of many terrorist assaults that training, whether given by the Arabs or by instructors from the operator's own movement, is not of a particularly high standard.

Western Intelligence

One important subject terrorists do pay attention to is the use of disguise. In successful groups international figures who had reappeared several times looked quite different on each occasion. For example, Carlos was recognised at first instance when he led the raid on OPEC in Vienna. He was bearded, thinner in the face and the colour of his dark hair had been altered. It is more than obvious that plastic surgery had been used to remove his heavy jowls and to alter the shape of the chubby face so well known to the French DST.

Western intelligence men believe that Prague has emerged the centre for plastic surgery to alter the appearance of known terrorists. Even without such expert specialist attention a terrorist can easily learn to alter his appearance enough to fool security men who have only out-of-date identity pictures. A moustache, a bottle of dye, and a slight gain or loss of weight is usually enough.

Both the 'territorial' terrorist groups acting in the Palestinian cause and the 'transnational' groups of which they later became one element received considerable initial help from Arab countries. In the early days of the present wave of terrorism Egypt and Syria were every bit as co-operative with the guerrillas as Lebanon, Iraq and Syria. All these countries helped to set up groups ready for action. In addition, they provided instruction in intelligence work and helped to furnish arms and fraud documentation. Before the Yom Kippur War in 1973, the Egyptian Army officered courses in special camps where the guerrillas learned side by side with Egyptian troops on six-month courses. Basic training was provided in intelligence, frogmen operations and commando work. But there were also special training lessons with heavy weapons, Katushka rockets, recoilless guns and mortars. Most of the weaponry was provided by the erstwhile Soviet Union. Such course were intended for the use of Palestinians serving as infantry with the Arab armies (there were some 8000 Palestinian regular infantry), but a number of exclusively terrorist Arabs also benefited from such instruction.

Since then both Egypt and Syria have shown more interest in trying to solve the Israeli - Arab conflict by diplomatic means with approval from the United States and to a certain extent from the Soviet Union. Their role as teachers of subversive warfare had been taken over by those who support the Rejection Front, for instance Libya, Iraq, South Yemen and Algeria, who believed that the Middle East problem can only be solved by force. But even there the Iraqi government showed more caution lately and now keeps the *fedayeen* under fairly tight control. The Lesson of Lebanon, where the aggressiveness and arrogance of the Palestinian outfits provoked a damaging civil war, has not been on neighbouring Arab countries.

That is the trouble with helping terrorists — a government can never be sure that they will not become overambitious and turn their weapons against the host state. Even the romantic and enthusiastic Colonel Gaddafi showed more circumspection in his dealings with international terrorists, though he had offered them facilities and a main PFLP training centre and base is to be found at Nahar-El-Barad near Tripoli.

To use explosive devices of any but the simplest kind needs a good deal of training, and it is bomb work which divides the men from the boys. To explode an infernal machine effectively demands not only technical ability, but a cool head and a steady hand. It has often been proved both by the Provisional IRA, and at least once by the Red Army Faction, that lack of experience results in what the British Army calls 'scoring an own goal'.

Lebanese Civil War

When the Lebanese civil war was at its height Wadi Hadad, former leader of the breakaway radicals of the PFLP and without doubt the world's most experienced terrorist leader, had set up new training centre in the People's Republic of South Yemen, earlier the British colony of Aden. Hadad was a doctor and an Orthodox Christian by upbringing just like George Habash, leader of the mainstream PFLP. Little is known of the personality of this skilled and ruthless man. At the time of his death, he was in his forties, of average height and a keen womaniser. With the approval of the South Yemen government he took over a former British Army camp at Khayat, fifteen miles from the port of Aden. Carlos joined him there to lecture and had instructed as the organisation's most practised field operator.

A good deal is known about the methods of this camp because the Israelis seized a Dutch girl who had arrived at Lod Airport on a reconnaissance mission in September 1976. Lidwina Anna Jansen, an attractive girl from Amsterdam, and a supporter of the leftist 'Red Aid' organisation in Holland had drifted by way of radical student activities into terrorism. In Aden she had attracted the attention of Wadi Hadad, who selected her for the mission after she had attended his training course. She was to reconnoitre the Air France route from Paris to Tel Aviv and Bombay as groundwork for a hijacking.

She had first gone to Aden with a team of fifteen like minded Dutch youngsters and was taken off to Khayat. The international nature of the training course was proved by information she had given later to Israeli security interrogators. They were put through their paces as cadet terrorists for six weeks by skilled instructors. The subjects were the familiar ones of weapon training, communications and strategies.

Miss Jansen was useful to PFLP, for after a brief stint in Holland at the end of her course she was able to fly into Israel, an impossibility for any of the Arab trainees. But she failed to play her role with any assurance and attracted the attention of the airport's ever-alert security guards. She was arrested and had promptly confessed. Another Dutchman from the same group was travelling with her, but he did not arouse suspicion and was able to sneak through Tel Aviv before being arrested in New Delhi as the result of the information she gave the authorities.

While on her trip back home to Holland before the mission had started Miss Jansen recognised in newspaper photographs two Arab fellow trainees from the terror school in Aden. They had been arrested at Istanbul after spraying bullets at passengers waiting for an E1 A1 flight. Four people were killed. The release of these two men was among the demands of the hijackers who had forced the Lufthansa Boeing to fly to Mogadishu in 1977 and this demonstrated even more clearly the international ramifications of the Hadad training camp in Aden.

A mental hospital in Heidelberg may appear the unlikeliest of places to set up a terrorist training organisation but that is precisely what Dr Wolfgang Huber and his wife Ursula did. In their 'Heidelberg Socialist Patients' Collective' they trained their mental patients to become terrorists in order to fight against modern society because, argued Huber, it was that society which had made his patients sick. They started by mixing small quantities of explosives then took their first bomb to the Odenwald Forest, exploding it by remote control and proudly taking snapshots of their success.

It was members of the Socialist Patients' Collective - SPK - who had occupied the West German embassy in Stockholm in April 1975 and cold-bloodedly murdered two of the diplomats. When it had become obvious that despite the killings the authorities were not going to surrender to the terrorists' demands — the freeing of the Baader — Meinhof leaders — there was an explosion inside the embassy and Siegfried Hausner, who had trained in bomb making with the Working Circle, was mortally wounded.

Another of Dr Huber's protegees was Friedericke Krabbe, a student of psychology and sociology who in the autumn of 1977 inherited the mantle of Ulrike Meinhof and Gurun Ensslin as the female leader of German terrorism. Her training had been complete, for the SPK had so-called working circles on dialectics, Marxism, sexuality, education and religion. On the more pragmatic side of things the students were also taught radio transmission, photography and judo and karate. They were instructed how to jam police radios and required to take picture of police buildings, officers and equipment.

No such system of higher education in terrorism was ever available to the Provos in Ireland, though they did enjoy another advantage — that some of their finest recruits had already been trained during service in the British Army. One sergeant from the Parachute Regiment took his skill with mortars to the PIRA, and breakaway soldiers from the Irish Guards, too, provided expertise for compatriots. Some IRA members were encouraged by their leaders to join the British Army in order to get a first-class military training. But in general the Provos lacked lavish resources whether in equipment or training. Because they needed to exercise in secret in Ireland, and therefore could only practise with their weapons and explosives in small groups on the lonely banks of the Shannon or on the Northern Ireland coast near the Giant's Causeway, where they had been under constant threat of detection by Irish or British security forces, the Provisionals often displayed signs of under-training. On numerous occasions captured Provos admitted, ' My gun jammed and I couldn't get it going again.' That is no doubt partly because most of their weapons, old model Stens and Thomson sub-machine-guns, were no longer effective — the costly Armalites had only been entrusted to the expert.

Training Organisations

Among the most effective training organisations for the formation of the new generation of transnational terrorists were those established in Cuba after Fidel Castro's success. After the Tricontinental Conference there in 1966 had proclaimed its faith in the struggle against imperialism, camps were set up under both Cuban and Russian instructors to arrange the training of young Latin Americans in guerrilla warfare and terrorism. Castro himself knew the value of good training. Before launching his attack on Cuba, both he and Che Guevara had been coached by Alberto Bayo, an elderly Spanish colonel who learned his trade in the Spanish Civil War. With fund supplied by Castro, Bayo bought ranch at Santa Rosa near Mexico City and equipped it as a guerrilla school.

Orlando Castro Hidalgo, a defector from Castro's DGI (Direccion General de Inteligencia) tells in his book, *Spy For Fidel*, how the training camps in Cuba were operated: 'One of the first functions of DGI was the running of special schools for the training of Latin Americans in guerrilla warfare and subversive techniques. At one time, early in the sixties, as many as 1,500 men were being brought to Cuba for training...' Those who could not get there by air arrived clandestinely either by Communist freighter or fishing boat. On arrival in Havana they were grouped by nationality, and although a squad already consisted of between fifteen and twenty-five members, sometimes there were as few as three. For security reasons national groups were usually kept separated. In any case the different factions received specialised training; Venezuelans concentrated on guerrilla operations and sabotage techniques. Chileans, who in pre-Allende period came from a country with a strong Communist Party, were trained in using political methods to further the cause.

Guerrilla warfare courses lasted between three and six months, but sometimes even continued for a year. And promising recruits received additional instruction to become intelligence agents back in their home countries.

When Carlos was at Camp Matanzas in Cuba, one of his professors was General Viktor Simenov of the Soviet KGB, who had been sent to Havana to help arrange the Cuban secret service. Another instructor was Antonio Dages Bouvier, an Ecuadorian expert in guerrilla tactics, who turned up again later in London and was involved in masterminding the hijack at Entebbe. Carlos indeed provides a thread through the maze of international training in his own career. Like other up-and-coming candidates from Latin America he was singled out for further instruction in Moscow by way of the Patrice Lumumba University. Carlos became effective because he attended all the formidable terrorist schools — Havana, Moscow and finally the PFLP in the Middle East.

Lumumba University in Moscow, which enlists students from all parts of the Third World, has many faces. It was set up by Khrushchev ostensibly to provide university education for the underprivileged, but it would be naive to assume that it was not also used for propaganda purposes. According to one defector who taught there 90 per cent of the staff are connected to the KGB, and the Russian students who provide a quarter of the 20,000 strength of the university are carefully picked and then briefed for their task of spreading the Communist word among the outsiders: Most of the foreign students complete their courses and then return home to start jobs as doctors, engineers and civil servants and take their place among the leaders of their country. It is only then that Russian fellow students turn up as diplomats and journalists to renew affinities and often to put friendly 'old boy' pressure upon them to perform some service to the Soviet Union.

But among the negligible presence of foreign students who show enthusiasm and aptitude for clandestine activities on behalf of the cause, there are further courses available. The nobility in this field go on to be trained by Department V, the KGB's Assassination and Sabotage Squad, where they learn the dirty tricks of the business.

A training centre for expatriate recruits was established some years ago by Colonel Kotov, who, after serving in Israel in the guise of diplomat, moved to Lebanon where he had connections with Palestine guerrillas. When he returned to Moscow the KGB had already formulated its own terror courses. After rigorous weapon training international intakes were instructed in surveillance methods, how to follow without being detected and how to escape when they were themselves being tailed. The final stage of the course was concerned with how to organise and then operate a terrorist network. The student also received instruction in the use of disguise, fake identities and how to establish escape channels. The Russians later set up special courses in the Soviet Union and in East Germany for students to learn how to handle heavier and more modern weaponry. In particular they acquired the skills needed to handle SAM7 hand-held missiles and how to fire anti-tank weapons. It is now known that Carlos had passed through no less than four specialised training establishments operated by the Russian secret police near Moscow.

Worldwide Terrorism

This raises the question of how far the Russians and the KGB are involved in worldwide terrorism. Theoretically the Russians do not approve of terrorism, and officially condemn it as individualist and adventurist. Obviously, the then Soviet Union has no wish to give too much support to terrorist extremists who deviate from the classic Communist line. Yet it was tempting for them to use such people as substitutes in the cold war against the capitalist powers, and in any case by providing training and weapons for such men they can at least keep a measure of control over them and prevent them turning their attention to action within the then Soviet world. Another advantage of limited participation is that it enables the KGB to keep itself abreast about subversive groups. Finally the time might come when terrorism would be useful to the Kremlin as an extra weapon against their ideological adversaries in Peking.

Whatever the reasons, it is certain that some help had been given to transnational groups by the Soviet Union. In 1975 two terrorists sent to prison in Holland for plotting to hijack a train and take Soviet Jews as hostages gave evidence that they had learned their technique at a village near Moscow.

It is through giving support to Arab groups acting against Israeli interests that the then Soviet Union was drawn into supporting some terrorist activities. On numerous occasions there had been mention of a Soviet training camp at Simferpol in the Crimea which can handle 400 trainees. There were also active training camps at Ostrova in erstwhile Czechoslovakia and at Pankow in East Germany.

In Latin America many a terrorist has taken this classic course into subversive activities; Lenin himself relied on 'expropriations' to sponsor the Bolsheviks and Ben Bella, the Algerian FLN leader, started out by trying bank robbery first. The truth is that only by participating in a raid and by having his baptism of fire can a terrorist prove himself. The same is true of soldiers. However realistic their training they need to go into real action in order to find out if they have got the 'bottle' for the job.

In several groups criminals have been welcomed into the movement for their technical acumen, and sometimes because the participation of genuine working-class outlaws gives the thing a satisfactory doctrinal feel. The growing sophistication of terrorist training in Europe, now under constant pressure from highly specialised security forces, can be esteemed from examination of a manual produced for the Red Brigades in Italy. Its owners had failed to comply with its final instruction which was, 'This book must not be left lying around'), and police found it in a hastily abandoned terrorist hideout at 96 Via Gradoli, Rome. *Security Rules and Work Methods* — the title of this loose-leaf pamphlet - gives accurate instructions about the comportment of terrorist groups. It advised them that, to avoid drawing attention to themselves, they should appear to be respectable, house-proud and in regular jobs, none of them easy tasks for student-type killers. Flats should be 'proletarian, modest, clean, neat and completely furnished'. From the outside everything should seem to be normal with curtains, entrance light and nameplate in place. Window boxes help to provide an extra touch of respectability. The pamphlet recommended great care in choosing a hideout to make certain that it was in a street where the police would find it difficult to keep vigil from such traditional urban look-out places as bars, public buildings and warehouses. It warned that dirty cars attract attention and advised terrorists to spend time cleaning their cars rather than in going to nearby cafes and bars where they might excite curiosity. In case all these precautions failed the terrorists had been ordered to retain as little compromising material as possible, keep their weapons and essential equipment in bags, and always be prepared for a quick getaway.

It seems that in the case of the occupants of Via Gradoli, the strain of following the training recommendations of each choosing his role as factory employee, teacher or salesman — married or not — and then sticking to the regular work hours and arrivals and departures of such people, had proved too much for the enthusiasts who helped with the abduction of Aldo Moro. For eventually they did attract attention during the great police search in Rome when a neighbour complained about a water leak in their apartment. They left behind enough compromising evidence in the shape of false car licence plates, wigs and unused stationery stolen from Rome police headquarters.

Even more significant was the fact that other documents revealed a good deal about the efficiency of their organisation, proving that the Moro kidnapping had involved the complicated co-operation of about sixty people, including twelve involved in the attack on the politician and his five-man escort, all of whom were killed. The group left behind banknotes relating them to ransoms collected from other kidnaps. Records found with the training manual showed that the group had spent $20,000 on the purchase of firearms. Once again it was manifested that terrorist operations are costly.

An interesting example of 'learn-as-you-go' terrorism is provided by Ulrike Meinhof. Until she took part in the Berlin operation to free Andreas Baader she had absolutely no experience of violent law breaking. While she was on the run, she observed with interest as another member of the gang demonstrated how to start the engine of a stolen Mercedes by short-circuiting. In the stolen car they drove to a provincial town and intruded municipal offices, and there Ulrike learned how to open a locked door with a screwdriver. A coded message had been sent to her with instructions on where to send them, but because she decoded badly they were sent to the wrong address and that particular mission failed.

But in most cases the training of terrorists has become so formalised that regular courses are taught with passing-out ceremonies held to mark the end of the curriculum. Any applicant wishing to join the Montoneros, for example, must first undergo a two-month indoctrination course, during which the romantics and ineffectuals are weeded out. Family loyalty is the first to be attacked because it is the most basic of the old ties and the most difficult to eradicate.

Eight

Religious Terrorism: Specific Meaning

Religious fundamentalism has a clear and relatively specific meaning in the West. It refers to the maintenance of age-old beliefs involving a literal acceptance of the creeds as fundamental, as well as belief in the interrancy of the Scriptures. It is a term most promptly associated with a distinct school of American Protestantism, although its usage has extended to embrace a much wider context.

Perhaps the single critical quality of fundamentalism is that the believer considers religion seriously. This is to say, not only is there is a sense of truth and error in their belief systems, but in recognising truth it is the duty of the believer to follow religious prescriptions because they represent truth. From a psychological viewpoint, the significant feature of 'taking religion seriously' is that it implies not mere belief, but also behaviour. A quality of the fundamentalist believer is, therefore, the expression of the specific fundamentalist priorities in behaviour of some form.

Islamic Fundamentalism

Because fundamentalism is associated with a referencing back to traditional beliefs and values, the liberal West has a tendency to view such movements as essentially politically conservative and reactionary. In the present climate, this also tends to result in regarding fundamentalism in a negative way, in the sense of it being a reaction against modernity and battling for a return to some earlier and (assumed) less liberal society. This assumption that the past is in some way less 'liberal' may well be incorrect when applied in Islamic contexts, however. It is also an inappropriate assumption to make about many contemporary Christian fundamentalists.

If we look at what are termed radical views on Islam, certainly its critical quality, as seen by the Western observer, is a desire to return to the founding principles of Islam, and particularly those that were linked to the creation of an Islamised society at the time of the Prophet. What we cannot necessarily imagine, however, is that this represents a movement 'backwards' away from what the West would regard as liberal social values and 'civilisation' towards a conservative, essentially negative, unvarying world. The renewal implied by seeking to return to the fundamentals of Islam can be seen throughout the history of Islam. What we observe in the contemporary Islamic world may be better regarded in terms of cyclical religious refreshment rather than social retreat.

What constitutes 'backwards' is, of course, a matter of judgement, and we must not forget the relativity such a judgement implies. Paradoxically, in the contemporary world the changes desired by the Islamic fundamentalist believer may, in many ways, be akin to those desired by the contemporary political radical, at least in terms of process. Both, for example, are searching for a new 'social formula' which requires renunciation of the *status quo* and seeks profound social change. These desired changes may, in addition, also be necessarily revolutionary, resulting in the destabilisation and ultimate overthrow of an established regime. Whilst the broadly secular political radical and the religious fundamentalist may ultimately desire different things, fulfilment of their desires might require common processes sufficient to create allegiances. We can see, therefore, why what might be thought to be paradoxical terms — radical and fundamentalism— come together in some aspects of contemporary Islam. This seems to be very evident in the contemporary Islamic world, regardless of the debate about whether Islam in origin can be described as a 'political' religion.

To understand this more comprehensively, it is necessary to examine the aspirations of Islamic fundamentalism within the particular social definition in which it occurs.

We will use here the term 'Islamic fundamentalism' to refer to the sense in which the believer does accept religion seriously, where there is a sense of truth and error which manifests itself in social and political activity, and where the framework for social change lies primarily in the word of God, rather than the present social and economic climate. We should note, however, that whilst we can identify the broad parameters of fundamentalist ideology, the social and political influences of fundamentalist thinking are considerably difficult to assess. The significance of Islamic fundamentalism lies not so much in the numbers of believers who cling strictly to the fundamentalist position, but rather that it provides the moral authority and ideological dynamism from which significant political influence might develop.

Economic Impediments

Despite colonialism, economic impediments and political upheaval, Islam continues to command widespread general support across a wide spectrum of citizens in Islamic countries ranging from the rural and urban poor to intellectuals. It may well be that a common denominator of all the fractions is a dissatisfaction with their contemporary political and economic situation. But the significance of Islamic fundamentalism lies in its capacity to influence and channel that dissatisfaction in specific directions, rather than in the total number of fundamentalist believers. Particular circumstances (such as a ruler or a war) may influence the precise qualities aspired to, and the pragmatic needs of the moment may restrain the political expression of fundamentalist ideology.

The reasons for the increase in influence of fundamentalist movements within Islamic societies are very complicated. They relate to both the external and internal dynamics of those societies, and analyses can be developed at a variety of levels. In contrast to this complexity for the outside observer, however, the situation from the standpoint of the believer is obviously much simpler. The believer would assert that his views represents the revealed word of Allah, and place any account of the resurgence of these distinctive forms of Islam within a theological framework. This simplicity of belief and explanation for the believer is a significant quality of the fundamentalist view of the world.

One set of factors that can be identified from a Western social and psychological proportion lies in a general feeling of discontent expressed by many Islamic commentators with the nature of contemporary Islamic States. This discontent is one trait that seems to relate the theological to the political and which may from time to time manifest itself on overtly political activity. This may then be sometimes associated, or perhaps more optly correlated, with left wing political movements; but it may also become evident in a theological context, and address primarily religious targets. At least in its early stages, the ferment in Algeria following the electoral victories of Islamic parties illustrate this. However, the all-embracing social nature of Islam necessarily means that religious activity will impinge on broader socio-political issues which draws together the theological and political. Indeed, the inclusive trait of Islam presents the Western observer with serious difficulties of understanding. Areas of social separation on which the West prides itself and largely takes for granted (such as the distinction between the law and due process, and social and political issues related to public wellbeing) are contradicted in Islamic societies. There are striking differences with Western legal views in assumptions about the nature of legal process, evidence and even the concept of truth, for example. Indeed, what we might characterise in the West as a retreat refuge theology from the problems of the world within Islam necessarily means a growing engagement with the world and an absorption of the political within the theological. This baffling juxtaposition of the political and theological lies at the very origin of Islamic fundamentalism.

Two broad classes of influence can be identified which seem to be associated with the general dissatisfaction in Islamic societies — those concerned with the relationship between Islamic states and the broader world, which we might characterise as external factors, and those concerned with Islam itself and its practices, which we might label as internal factors.

One significant external factor of relevance to the Islamic masses (although possibly of less relevance to the religious) is the respective failure of the Arab and Islamic states to rival Western material wealth and success. The Muslim world remains primarily a part of the Third World, despite very considerable natural resources (in the form of oil, for example). The major Muslim countries, such as Egypt and Syria, had generally failed to achieve substantial rises in living standards for the vast majority of their citizens compared to the West, and remain with mostly poor peasant economies. In the developed countries (such as the Gulf States) economic wealth has benefited a relatively limited few, and has not been distributed to poorer Islamic countries, nor to their immensely vast migrant communities. Indeed, despite the overt theocratic qualities of life in the Gulf States, to many devout Muslims, the effects of increased oil wealth have been to enhance the influence of the West, and challenge the social foundation of Islam, rather than to complement and enhance it.

Similarly, the impetus to modernisation, secularism and Westernisation which from time to time characterised both Nasser's and Sadat's Egypt, for example, has totally failed to produce much improvement in most people's lives. Furthermore whilst Western economic practices may have contributed comparatively little to public well being, much Western investment that occurs in Islamic countries is frequently linked to multinationals, whose loyalties are seen to lie largely with the West. Indeed, such economic benefits as they may bring are often considered as being of less significance than the negative effects of encouraging secularism and behaviour contrary to Islamic values.

Arabs vs Israel

A further significant factor in the current sense of unrest are the repeated humiliating failures of Arab armies to defeat Israel. At the popular level, this emotive issue probably serves to mobilise opinion more than anything else, and is a significant element in the appeal of Arab nationalism. This mass sense of failure to achieve what are perceived to be essentially Arab (and to a lesser extent Islamic) objectives in the face of a strong West is a potent and enduring force which can hardly be underestimated. Tourism and the Western media also add further to the sense of particular Islamic concern, through encouraging secularism and the adoption of hedonistic lifestyles. This results in a strange and unexpected paradox. Whilst the contemporary Western view of Islam may be one of buoyancy and disquiet at its advance (perhaps not without some justification), the Fundamentalist views a situation where Islam appears to be on the retreat from an increasing tide of secularism and associated Western values.

Internal features of Islam complement and interact with this general sense of discontent. In the context of concern to us, relevant features of Islam as a religion and as a social movement that sustain fundamentalist positions can be identified. These are its claims to universal validity; its theocratic demands extending to all aspects of life; the sanctification of Islamic law and its verdicts; and a general equation (at least within Sunni thinking) if the State with the implementation of Islam.

Islam claims that it is the perfect and final embodiment of God's law to the believer; it is thus essentially the preferred, obvious and appropriate religion for all people. Conditional tolerance of other religions is strictly restricted to 'people of the Book' (broadly speaking Christians and Jews) who share a common heritage, even though, from an Islamic perspective, incomplete and flawed. These religious factions can live within an Islamic state without conversion or coercion provided they accepted Muslim rule and payment of a special tax.

When Western and largely Christian states have confronted Islam, they have in recent times emerged victorious in all arenas of conflict. Whilst challenging to concepts of Islamic superiority in the short term, this is in itself not necessarily so critical when a broader perspective is taken. There are historical instances from the time of the Prophet of the retreat of Islam, only to rise again with renewed vigour. Retreat and the development of a temporary modus vivendi with the forces of secularism can be withstood by Islam as short-term responses to circumstances.

More problematic to contemporary Islamic believers in this context are the experiences of post-colonialism. Post-colonial Muslim aspirations to redress the wrongs of colonialism, and to re-establish the relative positions of Muslim versus Christian (from Muslim vistas) have generally failed, yet Muslim countries have, at least ostensively, been ruled by Muslims and presumably have had the capacity to make use of the full potential of the force of Islam. The contrast between the achievements of Islamic countries in the contemporary world and the glorious history of Muslim advance in the seventh to tenth centuries only adds to the woes. In the consideration of the Fundamentalist, therefore, Islam is challenged and compromised not only by discrepancies in material wealth, but also in terms of its capacity to withstand its own moral and religious authority.

Responses to these apparent challenges to the moral authority of Islam are a critical element of the fundamentalist stand. Themes such as these are reflected in critical analyses of the very nature of Islam, and in particular can be seen in the writings of Sayyid Qutb, who occupies a very position in the development of Islamic fundamentalist thinking. His writings provide the ideological basis on which many aspects of contemporary radical fundamentalist thinking have developed. Whilst there may be disputes within the different fundamentalist movements about the appropriateness of the solutions he offers, his ideological influence remains unchallenged. In his most influential book, Qutb analyses the present position of Islam with particular respect to the challenge to its moral authority. The tone of his analysis can be from the following extract:

> The leadership of mankind by Western man is now on the decline, not because Western culture has become poor materially or because its economic and military power has become weak. The period of the Western system has come to an end primarily because it is deprived of those life-giving values which enabled it to be the leader of mankind. It is necessary for the new leadership to preserve and develop the material fruits of the creative genius of Europe, and also to provide mankind with such high ideals and values as have so far remained undiscovered by mankind, and which will also acquaint humanity with a way of life which is harmonious with human nature, which is positive and constructive, and which is practicable.

Islam is perhaps the only system which possess these values and this way of life.

Problems Facing Islam

It is interesting to note that fundamentalist analyses of the problems facing Islam never express doubt the ideological bases of Islam. In a sense, of course, this follows from 'taking religion seriously', or at least taking seriously the original precepts upon which a religion is based. But a quality of the radical believer is that he goes beyond adherence to basic precepts, and makes no distinction between the general principles upon which Islam might be founded as seen from the twentieth century and the pragmatic responses to life as the 7th century followers of Islam might have found it; the relationship with the contemporary world does not impinge on the analysis. Perhaps as a result of that, fundamentalist analyses always locate the source of any problems in their world view externally to the ideological bases of Islam. Either the West is responsible for deflecting or distorting the inevitability of the proper progress of Islam, or Islamic leaders have failed either through being subverted (again by the West), or because they fail to follow Islamic precepts. What they believe as the fundamental tenents of Islam are never open to question. Parallels may be drawn here with some of the psychological bases of prejudice, which will be returned to later.

That is not to say, however, that there is no criticism of various perspectives on fundamentalism from within Islam, and indeed from within the various fundamentalist positions. But such discussion is largely concerned with strategy, rather than principle. It distinctively identifies three themes common to fundamentalist writers — the total debilitation of the *umma* (people), the Western cause of such debilitation and the flawed foundation of any solutions to this problem other than Islam. The final theme is never questioned.

There is certainly a strong predisposition among writers such as Qutb to stress the poor state of contemporary Islam. In this respect, the theory of modernity as the new barbarity (*Jahiliyya*), which has its origins in the writings of Maudoodi, has played a very significant role in the fundamentalist justification for the debilitation of the *ummah*. At its simplest, the theory of the new *Jahiliyya* refers to the very incompatibility between Islam and modernity (as represented by Western values). It echoes the struggles of the Prophet and his followers in the very inception of Islam, and draws on Qur'anic themes familiar to all Islamic believers. Striving against the state of *Jahiliyya* provides the focus and justification for the fundamentalist agenda, accepting both the assertion of and the reason for the debilitated *ummah*, and its remedy.

Qutb argues that Islam is compelled to battle with *Jahiliyya* both to protect itself ('... its (Islam's) very nature demanded that *jahili* societies would attack it...') and as an instruction from Allah because Islam is the total and only way of life for the believer. To battle against *Jahiliyya* fulfils the requirements of *Jihad* (sacred or holy war). It may be necessary in specific circumstances to reach a temporary accommodation with the world as it exists; but restriction and tolerance is '... a question of strategy rather than of principle;... a matter pertaining to requirements of the movement and not belief. To achieve its ends, and to fight against *Jahiliyya*, Islam '... has a God given right to step forward and take control of the political authority, so that it may establish the Divine system on earth....'

Millenarianism

The discussion above has emphasised on the Islamic context to fundamentalism. These issues can also be viewed from another more general context, which both begins to place them within a broader conceptual structure and makes them more accessible to psychological analysis. Many of the features of Islamic fundamentalist thinking reveal strong evidence of millenarian influences. Millenarianism describes a distinctive quality of the content of an ideology. But it may also have a psychological magnitude in that millenarianism can relate to the way in which ideology can influence behaviour. Millenarianism refers to expectations of the attainment of the Millennium, an expected utopian end. From a theological viewpoint, this may be associated with the arrival of the Messiah, or God's direct intervention on earth in some sense. From a political vista, it may be associated with the attainment of a secular utopian state or other means of utopian social organisation. Millenarianism had played, and continues to play an important role in the development of political and religious movements and can be argued to be one of the significant factors in the development of political violence.

Themes like these have recurred throughout the history of Islam. Indeed, millenarian thinking can be traced to the very inception of Islam, and especially within Shi'a contexts, to the martyrdom of Hazrat Ali. The confident expectations of the return of Hazrat Ali is a feature of many Shi'a factions but elements of millenarian influence also remain within more orthodox Sunni thinking. More explicit Shi's millenarian influences can be seen in the way the different Ghulat sects relate to the succession of Immans. The recurrent religious rebellions that have emerged from within Islamic communities to defy the existing order from the very beginnings of Islam tend to be expressed in millenarian terms, with varying degrees of specific reference to the Mahdi who would come to save his people. Whilst social and economic factors have undoubtedly played a part in these events, Islamic millenarian movements have remained typically religious rather than secular movements.

Many of the qualities of Islamic fundamentalist thinking correspond to the qualities of millenarianism outlined above. Fundamentalist analyses of the current position of Islam strongly emphasise the catastrophic nature of contemporary life. Much of Qutb's work, for example, lucidly demonstrates this, as do the content of innumerable sermons and pamphlets, based upon his and other fundamentalist thinkers work. The special quality of knowledge of the cause of the disastrous present can be clearly noticed in Maudoodi's concept of modernity as the new barbarity (*Jahiliyya*), where the influence of the West is very explicitly presented to the Islamic masses in diabolical terms. Through returning to the basic tenents of Islam and especially the implementation of the *Shari'a* (Islamic Law), the uniquely powerful forces of Islam can be mobilised against the new *Jahiliyya*.

Furthermore, a sense of timeliness and necessity is a prominent feature of fundamentalist thinking — the *ummah* must act now to avert catastrophe. All of these forces come together in the conviction that if implemented, Islam must come out victorious and must defeat the forces of *Jahiliyya*. The looking back to the Golden Age of Islam necessarily heralds the dawning of a new Golden Age, if society is perfectly Islamised and the *Shari'a* implemented.

The assassination of Anwar Sadat in October, 1981, fits properly into this framework. The assassins of Sadat appear to have strongly desired the foundation of an Islamic state in Egypt, and the assassination of Sadat was to be its herald. They adopted a explicitly millenarian outlook where it was argued that Sadat represented the apostate, the representative of *Jahiliyya*. So much were the assassins (but not others who were involved in the plot, especially Abdul al-Zumur) influenced by the millenarian Islamic ideology that they made little or no preparation for the coalition of power after the death of Sadat. Those directly involved in the assassination seemed to have believed that once they had heeded the call to *Jihad*, and assassinated Sadat the Unjust Ruler (*Hakim Zalim*) God would intervene; their action in assassinating him was to pave the way for the millennial event. One reason why the Faridah could be published in Egypt after the event in 1983 was that the assassination seemed not to have established God's intervention, at least in the terms of envisaged by Faraj.

The themes discussed above have exercised considerable influence over contemporary Islamic fundamentalism. Whilst they may emerge in varying contexts, and be subject to differences in emphasis, they set the scene for the moral and psychological appeal of Islam. What is interesting and relevant from our standpoint is the sense in which political and social issues are drawn into the theological argument. But the solution for the problems of Islam are not merely constrained by a special world of theology; they necessarily embrace the broader society in which Islam functions and specify certain kinds of behaviour. This ideological position is very lucidly developed by Faraj. In his discussion of the theological adversities of contemporary Islam in general, and Egypt in particular (very much in the style of Qutb), he accuses the existing political leadership of Islamic countries of apostasy. Whilst they were born Muslims, they do not run their States as religious Muslim States, with the use of *Shari'a* as the foundation for legislation and social intervention and planning To Faraj, the link between theology and behaviour is the 'neglected duty', the duty of *Jihad*, the result from which will necessarily redress the ills of Islam.

Process of Ideological Control and Lack of Public Space

There is a further perspective on this issue which needs mention here. Hannah Arendt, in her analyses of the atrocities committed by the Nazi's during the Second World War, developed the concept of lack of public space. This notion addresses the issue of how people who were in other respects normal could become involved in the appalling activities that characterised the Third Reich. Lack of public space leads to the inability of individuals to exchange and develop ideas in circumstances where extreme control is exercised over social living, most significantly evident to totalitarian states. She gives to this capacity to communicate a significance in both the political and moral domains, and in particular relates the degree of social control it implies to a loss of a sense of reality and morality, making possible the brutalities of the concentration camps.

The extreme degree of social control required by fundamentalist interpretations of Islam meet the requirements for lack of public space, in Arendt's terms, and in result we might expect to see the lack of regard for the restraints on behaviour towards enemies emerging within Islam (although this is a subject considerably dealt with in the Qur'an, where clearly defined and explicit rules are given to regulate conduct). In behavioural terms it can be argued that lack of public space relates very explicitly to the degree of control exercised by behavioural rules. Societies showing a lack of public space are characterised by both explicit articulation of rules governing behaviour, and their rigorous application and enforcement. Fundamentalist Islamic aspirations readily fit this view.

In a sense, the precise detail of religious observance required is of less significance than the fact that behaviour is under close control of the religious ideology, expressed as rules. The rigidity of purpose, the insensitivity, the focusing, the intensely personalised view of the world, the tolerance of what to the non-initiate is uncongeniality the simplification of the world view and the loss of critical judgement, all seem to be qualities of the religious fundamentalist. They are also qualities which might be perceived to illustrate behaviour subject to extreme rule governance, as opposed to contingency control.

Psychological Approaches

There are other psychological insights that extend our understanding of these issues. One such relates to the theory of

Conspiracy. As we have noted earlier, an important feature of fundamentalist thinking is the malevolence of forces opposed to Islam, which conspire to subvert its message, and undermine the allegiances of believers. Much of Qutb's analysis of the state of the World of Islam, for instance, hinges upon assertions of the West's desires to subvert the rightful progress of Islam as the superior religious and social system. How else can the exhausted state of the *umma* be explained? Sometimes the conspiratorial intention is deliberate, and results from explicit acts of policy (shades of this were seen in some Islamic critiques of the Gulf War), but sometimes the West is the unaware instrument of a diabolical power. We might note, for example, the tendency amongst the rebels in Lebanon to explain victory by reference to courage and patriotism and defeat by reference to plots. This is probably a more general process rather than one confined to the Lebanese experience, but it is particularly noticeable amongst the various Lebanese parties. The defeat of Saddam Hussein in the Gulf War has also sometimes been explained in this way, with frequent reference to 'conspiracies' of either imperialism or colonialism.

Equally, the concept of conspiracy is central to millenarianism. It is an element of the struggle to attain the millennium, and also might be perceived to be a factor in the notion of 'timeliness' of millenarian attainment. The central feature of conspiracy in whatever disguise it appears, is that forces (sometimes defined, sometimes undefined) conspire to subvert, entrap, or in other way destroy the positive functions of society. Therefore, when millenarian Islam embraces conspiracy theories, we might expect forces of great momentum and power to develop.

The psychological bases of conspiracy theories are complicated, but a factor that might concern us is the sense of undeserved suffering experienced when an individual fails to attain material or spiritual benefits despite living a humble life. We can see here echoes of the notions of psychological 'justice' as an element in the justification of terrorism. How can a devout Muslim in a necessarily superior society and who obeys God's laws and acts in an upright and moral manner experience the defeat, humiliation, and lack of material advance that has characterised Islamic societies? If you accept the premises, the believer is being subjected to an undeserved injustice which is of paramount importance, in that it challenges God's order. For the devoutly religious, because his or her way of life is decided by God, it can only fail to deliver its promises because it is being subverted through some conspiracy of forces opposed to it. Analyses of the conduct of international affairs suggests that sometimes, of course, there are both overt and covert conspiracies at work, and the observation of participants are accurate!

Leaving aside situations where there are genuine grounds for suspecting conspiracy, one way of perceiving the processes that might be involved in conspiracy is to refer to Festinger's Theory of Cognitive Dissonance. The cognitive contention caused by the juxtaposition of firmly held beliefs about superiority, and the evident failure to attain objectives is resolved by reference to the action of external agencies. A related explanation refers to processes of peculiarities, as a means of understanding the world as we experience it, and in particular to what has been termed actor-observer rivalry. This refers to the tendency of people to attribute the causes of their own behaviour to external factors, as opposed to qualities in themselves. In particular, a noticeable feature of attributional processes is that it is the world in which we live that gives rise to our defeats rather than the inadequacy of our own actions. Attribution of defeat to external causes that actively conspire and plot against us readily fits into this model.

However, we conceptualise the issue, the idea of conspiracy is a way of making sense of a complex and confusing world, where real or imagined disadvantage occurs. The practical significance and influence of the notion of conspiracy cannot be dismissed as a factor in the Islamic perception of the world, and as a support for the framework of fundamentalism.

Other social psychological processes seem relevant to this discussion and merit some short reference. The complex of issues discussed above with reference to conspiracy theories also have elements in common with processes of prejudice formation and stereotyping. Elements of both can be clearly noticed in fundamentalism. The images of the West presented by authors such a Qutb draw upon simple stereotypes, attributing largely simplistic negative characteristics to entire communities.

Anti-westernism

Indeed, in other contexts, the Anti-westernism so frequently advocated in fundamentalist sermons would attract the term 'racism' and probably be seen as examples of prejudice. The psychological and cognitive bases of the refusal of the believer to question the fundamental principles of Islam noted earlier might be thought to be related to similar processes observed in analyses of prejudice, where rigidity of view, despite substantiation to the contrary, seems to characterise the prejudiced individual.

The above leads to an analysis of religious fundamentalism in terms of a framework in which specific ideological priorities might be expressed. An important implication of this is that fundamentalism is not necessarily a primary, and therefore distinctive, feature of either ideology or religious active, although it may be that it is more likely in some forms of religious expression than others. Nor need we look for specific individual qualities that allow for the expression of fundamentalist views. Rather, fundamentalism can be perceived as an instrumental quality of ideology, its incidence being determined by the interaction of ideology as contingency rules, the particular content of ideology, local and close behavioural contingencies and situational factors.

Indeed, under some circumstances, what we regard as fundamentalism may simply be a rather minor element linked with, and subsidiary to, other more dominant controlling contingencies. The broader results of fundamentalism may, of course, be profound for the recipient, or the society in which it occurs. But as far as the individual is concerned, it may well be an incidental ingredient in the broader contingencies controlling behaviour.

The behaviour of the religious fundamentalist can be perceived as having qualities similar to those of normal people, differing along a continuum of some kind rather than differing in definite terms. Perhaps one way of characterising that continuum is in terms of the extent to which the fundamentalist's behaviour is closely controlled by a particular set of rules which are relatively constrained in extent and closely interrelated. This contrasts with the relative multiplicity of rules that might control normal behaviour, and the extent of control exercised by current circumstances.

If we express this difference in such a way, this is not simply an exaggeration, nor is it an elaborate version of mentalistic accounts. An individual can be 'fanatical' (for this is another way of describing the qualities that we are concerned with) about a variety of things — he might radically follow a sport or become wholly absorbed and involved in an aspect of work. All are examples of the control exercised by behavioural rules. The nature of the particular rule following behaviour will certainly determine the focus. The distinctive quality of fanatical religious behaviour (which might be an appropriate term for fundamentalism) is the extent of control which is itself a reflection of the all accepting qualities of religion, in contrast to the limited scope of sport related rules, for example. In describing ideologically controlled behaviour in this way, and in particular by relating it to the response of the religious fundamentalist, we are not therefore only describing the nature of behavioural control, but also describing the processes whereby such control develops.

We can identify a number of important qualities of religious ideology that can now be brought within a larger framework. In particular, distinctions may be made between the content of ideology (the particular kind of religion, the proper nature of religious rules), and the process of ideology, implied and influenced by an ideology's particular content. At least three prime factors can be identified:

1. The specific content of an ideology (in terms of militancy, injunctions at a micro-level, etc.);
2. A more diffuse and higher level aspect of content, particularly as it relates to millenarianism;
3. The process implied by extreme ideological control, which can be characterised as 'lack of public space', as discussed above.

Other factors may be relevant, and this area needs further exploration. In the following, we will examine 1 and 2 above in more detail.

If we examine the concept of specific ideological content, the precise day-to-day injunctions of a religion are conspicuously one important element in determining religious behaviour. The prescriptions to prayer, for example, or the performance of fasting during ramadan are instances of the control of day-to-day religious life. The five 'pillars' of Islam can be seen in this light, as an example of specific ideological content. Allied to this level of specificity are more general injunctions, perhaps even precisely related to violence. Nazi ideology was replete with reference to the Jews as negative objects, and it urged discrimination and violence upon them in a very explicit manner. The extent to which an ideology explicitly rejects a group, and expresses that rejection in militant terms, is apparently one aspect of the potential for violence within an ideology.

Fundamentalist Islam quite clearly develops as part of the content of its ideological prescriptions aggression against Western life and Western culture. Islam contains many qualities which can be used to sustain a militant approach, the most significant of which is the concept of *Jihad*. '*Jihad* in Islam is simply a name for striving to make this system of life dominant in the world', (Qutb) expresses clearly the combative nature of Islam, at least as seen by Qutb.

This ideological imperative for *Jihad* need not in any way reduce the peaceful aspirations of Islam seen from the perspective of the believer. A fundamental requirement of Islam is that a Muslim is required to establish the sovereignty of God on earth. *Jihad* is a medium of establishing this - '*Jihad*, then, is a means to achieve a universal change by establishing peace of conscience, domestic peace, national peace and international peace' (Qutb). Because, for the believer, Islam is essentially the only possible way to attain God's dominion on the earth, the establishment of an Islamic world must produce God's peace and justice. Islam might be labelled a self-contained religion - it contains within itself all that is necessary for the believer to attain salvation and God's peace. Not to accept this obvious and unchallengeable logic can only be the result of vindictive influences, which are working to oppose the establishment of God's law (an issue related to conspiracy theories discussed earlier).

Qutb argues at considerable length the tolerant nature of Islam, but the tolerance only extends to those who accept the logic. Enemies of Islam are given three choices — to adopt Islam, to pay the tribute (as an acknowledgement that the non-believer will not hinder the progress of Islam), or to fight (because they 'obdurately stand between men and Islam's righteous and peaceful principles'). Given these views, what might be termed the militant logic of fanatical and fundamentalist Islam will inevitably establish confrontation between Islam and the West.

In behavioural terms, what we might characterise as the logic of Islam is no more than an expression of behavioural norms that specify relationships between long-term ends and immediate behaviour. The rules have their origin in the bases of Islam and the *Shari'a*, (the Qur'an, etc.) and the more detailed relationships are made clear (and given a distinctive emphasis) by authors such as Qutb. They are further refined by various commentaries and at the local level by weekly sermons in the Mosques, etc.

A clearer example of behavioural rules is of course the concept of *Shari'a*, Islam equates the laws of human nature with the laws of the universe (what we might term physical laws). Both are aspects of God's will, both are immutable essence of life, and both must be obeyed. This extends as much to voluntary as involuntary behaviour — but for the former, God especially prescribed the *Shari'a* to ensure that man's 'life is in harmony with his very own nature' (Qutb). *Shari'a* is the divine expression of God's law, and is found in the Holy Qur'an, the Sunna and the Hadiths (the precise weighting and form given to each element of the Holy writings relates to specific emphases and traditions within Islam).

The refinement process in the development of religious behavioural rules can be noticed in the relationship between *Shari'a* and the sources of Islamic law. The only source of authoritative written law in Islam is the Qur'an. "It is the exact spoken word of God as reduced to writing by the Prophet_" The Sunna were recorded after the Prophet's death, and constitute more substantive forms of guidance. The other sources of law (analogical reasoning or, *qiya*, and the idea of consensus or *ijma*) allow more detailed working out of general propositions related to the particular social circumstances of the time. It is of some importance that the contemporary role of *qiya* and *ijma* in the determination of *Shari'a* constitutes one of the watersheds that divide fundamentalist thinking from other emphases within Islam. However, *Shari'a* provides to establish a common bond between all Muslims, and its divine origin places it in a unique position with respect to human affairs. Its application is an element of faith for the devout, as the clear, unambiguous and thorough expression of God's will.

The *Shari'a* specifies behaviours appropriate to situations at a variety of levels. In the West, we tend to be most aware of *Shari'a* when applied within the context of criminal law, and more particularly in terms of the system of punishments specified for theft (amputation) and adultery (stoning). But *Shari'a* extends far beyond these confines, and embraces all aspects of jurisprudence, social living, the relationship between people in business and commercial enterprises, and especially the relationship between states. The self-contained nature of Islam is apparent in this area as in others — 'One cannot enforce a part of Islamic law and neglect another for then it would not be Islam' (Qutb).

The detail of what is particularly meant by *Shari'a* is itself a matter of some debate, and as we noted earlier, its exact meaning and referencing to the Qur'an, Sunna and Hadiths represents one of the watersheds along which approaches to Islam divide. No matter what particular approach is taken, however, a necessary social expression of the necessary fundamental and total change desired by the fundamentalist believer is a demand to implement the *Shari'a*. This is generally regardless of the larger social contexts and religious allegiances of those subjected to it. It is this demand that embodies in many respects the particular ideological qualities of social control within contemporary fundamentalist Islam. Because most Muslim States do not apply *Shari'a*, the issue has become a tangible social aspiration which brings together both fundamentalist politics and theology.

For the Islamic fundamentalist, the *Shari'a* is essentially and expression of behavioural rules. We should note that it is expressed at a behavioural level, and set out explicitly and unambiguously (subject to whatever interpretation authority places upon it) what an individual should and must do in a given situations. If the fundamentalist does take religion seriously, and acts upon what religion requires, he implements and adheres to these rules in his day-to-day life. It is difficult to imagine a clearer example of behavioural rule-following than the fundamentalist believer.

Two other aspects of the 'content' of Islam merit attention in this context. These are the notions of *bai'a* and *taqiia*. Both address issues related to the relationship between behaviour and Islam. *Bai'a* relates to the notion of allegiance and homage of the faithful to their leader. In Sunni terms, precedents for its importance lie in the succession of Abu Bakr to the Caliphate, which was made legitimate by the concept of *bai'a*, where those present also pledged the absent. The idea extends beyond simple allegiance in any Western sense, however, and draws upon the relationship between the Caliph (or leader) and Allah. *Bai'a* implies, therefore, a bond of absolute association, which may ultimately be to death if necessary. Faraj extends this issue, however, by distinguishing between the Oath of Allegiance to the Caliph, and the Oath of Allegiance till death. The importance of this is that the strength and moral demands of the Oath relates to the Caliph as the representative of the God.

The requirement of *bai'a* can at times confront with the duty which both Qutb and Faraj stress of the appropriateness of *Jihad* under some conditions against the rulers of Islamic states. The conflict is resolved, however, if the ruler does not abide by the principles of Islam, and is therefore either an apostate or *Jahili*. In this case, the devout are needed to kill him, despite claims from the ruler of *bai'a*.

The essentially Shi'a concept of *taqiia* relates to piousness that requires deception. The Qur'an contains detailed accounts of how Muslims should behave, both to other Muslims and to non-believers, which generally stress propriety and respect for others. In conditions of *Jihad*, however, there are circumstances where the injunctions against such things as fraudulence may be waived to enable some eventual achievement. Qutb discusses this, but a clearer account is given by Faraj where he discusses the appropriateness of lying to the enemy. Faraj states that it is quite permissible to lie in the course of *Jihad*.

Actions of Faraj

The actions of the group to which Faraj belonged illustrated both the limits on *bai'a* and the notion of *taqiia*. The assassins of Sadat were army officers, who remained as a hidden group until the assassination itself. Whilst Sadat, as leader of the Egyptian

State, could command *bai'a,* his position as analysed by Faraj placed him in the domains of *Jihad,* where *taqiia* and breaking *bai'a* was appropriate. In one sense, *bai'a* clearly relates to the strength of rule control, and the behaviour of the conspirators associated with Faraj explicitly demonstrate this. But the ideological bases of fundamentalist thinking can also result in a shift of control, expressed as a limitation on the concept of bai'a vis-à-vis particular rules, and an extension of the concept to embrace the supra-ordinate demands of *bai'a* to the Almighty. Deception and *taqiia* then become appropriate.

The significance of this for analyses of radical behaviour should not be underestimated. In the capacity of Islam to sustain the suicide bombers, for instance, we can see at one level evidence of the strength of *bai'a.* Similarly, we can see that what might appear to be duplicity on the part of participants in some negotiation is entirely appropriate and moral from their view-point where it involves *Jihad.* There is another sense in which this is significant, however. Both *bai'a* and *taqiia* are concepts more freely associated with *Shi'a* thinking rather than that of Sunni. The stress Sunni fundamentalist authors (such as Qutb) place on these concepts, marks the introduction of a vital new factor into Sunni ideology through a re-examination and re-emphasis of these concepts. These are clearly articulated aspects of fundamentalist ideology, and in the terms of the analysis presented here, because they are apparently articulated we would expect them to play a part in determining the behaviour of believers.

It follows, therefore, that the actions of Faraj and his co-conspirators should not be perceived as isolated aberrations within Sunni thinking, but as markers of its radicalisation, or even, as some commentators have suggested, its Shi'atisation. If we are to take the content of ideology seriously, as is discussed above, then the following comments by Qutb encompass the fundamentalist agenda: "The foremost duty of Islam in this world is to depose *Jahiliyya* from the leadership of man, and to take the leadership into its own hands..." (Qutb). The grounding of fundamentalist Islam in its classical history, and the historical might of the Muslim empire provides a rich source for very worrying analogies with the present day.

Ideology can be seen as affecting behaviour at a variety of levels. An example of this can be seen in the previous discussion, where reference was made to the millenarian qualities of militant Islam. These qualities can also be located within a general framework emphasising behavioural norms. But of particular relevance to our discussion are the relationships in millenarian ideology between the expected end state and human agency, in creating the desired state. Many, if not all, religions are millenarian, in the sense that they allow the believer to look forward to a more prosperous, happier and probably more just life after death. The particular quality that brings millenarianism within our explanatory framework is the sense of imminence of millenarian attainment. It is also this characteristic feature that relates millenarianism to violence.

Whether imminence is a variable affecting the positive outcomes of behavioural rules, or whether it relates to notions of 'easy to follow' and 'hard to follow' rules, or indeed other factors, is unclear. There are, however, cogent arguments to endorse the notion that the timeliness of action, which is so much a feature of millenarian activity, relates to the impending attainment of the millennium, and that such a sense of timeliness is a significant factor in the development of violence and an associated sense of personal agency.

Millenarianism is at one level a facet of the content of ideology, but at another level of analysis it has certain features that relate to more general processes. As we have seen in our earlier discussion, fundamentalist thinkers vehemently emphasise the timeliness of action for the believer, given the apocalyptic features of the present, and the profoundly positive consequences of engagement with the apocalyptic forces. Coherent to the above discussion, we might note that the focus of the negative effects on the world is secularism, embodied by Western values and economic power. Thus, we can see a further behavioural pressure towards fundamentalist confrontation with the West, which we can conceptualise within the context of behavioural norms.

The nature of Islamic fundamentalism is yet to be properly understood by most citizens of the Western world. They would do well to study it and would then come to realise that it is a force of vast potential.

Nine

Facets of Jihad

I

While the Islamic movement in the West Bank and Gaza has made tangible gains by becoming a significant political force in Palestinian society, this movement continues to face a number of major challenges. It is not yet clear whether this movement will ever be able to make Islam a substitute to the PLO and what it stands for, as a frame of reference for the Palestinian people in the Occupied Territories. This kind of accomplishment will depend on the Islamists' ability to prove the validity of their conception and the feasibility of their positions and policies with regard to the achievement of legitimate national goals of the Palestinian people. It will also depend on the extent to which the Palestinians are intending to take an Islamic identity and give this identity priority over their nationalist identity, as well as the ability of the Islamic movement to rekindle Islamic sentiments and beliefs.

Role of PLO

In addition to distrust about the Islamic movement's ability to become a viable alternative to the PLO, the strict and conservative social outlook of the movement creates anxiety among large sections of the population. Palestinian society has a strong secular tradition. This tradition can act as counterbalance to the expansion of Islamic influence. Secularist tendencies in the Occupied Territories are executed through a large number of secular institutions, PLO factions, and the intelligentsia as a whole. There is also an active Christian minority that is centrally positioned in the cities of Jerusalem, Ramallah, and Bethlehem. Many members of this minority are frontline politicians, businessmen, academicians, journalists, educators, and community leaders. Furthermore, Christian schools and kindergartens, which are attended by large numbers of Muslim students and children, play a key role in defining Palestinian national and political culture.

The Islamic movement in the Occupied Territories has few prominent leadership figures. A number of the Hamas leaders and almost all known leaders of the Islamic *Jihad* have been expelled from the West Bank and Gaza. A leadership vacuum might open the way for a younger, less experienced breed of leaders who may be prone to internal divisions and splits or may be trapped in an untimely showdown with the Israeli authorities. This showdown could prove to be harmful to Hamas and the Muslim Brotherhood Society as a whole. The December 1992 deportation of 418 Hamas and *Jihad* leaders and activists by the Israeli authorities should be seen in this context.

Moreover, the Islamic movement is not a consistent whole. The two major groups comprising this movement have varying views and positions, and within each group homogeneity is far from being total. In Hamas, for instance, there are the fundamentalist, the political, and the opportunist. While still united vis-à-vis the PLO, no major differences within Hamas have yet emerged. But the threats facing the movement, and conflicting views as to the best way to handle them, may give rise to differences and bring them to the fore. However, active involvement of the Jordanian Brotherhood in Hamas and Hamas's major faith on the Muslim Brotherhood in Jordan may prevent the emergence of any significant crises within the movement.

Smaller factions have also break away from the Islamic *Jihad* movement. Splits are motivated primarily by personal differences or by competition. Following a dispute over the leadership of the Islamic *Jihad*, As'ad Bayoud al-Tamimi split from the movement and established a faction under his own leadership.

A second splinter group is headed by Ahmad Mahanna, who formed an organisation called "Hizbullah Palestine." Mahanna is believed to be the person who planned an attack on an Israeli tourist bus in 1989 on the road between Cairo and Isma'iliyya in Egypt, before his split from al-Tamimi's group. In this attack, twelve Israelis were killed and seven others were injured. It is not apparent what process of differentiation will take place within the Islamic groups, especially if the Islamic movement gains supremacy in the Occupied Territories.

Issues of democracy and pluralism have not till now been a matter of concern for the Islamic movement in the Occupied Territories. But failure to articulate acceptable positions on these issues may alienate prominent segments of the Palestinian society and consequently undermine the Islamic movement and its influence. The problems Islamists in some other countries (Tunisia and Algeria, for instance) are confronting may urge the Palestinian Islamists to address these issues. The Islamic movement in the Occupied Territories may be able to evade such issues for some time on the pretext that the pressing and primary concern of the movement is national liberation from the Israeli occupation, and not the seizure of political power in society. But despite that, the Islamists need to define the basis for their dealings with other political factions and with society as a whole.

From a theoretical and doctrinal point of view, Palestinian Islamists dismiss the concept of democracy as a Western notion that has no place in a Muslim society. The Islamists argue that the Islamic doctrine provides principles that are more just and comprehensive. In an Islamic order, political parties that do not accept Islam as a frame of reference will be prevented. But while the Islamic society and Islamic rule are not established, the Islamists favour the notion of democracy because they believe that Islam can thrive under democracy better than it does under dictatorship.

The PLO remains the major and more powerful challenge to the Islamic movement in the Occupied Territories. The Islamic movement does not have the solid nationalist record and genuineness which the PLO has earned as a result of more than twenty-five years of nationalist resistance to the Israeli occupation. The PLO is accredited with restoring and crystallising the Palestinian national identity and with defining the national rights of the Palestinian people. As long as the Islamic movement does not espouse a defined nationalist programme that responds to the aspirations of the Palestinian people and stresses their right to self-determination and statehood, the movement may not be able to become an alternative to the PLO or even a serious contender for the genuine representation of the Palestinian people. However, the Islamic movement will enjoy a larger measure of popular support if the PLO fails to achieve the national objectives it has defined for itself. The failing of the PLO to deliver will most likely translate into credit for the Islamic groups. Hamas gained the most when the PLO failed to deliver after all the concessions the PLO leadership has made. Hamas has been challenging the PLO to produce any concrete achievement as a result of these concessions. But these Islamic groups, especially Hamas, will be required to deliver and not to rely on the shortcomings of others as a means of gaining influence. While the maximalist stands of the Islamic outfits may be appealing to the Palestinians in the Occupied Territories, in light of increasing disillusionment with the PLO and its ability to offer tangible gains, the Islamists' high targets of establishing an Islamic state and society in Palestine, which are unattainable, at least in the short run, may produce the same kind of disillusionment.

The reluctance of the Islamic groups to work jointly with the PLO may estrange Palestinians who believe in the virtue of national unity. From the very start, the Muslim Brotherhood, and later Hamas, have refused to work with the PLO because of irreconcilable ideological and political differences. In the aftermath of Israel's deportation to southern Lebanon of 418 Hamas and Islamic *Jihad* leaders and activists in December 1992, Hamas had offered new conditions for joining the PLO. While no longer insisting on a specific number of seats in the PNC, Hamas requested the conducting of elections inside and outside the Occupied Territories to enable the Palestinians to elect their representatives in the PLO leadership bodies. The PLO had also declined to concede this demand, arguing that it is impractical under the circumstances. Hamas opposed the PLO's political design altogether. Joining a PLO that is secular and which has already recognised Israel would undermine the very raison d'etre of Hamas and the mother organisation of the Muslim Brotherhood Society. Therefore, it was not clear whether the Hamas had termed to join the PLO are genuine or if they are only meant to make it thoroughly difficult for the PLO to accept them. Perhaps Hamas had wished to place the blame on the other side and would relieve itself from Palestinian public pressure for rejecting national unity and cooperation with the PLO.

Iraq's Invasion of Kuwait

The reaction of Hamas to Iraq's invasion of Kuwait on August 2, 1990, and the impending Gulf crisis was not very much different from the reaction of the PLO factions in the Occupied Territories. While Hamas had opposed the Iraqi invasion of Kuwait, it strongly opposed the massive foreign military presence in Saudi Arabia and the "American occupation of lands sacred to Islam," and called on Iraq to "attack the heart of Tel Aviv if America attacked Baghdad.

The Iraqi invasion of Kuwait and the Gulf crisis came to preoccupy Palestinians in the Occupied Territories and to detract their full attention from the *intifada*. The crisis mitigated the internal Palestinian debate on a variety of issues, including the relationship between the nationalist and the Islamic camps. Initially, the imbroglio tipped the balance of popular support between Hamas and the PLO in support of the PLO, though temporarily. Hamas had to follow the lead of a nationalist, pan-Arab line, since the confrontation in the Gulf was perceived in the Occupied Territories primarily as one between the Arabs and the United States. Of course Hamas had chosen to define this confrontation as one between the Muslims and the West and take the lead itself.

The Gulf crisis was a critical test for Hamas. It confronted the movement with a dilemma. With the kind of position it took vis-à-vis the crisis, Hamas had risked alienating its allies and adherents in Saudi Arabia and the other Gulf states. The decline and loss of financial and political support may have cost the movement internal Palestinian popular support. Furthermore, it had been doubtful that Hamas was eager to fight such a major and uncertain battle with much at stake, let alone under the leadership of a man, Saddam Hussein, whose Islamic credentials are not very encouraging.

With the defeat of Iraq in the Gulf War, both the PLO and Hamas were held accountable by Kuwait and Saudi Arabia and their Arab and foreign allies for backing Iraq. Iraq's defeat created a condition of objective weakness in the Palestinian arena for all the Palestinian parties involved. While both the PLO and Hamas had been weakened in the aftermath of the war, it was expected that Hamas would survive the defeat and emerge with less damage than the PLO.

First, Hamas did not have a strict and well-defined political scheme. It could claim, for example, that while the liberation of "Muslim Palestine" remained the ultimate goal, and *Jihad* the ultimate means, the circumstances which the *umma* was going through required a temporary and tactical retreat. The Muslim Brotherhood had done that in the past and for many years, until the eruption of the *intifada* in 1987. Hamas could use the example of the *intifada* to support an argument that when the time was opportune, the Muslims would engage the enemy as they did during the *intifada*. Hamas could rely on an Islamic doctrine that provided itself to more than one interpretation to justify shifts in attitudes.

In the meantime, the PLO could not suggest to its following that self-determination, statehood on about 20 per cent of the land of Palestine, the right of return, and PLO representation were no longer feasible and need to be postponed until further notice, and that the Palestinians should settle for whatever the Israelis were willing to offer. After all, the above-stated objectives had been the raison d'etre of the PLO. The PLO would have a tough time making a case for a settlement that fell short of addressing its stated objectives or that did not have the prospects for achieving such objectives.

Second, unlike the PLO, Hamas had better prospects for reconciliation with the old Arab order, or even with a new one, in which the pro-U.S. Arab states had become dominant. The Muslim Brotherhood Society had Hamas's political and ideological flexibility had allowed that kind of reconciliation. In addition, Islamic movements in other Arab states would be inclined to press for a sympathetic view toward their Palestinian brethren.

Third, Hamas would also be amendable to some kind of relationship with Jordan. It is worth mentioning that the Muslim Brotherhood in the Occupied Territories had opposed King Hussein's disengagement from the West Bank in 1988. The Brotherhood and Hamas also had supported a Palestinian-

Jordanian confederation. In this regard Yasin argued: "Islam calls for unity. When we commit ourselves to Islam, we do not reject any unity, but this unity should be predicated on correct and equal basis." With the Muslim Brotherhood in Jordan enjoying considerable political weight, Hamas could be assured that a relationship with Jordan was not going to be detrimental to the movement. Rather, such relationship is bound to strengthen the Brotherhood vis-à-vis the PLO nationalists.

Fourth, one reason for the radicalisation of the Muslim Brotherhood in Palestine has been the contest with the PLO nationalist factions. If the nationalists had been weakened, Hamas would feel less pressed to adopt radical politics to keep up with the competition. It is true that the weakening of the nationalists will translate into a relative strength for Hamas, but it will not necessarily mean the further radicalisation of Hamas. A transition of Hamas from militancy to accommodation may not, however, be smooth. The movement may undergo segmentation of radical factions, as had been the case in 1980 when the Islamic *Jihad* movement split from the Muslim Brotherhood Society.

The most serious challenge the Islamic movement is considered to confront is the Israeli occupation. The way the Israeli authorities decide to deal with the Islamic movement will have a striking impact on the future of the movement. Israel has been subjecting the movement to harsh measures, especially when Islamic activists resort to violence in their conflict with Israel. As a result of these measures, the movement has been weakened. In May 1989, about 260 Hamas activists, together with Yasin and his close aids, were arrested. The Islamic *Jihad* activists had been subjected to similar treatment. Ever since that date, Israel had managed to abort every attempt by the Islamic movement to regather its full strength. Several Islamic leaders, activists, members, or sympathisers had been in Israeli jails or detention camps. The December, 1992 deportation to south Lebanon of many Hamas and Islamic *Jihad* leaders and activists had been the most dramatic measure undertaken by the Israeli authorities.

Fear of Israeli wrath is likely to have a sobering effect on the Islamic groups. Hamas in particular may have to mitigate its rigid political and ideological position and perhaps its violent tactics, since it is more exposed to the Israeli authorities than the secretive and smaller organisation of the Islamic *Jihad*. Because of this fear, and in the absence of any effective means to seriously threat the Israeli occupation, Hamas may shift back, perhaps tactically, to infrastructure-building and consolidation of internal influence within the Palestinian society.

Finally, the Islamic movement in the Occupied Territories is undoubtedly an integral part of the world Islamic movement. While this dimension may be an asset, since it would ensure different forms of support for Palestinian Islamists, it may also appear to be a liability. The world Islamic movement, as well as the Muslim Brotherhood Societies in the Arab region, mainly in Jordan and Egypt, may, for certain considerations, restrain the Islamic movement in the Occupied Territories. Since the Islamic outfits in the West Bank and Gaza lack decision making authority, especially with regard to strategic matters, these groups may have to abide by decisions that are taken outside the Occupied Territories.

New Threat

Terrorism is not new. It is as old as the social order, the rulers and the state. It has, however, undergone much sophistication. Terror is used as an instrument of change in the social or political order. Terrorism, however appeals to an alternative future. It assures the promise of realisation of some ultimate goal unattainable by peaceful legislative and legal means. An act of terror by itself is an act of coercion. Its aim is to create intense anxiety and fear on the part of others to reform their behaviour. Terrorists believe that Hell must precede the Heaven. The phenomenon of terrorism had given way to strategic debate whether not winning means losing or not losing means winning. It has left the target nation in a dilemma worrying endlessly over whether and how to respond to this category of political violence.

Facets of Terrorism

Irrespective of the cause espoused by any terrorist organisation, there can be discerned some common features. Cause of terrorists could be local, ethnic or religious diversity, international campaign, ideological or revolutionary radicalism or fundamentalist backlash, but the terrorist actors employ similar tactics and techniques. To understand the complex and growing phenomenon of terrorism, it is necessary to lay focus on its various aspects. Terrorist outfits have undoubtedly succeeded in getting ransom money and also have successfully obtained release of their companions from government's jails. Their record of changing the political system has been utterly dismal despite their protracted struggles involving heavy loss of human lives. Terrorism leaves psychological scars as can be discerned in Punjab now. Some of the salient facets of terrorism are given in succeeding paras.

Cult of Violence

Terrorism is violence for effect, not essentially on the victims of terrorists. Fear and shock are the intended effects. Terrorism is mindless, senseless, bestial and irrational violence. If the terrorist outfits do not commit acts of violence and destruction, they lose their meaning, impact and relevance. The violence of terrorists is addressed to the leadership of the nation who they want should capitulate to their demands. The objective of terrorists is not to kill or destroy government or private property but to break the spirit of the opposition. As such, to most of the victims, acts of terrorism come as unexpected, unprovoked and unjustified. The psychologically grieved Sikh terrorists, in the Fright Decade of Eighties in Punjab, bombed, burned, robbed, kidnapped and killed with a dazzling display of nerve, skill, discipline, inventiveness and bravado. Their quasi-judicial retaliatory executions and disgrace on their alleged opponents were mind-boggling.

In the terrorist environment, security officers and men are bound to witness terrorist violence of such apparent brutality as at first will defy understanding. It may rightly cause revulsion at the methods employed by terrorists for bringing about change in society. Terrorism is a power response and there is no chance of communication with the invisible enemy. Terrorists in states like Punjab, Assam and J&K showed no inclination for entering into any negotiations with the governments. LTTE terrorists of Sri Lanka have the notorious distinction of popularising suicidal violence through use of cyanide capsules and human bombs.

Enemy Status

Once the government and Security Forces make terrorists into a generalised enemy, it tends to legitimise the belief of terrorists that they are at war with the state and they have become its moral equal. We often observe terrorist movements declaring establishment of parallel governments and institutions. Unlike a war between nations, the terrorists do not follow any conventions and agreements of civilised nature. As such, terrorists often attack soft undefended civilian targets with an easy conscience.

Disorientation of Target Society

Terrorist outfits aim to disrupt the inertial relationship between the ruling regime and the general masses. The ruler has to be made to look inefficient, inept, corrupt and illegitimate. This state of society makes the general public responsive to terror itself. Terror does not permit any feedback from the society which blurs the sensitivities of the government and its Security Forces. Terrorism to be successful in its political ends needs to remove the structural supports that give strength to the society.

Targets of Symbolic Value

Terrorism is for psychological significance on the society at large and the ruling elite. The uncommitted masses are very 'resonant' and they respond actively to acts of terror. Terrorist groups, therefore, attack targets with lot of symbolic value in spite of their material value. They often kill ordinary and innocent citizens in a spectacular and primitive manner. Sikh terrorists often massacred innocent labourers living in road-side tenements thus sending shock-waves in the remote corners of the country. In a way, terrorists conveyed that government failed to protect its citizens and its own property. When a soldier is killed in the unequal war of terrorism, others take a disquieting note of such incidents.

Sensation and Publicity

Terrorism survives and feeds on sensation and publicity. Sensation value of terrorists attacks is out of all proportions to the actual physical damage caused and the numbers killed. Terrorist spectaculars are the result of a well-considered. Terrorism is a bloody drama where all members of the society are to some extent unwilling and unwitting participants. Terrorists try to publicise their acts of atrocities and repression. They lack resources to put issues in mass consciousness but government's rhetoric, political leaders' denunciations and claims of security officers keep the pot boiling after a terrorist incident. Moreover, the hostile country exploits the situation by focused alleged violations of human rights, suppression of minorities and attempts at so-called ethnic cleansing.

Modern world is violence-ridden and news of violence in any part of the globe travels fast. Terrorists have a ready audience who are willing to know the number killed every morning. Terrorism is theatre. Violence is aimed at the people watching and not at the actual victims. Black September terrorists achieved the ultimate in publicity and sensation during the 1972 Munich Olympics killing of 11 Israeli athletes. The gruesome incident brought the issue of Palestinian rebels to the notice of the whole world in a vividly smiting manner. In certain Western countries, terrorism has presented itself as a type of propaganda action aiming to promote a certain principle or set of demands, using the modern techniques of publicity. Moreover, media has also assumed an activist role in terrorist situations. Publicity does not spawn terror in the same extent terror leads to publicity.

Creation of Fear

Terrorists aim at creation of a general environment of fear and anxiety. It is achieved by both violence and threat of violence. Once the common public gets frightened, it withdraws its support to the ruling government. Fear and anxiety are transient phenomena. As such, terrorist outfits have to indulge in repeated acts of violence to maintain a paralysing level of fear in society. The very essence of terrorism lies in always presenting the unique danger of a readiness to kill at random to produce a shockwave. At the same time, the terrorists know that their target can be achieved by jeopardising the general security of the society and not by killing some selected persons. Terrorist incidents are useless if these do not generate emotional trauma and social effects. Level of mass harassment is the area of concern for the government and Security Forces.

Element of Indiscrimination

No doubt, the terrorist outfits try to kill persons of importance amongst the ruling elite. When the society is sought to be divided on communal lines, the persons of the opposing community become clear targets. Sikh terrorists killed Hindus in Punjab with the grand design of creating a communal wedge. If there is no element of indiscrimination in a terrorist campaign, it becomes predictable. Targets can be identified and necessary protective measures can be taken. Terrorists in Jammu and Kashmir were able to flush out the Kashmiri Pandits from Kashmir Valley by targeting them selectively. Hindu population in districts of Doda, Rajouri and Poonch in Jammu region has been put to immense anxiety and trauma by the mindless massacre of Hindus living in remote villages. Terrorists, however, believe that differentiation between those who are relevant to the achievement of their goal and those who are acting as obstacles determine their actual selection of targets. Tactics of terrorists is to look indiscriminate while being actually discriminate on the ground. Indiscriminate violence frustrates and disorients the individuals, atomises the society and disrupts the socio-physiological ties of all members of the target society.

Inciting Counter-terror

Terrorism by design is highly provocative. Acts of terrorism provoke severe counter-measures by the ruling regime and its Security Forces. Governments faced with the intractable problem of terrorism react legislatively by imposing strict preventive laws. These laws affect both the best and the worst in society. Extreme laws are also unjust laws. Ruthless and indiscriminate counter-measures involving searches, preventive detentions, encounters and physical checks cause untold inconveniences to the general public. The effect of these terror-provoking counter-measures is that the public loses confidence in the ruling government and its security agencies. On the other hand, terrorist outfits sometimes do not kill some prominent person to avoid massive response from Security Forces in the form of more deployment and security checks. Lenient approach by Security Forces leads to more lives endangered. Security Forces have to compulsively operate at the dangerous mid-level of coerciveness. It has now been proved beyond doubt that restraint of Police and Security Forces has compounded the difficulty in combating terrorism. Case of Punjab is an apt one.

On disquieting feature of terrorism is that terrorist groups react violently to proclamations of the government and Security Forces of success against their agitational schemes. It was often witnessed with dismay that terrorists in Punjab and Jammu and Kashmir selected a very soft target to unleash mindless violence and destruction within hours of government's claims of spectacular successes against the existing terrorist campaign. Government needs to replace rhetoric with a claim inscrutability. Junior leaders of Security Forces should evade boastful claims of encounters, intelligence collection and captures.

Terrorism is calculating, callous and cold-blooded. Terrorists know the limits of acceptability in a social order. They consciously flout these limits and norms of acceptability and this gives them the desired impact and resonance. The task of the terrorist is to goad the government to an inflexible attitude. Security Forces have an indiscriminate response. Provocative strategies of terrorists result in injustices and inconveniences to general public on account of reactive operations of Security Forces. The self-same public becomes alienated. Atrocities are then alleged by sympathisers of terrorist outfits and the Human Rights organisations and activists. Like Pakistan media and government agencies are doing for J&K terrorist groups, exaggerated reports of atrocities of Security Forces are published. No doubt, provoking of repression is one of the primary aims of terrorism. Terrorist groups make deft use of 'the rationality of the irrational.' By seeming to be irrational time by committing unrelieved violence on innocent victims, the terrorists manage to gain an edge over the forces of government. Government and its Security Forces feel compelled to act with reasonable restraint to avoid an unmitigated disaster.

Weapon of the Weak

It has been truly said that terrorism is a weapon of the weak pretending to be strong. Terrorist groups are small and they take on the massive strength of the state. Terrorism as weapon for political change has its strategic strengths. Terrorists all the time tend to give the impression that in utter desperation they are driving themselves increasingly toward the adoption of a policy of consuming the tranquility of the world. Palestinians fighting for a separate homeland against the Jewish State of Israel have shown it in good measure. Rebels now do not want to remain obscure fighters in the jungles. They want to appear on the world stage of television and radio. Terrorism remains to be only a desperate response of the growing number of weak and powerless groups challenging the system of the state. It is a fight between a force without authority against a force with authority. Terrorist is fully aware of the fact that he is at the wrong end of this asymmetrical conflict. He knows that he is employing the doubtful strategy of pitting the power of impotence to expose the impotence of power. Perceived injustices and exploitations are the breeding ground for terrorism. In liberal democracies, there is an increasing number of young people who are critical of the injustices and dishonesty of the country. Terrorism, therefore, is an attraction for desperate and radical groups that are otherwise unable to win outright political and military victory.

Security of Terrorists

Terrorist groups are small and they cannot accept casualties on a regular basis by running into fire-fights with Security Forces. Recruitment to terrorism is small as young entrants know that death is a virtual reality in the wake of operations of Security Forces. Entry in the terrorist environment may be easy but exit is via the graveyard. Terrorists select their targets with utmost care and caution. They often employ over-ground workers for planting bombs and for other hazardous missions. Terrorist groups keep moving from place to place to avoid being traced. Terrorism is highly mobile for tactical reasons also. Organised terrorist groups in Jammu and Kashmir like Hizbul Mujahideen, Lashkar-e-Taiba or Harkat ul Mujahideen are equipped with highly sophisticated communication sets. This capability makes them secure and elusive.

Terrorists do not take their targets in haste. They wait with patience for the target to become vulnerable and their 'get-away' secure. If a suitable targets does not appear, the terrorists shift to an alternative target with a sense of petulance. There is no immunity for innocent civilians, non-combatants, children, women, old and sick. While government forces can take casualties as they are staffed with ambitious professional people, the terrorists cannot absorb heavy losses. When one terrorist is killed, others tend to go into hibernation. Protracted nature of terrorist campaign also snuffs out the initial revolutionary zeal.

Universal Vulnerability

Terrorists can take any target, animate or inanimate. There is no target which is inaccessible. No person in the society is invulnerable. The newest trend of employing the 'human bomb' and car-bomb for destroying the target person or property has opened floodgates of sensational violence. Security Force cannot protect everybody always and constantly. Hitler once said that even a resolute outlaw could prevent an honest man from carrying out political activity. A policy of terror assumes the social system to be inherently law-abiding not only as a rational goal but also as an existing functional pre-requisite. So the terrorist is assured of a strong reaction to his violations of social norms especially done with use of violent force. The state cannot allow anybody including the terrorist to take any human life in the name of social justice.

Suicide Terrorists

Terrorists behave differently when they face certain capture, death or incanceration. Japanese revolutionary youths have traditionally been doing 'hara-kiri' for achieving tactical ends or escaping capture by the enemy. In the last one decade, Sri Lanka's LTTE rebels have embraced suicidal death often for carrying out the ends of their movement. Sikh terrorists also consumed cyanide capsules to escape capture by the dreaded Punjab Police. They are dying in sizeable number as the local terrorists are getting cold feet after paying heavy price in the last one decade or so. Some of these mercenaries are not only willing to die but actually desire to die for achieving martyrdom. Shiite terrorists of Lebanon are leading the rest in this trend. Anyway, 'human bomb' has appeared as a dreadful development in the broader framework of political violence movement and needs to be taken seriously. There is no dearth of frustrated youths who may like to go down as authentic heroes in an otherwise unheroic world. Nihilistic groups like the Japanese Red Army Faction have even indulged in death-defying terrorist acts like the one of massacre at Lod Airport in Israel.

Culpability of Target

Terrorism has been called a phenomenon that happens to other people. This is the strategic strength of terrorism. Common wisdom says that all members of society should take some minimal precautions so that terrorists may find it difficult to survive. As terrorists groups have a wide option for selection of targets, it is difficult to deter their assault on the social order. Western countries and USA have hardened their targets by spending huge amounts on security infrastructures and special operations forces. Potential human targets should not leave their security to the care of others. There is always some culpability of the target, animate or inanimate.

The contagion effect of terror is immense. Terrorism spreads by its sheer momentum. Terrorist incidents may occur at places far apart from each other. Terrorism has no front, no operational bases, no specific tactical objectives, no order of battle and no fixed techniques. Its variety of weapons, targets and modes of unleashing violence is immense. Terrorists aim to grip the target society with paralysing emotive fear and this joins their battle with the ruling government.

II

The Founding of the Islamic Jihad

The Islamic *Jihad* movement started as a splinter faction of the Muslim Brotherhood Society. The 1967 war was a pivotal point in the evolution of the Muslim Brotherhood Society and the transformations it went through. This war, from the standpoint of one of the Islamic *Jihad* founders, did not put only nationalist and secularist ideological orientations into a self-questioning disposition. It also put the conventional religious orientation, led by the Muslim Brotherhood Society, in the same posture of self-questioning. The Muslim Brotherhood Society was held accountable and was not exonerated of the burden of negligence and defeat. Despite the overwhelming influence of Islam in Arab culture and society, the Brotherhood, which was established in 1928 in Egypt, was not successful in resisting the nationalist and secularist trends, or in preventing the defeat.

According to the Islamic *Jihad* movement in the Occupied Territories, the Muslim had gone through three stages. The first was the Hasan al-Banna stage (1928-1949), known as the "stage of insurrection." The second was the "stage of ordeal and retreat"(1949-1967). This phase witnessed the development of the society after Hasan al-Banna, the rise and fall of its influence, and the alterations in its domestic and external relations. The third stage was the "stage of differentiation" within the society (1967-present).

Following the 1967 war, intellectual and ideological differentiation within the Muslim Brotherhood Society began to crop up in a limited way, at least on the individual level. This war caused a severe upheaval within the Brotherhood and posed several questions pertaining to the stalemates of the society that were still unanswered. The search for solutions and alternatives continued for more than a decade. The Islamic revolution in Iran in 1979 came to offer an Islamic pattern that could be emulated. The Islamic *Jihad* movement in the West Bank and Gaza was the product of these factors. The Islamic model in Iran had considerable influence on the movement but it was not the only one.

The Beginnings

The official founding of the Islamic *Jihad* movement in Palestine took place in the midst of differences of opinion and the emergence of certain trends within the Muslim Brotherhood Society in Egypt. The founders of the Islamic *Jihad* were very much conscious of these trends. While attending university in Egypt, the founders of the Islamic *Jihad* were exposed to militant Islamic outfits such as *al-Takfir wal-Hijra* [the Atonement and Holy Flight] and the *Tandhim al-Jihad* [the *Jihad* Organisation], both of which emerged from the Muslim Brotherhood ranks in the mid-seventies.

One of the first Islamic figures in the Occupied Territories to call overtly for *Jihad* against the Israeli occupation was Ya'qub

Qirrish, who was linked with the Fatah movement. Qirrish tried in 1977 to set up an organisation to resist the Israeli occupation. He was arrested in early 1979 and was expelled to Jordan. Although Qurrish's efforts were not sufficient to crystallise the new trend of thought in Islamic ranks, his endeavour contributed new ideas and set a precedent. Other Islamic figures followed suit later.

In Israel itself, a trend calling itself *Usrat al-Jihad* (the Family of *Jihad*) emerged from within the Muslim Brotherhood Society. This trend emerged in 1979, the year the Islamic revolution erupted in Iran. Sheikh 'Abdallah Nimr Darwish, the spiritual leader of the Family of *Jihad*, led this new trend. After he was imprisoned for three years on charges of belonging to an organisation hostile to the state of Israel and carrying out several military operations, Darwish gave up his Islamic revolutionary notions and visions. He returned to advocating religious education as a means of spreading the Islamic call and thereby came closer to the traditional ideas of the Muslim Brotherhood. Darwish relinquished the idea of establishing an Islamic state in Palestine and criticised the ideas of Sa'id Hawwa, which call for an Islamic revolution, describing these ideas as inappropriate for the Muslims in Palestine.

The establishment of the Family of *Jihad* in Israel might have some relationship with the emergence of the Islamic *Jihad* in the West Bank and Gaza Strip, but there is no substantial evidence to indicate that there was a direct connection between Darwish and the founders of the Islamic *Jihad*. Darwish might, however, have offered another example to emulate for those who later founded the Islamic *Jihad* in the Occupied Territories.

After 1970, a group of Palestinian students from the West Bank and the Gaza Strip went to attend Egyptian universities. These students included members of the Muslim Brotherhood. The presence of these students in Egypt, intimate to the Muslim Brotherhood's mother organisation, played an important role in crystallising new ideas in their minds.

In the period between 1967 and 1970, questions arose within the Brotherhood about the society's stance towards the Israeli occupation and how to face it. The issue of armed resistance was also debated. The Brotherhood leaders' response then was that the society should focus on the raising of an Islamic generation and also justified non-involvement in armed resistance against the occupation on the grounds that "the leadership of the struggle was not in Islamic hands." Such answers failed to impress dissenting young Muslims.

In addition, there were other factors that inspired the breakaway from the society. The young Muslims believed that the society was ridden by "moral bankruptcy," notably the absence in the society of the spirit of criticism and new thinking and conspicuousness. According to the *Jihad*, the Islamic revival that started in the mid-seventies came partly as a reaction to the shortcomings of the Islamic movement and was the "natural and practical response to the earlier stages, which had led our *umma* to two terrible catastrophes in less than 20 years," the catastrophes of the 1948 and 1967 defeats.

Ceremonious Emergence

The year 1980 is considered the official year of the founding of the Islamic *Jihad* movement in Palestine. The founders of this movement were two persons from the Gaza Strip, Fathi al-Shaqaqi and Abd al-'AzizAuda. Al-Shaqaqi is one of the movement's most important thinkers, while 'Auda is the movement's spiritual leader.

During his university studies in Egypt, al-Shaqaqi was arrested twice in 1979. He was also imprisoned in Gaza in 1983 for eleven months. In 1986, he was again incarcerated and sentenced to four years of actual imprisonment and another five years of suspended sentence on charges of instigation against the Israeli occupation, transporting weapons to the Gaza Strip, and belonging to the Islamic *Jihad* movement.

Prior to 1967, al-Shaqaqi was a Nasirite. The 1967 defeat had such a far-reaching impact on him that he changed his orientation and joined the Muslim Brotherhood Society. However, by the end of 1974 and the beginning of 1975, al-Shaqaqi began to differ with the Muslim Brotherhood. His different political and ideological vistas were expressed in his book, *Al-Khomeini: al-Hall al-'Islami wal-Badil [Khomeini: The Islamic Solution and Alternative]*, published in 1979.

'Abd-al-'Aziz 'Auda's family came to the Gaza Strip from the Wadi al-Hasa area in the Bersheba district of Palestine in 1948.

They subsisted in the Jabaliya refugee camp in the northern part of the Strip. 'Auda earned a degree in Arab and Islamic studies from Daral-'Ulum in Cairo, as well as a diploma in the Islamic *shari'a*. On his return to the Gaza Strip in 1981, 'Auda worked as a lecturer in the Islamic University in Gaza. In 1984, the Israeli authorities arrested 'Auda on charges of incitement and sentenced him to eleven months in prison, and in November 1987, the Israeli authorities deported him to Lebanon. While still in Gaza, 'Abd-al 'Aziz 'Auda earned the respect of many people in the Occupied Territories. Until their deportation, al-Shaqaqi and 'Auda were considered the two leading leaders of the Islamic *Jihad* movement in the Occupied Territories.

Leadership and Following

The leaders of the *Jihad* usually hail from a new Islamic generation; they are young men in their thirties or early forties. The founders and leaders of the movement, like 'Auda and al-Shaqaqi, hailed from the ranks of the Muslim Brotherhood, while others were originally members of the PLO factions and were recruited by the Islamic *Jihad* inside Israeli prisons. This group had also set the stage for the emergence of the Islamic *Jihad* tradition in Palestine. 'Ammar was arrested in the early seventies and was sentenced to life imprisonment. He was released in a prisoner exchange in 1983 and afterwards was sent to Egypt. However, it was not long before he was deported from Egypt because of his sedition-related activities.

Another leader of the Islamic *Jihad* is Ahmad Mahanna, a former officer in the PLF. Mahanna was one of the leading *Jihad* leaders in the Israeli prisons. He was sentenced to life and then was released in a prisoner exchange in 1985, but he was arrested again in 1986, on the charge of leading one of the Islamic *Jihad's* military groups. Other leading figures were Muhammad al-Jamal and Misbah al-Suri, who were former members of the PFLP and the PLF, respectively. Al-Jamal and al-Suri were appointed by the *Jihad* during their imprisonment in Israeli jails.

Some *Jihad* leaders were even secularists before they converted to fundamentalism. Among those topnotch leaders were Ramadan Shallah, Suleiman 'Auda, Fayez Abu-Mu mmar, Nayef

Azzam, Fayez al-Aswad, and Ahmad Mahanna. A small number of the *Jihad's* founders were former activist students who had been banned from Egyptian universities because of their underground activities there.

The Islamic *Jihad* members are known for their good organisation, strict discipline, and absolute secrecy, especially with regard to armed activities. They are young Palestinians who were fascinated to the militant positions embraced by the Islamic *Jihad* and were impressed by its violent activities. They were adherents to a new way of thinking characterised by enlightenment, debate, and sublime awareness. The Islamic *Jihad* followers go through hard ideological indoctrination and training.

Islamic *Jihad* leaders in the Israeli jails were successful at recruiting many new members. Perhaps this was one reason why the Israeli authorities began to expatriate the *Jihad* leaders instead of keeping them in jail. Members of the Islamic *Jihad* are religious fundamentalists who do not hesitate to carry out actions even if these are dangerous.

The majority of *Jihad* followers come from humble social background and live in poor neighbourhoods and refugee camps. This following is primarily concentrated in the Gaza Strip. But the movement's small presence in the West Bank is constantly on the rise. Israeli security sources announce, from time to time, discovery of secret cells of the Islamic *Jihad*.

In the Islamic University in Gaza, the Islamic *Jihad* has a few hundred supporters among the student body, and it has a small but increasing number of supporters in other universities of the Occupied Territories. There are also a number of Muslim Brotherhood members who have strong inclinations towards the Islamic *Jihad* movement without openly declaring their weakness.

In the West Bank, the Islamic *Jihad* movement was responsible for the famous Gate of Moors operation on October 15, 1986. In this operation, three hand grenades were hurled by Islamic *Jihad* members at Israeli troops.

In August 1988, cells belonging to the Islamic *Jihad* had been discovered in the Hebron area. In the following years, Islamic *Jihad* supporters, despite their small numbers compared to Hamas, were found all across the West Bank and Gaza. In any case, it is arduous to determine the actual size of the Islamic *Jihad* following and their areas of concentration because of the secrecy of the organisation.

Principle and Ideology

The Islamic *Jihad* movement derives its ideology and political notions from the Islamic tradition in general. Nevertheless, there are three Islamic figures who enjoy distinguished status among the leaders and followers of the Islamic *Jihad* and are considered worthy of following. They are Hasan al-Banna, Sayyid Qutb, and 'Izz-al-Din al-Qassam, in addition to the Ayatollah Khomeini, the leader of the Islamic revolution in Iran.

The Islamic *Jihad* consider Hasan al-Banna as an Islamic leader who founded an Islamic renaissance movement by the reconciling two Islamic orientations, one Salafi and the other reformist, Al-Banna's significance, from the Islamic *Jihad's* point of view, lies in three aspects that he emphasised in his attempt to revitalise the Islamic call. They are revival, organisation, and upbringing.

Sayyid Qutb enjoys a special status for the Islamic *Jihad* movement. He is credited for his intellectual and ideological qualities and his ability to materialise the aspects of the challenge that Muslims face, as well as his ideas regarding the way to face that challenge. Qutb embodies the position of active opposition to, and non-cooperation with, the prevailing order, in contrast to Hasan al-Banna, who is known for his moderation. Qutb is a model for the Islamic fundamentalist leader and is considered by the Islamic *Jihad* movement a genuine symbol of revolutionary Islam. Qutb talked about an "Islamic vanguard," without which the Islamic renaissance will not be achieved.

Sayyid Qutb's books are sources of education and indoctrination for the Islamic *Jihad* movement. His book, Ma' alim 'ala al-Tariq [Signs along the Way], is a piece of revolutionary analysis preaching a new Islamic way, different from the conventional one: ("Today, we are in an age of ignorance like the ignorance which existed prior to the coming of Islam, and even worse. There is ignorance all around us, in the ideas of the people and their beliefs, customs and traditions, the sources of their culture, arts and literature, and their religious and secular laws. Much of what we regard as Islamic culture, Islamic philosophy, and Islamic thought is derived from this ignorance.")

The distinguished Egyptian writer Hasan Hanafi refers to Ma 'alim 'ala al-Tariq as a basic turning point in the development of Muslim Brotherhood thought. This book emphasises the existence of a "severe contradiction between two thoughts, two notions, two societies, two systems, and two truths: Islam and ignorance, belief and heresy, truth and falsehood, good and evil, the rule of God and the rule of man, God and Satan.... The existence of the one requires the destruction of the other. There is no way to compromise or mediate between the two." According to this book, change cannot transpire except through the overthrow of authority, the destruction of the imams of non-belief, and putting the imams of belief in their place. There are no stages and no gradual progress in the process of change: "As the revolution in the person occurs through divine guidance, it occurs in society through the change of authority."

Egyptian writer Muhammad Ahmad Khalafallah wrote that the notions and beliefs of Sayyid Qutb "are the foundation of Islamic consciousness and are the cause for the rifts within the Muslim Brotherhood Society and the emergence of splinter groups from it."

Sheikh 'Izz-al-Din al-Qassam is the prime source of inspiration for the Islamic *Jihad* movement. Al-Qassam is considered the movement's trailblaser. He is perceived as the first leader of the Palestinian armed resistance in the history of modern Palestine and the true father of the armed Palestinian revolution. Al-Qassam is a sublime and revered symbol. The Islamic *Jihad's* supporters have elevated him almost to a saintly status.

Sheikh 'Izz-al'Din al-Qassam was a Syrian who received his education at al-Azhar, Egypt, where he was a student of Sheikh Muhammad Abdu. Abdu left his mark on al-Qassam's philosophy. From the beginning, al-Qassam called for resisting British colonialism and Zionist settlement in Palestine. His message was pretty simple. "*Jihad* against Britain and its Zionist agents."

There are a number of similarities between what al-Qassam and his supporters did in opposing Britain and what the Islamic

Jihad is doing in its clashes against the Israeli occupation. Al-Qassam, who is thought of as a symbol of belief, consciousness, and revolution, combined the call for *Jihad* for the sake of God with the call for *Jihad* for the interest of the country, raising the slogan "God's book in one hand, and the rifle in the other." Al-Qassam believed that blood and revolution are the ways to freedom and independence; therefore, he raised the banner of armed combat instead of passive resistance.

The Islamic *Jihad* movement has emulated al-Qassam by selecting its followers with utmost care. A prospective member is carefully observed and put on probation before he is placed in a secret cell, composed of a small faction of individuals who do not know one another. Al-Qassam believed that the peasants and other backward classes in Palestine were the ones to be entrusted with carrying out the *Jihad*.

Just as "Izz-al-Din al-Qassam embarrassed the traditional leaders of his time with the pursuit of the *Jihad*, the Islamic *Jihad* had distressed the Muslim Brotherhood Society before the *intifada*. The Islamic *Jihad* has engaged the Israeli occupation in armed resistance, while the Brotherhood avoided this. Al-Qassam, who was martyred in a confrontation with the British forces in 1935, understood that the pursuit of the *Jihad* would end with his martyrdom. This is the same spirit that overrules the young men who join the ranks of the Islamic *Jihad* today.

Al-Qassam saw Britain and Zionism as two faces of the same coin, and the Islamic *Jihad* sees Israel and America in the same way. He believed that the Muslim Arabs in neighbouring countries were a strategic depth for the Palestinian masses and their revolution, but that the Palestinian people must depend on themselves first because those countries were under the oppression of imperialism. In the same way, the Islamic *Jihad* movement believes that *Jihad* for Palestine must be waged by the Palestinians without waiting anymore for the prior victory of the Islamic call.

There are other similarities between al-Qassam's movement and the Islamic *Jihad*. Just as the battle of Ya'bad in Jenin was the real spark for the revolution that broke out in 1935 and continued until 1939, supporters of the Islamic *Jihad* were of the view of that the daring operations that they had carried out against the Israeli occupation shortly before the *intifada* were the spark that ignited this *intifada*. And just as al-Qassam and his colleagues renounced the principle of dialogue with Britain, in contrast to other nationalist factions and traditional political parties in the thirties, the supporters of the Islamic *Jihad* refuse dialogue with Israel and the United States.

As it was not possible to figure out the true number of Al-Qassam's followers because of the secrecy of his organisation, so too it is not possible to learn the number of the Islamic *Jihad's* following. Al-Qassam's adherents were active inside prisons, and so was the Islamic *Jihad*, whose members recruited palestinian prisoners in Israeli jails to their movement's ranks. Despite the fact that Islam is the leading and ultimate frame of reference for both al-Qassam's movement and the Islamic *Jihad*, the two movements manifest a unique relationship between religion and nationalism. There is no doubt that al-Qassam's character, experience, and leadership left a listing effect on Palestinian political culture.

Al-Qassam was admired by non-Islamists for being a symbol for the downtrodden and for embodying what they believed to be the path to salvation for the majority of the Palestinian people. He also personified two other dimensions, one nationalist and the other socialist. Al-Qassam was a Syrian Arab who stood firmly against British imperialism and Zionism in Palestine, just as he had resisted French colonialism before in Syria. On the other hand, Al-Qassam was a champion and ally of the poor. He saw "the workers and peasants to be the most sincere groups, who were willing to work and sacrifice."

The Islamic *Jihad* movement rejects putting a social class impression on al-Qassam's notions and practices: "We must forget the idea that the main motive behind the actions of al-Qassam and his followers was economic; they did not come from the most economically grieved class. He who can arm himself is economically able, and al-Qassam himself enjoyed a stable economic condition".

With regard to the fallout of the Islamic revolution in Iran on the doctrine and ideology of the Islamic *Jihad* movement, this revolution was a source of inspiration in terms of ideas and practice.

From the outset, the *Jihad's* founders revered Ayatollah Khomeini as a symbol and leader of the Islamic revolution and revival, not just in Iran but everywhere. They tried to learn lessons from the Iranian revolution and to apply its lessons in the Palestinian context. Until the eruption of the Islamic revolution in Iran, Islam was, from the Islamic *Jihad's* viewpoint, absent from the battlefield. This revolution proved to the Islamic *Jihad* that Islam was the solution and that *Jihad* was the way.

In addition to al-Qassam's experience, the Islamic *Jihad* also received inspiration for its position on the issue of *Jihad* in Palestine from the Iranian revolution, the Muslim Brotherhood tradition, and the experience of the *Jihad* Organisation in Egypt. Islam, according to Khomeini, is ("the religion of the *Mujahidin* who want truth and justice. It is the religion of those who demand freedom and independence".) The pioneers of the Islamic *Jihad* in Palestine have been influenced by the *Jihad* Organisation's experience in Egypt, by virtue of having this experience from close range. The *Jihad* Organisation in Egypt believes that *Jihad* is the only means of achieving the Islamic state. The Muslim Brotherhood's experience in the war of Palestine is remembered, but the articulations of Sayyid Qutb regarding *Jihad* are considered a frame of reference.

Muhammad 'Abd-al-Salam Faraj's book *Al-Farida al-Gha'iba [The Absent Duty]* is considered the most prominent of the *Jihad* literature. Faraj was the leader of the *Jihad* Organisation and was responsible for issuing the order to assassinate President Sadat. In the words of Hasan Hanafi, this book has had considerable influence on youth, because it reinforces the "self-confidence versus loss, pride versus submission, dignity versus humiliation, and power versus failure." Among the ideas contained in this book is that ("learned men of religion today have ignored *Jihad*, despite their knowledge that it is the only way to restore and raise the edifice of Islam again, and despite their awareness that the idols on this earth can only be removed by the power of the sword."

The Islamic *Jihad* theoreticians perceive that the danger of Israel lies not only in its occupation of Palestine, which is part of "Dar al-Islam (House of Islam), and the humiliation of its people, but also in the spread of Jewish corruption in it. Israel is an essential part of a plan to fragment the Islamic *umma*, to westernise it, to subjugate it, to enslave it, to incapacitate its will, and to cast an eternal yoke over its neck.... The planners wanted Israel to be a military force from which the [Arab] governments of partition will recoil and will wish to have a truce with, so these governments would surrender leadership to America to avoid Israel's evil....until this surrender invites subjugation and subordination and even leads to implementing the plans of the East and West in fighting Islam and the Muslims."

From the point of view of the Islamic *Jihad*, Muslims who have rejected Israel from South Lebanon are the best Muslims. Fighting the "Torah adherents to the bone" can only be done through the "Islamic doctrine and the war of popular liberation." Islam alone as a religion, as a culture, as a way of life is "capable of withstanding the crises, of understanding it, of leading the struggle, and concluding it.....Islam represents the awareness of the *umma*." In his book, *Khomeini: al-Hall al-Islami wal-Badil*, Fathi al-Shaqaqi mentions a *fatwa* issued by Khomeini indicating that the endeavour to eliminate the "Zionist entity" is a religious duty.

According to the Islamic *Jihad*, suicidal attacks are acts of martyrdom. These attacks comprise one of the principal ways in the tradition of *Jihad*. They assume a special significance because of their symbolism as well as the other effects they have: "Perhaps it is a blessing of God Almighty bestowed upon one *Mujahid* or two *Mujahidin*, enabling him or them to indict against the enemy's position, or against a concentration of enemy military forces on a martyrdom mission, assaulting with explosives, smashing down everything around them, imposing the heaviest losses, breaking down the enemy's morale and determination in the face of this Islamic spirit of martyrdom which cannot be resisted. At the same time, it compounds fear of the Muslims after a long period of weakness and humiliation, and it increases the outpouring of new bloods which seek *Jihad* for the sake of God".

As for Palestine and its liberation, the Islamic *Jihad's* philosophy is a clear one, which does not restrict Islam's role to the mosque, as is the case in traditional Islamic practices. The Muslim Brotherhood, from the Islamic *Jihad's* point of view, concentrates on religious upbringing and education, unlike the nationalist factions of the PLO, which concentrate on struggle. The Muslim Brotherhood has chosen the "path of belief", and did not choose the "path of *Jihad*." The nationalists close the "path of *Jihad*," and as a result, have avoided the "path of belief". The uniqueness of the Islamic *Jihad* movement lies in forging a dialectical relationship between the path of *Jihad* and the path of belief. In this sense, the Islamic *Jihad* synthesises religion and nationalism in its endeavour to annihilate Israel, combat Zionism, and establish an Islamic state in Palestine. These ideological positions are reflected in the *Jihad* movement's practices and functions. On one occasion, the flag of Israel was discovered in Gaza with "*allahu akbar* [God is great], death of Israel, the destruction of Israel is a Koranic imperative" written on it.

Unlike the Muslim Brotherhood Society, the Islamic *Jihad* is not a transnational movement in the organisational sense. However, the movement does have much organisational following outside Palestine. It also has political and ideological affiliations and certain forms of coordination and cooperation with other Islamic outfits.

The Islamic *Jihad* does not have major local publications in the West Bank and the Gaza Strip. On specific occasions, the movement issues statements or pamphlets to clarify its position regarding a particular issue. However, there are certain Islamic publications which, to a considerable extent, reflect the Islamic *Jihad's* points of view. These are published abroad, but they find their way to the Occupied Territories. Among these publications is *Al-Tali'ah Al-Islamiyya*, a monthly magazine published in London and revealing the line of the Islamic revolution in Iran. This magazine began publication in 1982 but ceased to appear a few years afterwards. Another publication is *Al-Mukhtar Al-Islami*, also a monthly magazine, published in Cairo, expressing the opinions of the fundamental Islamic trend in Egypt. A third publication is entitled *Al-'Islam wa-Filastin* and is published in Cyprus. After the eruption of the *intifada*, the Islamic *Jihad* started publishing its own bulletin, *al-Mujahid*, which comes out of Lebanon.

With the founding of the *Jihad* movement, a new kind of political Islam and Islamic leaders began to emerge in the Occupied Territories. From the very inception, the Islamic *Jihad* and its leaders provided a new formulation in which religion and politics were directly and practically linked. Therefore, the *Jihad* movement posed a challenge, not only to the Muslim Brotherhood Society, but also to the rest of the Palestinian nationalist factions inside the Occupied Territories. The Islamic *Jihad* was able, by displaying Islam as a force of resistance, to attract the sympathy and acceptance of a growing number of people.

The special characteristic of the Islamic Jihad movement lies in its being an organisation that was founded and developed inside the Occupied Territories. By virtue of its ideology and the nature of its leaders, membership, strategy, and tactics, the *Jihad* movement seemed to have had no other group had. In contrast to the Muslim Brotherhood Society and the PLO factions, the Islamic *Jihad* movement does not subject itself to the political and diplomatic-considerations to which the rest of the organisations do. It does not receive instructions from abroad that might contradict reality at home. However, the Islamic *Jihad* has not so far achieved the desired takeoff. The rise of the movement was curbed essentially by harsh Israeli measures and by the emergence of Hamas as a competitive militant force.

Strategy vis-a-vis Palestine

The Islamic *Jihad* movement considers Palestine its core issue, in contrast to the Muslim Brotherhood Society, which regards the victory of the Islamic call as the cardinal issue and the prelude to resolving the Palestinian problem in an Islamic way. In the words of Sheikh *'Abd al-'Aziz 'Auda*, "I am a Palestinian Muslim; I consider Palestine the most important nation in the Islamic world. I hope that an Islamic state will be established there; we dream of this." Like the Muslim Brotherhood, the Islamic *Jihad* also sees the Palestinian problem as an Islamic problem and not a national or pan-Arab nationalist issue that concerns the Arabs only, but rather a problem that concerns the entire Islamic nation. As for the most pertinent solution to this problem, the Islamic *Jihad* believes in an Islamic popular war of liberation, resulting in the annihilation of Israel and the creation of an Islamic state in Palestine.

The Islamic *Jihad* thinks that Palestine has come to its present condition because of the role of "the opportunistic non-Islamic leaderships, which successively led the people, or which seized power following the defeat of the Islamic state at the beginning of this century." The Islamic *Jihad* assumes that the Arab nationalist movement "was a legitimate son of the Western assault against the Islamic nation," and the Zionist movement also began "as a genuine part of that attack." The failure of the non-Islamic leadership, according to the Islamic *Jihad*, was repeated in 1948 and 1967 and is reflected in the inability of these leaderships to pursue further, and to properly understand, the struggle. This failure is evident today in the practices of "those who claim to lead the Palestinian people" and in the plans that they put forth to solve the Palestinian issue.

In his booklet *Ma ba'd al-Nakbatayn [After Two Catastrophes]*, published in 1968, the Islamic writer Tawfiq al-Tayyib wrote that the disaster of 1948 was a humiliation for liberal Arab thought, whereas the rout of 1967 was a defeat for Arab socialist and revolutionary ideas. This booklet is considered by the Islamic *Jihad* leaders in Palestine as one of the most influential Islamic documents to be published after the 1967 defeat. Al-Tayyib believes that the Arab debacle was in essence an intellectual catastrophe, a catastrophe of modern Arab thought: "The disaster in our ideas came before the disaster in our land....and was the prelude, and the long-term cause, for the disaster in the land." The Zionist existence in Palestine, according to al-Tayyib, is "an embodiment of the modern Western challenge, and an evidence that this challenge still exists. .....The natural feedback to the challenge lies in the Islamic trend which constitutes the defence line. And despite our harsh criticism of this trend, it has played a historic role in the restoration of the psychological balance of both the Islamic community and of the educated Muslim." According to this stance, the Islamic solution continues to be the final and divinely guided solution, which is bound to fill the vacuum in the continuing ideological and political struggle.

The Islamic *Jihad* movement believes in the armed struggle as a strategy for political action. Contrary to the Muslim Brotherhood's point of view, the Islamic *Jihad* does not harp on the Islamic transformation of society as a prerequisite to the liberation of Palestine and the establishment of an Islamic state in it. The Brotherhood believes that Islam must exist in society before the struggle for Palestine starts. The Islamic *Jihad's* position gives priority to the elimination of Israeli rule. This goal can only be achieved through *Jihad*, which cannot be delayed under any semblance. Like the Brotherhood, the Islamic Jihad rejects any form of recognition of Israel and took a stand against all proposed political settlements.

The Islamic *Jihad* has focused its activities on armed struggle against the Israeli occupation. The *Jihad* differs in this context from the remaining factions that adopt this strategy. When it started its operations against Israeli targets, the Islamic *Jihad* refrained from claiming responsibility for these operations, in order not to give the Israeli authorities any justification to indict its members. Despite that, the Islamic *Jihad* left its special mark on the operations it undertook. The Islamic *Jihad* offensives were usually noted for their effectiveness and success. After repeated Israeli blows prior to and following the outbreak of the *intifada*, the Islamic *Jihad* began to claim responsibility for operations it undertook in order to prove its endured existence.

Among other spectacular operations of the Islamic *Jihad*, in addition to the Gate of Moors attack, was the successful evasion from the Gaza Central Prison of six *Jihad* members, the killing of Captain Ron Tal, commander of the Israeli military police in the Gaza Strip on August 2, 1987, and the violent confrontation between *Jihad* members and the Israeli security forces in the al-Shija'iyya area of Gaza city on October 6, 1987, which resulted in the expiry of an Israeli security officer, in addition to the four members of the *Jihad* cell.

Members of the Islamic *Jihad* are usually subjected to the severest punishments. They are perceived by the Israeli authorities as highly dangerous. Before the outbreak of the *intifada*, there were fifty to sixty members of the Islamic *Jihad* incarcerated in Israeli jails for carrying out armed actions or attempting to carry out similar actions against the occupation.

Despite severe Israeli punishment, which included long-term imprisonment, banishments, and in a few cases, killings, the material presence of the movement, contrary to some expectations, has not been destroyed. On the first anniversary of the famous al-Shija'iyya operation, the *Jihad* adherents distributed a statement in the Gaza

Strip calling on the people to observe a strike. This appeal received a widespread response from the various nationalist quarters and the population at large. On the same day, *Jihad* members lobbed hand grenades at an Israeli military patrol in the Sheikh Radwan neighbourhood in Gaza, and injured two Israeli soldiers.

Subsequently, the Islamic *Jihad* movement in Palestine claimed responsibility for a series of operations against Israeli targets. There was also the firebombing in Ramallah on August 14, 1989, of an Israeli Civil Administration vehicle, in which four Israeli tax collectors were injured.

As described by an Israeli journalist, "the Islamic *Jihad* is a plant that, as soon as it is cut off, it grows bigger and stronger once again."

Islamic *Jihad* and the PLO

Until the *intifada*, there was no direct synchronisation or cooperation between the Islamic *Jihad* movement and factions of the PLO, with the exception of the Fatah movement. Islamic *Jihad* supporters do not agree with the secular assimilation of the various PLO factions, especially those factions with Marxist beliefs. The Islamic *Jihad* regards the PLO's aim of establishing a secular democratic state in Palestine as incompatible with the Islamic view of history. However, the Islamic *Jihad's* stance toward the PLO and its factions can generally be described as ambiguous and two faceted.

The Fatah movement is the closest of the PLO factions to the Islamic *Jihad*. The fact of the matter is that there is some affinity between the two organisations. Fatah's ideological perception of the Palestinian issue is closer to the Islamic *Jihad's* view than it is to the Muslim Brotherhood's.

As for those who are in charge of Fatah, the Jihad argues that all of them were the sons of the Islamic movement: "Yasser Arafat, Khalil al-Wazir, Salah Khalaf, 'Abd-al-Fatah al-Hmud, Kamal 'Udwan, Muhammad Yusef al-Najjar, Mamduh Saydam, Mahmud Abbas, and Salim al-Za-'nun. One should not forget that the first military communique issued by al-'Asifa forces [military wing of Fatah] opened with the mention of the name of God, followed by a verse from the Koran."

According to the Islamic *Jihad*, Fatah embodied the endeavours of the Palestinian masses. ("The Fatah Movement is not only the largest of the Palestinian movements, and not only the mother of the contemporary armed revolution (since its inception in 1965), but it is also a microcosm of the Palestinian people at home and abroad, in all their past and present interactions, struggles, sensitivities, and contradictions.... Because of that, Fatah is constantly at the centre of the concerns of the Palestinian people of all affiliations."

However, the Islamic *Jihad* does not hesitate to criticise Fatah. This is reflected mostly in voicing differences on the ideological and political levels, especially after Fatah had transformed into a "mixture of Islam, nationalism, liberalism, and finally leftist ideas." After the Fatah leadership changed into "a nationalist leadership of the same mould as other liberation movements in Third World countries, and began to fluctuate between Islam and nationalism, it became a blend of tradition, liberalism, and nationalism, and turned away from its Islamic essence. This change has forced Fatah to adopt a policy of manoeuvres, parallel positions, balances, and domestic and foreign bargains to maintain equilibrium and safeguard itself and the accomplishments it achieved! This policy has prevented any likelihood for an Islamic evolution within the Fatah movement, and has changed those who some time ago were Muslim leaders into professional politicians, and dignitaries competing for influence and status."

In a conscious reference to Fatah, Sheikh 'Abd-al-'Aziz 'Auda wrote: "We do not accept the slogan raised by the PLO's main faction with regard to non-interference in the internal affairs of the Arab countries. But our political and ideological differences with the PLO do not justify the use of violence against the nationalist forces. We respect the viewpoints of the main faction [Fatah] and all nationalist forces, because we believe in dialogue as the only means to reach a mutual understanding. Our main dispute is with the Israeli occupation."

It is not easy to ascertain the nature of the relationship between Fatah and the Islamic *Jihad* and whether this relationship does in fact exist as a coordinated strategy, or just a functional relationship between factions or wings in the two movements.

The Islamic *Jihad* rejects Fatah's claims about its relationship with the *Jihad* and points out that Fatah and others try to gain credibility through linking their names with the Islamic *Jihad*.

But Fatah sources define the relationship with the Islamic *Jihad* as one of sheer cooperation. These sources suggest that the Fatah leaders, especially Abu-Jihad, encouraged the notion of Islamic *Jihad*, particularly after the Islamic movement had become an effective force in the Occupied Territories. Abu-Jihad was conscious of the religious propensity of the Palestinian people and fully understood the role of Islam as a driving force in society. Abu-Jihad believed that if Islam could be manipulated, it would become a force to be reckoned with in confronting the occupation. During the *intifada* in particular, the Islamic character of resistance to the Israeli occupation became more apparent. The nationalists had become aware of that, and the leaflets of the United National Leadership of the *intifada* began to include various religious references.

Even before the *intifada*, Abu-Jihad tried to win over a group of young Muslims who were disenchanted with the nationalist outfits as well as with the Muslim Brotherhood. Since 1982, he encouraged a trend within Fatah to extend all forms of support to those Palestinian Islamists who believed in the notion of *Jihad* in Palestine. This trend was led by Muhammad Basim al-Tamimi (Hamdi), who is considered one of the leading military leaders in Fatah. It may be mentioned here that Hamdi was one of the three Palestinians assassinated in Cyprus on February 14, 1988. The Israeli Intelligence was accused of this assassination. It is considered that Fatah did provide military and logistical support to the Islamic *Jihad* before the movement diversified its sources of support to include Iran and Islamic factions in some Arab countries.

While the Islamic *Jihad* received support from Fatah and maintained a relationship with it, the movement, at the same time, was eager to maintain its independence and its distinct ideological and political views. However, after the outbreak of the *intifada*, the Islamic *Jihad* was more willing than the Muslim Brotherhood to coordinate with Fatah and the Unified National Leadership of the *intifada*, despite its refusal to join the UNL formally.

Like the Muslim Brotherhood, the Islamic *Jihad* had called

upon Fatah to return to Islam before it was too late. The movement states that the revolutionary Islamic position "makes it incumbent upon us to be concerned about Fatah so it does not become a scapegoat for Arab and international intrigues, which would force the movement to drop the rifles which it is raising against the enemy." The *Jihad* movement goes on to assert: "Once again the region looks as if it is returning to the time of the collapse of the Army of Salvation, and the battalions of the Holy *Jihad,* in 1948. The only solution from the Islamic Jihad's point of view lies "in the advance of the forces of revolutionary Islam to occupy the lost space, on the basis of *Jihad* against the enemies....Between the end of the 1940s and the beginning of the 1980s are thirty years, a thousand experiences and another generation on the move."

The Islamic *Jihad's* stance towards the PLO faction is defined in a book published by one of the movement's leaders in Palestine. The book indicates that these factions, which have damaged "our people, our cause and our *umma,*" because of their leadership of the Palestinian people, were able to do so as a result of "the Islamists' absence."

The book also states the following :

We Islamists neither hate nor reject these organisations, groups and political parties, nor oppose them because they are carrying arms against the Zionist foe, but because they are not carrying Islam, nor ruling by the Qura'n....We want these organisations and groups to discard all the anti-Islamic ideas, doctrines, programmes, and slogans.....We want them to be committed to Islam, to the Koran and the Sunna, in word and deed, in everything, small and large, and to adopt the Islamic doctrine and carry weapons simultaneously. However, and regrettably, we note that these organisations have categorically rejected, and still reject commitment to Islam, from their inception until today. They have adopted constitutions, principles, charters, and manmade doctrines which have no relationship to Islam. Based on that, we will not accept, and our Muslim people will not accept, and our *umma* will not accept the leadership of these organisations.

Other PLO factions may perceive the Islamic *Jihad* with anxiety. The daring attacks of the *Jihad* on Israeli targets have embarrassed those factions that could not match the movement in this sphere. It was therefore natural for some of these smaller groups to cast doubts on the Islamic *Jihad*. A publication reflecting the views of a marginal Palestinian Communist group, the Revolutionary Workers party, which is supported by Fatah, asserted:

> Despite the tangible progress in the Islamic *Jihad's* positions, particularly in its struggle against the occupation which, from the political standpoint is inspired by the Palestinian nationalist position, the *Jihad's* tactics towards the United National Leadership and consequently, the PLO, allude to what these tactics hide. The position of the Islamic *Jihad* is still one of opposition to the democratic and secular nature of the PLO. The *Jihad* attempts to Islamise the PLO, even though it does not state this goal explicitly. On this basis, the leaders of this movement express their willingness to cooperate and coordinate only with Fatah and not with the other Palestinian organisations. This position reveals the attempt by this movement to attain a level of achievement that would enable it to compete with the democratic nationalist orientation which the PLO represents.

The leftists believe that the ideological standpoint of the Islamic *Jihad* does not differ from the Muslim Brotherhood's stance, especially with regard to the PLO. While the *Jihad* does not object to cooperation with Fatah, it, like the Muslim Brotherhood, declines to join the PLO.

The Islamic *Jihad* movement argues that there is room for all to continue the struggle: "The Islamic *Jihad* is keen on avoiding any clash with any other Palestinian force, whether Islamic or secular, and considers that the battlefield is wide enough for all." In a clear reference to the Muslim Brotherhood and their position regarding secularist groups, one Islamic source wrote that the Islamic *Jihad* has "efficiently and consciously sidestepped a trap into which other Islamists operating in Palestine have fallen, by getting involved in unfortunate skirmishes with some Palestinian secularist factions."

But the most important nationalist endorsement for the

Islamic *Jihad* came from George Habash, the leader of the Popular Front for the Liberation of Palestine, the second largest outfit in the PLO after Fatah. He differentiated between the Islamic *Jihad* movement and the Muslim Brotherhood. He stated that while the Islamic *Jihad* focused its attention on Israel and conducted its military attacks against it, the reactionary trends in the Islamic movement intentionally manufactured confrontations with nationalist and progressive forces. Regarding the future of the Islamic tendency in the Occupied Territories, Habash said: "I believe that the religious trend will be able to take over in the event the PLO ceases to pursue armed struggle and continue to proceed on a course of deviation and capitulation. In this event, the Palestinian masses which seek the liberation of Palestine will rally behind those forces that they feel are capable of continuing the struggle to achieve this goal."

The *Intifada*

Islamic *Jihad* members were among the first elements to participate in the *intifada*. There is sufficient proof to suggest that they were extremely active in ensuring its continuation, especially at its growing stages. However, the active participation failed to continue for long, because of the repeated blows they suffered at the hands of the Israeli authorities. These blows prevented the *Jihad* from attaining more substantial influence among the population, despite the clear sympathy the movement had won. The Islamic *Jihad* resorted to violent stratagems to make up for the decline in its participation in the activities of the *intifada*.

In the early pamphlets it had issued, as well as in its graffiti, the Islamic *Jihad* had avoided taking any step against the positions of the Unified National Leadership. In fact, some sort of coordination took place between the *Jihad* and the UNL, especially during confrontations with the Israeli troops. In contrast to the Muslim Brotherhood, the statements of the Islamic *Jihad* did not initially reject the idea of a Palestinian state. These statements also refrained from making any mention of the PLO. Without a doubt, the *Jihad* movement's initial participation in the *intifada* strengthened its status, especially in contrast to the Muslim Brotherhood Society. The *Jihad* was taking a middle-of-the-road position. An Islamic *Jihad* leader said: "The *Jihad* is the only organisation capable of bring the traditional Muslim trend into the *intifada*. Even now, the Israelis are doing everything in their power to create opposition between the Islamists and the nationalists, especially in Gaza."

The incompatibility between the positions of the Islamic *Jihad* and those of the PLO began to appear more clearly during and following the resolutions of the PNC's nineteenth session. While the council was in session, the *Jihad* issued a statement in which it opposed the political plans submitted to the council. After the resolutions were adopted, the Islamic *Jihad* issued another statement castigating the acceptance of UN resolution 242 and stating that the acceptance of that resolutions meant conceding an important part of Palestine. This "comes after years of appeasing and deceiving the people, even at the last minute, since the Document of Independence [issued by the PLO] is merely a show."

The *Jihad* statement further added that acceptance of resolution 242 "shifts the future of the battle from a battle against the enemy to a battle on the Palestinian scene itself", and that the Palestinian state, if established, "would not only be divided from the rest of Palestine, but rather, would not be a state for all the Palestinian people, especially those who are scattered in the diaspora or who are still within the 1948 borders [Israel]....Finally it would form a true bridge for the expansion of Zionism throughout the whole region." The statement added that the recognition of resolution 242 comes in the absence from the council of the fighting groups, and in the absence of a significant segment of the Palestinian people, the segment of political Islam "which is always present on the Palestinian battlefield." The Islamic *Jihad* also warned against transforming the *intifada* from a means of liberation into a tactical manoeuvre to stir the Palestinian issue, as happened after the October 1973 war, when Egyptian president Anwar al-Sadat exploited the results of the war to agitate the Arab-Israeli issue, and not to liberate the land.

The Islamic *Jihad* regards the actions of the PLO leadership as similar to political suicide: "The political suicide into which the PLO leadership is plunging is similar to the step-by-step approach that begins with exploiting the *intifada*, and ends with nullifying it through the undoing of the elements of its strength, unity, and cohesion, and the use of its remnants to sign an agreement that, in the best of cases, will not surpass autonomy which is included in the Camp David Accords." The *Jihad* also expressed its hesitation over the attitude of the PLO leaders toward the Palestinian issue in the aftermath of the PNC resolutions: "This attitude continues to be known today in the official political dictionary of the Palestinian leadership as realism and rationalism. It obtains its strength from the weakness of the *umma*. The weakness of the *umma* is being used as a pretext to emphasis this official position. And instead of looking at the weakness of the *umma* as a strong reason to pinpoint the causes of this weakness...[that] weakness was made a strong pretext to carry through the policy of the *fait accompli*."

In a subsequent statement, distributed by the Islamic *Jihad* on March 20, 1989, the movement declared that it was "innocent before God of all bargaining over our rights in all of our homeland, or of willingness to reject any inch of our holy land....We are innocent before God of any call for the so-called elections or for the so-called international conference or any formula that overturns on the owners of those rights the curse of conceding their rights." Lastly, the Islamic *Jihad* movement wonders whether it was possible to remove or wrest away the representation the PLO leadership has exercised throughout the last two decades. The *Jihad's* reply was that the PLO leadership is "like the cat which licks the wound...While it was enjoying the taste of its own blood, it believed that it was drinking the blood of someone else."

Undoubtedly, the Islamic *Jihad* movement, as a concept and as an organisation, has dug its roots inside the Occupied Territories as a political force. This movement signifies a form of political Islamic resurgence more than it embodies a revival of religious practices or moral conduct. By its daring actions against the Israeli occupation, the Islamic *Jihad* claims that it played a role in restoring confidence among the people following a period of decline, indifference, and recess of Palestinian nationalist unrest.

However, the future of the Islamic *Jihad* movement does not depend solely on the quality of its own performance. Rather, this future will also be determined by four other factors. The first factor is the Muslim Brotherhood's position toward the Palestinian issue and the changes that may emerge in this position. The second factor relates to the performance of the PLO outfits and their success or failure in maintaining their support among the Palestinians of the Occupied Territories. The third factor is the reaction of the Israeli authorities and the capacity these authorities will use in dealing with the Islamic *Jihad*. The fourth factor is the level of support the Islamic movements outside Palestine are intending to give the Islamic *Jihad*.

Role of Muslim Brotherhood

The Islamic *Jihad* movement and the Muslim Brotherhood Society share the broad lines of the Islamic ideology. Both factions seek to establish an Islamic state and apply Islamic principles in an Islamic society as an ultimate goal. The differences between the two outfits are not epistemological or doctrinal, but rather emerge from their different understanding and interpretation of the doctrine in the way it deals with the various Islamic issues, in particular, the political and the social.

Islamic writers who are sympathetic to the notion of the Islamic *Jihad* argue that the Muslim Brotherhood has lost the living and correct perspective of history and deals with this history as if it were scattered events, not supervised by a framework or law. Consequently, the Brotherhood does not understand the reality around it. It is not totally aware of how to define the basic features of history and sometimes does not understand the need to search for them. The society has lost the correct viewpoint and does not "sense the Israeli era which is creeping everywhere. It inflates small issues while the large issues are marginalised."

In its criticism of the Muslim Brotherhood, the Islamic *Jihad* depends on the writings and ideas of Islamic writers such as the prominent Muslim thinker Fathi Yakin. Yakin writes: "The battle that is going on today between Islam and the *Jahiliyya* [pre-Islamic age of ignorance] is more waged on the level of pure scientific discussion or within the bounds of purposeful, intellectual debate ....The struggle has become bloody and fierce in the real sense of the term." He adds: "The Islamic movement ought to be the academy that produces the *Mujahidin* and heroes, before being an intellectual academy promoting culture and pure Islamic notions among the people....We need consciousness, profoundness, and wisdom, just as we need courage, sacrifice, and boldness.....The tyranny of the principle of seeking safety and exaggerating this principle and adopting it as a permanent policy at all times and in every situation and on all levels, will only result in the permanent killing of the spirit of sacrifice in individuals and will transform the Islamic movement into a theoretical school or simply into one assimilation of thinking."

Yakin also writes: "In order for the Islamic movement to shoulder its responsibilities, it must reconsider its basic principles....its internal structure, educational programmes, direction, means of operation, and methods of conflict...." Because "the methods the Islamic movement had relied upon throughout the past years always lacked the exploration and evolution required to cope with the Islamic cause and the events and circumstances that encompassed it. If the Islamic orientation needs to develop its methods and programmes, it is even in greater need to explore the value of planning and its role in enabling the Islamic cause and the Islamic movement to achieve their aims and objectives....The failure and the setbacks that afflicted the Islamic movement stemmed in particular from confusion in the manner of learning and the negligence in the areas of planning."

Fathi Yakin concludes: "There is another justification that necessitates the establishment of one international Islamic movement. The challenges confronting Islam come in fact from international movements, such as Zionism, Masonry, communism, and the crusading missionary movements....These international movements, with their enormous human, material and technical capabilities and resources, cannot be matched except by equivalent means and levels. Failing to do so will mean nothing but retreat and destruction."

Al-Shaqaqi held the Muslim Brotherhood responsible for the indifference of the Islamic youth, putting the blame on the methods of formation the Brotherhood adopts. These methods are, in several cases, "static and detached from the ever changing social, political, economic and intellectual reality." Al-Shaqaqi questions the ability of the conventional Islamic movement to "tear up its methodological, ideological, and political covering, in order to catch up with the movement of history, and join with the masses in their daily pre-occupations and in all their small and large concerns."

The Islamic *Jihad* movement contemplates Hasan al-Banna, the founder of the organisation of the Muslim Brotherhood Society, a frontline leader and a symbol for *Jihad* as well as the inventor of new Brotherhood principles. In this respect, reference is made to the Brotherhood volunteers whom al-Banna dispatched to Palestine in 1947-48. But the Islamic *Jihad* movement condemns the Muslim Brotherhood for not having a proper understanding of what Hasan al-Banna represents, and for not being committed to the essence of his notions and positions.

The Islamic *Jihad* stresses the difference in its interpretation of Islam in comparison to the Muslim Brotherhood's interpretation. Sheikh 'Abd-al-'Aziz 'Auda says: "Our interpretation of Islam is not engulfed in ambiguity. It is based on our understanding of the social, political, and economic dimensions of the lives of the people.

From the Islamic *Jihad's* point of view, the problems of the Arab society cannot be solved by gradual reform. Therefore, the Islamic *Jihad* renounces the Muslim Brotherhood's traditional notions and practices in all aspects of daily life and argues that the alternative to that reformist attitude is revolutionary action by an Islamic vanguard, capable of imposing an Islamic system that can launch a no-holds-barred war against Israel.

Generally the Islamic *Jihad* movement regards itself as the anti-thesis of the reformist assimilation of the Muslim Brotherhood Society. It represents a trend of "decisiveness and revolution," in contrast to the trend of "truce, patching and reform." The Islamic *Jihad* perceives itself a source of challenge to the Brotherhood, because of the latter's lack of commitment to an extensive battle against Israel. The *Jihad* movement blames the Brotherhood for its moderate stance and policies in this regard. The *Jihad* supporters wonder how the Brotherhood, which considers *Jihad* to be one of the pillars of its doctrine, did not engage in armed rebellion, while the secular nationalist factions engaged in this kind of struggle.

The Muslim Brotherhood can justify its position in the words of Hasan al-Banna, founder of the mother society:

> Many people ask: does the Muslim Brotherhood Society intend to use force to achieve its goals and attain its objectives? Does the Muslim Brotherhood think about the preparation for a general revolution against the political system or the social system? I do not want to leave these questioners in any doubt. I will take this opportunity to remove the veil from the straightforward answer to these questions, and say it clearly for those who wish to listen. As for force, it is the motto of Islam in all its rules and regulations....but the Brotherhood's thought is too deep and farsighted to be lured by the superficiality of ideal and deeds, instead of diving into the depth of things and weighing their results, meanings and purposes. The Brotherhood knows that the ultimate degree of force is the force of doctrine and belief; the force of the arm and weapons comes second. It is incorrect to attribute force to a group until all meanings of the word are acquired. If the force of the arm and weapons is used while the group suffers from incoherence, disequilibrium or weakness of doctrine, then the fate of that group will be destruction.

The views of the *Jihad* movement and the Muslim Brotherhood differ concerning several issues, but the main differences between the two factions revolve around the Palestinian issue, the position that should be taken toward the existing Arab order, and the attitude toward the Islamic revolution in Iran. The Islamic *Jihad* believes that the Brotherhood's stance toward the Palestinian issue is erroneous. It argues that the Brotherhood's position lacks criticism and analysis, particularly the society's perception that the "establishment of an Islamic state in the region would end the problem completely, resolve the long conflict, and restore Palestine to its people within hours. 'It is not our concern to think about it, or plan for it. We must work and work only.' Regrettably, the Brotherhood is ignorant of this stage and of its weapons, because the Society is ignorant of the essence of the struggle that is now taking place on the Muslim homeland, and of the relationship of the Palestinian issue, and its position in this phase, and in the circle of struggle."

The Islamic *Jihad* rejects the position of the Muslim

Brotherhood Society toward the Palestinian issue and describes this as being emotional, depending on rhetoric instead of the actual fight for the liberation of Palestine. The *Jihad* considers this position as alien to the heritage of the Islamic movement, and incompatible with Hasan al-Banna's work, since he had emphasised actual struggle by dispatching Brotherhood members to fight in Palestine. When the Muslim Brotherhood had sent its youth to Palestine between 1947 and 1948, it reinforced the awareness of the Palestinian issue as the Islamic movement's central issue.

Al-Shaqaqi attributes the Muslim Brotherhood's crisis, regarding the attitude toward the Palestinian issue, to the society's slip-up to engage in the armed struggle: "Was not the withdrawal of the Palestinian Islamic leadership from the Palestinian battlefield, and their disavowal of 'national paganism' a reason for alienation and hostility between the youths of the Islamic movement and the majority of our people?....It is ironic that the theoreticians and writers of the Islamic movement, some of whom are Palestinians, are the ones who talk most, and sometimes exaggerate the Jewish plots and plans....yet, the Islamic movement in recent years has remained most distant from the clashes with the Jewish entity in Palestine."

In a clear reference to the Muslim Brotherhood, the following was published in one of the periodicals that reveal the opinions of the Islamic *Jihad* movement: "Even in the ranks of Islamic movement, there are major tendencies and forces that pursue the same policy of Arafat: respect for the international game, the balances, the alliances, liberalism in practice and relations, financial and media power, status, and influence as an alternative to the continuing jihad and reliance on God and the power of the conscious Muslim masses."

With regard to its position vis-a-vis the Arab regimes, the Islamic *Jihad* movement considers the Arab governments as an "actual security belt for Israel," and believes that these governments are hostile to the concept of *Jihad*, because *Jihad* would reveal the "falsehood of these governments and their slogans and ideas and would reveal their collusion, dependency, and connections with the Jewish and colonialist enemies of Islam. The exercise of *Jihad* would divulge the true features of these governments, which only serve the Zionist entity. The *Jihad* would leave these governments unveiled before the masses which would see with their own eyes these governments' positions in light of our *Jihad*, and the clash with the Zionist enemy that will result from it. The masses would recognise that these governments are the real guardians of the security of the Zionist enemy and that they are the real tools, which the Jews and colonialism used, and still use, to inhibit the *mujahidin* movements." The Islamic *Jihad* criticises the Muslim Brotherhood for its position of truce and co-existence with these regimes, especially those which have strong affinity with the West, such as Saudi Arabia, Egypt, and Jordan. One *Jihad* leader points out that the Muslim Brotherhood's coexistence with these regimes reflects the fact that the Brotherhood is out of touch with history, as well as the society's inclination to deal with the status quo.

The Islamic *Jihad* declines conciliation with Arab regimes and believes in the comprehensive struggle. It regards "the Arab regimes and Israel as two faces to the same coin; they are both the fruit of the Western invasion of the Arab world. The political agenda of these regimes represent a peripheral challenge and a marginal struggle with this invasion. Islam is the real opposition."

It is worth mentioning that the Islamic *Jihad* movement views Hafiz al-Asad, Mu'ammar al-Qaddafi, King Fahd, King Hussein, and Saddam Hussein in the same frame of mind. After the deportation of its leaders from the Occupied Territories, the *Jihad* ceased to attack Hafiz al-Asad, since some of these leaders and some of their followers reside in, or operate from, Syria and Lebanon.

In the Occupied Territories, the Islamic *Jihad* accuses the Brotherhood of direct collusion with Arab regimes. One of the pamphlets issued by a pro-Islamic *Jihad* student outfit in the Islamic University in Gaza claimed that the university's administration, dominated by the Muslim Brotherhood, was seeking, with the assistance of Jordan, to create centres of influence for Jordan in the Gaza Strip. The pamphlet also pointed out that "the American-Jewish-Saudi axis" was controlling the region. In another statement, supporters of the *Jihad* movement held the Muslim Brotherhood in the Gaza Strip of trying to link the Strip to the Jordanian regime, "as a card in the Jordanian king's hand with which to enter the tarnished American peace." Moreover, they indicated the Islamic University's administration of working to "liquidate the aware and committed Islamic trend and every honourable Palestinian Muslim rejecting the administration's conspiracies."

The Muslim Brotherhood, on its part, charged the Islamic *Jihad* movement of being a Shi'ite movement allying itself with the Communists. The *Jihad* refuted such charges: "While everyone knows that in all of Palestine, from the river to the sea, there is not a single Shi'ite, we find those who lie to God and who lie to you, labelling the chastised youth who are willing to give up this life and give themselves to God and to death on His path....of being Shi'ite in an attempt to exploit the ignorance of some, and to besiege this Muslim voice....They talk falsely about alleged alliances with other forces, exploiting the simplicity of some Muslim youth. But God knows, and they know, that they are lying."

Regarding the attitude toward the Iranian revolution, the Islamic *Jihad* viewed this revolution as a beginning for comprehensive revolutionary change. The Muslim Brotherhood does not share this view, although it initially considered the Iranian revolution favourably, but soon changed its position with the start of the Iran-Iraq war. The Muslim Brotherhood believes that despite the fact that this revolution stemmed from Islamic principles, it started to lose its Islamic appeal. The society argues that while the revolution succeeded in overthrowing the Shah's regime, it was "unable to claim that it had established an exemplary Islamic state that is founded on firm institutions....An Islamic state which strives to absorb all Islamic potentials is supposed to embrace Islamic principles that would go beyond sectarian differences. However, all can see the sectarian nature of the state, which is confirmed day after day through words and deeds inside and outside Iran."

The *Jihad* movement believes that specific Arab antirevolutionary regimes could not openly stand against the Iranian revolution at the outset and that these regimes remained silent or even expressed support until the outbreak of the Iran-Iraq war, when campaigns of incitement and scheming against the revolution then began. The *Jihad* indicates that the regime in Jordan played a role in pressuring the Muslim Brotherhood in Jordan to persuade the Brotherhood in the Occupied Territories to change its position toward the Iranian revolution. The Islamic *Jihad* argues that the Brotherhood inflamed the issue of the dispute between Shi'ites and Sunnis as a pretext to embrace a hostile position toward the Islamic revolution in Iran.

The Islamic *Jihad* movement points out that the Muslim Brotherhood Society in the West Bank and the Gaza Strip held a hostile stance toward the revolution, while the other Islamic movements did not take a similar one. In this regard, the Islamic *Jihad* refers to the attitudes of 'Issam al-'Attar, a Syrian Muslim Brotherhood leader, and of Fathi Yakin, a prominent Islamic thinker. It also refers to the position of the Muslim Brotherhood's International Organisation and to al-Azhar's stance in Egypt, as well as to the positions of the Islamic outfits in Pakistan and the prominent Islamic educator, Abu-al-A'la al-Mawdudi. All of these positions were cordial and reflected no hostility to the Iranian revolution.

The Islamic *Jihad* is condemned by the Muslim Brotherhood for various reasons. The *Jihad* is accused of being part of the Fatah movement, the "Islamic Fatah," which suffers from duplicity in principle. The *Jihad* movement is also criticised for concentrating on the political matters, while ignoring the significance of Islamic education. The Brotherhood accuses the *Jihad* of following Iran's path and of being unwaveringly linked to it. The *Jihad* is also labelled as a Shi'ite faction, carrying out Iranian policies, which the Muslim Brotherhood rejects.

The Islamic *Jihad* has defined its relationship with Iran in the words of the movement's spiritual leader, Sheikh 'Abd-al-Aziz 'Auda: "The Iranian revolution is a momentous and important attempt to achieve the Islamic awakening. Iran is now trying to unify the Islamic *umma* and unite the Sunni and Shi'ite schools of thought." As regards the *Jihad* movement's stance toward the Iran-Iraq war, Sheikh 'Auda stated: "Khomeini's decision to continue the war against Iraq was a wise decision....We see the Iran-Iraq conflict as a classical war that will bring about unusual results and will alter the face of the entire region. Based on that, we believe that the continuation of the war will do good to the Palestinian cause."

The Islamic *Jihad* believes that Islamic Iran is the state that is most committed to the Palestinian issue and that its victory over Iraq would create a new scenario in the region on the way to the establishment of the Islamic state, which will in turn be an asset in the battle against Israel. The *Jihad* leaders draw an equivalence between Sheikh 'Izz-al-Din al-Qassam and al-Hussein, son of 'Ali, who is revered by the Shi'ities: "Like al-Hussein in the dawn of the first movvement, al-Qassam was, in the twenties and thirties of this century, a symbol of belief, consciousness and revolution."

Sheikh 'Abd-al-Aziz 'Auda points out that the campaign of siege which the Muslim Brotherhood launched against the Islamic *Jihad* since 1981 has hampered the movement's efforts to take up armed action against Israel in an earlier period. 'Auda attributes the Brotherhood's negative stance toward the Islamic *Jihad* to the society's fear that the *Jihad* may become an alternative to the Brotherhood.

The Islamic *Jihad* notes that the Brotherhood's refusal to go into alliances with the nationalist groups stems from the Brotherhood's belief that such alliances would weaken the Brotherhood's influence as a distinct movement. Moreover, this refusal also stems from an inability to comprehend and analyse, and is a result of the type of mentality that dominates the Brotherhood. The Islamic *Jihad* mentions the example of how the Syrian Muslim Brotherhood joined the National Front for the Liberation of Syria along with secular forces, while the Brotherhood in the Occupied Territories declines to ally itself with similar nationalist forces, using the pretext that "the Muslim *ulema* of Syria are erudite men and are better judges of their own situation." From the *Jihad* movement's point of view this kind of attitude reveals the uncritical mentality of the Muslim Brotherhood.

Until the eruption of the *intifada*, the relationship between the Islamic *Jihad* movement and the Muslim Brotherhood Society could be narrated as negative and incompatible. No attempts until then were made at unification, serious reconciliation, or narrowing of large-scale differences. Disputes between the two groups had at one point of time turned into violent clashes. The last of these clashes broke out when a group of pro-Brotherhood youths in the Islamic University attacked, a few days before the *intifada*, supporters of the Islamic *Jihad* in the university. The latter were demonstrating within the very vicinity of the university protesting the Israeli authorities' decision to banish Sheikh 'Abd-al-'Aziz 'Auda. Before that, other incidents and confrontations occurred between the two sides. The Islamic *Jihad* censured the Muslim Brotherhood of attempting to assassinate 'Auda on January 16, 1983, but the Brotherhood denied the charge.

While considering the future relationship between the Muslim Brotherhood and the Islamic *Jihad* and the possibilities of unity between the two factions, the brotherhood sees itself as the primary Islamic power and believes that cooperation with the *Jihad* would be acceptable only if it is done according to Brotherhood's terms. As an independent organisation, the Brotherhood can make its own decisions and has no need to give concessions. On the other hand, the Brotherhood looks suspiciously at the *Jihad's* links with Fatah and Iran. The Brotherhood still recalls that the Islamic *Jihad* is a splinter faction from the society and that it may still expect to dominate the Islamic movement in the Occupied Territories. But prospects for mutual understanding became improving during and in the aftermath of the Gulf crisis. The prevailing mood in the circles of both the Brotherhood and *Jihad* favours a rapprochement between the two factions.

The Brotherhood's participation in the *intifada*, the formation of Hamas, and the application by Hamas of violent tactics against the Israeli occupation have narrowed the disparities between the Brotherhood and the *Jihad*. During the Gulf crisis, the Brotherhood's attitude toward Arab regimes, especially Saudi Arabia and the Gulf states, has become closer to the critical standpoints of the Islamic *Jihad* toward these regimes. The Brotherhood, like the Islamic *Jihad*, has established links with other Muslim fundamentalist outfits in the Arab countries.

Ten

Pre-requisites of Terrorism

Inherent Limitation

No terrorist movement can hope that the ruling regime will collapse as soon as the terrorists unleash their terroristic activities. On the other hand, it can expect stiff resistance leading to massive loss of lives on both sides. Often the terrorist outfits have political objectives including secession. No government, howsoever inept and unpopular, can take the affront of a terrorist group challenging its legitimacy. It, therefore, brings into effect into all its means of power and influence to crush the movement.

Terrorists know that they cannot achieve outright victory over government forces. They want to undermine the morale of the government and its fighting forces. The aim is to erode the integrity of society by loosening its institutional props so that it caves in on itself, its structure too weak to support the weight pressing on it. These terrorist outfits expect that fluidity of events and involvement of others will see the end of the unpopular regime.

Critical Preconditions

Terrorism struggles are special. For terrorism to progress satisfactorily, some minimal conditions, resources and pre-requisites are necessary. While the armed conflict with the state throws up many critical constraints and openings for terrorist groups, the succeeding resources are needed for the initiation and progress of a political violence movement.

Organisation

A terrorist movement needs to put a substantial organisation on the ground. Its main requirements are a direction-giving body at the helm of affairs, the strike groups and the intelligence set-up. As terrorism in a specific geographical region gains predominance, the need for a full-fledged political wing also crops up. This wing is responsible for making clear the demands of the violent movement to the ruling regime. In any case, the bulk of the volunteers in a terrorist outfit remain busy in planning and executing violent incidents to create a paralyzing level of fear in the target society.

Charismatic Leader

Terrorism is a very unnatural method to acquire or maintain power or control by intimidation. It tries to instil fear of destruction or helplessness in the objects of terrorism. Such a movement needs a charismatic leader with a magnetic personality. A person is needed who can instigate the imagination of young people to join this highly risky venture. Such a leader may have religious or political background. He may be an intellectual rebel, a radical ideologue or even a plain rabble-rouser. He is one who displays unflinching self-confidence and voices his opinions and concerns with absolute certainty. A charismatic leader has to act as a guide to those who need his guidance. He should, above all, be an object of worship for the common people especially the youth. A terrorist movement needs a leader who should highly inflexible and should be ready to lay down his life for the cause espoused by him. Ayatollah Khomenei of Iran and Sant Jarnail Singh Bhindranwale were such leaders with magnetic personality. The charismatic leader controls the pulsations of the terrorist movement. Absence of a charismatic personality in a terrorism struggle is a debilitating factor in its effort at successful culmination.

Motivation Resource

The progress and popularity of a terrorist movement will be considerably affected by the resource of motivation for its volunteers. Religious identity especially its fundamentalist sentimentalities is a potent resource of motivation. Ideological trends have unleashed a series of terrorist outrages whose justification is based on patriotism, nationalism, racism, cultural intolerance, religious fanaticism and political dogma. The intensity of any terrorist movement and the zeal displayed by the volunteers depend upon the motivation resource selected for the movement. A terrorist campaign may use more than one ideological impetus for broad-basing its network.

Discipline

Terrorism is a disciplined endeavour. It trades in death and destructions. Violations of moral nature are unpardonable. Clandestinity is a principled choice and any indiscretion to breach it can jeopardize the very existence of the terrorist outfits and strike groups. There is no place for 'doubters' and 'ditherers' in any terrorist organisation. Utter loyalty and dedication to the cause and the central leadership are vitally important. Che Guevara got rid of some very close aides as they started dithering midway during the Cuban Revolutionary War. Terrorism actors need to exhibit total commitment and renegades are not allowed to live.

Outside Support

Terrorism struggle cannot depend upon local support as it is obtained at the point of gun. Society is crippled by fear of death and destruction. Support to terrorism is directly proportional to the level of fear and feeling of repression felt by the target society. Terrorist outfits require outside help for their survival.

Terrorist campaigns get lot of sustenance if the geographical area of their movement touches some other country. Terrorist movements in Punjab, J&K and Assam enjoy this unique advantage. Prov IRA of Northern Ireland also had this overwhelming factor in its favour. ETA of the Basque region of Spain touching France made use of the favourable terrain across the border and the sympathetic attitude of ethnic Basque community.

In seeking outside support, the leader of a terrorist campaign shows no moral qualms. They have no treaties to follow or any international norms to observe. They require help for immediate assault against the target country. They use their manipulative skills to involve the supporting country in an irretrievable situation.

Publicity

Terrorism needs active interference of media for its impact. Modern world is highly dependent upon mass communication and information technology. As terrorism is pre-eminently a psychological warfare, it needs to rely on television, telephone, radio, print media and cinema. Internet, Fax and e-Mail are too piaying active part in projection of terrorist activities. By its very nature, terrorism is sensation-inducing and as such is a favourite field for news-seekers. Its news-worthiness is unique and unending. Publicity is the oxygen of terrorism. Terrorist leaders plan meticulously for achieving maximum coverage of their violent deeds. They also choose resonant targets for this purpose. Human bomb is the total terror employed for getting world-wide coverage as several PLO and LTTE terrorists could manage to do. The very survival of the terrorist campaign draws extensive publicity through political rhetoric and self-congratulatory pronouncements of commanders of Security Forces.

Funds

A terrorist movement needs staggering amounts of money for different requirements. Money is required for procurement of arms, ammunitions, explosives, equipment and foodstuff. One very frequent demand on funds comes from people who supply daily information about the activities of Police, Security Forces, political leaders and the selected goals. This omnipresent network of agents of terrorist outfits can made to operate if regular supply of money is ensured at the front end. Sophisticated arms, explosives and wireless sets cost a lot. As gun-runners are available everywhere, it is an ideal situation for a terrorist campaign like the one run by Pakistan in J & K.

Evidently, terrorists do not have funds or any legal sources of funds. They belong to the weaker sections of society and are generally economically deprived. Mostly it is economic hardship that drives a young man into the terrorist fold. Terrorists have to commit extortions, blackmail, thefts, bank robberies and kidnappings for ransom money. Terrorists have indulged in smuggling of narcotics and arms for earning money for the outfits. They also take commission from traders, contractors, government officials and other civilians working in different institutions. Big multinational firms pay 'protection money' to terrorist leadership. Some terrorist states also contribute huge amounts of money to bolster the morale of terrorists engaged in religious war. PLO, Prov IRA, Talibans and several fundamentalist militia in J&K have been getting massive financial aids from their foreign masters. For Munich killings of 11 Israeli athletes in September 1972, Black September got seven million dollars.

Cooperation with other Terrorist Movements

Nothing gives more encouragement to a terrorist movement than the success of another struggle in some other land. Terrorist outfits pursue similar goals. Their interests and needs often coincide. They help out each other with funds, weapons, explosives, communication facilities, safe houses, cars with false number plates, fake passports and surveillance elements. Terrorists from Japan have cooperated with PLO. Similarly, Prov IRA have joined hands for taking on targets in London and various countries in Europe.

The startling feature of this trans-national cooperation has been noticed in South Asia. Courtesy the terrorism-sponsoring state of Pakistan, Taliban of Afghanistan are actively cooperating with fundamentalist Islamic militias operating in J&K from Pakistan territory. Besides sophisticated weapons, explosives and state of the art wireless sets, Talibans are sending hordes of trained Afghani Mujahideens waiting for green signal from Pakistan's ISI to walk into the terrorist cauldron of Kashmir Valley for embracing martyrdom. Pakistani leadership is so gleefully hoisted on its petard of Pan Islamic movement that it is interfering unabashedly in Afghanistan and Chechenya, a Republic of Russia. Earlier, it was protesting against fervently atrocities on Muslims in Kosovo and Bosnia. While discerning the strategic dimensions of any terrorist movement, its existing and potential connections with other similar movements and countries need to be identified.

Accommodation and Hideouts

Terrorists are not guerrillas of the bush. Both urban and rural terrorist cadres need accommodation for dwelling and storage of arms, explosive and ammunitions. Terrorists prefer to hibernate when they are not in some specific mission. They are highly vulnerable to checkings and interceptions when they are on the move. They prefer to merge with the indistinguishable mass of society. Under pressure the terrorists go into forested areas to escape easy detection and apprehension. Sikh terrorists had rural background. They did not make use of the cities and preferred to stay in farm-houses in the countryside. Some preferred to remain slowed away in religious places. Officers of security communities should exercise their minds to detect the possible pattern of terrorists' possible hideouts. In J&K, while foreign mercenaries prefer to live in forests and high mountains for operational reasons, the local Kashmiri Mujahideens swing toward the inhabited areas. Need for a civilised-looking dwelling place by terrorists is a vulnerable attributes which the field officers of Security Forces need to keep in mind. Several insurgents in North Eastern states of India betrayed this weakness. Travails of life or rebellion are too harsh even for the highly motivated terrorists.

Mobility

Development strategies in all corners of the country have made remote areas accessible. Observation capabilities from the ground and air have improved reducing the load on mobility elements. Excellent network of roads in Punjab contributed immensely to the quick movements of strike factions in the area of operation during counter-terrorist operations. Leaders of Security Forces need to integrate the mobility elements with deployment grid for effective coverage of the terror-scape under their respective jurisdiction. Mobility is a two-way asset for both terrorists and Security Forces.

Communications

Terrorists, most of the time, operate in small groups for reasons of security and operational necessity. A terrorist group has not to fight a pitched battle. It needs to exercise maximum secrecy and surprise for executing its mission. Normally, it is a single phase or single action strike on a human target. Terrorist groups are in no hurry and they can take their time. Such an operational field needs excellent system of communication. There is need for continuous communication as the group may have to be rescued. Availability of telephone facilities in villages has opened floodgates of information-sharing. Internet has allowed a method of communication which has given a quantum leap to terrorist organisations for their projections to the outside world. It is a multiplier for the terrorist side.

Recruitment

A terrorist rarely enjoys a long life. After the initial vigour of enthusiasm, every terrorist movement gets into an even keel. When terrorists get killed, potential young recruits take notice. Many give it a second thought. The movement looks bogged down and the declared target seems remote and unachievable. Regular and adequate recruitment of young volunteers is essential for the movement to go on. When the new terrorists do not come forward, the campaign loses its steam and comes to a standstill. Call it violence fatigue or fluidity of events or sheer revulsion to prolonged violence of years, the 'fighters' do not appear anymore as happened in Punjab.

Weapons and Explosives

Cuban Revolutionary War started with Fidel Castro and Che Guevara possessing just a dozen weapons. They went on plundering weapons and ammunitions from Batista's corrupt and incompetent Police and Security personnel. That was more than 40 years ago. Times have changed now.

Terrorist movements of the Fright Decades of Twentieth Century did not face many problems in getting weapons. Proliferation of illegal weapons has gone apace in developing countries. Erstwhile Soviet Union's invasion of Afghanistan in 1979 and US aid to Pakistan for bolstering the strength and fighting ability of Afghan Mujahideen brought millions of weapons in the region. With the rise of Taliban, the withdrawal of Russian force from Afghanistan, the victory of Taliban and its taking over of control of Kabul and Pakistan's interference in the internal affairs of Afghanistan, the availability of weapons of revolution in this region has become much easy. These weapons have found their way into Pakistan and J&K state of India, the latter being in the grip of high intensity terrorism sponsored by Pakistan. This background of region's turmoil is a proof enough that the requirements of terrorist outfits and movements will be fully met for years to come.

Every terrorist movement requires light and small arms such as rifles and pistols. For well-entrenched groups who can exercise some freedom of movement, weapons like Light Machine Gun (LMG), Medium Machine Gun (MMG) and Rocket Launchers (RL) are also required. Similarly, explosives of various kind are needed for causing destruction of human lives and property. Normally, these items cannot be purchased from the open market as these are not available. In the context of terrorist movement in J&K, the entire issue is pointless and irrelevant. Pakistan's Inter Services Intelligence (ISI) is coordinating the arming and furnishing of various terrorist outfits. All the fanatic zealots of Islam who want to embrace martyrdom are trained in Pakistan and Afghanistan in training centres. Rigorous arms training and motivational indoctrination are done and they are then nose-led into J&K for waging terrorist campaign against India. A stage has now reached where the terrorists possess very sophisticated and destructive weapons. As procuring weapons and explosives has become easy, the Islamic terrorists are not overly worried about loss or capture of their weapons as revolutionaries of earlier era used to show.

Planning and Information

No terrorist movement can hope to coerce a regime to yield its demands if it hits out blindly. While violence and threat of violence are the significant means of demoralising the society and government, all killings and destructions have to be planned for impact. The indiscriminateness of violence is also meant to confuse the adversary about the pattern of movement's targeting. Terrorist activities should force prohibitive cost on society and government forcing the latter to react in anger and petulance. Terrorists want to draw repression on the innocent mass of people.

There is a striking element of central planning in terrorism. Tight central control on the activities of terrorist groups is a functional pre-requisite. It is through central planning that issues of foreign support, political assassinations, regional responsibility, distribution of funds, arms, ammunition and explosives are resolved. A wide network of overground and underground operatives is needed to provide regular information about Police movements and Security Forces operations. Information is the life-line of terrorists in the field. Terrorists are highly romantic youths who remain hoisted on their egos. They have to be kept under leash or they can go hastily into a destructive spree or self-immolation. Even for small ambushes of armed Police and Security Forces personnel, exhaustive coordination and planning need to be done to reduce own losses.

Tactical Superiority

Clandestinity at the tactical level is indispensable for the terrorist actors. In excessive secrecy, the terrorist fails to enjoy any authority but it is needed for his security. Terrorists cannot operate freely. They have to show tactical superiority by making effective and intelligent use of time, space, choice, of target and intensity of operation. A terrorist group hits out when the opportunity occurs. He needs to thunderclap his adversary and leave him stunned and confused. The regime's security apparatus should look inadequate. People should feel that the government cannot protect them and their assets. Terrorist groups need to develop high degree of intelligence about government's projected activities. Government's informers and agents have to be eliminated in a merciless manner. Lapses and acts of negligence of Security Forces have to be punished with a sense of vengeance.

Exploiting Weaknesses of open Societies

A terrorist campaign can make progress if it exploits the freedoms of an open liberal democracy in a systematic way. This is the Achilles' heel of a democratic society. A liberal democracy permits its citizens lot of freedoms. Press enjoys undiluted and unhampered freedom. Random arrests and detentions can be easily challenged in the courts of law. Freedom of expression is also guaranteed. There is freedom of movement. Various social, political and economic institutions ensure active participation of people in development processes. These conditions are exploited by the terrorist outfits. They can travel freely using normal means of transportation. If the government introduces too many checkings and screenings, the inconveniences alienate the people from the ruling regime.

By systematic exploitation of freedoms of a democratic free society, the terrorists can force the rulers to close down the society. Military regimes, monarchies and totalitarian states do not permit open dissent leave aside a terrorist movement. It is in this field that the planners of terrorism have to work hard as to how to continue their struggle beyond the limits which constrain the majority of citizens from protest or direct action whether they are malcontents or not. A terrorist is one who knows the limits, it is the calculated violation of the barrier of acceptability which gives terrorist violence its impact. If the terrorist group does not hit out when an opportunity comes up, it has lost its meaning. The common belief of government officials giving a civilised response to terrorist activities must be exploited by the terrorist groups.

Using Society as Cushion

Terrorism has been condemned as cancer of the social order. A terrorist is one who does not accept the norms of his present social order. He wants to demolish it by flouting the norms of civilised behaviour. His convoluted logic makes no sense through he indicates that he will come back to his law-abiding ways. A terrorist gets enmeshed with the society. He uses its indistinguishable mass for keeping his identity concealed. He exploits the assests of society telling its members that he is fighting for justice. He tells the people that he is fighting for a higher cause. His morality surpasses the common moral code. He holds the victims of injustice and indignities as responsible as the perpetrators of atrocities.

The terrorist cannot operate without active support of the people but this support comes on account of the widespread fear created by indiscriminate killings. Terrorist groups progress their movement with the clear premise that they shall be able to retain society's support in their favour. Terrorist groups have to study closely the pattern of population and their attitude for mounting terrorist operations with a view to carving out an area of influence.

Gradual Inflammation of the Area

Terrorist campaign leaders do not make ambitious plans to inflame the entire area of interest by simultaneous terroristic incidents. They are not very sure about the reaction of the population and the ruling regime. This tactics is essential on account of several reasons. Terrorist movements do not have adequate number of armed volunteers and strike groups. Terrorist leaders are not very confident about their own fighters once the casualties start occurring. There is uncertainty about selection of targets and the intensity of reaction. Foreign support may not flow in at the required speed and quantity. Terrorist movements in Punjab, J&K and Assam started from border districts and advanced towards the interior areas in an irrevocable manner. Terrorists prefer to bite that much as they can chew. Containment strategies of Security Forces should be based on this trend.

Terrorism is an interpretable phenomenon. Anti-terrorist agencies of the state should not abandon restraint. Innovative approaches from reconciliation efforts to individual de-indoctrination of leaders can be tried through parents, friends, priests and teachers. Government may get unexpected assistance on account of occurrence of some overwhelming political events or some other fluidity of circumstances.

Eleven

The Stalemate of Ideology

The Theoretical model has broken down. It has stopped functioning, first, in terms of texts: since the founding writings of Abul-Ala Maududi, Hasan al-Banna, Sayyid Qutb, Mustafa al-Siba'i (Syrian MB), Ali Shariati, Ruhollah Khomeini, Baqir al-Sadr, Murtaza Mutahhari, all prior to 1978, in all the languages of the *umma* there are nothing but brochures, prayers, feeble glosses and citations of recognised authors. It has broken down, next, in terms of concepts, which are reaching a dead end: for the Islamists, Islamic society exists only through politics, but the political institutions function only due to the virtue of those who run them, a virtue that can become widespread only if the society is Islamic beforehand. It is a mean circle. Finally, it has broken down in terms of action, the success of which might have made people to forget the impoverishment of the discourse; but neither the Islamic revolution in Iran, mired in economic catastrophe and in fighting among factions, nor the liberated regions of Afghanistan, torn apart by clannish and ethnic conflicts, furnish a model for what an Islamic society should be. And the FIS's Algeria will do nothing more than place a chador over the FLN's Algeria.

The Concept of Islamic State

Virtue, the only Foundation for Institutions

Aside from the Iranian revolution, which generated a complex and effective constitution, the poverty of Islamist thought on political institutions is noticeable, considering the emphasis Islamism places on politics. One the one hand, all Islamists agree on one point: political power is indispensable to the formation of an Islamic society. "The reforms that Islam wants to bring about cannot be effected by sermons alone. Political power is also essential to achieve them," writes Khurshid Ahmed; Maududi is unreservedly of this opinion, stating that it is impossible for a Muslim to observe successfully "an Islamic pattern of life" under the functioning of a non-Islamic system of government. But on the other hand, the plans for the creation of institutions are terminated while still on the drawing board in favour of a discussion of the qualities and virtues of their leaders.

How can one translate into concrete political institutions the notions of the amir and the *shura*, which, as we have seen, are the fundamentals for the Islamist vision of politics? The question is explicitly rejected as irrelevant. Maududi asserts right from the start: ("Islam does not prescribe any definite form for the formation of the consultative body or bodies for the simple reason that it is a universal religion meant for all times and climes") He maintains that the tenets of political Islam can be embodied in a variety of constitutional formulas (including something that resembles Western democracy, with a parliament and elections). What counts is neither the form nor the might of the institution, but rather the manner in which the institution effaces itself before the establishment of Islamic tenets, which then must govern the heart and actions of men. The key to politics is in a "social morality".

Neither the people nor the parliament nor the sovereign can be sources of law. The state has no positive power in and of itself. What is the point of actually defining political institutions, when in any case the executive, legislative, and judicial powers have very little room to manoeuvre? Sovereignty lies with God alone, and the law has already been given. "Whatever human agency is constituted to enforce the political system of Islam in a state will not possess sovereignty in the legal and political sense of the term, because ... its powers are limited and circumscribed by a supreme law which it can neither alter nor interfere with."

Thus, the important thing is that men, beginning with the leaders, fade themselves before the divine law. For Islamists, a discussion about institutions quickly turns into a discussion about determining the virtues and personal traits of those qualified to fulfil the various functions. Aside from a number of "objective" criteria (the head of state must be male, a Muslim, sane and an adult), the qualities are largely subjective, for they rest entirely on virtue, faith, and knowledge. The priority accorded to personal attributes over the definition of duties prevents the emergence of any thought on the subject of institutions. Institutional functions are only as effective as the virtue of those who exercise them.

In speaking of "those who bind and unbind" (*ahl al-hall wal-aqd*), that is, of political personnel, Maududi tells "they should be such whose sincerity, ability and loyalty [are] above reproach in the eyes of the public." Turabi builds on this: "The prevailing criteria of political merit for the purposes of candidature for any political office on moral integrity as well as on other relevant criteria. The discussion of who should be the leader consists in the portrayal of the ideal sovereign according to Quranic norms. Similarly, reflections on administration are reduced to discussion of the virtues and veracity of the functionary.

Institutions exist to oblige the individual to be a good Muslim (it is the duty of "ordering the good and chasing the bad"); once the members of the community are steadfastly virtuous, there will be no need for institutions. Islamist authors escape any definition of institutions, which they essentially mistrust, in favour of reflections on virtue (*taqwa*). The tenet of nonseparation between religion and politics (*din wa siyasa*), which for traditional ulemas amounted to casting politics into the domain of the empirical and the contingent, becomes, ambiguously, for the Islamists, a negation of politics itself in favour of an impossible pursuit for a virtue that can never be attained. The Islamist political model being attainable only in a man, and not in institutions, it solely makes the creation of a *polis*, an Islamist "polity," impossible.

A successful re-Islamisation would bring an end to political society. If everyone is virtuous, then why are institution necessary? Institutions, which are always discredited in Islamist thought, are accorded a simple pedagogical role—that of providing a permanent constraint that, on the one hand, removes any possibilities for sin and, on the other hand, establishes a system of punishment that aims to reestablish the purity of the community, to eradicate sin. The advent of genuine Islamic society would thus cause a withering of the state, because then social relationships would be an outgrowth of individual virtues and would require no institutional mediation. The goal is not the state, but devotion, which is at the same time both an individual and a social practice.

"An Islamic form of government exists when its members are Muslims, abide by their own Islamic duties and religious obligations, and do not disobey the Islamic laws." For Islamists, what actually propels the Islamic society is man, the believer. To become a true believer, a *homo islamicus,* he must destroy the old society through political action. But once the Islamic state comes into being, justice results not so much from state actions as from the convergence of men who are virtuous at last, who spontaneously match to the *sharia* without any external pressure. Social relationships are degraded to the horizontal relationships among individuals, in which the state intervenes only when there has been a fault against religious principle. The state has a purely pedagogical role: to make men virtuous. Its success is its own demise. If everyone is virtuous, then harmony certainly exists among men. The state is not a mediator between individuals and citizens; it does not construct a civil society. The more virtuous the society is, the more the state decays. The society exists in and of itself and results from the interaction of men among themselves: this interaction is very simply the *sharia;* no longer a simple catalogue of instructions, as it was considered among traditional jurists, the *sharia* becomes the differentiated expression of this totality that is the creature of God acting with the fear of God as his primary consideration. Because there is no hypothesis of original sin in Islam, man can create God's kingdom on earth.

The issue is not one of a state or on a democracy. The fact that divergent opinions exist is not denied, but general agreement remains the ideal. That is why the debating of ideas must be sustained among individuals, and not be embodied in different parties. ("While there may be a multiparty system, an Islamic government should function more as a consensus-oriented rather than a minority/majority system with political parties rigidly confronting each other over decisions").

The paradox is that the Islamists, who began by concerning themselves with politics, can at this point condemn the autonomous space of politics that the ulemas accepted: specifically, the possibility for the state to elaborate a positive law to legislate in areas not veiled by the *sharia* (this type of legislation is called *ta'zir* and *qanun*). Having begun with criticism of the overly legalistic and casuistic sprit of the ulemas as well as their disinterestedness to politics, the Islamists arrive at an even more radical negation of the political sphere: "In a tawhid society, there is no place for *ta'zir* and *qanun*". The state effaces itself when it has accomplished its historic task: to establish the exclusivity of the *sharia*, the only norm for social relations; "for the people to be just and happy, it is necessary and sufficient for the *sharia* to be implemented". But of course this *sharia*, as we shall see, no longer bears any similarity to the casuistry and formalism of the ulemas: it is a dynamic *sharia* (*haraki*), an active *sharia*, for it is internalised, lived, essentially becoming one's religious practice. The circle is closed: political action leads to religion, but to a religion of a mystical order.

Holiness versus Anthropology

The Hidden Dimension

At this point the return to fundamentalism, the *sharia* is no longer perceived as the finicky casuistics of the ulemas: it reveals a new being, the born-again Muslim. Society cannot be changed without a change in men. This hypothesis of a "spiritual revival" runs throughout the work of al-Banna; Muhammad Qutb, brother of Sayyid, writes: "Islam, in its general and wide sense, means that man should give himself up to God, surrender his soul completely to Him and leave everything, however small, in His hands". This position only appears to contradict the political activism characteristic of the Islamists.

For Islamists, the political detour is not an illusion, resulting in a return to the point of departure: it is the means by which a new conversion of the individual will appear. The political phase is the experience of total commitment, of a militancy inscribed within a psychological agenda. Respect for the *sharia* is not the mechanical application of a formalist legalism; it is the translation of genuine virtue into human behaviour. Thus, on the subject of the Christian and Jewish *dhimmi* living in Islamic territory, Hassan al-Turabi narrates "It is more than a matter of tolerance or legal immunity. Muslims have a moral obligation to be fair and friendly in their person-to-person conduct with non-Muslim citizens, and will be answerable to God for that". In a word, beyond the text of the *sharia* itself, exist virtue and fear: the issues of formal law and of institutions could not be more perfectly dismissed. The acquisition of this virtue presupposes a true mystical experience.

The ultimate experience is of course jihad, which, for the Islamists, means armed battle: against communists (Afghanistan) or Zionists (Palestine) or, for the fundamentalists, against renegades and the impious. But the literature of jihad places less importance on the objective (to create an Islamic state) than on the transcendental dimension (to sacrifice one's life); it is the act of supreme devotion. The fact that jihad is not part of the five pillars of the religion disturbs fundamentalist Islamists, one of whom, the Egyptian Farag, made it the sixth, absent obligation.

At the same time, devotion is opposed to organisation: martyrdom has more significance than victory. There is no "obligation to produce a result" in jihad: it is an affair between the believer and God and not between the *mujahid* and his enemy. Jihad does not operate within a territorialised state, but within the *umma*. One can perform one's jihad anywhere and within any institutional framework. We will see later on how this conception led thousands of young Arabs to engage in battle in Afghanistan, even though they were completely uninterested in the ethnic and political context, with all negative results one can imagine.

This concept of jihad, in which the individual act has more value than collective action, also goes against the organisational model borrowed from the Third World liberation wars, based on the encadrement of a large-scale movement within a single Leninist-type party. As Mohammed Arkoun notes, "The debate with the colonialist West transforms religious language into an ideological language, that is to say, the mythical intention into an immediate historical objective. Nevertheless it never attains the Marxist level of efficiency, for ... the ideological discourse remains ensnared in a subjective imagery of the past and present." Nonetheless, it is not fatalistic, for action, or activism, is valued, but victory is not perceived to be the result of a series of human acts: it is a gift from God, which may or may not be granted. One of the most commonly employed slogans in jihad propaganda is *tawfiq min Allah*, "success comes from God".

This hidden dimension naturally became highly visible in the Afghan underground forces and among the Iranian Revolutionary

Guards of the first Gulf War. It is always hard to establish the political sociology of mysticism, because in such circumstances we are dealing with "the institutionalisation of charisma," to quote Weber (again!). One loses the *moment*, the kind of moment that generally occurs only in literature. These periods of exaltation are transient: the same individuals who were prepared to die on the Iranian or Afghan front may now be local chiefs demanding their due. But this fall to earth is considered to be unscrupulousness by the actors themselves, who dream of the past moment of purity instead of attempting to build institutions capable of handling the shortcomings of men. Failure brings a setback to square one. Failure is scandalous. Either God has forgotten men, or men have forgotten God. Certainly, it is the latter proposition that is adopted. Far from militants' questioning their religion, political failure pushes them to leave toward forms of quietism (neofundamentalism) or despair (the martyrdom of Shiite combatants).

No doubt one should see in the individual's transition to terrorism the suicidal pursuit for an unattainable virtue. It is curious that almost all Western reflection on Islamic terrorism traces it back to the Ismaili "Assassins" (*hashashin*) of the twelfth century, without noticing its continuity with the Western terrorist tradition, which dates back to the Carbonari, the anarchists, and the Russian populists, a terrorism whose ethical and hidden aspects have been amply described by novelists (Camus, Malraux): suicide when faced with the impossibility of perfection, and the abolition of man's split between good and evil through one individual's sacrificial death.

After the mystical moment, Islamist thought undergoes a characteristic turnabout: beginning with politics, it returns to a form of neofundamentalism, that is, a negation of politics: "You cannot have an Islamic state except insofar [as] you have an Islamic society," writes the same Hassan al-Turabi who emphasises: "States come and go; Islamic society can exist and has existed without the structures of a state for centuries".

From Party to Faction

How can one escape the cycle: no Islamic state without virtuous Muslims, no virtuous Muslims without an Islamic state?

This is the function of the party: a training place for the pure, a synthesis between a political actor and a moral instructor, the party functions more as a splinter than as an instrument for obtaining power. Within the Muslim Brotherhood and the Pakistani Jamaat, it is explicitly asserted that the party is reserved for an elite.

The strictly Leninist model of the party never really caught on in Islamism. In Iran, where the revolution was nearer to the great revolutionary movements of the Third World, the single party, which could have been personified by the Islamic Republican Party (IRP), never really functioned, and the IRP was dissolved by Khomeini himself; politics were overrun by political factions and more informal associations, formed around networks of personal relationships. The Arab MBs have remained influence groups and have never converted into true political parties. The most Leninist of all the Islamist parties is unquestionably Hikmatyar's Hizb-i Islami in Afghanistan, which was strongly influenced by the communist organisational model as a result of the long history of interaction between Islamist students and communists and the affinities uniting the two groups. But the HI remained very much in the minority in the Afghan resistance.

Nonetheless it is clear, from a straightforward reading of the available statutes of these parties and associations, that their way of functioning anticipates, in the eyes of their founders, the creation of the Islamic society. The institutions (the amir and the *shura*) and tenet for the party's functioning (the *sharia*) are the same as those that would govern the ideal society. The party's hierarchy corresponds to degrees of introduction and purification — chiefly to an initiation process for militants, who must ultimately assimilate the Islamic principles within themselves. Membership being voluntary, the militant must internalise the party's principles and attain, through participation in the party's actions and the training he obtains in his heart, the state of virtue that is the condition for the advent of any Islamic society.

The militant must be separated from "ignorant" society (*jahili*) and live according to purely Islamic criteria. The party is an island of purity in an ocean of naivety and corruption. Militants are generally invited to live as much as possible among themselves, as indicated by the Egyptian MB's use of the term *usra* (family) to designate the basic cell. For the most radical organisations, endogamy is required, accentuating the impression of a sect. The members of this counter-society, nonetheless live among human society (which is reminiscent of the old Sufi principle: *khalvat dar anjoman*, "solitude in the midst of society").

The degrees of affiliation to the party correspond to stages of personal conversion, of psychological internalisation, and not to the simple acquisition of knowledge and techniques. The career of the militant is thus a kind of ladder of virtues, the quintessence of which is manifested in the one who stands at the summit, the amir. The members of the party advance on this scale as a function of their degree of initiation and purification, the criteria for their position in the hierarchy. The same type of organisation is found in the Egyptian, Jordanian, and Palestinian Muslim Brotherhoods, as well as in the Afghan Hizb-i Islami, many of whose statutes are plain translations of Egyptian MB texts, such as the *Risalat al-ta'alim*, written by al-Banna.

There are generally four stages to the initiation-membership process; the list for the Afghan Hizb-i Islami is as follows: sympathisers, members, "pillars," and *shura-ye markazi* (the "Central Council"), which elects the amir, assisted by an Executive Committee (*komite-ye ijra'iyya*). The degrees of "initiation" are vividly likened to a mystical initiation: "From the point of view of morality, this party is an avant-garde founded on spirituality [*ruha-niyya*] and Sufism [*tasawwuf*]." The new member must purify his soul in order to achieve a "spiritual education" (*tarbiya-ye irfani*) (page 83 of the HI statutes). Initiation includes three degrees, which correspond to the three first stages of membership: *ta'arruf* ("the search for knowledge"), during which the candidate must gather knowledge of the society, preaching, and the Islamic books; *takwin* ("genesis"), during which the candidate must acquire thorough obedience to the principles of the party, the better to purify himself; and *tanfidh* ("implementation"). During which the candidate can finally put the politics of the party into a genuine practice.

More than an instrument for attaining power, the party, or rather the "society", the association, is the place where an individual is transformed. It is a mirror of what the *umma* in general should be. The militant must convince others by the instance he offers in his personal actions rather than in his political activity per se. There are two possibilities for procuring power: either through the indefinite expansion of the party, conceived of as a counter-society that ends up attracting the bulk of the population and gradually incorporating those who have fallen into ignorance (*jahili*) — in this scenario the society becomes Islamised without a violent takeover of state power; or through a putsch that aims to slay the "Pharaoh" (the renegade sovereign), hoping, in the nineteenth-century Russian socialist revolutionary tradition, to revive the "consciousness" of the masses and bring about a spontaneous uprising. The practices of the Islamist movements oscillate between these two notions. In reality there is no precise theory for the seizing of power, aside from the idea that the party, by the influence of its members, will be ushered in rather than take power.

Preaching (*da'wa*) is the instrument of the march to power. The difference between preaching and propaganda is that the first assumes the immediate creation of an Islamist model: the militant must behave like the Prophet, dress, eat, express himself like the Prophet. By achieving in his person a model that is ethical and no longer political, he can hardly guide a genuine political action, for he demands conversion, and not membership, and replaces political action by the display of his very own behaviour.

The party thus becomes a sect, a counter-society, as its name often indicates (*jam'iyya, jama'a*: "society, association"), a refuge for pure believers who endure a kind of internal hegira (*hijra*) to shelter themselves from the impious and from corrupt Muslims, thereby developing means of avoidance that are apparently inconsistent with political action (endogamy, refusal to associate with nonmembers, and so on).

Mystified Anthropology

There is no true Islamist political thought, because Islamism rejects political philosophy and the human sciences as such. The magical appeal to virtue conceals the impossibility of defining the Islamist political programme in terms of the social reality.

Because it sees social segmentation as negative, Islamism can foresee its return to the political arena only as sin ... or a plot. The ideal Islamic society is defined as *umma*, an egalitarian community of believers. The political notion that expresses *umma* for Islamists is thus *tawhid*, "oneness," the negation both of social classes and of national, ethnic, or tribal divisions. All differentiation is inherently a renunciation of *umma*. At the very worst, this leads to *fitna*, a rupture, separation, splitting of the community: this, no doubt, is the major political blunder. Segmentation is perceived as a sin and not as a sociological fact. Which is why Islamist thought denies whatever may result from splits, first and foremost the division of religious schools (the four traditional Sunni schools — Hanafi, Maliki, Shafii, Hambali — as well as split between Shiism and Sunnism), but also the divisions between countries, ethnic groups, tribes, classes, social categories, interest groups, and so on. The interest in Ibn Khaldun — the inventor of the notion of *asabiyya* ("solidarity group") — in the West, where he is considered as an outstanding sociologist, strikes the Islamists as highly suspect.

Good cannot be analysed or broken down into elements: for Islamist theoreticians, Islam has no history, *umma* has no divisions. As the instrument of political analysis and thus of action, the human sciences are pushed back into the domain of the unthought or the unsaid when it comes to Islamic society.

"[Islam] comprehends every aspect of the human soul because it is manifested for every single person living on this earth irrespective of his race, colour, language, location, environment, historical or geographic circumstances, intellectual or cultural heritage ... It comprehends and accomplishes all the requirements of life, past and future ... whether these requirements are spiritual, material, political, economic, social, moral, intellectual or aesthetic". The universality of the message compensates for the great barrenness of its anthropological object: a universal human nature perceived as an ensemble of needs desires, and physical capacities, concentrated on the primordial fact of the biological difference of the sexes, upon which culture and history merely skim the surface. The pursuit for the "pure Muslim" presupposes that man will tear himself away from social and cultural determinisms, in particular from any of the reference points that define identity (other than Islamic) and that build the society in the realm of the unsaid (ethnic, tribal, social, national, or other segmentation), in order to return to and spiritualise the initial anthropological model.

Role of Human Sciences

The human sciences, which bring to light the objective foundations of differentiation and segmentation and thus consider the accomplishment of a "universal man" to be an illusion, are seen as instruments of cultural Westernisation and the perpetuation of divisions in the *umma*. Beyond criticising the values and ideology peddled by the human sciences (the idea that the intellectual practices of sociologists carry the prejudices of their own society is not new and has even been used by Marxist intellectuals), Islamist intellectuals question the very procedures and methodology of these sciences, which are by definition "reductionist": these sciences deconstruct the totality (the *umma*, for example, finds itself split into the *madhahib*—legal schools - ethnic, tribal, and other cultural entirety, the Revelation itself is historicised). They make totalities like Man and God into myths or secondary, peripheral constructions with respect to the structures. They denounce the Revelation.

The general criticism of the human sciences, particularly sociology and history, by Islamists who place value on the "hard" sciences and rationality, is problematic, whether this critique demands a total rejection of these disciplines or the desire to elaborate new human sciences that are Islamic not only in their values but also in their methodology. In this sense, an "Islamic sociology" is not one that would embrace an Islamic perspective and values, but one that would disown itself a methodological deconstruction of its object: it is a contradiction in terms. An Islamist will speak more comfortably about the concordances between the Quran and nuclear physics than about those between the Quran and structuralism. Exact sciences, not the human sciences, fascinate the Islamist, largely because the human sciences are a deconstruction of total Man, of Man in general, to which the exact sciences make no pretension.

The paradigm of man is the Prophet; the pattern of society is the community at the time of Medina or at most during the first four caliphs. Good militants aim to reestablish the model of the Prophet in their very person, in their bodies, their gestures, their dress, their table manners. Imitation of the Prophet replaces revolution.

Thus, there is no history, since nothing new has happened barring a return to the *jahiliyya* of pre-Islamic ages, nor anthropology, since man is simply the exercise of virtue (there is no depth psychology in Islam: sin is not an introduction to the other within), nor sociology, since division is *fitna*, splitting of the community, and thus an assault on the divine oneness the community reflects. Anything, in fact, that differentiates is seen as a threat to the unity of the community, and thus as *fitna*.

Differentiation is thus either attributed to nature (man/woman) or denied in favour of the sublimated anthropological model represented by the Prophet and the sociological model of the ideal community of Medina applied to the entirety of the *umma*. Differentiation is explicitly and wilfully rejected: it is even presented as proof of the superiority of Islam. Rationalising apologetics (Islam is the best religion because it is the best adapted to the nature of man) regularly punctuate today's popular sermons.

Refusal of History

"Secular history is obviously present, especially among the Muslim Brotherhood, whose armed commitment to the political struggle we know; but it is contingent and entirely subordinate to the history of salvation by God," writes Arkoun. For Islamists, the supposed Muslim world of today have fallen into a state of *jahiliyya*, the state in which they found themselves before the Revelation: there has never been an Islamic state or society in truest term except during the time of the Prophet and his four successors. Thus, history, far from being the means of the advent of modernity, is just parenthesis, a perdition, which will be cancelled out by the advent of a new Islamic society. All that has been created during this parenthesis of nearly fourteen centuries, that is to say, Islamic culture (literature, philosophy, mysticism), must also be renounced, since everything that has happened since the death of the last "just" caliph (Ali) has been both decline and descent into ignorance, aside from the appeals to this return (the works of Ibn Taymiyya, for example). History is but a repository of paradigms and anecdotes.

At the same time, the "fall", or more precisely the second fall that followed the four caliphs, remains incomprehensible: why did God allow His community to fall into decline?

Twelve

Terrorism in Jammu and Kashmir

Inherent Delay

One question is persistently asked by sensitive members of society, how long will it take government or its Security Forces to terminate terrorism in J&K? It is indeed a moot question but belies an easy reply. Wherever terrorism has struck as a political violence movement, it has defied time-frame resolution strategies of popular democratic governments despite the abysmal level of achievements by the violent non-state actors. Terrorism movement aided and encouraged allegedly by Pakistan in J&K is no exception. This mystifying factor of the indeterminable time-line also underscores the management function of both the terrorist groups and anti-terrorist response agencies and inputs. Inherent delay in controlling terrorism is further intensified by the fact that the realist group describes terrorism as something that happens to other people. All members of society do not feel affected to the point of action. Far too many people prefer to keep silent. This approach rather the ground reality is also indicative of the unilineal strategy to control terrorism by coercive physical operations with the help of Security Forces. Terrorism, on the other hand, needs a multi-disciplinary application encompassing political, economic, psychological and sociological inputs. These counter-terrorism strategies are complex, time-consuming and need high degree of co-ordination for implementation.

Pakistan's Confrontationist Attitude

Pakistan has allegedly turned Kashmir Valley into a hell of death, destruction, despair and dread for the last over 10 years. Nowhere in the world has any country so blatantly interfered in the internal affairs of a neighbouring country by sponsoring large-scale terrorism in its sensitive border states. Pakistan's grand plan of destabilising India goes beyond Kashmir and has several complex connections and manifestations. Realising that it cannot grab Kashmir through an overt aggression, it has resorted to a proxy war. By taking up Kashmir issue, military or political rulers of Pakistan can seek all types of assistance from Muslim countries. Kashmir is a rallying point for Pakistani leaders and they use this blinding obsession for the consolidation of their own misrule. Of late, terrorism of high intensity is being effectively used for flash pointing the issue with the aim of intimidating the Western world. Kargil Conflict of 1999 has revealed the sinister plan of Pakistan to the world as it fell on its face on account of lack of diplomatic support for its military adventurism.

The facets of proxy war in J&K perpetrated by Pakistan are now clear. Pakistan is unabashedly indulging in sending terrorists to carry flag of Jehad in Kashmir Valley. It is openly extending moral, political, diplomatic, military and financial support to terrorist outfits operating from Pakistan-occupied Kashmir and Indian State of Jammu and Kashmir. A large number of armed volunteers from other provinces of Pakistan are fighting a bloody warfare in India's sensitive state for destroying the identity of Kashmiri masses. To their utter dismay and disillusionment. Kashmiri Muslims know that their cultural ethos cannot flourish in Punjabi-dominated Pakistan. Religious leaders have only been able to sway the hearts of the young Kashmiris but not their minds. Pakistan has made frantic efforts to internationalise Kashmir issue by dragging it in various regional and world fora. Nuclear tests conducted by India and reply tests Pakistan in May 1998 also furnished a chance to Pakistan to flashpoint Kashmir into the minds of the world leaders. Kargil Conflict brought it on the front-burner.

Zia-ul Haq's 'Operation Topac'

It was General Zia-ul Haq who took humiliation of Pakistan Army in East Pakistan in 1971 very seriously. He undertook extensive plans to rebuild and refurbish his Army to avenge this historic humiliation. It is now common knowledge that every passing out cadet of Pakistan Military Academy takes a vow to average his Army's defeat. Pakistan Army still smarts under the shabbiest insult of a comprehensive military defeat in December 1971 at the hands of Indian Army. General Zia-ul Haq gave substance and the motive force to his self-selected resolve of taking revenge on India and Indian Army. He selected the issue of Kashmir in this regard. A few months before his death, General Zia-ul Haq addressed a lop-level meeting in April 1988 which was attended by some selected Corps Commanders and ISI officers. The contents of this meeting have since been made public through publication in newspapers. To understand the genesis and cancerous growth of the ongoing terrorism in Kashmir, it is necessary to read between the lines of Zia's diktat to his trusted officers. General Zia-ul Haq was master of manipulation and ruled the ungovernable Pakistan for 11 long years giving Pakistan Army the invidious task of defending the ideological frontiers of the ever-beleaguered state of Pakistan. Some salient aspects of his historic address of April 1988 which brought disaster to Kashmir Valley are reproduced below :-

"Gentlemen, I have spoken on this subject at length before; therefore, I will leave out the details. Let there be no mistake, however, that our aim remains quite clear and firm, the liberation of the Kashmir Valley, our Muslim Kashmir brothers cannot be allowed to stay with India for any length of time now.

In the past, we had opted for hamhanded military options and, therefore, failed. So as I have mentioned before, we will now keep our military option for the last moment as a coup de grace, if and when necessary. Our Kashmiri brothers in the Valley though with us in their hearts and minds are simple-minded folks and do not easily take to the type of welfare to which say a Punjabi or Afghan takes to naturally against foreign domination.

The Kashmiris, however, have a few qualities which we can exploit. First his shrewdness and intelligence, second his power to persevere under pressure and the third if I may say so, he is a master of political intrigue. If we provide him means through which he can best utilise these qualities, he will deliver the goods. Sheer brute force is in any case not needed in every type of warfare, especially so in the situation obtaining in the Kashmir Valley as I have explained earlier.

Here we must adopt those methods of combat which the Kashmiri mind can grasp and cope with, in other words, a coordinated use of moral and physical means, other than military operations which will destroy the will of the enemy, damage his political capacity and expose him to the world as an oppressor.

In the first phase which may, if necessary, last a couple of years, we will assist our Kashmiri brothers in getting hold of the power apparatus of the state by political subversion and intrigue. We must, therefore, ensure that certain favoured politicians from the ruling elite be selected who would collaborate with us in subverting all effective organs of the state. In brief, our plan for Kashmir which will be codenamed as 'Op Topac' will be as follows:—

(a) A low level insurgency against the regime so that it is under siege but does not collapse as would not yet want Central rule imposed by Delhi.

(b) We place our chosen men in all the key positions. They will subvert the police forces, financial institutions, the communication network and other important organisations.

Kashmir Obsession

Pakistan never got reconciled to the reality of Kashmir Valley being an integral part of India. It made two abortive attempts to grab it. After Zia-ul Haq assumed power in Pakistan in 1977, he put into action a plan of subversion in Kashmir Valley. The foundation of this subversion plan was to render clandestine financial and moral support to Jamaat-e-Islami to initiate fundamentalist Islamic education in schools run by it under the cover of religious education. Hindi-speaking Muslim clerics were recruited for this purpose ostensibly helped by generous financial grants from some Muslim countries especially Saudi Arabia. Use of religious places for anti-India propaganda was a routine feature in Kashmir Valley in the 1980s.

Secret consignments of weapons also started pouring into Kashmir Valley once the fighting in Afghanistan erupted in 1979 in the wake of USSR's military intervention in that beleaguered country. Soon Pakistan was flooded with weapons as a result of massive assistance doled out by USA to strengthen the Afghan Mujahideens to fight against the occupation forces of USSR. Afghan refugees taking shelter in NWFP region of Pakistan brought a huge quantity of weapons which literally flooded the social scene. This single development in the region became the cause of rise of terrorism in the sensitive states of Punjab and J&K. Pakistan was similarly caught in the vicious grip of parochialism.

Zia-ul Haq was very hopeful of favourable conditions in Kashmir Valley at a future date for a spontaneous insurrectionary strife. He knew that some sections of society basically minority groups will always have some grievances real or perceived. Young people who feel marginalised and deprived on account of economic hardship and unemployment can then take to direct armed action if they are led by some charismatic leaders supporting radical political changes. In the grand design of subversion and betrayal, Islamic universities at Islamabad and Karachi were to be used as motivational agents for poisoning the minds of thousands of young volunteers in Pakistan especially in Pakistan-occupied Kashmir. Zia-ul Haq could not live to see the fruition of his design of grabbing J&K from India. The proxy war initiated by the great dictator has already taken thousands of lives and has put India and Pakistan on an irrevocable mutually-destructive confrontation.

Other Causes of Trouble

Some other developments and conditions that instigated Pakistan to unleash a violent grinding 'proxy war' in the most sensitive border state of India are as under:—

(a) Lack of socialisation between J&K Muslim community and Indian mainstream Muslims was exploited by impersonating the latter as a minority community under subjugation. Intriguingly, Muslim leadership in other states of India has not been able to exert sedating influence on the rebellious groups who have been spouting venomous propaganda harmful to communal harmony in other parts of India.

(b) Afghanistan crisis since 1979 has influenced happenings in Punjab and J&K on Indian side in more than one way. Besides the inflow of weapons, the successful termination of Russian exploits in Afghanistan by Islamic Mujahideens by 1989 triggered insurrectionary atmosphere in J&K spurred by ISI's deft moves.

(c) Kashmiri Pandits livings indissolubly with Muslim majority in the salubrious Kashmir Valley for centuries failed to face the turn-about terrorism of native Muslim youths. Their extermination was easy and did not evoke any international condemnation. Poor rural population proved fragile and highly vulnerable.

(d) Other existing insurgency movements in some North-Eastern states and sub-national movement of Sikhs in Punjab gave impetus to secessionist aspirations of terrorist groups that mushroomed in Kashmir Valley in the later years of 1980s.

(e) On account of a significant diplomatic and external policy failure of India, Pakistan's hawkish political leadership could successfully portray Kashmir as a flash point of conflict and tension between the two adversaries alleging brutalities of Security Forces of India on Kashmiri Muslims. Kashmir is no more a moribund issue of disputed legacy of partition of India though Pakistan is pleading incessantly for its resolution as per UNO's previous directions.

(f) An over religio-political body called All Parties Hurriyat Conference based in Srinagar has been blatantly preaching violence and secessionist strategy besides coordinating the subversive activities of a large number of terrorist outfits in Kashmir Valley. It is also working as a conduit for financial support to terrorist groups after mobilising the same from Pakistan's ISI and foreign agencies. It has thus exploited the freedoms available in the liberal democracy practised by India.

Terrorist Activities

Terrorist groups especially those led by mercenaries inducted by Pak ISI from its trained reserve of Afghanis commit acts of violence with an undemanding conscience both against Security Forces and co-religionists. According to Harkat-ul-Ansar, Hizbul Mujahideen, Al Badr and Lashkar-e-Taiba, even innocent bystanders are equally responsible for the injustices of the state oppressors. Deaths of such innocent people do not evoke any sympathy. Such is the convoluted logic of terrorists who have committed dozens of carnages of Hindu population shocking the minds of civilised world. One dominant sentiment of terrorist frenzy is to shock the world to force it to attend to their plight. Pakistan has been able to popularise Jehad for liberation of J&K and its repeatedly maddening calls for volunteers have yielded results.

Terrorist groups in both Kashmir and Jammu region know that prospects of success against the might of Indian forces are dim. At the minimum, they expect that their violent drama which has claimed thousands of lives will gain international attention. Sheer volume of state's security apparatus, rhetoric and reaction guarantees an international audience to terrorist strategies. Government pronouncements and statements of commanders of Security Forces provoke terrorist groups to strike at random at unprotected targets. Carnages of Wandhama and Chitti Singhpura are gruesome reminders of the fact that terrorist groups will not allow Security Forces to gain the impression that the terrorists have been routed and quietened.

No Alternative Strategy

Pakistan's political leadership, whatever be its complexion, civil or military, is convinced on one issue that liberation of Kashmir can be achieved through a 'proxy war' which it can continue for long and thus bleed India white. Terrorism can keep the pot boiling and the outside world can be made to take notice of the loss of human lives. With the nuclearisation of both India and Pakistan, an outright conventional war is not likely to take place in the foreseeable future. Pakistan probably also thinks that it is suicidal to involve itself in an arms race with India with the ultimate goal of achieving a military victory. Another Kargil-type conflict cannot be ruled out as a frantic action for drawing the attention of the outside world.

Terrorism campaign inside Indian territory of J&K does not hurt Pakistan militarily, politically and economically. It does not cost much as ISI is running various drug cartels and enough money is available from Muslim countries. Saudi Arabia, UAE and Qatar are sending bagfuls of money for waging *Jehad* in Kashmir. Spare weapons, ammunition, explosives and wireless sets of Russo-Afghan War (1979-1989) are enough to last another 10 years. Foot-loose mercenary Islamic Jehadis are available in large number both in Pakistan and other countries for martyrdom. Kashmiri people are too weak to combat the onslaught of fundamentalist forces in the otherwise tolerant culture of Jammu and Kashmir. Having come so far, Pakistan, meanwhile, is caught in an existential dilemma. If it fails to grab Kashmir by this method, it is bound to disintegrate. That is the bottom-line on this issue. India knows it too well and has jacked up its riposte to a level where it has started hurting Pakistan on all fronts.

Violations of Line of Control

Kargil Conflict almost sanctified the Line of Control (LoC) as India deliberately exercised restraint and did not violate its sanctity while flushing out the infiltrating Pakistani Army elements and terrorists during 2 month long armed showdown. But the LoC is being violated on a daily basis by Pakistan who pushes in trained Mujahideens of various outfits by giving them guides and covering fire. The significance of sealing the borders and LoC against Pakistan has come to fore. It cannot be over-emphasised as Pakistan is bound to exploit every chink in the arsenal of India. Nothing would serve India's interest better than Indian Security Forces having pitched encounters with terrorist groups on LoC and border denying them unopposed entry. The population, mostly favourable to the machinations of Pakistan, then will not come into play as a cushion for survival of terrorists. With local terrorists reaching a barrier of 'no win' situation, this strategy for termination of terrorism in this volatile state is very relevant. A fierce and relentless battle needs to be fought at the front line besides making it physically unnegotiable.

In 1999, there were alarming reports that the local Kashmiri terrorists had been comprehensively sidelined from active command by hard-core elements belonging to Pakistan and Afghanistan. Kashmiri youths became disillusioned with the struggle and adopted a sullen attitude. Successes of Security Forces further unnerved the ISI bosses and Pakistan's military rulers. To his chagrin, the Chief Executive found that the movement was plunging to an inconsequential end. He ordered that new life be injected into the ongoing terrorist movement by organising death-squads and Fidayen groups to hog limelight once again. It was also aimed at reducing the devastating effect of Kargil defeat on the morale of Pakistani people, Army and terrorist outfits.

Role of All Parties Hurriyat Conference

This overt conglomerate of leaders of several anti-national political outfits in Kashmir Valley has played dubious role in the rise and progress of terrorism in J&K. It comprises representatives of several Muslim political outfits who do not wield any influence at the grassroots level and have always avoided participation in electoral processes. They exert considerable influence through the use of gun which their favourite terrorist outfits are always ready to do at their bidding. This group has worked as the mouthpiece of terrorist outfits and has openly indulged in manipulating the developments in favour of Pakistan. It has been plentifully financed by Pakistan, Saudi Arabia and some other Islamic countries. It is deeply involved in distributing funds to various terrorist outfits and coordinating their routine terrorist incidents. For their highly dangerous pursuits, most of the activists were put behind bars in 1999 but were released in 2000 with the understanding that they would open constructive parleys with Indian leaders. They openly promote forces of secessionism in J&K.

The All Parties Hurriyat Conference stands for strikes, bandhs and series of protests. It has brought lot of misery to common people in Kashmir Valley. They have exploited the religious sentiments of the people in a primitive fashion. They are very fearful of Pakistan's ISI and know that the agents of that organisation can create mayhem with their fragile set-up. Similarly, they show lot of fear when it comes to dealing with active terrorist outfits. They are literally stooges in the hands of Pakistan's ISI and the powerful terrorist outfits. This conglomerate has no political base. But surprisingly, it has emerged as the unchallenged mouthpiece of all the disruptive forces operating in Kashmir Valley against the political interests of India.

After the military takeover in Pakistan on 12 October, 1999, there has set in a sort of rethinking in the minds of All Parties Hurriyat Conference and the terrorist outfits. While the 'desperation phase' actions have been launched in the form of Fidayen groups and other suicide squads, the terrorist movement has not been able to cause the expected 'climate of collapse'. Response of India's Security Forces has been very matching and back-breaking for terrorist outfits. Pakistan's 'flash-point strategy' has been defeated for the time being. The All Parties Hurriyat Conference and terrorist outfits specially the most dominant outfit Hizbul Mujahideen have been forced to put on their thinking cap. Terrorist outfits cannot take undesirable losses which the Security Forces inflicted on them in the year 2000.

Sensing the change in terror-scape of Jammu and Kashmir, All Parties Hurriyat Conference lost no time and declared that it was too ready to resume parleys with Indian Government. Earlier, this self-styled organ of people's aspirations had been dodging the issue of holding talks with Indian leaders under seeming pressure from Pakistan's military leaders. So right at the end of July 2000, hardliner terrorist outfit Hizbul Mujahideen and the supporting umbrella political mouthpiece of all violence-inducing terrorist outfits namely All Parties Hurriyat Conference have expressed their willingness to break the ice for negotiations on the contentious issue of Kashmir. Can this development lead to some constructive parleys? Much depends upon how Pakistan's military leaders act in this juncture. Apparently, they would adopt an obstructionist attitude as they would never like to abandon the path of cheap proxy war. How the drama really unfolds will be seen by the reader in the next couple of years. Prolonged nature of terrorism earlier in Punjab and now in J&K has definitely perturbed the morale and operational effectiveness of all forces involved in anti-terrorist operations. Political agitations in Assam, Manipur and Tripura are also assuming dangerous proportions. It is the foreign hand behind these disruptive movements that has complicated the task of both government and Security Forces. There seems to be virtually no end to the volunteers for Islamic *Jehad* especially when Pakistani leadership is constantly fomenting the passions of the illiterate masses in their country. Death is not much of a deterrence for these terrorists as they hope to go to Heaven.

Grim Situation

Security Forces in J&K are facing a very dangerous situation. On account of the religious character of the terrorist movement, the people are rendering lot of help to terrorists both foreign and local. Security Forces cannot assess the dangers in the workspace. Foreign terrorists have attacked Security Posts in a desperate bid to keep the secessionist movement alive. Use of IEDs has been done comprehensively and several officers and men of different forces were killed or wounded putting Security Forces into defensive position in urban areas. In rural areas, both plain and mountainous, ambushes are quite common. Unlike the local terrorists, the foreign mercenaries give stiff resistance when they are pitted against any party of Army, Rashtriya Rifles, BSF or local Police. Some foreign terrorists when enmeshed in a holed-up position in some building or inhabited area, have exhibited extraordinary courage and tactical acumen. Security Forces can no more take any group of terrorists lightly as the latter try to kill soldiers before embracing death.

The intensity of terrorist activities and the high level of risk in undertaking offensive strikes are psychologically depressing for soldiers trained for compact operations against a visible enemy. Terrorists employ too many stratagems to surprise and kill soldiers. The terrain in J&K and the day to day keeping an eye on of terrorist activities by Pakistan's ISI bosses from Muzaffarabad are factors that ensure a continued state of violence in the state. Kashmir Valley is sentenced to a long period of turbulence, destruction and death. State of human ecology is going to get worse.

Thirteen

Unabated Insurgency in the Valley

The successive rulers imposed by the Centre, the arbitrary dismissal of Farooq's government and subsequent arm-twisting to share power with the Congress, and the blatant manipulation of the electoral process in 1987 led Kashmiris to consider that they would remain permanently marginalised under the current political dispensation. Hence rose the demand for secession. Three conceptions of Kashmiri identity, the secular, the Islamic, and the Pan-Islamic, emerged with different political objectives and different mobilisation strategies marked with an extraordinary degree of political violence.

Farooq Abdullah was discredited and deprived of a patron, the mantle of safeguarding the political interests of Kashmiris fell upon the new generation of Kashmiri youth. When the attempt by the young protagonists to seize state power through constitutional means was scuttled by rigged state elections, they felt that 'the bullet will deliver where the ballot had failed'.

It was in the police control rooms and Kashmiri jails that the first generation of Kashmiri militants was born. The first batch of youth crossed over the Pakistan for arms training in 1987-88. The Kashmiri separatist movement can be grouped into five phases. Each phase focuses on dominant trends, but the dominant voice should not be misconstrued to mean the only voice, nor were these mutually exclusive or necessarily sequential.

First Phase

The first phase (1988 to 1990) may be classified into two parts: the underground militant movement (1988-89) and the mass political movement (1990). Kashmiris, spearheaded by the Jammu and Kashmir Liberation Front (JKLF), demanded independence through a lonf-drawn-out armed struggle.

Underground Militant Activities

The militants used violence most effectively to achieve the immediate political objectives of paralysing the state apparatus and de-legitimising the political institutions which had appropriated the space for articulating the political aspirations of Kashmiris. They sought to defy the state authority; transfer people's support and loyalty to themselves; attack the state symbols; and render every state institution that could potentially meet their political challenge dysfunctional. A series of violent demonstrations brokeout on various issues, such as the hike in the power tariff and the demand for a ban of Salman Rushdie's *Satanic Verses*.

The systematic campaign in 1988-89 challenged and replaced the official state symbols with an alternative calendar of public events. *Bandhs* were organised on Indian Independence Day and Republic Day and 'civil curfew' (as opposed to government-ordered) was imposed with a ceremonial burning of the Indian flag while Pakistan's Independence Day was celebrated with utmost fanfare. The Accession Day, 20 October, was denounced as the 'day of occupation' and Nehru's birth anniversary on 14 November was observed as a 'black day'. Even the death anniversary of the founder of the JKLF, Maqbool Butt, was celebrated, in glaring contrast to Sheikh Abdullah's death anniversary which was termed *Yome-i-Nijat* (day of deliverance).

A symbolic drive was launched to remove the 'India' signs of the State Bank of India, Air India, Indian Oil, Bharat Petroleum, and Indian insurance companies. People were even ordered to transfer money from Indian banks to the J&K Bank. The militants' writ ran large. Their order to observe Friday instead of Sunday as a holiday was tacitly complied within public offices, including the civil secretariat and banks.

The militants first targeted the police, CRPF and intelligence organisations. They sought to neutralize the police force by attacking police stations in Srinagar with impunity and killed police officers in utterly barbaric manner. Stigmatised as 'traitors', ostracised by society, and neglected by senior officers who did not mourn their colleagues' deaths nor accord any state honour, these massacres played havoc with the morale of the police force which became openly critical of the poor leadership of the Director General of Police, Ghulam Jalani Pandit. Attacks on the CRPF personnel and killing of intelligence officials followed in quick successions, the militants were apparently targeting the institutions responsible for the state's internal security. Next, all political activities were halted and political institutions were undermined. Militants very particularly killed prominent workers of the National Conference, the only pro-Indian local political force in the Valley. An open ultimatum was issued to its cadre in August 1989 to publicly break association with the party. The compliance was so supreme that the Kashmir daily *Aftab* carried a special column *Izhar-e-Latalugee* (declaration of disassociation) for this purpose. Rife with internal dissension, political parties such as the Congress and the Muslim United Front (MUF) had practically stopped functioning. Former Chief Minister G.M. Shah then remarked: "We [politicians] are not relevant at all. No one talks to us. No one listens to us. You are all up against in idea, which is supported by the gun and believed by the people."

In response to the militants' call for a boycott of the Lok Sabha by-elections in November 1989, a large number of polling officers (nearly 5,000 according to one estimate) refused to perform their duties, and government school buildings used as polling stations were set on fire. A 'civil curfew' was clamped on the polling day and a coffin was placed outside the polling booth in Baramulla with a placard which said, 'It is for the first man who casts his vote.'

The administration absolutely did nothing. Official estimates of average voting in Anantnag and Baramulla were 5.11 and 5.47 per cent respectively, although the local media reported it at 2 per cent. In some polling centres, no votes were cast. By discrediting the political parties and nullifying the electoral process, the militants had monopolised the space of state politics.

People took pride in the militants' exploits because the 'boys' had somehow brought back Kashmir's pride. Mirwaiz Maulvi Farooq observed:

People have realised that the secular, nationalist parties are all lies. They are not in power to help the *quam* or *awaam*; they are here only for self-aggrandisement and for power ... People had lost faith in democracy and were more attracted to the militants and their armed solution to the problem, because they felt that they at least were prepared to die for Kashmir.

Initially, the movement was driven by a well-planned strategy. Pakistan's role in this context need a close observation. While the impulses of Kashmiri separatism were generated internally, Pakistan was quick to capitalise on the situation. Significantly, Pakistan used the 'Kashmiri card' as distinct from the 'Muslim' or 'Islamic card' to empathize with the struggle of the militants. Differing opinions, however, persist regarding the timing of Pakistan's organisational and armed support to militants. Hasim Qureshi, a leading JKLF leader, disclosed that they were approached by the Pakistani military to prepare for the new phase of 'Kashmir's liberation' in 1984. Amanullah Khan, the JKLF's supremo, reiterated that the 'JKLF had actually started political planning in 1986 and continued till the end of 1987 ... and it began in July 1988 ... the boys who originally belonged to that area [Jammu and Kashmir state] are actually fighting ... boys were trained here [Azad Kashmir], then went back and trained others ... Interaction with JKLF militants confirms this point. Some considered Pakistan as an ally, while others justified taking support of the people of Azad Kashmir because 'Azad Kashmir is our part [of Kashmir] only'.

Government Response

The Centre and state governments' initial response to Kashmiri militancy varied from utter helplessness and confusion to sheer inertia and culpable negligence. Former Prime Minister Rajiv Gandhi was too embroiled in the Bofors corruption charges to pay attention to Kashmir. Farooq had justified the compromise of Kashmir's political autonomy on the single plank of central aid worth Rs. 2,000 crore for economic development. When nothing materialised, the casualty was not only Farooq's government; it was a serious blow of Kashmiris' faith in the Indian State.

The absence of a clear, firm and effective state response from either its political or administrative leadership helped the militants to neutralise the police and intelligence. The alarming reports from Srinagar were dismissed as mere panic reactions, and a top central civil servant rationalised the drift with a theory of a 'tolerable level of violence'. It was further admitted that 'New Delhi was aware of the developing situation but did not quite appreciate the urgency of dealing with it and militancy was indeed allowed to dig deep roots in the Valley' (emphasis added). There was overall failure of intelligence. The Research and Analysis Wing (RAW) and the Intelligence Bureau (IB) had little information about the inflow of arms and trained youth from across the border. Poor coordination among intelligence agencies was attributed to 'absence of culture of sharing information' and 'different bureaucratic structures and hierarchies'. There was a sense of disbelief when the first Kalashnikov was seized in the Valley.

Stripped of political legitimacy, Farooq's government was virtually under siege by the banned militants when they kidnapped former Union Home Minister Mufti Mohammad Sayeed's daughter, Rubaiya Sayeed, on 8 December 1989. The government's mishandling of her kidnapping proved to be a turning point. Despite Farooq's stern opposition and senior officials' warnings that meek surrender would have grave repercussions in boosting militancy, the decision of the Central Government prevailed. The release of the militants resulted in a mass upsurge. The streets of Srinagar were filled with victory processions of elated crowds demanding *azadi*. The government's abject surrender was widely perceived as the ultimate proof that the mighty Indian State had caved in and *azadi* was round the corner.

Worldwide Developments

The heady sweep of contemporary liberation history—from demolition of the Berlin Wall and overthrow of Romania's tyrannical rule to the alluring echoes of freedom along the trans-Caucasian Pamir—marching nearer home also made *azadi* appear as a plausible alternative to Kashmiris. The common Kashmiris were very conscious about the 'malleability of borders' and the birth of new nations causing euphoria that it would be their turn next.

The resurgence of Islam following the Iranian revolution, the

Palestinian intifada and the mujahedins' success in driving the Soviet Union out of Afghanistan provided greater impetus to the Kashmiri youth. Kashmiri Muslims, it was argued:

> could now seek ideological sustenance from a trans-national Islam, while simultaneously basking in the quarantiral revolution in Iran, the mood of Islamic re-assertion in the Far reaches of the world of Islam—from Palestine to Pakistan, the Soviet Central Republics and Sinkiang to the Far East, has provided an awareness of faith and collective power that can rarely escape Muslims especially those who live under conditions of subordination and find the alternative secular mode of being, lacking in material or moral fulfillment. How can Kashmiri Muslims escape the reach of a trans-national awareness?

Mass Political Movement

Farooq Abdullah's resignation and Governor Jagmohan's policy of quelling the movement finally caused it to explode. A massive crackdown and the Gawkadal incident, in which a large number of unarmed civilians including women and children were massacred, proved to be a watershed in transforming the underground militant siege into a popular mass movement. Kalashnikovs replaced black flags and the 'boys' became 'mujahedin' overnight. The Valley witnessed a series of protest rallies of several thousands of people demanding *azadi*, causing total collapse of state authority.

Governor Jagmohan's recipe was to unleash the coercive arm of the state to curb terrorism and force Kashmiris into submission. He believed: *The bullet is the only solution for Kashmiris*. Unless the militants are fully wiped out, normalcy cannot return to the Valley' (emphasis added). Thus, began a long spell of state repression in the form of cordon-and-search operations or crackdowns, extended periods of blanket curfews in major towns, specially Srinagar, lasting for weeks without any provision for essential food supplies, road block checks involving atrocities, intimidation, verbal abuse and humiliation, widespread torture, rape, arbitrary detention of scores of youth suspected of being militants and shootings by the security forces at public processions and crowded market areas, often in a panic response to the militants fire.

Kashmiris' Secular Identity: A New Definition

The JKLF was at the forefront of the secessionist movement though militant outfits such as Allah Tigers, People League and Hizb-i-Islamia were also active. It redefined the Kashmiri community as including the entire populace of the Indian and Pakistani parts of the Jammu & Kashmir state. The JKLF's political objective was 'liberation of Jammu & Kashmir state from India and re-unification of territories of the original Dogra State of Jammu & Kashmir'. It questioned the legality and authenticity of the Instrument of Accession signed, as they claimed, by the fleeing Maharaja. Nehru's promise to honour Kashmiris' right of self-determination and UN resolutions to hold a plebiscite were also revived. Ideologically, the JKLF's secular Kashmiri nationalism was in keeping with the traditions of Sheikh Abdullah's National Conference, but, disassociating itself from the Sheikh's political heritage, it denounced him for surrendering the demand for plebiscite in the 1975 Accord.

The JKLF articulated the vision of an independent state based on a federal, parliamentary and democratic political system. Each of the five federating units, such as Kashmir Valley, Jammu Province, Ladakh, Azad Kashmir, and Gilgit and Baltistan would enjoy internal autonomy with elected provincial governments. The members of the lower house of Parliament would be proportionate to the population of each unit elected through adult franchise, and the upper house would have an equal number of elected members from all units. The constitution would provide equal social, economic and political rights and status to religious and ethnic minorities. A neutral position was advocated for the proposed independent Jammu and Kashmir state on the Swiss pattern, with friendly relations with both India and Pakistan.

Strategies and Tactics

The JKLF's strategy is believed to be divided into four components: establishing an organisational base and devising military strategy; pursuit to international support; mobilising popular support; and its rationale of resorting to violence. Kashmiri youth leaders such as Ashfaq Majid Wani, Hamid Sheikh, Yasin Malik and Javed Mir led the JKLF in the Valley. Amanullah Khan, the chairman headed the central committee, the supreme policy-making body, based at Muzaffarabad. Three sub-committees supervised military, political and diplomatic activities. The organisation was divided into three zones: Jammu and Kashmir wing, Azad Kashmir wing, and the Overseas wing. A chief commander, followed by zonal, district and *tehsil* commanders, headed the entire command in the Valley. A joint revolutionary council coordinated the activities of all zones.

The military strategy was devised jointly by the JKLF leadership in the Valley and Muzaffarabad. Azad Kashmir supplied weapons, held training camps and provided sanctuary. Amanullah Khan and Javed Mir candidly admitted smuggling of weapons across the Indo-Pakistani border to militant ranks in the Kashmir Valley. Sardar Abdul Qayyum, President of Azad Kashmir, described it as the 'base camp of the Kashmiri freedom struggle'. Militant operations in the Valley were confined mostly to urban areas. A favourite tactic was to shoot security forces' personnel in crowded areas, provoking retaliation and killing of innocent civilians. Every new 'martyr' merited a *namaz-e-janaza* (funeral prayer) from the *mohalla* mosque, which infailingly resulting in more firings, more martyrs and more mobs, all feeding a vicious circle. The militants ran a highly sophisticated parallel media machinery. Video cassettes of protest marches and atrocities by the security forces were available and circulated.

Beyond holding the security forces to ransom the militants had no long-term strategy to compel the Indian State to withdraw from Kashmir. The absence of an effective state response was critical to the militants' success in paralysing the state administration throughout 1988-89. A naive belief that 'the Indian State had lost the will to govern' was backed by high hopes that once the 'uprising' started, Pakistan would invade India to secure Kashmir's liberation. Both were utterly grave miscalculations. Pakistan did not attack and India did not hand over *azadi* on a platter. The real threat to the Indian State emanated not from the militancy but from mass processions symbolising complete rejection of state authority. It may be charitable to characterise the mass rallies purely as a product of the militants' strategy but they were more in the nature of spontaneous outbursts that part of military tactics and strategy. In fact, militants were overwhelmed by the mass response but could not purposefully and effectively channelise it for achieving *azadi*.

Support from Various Quarters

The JKLF mobilised international support for Kashmiris' right of self-determination by concentrating on human rights violations. It had raised funds through front organisations in the Middle East, UK, Europe and USA since 1977. Pakistan embarked on a massive diplomatic exercise to internationalise the issue and raised Kashmir at the UN, Non-Aligned Movement (NAM), Commonwealth Heads of Government Meeting (CHOGM), Organisation of Islamic Countries (OIC) and so on. Kashmiri Muslims, including intellectuals, trade unionists, peasants, students and government employees, whole-heartedly supported the JKLF. Some sections in the Mirpur district of Azad Kashmir were also committed supporters of independent Kashmir. The absence of a charismatic leader posed little difficulty in mass mobilisation. 'The masses needed no convincing', a militant leader said, 'only a spark to ignite their reaction ... [which was] provided by none other than Jagmohan'. Even a senior civil servant, Ashok Jaitley, admitted that 'what Jagmohan did in five months, the militants could not have achieved in five years'.

Jagmohan's policy of inflicting 'collective punishment on a disloyal population' backfired. He could not observe a thin though vital distinction between *militants*, *symphathisers* of militants, and *innocent civilians*. His policy seemed to be, 'If you are a Kashmiri, you are a Muslim, you are pro-Pakistani and you have to be dealt with accordingly'. This proved to be disastrous; it pushed the populace to becoming anti-Indian and turned the most apolitical Kashmiris into staunch supporters of militancy. A senior police official noted, 'People have lost their fear. This is a defiant new breed of Kashmiri'. Even the CRPF officials used to fighting pitched battles with irated mobs in other parts of the country admitted,

'Today you kill one demonstrator, then a second and yet the mob keeps coming at you. Finally you withdraw. The popular slogan: *Jo kare Khuda ka Khyauf, Utha le Kalashnikov* (All god-fearing men should pick up the gun) reflected the Kashmiri mood.

Reasons for Violence

Kashmiris devised new social norms and social sanction for justifying political violence. The women would put *mehendi* (henna) on their sons going to Pakistan and daughters accorded them a hero's welcome on return. Having a *mujahideen* in the family became a status symbol. The families and the peer groups competed for crossing the border to get arms training. Children carried placards saying 'Indian Dogs go Home' or '*Mujahideen Qaum Zindabad*'. A new vocabulary of violence depicted militants as 'freedom fighters' and the security personnel as 'occupation forces'. Curfews were considered as 'martial law' and martyrs' graveyards became 'places of pilgrimage'.

Contemporary political practices and state violence were used to justify the Kashmiris' stand to violence. Militant violence was explained as 'response to injustice' and committed on 'behalf of the community'. Many shared the view: "When the government has taken the gun against the people, why should not we take up a gun?' or 'If we have to die like this, why not pick up the gun?' The rationale of violence was purely contemporary because Kashmiri cultural heritage, shaped by the pacifist and non-violent Rishi Order, did not offer mythological elements for sanctifying political violence. Kashmiris did not have a history of valour of militarily resisting hordes of foreign rulers, nor did traditions and folklore have a reservoir of stories eulogising heroic conquests and victories against the enemy. The modern history of Kashmiri political movements from the anti-monarchy unrest in the 1930s to the Plebiscite Front's demand for self-determination in the 1960s had also been fought through political and constitutional means. If at all, Kashmiris were stigmatised as cowards who could not think beyond 'throwing *kangris* (small earthen pots with glowing embers held under an outer cape—firan—for warmth) at each other as the ultimate act of violence'.

When the 'Kashmiri' component of the past did not help,

many looked to Islam for an entirely new rationale. 'Islam teaches us to fight for rights and justice. Our activities are in accordance with the Islamic precepts. We have thus complete moral basis in our activities.' Significantly, Islam's sanction of violence was used to defend their political and militant struggle for 'justice'. 'Jihad' (holy war) did not figure in the militants' political vocabulary but a growing emphasis on Islam for mobilisation and emergence of mosques as the 'new power centres', used as community centres and refuges for militants, was unmistakable. Some popular slogans were, *Azadi ka matlab kya, La Illahililillah* or *Hum kya chahte hain - Nizam-i-Mustafa*. The JKLF's manifesto of the early 1990s had distinct Islamic flavour in defining its objectives as complete independence of Jammu & Kashmir, system of Islamic democracy, safeguarding rights of the minorities as prescribed in the Koran and Sunnah and an economy of *Islamic socialism*.

Mass Exodus

The shift from Kashmiri Islam to Islam sharply increased the social, cultural and political distance between the Kashmiri Muslims and Kashmiri Pandits. Selective massacres of Kashmiri Pandits in late 1989, followed by mass rallies and mosque loudspeakers shouting slogans of *Nizam-i-Mustafa*, and a planned campaign telling Pandits to leave the Valley had created an atmosphere of fear and insecurity in the community. The state government's inability to provide security and its tacit encouragement to them to leave the Valley exacerbated the situation. While Jagmohan's contribution in organising the exodus of Kashmiri Pandits continues to be hotly debated, it is clear they left enmasse within days of his arrival and appear to have been assisted logistically in the exodus. The Kashmiri Pandit exodus would prove to be a milestone in changing to nature of the Kashmiri identity in terms of imminent bifurcation between Kashmiri Muslims and Kashmiri Pandits.

Official Stand

There was no clear and coherent policy direction from V.P. Singh's minority government which was hamstrung by opposing pulls of the left and the Bharatiya Janata Party (BJP). The BJP, symbolising revival of the 'Hindu' notion of the Indian nation, had appeared as a powerful political force in the late 1980s. The Hindutva brigade's attempts to transform the multifaceted religious system of Hinduism into a monolithic brand and to pave the way for a Hindu vote bank had grave long-term implications. The BJP sought to subsume different layers of community identity in terms of culture, language and caste under a single overarching category of religion, and by making Hinduism central of Indian identity denied political space to sub-national identities woven around linguistic, caste, regional or cultural affinities. Significantly, Kashmir has always been central to the Hindu belief of *rashtra-rajya* and the secessionist demands are viewed as reinforcing its belief in Muslim disloyalty to India'. Accordingly, the BJP favoured abolition of Article 370 and reversal of the 'state-subject' definition, consciously settling Hindus in the Valley to change the population balance. There was, however, no sufficient evidence of BJP influence on the government's Kashmir policy but its political ideology did impinge upon the Kashmiri psyche.

Governor Jagmohan was a one-man crusader, and instead of revitalising and mobilising the governmental and political institutions, he centralised all important decision-making powers himself. Firm in the conviction that 'every component of the power structure had been taken over by the terrorists', he consciously and deliberately marginalised and undermined them. For instance, he denied funds for medical supplies to government hospitals, banished the foreign media, staunchly restricted the local media, and scuttled local Doordarshan (TV) programmes because these had been infiltrated by the militants.

This also created serious dissension in the state police hierarchy between 'local' and 'outsiders' (meaning IPS officers), and a sharp divide between the Jammu & Kashmir Armed Police (JKAP) and paramilitary forces. A senior police official argued, "If you come from Delhi and tell a local officer that he is "mixed up" with the militants, where is the morale for him to work for the state?" The splits ran so deep that a false rumour of JKAP personnel being shot by the CRPF resulted in a police revolt on 22 January 1990.

Jagmohan's decision to dissolve the state assembly on 17 February 1990 without taking his advisers and the Centre into confidence closed all doors for reviving the political process. This caused a rift between the Governor and the Central Government, and the BJP and other political parties. New Delhi decided to cut Jagmohan to size by setting up an All-Party Advisory Committee and sending an all-party delegation to Srinagar.

In contrast, Fernandes offered compassionate understanding of militants with a healing touch for the Kashmiris. He explored different options of starting a political process through restructuring the National Conference under Farooq Abdullah; amalgamating the JKLF, the MUF, the Peoples Conference and the Peoples League into a new political party led by Shabir Shah; and initiating dialogue with Mirwaiz Maulvi Farooq. With Jagmohan and Fernandes castigating each other for the 'mess' in Kashmir and Home Minister Mufti Mohammad Sayeed introducing a third tangent, an impossible situation was created by the three power centres working at cross-purposes. Serious dissension between the Governor and the Central Government, the state bureaucracy and police with the Governor, and local police with the army and paramilitary forces paralysed the policy-making apparatus. The Indian State was on its weakest footing. Internationally, too, the government was on the defensive, warding off external pressures, defending the human rights record and blaming Pakistan squarely for inciting trouble in the Valley. The Benazir Bhutto government's belligerent statements from Islamabad matched by V.P. Singh's warnings against misadventure in Kashmir created an utterly volatile situation across the Line of Control in March-April 1990.

Second Phase

By late 1990, the movement was at its prime and then its decline set in as the character of militancy gradually changed. From mid-1990, the JKLF began losing its leadership role, partly because the security forces were better prepared. By the end of the year, most of the JKLF's top leadership had either been killed or nabbed and later, imprisoned.

Marginalising JKLF

Pakistan realised that the 'Kashmiri card' had served its purpose and if allowed to persist to its logical conclusion, it might backfire on Pakistan because 'independence and re-unification of the divided Kashmir and not accession to Pakistan' was the JKLF's political objective. Consequently, a 'conscious political decision appears to have been taken very quickly in Islamabad to eliminate the *independence* sentiment'. Robert Wirsing quotes a Kashmiri observer based in Pakistan:

> When the People's Party was yet in power, Pakistani leaders became aware of the need of assert more Pakistani control of the uprising. The movement was getting huge in size and the cry of azadi—independence of both India and Pakistan—was growing loud. In early February 1990, a meeting was held in Islamabad, with Prime Minister Benazir Bhutto in the chair, and with the Chief of Army Staff General Aslam Beg, and the President and Prime Minister of Azad Kashmir in attendance. They considered the possibility that the uprising could boomerang on Pakistan, and that Pakistan could lose not only Jammu and Kashmir but the Northern Areas as well. They decided they *had to curb the azadi forces, meaning they would not equip them and not send them into the valley.* It was decided that the Pakistan army should take over the private camps that had sprung up. Bhutto addressed a press conference later that month ... and said that accession to Pakistan was the only option open to Kashmiris. (emphasis added).

Amanullah Khan corroborated that during Benazir Bhutto's tenure several pro-Pakistan outfits were raised as rivals to the JKLF. Nawaz Sharif's government subsequently pitted the new groups against the JKLF, which was accused of being 'terrorists' and to destabilise its campaign. My interactions with the Valley-based leadership of the JKLF confirm this point. By early 1991, the JKLF leadership realised that Pakistan had used it as a pawn for serving its own political interests. Hasim Qureshi's disclosures proved to be prophetic.

With a sudden and total cessation offends and arms supplies from Pakistan, the JKLF's calculations went completely awry. They not only had difficulties in new recruitment and training of cadres but, more important, faced a new lethal enemy in the Hizbul Mujahideen, 'a militant organisation created only to eliminate JKLF'.

Islamisation and its Agenda

The Hizbul Mujahideen's ascendancy and its agenda for Islamisation was the hallmark of the second phase of militancy (1991-93). Using the prism of religion, the problem was articulated in terms of the *Muslim Valley waging a war against the Indian State* in order to accede to Pakistan. The Hizbul Mujahideen faced three challenges in the Valley, namely, the JKLF's secular ideology, Mirwaiz Maulvi Farooq's articulation of Kashmiris' Muslim identity, and the Kashmiri Pandits. Pakistan and Azad Kashmir's Muslims regarded as a part of the *millat* (the Islamic community world-wide). Interestingly, the Hizbul Mujahideen never mentioned Indian Muslims as a part of this *millat*, it single-mindedly favoured Kashmir's accession to Pakistan and demanded plebiscite according to the original UN resolutions (1948-49). It staunchly opposed an independent Kashmir based on secular nationalism because nationalism, according to Islam, was based only on religion.

Inspired by Islamic ideology, Kashmir's history was written afresh in which the 1931 movement was characterised as a movement by the Muslim-majority populace 'to free Kashmir from Dogras and to make it a part of the Islamic world'. Sheikh Abdullah was projected as a 'willing victim' of the Hindu Congress' conspiracy and the National Conference, under the clout of Communists and Qadianis, forced the Valley Muslims to accede to India.

Organisational Foundation

The Hizbul Mujahideen was a large organisation with an estimated strength of 13,000-20,000 men. Its political patron, the Jamaat-i-Islami, nominated Syed Salahuddin as the Supreme Commander—*Sarparste Alla*. Each wing of the organisation had a leader for military and ideological training, intelligence, supplies, logistics and funds. All positions together formed the nucleus of the larger body, the *Majlis-i-Shoora*, which was the chief command of the Hizbul Mujahideen.

The organisational networks of the Hizbul Mujahideen spread down to the divisional and district levels in the Valley. Their cadre was better equipped, more disciplined, and better trained with considerable combat experience in Afghanistan. The Jamaat-i-Islami and the Hizbul Mujahideen also had front organisations such the Jamiat-ul-Tulba, its student wing, and the Dukhtaran-e-Millat (Daughters of the Faith), the women's wing led by Aasiya Andarabi whose organisation also ran the Islamic Relief committee and the Islamic Blood Bank.

Inspired by Pakistan's Inter-Services Intelligence (ISI) experience in Afghanistan, the Hizbul Mujahideen's theory was to make the economic, military and political costs of retaining Kashmir too prohibitive for India. This had two components: to raise military costs by tying down large numbers of the Indian Army in the Valley; and to expand, the area of operations to other parts of the state, and indeed, the rest of the country. The Hizbul Mujahideen leader, Salahuddin, said, 'We want to hit India economically ... and strike in every nook and corner [of the country].'

The Hizbul spread out to the rural areas, which served as useful hideouts, and village madrasas were a valuable source of recruitment of militants. Gradually, they moved to the Doda district of Jammu, perhaps because of the growing pressure of the security forces in the Valley. Doda's rugged mountainous terrain enabled a small number of militants to tie down disproportionately huge numbers of security forces, and its contiguity to six districts—Kathua, Udhampur, Kargil, Rajouri, Anantnag and Chamba in Himachal Pradesh—served as an ideal springboard to spread out further. Their military tactics included hit-and-run attacks with sophisticated weapons and by late 1991-92, they were creating 'liberated zones' in some pockets of Baramula, Srinagar and Anantnag districts.

Outside Support

The Hizbul Mujahideen was clearly the organisation most patronised by Pakistan in arms, training, logistics and funds. Islamic political parties led by the Jamaat-i-Islami strongly favoured arming Kashmiri militants, and open camps were organised in Pakistan for recruiting Mujahideen and collecting funds for the 'Kashmiri jihad'. The ISI its arm, the Field Intelligence Unit, provided critical organisational support.

In 1992, the ISI established the Markaz-Ud-Dawa-Wal-Irshad,

ostensibly an international centre to coordinate Islamic militant activities worldwide. Located at the outskirts of Lahore, the centre trained fighters and filtered weapons left over from the Afghan conflict to Kashmiri militants, specially the Hizbul. Pakistan also played a pivotal role in garnering international support of Islamic countries and got several anti-Indian resolutions condemning human rights violations passed by the OIC.

Mobilisation

The Hizbul cadre was recruited by the Jamaat-i-Islami which had done systematic basework by introducing a Sunni Islamic culture and literature through madrasas and about 2,500-3,000 mosques teaching the Koran and Hadith (interpretation of Islam) since the 1970s, and preparing young Kashmiri Muslims for a truly Islamic revolution. The Dukhtaran-e-Millat's 10,000 members imparted ideological training to women. Aasiya Andarabi affirmed: "We are uniting our women and urging them to give their men the courage to fight ... we don't mind paying with our blood. We have told our brothers to return only after Kashmir has been liberated." The Hizbul Mujahideen mobilised the cadre in the name of Islam and introduced the highly emotive terminology of jihad to justify political violence. A popular slogan was *Na guerrilla jang, na quami jang: al jihad, al jihad* (It is neither a guerrilla war nor a national war: it is a holy war).

The motivational literature mobilising the cadre used symbols and metaphors of Islam extensively. Carefully selecting militant strands of Islamic history, allusions were made to the heroic deeds of Prophet Muhammad. For instance, 'Badr', signifying Prophet Muhammad's spectacular victory over Arab pagans of Mecca, was referred to eulogise Islamic heroism, and exhortation to violence were skilfully done for another jihad in the light of the Prophet's teachings.

Several leaders used Islamic fables for mobilising the people. For instance, popular leader Shabir Shah's appeals, posters, and pamphlets started with averse of Iqbal. The gist of his speeches was:

> The enemies of Islam are uniting on all fronts to frustrate our mission. An example of this is the occupation of

> Kashmir. But now the Kashmiri nation, inspired and guided by Islam, was woken up. The sun of Islamic revolution is rising. The children of faith should now unite and come to the forefront to secure freedom from Bharat [India]. *Allah will be our guide, Quran is our constitution, jihad is our strategy and martyrdom is our aspiration*. (emphasis added).

However, it was precisely as a result of strict adherence to Islamic ideology that the Hizbul lacked popular support in the Valley. Kashmiri Muslims supported the Hizbul in 'the fight against India', but its pure Islamic notions which considered Kashmiri practices of offering prayers at Sufi shrines and *pir's mazars* as idolatrous, soon alienated the masses. The Hizbul Mujahideen faced a formidable ideological adversary in the JKLF, whose nationalist and secular ideology was antithetical to Islamic ideology. Supported by Pakistan, they attacked and killed JKLF militants and leaked information about their hideouts and action plans to the Indian Army. The Pakistani troops opened fire on unarmed JKLF activists to stop them from crossing the Line of Control in February 1992. This marked the collapse of reluctant accommodation between the JKLF and Pakistan and made its leader Javed Mir to declare, 'Now we have two enemies—India and Pakistan'.

Another powerful potential rival was the Mirwaiz, Maulvi Farooq, who had inherited the mantle of the Muslim Conference and enjoyed an utterly independent power base in the Valley. The Mirwaiz had pursued Muslim politics as distinct from the Jamaat's Islamic ideology, and was a critical hurdle in the latter's Islamisation drive. He was not extremist, nor amenable to accepting orders from across the border; and that is why he had to be curbed. The Mirwaiz's attempts to open a political channel of negotiations with George Fernandes sealed his fate. Hizbul Mujahideen militants killed him on 21 May 1990.

Third, Kashmiri Pandits did not fit the Hizbul's gameplan of 'Muslimising the Valley' to facilitate accession to Pakistan. Although the Pandit exodus was more or less complete before the Hizbul came to dominate the Valley, its dire warning—'Kashmiri Pandits responsible for duress against Muslims should leave the

Valley within two days' published in the Urdu daily *Alsafa* on 14 April 1990, was the driving force triggering the exodus

Subsequently, it warned the Pandits against returning to the Valley because 'they had joined hands with the enemy forces [read Indian government]'. Salahuddin declared, 'Pandits would not be allowed to return until they had proved themselves to be an integral part of their movement by making their own contribution'. The Hizbul's simultaneous threats to auction the Kashmiri Muslims' properties unless they returned immediately gave away the blueprint of what has been termed as ethnic cleansing of the Valley.

The Hizbul Mujahideen's operations in Doda were also designed to create a communal polarisation between its Hindu and Muslim populace. The militants targeted the Hindus. The situation became further complicated when the BJP systematically scuttled all efforts for joint community initiatives and preferred to create armed village defence committees imparting arms training to the villagers in Hindu-majority areas, and demanded Doda to be declared as a disturbed area to be handed over to the army.

Government Reaction

The state administration as well as the Central Government continued to be a divided house. In the aftermath of Mirwaiz Maulvi Farooq's killing, Governor Jagmohan was replaced by G.C. Saxena, a former head of the Research and Analysis Wing (RAW). He reined in the security forces and escaped public showdowns by not imposing curfews on Fridays and ordering crackdowns only on specific intelligence. But Saxena failed to win the confidence of his administrative team. His adviser Ved Marwah attribute it to his 'highly secretive' style of functioning and said that, 'Saxena did have a "game plan" but he never shared it with us'. Saxena's handling of senior IAS officers' petitions against the functioning of the government and security forces and an indefinite strike by government employees came under staunch criticism. His initial tough stand of 'no work, no pay' ended in tame acceptance of virtually all their demands, with the net effect of turning the bureaucracy against him.

Frequent changes in political equations at the Centre further worsened the situation. Every time anew government took charge, the predecessor government was blamed for the impasse followed by drastic changes in the top administration. Consequently, the Governor was pulled in different directions. For instance, Saxena and Farooq Abdullah had locked horns on the government employee's strike as the latter was putting pressure on the Centre of intervene. When Chandra Shekhar replaced V.P. Singh, the National Conference gained prominence in the Centre's calculations and forced the Governor to accept the employees' demands.

Rifts within Militant Ranks

The ideological polarisation between the JKLF's goal of *Kashmir banega Khudmukhtar* (Kashmir will be independent) and the Hizbul Mujahideen's demand of *Kashmir banega Pakistan* divided the militant ranks sharply and set in motion the division of the movement. The Valley witnessed a mushrooming of groups between 1990 and 1993. Governor Jagmohan had listed 44 active 'terrorist organisations' in January 1990; in 1991, Amanullah Khan put their number at 60 to 70.

At one point, the army authorities had listed 177 militant outfits. Most of these organisations were splinter outfits moving in and out of coalition and mergers with other groups'.

Although the Hizbul Mujahideen continued to be Pakistan's favourite, the latter had deliberately created a large number of militant outfits. Pakistan's strategy of patronising a multiplicity of organisations was twofold. It ensured that the movement was not amenable to centralised control within the Valley, and by playing one against the other, they could counterbalance different groups. No single organisation could claim the political and moral leadership of the movement to negotiate a deal with the Indian government. Pakistan's subsequent efforts to unite the pro-Pak outfit under an apex organisation called the Jihad Council failed to stem inter-group clashes, particularly between the pro-accession and pro-independence outfits.

Popular Disenchantment

With growing realisation that *azadi* was not round the corner, people were becoming disillusioned. The much-anticipated

Pakistani attack had not materialised, nor did the support of the Islamic countries offer any great solace. Militant factions began turning the guns on each other, and new recruits entering the fray were driven more by the glamour and power of the gun than ideology.

Many militants extorted 'donations' from people (particularly from businessmen), forced people to offer food and shelter at gunpoint, and also abused the womenfolk. Some were engaged in illegal sale of timber and contract killings. The mass rallies demanding *azadi* had long ceased and increasing criminalisation and degeneration of militancy disillusioned the people. The militants were then feared, there was no affection or respect.

Third Phase

The Hazratbal siege and surrender of the militants in April 1993 marked the beginning of turnaround. Militants lost face and people were enraged for having undergone severe hardships for nothing. Pakistan perceived it as a sign of fatigue among the Kashmiri militants, and in order to keep the militancy alive, a conscious policy decision seemed to have been taken to push more Afghan veterans, Pakistani nationals and foreign mercenaries into the Valley. Political analysts argued that after forcing the Soviet withdrawal, many Afghan veterans were bringing back the large battle of establishing 'truly' Islamic governments and were pushed into the Valley to wage a new form of war lest they start creating trouble within Pakistan.

Pan-Islamic Agenda

The induction of foreign mercenaries into Kashmir radically changed the character of militancy into complete Islamisation and total negation of the Kashmiri component. They sought to forge a Pan-Islamic identity in which the Muslim-majority Kashmir Valley was only a tiny element whose struggle was a part of the worldwide religious crusade. The proponents of the transnational Islamic identity defined the *millat* to include the world's entire Muslim populace. They were fighting against various governments accused of terrorising 'true Muslims' in Islamic states and Muslim minorities in the secular states of the world.

The self-professed objective was to establish a grand Islamic state stretching from Kashmir to Pakistan through Afghanistan, Iran and Central Asia, similar to the Islamic Caliphate of medieval times. Some factions defined it as the first step towards converting the universe into *dar-ul-Islam* (land of Islam), while others focused on the immediate target of establishing Islamic governments in moderate Arab nations such as Egypt, Algeria, Tunis and Jordan and fighting against non-Muslim governments in Bosnia, Chechnya, Tajikistan, Myanmar, the Philippines and India. They believed in one supreme leader and were not only committed to separating Islamic countries, but also justified armed interference in another country because Islam was, according to them, under threat.

Organisational Foundation

Who were these Islamic warriors? They comprised Pakistanis, Afghans, Sudanese, Lebanese, Turks, Arabs, Central Asian and Afro-American nationals who regarded themselves as genuine 'Jihad Mussalmans'. Organisationally, these included the Harkat-ul-Ansar (HUA), the Harkat-ul-Jehad-Islami, the Harkat-ul-Mujahideen, the Jamiat-ul-Mujahideen and the Lashkar-i-Toiba. Most of these organisations had a Wahhabi orientation with a virulent militant outlook. The Harkat-ul-Ansar, for instance, is a Sunni organisation close to the Deobandi school of thought, while its recruits came from the Tablighi Jamaat.

The HUA is an international network of Muslims who believe that 'frontiers could never divide Muslims' and offer their services for Jihad anywhere in the world. It started with an elaborate organisational structure with separate cells for fund raising, training and operations. The Harket's members are committed Islamic Militants who first received training in Paktia province from the Hizb-i-Islamia (Khalis) commander, Maulana Jalaluddin Haqqani, and gradually its commanders opened training camps inside Afghanistan, just across Miran Shah in the North-West Frontier Province (NWFP).

Another organisation, Markaz-Ud-Dawa-Wal-Irshad of the Ahle Hadith sect, had a military wing, Lashkar-i-Toiba, that supplied shopkeepers, office workers, students, ex-servicemen and unemployed youth from centres in Afghanistan as volunteers in Kashmir to wage jihad. By end-1993, the number of foreign mercenaries was estimated at about 1,200. Their infiltration continued throughout 1994-95. The battle hardened Afghan war veterans were highly trained in sophisticated weapons; they changed the militant strategies by directly engaging the army through attacking pickets, checkpoints and patrol parties.

Negation of Kashmiri Upsurge

Such Islamic militant organisations completely negated the Kashmiri ethos, for them Kashmiris' independence struggle and the right of self-determination were irrelevant. The Jamiat-ul-Mujahideen asserted:

> The slogan that Kashmiris should decide the future of Kashmir has given rise to an *evil, which was distorting the Islamic identity of the present movement and reducing it to a mere democratic movement. From [the] Islamic viewpoint, the people's opinion has no importance.* God and the Prophet (Peace Be upon Him) law is the supreme one and should be obeyed. Barring this, no group and no individual can decide everything. (emphasis added).

The Harkat's pan-Islamic philosophy was least concerned about the Kashmiris' preoccupation in staying independent or acceding to Pakistan. Kashmiriyat was debunked as Islam did not recognise territorial nationalism. The only real ideology was the ideology of the Islamic Caliphate transcending race, gender and territorial boundaries. The Jamiat-ul-Ulema-Islam reiterated that, *Islam and independence were two contradictory slogans* and announced 'establishment of Caliphate' as the ultimate goal of Kashmiris' struggle.

Labelled as 'guest militants' by the Hizbul Mujahideen and the Jamaat-i-Islami, the foreign mercenaries' extremist Islamic orientation was alien to the socio-cultural characterising of Kashmiri society. The people strongly resented the political movement being hijacked by the Islamic warriors who had no respect for the religious beliefs of Sufi Islam and who debunked their political objective of independence.

The increasing disillusionment of the people with the

degeneration and Islamist orientation of the militant movement opened a window of opportunity for the government. But the new Congress government, led by Narasimha Rao, pursued the old theories of outplaying the extremist elements through military pressure, opening negotiations with the moderates, and holding elections. Little effort was made to assuage Kashmiris' hurt sentiment.

Rajesh Pilot, the then Union Minister of State for Home, tried to break new ground by shifting from a law-and-order strategy to a political approach. The first step was to focus the human face of the administration by replacing key personnel in civil and military positions in Srinagar. A new team espousing a soft approach, including Governor Krishna Rao, two senior IAS officers (Ashok Jaitley and Wajahat Habibullah) and Lieutenant General M.A. Zaki were appointed.

Governor Rao's gameplan was to win over the public by stopping random cordon operations alienating innocent civilians, meeting common masses and addressing their complaints, and better discipline among the security forces. The government announced a package of preventive procedural rules to curb excessive hostility against the militants and to expedite the release of innocent persons. Besides, democratic politics needed to be rejuvenated by encouraging the grass-roots politicians to start communicating with the people.

A Unified Command to improve and institutionalise the coordination of counter-insurgency operations between the security forces and the civil administration was created in May 1993. Chaired by the then Lieutenant General M.A. Zaki, the senior commanders of the security forces met daily while the overall charge of internal security was entrusted to the Ministry of Home Affairs. The Army's role was expanded, although the paramilitary forces retained paramount responsibility for internal security.

The Centre announced an economic package including expansion of higher education facilities, public works projects (repair and construction of roads and bridges), opening rehabilitation centres for training detained militants, restoration of the Governor's Advisory Council, and re-opening of Srinagar's Passport office, All India Radio and Doordarshan stations. These attempts were severely flayed for offering 'too little, too late'. The state administration was disappointed because the package failed to address the unemployment problem, shrunken revenues, and huge deficit while the militants objected to the government's attempts to pave the way for elections. Massive strikes paralysed the Valley.

Operational handicaps ensuing from personality clashes and instable coordination among different wings of the government and security forces derailed other administrative measures. In the Ministry of Home Affairs, the erstwhile Home Minister S.B. Chavan and his deputy, Rajesh Pilot, were at daggers drawn on issues ranging from appointment of advisers, the Hazratbal siege, negotiations with militants, retention of TADA, to the timing of holding elections. Chavan did not favour Pilot's efforts to bring Farooq Abdullah back in the Valley's politics and disagreed openly with the latter's position on considering grant of autonomy before the polls.

Governor Krishna Rao developed differences with both Chavan and Pilot and insisted on reporting directly to the Prime Minister. Krishna Rao's inaccessibility to the Central Government as well as his advisers and the state administration came under sharp criticism. Between 1993 and 1995, four of his advisers quit and the state Chief Secretaries were shuffled twice. The Unified Command never worked effectively.

The Army and paramilitary forces distrusted each other and crucial intelligence information was withheld on prime occasions. Although Lieutenant General Zaki was supposed to coordinate counter insurgency operations, the security forces were acting on their own. The whole system was in disarray. One organ of the government did not know what the other was doing, or worse, they were working at cross-purposes.

Pilot's political initiatives fared marginally better. His strategy was two fold: to bring Farooq Abdullah back into state politics, and help revive and mobilise the grass-roots cadre of the National Conference; and open a dialogue with Kashmiri militants, specially the moderate elements like the JKLF. Floating Farooq's name backfired; he remained anathema to Kashmiris because they believed that the rigging of the 1987 elections was directly responsible for triggering the militancy, nor was he forgiven for deserting the Valley during its all-time worst turmoil. Talks with the JKLF were too transparent and failed to take into account the Hizbul Mujahideen's determination to derail any initiative for reviving the political process. The brutal massacre of Dr Abdul Ahad Guru, a highly respected cardiologist, and a JKLF ideologue, on 31 March 1993 sent a chilling message that breaking ranks with the militants would be punished swiftly.

Fourth Phase

The fourth phase (1994-95) was marked by retracing steps in pursuit of political avenues for negotiations, growing instances of people"s resistance, increasing misuse against militants' 'misuse of the gun', and determined efforts to regain Kashmiri control over the movement.

Mass Resistance

Popular disillusionment with increasingly fragmented and criminalised militancy was the most critical factor in reversing direction. The gun for jihad had backfired. A Srinagar resident said, 'Militancy had a charm earlier but now it is a punishment.' In the first reported incident of a full-fledged public protest against the militants, 5,000 women demonstrated in protest against the slaughter of Pandit family in April 1992. A year later, kidnapping of Nahida Imtiaz, daughter of National Conference MP Saifuddin Soz, was criticized because 'abduction of a woman was against their religious tenets' and it evoked appeals from JKLF leaders for her immediate release. The metamorphosis in public response as compared to Rubaiya Sayeed's abduction only three years earlier was unmistakable.

In 1994, people actively resisted the militants. On 13 May 1994, a bid by militants to kidnap Yasmeen, daughter of National Conference leader Ali Mohammad Sagar, was foiled by a strong crowd of 2,000 people. In another incident, Muslims brickbatted the militants on shooting of two Hindu shopkeepers in downtown Srinagar. The militants still enforced their writ and the fear of the gun was all-pervasive, but the tide had already started to turn. The message was not lost on the militants.

Exploring Political Avenues

Introspection in the militant ranks led some leaders to reconsider political solutions. The Central Government had earlier released five top-notch leaders—Syed Ali Shah Geelani of the Jamaat-i-Islami, Abdul Ghani Lone of the Peoples Conference and Maulana Abbas Ansari, Qazi Nissar and Abdul Ghani Bhatt of the MUF — hoping that they would unit the disparate militant factions and prepare the ground for a negotiated settlement.

An All-Party Hurriyat Conference (APHC) comprising 30-odd political groups and militant outfits and an executive council from seven parties was formed. Chaired by the young Mirwaiz, Umar Farooq, the Hurriyat sought to bring different ideological strands into a common alignment.

With a broadly pro-Pakistan and pronounced Islamic orientation, a common minimum position was evolved in 'demanding plebiscite to allow Kashmiris to exercise self-determination as per the UN resolutions including the right to independence.

The Hurriyat's constitution was committed to waging peaceful political war although it included several militant outfits engaged in the armed struggle. It ruled out a negotiated settlement within the framework of the Indian Constitution and yet sought recognition from New Delhi as a legitimate mouthpiece of moderate Kashmiri opinion.

The Hurriyat's internal contradictions, ideological divergences, subservience to Pakistan and failure to exercise political command over the militant outfits did not allow it to become an effective instrument for imparting political direction to the militant movement. The militants' open threat, 'We will liquidate them if they talk of anything other than self-determination under the UN resolutions', gave little scope for manoeuvre.

The process, however, survived with the release of the JKLF leader Yasin Malik in May 1994, and that of the People's League chief, Shabir Shah, in November 1994. These two leaders of the old guard enjoyed credibility in the militant ranks and mass support in the Valley. The JKLF had never toed Pakistan's line, and Shabir had come a long way from a pro-Pakistan standpoint to adopting a pro-people approach. Both were acutely well-informed of the movement's loss of direction. Yasin declared that the first priority was to 'purify' the movement by weeding out the 'undesirable elements—criminals and Indian agents', and strongly lashed out against the 'black-sheep who have been misusing the gun taken up for a sacred cause'. Shabir Shah also acknowledged infiltration by criminal elements who were 'bent upon destroying the struggle'.

Several militant leaders joined the fray in protesting against the prevailing 'gun culture' and favoured exploring political options. Ghulam Nabi Butt, younger brother of Maqbool Butt said: 'Only the gun cannot get us *azadi*. The solution lies in talking across the table.' This view was also echoed by JKLF leader Javed Mir: 'We can hold talks with the centre provided the centre around independence. *The gun after all is not the answer.*' Even Amanullah Khan reiterated, 'I would be a fool if I thought we could shunt out Indians only with the gun ... The fight is also political and diplomatic'. Yasin Malik had undergone a dramatic transformation in forswearing the gun to adopt Gandhian methods of observing indefinite fasts. He announced a unilateral ceasefire and was all set to hold talks with the Indian government provided 'there were no pre-conditions and we are treated equally'.

Re-establishing Kashmiri Command

A critical feature of this phase was conscious and sustained efforts to wrest the initiative from pro-Pakistan and foreign 'Islamic warriors', and re-establish Kashmiri control over the movement. Charting a secular course, Shabir Shah stressed that 'it is not a fight between one and the other religion but a war between oppressed and oppressors'. He redefined the Kashmiri movement:

> We demand right of self-determination to make it unambiguously clear to India that *we are a quam, a respectful and courageous identity* with a determination to march in step with others in the comity of nations. We are not a herd, which can be pushed around by India or Pakistan ... We will lay down our lives but will not permit any division of the state by the people in Islamabad or New Delhi ... The issue concerns 1.25 crore inhabitants of Jammu & Kashmir and a solution has to be acceptable to the three parties—India, Pakistan and the people of Kashmir. (emphasis added)

The Mirwaiz, Umar Farooq, characterised the movement as 'not an Islamic movement but a movement of Kashmiri people. Yasin Malik foiled the Harkat-ul-Ansar's attempts to appropriate the Hazratbal platform, a secular symbol of Kashmiri identity which had no scope in the pan-Islamic philosophy. The Harkat's and Hizbul's ban on the Amarnath Yatra (pilgrimage) and their demand for the removal of bunkers around Hazratbal had alarmed the JKLF which could not surrender the initiative of protecting the Kashmiri ethos and allow the Harkat to hijack the Hazratbal shrine for serving Pakistan's territorial designs of Kashmir. The JKLF called a general strike, and Yasin Malik started an indefinite fast to focus on the issue. On receiving an assurance from the government, he persuaded the Hurriyat to appeal to all militant outfits to lift the ban on the yatra.

Yasin Malik had, by that time, refused to play second fiddle even to the Azad Kashmir leadership of the JKLF. His remarks on the eventual split from Amanullah Khan in October 1995 were significant as he asserted that, the 'movement cannot be run by remote control as Khan was doing [from Azad Kashmir]. We have ended the remote control of the JKLF'. Finally, Yasin and Shabir tried building bridges between Kashmiri Muslims and Pandits. Stressing that 'Kashmiris are incomplete without Kashmiri Pandits', they visited refugee camps and appealed to the Pandits to return. Shabir went a step further and sought the support of the people of Jammu and Ladakh for the common cause of the 'right of self determination'.

Both Yasin and Shabir, however, failed in uniting militant outfits because Pakistan directly controlled the powerful ones like Harkat-ul-Ansar and Hizbul Mujahideen. The Hizbul Mujahideen's political patron, the Jamaat-i-Islami, called the shots in the Hurriyat Conference and scuttled all attempts to secularise the movement and strengthen the independence option. Yasin was condemned for the un-Islamic practices of observing fasts, while Shabir's stand to involve the Kashmiri Pandits, Buddhists and Sikhs and to ensure representation of Jammu and Ladakh in the APHC evoked utmost discomfort. Both leaders lived under constant threat of liquidation, but they received overwhelming public support.

Mass Reactions

Kashmiris resisted the Jamaat's efforts to impose Islamic ideology and often flouted the Hizbul Mujahideen's strictures against observing centuries-old Kashmiri practices and festivals. The resistance of the people in Batamaloo in Srinagar on being restrained by militants from celebrating the annual *Urs* (a birth or death anniversary of a saint or rishi) of Batmoal Rishi, the burning down of part of Khanqah adjacent to the mausoleum of Baba Payamuddin Rishi in Tangmarg, and a clash in Aish Mugam when militants made an attempt to prevent the local villagers from celebrating the Urs of Baba Zainuddin Rishi, are some examples. At the Zain Shah Sahib near Gulmarg, more than 20,000 peasants congregated in defiance of the Jamaat and Hizbul to observe the festival of lights heralding the sowing season in the Valley. Clashes between the assembled peasants and the Hizbul militants resulted in the killing of the innocent.

In July 1994, the Hizbul's killing of Qazi Nissar for his pro-independence sentiments marked a significant milestone in the people's alienation from Pakistan. Thousands of Muslims participated in rallies and processions condemning the assassination and publicly condemning Pakistan. The popular slogan *Jo mangega Pakistan, Usko Milega kabristan* (Whosoever demands Pakistan shall be put into a grave) captured the public mood. The Jamaat-i-Islami leaders were unnerved and 'went into hiding for weeks together and the Hizbul militants were literally on the run in Anantnag, Shopian, Pulwama and Kulgam apprehending people's wrath. The Hizbul Mujahideen could then enforce its writ only through terror, as many admitted, 'if anybody protests, the answer is [a] bullet.'

Centre's Stand

The government continued to drift and failed to cash in on the situation to win the confidence of the people. Internal dissension dogged the decision-making apparatus. While Governor Krishna Rao survived a long-drawn-out campaign to oust him, many senior officers quit. In order to end the tussle between S.B. Chavan and Rajesh Pilot, Prime Minister Narasimha Rao divested the Kashmir Affairs Department from the Union Home Ministry and brought it under his direct command. This eliminated a valuable buffer between ministerial pronouncements and state policy and exposed the Prime Minister's stewardship to the risk of operational disability because his engagements did not allow enough time to conceive meaningful political initiatives for Kashmir.

The one-point gameplan of holding elections was criticised as an ill-timed attempt and met with stiff resistance from across the political spectrum ranging from the BJP to the CPI-M at the centre, and the National Conference, the Hurriyat and migrant Pandits, as well as government officials. People's reaction to elections ranged from apathy to antipathy, depending on the domination of militants in various places.

What compelled the government to postpone elections was the Charar-i-Sharif crisis in April 1995. Following a prolonged military stand-off between militants and security forces, Kashmir's most revered saint Sheikh Noordin's shrine, Charar-i-Sharif, was razed in a massive fire that embittered the people and deepened their alienation.

Significantly, for the first time, regional and national political parties joined people of all hues and colours in the state in condemning the government's failure to protect the shrine. The Hurriyat launched a fresh anti-election propaganda from Pulwama and torched more than a hundred government buildings which were to be used as polling stations.

Paradoxically, the Charar-i-Sharif tragedy proved to be a turning point in exposing the Islamic designs of Afghan mercenaries who had occupied the shrine. While the Army was held responsible for its destruction, privately many Kashmiris and the people of Charar-i-Sharif, in particular, were incensed at the total disrespect and contempt of Mast Gul and other foreign mercenaries for the Kashmiri shrine. The slogans of fighting Jihad and *Kashmir Banega Pakistan* written on the half-burnt walls of the shrine of a rishi who had always spoken against religious principles dividing the people spoke volumes. People acceptance of government relief for rebuilding homes and properties, in defiance of the Hizbul Mujahideen and the Jamiat-ul-Mujahideen's directives, sent the message home.

Fifth Phase

In the Valley, the hallmark of the fifth phase (1995-96) was continuing downturn of the militant movement, specially the 'Kashmiri component', voluntary surrender of militants and emergence of counter-insurgents or pro-India militants. Popular disillusionment, rethinking of the gun option by important leaders, and a high level of militant losses, with more than 4,000 killed and arrested in 1995 alone, had sharply reduced fresh recruitment to the militant ranks. Many surrendered.

The Kashmiri component of the militant struggle earlier marginalised by Pakistan's ISI was on the retreat. Foreign mercenaries increasingly replaced Kashmiri militants. The pro-Pakistan militants were also alarmed at the new turn of events, 'rendering Kashmiris irrelevant in Pakistani calculations and making the so-called "guest militants" not only the key force in the movement against India but virtual masters of the scene'. The security forces had gained a clear edge. A senior army officer commanding counter-insurgency operations in northern Kashmir stated 'No one now fights, except foreign mercenaries, who know we will show them no mercy.' Thus, success of the Kashmir Police's Special Operations Group in eliminating and arresting 60 top leaders indicated better local intelligence.

Counter-insurgency

Many militants who had surrendered switched loyalty and were by this time fighting to 'liberate Kashmir from agents of Pakistan'. Termed 'friendlies' by the security forces, these pro-Indian militants earned the epithet of 'renegades' by the other side. They became united with the Army and the Rashtriya Rifles in particular which protected, funded, and armed them in return for fighting the Hizbul Mujahideen. Kukka Parrey became the symbol of this phenomenon, a local product, offspring of the criminalisation of militancy. They exploited people's anger at excesses committed by the militants and were particularly successful in the Hizbul-dominated areas. A proliferation of pro-Indian militant outfits led them to immediately assert dominance over large parts of the Valley. Initially welcomed by the people, soon their ranks were also corrupted by the lumpen elements involved in the outlawed trade of timber, extortions and looting.

Steps Against Violence

A widespread revulsion against violence and the realisation that *azadi* remained a far cry gave rise to votaries of 'peace with honour'. But Kashmiris lacked an effective political leadership which could understand the people's mind and respond to the changing situation with creative alternatives. The Hurriyat's rigid, negative and conditional stand in not negotiating with the government until Pakistan was involved in tripartite talks and rejecting to participate in the elections only marginalised it further. Shabir Shah acknowledged the disillusionment of the people with the Hurriyat and their simmering resentment for 'its inability to fulfil their expectations' when he stated 'we asked them for their sons, they willingly sacrificed; we asked them for their money, they donated generously. Now, if they don't get what [they] expected, their disgruntlement is not unjustified.'

But his attempts to break ranks and willingness to 'participate in the electoral exercise if they were perfectly organised in order to determine the real representatives of the people' was promptly rejected by the pro-Pak factions of the Hurriyat as well as the Indian government. The popular mood was captured by a faction of ex-militants who decided to shun violence and hold unconditional talks with New Delhi. As top former brasses of the militant movement, including Babar Badr (chief of the Muslim Janbaaz Force), Imran Rahi (deputy chief of Hizbul Mujahideen), Bilal Lodhi (ex-deputy of the Hurriyat leader Abdul Ghani Lone) and Mohinuddin (chief of the Muslim Mujahideen), their credentials were above board.

In a significant departure, they did not insist upon Pakistan's involvement in negotiations. This political initiative offered an alternative platform to the Hurriyat, which was criticised sharply for pursuing rigid policies and 'zero achievements'. Its frequent calls for hartals had ruined the Valley's economy and the leaders' 'five-star life style' when the 'armed youth were laying down their lives' was denounced. A conspicuous absence of mass protests against the militants' offer for talks showed they were only voicing people's compounded enchantment with the Hurriyat.

The Central Government responded positively and invited their 'Forum for Peaceful Resolution of J&K' for talks at New Delhi.

The then Home Minister S.B. Chavan constituted a committee to consider the Forum's proposals for building confidence by releasing all detainees (specially those who were not charged with particular crimes), restraining the security forces, calling off offensive operations and disarming the 'renegade militants'.

Although the Forum's initiative was soon overtaken by the government's decision to hold the Lok Sabha elections, it definitely acted as a catalyst in bringing several militant leaders to the negotiating table. The Hizbul Mujahideen's former chief, Ahsan Dar, and Azim Inqalabi hailed the initiative and later three other militant outfits wanted to be invited by New Delhi for similar parleys. The movement had undoubtedly undergone a sea-change.

Revival of Political Process

Elections dominated the government's agenda for reviving the political process in the Valley. Farooq Abdullah demanded an autonomy package, reviving the pre-1953 status, before the polls. Prime Minister Narasimha Rao's half-hearted offer to re-examine the Kashmir Accord (1975), announced from Burkeina Faso, a small country in western Africa, dashed hopes of earlier promises of 'maximum autonomy short of *azadi*'. It was 'too little, too late', but it did help in reintroducing the agenda of Kashmir's autonomy.

The new decision to hold parliamentary elections in Jammu & Kashmir state was an important step. The odds were high. The Hurriyat's boycott was expected, and some moderate militant leaders also perceived that elections were redundant. Without any meaningful offer of autonomy, the National Conference decided to stay out. The fear of the gun was predominant. The counter-insurgents' entry into the electoral fray had raised fears of political parties. The real issue, however, was the participation of the people. Contesting the 6 parliamentary seats were 152 candidates. An impressive turnout of 39 per cent in the Valley carried the day.

Media reports attributing it to 'coercion' by the security forces had cast a shadow, but the fact that only 7 per cent of the votes cast were invalid pointed in the other direction. The government appeared to have crossed the Rubicon. The elections helped restore the legitimacy of political mechanisms and revived a democratic channel for articulating people's aspirations.

The political equations in the Valley changed rapidly. The Hurriyat was further marginalised. The Common Minimum Programme of the Unite Front, a new coalition government at the Centre, assured maximum autonomy to Jammu and Kashmir. The National Conference quickly realised that not contesting assembly polls would leave them in the wilderness.

Kashmiri Identity: A New Definition

After nine years of political oblivion, the National Conference mobilised Kashmiris as part of the Indian nation. Farooq Abdullah reiterated: 'We are a part of India. *It is only with India that we will progress and our Kashmiriyat survive*. Our identity cannot sustain in any other way. That is my belief' (emphasis added). He sought to revive the Delhi Agreement (1952) to give due honour and dignity to the Kashmiris and even promised that the Pandits would be brought back 'with respect and honour'.

With voter turnouts ranging from a mere 15 per cent to as much as 60 per cent in what most observers described as free and fair election, the National Conference emerged as the primary regional political force with an overwhelming two-thirds majority of 59 out of 87 seats.

More important, for the first time in the post-Independence history of Jammu & Kashmir state, it managed to win the mandate from all three regions. A badly divided Congress lost both in Valley and the traditional strongholds of Jammu, reducing its strength from 26 to 7. The BJP raised its tally from 2 to 8 seats, all in Jammu.

But the Kashmiris' vote for Farooq's government was at best qualified support. People had voted against the militancy and to replace the 'repressive and bureaucratic' regime with democratic channels for redressing grievances. The slogan of *azadi* had not lost appeal. But realising that *azadi* was not feasible, and with grudging respect for the coercive power of the Indian State, Kashmiris had sought a compromise. The battle of bullets was superseded, but the war of winning the hearts and minds of Kashmiris had just begun.

Why did Kashmiris fail to achieve their political objectives? I shall discuss three key factors: the limited and divided social base, lack of effective external support, and flawed political and military strategies.

Social Base

The JKLF demanded *azadi* for *all* the people of Jammu & Kashmir state, but indeed articulated the political interests of only the Valley Muslims. Kashmiri Pandits were alienated, and Jammu and Ladakh bitterly opposed its separatist agenda as well shall discuss in detail in the next chapter. The Jamaat and Hizbul Mujahideen's articulation of Kashmiris' Islamic identity was not supported by a majority of Kashmiri Muslims. After the romance wore off, Pakistan too had little appeal. Finally, the pan-Islamic identity was a new concept to Kashmiri Muslims, an extraneous imposition with no social base in the Valley. Kashmiris and their political aspirations counted little in the foreign mercenaries' worldwide religious crusade.

Inadequate External Support

Kashmiri groups had singularly failed in mobilising the national political parties, regional political groups and the Indian intelligentsia to assist their cause. The human rights organisations were the only exceptions. Nor could Kashmiris effectively campaign through the media. The stand of Indian Muslims needs special mention. While the Muslim leaders in Bihar, Uttar Pradesh, Delhi and Hyderabad criticised the Centres handling of Kashmir, no one supported its right to secede. The Indian Urdu press objected to holding the Indian Muslims hostage to the fate of Kashmir rather than the Kashmiri issue.

In contrast, the Kashmiris—backed by Pakistan's diplomatic machinery—had been successful in drawing the world's attention to their cause. But after the initial barrage of criticism of the Indian government for human rights violations in the Valley, the Kashmiris' plank of self-determination found minimum support even among the OIC members. The Shimla Agreement remained the buzzword in world capitals, for no country seemed to be prepared to hold its relationship with

India hostage to the Kashmir issue. In fact, by 1993-94, the tables had turned on Pakistan. As the Indian government improved its human rights record and opened the Valley to diplomats and the foreign media, the submissions of the Pakistan's armed support to Kashmiris gained credence. The induction of foreign mercenaries into Kashmir and the recognition of the increasing pan-Islamic character of the militancy caused consternation among many who had by then become victims of international Islamic terrorism. Pakistan came close to being blacklisted as a terrorist state by the USA in 1993.

Pakistani attempts to internationalise the Kashmir issue had also failed. Pakistan was persuaded by 'Islamic' Iran and its 'friend and ally' China against moving any resolution against India at the UN Human Rights Commission in Geneva in 1993. The following year, even the OIC Contact Group decided to drop the resolution on Kashmir in the UN International Security Committee for lack of support among its members.

Overall, beyond expressions of sympathy, the much-anticipated international support for the Kashmiri cause did not materialise. The international situation itself had undergone a sea-change dashing the early hopes of Kashmiris. Afghanistan had degenerated into a civil war between warring factions of mujahedin, and by 1995-96, the Taliban's imposition of medieval anarchic Islamic practices had brought home the dangers of Islamising their own society. The break up of the Soviet Union and Yugoslavia resulting in several international ethnic conflicts had made world leaders apprehensive of disturbing international boundaries and creating new states.

The most critical source of external support was Pakistan. Kashmiris' romantic conception of the 'Promised Land of Pakistan' died quickly. Pakistan support for the right of self-determination had come with a rider—that of *Kashmir's support for accession to Pakistan*. An independent Kashmir was, however, ruled out. Since Pakistan controlled key levers of the militant movement, every militant outfit which did not serve Pakistan's interests was systematically marginalised.

The JKLF leadership had failed to see through Pakistan's

gameplan and miscalculated gravely in depending solely on Pakistan for funds, arms and training. By the time the goal of *azadi* caught the people's imagination, the JKLF had been marginalised and replaced by the pro-Pak Hizbul Mujahideen. When the latter began to lose momentum and failed to recruit more Kashmiri militants, they too were superseded by foreign mercenaries of the Harkat-ul-Ansar. Gradually, all militant groups realised that Pakistan did not have the military wherewithal, nor any intention, to risk a long-drawn-out war with India to liberate Kashmir. Many believed that Pakistan was using Kashmir merely as a pawn for 'bleeding India'. The Pakistan government's manipulation of Azad Kashmir elections suppression of people in the Northern Areas, and the suppression of *mohajirs* in Sindh exposed its brutal face. The honeymoon with Pakistan was over.

Miscalculated Strategies

The militant movement also failed because it lacked a coherent and effective military strategy. Militant violence was most effective in 1989-90. At the prime of militancy in 1990, there was a general belief that the Indian State would soon 'withdraw', granting Kashmir independence, rather than continue with a well-planned and long-term military strategy of 'liberating Kashmir'. The militants were overtaken by frequent the mass processions demanding *azadi*. The real threat to the Indian State was not as much from Kashmiri militant struggle as from mass demonstrations which symbolised total rejection of state authority.

The Indian State has considerable experience in successfully combating insurgency in the North-East and Punjab, but has rarely faced mass movements demanding secession. When the militants failed to channelise the mass demonstrations for their cause, nor sustain them, the battle was clearly lost. None other than its patron, Pakistan, quickly neutralised the military might of the JKLF. Devoid of sophisticated weapons, cadres and funds, the JKLF was no match for the massive military power of the Indian State.

Moreover, it also faced the lethal challenge of the Hizbul Mujahideen which had Jamaat-trained, highly disciplined cadres, better equipment and better military strategy. Their objective of joining Pakistan or their Islamic ideology failed to convince people in the Valley. The average Kashmiri militant was driven more by economic and political frustration and a radical sense of taking revenge against the perceived oppression than by ideological zest. Religion was simply not an important motivating factor; he never considered himself a holy warrior.

Without mass support, the battle-hardened foreign mercenaries were also doomed to failure. Thus, the JKLF enjoyed popular support but lacked weapons and a military strategy, while the Hizbul Mujahideen was much better equipped but also lacked popular backing. Without each other's support, both failed. Shabir Shah and Yasin Malik tried to impart a new direction, but under Pakistan's pressure, both were soon forced to retrace their steps.

The militant movement was ideologically graded into pro-accession and pro-independence camps and fragmented deeply among several outfits. The Hurriyat Conference also lacked a clear, consistent and consensual strategy of achieving its political objectives. Rife with ideological differences, factionalism and personality clashes, it could hardly agree on beyond the common minimum position of 'plebiscite under the UN auspices' and was totally isolated due to its rigid stand on 'no negotiations without Pakistan'.

Finally, criminalisation and degeneration of the militancy alienated the masses. The gun had backfired, brutalising the entire Kashmiri society. A complete generation of youth had gone astray and the children were becoming desensitised to violence, which many feared may well lead to de-humanisation in due course.

On the other side, the Indian State had fended off Jammu and Kashmir's secession, but the political battle of weaning Kashmiris back into peace and the Indian mainstream had concluded in a stalemate. Secessionists had been crushed, but pro-*azadi* sentiments had not lost grounds. The people seemed to be resigned to their fate under the existing political dispensation. Kashmiris' collective sense of disenchantment with the Indian State prevailed. State elections and a popularly-elected government could only be termed as a good beginning.

Fourteen

Islamic Economy: Illusions and Rhetoric

The concept of an Islamic economy appears to be a twentieth-century phenomenon. In the earlier Islamic tradition, the economy was not considered an autonomous agent: the economic action (buying, selling, owning) was merely a single aspect of human activity in general, and as such was regulated by the *sharia*. The *sharia* sets forth a definite number of concepts with an economic impact: the *zakat* (taxing of certain goods, such as harvests, with an eye to allotting these taxes to expenditures that are also explicitly defined, such as aid to the needy); the interdiction of chance (*gharar*), that is, of the existence of any element of uncertainty, in a contract (which excludes not only insurance but also the lending of money without participation in the risks); and, finally, the restriction of what is referred to as usury (*riba*), all of this defines the permissible use of money to buy goods. The *sharia* also declares inheritance, property, usufruct, booty, community rights, and so on. As always in Muslim Law, these concepts are designed on the basis of isolated prescriptions, anecdotes, examples, words of the Prophet, all gathered together and systematised by commentators according to an inductive, casuistic method.

For traditionalist ulemas, these prescriptions are elements of Muslim law among others: in no way do they carve out an autonomous area that could be called "commercial law" or on economic theory, even if they have influence on economic activity. A good example of this process can be found, curiously, in the writings of Imam Khomeini: in his work *Tawzih al-masa'il* (the explanation of problems) he catches up with the economy as the classical ulemas do; the term "economy" does not appear; the chapter on selling and buying (*kharid o forush*) comes after the one on pilgrimage and presents economic issues as individual acts open to moral analysis: "To lend (without interest, on a note from the lender) is among the good works that are specifically recommended in the verses of the Quran and in the Tradition."

As we have seen, the Salafist reformers were generally uninterested in socioeconomic issues. Reflection on the Islamic economy is thus an Islamist novelty despite the recent appearance of the conservative technocratic trend (especially in Saudi and Pakistani milieus) that endeavours to adapt modern banking practices to Quranic norms.

An Ideological Construct

As in the case of politics, the Islamists took a category, the "economy", that had been isolated and defined by Western modernity: the "economy" (*iqtisad*) is becoming the purpose of specific research, as indicated by the large number of books or articles devoted exclusively to it in the past half-century, instead of being integrated into generalised treatises on law. The Islamists have undertaken the systematisation and conceptualisation of basic shariatic prescriptions in order to construct a coherent and functional entirety that would offer a middle ground between the two systems of the twentieth century, Marxism and capitalism. Capitalism never having been an economic doctrine, it is Marxism that is the mirror and foil of the Islamist effort. Whatever the amalgamation created in the name of an Islamic economy, it is above all an ideological construct.

The point of departure for the economy according to the Islamists lies not in the doctrines of the *sharia* (usury, and so on), as it does for the ulemas, but in an anthropology like the one we have already faced in Chapter 3: a "theological anthropology" in which man is defined as a creature of God, gifted with reason, evolving in the realms both of need and salvation — in brief, as a goal-oriented, teleological "nature" (with its physical needs), oriented toward the goal of its salvation. The economy exists because man is a creature of needs; it therefore aims to suffice these needs. But because man's superior aim is salvation, his economic activity must be exercised within the ethical structure defined by the Quran. The economy is a means, not an end.

Islamist theoreticians do not praise asceticism: respecting values allows the believer not only to enjoy the goods of the earth, but certainly brings about the prosperity of the community as well as economic progress.

Evil is a logic that causes man to forget his goal in the satisfaction of his needs: it is excess, bloating (tavarrum). It is therefore imperative to strike a balance between consumption on the one hand, and redistribution to the poor on the other.

Sometimes more fundamentalist Islamists draw the philosophical and anthropological definition of the economy (such as the extension of man conceived of as a creature of needs) from the analysis of Western classics (mostly Rousseau and Marx), and explain it with Quranic citations; they position Islam as the solution to the aporias of Western thought, but within a conceptual framework established by Western philosophy. Thus, Abdul Hasan Bani Sadr embraced a Marxist-leaning anthropology ("work and only work is the basis of the relationship between man and God, between man and others, between man and things"), but based it on a excerpt from the Quran: "man will possess only what he acquires through his own efforts" (sura 53 [The Star], verse 39), concluding with the statement that the right to property depends above all on work.

A Social-Democratic Vision

Even among the most hardcore Islamists, there is no communist interpretation of the Islamic economy. The notion of "social justice," even of "Islamic socialism," however, does appear among the MBs and the Iranians; this socialist tendency tends to highlight areas of Islamic law that allow for the limitation of property, whereas the conservative current makes are right to property the cornerstone of the Islamic economy. Generally the radicals form a "social-democratic" vision of the economy: they recognise private property, but want the State to ensure social justice through limiting the accumulation of wealth and through its redistribution, systematising the scattered economic principles in the *sharia* (zakat, and so on). In keeping with the logic of legitimating neologism by returning to the sources, they hark back to the first Islamic society, at the time of the Prophet, whose companion, Abu Dharr, is considered a harbinger of Islamic socialism.

The limitation on growth is implemented by condemning whatever goes beyond the satisfaction of needs: luxury, amassing wealth, certain types of income — in brief, any income that is not earned through work or running a risk, basically, hoarding (*ihtikar*). Thus, it is necessary to begin by placing limits on the thirst for possessing; the first limit is the ethical model of a good Muslim, the paradigm of the Prophet, who offers an image of self-control and moderation. But radical Islamists do not consider this ethical exhortation to be sufficient; they interpret the Quran's prescriptions as a system that authorises the State to organise the redistribution of wealth. The first limitation is on ownership, even if it is lawful in doctrine. This limitation has a theological basis: man has only usufruct of the earth and its goods, the highest ownership of which is God's alone. This highest level of ownership can successively consign to the *umma*, then to the Islamic state, embodied for Shiites in the imam. Thus, a policy of nationlisation and state ownership is justified, reinforced by the Quranic interdiction of the appropriation of certain "primary goods": water, mines, pasturage and combustibles.

Next one must ensure redistribution, primarily because it averts accumulation, second because it allows one to fulfil the legal obligations of the religion (*sadaqa* and *zakat*). *Zakat* meets both requirement: it deals with capital and serves to check accumulation, but must benefit specific categories of the population, including the needy, as well as defend the religion and the community. The laws of inheritance, by favouring the breaking up of patrimony, also work against growth, for in Islamic law there is no privileged successor: parents, descendants, and relatives inherit equally as a function of their nearness to the defunct and of their sex (a half-share for women).

This delegation from God to the *umma*, and from the *umma* to the Islamic state allows staunch Islamists to consider the state an engine of economic planning, justifying a policy of bank nationalisation and of centralised economic development, which would turn out in particular to be the credo of Iranian governments under the authority of Prime Minister M.H. Musavi (1981-1989).

But many Islamists renounce this socialist-leading reading of Islam; they emphasise instead all that is compatible with capitalism in Islam (the right to ownership and a market economy) while assigning the state a relatively significant role in planning, fighting monopolies, and acting as an engine for industrialisation and social action; this is the line of thought of the Turkish Prosperity Party, the Iranian Hujjatiyya group, and the Algerian FIS. The last two examples indicate that there is no systematic connection between radicalism in politics, ideology, and economics.

One point is generally missing from Islamist economic thought, whether moderate or radical, except in the writings of Sayyid Qutb: it is the issue of agrarian reform. On the one hand, such reform would imply a reanalysis of the concept of ownership, but most of all it would throw into question the *waqf*, endowments whose revenue certifies the functioning of religious institutions. Thus in the Iranian province of Khorasan, 50 per cent of the cultivated lands belong to the religious foundation Astan-i Quds, which oversees the mausoleum of the Imam Reza in Mashhad. Questioning *waqf* property, therefore, would mean questioning the basis of the financial autonomy of the mullahs and mosques. Even during the most Third World period of the Islamic revolution in Iran, there was no agrarian restoration. Opposition to agrarian reform has even played a role in Islamist uprisings (Iran, 1963; Afghanistan, 1978).

Primacy of Ethics

In the Islamist conception of the economy, the ethical model is pivotal. Even if the Quranic prescriptions must be implemented by institutions like the state, they also rest on an anthropology in which man, a creature of needs, must organise his activities according to a moral model, which is that of the Prophet. According to Bani Sadr, the principle in an Islamic society is "to produce according to one's capacities, to consume according to virtue (*taqwa*)," for only this limitation of consumption can ensure an excess and its redistribution—voluntary and automatic for those who follow the path of virtue, forced for those who do not. Virtue is self-limitation. Redistribution ensures that everyone's needs will be fulfilled, since God could not have put his creature into a world of scarcity: scarcity is a consequence of hoarding, thus an absence of virtue. The satisfaction of needs allows one to devote oneself to the essentials: "Material self-sufficiency is an opportunity to advance toward virtue." Institutions exist only to lead man to the ethical form. If each man followed the Prophet's ethical model on his own, there would be no need to legislate it from without. Even in as political an author as Bani Sadr, state authority disappears in favour of the figure of the imam, defined as someone who does not govern, but who symbolises and unifies a society that has finally become "one" (*tawhidi*); his mere presence at the highest point of the system prevents the constitution of a separate ground of power, capable of appropriating the surplus to maintain its power. The imam is the "symbol of consensus" and "the mirror that reflects the image of *towhid*."

Respect for ethics is considered as a way to enjoy the goods of the earth, unlike in Christian asceticism. A leitmotif of the "Islamic economy" is the blend of the respect for ethics and prosperity. The world is not a "vale of tears", but was entrusted with a sense of pleasure, for everlasting enjoyment, to man. In every case, the basic economic actor remains the individual, who behaves in conformity with the norms of the sharia, which are implemented by the state.

The image of the "left-wing Islamist," incarnated in the Iranian revolution, was gradually supplanted by a less state-oriented and more liberal image, at least with respect to the economy, in Iran as in the rest of the Muslim world. This evolution juxtaposes both with Islamism's shift toward neofundamentalism and with the diffusion of the Islamist message to a much broader audience (businessmen, students of economics, and others). In any case, the Islamist scheme has never been collectivist, unlike Christian liberation theology, which attempts at times to make the base communities the economic actors. Although one can notice a certain associative or cooperative spirit among the Islamist left (for example, the militants of the "reconstruction crusade" in Iran), the usual attitude of the Islamists, and even more so of the neofundamentalists, is favourable to individual free enterprise, balanced by a moral discourse regarding the preferred practices of the economic actors. Both the Algerian FIS and the Turkish

Prosperity Party (the reference to materialistic pleasure is no accident) support individual initiative and privatisation: here political fundamentalism (for the FIS) or technocratism has no fascination with a socialist model (which is, besides, rapidly losing viability).

Khomeini's Iran

In Iran, the slogan "Islamise the economy" had two different meanings, depending on who said it. For the Islamists, it meant above all introducing state control and redistributing wealth toward the masses; this vision, which was that of all Third World models of state socialism, prevailed in Iran until Khomeini's death. For the conservatives (the high clergy, the market), it was a matter mostly of protecting private property and granting a legal religious framework for seeking profit. This permanent conflict resulted in the blockage of all important decisions: those in favour of state control sat in the parliament, which has influential power over economic matters (voting on laws, but also the censure of ministers), while the "liberals" occupied the Supervisory Council, governed by the high clergy and responsible for verifying the conformity with Islam of the laws passed by parliament. There is no automatic correspondence between political fundamentalism and state socialism: economic liberals, such as the group constituted by Ayatollah Azari Qumi around the newspaper *Risalat* or the association Hujjatiyya, are highly categorical on a theological level.

For the most part the Supervisory Council has opposed laws that would have had an economic influence (like agrarian reform) but has never tried to define positively what an Islamic economy would look like. In fact, under the pretext of allegiance with Islam, the Council constantly defended a liberal vision of the economy, in opposition to the state-controlled Islamo-socialist vision of the parliament, which translated into a series of procedures that had nothing Islamic about them in and of themselves, but were in keeping with a Third World socialist view: control of imports through licensing, setting of foreign exchange rates, a state monopoly on some activities, obstacles to the development of national capitalism in favour of the state sector, and so on.

On balance, the Islamisation of the Iranian economy is

superficial. The *waqf,* which the Shah had attempted to control without totally eliminating, have been entirely reestablished but are often managed in a perfectly technocratic fashion: the Astan-i Quds, which oversees considerable waqf linked with the mausoleum of the Imam Reza, is closer to a modern financial holding company than to a religious foundation, except insofar as it maintains a role of philanthropic sponsorship. Similarly, the revolutionary foundations ("Foundation of the Disinherited," "Foundation of Martyrs") are patronage-oriented holding companies that ensure the course of revenues to groups and milieus supporting the regime (but not to specific classes or sectors of the population). The diversion of revenues (the malnourishment of salaried employees, the enrichment of those who are in an intermediary position between the state and the market) is common to all regimes of the Third World, where a centralised state dominates the market economy in a system short on currency. This has nothing to do with a redistribution based on the pursuit for social justice.

More surprisingly, the financial system has barely been Islamised Christians, for example, are not subject to a poll tax and pay according to the common scheme. Insurance is maintained (even though chance, the very principle for insurance, should theoretically be excluded from all contracts). The contracts signed with foreigners all accept the matter of interest. The cardinal mechanisms of the economy oscillate between capitalist liberalism and state-controlled socialism.

As for the financial and banking system, it works essentially on speculation. In Iran, 1300 Islamic credit unions "became usurers' dens"; under the influence of the market, they were regrouped into an "Organisation of the Islamic Economy" and pay annual interest rates of from 25 to 50 per cent that are designated as "participation in the profits of enterprise"; they thereby pull into the speculative sector savings that the state banks, more concerned with investment, can remunerate at only 9 per cent. In any case, the principles controlling the Iranian banks are the same as those of the Sunni Islamic financial institutions that sprang up in the 1980s.

Islamic Bank

Today there are two forms of an Islamic economy. The Islamist, socialist, and state-run version existed in Iran only during the Khomeini era (1979-1989). The technocratic, conservative version was partially existing in Pakistan and in some Islamic banks or financial institutions in the Middle East. The two endeavours occurred during the same period, starting in 1980. If we observe closely, we see that in all cases the establishment of an "Islamic economy" concerns the banking system thoroughly, and that on this point there is essentially no difference between the two visions. Curiously, despite their penchant for productivity, the Islamists seem quite reluctant in developing an Islamic system of production. The Egyptian MBs under Hasan al-Banna created a "Company for Islamic Transactions" (*sharikat al-mu'amalat al-islamiyya*) in 1938, an investment company based on Islamic tenets (the distribution of profits), as well as small industrial enterprises; but these institutions could not escape the political crisis of 1948. In fact the Islamists have contented themselves with preaching the Islamisation of the financial and banking systems on a far from revolutionary basis.

The concept of an "Islamic bank" rests on a technocratic and non-ideological conception of the Islamic economy, one that does not extend beyond the financial and, occasionally, fiscal sphere. The mechanism aims, in countries such as Pakistan and Saudi Arabia, to Islamise the current practices of the modern economy in the fiscal and banking areas, without calling into question the social and political order: we are dealing here with a "technocratic" extension of traditionalist fundamentalism, which intends to enable a good Muslim to participate in a modern economy. The end result of economic activity, not to mention its social impact, is ignored: this is a far cry from political Islamism. Yet this technocratic view governs both the Iranian banking system and the Islamic financial institutions associated with MB circles.

The target of the Islamic bank is to make depositors' money bear fruit according to a system that complies with the *sharia*; the concept is far from the moral conception of the loan, according to which it is a pious act to refuse any growth in the sum. Lawful profit is profit in which the borrower participates in the financial operation and thus shares the risks, losses, and profits. The two main types of contracts provided for are: the joint venture (*mudaraba*, or *muzarebe* in Persian pronunciation), in which the bank grants the capital, receives its share of the profits, and bears its share of the losses; and the partnership (*musharaka*), in which the bank cannot invest more than its private partner and owns shares that can be resold.

It is interesting that there is no deviation between Shiites and Sunnis on this matter of the Islamic bank. Iran developed a banking system on the same bases as the one setup by Pakistani or Saudi theoreticians. The "Islamic banking system," the object of a 1983 order, is in fact a reconciliation of capitalistic practices and the Islamic taboo against interest. There are joint venture (*muzarebe*) and partnership (*musharaka*) contracts in Iran, as well as the notion of the "anticipated sale" (*salaf*), a legal form of loan. Banks are required to make interest-free loans, but fees are deducted. Banks can also invest directly according to complex terms and conditions that are rigidly controlled by the state. There are two types of deposits: *qard hasan*, a bank deposit made by individuals that bears no interest, but on which the bank is authorised to offer bonuses or various incentives to depositors; and the term investment, in which the bank and the depositor share the risks and profits.

Regarding the matter of taxation, Pakistan introduced the *zakat*, the Islamic tax, in the form of an automatic and obligatory tax on bank accounts; the sums collected are given to a special committee entrusted for distributing them among the beneficiaries provided for in the *sharia* (including the collectors themselves).

Manifestations Outside Iran

The Islamisation of the economy consists primarily in installing "Islamic" windows that open onto a reality that is far less Islamic, but are based on the model one could call "conservative technocratic": the target is to offer the believer a means of making his money grow without violating the *sharia*. These enterprises are always private. The large Islamic banks (Dubai Islamic Bank, founded in 1975, Faysal Islamic Bank, Kuwait Finance, Al-Taqwa

Islamic Bank) are totally separate from the Islamic states: they serve essentially to make the capital of high-level shareholders bear fruit and to attract popular savings. The creation of an Islamic bank is not proof of an Islamist state. Saudi Arabia has never Islamised its official banking system. Private Islamic banks do not aim to change the society, but to capture a definite new clientele.

The theory behind Islamic banks is that they avoid sin while yielding more than ordinary banks. Established in countries with unsettled, high-inflation economies (Iran, Pakistan), the banks cannot draw their profits from industrial production, yet they must pay higher than inflation. The necessity of producing profits to seem more attractive than ordinary banks implies a certain economic adventurism, thus speculation. The concept of sharing risks and profits, even when applied honestly, stimulates the banks to get involved in only short-term operations. No matter where Islamic banks have been set up, or where "normal" banks have created an "Islamic division" (such as the BCCI, with Pakistani management and Dubai capital), they have functioned essentially on speculation and short-term investment.

Sooner or later, speculation entails a crash. The examples of crashes of "Islamic" financial institutions are legion. In Egypt, the Al-Rayan Bank, founded in the early 1980s on the notion of sharing profits (which introduces the concept of sharing risks, which is essential in order to distinguish genuine profit from interest), boasted profits between 24 and 30 per cent, while the state banks were offering 13 per cent. It soon came to light that such revenues were drawn from speculation on international markets: the temporary success of the Islamic banks was founded on playing the most unstable elements of Western markets (the gold market in New York in the case of Al-Rayan); when situation changed (the Wall Street crash of October 1987), bankruptcy loomed.

The economies of the Middle East are quite often economies of speculation, because of the fact that the state is the primary intermediary of economic impetus (nationalism, protectionism, control of import and export licenses as well as of currency); the state turns out, generally, to be opposed to national capitalism (Iran, Syria, Algeria), but it maintains a relationship of patronage between bureaucrats and speculators. It is the state machine that allows the appropriation of surplus; thus the image of the "functionary-prebendary," in Michel Seurat's apt term. Money is invested in speculation and not in production: despite its boastful discourse, the "Islamic economy" is no different from the economies of speculation that assist social groups who have attached themselves to a particular state apparatus. Islamisation often merely provides more ample, "whiter" garb for these speculation and patronage-oriented relationships.

The lack of real impact of an Islamisation policy on the economy and the society can be seen in Pakistan, where the establishment of *zakat* has had no serious impact on the redistribution of income, if one assumes that the *zakat* is being honestly divided up.

Thus, Islamic banks are not institutions used to fund Islamist movements. Behind these bank, we are likely to find Saudis, Kuwaitis, and Pakistanis. It is true that a certain number of Islamic bank founders, such as the Saudi Salih Kamil who directs the Baraka groups, are ardent Muslims, personally concerned with offering an Islamic alternative to the existing banks.

The goal is to tap into a type of savings among "Islamic" depositors and not to finance Islamic movements or even to contribute to the creation of Islamised spaces. The "Islamic bank" is a marketing tool and not a scheme for a new economic order. That Islam is an inviting product is confirmed by the fact that several banks, without changing their commercial operations, have opened an "Islamic" branch, or even just a window, or provide "Islamic" interpretations of their practices. The following example, which is quite conventional, appeared in a bilingual French-Arab monthly:

> The Winterthur Company... is offering very favourable conditions for the insurance of your possessions; and we are doing even more. For moral reasons connected to religion, it is not desirable to speak of life insurance. Winterthur has established a savings account to be withdrawn by specified parties. The name of this contract is *Cap Retraite*. The idea is this: by signing this contract, you open a savings account that is remunerated, for several years, at an annual rate of 12.5 per cent. As you will see,

> Winterthur pays its clients a share of 95 per cent of the profits....

In brief, it is a matter of translating into Islamic terms (no speculation on death, share in the profits) a financial product defined by the French minister of finance and unrelated to a Quranic exegesis. The financial facts do not change; the presentation does.

An Impossible Islamic Economy

The Islamisation of the economy is thus broadly rhetorical. The failure of the Iranian revolution to transform the society chips away at the dream of a purely Islamic economic. All a ardent Muslim can do is bring his activities into conformity with the *sharia*: to do so, he can either withdraw from the modern world or utilise the instruments for the purification of profits, the Islamic banks and windows. But as far as the economy advances, these institutions function between two models, neither of which is specifically Islamic: the declining model of the centralised, socialist-leaning state, or the triumphant model of liberalism and capitalism.

The "Islamisation" of the economy is, to borrow a terms from computer terminology, an interface between two systems: one ethical and legal (the *sharia*), the other the reality of the global economy. The conversation works in only one direction; it is a simply transference, with hardly any effect on the reality. This interface can function not only in terms of rhetoric, but also through the "ruse" (*hile*) that prepares one to get around interdictions, particularly the one regarding interest: the ruse can be considered legal if appearances are sound.

The economic institution is never considered as such: everything stands on individual virtue. But the economies of modern societies assume that whatever the motivation and the goals of each individual, mechanisms are in place that meld the incongruity of the actors and their actions into a whole, the market, independent of their individual wills, but more or less regulated by institutions (states, stock exchanges). The notion of building a modern economy that would function only through the virtue of the economic actors is an illusion, one to be sure in terms of collectivist utopias, but for this reason totally nonfunctional, as various attempts have shown. And, in economics as in politics, when virtue doesn't function, its opposite appears: the abuse of power, speculation, and corruption, the banes of "Islamised" economic systems.

Here again the social sciences are unregarded. Islamism is distinguished by a sheer absence of socioeconomic analyses (causes of inflation, definition of economic agents, and so on) except in the rare instances in which a recent university graduate sets himself the task of translating his final honours paper into vaguely religious terms.

The object of the reflection is never the society, but man and the revealed text. We are thus still within the framework of the meeting of anthropology and ethics: if the economic agent acted properly and with the *sharia* in mind, then the society (and he himself) would be just and prosperous. Disorder come from transgressing the rules set forth by God, which attempt to keep man at a happy medium between the satisfaction of his needs and his ethical goal. Like politics, the Islamic economy is the summary of a matrix borrowed from the West with legal terminology based on an ethical anthropology.

Fifteen

New Masterminds

We have briefly discussed the sociology of the Islamist movement and have noted that the militants of political Islam came invariably from the modern educational system, but found themselves in a position of degraded social status. They reject the ulemas, whom they accuse of making compromises with modern society, but do not possess their theological knowledge. They also reject as "Christian" or "colonial" the analysis of their very own society in terms of the human sciences. They have thus broken with the ulemas and with the Westernised Muslim intellectuals who, whatever their political positions, accept the idea of modern, universal intellectual knowledge unconnected to religion. We are now going to examine the relationship to knowledge that marks contemporary Islamist intellectuals with respect to these two other categories. This undertaking appears useful in order to mark the ways in which the premises of political Islam also correspond to a kind of existential premise, a gap between two cultures and sometimes between two languages an incongruity between the Islamist's sociological origins and the mythical origins of the society of his dreams, between a body knowledge he hasn't mastered and the categories in which he conceives of it, between an image of himself as an intellectual and a society that offers no future — in brief, the discomfort of the Islamist and neofundamentalist lumpen-intelligentsia, those whom I will call here the "new intellectuals." For, as we have noticed the age of thinkers has finally come to an end. Now it is the era of reassessment or emigration.

Relationship to Knowledge

It is their relationship to knowledge that allows us to distinguish between clerical scholars (the ulemas), Westernised intellectuals, and "new intellectuals". These three figures do not belong exclusively to the Muslim society (we also find them in Western cultural history), but they coexist today in an original configuration. Four criteria characterise the relationship to intellectual knowledge (as opposed to technical or mythical knowledge): the definition of a compilation of texts; the position of a universal principle that explains the world, which makes sense by unifying the social field through a practice of values (religious, ethnic, political, or simply "rational"); a discursive instrument, language as a principle of rational explication; and ultimately the designation of an "other" (the secular man as opposed to the cleric, the illiterate as opposed to the educated, or common sense as opposed to the philosopher), whether this distinction is institutionalised (by a diploma, membership in a group, or the exercise of a profession) or experienced as a value.

Clerical scholars and Western-style intellectuals initially distinguish themselves by their respective relationships to the corpus. For the clerical scholar, the corpus is closed, it is a fact that one comments upon; it is anchored with supreme authority, and the relationship one maintains with it is a religious, and thus not a critical, one. The compilation is first and foremost a library, and the ulema's curriculum consists in memorising and commenting of a finite number of books, which are themselves commentaries on *the* Book. The compilation is homogeneous, even though this homogeneity may be a creation after the fact. The discourse is gloss: it aims to make clear and explain rationally something whose base is beyond reason.

For the Western-type intellectual, on the contrary, the text loses its sacredness. It is resituated in its historical actuality and contingency; it is open, for one can at any moment introduce new breaking points and add fresh elements, it is heterogeneous, in the sense that it juxtaposes elements of different cultural and historical origins. The intellectual assumes the desacralisation of the corpus and of the world. Thus, historicisation brings up the matter of politics, which no doubt most clearly separates clerics and intellectuals of today.

The passage from the clerical scholar to the intellectual does not seem to have been a historical course. Certainly, one can present Western history as a passage *sui generis* from the cleric to the intellectual; but just as the cleric may reappear beneath the intellectual, so the figure of the intellectual was already present in Greek philosophy, which was obsessed with politics, or in the medieval jurist, whose nominalism was a manner of desacralising the text and bringing forth the law of will, thus of politics, and not of the text, thus the sacred. The disappearance of the cleric in the West has not caused the sacred relationship to the text merely to disappear: the definition of a closed corpus that is beyond criticism, the historicity of which is rejected and which cannot be commented upon, is found in classical mythology, in Marxism, and even in a certain Freudianism: the "returns to ..." that have occurred in France over the last twenty years are returns to the behaviour of the cleric on the part of intellectuals; the teaching of Marxism in socialist countries was also based on a cleric's perception.

Institutionalisation of Clerics

Only for the intellectual do politics exist, since for the clerical scholar politics remain contingent as compared to the ethics deduced from the text. For ulemas, the rejection to distinguish religion from politics indicates a devaluation of politics and not their elevation to the rank of the universal. The cleric can express opinions on political issues in the name of the ethics derived from the corpus, but his conception of politics boils down to an imitation of the founding model or an expression of the leader's virtue. Politics in this sphere always lie between the empirical reality and ethics. The cleric who gets involved in politics is either an adviser to the prince or an exile.

In contrast to the cleric, who wonders about the reasonableness of the sovereign (is he fulfilling his role? Is he a good Muslim?), the intellectual wonders about the legitimacy of the state. He considers himself as bringing some distance and reflection to the foundations of this legitimacy: legitimacy cannot be summarized to the state's capacity to put an ethical or religious model into practice, but has to do with its very origin. The intellectual thus appears at a moment when the model of the state exists as separate and distinct from the person of the sovereign and as a historical process: History replaces the ruler. History is the intellectual's universal principle.

Western-style intellectuals and clerical masterminds have one point in common: their social status is promised by processes of investiture and authorisation that distinguish them from the masses. The clerical scholar is a former student of the religious schools and is admitted by a master or a chapter. The intellectual has a university diploma, whose curriculum has in many cases been completed in the West. Both have a vocation to exist as a "profession," the intellectual mostly within the limits of university, the ulemas within a judicial system. The contemporary breadth of the state apparatus turns them primarily into functionaries and occasional competitors — both for certain posts and for control of the commanding ideology — but in solidarity as representatives of a state establishment.

In the Muslim world, the eternity of the clerical scholar is significant: the ulemas maintain legitimacy if not power. Unlike the procedure within the Catholic church, they exist as association and not as a clergy; that is, they derive their status not from an institution in which they are members, but from a relationship to knowledge attained according to procedures that are defined and controlled by the corporation — at least until the recent efforts by various states, from Morocco to the former Soviet Union, to create a bureaucratised clergy, on which the state would henceforth bestow investiture. The corporation of the Muslim cleric has its own network of self-perpetuation (the *madrasa*), but it is presently experiencing a problem of social and economic insertion: what do ulemas do, and who pays them? The ulemas are becoming "modern" rather than marginal. At the very top, the great *madrasa* resemble universities, and the ulemas are now functionarises, all of which brings their status closer to that of Westernised intellectuals. On the bottom, there is an increasing "lumpenisation" of smalltime mullahs, who must find a second profession, as immigrant workers or peddlers, in the manner of the "new intellectuals," whose journey in the reverse way leads them to become mullahs.

The New Intellectual

What permits us to speak of "new intellectuals"? First a sociological change, as observed in Chapter 2: the advent, in a period of population explosion, of a new category of educated individuals produced by the recent expansion in state-funded education established on Western lines. These young people are hard pressed to find positions or professions that correspond to their expectations or visions of themselves, either in the state mechanism (the administrations are saturated), in industry (national capitalism is weak), or, for that matter, in the traditional network (devaluation of religious schools) or new universities (where Westernised intellectuals feel a loss of social status themselves). Whereas Western societies were able to unite the new lower middle classes graduating from the mass educational system with a differentiated "trade" or "professional" status, the newly "educated" of the Muslim society find no social ratification, either genuine or symbolic, for what they perceive as their new status. Note the persistence of the term "educated" (*muta'allim* in the Arab World, *ta'lim kardi* in Afghanistan, or simply "educated" in Pakistan), designating a class that is no longer distinguished in the West, where the terms "high school student," "college student," and so on prefer to designate states, not results. The boundaries that mark the differences between "people of the pen" (ulemas, scribes, university professors) and the *vulgum pecus* are growing indistinct through the combined effects of mass literacy, the democratisation of the means of transmitting knowledge (television, offset-printed brochures, cassettes) which facilitate access to a popularised discourse, and the impoverishment of the middle classes. The corpus is no longer defined by a place and a specific process of acquisition: anything printed or even "said" (cassettes) is the compilation. This lack of definition of the field of knowledge results in a lack of definition of the status of the "educated". The new intellectuals live in continuous tension: they repeatedly demand the right to manipulate, even to monopolise symbols (especially since they disqualify Westernised intellectuals for their lack of authenticity, and ulemas for excessive traditionalism and compromise with unlawful powers), while their weak separation from the other, the "uneducated," is patent in terms of social and professional status. The educated also live from small trades, also work as taxi drivers or night watchmen. Education provides them neither knowledge nor power nor status.

It is thus all the more important to distinguish oneself as "educated" because there is no evident sign of this condition: neither social status, nor operational knowledge (like that of the technician), nor income, nor institution, like the mosque. The new intellectual identifies himself by his attire (the Islamic "look" combines an often anachronistic return to traditionalism with marks of modernity, like pens and parkas), by his language (use of a language and not a dialect, with an affluence of neologisms and borrowed terms), as well as, and particularly, through political contestation or, as a last resort, withdrawal to a sect. The marking of a difference with respect to the other, is based on the way one presents oneself, since neither the state nor the society furnishes institutional criteria for recognising the category.

Trifling and Mysticism

Behind the sociological mutation, a new mode of acquiring knowledge is being sketched out, which in turn is creating a new sphere of knowledge. In this mode of acquisition, we find both a quasi-mystical and ontological perception of knowledge — which acts in a sense by proxy, outside any normed and discursive acquisition — a true autodidactic practice.

For the new breed of intellectuals, neither the transmission of knowledge nor the place of this transmission is institutionalised. Everyone is "authorised". The modes of authorisation of the cleric and of the Westernised intellectual (investiture by a master or an exam) are refused for they occur within the framework of the institution. Instead the new intellectuals approach knowledge with the attitude that the state, the institution, and even the society have lost their genuineness; they are perceived as steeped in ignorance and sin (*jahiliyya*). There is no "body" of new intellectuals. Although the Western-style intellectual has always claimed the individualisation of thought as his privilege (as well as freedom of thought and independence with respect to the state), he is every bit as defined by membership in the body to which he belongs as the ulemas, a body with its own schemes of acceptance and legitimation. The Western-style intellectual insists that the state itself organise a free zone within the institution (university charters, autonomous hiring and promotion procedures, freedom of expression).

The state has no means by which it can command the new Islamist intellectual in his social function. His thought does not correspond to his social status, he does not live from his profession, the networks of his activities are on the fringe of institutions, when they are not entirely secret. He operates in remote places (meeting houses, sites of worship, educational centres) and in spaces outside the traditional society that the state has not resocialised (the new suburbs). For the state, better a Marxist university professor than a sermonising, vagabond new intellectual. The problems for the police has always been to create a setting, whether it be mafia or criminal, red-light or university: they wish to place, check, anchor, the better to control. There is a very distinct relationship between the configuration of the new intellectual's knowledge and the form he assumes socially. The new intellectual is voluntarily outside the existing norms, although he may dream of a new society.

Of what does the new intellectual's corpus consist? It is fragmented off and borrowed from different matrices (Western-style curricula, the religious corpus, educational manuals assembled by the state as a function of its ideological imperatives of legitimation ...); this corpus is accessible in a popularised, fragmented form. The new intellectual juxtaposes the educational programmes of the "modern" establishments he attended and the religious tradition, to which he has had indirect access (through a religious school he may have attended during his childhood or through a member of his family while waiting for the preacher to come knocking at the door). In both cases, the corpus is differing and fragmented, never grasped as a whole. In both areas, the techniques of apprenticeship are identical, based on memorisation and repetition: the student learns snatches of information by heart. Yet this obvious symmetry does not produce the same effects. These modern schools lack a progressive pedagogical approach, as well as the unifying figure of the professor (who is overworked, poorly paid, and who therefore must be paid to make himself available). The *madrasa*, on the contrary, constitutes a social, intellectual, effective "milieu"; the master is approachable, and there attaches to him the image of unified body of knowledge, which the student has yet to master. The cleric, finally, is certain of the collection and of its closure, even if the content is infinite; the excerpt refers back to the original. This corpus is guaranteed by the Tradition and History; it is sealed by an act of faith, by belief in a Revelation developed in its analyses. But how can the new intellectual recreate the universal from a corpus that has been broken to pieces?

The new intellectual has an autodidactic relationship to knowledge. Knowledge is obtained in a fragmented (manuals, excerpts, popular brochures), encyclopedic, and immediate manner: everything is discussed without the intervention of an apprenticeship, a method, or a professor. Popularisation implies direct access to material that has become dogmatic through the confusion of the procedures by which it emerged. The new media, such as radio, television, cassettes, and inexpensive offset brochures, make snatches of this content available. The new intellectual is a tinkerer, he prepares a montage, as his personal itinerary guides him, of divisions of knowledge, using methods that come from a different conceptual universe than the segments he recombines, creating a corpus that is more imaginary than theoretical. The absence of a genuine, purely mastered corpus is compensated for by reference to an emblematic knowledge, which one may display but may not study, for the alternative step would imply becoming a scientist or a clergyman, which the "modern" educational network that produces the new intellectual would not allow. It is evident that Science with a capital "S" (the type that allows us to say: "modern Science has shown that ..."), the Quran (with which they are not so much familiar, but which they know has an answer to everything) or historical materialism (in the past ...) would serve as frames of reference and not as objects of knowledge, for the more inestimable and transcendent the domain is considered to be, the less one has to answer to its content.

The field of knowledge evoked in this way is enormous, with neither closure nor norm: one can speak with equal authority of sociology, nuclear physics, economics, or theology. It is true that such a configuration is similar to a French high school senior-year philosophy textbook, for example, but the methodology is lacking, or rather the notion of methodology and the unifying figure (the "professeur," in the case of French secondary schools).

What is gone is the ritual of transmission, which is as important for clerics as it is for intellectuals: the corpus appears immediately accessible, available. Thus, one of the elements of the new Islamist intellectuals is: "Everything is in the Quran," followed by an immediate offer of demonstration regarding any theme proposed.

For want of mediators, the reconstitution of this knowledge as totality and truth happens on the basis of a religious position: this point (along with the weakness of social insertion) separates the new Islamist intellectual from his European counterpart, who is also a product of the mass educational system, who appropriates a corpus in an autodidactic and ideological fashion, and who has equipped the mass of post-1968 "leftist" militants. The new Islamist intellectual borrows from religion the unifying figure that is absent in the knowledge proposed by the school. Fragmentary modern knowledge, acquired autodidactically, is integrated within a Quranic intellectual structure, developing, on the one hand, the image of a transcendent totality, the *tawhid* (the oneness of God, which extends to His Creation), in which all knowledge comes together, and, on the other hand, a terminology taken from the Tradition, supported by the citation of verses, but often positioned as the equivalent of concepts issued from modern ideologies. The two multitudes of knowledge (modern through brochures and manuals, Quranic by citation) in fact cover a "do-it-yourself" creation, the juxtaposition of segments of knowledge into a whole whose logic cannot be curtailed to the sum of its parts. Yet the new intellectual's segments of knowledge also include ready-made ideological schemes, such as Marxism. The synthesis takes different forms depending on whether one is talking about a politicised Islamist or a neofundamentalist. The former gives priority to the conceptual space of the borrowed ideology, with the Quran decorating only the language to enable the rewriting of Marxism: this was the case of the Iranian Islamists (with the term *mustadafin*, for example, "damned of the earth"), who retain the unifying status of the *tawhid*, the mythical site of the montage's unity. The approach is reminiscent of Christian "liberation theology." The neofundamentalist, on the other hand, will simply insert popularised scientific information within the strands of a religious sermon: less politicised, less preoccupied with the matter of the state and the revolution, he conceives of the formation of a truly Islamic society more through the re-Islamisation of Muslims in contact with the Western world than through an Islamic revolution. In this he agrees with the traditionalist clergy.

Rejecting Methodology

Let's return to a seemingly unobjectionable point, but one in which the conception of knowledge and its position with respect to the state and institutions come together: the general objection against school and university exams, and not only among Islamists. The rejection of examinations implies the rejection of access to knowledge as a compelled, normalised reading process. The exam simultaneously denies self-proclamation, the figure of the master, and the image of knowledge as truth founded in transcendency. On an exam, the relationship to knowledge is analytic and presumes a graduated progression that can be measured in years. The rejection of examination is a challenge not to the concept of the progressive acquisition of knowledge (nothing is more gradual than a Sufi initiation), but rather to the idea that knowledge can be decomposed, classified—in brief, that it is a process of reduction not grasped all at once as a whole. The image of knowledge that is resurfacing underneath this challenge is, on the one hand, that of the traditional *madrasa*, where acquisition occurs at the student's own pace, and on the other hand that of Sufism, in which access to complete knowledge (to the state of total man) retrospectively devalues the path of access. As in the Platonic myth of the cave, there is a qualitative escalation between apprenticeship and knowledge, while according to the Western, Cartesian conception of knowledge, science is the set of its methods of acquisition. In the human sciences, the methods of learning about reality are ultimately richer than the reality, and in any case are never meant to fade before the result. Herein lies the major difference: the methods of access to knowledge are valid in and of themselves in modern Western science, whereas they negate themselves in access to the One. The university exam shows that access to knowledge depends on the process in which an institution has decided to break up the knowledge (especially since exams are made up of questions and answers that must be learned by heart), not on the essence of the knowledge: it is the rejection of knowledge as oneness. And this oneness is the assumption of all autodidacticism, but also of all religion.

The negation of institutional validation emphasises the process of delegitimation of the state, which is always present in Muslim countries, and again raises the problem of authority: who is the master? For, to return to our previous criteria, one's contrast with the "other", those who don't know (whether the ignorance is that of the "illiterate" or of the *jahiliyya*), can be established only through a decisive, even hostile act, for want of set procedures recognised by the new intellectuals. This is the violence of the new intellectual faced with the violence of the state.

A Perfect Man

If we take it that all knowledge can be combined in the figure of the divine *tawhid*, how can this unity occur in man? Here we find that the new intellectuals readopt, more or less explicitly, one of the Muslim mystic's traditional figures, that of Perfect Man (*insan-e-kamil*), which is the place where all knowledge merges, not because perfect Man has systematically acquired it, but because he himself is the image of God. Knowledge, seen as a transcendent totality, cannot be acquired by a quantifiable, normative accumulation, but only by the transformation of the individual being, by a change. It is in the reality of the complete and Perfect Man, as also in a corpus or in History, that one can read the universal, that all knowledge seems reasonable and that the return to the golden age — the time of the Prophet — is foreshadowed. It is with this mystical notion of knowledge that the new intellectual completes his indigenous construction. We have here the primary ethical and mystical concept that in fact conditions all Islamist thought.

Access to truth suggests a break with *jahiliyya*, ignorance composed more of false knowledge than of emptiness, or rather, belief that this false notion is enough to fill the world. Just as *jahiliyya* is as much baseless scientific position as it is "sin," so true knowledge is first and foremost a matter of ethics and faith. The constant citation from and chanting of the Quran regarding every topic — using the *bismillah* to introduce all discourse, for instance

- whether it has to do with politics or with nuclear physics, is the magical act that subsumes incomplete knowledge into the divine unity and makes whoever pronounces it more than just a scientist, who may say the same thing, but not situating it within the absolute.

According to the myth of Perfect Man, insan-e-kamil, it is the ethical disposition of one's soul that gives unity to one's knowledge and practices. The hidden assumption is that one can have access to knowledge beyond the methods of acquisition, which are confronted on the levels both of methodology and of the institution. The first is seen as an importation of Western thought and ideology, which boils down to rejecting the transcendency and the basic totality of the sacred; the second is seen as a tool of an integrationist and *jahili* state, which denies the ultimate goals in favour of self-perpetuation. These two points mark the break with the Westernised intellectual: the latter accepted the validity of the methodology and organisation of Western knowledge (but not the underlying values and philosophy), and sought to ensure the autonomy of the university with respect to the state, without denying the justification of associating the goals of knowledge and the aims of the state (the problem was thus that of the "good state"). The new intellectual questions the university in and of itself, in its methods as in its relations with the state.

This emphasis on "oneness" devalues partial knowledge as such (research is not highly regarded), but does place value on its use for defensive purposes or for winning over society; both the cultured advocate and the Islamist engineer find meaning here in the autodidactic method of acquisition: in their eyes, trifling with pieces of knowledge is not a sign of ignorance, but indicates the fundamental relationship between partial bits of knowledge and truth, God's transcendency. Knowledge is not the result of methodical reasoning, but a mystical object, which is refracted and fragmented into the many facets of the world.

Although Sufism is generally devalued by the new intellectuals, the notion of Perfect Man that conditions their relationship to knowledge, action, and leadership is of mystical origin. But this mysticism harks back to militant, conquering Sufism, defender of the *sharia,* more than to popular maraboutism. Islamist vocabulary is often procured from the Sufi world: *da'wa* ("call"), *muballigh* ("preacher"), and so on.' The objective is to create a total, wise, fighting man, and especially one who has experienced a kind of "mental conversion": beyond education, this conversion consists in a new vision of the world. Ideological formation is more important than deriving knowledge.

The reality of Perfect Man implies a negation of differences (except between the sexes). There are neither ethnic groups, tribes, classes, nor *madhahib* (schools of jurisprudence), and History is but a parenthesis, a moment of instruction before the return of the golden age. Hence the difficulty in conceptualising fragmentation, differences, distances, as well as failure. All differentiation not founded on a moral or metaphysical essence (*batil* versus *haqiqa*, "false" versus "true": this is how Iran displayed the war against Iraq) becomes the product of a plot, an external interference against what is one. The subject-matter of the oneness of the political party is expressed in this way: *la hizb illa hizb Allah*, "no other party than the party of God."

Praise of Science

Should we see this "tinkering" as an effect of the cultural and social crises or as a desire to reconstitute the field of knowledge, to recreate an order? Both Islamists and neofundamentalists praise "science" (ilm), which is first religious knowledge, but also general knowledge, an indication of the absence of borders between the areas of knowledge. We have seen (Chapter 4) Islamism's profound renunciation of the human sciences, which are always accused of deconstructing All — the world, society, the human psyche, reality itself — and thus of rejecting divine oneness. Ethical, religious, or anthropological knowledge can only be commented upon, since they are given by the Revelation. For all the Islamic reformers of our century, the very sciences pose fewer theological problems than the human sciences: God gave man the physical world for man "to discover" ("seek science all the way to China," says a famous *hadith*); as for the fundamental principles of modern science, they are already present in the Quran in metaphorical form. While men at the time of the Revelation failed to understand this knowledge, the study of these basic principles can only lead back to unity: the unity of creation.

The pure or applied sciences are presented as the illustration of the congruity of All, of divine will, of the rationality of the One. Popularisation plays a role here. The new intellectual's reinvesting of technical knowledge with broader significance (a process disdained by Westernised intellectuals) is characteristic of this perception of integrity which though disparaged by the human sciences is on the contrary re-established, in paradigmatic and defensive fashion, by the "exact sciences": one seeks in the Big Bang theories, for instance, proof of God's instantaneous creation of the world. The engineer is more an advocate than a militant: his profession gives him a wealth of paradigms and explanations of God's greatness. Scientism and religion work hand in hand.

In seeking a status, it is fitting to distance oneself from the "people". Since this distance is not adequately clear, the new intellectual recreates one by analysing popular religious practice, adopting the *salafiyya's* rationalist discourse against the marabout, against the cult of saints and superstitions. The access to reason and science finds new meaning here: rationalism, or ratiocination, is the common ground between the cleric, the Westernised intellectual, and the new intellectual.

Illusory Exercise of Interpretation

The new Islamist intellectual thus demands the right to manipulate a meandering and rational instrument. Resolutely rationalist (herein lies his rupture with Sufism), he demands the renunciation of *taqlid* (the tradition of exegesis) and a return to *ijtihad*, the sole way to get around the body of ulemas. In effect, the return to *ijtihad* devalues the corpus, insofar as its commentary is no longer the essential task of the learned, and especially insofar as the corpus becomes a simple point of departure, even just a reference, ever susceptible to being transformed into rhetoric, proverbs, epigraphs, and interpolations—in brief, into a reservoir of quotes. For the new Islamist intellectual, it is a matter of reclaiming religious legitimacy, in opposition to Westernised intellectuals, while also claiming rationality and science. A political speech will begin with a Quranic hook, a few verse meant not to explain, but to anchor the speech in superemacy, even if what is said is purely secular, even Marxist. The two worlds, that of the

Tradition (the Quran) and of modernity (political discourse) mirror each other, complementarily illustrating each other in a rhetoric that may be hair-splitting but is never inventive. The call to relaunching *ijtihad* does not bring innovation, but tinkering. Since the corpus (whether borrowed from the religious world or from the library of the Westernised intellectual) is above criticism, political discourse remains on the level of defensive advocating. One aims to demonstrate what is true prior to the demonstration, so that the new intellectual is always seeking some form of intervention toward this knowledge: hence the importance of the party, the leader, or the guide. The leader can speak about everything, he has enlightenment on each and every subject and it is only because he is called to higher tasks that he doesn't have time to produce particular knowledge. It is in the spirit of *taqlid*, simulation, that one demands *ijtihad*, critical innovation.

Institutionalisation of New Intellectuals

Although the new intellectual is the result of a process of marginalisation from and maladjustment to the state, institutions and models of knowledge, he is nonetheless being granted institutional status today thanks to petrodollars. During the 1980s a movement to give birth to a new kind of Islamic school or institute (between a *madrasa* and a university) began moulding in the Muslim world: in Nigeria, in Iran and Shiite Lebanon, in Saudi Arabia and in France. These new institutions, both state-run and private, endeavour to return to the corpus and the projects of the new intellectuals, to turn out "militants" or preachers, even bureaucrats. It is noteworthy that in places where the state has taken charge of this institutionalisation, it is occurring in the form of institutes or centres of militant training, never as a reorganisation of the educational system, which continues to function according to the dichotomy between Westernised systems and Quranic schools (whether in Nigeria or in Iran).

The project is most organised and developed in Iran. The goal is to train *homo islamicus*, a modern technocrat who thinks according to Islamic ideology, captivating modern science without being corrupted by Western values. Perfect Man is a polyvalent, ideologised man. It is because knowledge is grasped within the framework of a globalising ideology (explicitly called "Islamic ideology") that it is assumed to be total by association. The explicit expression of this perfection depends in fact on breadth of education, which extends from theology to living languages, from weapons handling to the study of Islamic "psychology". An instance of this training is found at the Rizayi University of the Astan-i Quds (a pious foundation that manages the sanctuary) in Mashhad, set-up by the Islamic Republic of Iran. Here one finds both the religious structures of the *madrasa* and the pedagogical frameworks of the modern university: the curriculum is counted in years and not in books read; subjects taught include more modern disciplines than customary ones; the rooms are laid out in amphitheatres, even though the students prefer to sit in circles, cross-legged, at the foot of the tiers; the equipment is modern, with audiovisual courses and libraries managed by computers. It is a university setup both for mullahs and for the secular, where specialisation begins only after a common core of study; at which point one chooses to become either a mullah or a multipurpose technocrat (an Islamist higher civil servant).

These institutes are still in operation, but they provide few high-level executives, and their impact remains marginal.

Other educational networks exist in purely neofundamentalist context: they are financed directly or indirectly by the Saudis, often within the framework of the World Muslim League. These institutes have the advantage of up-to-date technology (in computer science, for example), but the content of the teaching is based entirely on the reformist fundamentalism particular to the Salafists and Wahhabis. Many of the students are "new intellectuals" who are thus transformed into preachers and mullahs. Their approach to the modern world is similar to that of the old-time Christian missionaries: "learn the other's culture the better to fight against it". Languages and science are taught to apologetic ends: to show the excellence of Islam and it, capability to respond to the challenges of modernity, not by adapting, but rather by returning to its true foundations.

These institutes and research centres have become bustling sites of intense activity, with publications, conferences, colloquia and seminars. The production of the network differs from the

Islamist message in that it escapes the question of state legitimacy, out of consideration for the Saudi financial backers, but deals with the whole of society; the message is thus distinctively neofundamentalist. The issues of both the Islamic bank and the relationship between the Quran and modern science are discussed. This network permits the new intellectual elite to find easy funding for any discourse that bolsters Islam, any programme of Islamisation, any rereading of science or of history in Islamic terms; plagiarism and pirating of other texts are frequent. An autodidactic literature, turned academic in one fell swoop, thus propagates within a modern system of production and distribution.

This intellectually weak production aims for a broad public, circulating among the "new intellectuals" as well as representing a legitimate area of knowledge for sections of the population that have received little education, who are cut off from quality teaching in their own language yet nostalgic for "culture": this is persistently the case among Muslim emigrants in Europe, who are literate yet not harmonised into the culture of the host country, and who work in manual or commercial jobs (the Pakistanis in England). Thus a lumpenintelligentsia perpetuates itself.

Sixteen

Sociology of Islamism

Beginning in the 1960s, demographic increase and rural exodus in the countries of the Middle East swelled the population of cities, where the state was unable to ensure the functioning of public services or even simple urbanisation. At the same time, the development of education, combined with budgetary restrictions, and thus a relative decline in jobs offered by the state, increased the number of intellectuals forced into the lower classes. Not only were there no jobs to meet their aspirations, but conditions at the universities worsened, disposing them to participate in various forms of protest.

The educational systems follow a Western style of teaching. They are generally coed (except of course in Saudi Arabia) and experienced marked development between 1950 and 1980, followed by stagnation and decline. If one considers the case of Egypt, the cradle of the extremist groups of the 1960s, one observes that during this decade the number of students doubled, while demographic growth was at 2.8 per cent a year. Today in Egypt there is one doctor for every 770 inhabitants: in most cases their status is that of underpaid bureaucrats (the equivalent of about thirty-five dollars a month for someone starting out in 1989); in the same way, the country produces more engineers (3000 per year in 1989) than it needs. Literacy is around 50 per cent. In Iran, at the time of the revolution 1979, 65 per cent of the urban population was literate, climbing to 83 per cent for men aged fifteen to thirty — the main participants in the revolution. In 1988 in Tunisia, 54 per cent of the population was literate.

At the same time, these hard-won diplomas were devalued for want of openings. The states were incapable of absorbing the fresh graduates, despite a kind of "right to employment" policy (in Egypt, in Afghanistan before 1978, and in Saudi Arabia) by which the state systematically offered jobs to the new graduates; but this policy had another ill consequence: the state became the graduate's sole horizon. An intellectual was a bureaucrat. In the meantime, the various policies of liberalisation and government cuts instituted in the 1970s under pressure from the International Monetary Fund (the policy of *infitah* — opening up — in Egypt, beginning in 1971; the policy of President Chadli Benjedid in Algeria) led to devalued status for the intellectual-bureaucrat. Liberalisation of the economy essentially favoured the private sector; salaries were consumed by inflation and declined relative to the new rich; the bureaucrat had to take a second job in order to survive (taxi driver, night watchman at an international hotel); the business sector became politically more important than the intellectual one. The state forgot the intellectuals, and they could not adapt. Indeed, university education is largely bookish, even in medicine, and out of synch with the social and economic realities. A graduate sees himself as a member of a caste; he assumes that he should no longer be subjected to physical labour, or even to physical contact; he strives to mark his difference on his physical person, in his clothing for instance. He is thus not very receptive to his new proletarian status, to which he responds by ideologising his condition and dreaming of a revolution and a new, strong, centralised state.

Cadres of the Islamist Party

The cadres of the Islamist parties are young intellectuals, educated in government schools following a Westernised curriculum and in many cases from recently urbanised families. At the university, the Islamists recruit more from engineering than from philosophy departments, with one exception: the teacher's training colleges. The pattern of the Islamist cadre is an engineer, born sometime in the 1950s in a city but whose parents were from the country. Some, the elite, have even completed their studies in the West. The Council of Iranian Ministers is an instant example of this sociological tendency (Vilayati, the minister of foreign affairs, is a pediaetrician educated in the United States; Nabavi, formerly minister of industry, is an engineer also educated in the United States). This is equally true of the former Turkish president Turgut Ozal, who once militated for an Islamist party, Erbakan's National Salvation, after pursuing his engineering degree at the Massachusetts Institute of Technology; in the 1970s, one-fourth of the deputies in this party were engineers. Abd al-Salam Yasin, the Moroccan Islamist leader, is an inspector for French language teaching in the national education department.

Thus the emergence of contemporary political Islam is in no way the return of a medieval, obscurantist clergy crusading against modernity. Muslim revolts today are urban: Tehran in 1978-1979, Hama (Syria) in 1982, Asyut in a frequent manner in Egypt, Gaza in Palestine, Algiers, and, in Lebanon, southern Beirut and Tripoli. The only recent armed peasant revolt in the name of Islam occurred in Afghanistan and owes its strength to the need to resist foreign invasion; but its cadres also come from the city and in many cases match the profile of the Islamist militant: Ahmad Shah Masud, the great leader from the north, is a former student of the Kabul Polytechnic; Gulbadin Hikmatyar, director of the Hizb-i Islami, was a student of the engineering school. In Algeria, the spokesperson for the FIS in 1991, Abd al-Qadir Hashani, was an oil engineer. All sociological studies regarding the Islamists lead to the same conclusions: they recruit from intellectual, urban milieus. It is a group that is sociologically modern, issued from the modernist sectors of the society. Rather than a reaction against the modernisation of Muslim societies, Islamism is a product of it.

With the beginning of 1970s, however, a new generation of Islamists emerged, less intellectual than the former. Student over-population, the weakening of the general norms of education, and the replacement of colonial languages (English and French) with national languages, which in some places are under the impediment of not being the normally spoken language (like modern Arabic in Algeria, as opposed to the dialect), brought about the rise of a young "lumpenintelligentsia"; they've spent enough time in school to consider themselves "educated" and not to want to return to the country or work in a factory (if these possibilities existed, which isn't the case), but they haven't pursued higher education. Spending on education took a downward trend in the Maghreb in the years 1980-1985 as compared with 1975-1980, while in Algeria

100,000 young people leave secondary school each year without being able to pursue their studies. Meanwhile, in the 1980s the Islamist movements recruited more from secondary schools than from universities: the change was noticed in 1983 in Pakistan. Unemployment among the educated is the main resource of the Islamist movements: the policies of "Arabisation," like the one implemented in Algeria in the 1970s, accentuates the phenomenon in that young "Arabists" who no longer even have the possibility of emigrating. This new generation is more neofundamentalist than Islamist, for it is intellectually less "Westernised" than the preceding generation.

The Islamists made progress everywhere, first on campuses and then, more solidly, among the recently urbanised masses. University elections reveal an Islamist breakthrough on campuses beginning in the early 1970s in Egypt, Pakistan, and Afghanistan. During the 1980s it was the Palestinians and the three North African countries that were most affected by the re-Islamisation of student milieus: a certain delay can be noted generally in the Maghreb with respect to the Middle East proper in the spread of the movement.

One of the reasons for this success is that the ideologies or groups (secular, nationalist, or Marxist) that fulfilled the need for protest were gradually losing momentum. Militant Arab nationalists, who are often socialist leaning, were absorbed by the state bureaucracies, from Algeria to Egypt to Iraq. The Palestine Liberation Organisation embarked on a process of international negotiation and recognition that brought no results for local people. The communist parties were unable to break out of their ghettos among the newly formed working classes, ethnic and religious minorities, or on campuses. Paradoxically, the communist or secular (ba'thist) parties have a more rural than an urban base (Hafiz al-Asad and Saddam Husain are from the country). In Afghanistan, Iraq, South Yemen, and Syria, the armies, vehicles of secular state coups, have officers of peasant origins.

Islamist gains in intellectual milieus can also be explained by a crisis in ideology. The general loss of prestige of progressive ideologies and the failure of the "Arab socialist" model have left room for new protest ideologies to appear in destructured societies in which the theories of roots and identity have suddenly resurfaced, in a quest not for a return to the past but for the readaptation of modernity to a newly-rediscovered identity. As a result of which the Islamists everywhere favour industrial development, urbanisation, education for the masses and the teaching of science. What they offer the oppressed and subjugated (*mustadafin*) of all countries is the dream of access to the world of development and consumption, from which they feel excluded. Islamism is the *sharia* plus electricity.

But the young Islamists are blocked by often archaic political systems in societies that are broadly modern. Power resides in patronage networks, in which nepotism and corruption are the exiting norm. In a country as developed as the Shah's Iran, for example, the summits of power functioned in the archaic ways of the seraglio and the court. In Syria and Iraq, power is held by *asabiyya*, solidarity groups founded on ethnicity, clan, and family. Following the riots of October 1988 in Algeria, the sole strategy of the party in power, the FLN (National Liberation Front), was to stay in power, which it did through a series of manipulations of electoral law. In Pakistan, both the conservative party and the Bhutto family's People's Party were arms of large families with industrial and land holdings. In Afghanistan and Lebanon, Islamism is slowly entering into open confrontation with the great tribal families: the Amal movement, founded by Imam Musa al-Sadr, established itself in the Lebanese Beka Valley against the influential Jaffar clan and assembled the new generation of educated youth around two religious families, the Musawis and the Husaynis. Finally, in countries such as Lebanon, Iraq, Afghanistan, and Pakistan, the simple fact of being a Shiite made a career in the army or government nearly impossible.

Deprived of a political future within the framework of the system, young intellectuals have minimal hope of finding a post equal to their ambitions either in an overcrowded state bureaucracy or in a national capitalist framework less concerned with development or in a national capitalist less concerned with development than with shady business and financing. For them the revolution suggests social integration and upward mobility. The revolution is being waged in the name of civil society, of the

Muslim *umma*, that is to say, for the universal good, against a state viewed as particularist, issuing from and hostage to an individual group.

Islamist Masses

You can't create a revolution solely with party cadres. You need masses. The masses of revolutionary Islam are also a product of modern society. Islamist themes resound little in the countryside, where people are often faithful to a popular, marabout-type Islam that includes few clergy. The modern masses are the new urban arrivals, the millions of peasants who have almost tripled the populations of the great Muslim metropolises in the past twenty years (Tehran's population increased from three to nine million between 1970 and 1990). It is not by chance that the Iranian revolution occurred the very year the proportion of city-dwellers in Iran crossed the 50 per cent mark. By 1988, 44 per cent of the populations of Algeria, Morocco, and Egypt were urbanised; in Tunisia, 54 per cent. Urbanisation and social problems are exacerbated by population growth, which exceeded 3 per cent annually in many countries (Algeria, Iran, Pakistan). It is true that the fertility rate (number of children per woman) is declining today (from 7.4 to 4.8 in Algeria between 1965 and 1987), following the dissemination of the Western cultural model, but it will take two decades for this downward trend to affect the rate of population growth. There is thus a mass of young people with minimal prospect for social mobility.

But these urban populations are different from the inhabitants of the traditional Muslim city, unlike a common analysis that sees Islamism as the bazaar's reaction against active industrialisation. The traditional Muslim city defined by the bazaar, the old city, the palace, professional organisations and trade guilds, neighbourhoods, and the absence of public space has disappeared. The Kasba in Algiers is crumbling; the old city of Fes is collapsing due to overpopulation. Everywhere the important families are leaving the bazaar and the centre; they are being replaced by an uprooted class that does not possess an urban culture. The traditional city is no more even though its memory still structures the surface appearances, as in the case of the bazaar in Tehran, which seems to be organised according to guilds, each with its own street and mosque; but what counts is the telephone that connects the store to New York and to the circle the shop owner frequents when he returns home at night, to the neighbourhoods in the north of city, far from all the pollution. A new space is being created, divided by avenues and squares where mass demonstrations can be staged; these cities are organised along social lines (in Tehran, north versus south; elsewhere, suburbs versus the inner city) or denominational divisions (in Beirut, west versus east). The urban explosion is causing shortage in housing and transportation. In Algeria in 1990, 80 per cent of youth aged sixteen to twenty-nine still lived with their parents, with an average of eight inhabitants to a room. The distant suburbs are connected to the centre by overcrowded buses. The city no longer offers places for socialising.

These new populations are squeezing into an urban space that the state has been unable to organise either with respect to infrastructures (water, sewers, transportation) or in terms of cultural or political structures. New neighbourhoods spring up in a mixture of squatting and real estate speculation, while the state is unable or reluctant to impose a strategy for urban development. They are not really shantytowns, but a juxtaposition of small houses constructed with makeshift materials, reproducing as well as possible the traditional Muslim home (rooms opening onto a small interior courtyard). The old clan or ethnic camaraderie, the clout of the elders, and family control are fading little by little in the face of changes in the social structure: uprootedness, absent fathers (emigration, long commutes, straining of the family fabric and a divorce rate unprecedented in the country), population explosions, unemployment, and so on. The crisis is constantly getting worse: in 1990 in Algeria, for example, economic growth was lower than population growth (2.4 per cent versus 2.7 per cent), unemployment affected 23 per cent of the active population, but especially the young. The repayment of foreign debt and the demands of the International Monetary Fund are leading to a notable increase in the price of staples, which had previously been subsidised. Salaried workers and bureaucrats are growing poorer and must often take on second jobs, which naturally leads to a downgrading in public services, beginning with education, and to the spread of corruption.

The unions and leftist movements, which are more bourgeois, have been unable to penetrate these new locales, where small trades and odd jobs are more common than true working-class jobs, considered the realm of the privileged.

Consumption and Frustration

The cultural models of consumption in these modern cities are those based on Western society; people dream of videos and cars, signs of success, ways of conspicuously displaying one's place in a new social hierarchy based on money. Shops and black markets are obliged to offer Western or Japanese "musts". Even the forms of leisure tend to be a compromise between the traditional way of life (centred upon the family) and a modern mode of consumption. The traditional society no longer furnishes a model for pleasure, aside from that of the ostentatious banquet, which in any case needs significant funds (and which the wealthiest segments of the population hold in large international hotels). Fast-food joints are flourishing, especially in places where cafes are banned (Iran). Modernisation involves the juxtaposition of conspicuous consumption on the part of the new rich with the new needs of the poor. Hence the riots over prices and the attacks against symbols of wealth and Westernisation that began in the 1970s: the "bread" riots in Cairo in January 1977, with attacks on the famous nightclubs of Pyramids Streets; the Casablanca riots which took place in 1983.

One minor but significant aspect of the success of Islamism is precisely that it offers frustrated youth a justification for their frustration. Western adoption in terms of culture has not freed up mores, or else has made pleasure financially inaccessible. Value is still attached to a girl's virginity, but age at marriage is rising, and the young are more licentious than they ever were in traditional society: everything is coed, from schools and universities to housing and transportation; temptation is reinforced by the model of sexual freedom conveyed through media like television, films, and magazines, but also by experiences of and stories about life in the West. Overall ruin and overpopulation make it difficult for young people to have independent lives. Pleasure is only reserved for the rich. The Islamists present a defense of chastity and virtue, a defense that is in fact widely divergent from a certain *art de vivre* inherent in Muslim civilisation. They transform what was previously a reflection of one's degraded self-image into a source of dignity.

Implantation and Preaching

The Islamists have endeavoured to "resocialise" these new urban spaces. In Iran, as in south Beirut and the Shiite sections of Baghdad it was the Shiite clergy, often aided by young Islamist militants, who performed this work of resocialisation, using the mosques as their bases of operation with sports clubs, mutual aid cooperatives, foundations to provide dowries for impoverished young girls, reading circles, political sermons, and so on. All this occurred in an ambience of puritanism that highlighted the alleged corruption of the ruling classes. All revolutions are puritanical (which is why May 1968 in Paris was not a revolution): the emergence of Islamic dress is merely a sign of this puritanism and of the anxiety of the neo-urbanised faced with the sudden and apparent degradation of values incarnated in the city. Only in Iran has there been a revolution, because only in that country could the *mustadafin* ("those who have fallen on earth," a category that corresponds to the newly-unbanised) be incorporated into this new framework, owing to the autonomy and free rein given to a well-organised Shiite clergy.

Militancy, strictly speaking, results more from religious preaching than from political training: the term used is da'wa, "call," "invitation," in fact "militant preaching"; Hasan al-Banna wrote a treatise titled *Da'watuna* (Our militant preaching). We find here the old tradition of the Ismaili da'i or of the Sufis, preachers of combat. But in this case the preaching emanates from the mosques, although it reflects a sensitivity to social issues and the influence of the Marxist model. It is addressed to specific groups (peasants, students, workers, members of the military). Social differentiation is taken as a basic fact, even if it is supposed to disappear in the archetype Islamic society. "Cells" are created at universities, in factories, in administrations. A socialisation process that was derailed by the weakening of the traditional solidarity networks is reinvented: clubs, libraries, night classes, mutual aid. In the 1940s, the Egyptian Muslim Brotherhoods started a network of schools, clinics, and even small industries. They created student and professional sections, geared in fact toward modern professions (lawyers, engineers, doctors, teachers, bureaucrats), as well as worker sections in which they encouraged unionisation. In south Lebanon, Imam Musa al-Sadr also developed social action to detach the Shiite population from the patronage of the influential families. The Islamists take into consideration the rural exodus and the break with traditional village, clan, or family support.

But the resocialisation is based on popular values, on a social rereading of Islam and the use of a language of moralisation and solidarity accessible to the people. No mention is made of the proletariat, but of the little person — the impoverished, the humiliated — to whom dignity and pride must be restored.

The Islamists take advantage of a popular religiosity that the ulemas do a poor job of exploiting, while lambasting its "deviations" (cults of saints). Young militants come to play the role of the sympathetic imam or mullah in the poorly-served or improvised mosques of newly-urbanised areas. We find here the "implantation" so dear to the French Maoists of 1968. The lines grow hazy between low-level clergy habitually co-opted by the base communities, and militants turned self-proclaimed mullahs, who portray and appropriate the new social spaces abandoned by the state (suburbs, university campuses, the new intelligentsia—) and by the traditional mullahs. The problem accordingly becomes one of expressing an often abstract discourse and radical practice in terms of a popular religious practice at times tainted by the very beliefs the Islamists castigate (Sufism, maraboutism), especially since this popular religious practice is presided over by a body of mullahs generally unsympathetic to Islamism.

Thus, the Islamists come to reassume certain functions that traditionally belong to ulemas and mullahs, despite their inherent anticlericalism. Maududi created his own *madrasa* in Mansura, in the suburbs of Lahore, which would gain the official recognition of the Pakistani state. In Afghanistan the government school of theology set-up in 1951 by the monarchy to check the tradition, alism of the *madrasa,* would become the training ground of the Islamists. Products of secular milieus, the Islamists would first rally and then produce their own ulemas, who would form or rejoin the moderate stream of the Islamic movements (Rabbani in Afghanistan, Hudaybi and Talmasani among the Egyptian MBs), while the fanatic sphere would lie in secular hands (Hikmatyar in Afghanistan).

Women

The Islamists have often recruited among women, especially in Iran. The issue of women, as we have seen, is one of the points on which Islamism parts with traditionalist fundamentalism. The Islamists consider women's role as an essential feature for education and the society. They see women as people, and no longer as mere instruments of sexual pleasure or reproduction. They are opposed to excessive dowries and divorces of convenience. Islamist organisations include entire women's sections, the "sisters", the first of which was formed in Egypt in 1944 (*al-akhawat al-muslimat,* "the Muslim sisters"). As early as 1933, al-Banna started a school for "the mothers of believers." Observers have all noted the presence and involvement of women in the Islamist movement: recall the demonstrations of armed and curtained women in Iran. Both Iran and Egypt boast and elite class of Islamist intellectual women who write and are published.

The Islamist woman militates and studies; she enters into politics, although she is excluded from certain posts: she cannot be a judge or a head of state. The Islamists' obsession is not that women should return to the home, but that the sexes be separated in public. The Islamists designate particular areas for women in mosques and public places. The invention of a new mode of dress (scarf, raincoat, gloves — basically a nunlike attire) allows women to achieve two contradictory objectives: to come out of virtual reclusion (*purda* in the Irano-Indian world) and to maintain a sense of modesty (through *hijab,* wearing the veil). *Hijab,* then, is not a modern adaptation of the traditional veil; it marks a new position for women in the social order, where the Western model would entail discarding of all traditional values. It is true that the position of women is still secondary: Islamists always highlight the weakness of women as inherent in their nature ("her sensibility is greater than her reasoning power; she is physically weaker"); similarly, they insist that family and motherhood are the natural spheres of women. But the main taboo is that of coeducation (*ikhtilat*). It is to be mentioned that in Iran women vote and drive cars, which would be unthinkable in traditional fundamentalism of Saudi variety. Those most radical in their politics are often the least inegalitarian.

The tendency of Islamism toward neo-fundamentalism has translated into a regression regarding the issue of women: the Algerian FIS disputes women's right to vote and presented no female candidates for the 1991 elections.

We see then that as much by the sociology of their origins as by the manner in which they are attempting to construct a new urban space, in which relationships would no longer be mediated singularly by family or guild bonds, the Islamists are products of and actors upon the modern urban space. But what has their political project achieved?

Seventeen

Notions of Islamism

The origins of the present-day Islamist thought and organisations today can be traced to the Society of the Muslim Brotherhood, created by the school teacher Hasan al-Banna in Egypt in 1928, and the Jamaat-i Islami of Pakistan, formed by Abul-Ala Maududi in 1941. Although the two movements developed independently, the overlapping of their themes was significant and intellectual contacts were soon established: it was a disciple of Maududi, the Indian Abul Hasan Ali Nadvi, who undertook the translation of Maududi into Arabic and who met with Sayyid Qtub.

On the Indian subcontinent the Jamaat-i Islami received little challenge from more fanatical movements, while in Egypt the MB spawned radical Islamist groups in the 1970s, inspired by the thought of Sayyid Qutb (an MB himself, executed by President Gamal Abdel Nasser in 1966).

We will therefore study the common socio-political conditions, in terms of ideas and of organisation, of contemporary political Islamism.

Islamism was created both along the lines of and as a break from the *salafiyya*. The Islamists generally adopt Salafist theology: they advocated a return to the Quran, the Sunna, and the *sharia* and rejected the commentaries that have been part of the tradition (the gloss, the philosophy, but also the four major legal schools, the *madhahib*). They therefore demand the right to *ijtihad*, individual interpretation.

Three points clearly separate the Islamists from the fundamentalism of ulemas: political uprising, the *sharia*, and the issue of women.

Islamists consider that the society will be Islamised only through social and political action: it is necessary to leave the mosque. The

Islamists movements intervene directly in political life and since the 1960s had attempted to gain power. The economy and social relationships are no longer perceived as subordinate activities that grow out of pious acts or the *sharia*, but are considered cardinal areas.

The Islamists pose the question of politics starting from the principle that Islam is a global and synthesising system of thought. It is not enough for society to be composed of Muslims; it must be Islamic in its foundation and its structure: a difference is therefore introduced between what is "Muslim" and what is "Islamic," a distinction that legitimates the use made here of the word "Islamism." From there it follows, but only for the most fanatic of the Islamists (disciples of Sayyid Qutb and of Khomeini, but not of Maududi), that one has a duty to revolt against a Muslim state judged to be corrupt: it was over the duty to excommunicate (*takfir*) the sovereign considered apostate and to undertake violent action (terrorism and revolution) that a considerable difference would develop within the Islamist movement between revolutionaries and "neofundamentalists."

The Islamist movement is not led by clerics (except in Iran), but by young secular intellectuals, who cordially claim to be "religious thinkers," rivals of or successors to a class of ulemas who have compromised themselves with respect to those in power: "Because all knowledge is divine and religious, a chemist, an engineer, an economist, or a jurist are all ulemas." There is an Islamist anticlericalism, which led the most fanatical elements to assassinate ulemas judged to be near power (such as the Egyptian minister of the Waqf, Muhammad al-Dhahabi, in 1977; and the director of the Waqf in Aleppo, Syria, Muhammad al-Misri, in 1979). The Sunni Islamists reject both the bureaucratised clergy and the clerical state in which ulemas have power. Even among the Iranian Islamists, an anticlerical tendency has largely existed (Ali Shariati adopted the term *akhund*, which in the Iranian tradition is a pejorative way of referring to the mullahs). The Islamist movement was created outside the body of ulemas and the large religious universities, namely Al-Azhar in Egypt, which it opposed although over time moderate Islamists have gained ground within these establishments and recruited from among the ulemas. The demand for the right to interpretation and the condemnation of the nitpicking legalism of the mullahs who specialise in *fiqh* (Islamic jurisprudence), which is timeless and indifferent to the social and political context, is also a means for the Islamists to contest the very foundation of the ulemas' and mullahs' genuineness, their religious knowledge and their function as judges.

The Islamists reproach the ulemas for two things. One is their servility to the powers in place, which leads them to accept a secular government and laws that do not adapt to the *sharia*. The other is their compromise with Western modernity: the ulemas have accepted modernity where the Islamists refute it (acceptance of the separation of religion and politics, which necessarily leads to secularisation) and maintained the tradition where the Islamists renounce it (indifference to modern science, rigid and casuistic teachings, rejection of political and social action).

Islamism adopts the classical vision of Islam as a complete and universal system, one, therefore, that does not have to "modernise" or adapt. But it applies this model to a "modern" object: to society, or more exactly, to a society defined in modern terms (that is, one in which the distinction among social, political, and economic authorities is recognised). Whether the Islamist ideal aims to bring these different sections of society together to recreate the unity of the original community, or whether it views history as decadence and not as an agent of modernity, the Islamists make modern society the crux of their actions, a society of which they themselves are products. As a result, one finds an important body of literature concerning social problem (*ijtima*, the social) and economics (*iqtisad*, the economy): Ayatollahs Baqir al-Sadr and Taliqani both wrote Islamic economic essays, Sayyid Qutb wrote a book titled *Social Justice in Islam* (*Al-adala al-ijtima'iyya fi al-islam*), which was also the title of a series of radio broadcasts by the Syrian MB M-al-Siba'i in 1950.

Two other issues separates Islamists and fundamentalists *stricto sensu*: the *sharia* and women. Islamists generally tend to favour the education of women and their participation in social and political life: the Islamists woman militates, studies and has the right to work. Islamist groups also include women's associations. The Iranian constitution recognised the right to vote for women without provoking much debate among constituents.

Islamist movements insist less on the application of the *sharia* than do the fundamentalist ulemas. Whereas moderates and neofundamentalists see the application of the *sharia* as a key to the Islamisation of society, the radical Islamists, without questioning the principle of the *sharia*, tend to consider it more a project than a corpus. Indeed, for radical Islamists, institution of the *sharia* presumes a transformation of society if it is not to be sheer hypocrisy. The real gamble is to redefine the social bond itself on a political basis, and not simply to apply the *sharia*. Imam Khomeini, in a famous declaration of January 1989 pronounced, in opposition to the president of the Khomanei Republic, that the logic of the revolution took precedence over the application of the *sharia*. Sayyid Qutb spoke of an "Islamic law in motion" (*fiqh haraki*), as a result of the interpretation of those who fight for Islam and established in accordance with social conditions — as opposed to the fixed, rigid and casuistic law of the ulemas. This notion was adopted by the Moroccan Islamist Yasin, Islamic law — beginning with punishment by amputation — cannot be applied in a society that is not yet Islamic. The same issue is invoked by Iranian militants, particularly by Islamist women. On the other hand, in a genuine Islamic society, the state can innovate on technical subjects not provided for in the sharia or make use of the right to interpretation by its leaders on other issues, such as the creation of taxes and all ad hoc legislation. For Islamists, to recognise the current states' right to innovate as do the ulemas, is to recognise a secular space; on the other hand, to recognise this right to innovate in perfect Islamic state is to inscribe the *sharia* in a broader whole: that of the Islamisation of the entire society and not only of the law. For Islamists, Islam is more than the simple application of the *sharia*: it is synthesising, totalising ideology that must first transform society in order that the *sharia* may be established, almost automatically. The Islamic nature of the state is more important than the rigid application of the *sharia*, which is meaningful only in a truly Islamic society — a society that can then move beyond this application, even to the point of innovation.

These three elements (the place of politics, women, and the *sharia*) are good criteria for distinguishing fanatic Islamists from conservative fundamentalist regimes or even from modern neofundamentalist movements (the Algerian FIS), although the definition, at this point, lacks detail and nuance.

The Islamist movement thus conceives of itself clearly as a socio-political movement, founded on an Islam defined as much in terms of a political ideology as in terms of a religion. One evidence of this is the symmetrical comparison the Islamists regularly make between their thought on the one side and, on the other, not other religions, but the main ideologies of the twentieth century (Marxism, fascism, "capitalism"). It is within this framework that we will study their conception of society and politics.

Political Reading of the Quran

The Islamists fill a conceptual matrix borrowed either from Marxism or from categories of Western political science with Quranic terminology or neologisms meant to Islamise the grid.

From the Quran come the terms: *shura* (advisory council), *hizb* (party), *tawhid* (oneness), *mustadaf* (oppressed), *umma* (community of believers), and *jahiliyya* (ignorance), which are explained in a modern political context (democracy, political parties, a classless society, social classes and so on. We also find neologisms (the roots exist, but not the meaning): *hakimiyya* (sovereignty), *thawra* and *inqilab* (revolution); and, finally words that are borrowed terms or calques: the word "ideology" is copiously used either as a borrowed term (*ideolozhi* in Persian), or as a calque (*mafkura* in Arabic and Persian, *fikra* in Arabic), as if the term "religion," *din* were perceived as insufficient.

The Islamists engage in a political and social rereading of the Quran, made possible distinctly by the distortion of Muslim tradition. Maududi and Hassan al-Turabi, for example, are careful to categorise the concepts of political Islam as functions of areas of law and of Western political science, as if they were universal. The Iranian ideologues, such as Bani Sadr, match *tawhid* with a classless society and *mustadaf* with the proletariat; in the work of Ali Shariati, Shiite eschatology shifts toward a revolutionary mould. But at the same time, Islamists refuse to strike the defensive, conciliatory, and apologist note of many Muslim "modernists," who attempt Islam's modernity by the yardstick of Western values and concepts.

For Islamists, it is a matter of showing not that Islam perfectly realises universal values, but on the contrary that Islam is the universal value and need not be compared with other religions or political systems.

Islam: An "Inclusive Order" and an Ideology

Islamism begins with a theological concept that is the very basis of the Muslim religion: divine oneness or *tawhid*, which says that God is transcendent, unique, and without associates. The Islamist contribution (or rupture) with respect to its tradition consists in applying this theological concept to society, whereas previously it was related exclusively to God. Society is, or rather must be, a reflection of divine oneness, of *tawhid*. While "oneness" is the basic fact of divine spirits, in a human society it is something that must be constructed as well as created. A *tawhidi* society (an adjective in use among Iranian ideologues) cannot tolerate either inner segmentation (social, ethnic, tribal, or national) or a political authority that is autonomous with respect to the divine order, even in complement manner. God's absolute sovereignty, *hakimiyya*, will then prevail, governing all aspects of the life of the individual as well as of society.

Islam is thus not only an entirety of beliefs but an "inclusive order," a "total order," *nizam*: "Islam is an inclusive order that pertains to all aspects of life." This new order excludes any secular space, even a contingent one.

Rupture to Revolution

But how can an Islamic society be established? Disagreement between moderate and extremist Islamists has existed on this point throughout the history of Islamism. The moderates are partisans of re-Islamisation from the bottom up (preaching, establishing sociocultural movements) while pressuring the leaders (in particular through political alliances) to promote Islamisation from the top (introducing the *sharia* into legislation): this was the politics of the founding fathers, al-Banna and Maududi, who accepted the concept of revolt only if the state took a resolutely anti-Islamic stance and if all norms of peaceful protest had been exhausted: "If the government should become so alien as to surpass the *sharia*, then (the individual) has the right and obligation to revolt. This is the revolutionary element of Islam."

Meanwhile, the radicals consider that no compromise with current Muslim society is possible: they advocate political fragmentation and introduce the concept of *revolution*, another borrowing from the century's progressive ideologies. It was Sayyid Qutb, an Egyptian Muslim Brother (executed in 1966), who typed himself as the theoretician of rupture and inspired the revolutionary groups of the 1970s. His analysis turns upon two notions: *jahiliyya* and *takfir*.

Jahiliyya, a Quranic term, refers to the condition of pre-Islamic society, combining ignorance and savagery. Islamists assert that present Muslim societies have reverted to *jahiliyya*, a theme that is also contemporary to revolutionary Iran in the expression *taghuti*: society, spirit, or individual, the taghuti (the name of an idol in the Quran) is everything that refutes the divine order. In such a case, jihad against governments who are Muslim only in name is lawful. Their leaders can be declared to be in a state of infidelity: *takfir*, or excommunication, is the act of pronouncing that someone who professes Islam is in fact an infidel, *kafir*. Moderate Islamists reject the notion of excommunication, considering, in the tradition of the ulemas, that an unjust power is preferable to segmentation of the community (*fitna*).

Whereas moderate Islamism maintains a reformist position, radical Islamism reappropriates the concept of revolution: the forceful ousting of a political regime in order to replace it with a system founded on a different ideology.

The State and the Institutions of Islamist Thought

"The Quran is our Constitution" is the slogan encountered from the Egyptian Muslim Brotherhood to the Afghan Islamists. But what institutions are to be derived from this generality? Two theories recur constantly among most Islamist theoreticians: that of the leader (*amir*) and that of the advisory council (*shura*), based on which both the Islamic political party and the future Islamic society are structured.

The terms that appoint the leader vary: *murshid* among the MB; amir for Tunisians, Pakistanis, Afghans and Soviet Muslims;

imam in Iran (but this concept has specifically Shiite connotations). The term *khalifa*, caliph, sometimes used in the 1950s, has actually disappeared. The amir is both the political and religious leader of the community. For Islamists, the challenge is to end the division of power that has historically existed in the Muslim world between the *de facto* sovereign and a class of ulemas who oversee the law without involving themselves in matters of power.

Early on, Islamists replaced the notion of the *caliphate* (surviving mainly in the writings of Hasan al-Banna) with that of the amir. One reason for this is that according to the classical authors, a caliph or a religious leader must be a member of the tribe of the Prophet (the Quraysh), which would not correspond to the emergence of a new elite; moreover, caliphs ruled societies which the Islamists do not consider to have been Islamic (the Ottoman Empire). Next, Islamists wish to establish a political organisation that can become visible at once in the first country in which an Islamic revolution succeeds, without waiting for a supposed reconstitution of the political *umma*. Finally, before being society's guide, the amir has the advantage of being a party leader, a new concept that is totally unrelated to the medieval debates on the nature of the caliphate.

Who appoints the amir? Little is said in Islamist literature about concrete procedures for designating the amir or about the extent and limits of his power. To many Islamists (with the exception of the Iranians), the idea of voting and of elections seems to weaken the unity of the *umma* and to relativise, "humanise," that which proceeds from God alone. The ideal solution, which runs throughout the debate, would be for the amir to be *index sui*, his own indicator; that is, by merely appearing he would be instantly recongnisable. Hence, no doubt, the incessant quest for a charismatic chief, which is transformed in political life into a quest for a leader. The only criterion for appointing an amir would therefore be the man himself, his virtue, his personality.

The quest for the amir is often reduced to a description of the qualities he should exhibit. Thus, for Maududi, who generally is very concerned with enlisting political Islam into a modern constitutional framework, the political leader must meet the following conditions: he must be a Muslim, a male, an adult, healthy, and have performed *hijra,* that is, he must belong to the section of followers who have separated themselves from a corrupt society; he must fear God, be wise, worthy of trust, and .... he must not aspire to the position. According to the Afghan Hizb-i Islami's programme the amir must abstain from sin and from all that is "religiously forbidden," must personify "sincerity, equity, justice, purity" and "surpass all members of society in the qualities that are required of a believer." Although the amir is obviously never matched with the Prophet, it is clear that he is considered a model for behaviour. He is as much a religious chief as a political leader; many theoreticians bestow him the right to *ijtihad,* which places him above the ulemas, although no Islamist text requires that he come from the ulemas' milieu.

General view suggests that the more radical the party, the more central is the figure of the amir. In the programme of the Hizb-i Islami, which often simply paraphrases the texts of Hasan al-Banna, it is written that the director must be considered "a spiritual leader" by party members. The amir is thus a "doctor of law," a political leader as well as a model of behaviour. One must pledge him allegiance (*bay'a*). The right to interpretation is explicitly accorded to the amir in the programme of the Afghan Hizb-i Islami, although the current leader, Gulbadin Hikmatyar, is an engineer with no particular religious training; the primacy of politics over religion is broadly apparent here, as is the resulting paradox: the amir is supposed to have greater religious competency than the ulemas. Meanwhile, the more moderate groups restrict the right to interpretation to an amir who has proper religious training, at the risk of reintroducing the pre-eminence of the ulemas that the Islamists have so decried.

Nevertheless, there has been a weakening of the figure and the concept of the amir among recent Islamist uprisings, which tend to be more neofundamentalist (the Algerian FIS, the Soviet Islamic Renaissance Party).

Elections and the Advisory Council

Since sovereignty belongs only to God, the Islamists reject the concept of popular sovereignty and endow only contingent value to the elective principle. If no individual comes forward as the evident amir, then he can be elected by an advisory assembly (the *shura*) or even by universal suffrage, both of which, in this case, do not express sovereignty, but simply the principle of community consensus (*ijma*).

The *shura* only "counsels": sovereignty effectively arising from God alone, the only power the community has is to advise (and admonish) the amir in the name of Islamic principles. In short, the *shura's* function is superfluous: to reiterate divine principles, to help the amir make decisions in the name of these principles, and ultimately to criticise the amir if he strays from them. The *shura* can take the form of a parliament. What matters is that the function of "counselling" (and not legislation, since God alone legislates) be provided for, whatever the specific modalities may be. "This consultative process... could very well be formulated through a parliament, a council, or a *majlis-i-shura'* (consultative council)." This is a good indication of the disregard of Sunni thought to the concrete form that institutions may take. Once the principles are agreed upon, the details can be worked out when the need arises.

But who sits on the *shura*? Here one finds the same problem as for the designation of the amir. Islamist thought refers to those who, following a Quranic verse, are called the *ahl al-hall wal-aqd*, that is "those who have the power to bind and unbind." Three factions, in contemporary writings, are in competition:

The clergy, that is, the ulemas, which reintroduces the dichotomy that the Islamists have always wanted to abolish between clerics and the society.

The entire community, which justifies universal suffrage by which today implies a reference to the "Western" democracy reviled by many Islamists.

"Islamists intellectuals," that is, the intellectuals and militants of contemporary Islam, who are almost always secular from a sociological point of view.

The debate forms an unprincipled circle, since the choice of those who decide the question implies the answer to the question. As for the amir, it is expected that "good men" will appear through a natural process, which may or may not take the form of elections.

All Sunni Islamist thought in fact expresses a strong aversion for translating the notions of the amir and of the *shura* into terms of autonomous institutions capable of impressively producing a stable political practice independent of the individuals who compose it: in other words, into the form of a constitution. The Sunnis stop at the slogan "The Quran is Our Constitution." What precise form the executive and "legislative" branches will take does not seem essential, for, as Turabi notes, "Whatever form the executive may take, a leader is always subject to the *shariah* and to the *ijma* (the consensus) formulated under it." Unlike the Iranians, the Sunni Islamists remain apprehensive of the state in general. (In fact in this same text, Turabi speaks of the Islamic state as a very limited government.)

Association, Party, or Sect?

Unlike the ulemas and the Salafists, Islamists give preference to political action. They have established movements that operate outside the structure of mosques and strictly religious activities, the form of which oscillates among three models:

A Leninist-type party presenting itself as an avant-garde aiming to conquer power and denying the legitimacy of all other parties; the Hizb-i Islami in Afghanistan is a case in point.

A Western-style political party, seeking, within an electoralist and multiparty structure, to get the maximum number of elements in its programme adopted; an example is the Prosperity Party in Turkey.

A religious militant organisation, aiming to promote Islamic values and to modify society and mentalities by giving rise to associations and by permeating the elite, but without direct political ambitions; examples include the Egyptian Muslim Brotherhood, which insists on mass action; and the Jamaat-i Islami of Pakistan, more given to penetrating the elite. The two parties occasionally present their own candidates at elections.

There is constant wavering among these three forms. For example, in Egypt, when the decree of September 9, 1952, invited political parties to register themselves, the current head of the MB, Hydaybi, opposed registration as a party but was ruled out by the Advisory Council. The Algerian FIS has successively claimed to fit each of these moulds, depending on whether it is denouncing or playing the political game. Generally, words suggesting the notion of a "society" (*jama'a, jam'iyya*) tend to be used by moderates, while the radical groups more readily call themselves parties (*hizb*), under the influence, no doubt, of Marxist-leaning movements (Hizb al-Tahrir, Hizb-i Islami, Hizbullah). If the choice is intricate, it is because for the Islamists the party is both a means of political action and a countersociety in which the militant can start to live right away according to the true Islamic model.

The very concept of a party is problematic to Islamists. In the *umma* there is "no other party than the Party of God": *la hizb illa hizbullah* was the chant of the Iranian militants as they lashed on other parties' headquarters and demonstrations during the first year of the Iranian revolution. Hasan al-Banna asked King Farouq to dissolve the *hizbiyya,* that is, the very fact that political parties could exist. The fundamentalist Egyptian leader Farag critcised those who wanted to establish an Islamic party as a party among others to compete in the political arena.

The Islamists' difficulty in situating their party within the framework can be explained by the party's very specific nature. A reading of the statutes of the different movements makes it evident that the Islamist party prefigures the Islamic society, first in that it demands an individual "re-Islamisation" of its members (what one might call a born-again Muslim), and then because the institutions it provides for within itself (the amir, the *shura*) have alikeness with those of the future Islamic state. The party is a cross between a Leninist structure and a mystical order based on personal induction under the auspices of a Guide. The vocabulary can be read in two ways: guide/secretary-general, brother/comrade, council/central committee, advisory duties followed by allegiance, *bay'a*/democratic centralism, and so on.

Most of the movements adopt the model developed by the Egyptian MB. The chief (amir, guide ...) is elected but then becomes quasi irremovable unless disqualified by the *shura*. He is backed up by an executive committee or council, over which he normally exercises supervisory authority. The party has at its disposal an administration in the form of specialised committees, including those of preaching and propaganda (*da'wa*). Specialised sections cover the professional sectors (peasants, workers, students, and others). The party sometimes also includes a secret paramilitary or special service organisation. Almost all Islamist parties include a women's association.

It is noteworthy that there is almost never a council of ulemas in Islamist parties (with the exceptions, in Central Asia, of the Afghan Jamaat-i Islami and the Soviet Islamic Renaissance Party).

Thus, despite the difference in emphasis between moderates and radicals, Islamist movements offer a logical doctrine and a new organisational model. As we shall soon see, they have taken root in areas that are sociologically modern, breaking with the intellectual and social universe of the traditionalist ulemas.

Eighteen

Journey from Tradition to Reformism

Mullahs and Ulemas

There is no clergy in Islam. Yet there is a multitude of lettered men, doctors of law — the ulemas — whose entirety and curriculum display remarkable stability in space and time, and who have had a quasi-monopoly on intellectual production and teaching, at least between the end of the great era of philosophic creativity in the Middle Ages and the emergence, in the nineteenth century, of intellectuals of secular culture. The places where they perpetuate themselves are called *madrasa*, theological schools or universities. The oneness of this body results from the teaching that is dispensed there and from the techniques used for the transmission of knowledge (repetition, access to texts through commentary, loyalty to a master). But ulemas are capable of fulfilling various functions: teachers, judges (*qadi*), imams in mosques. They do not have a monopoly on houses of worship: many mosques, especially village or neighbourhood mosques, are served only by simple mullahs, who have no higher religious preparation and are mainly "ritual practitioners"; they do not answer to any higher authority (except in Iran). These mosque mullahs are referred to by terms that vary depending on one's location in the Muslim society (mullah in Iran, Turkey, central Asia, and the Indian subcontinent; imam in the Maghreb and therefore among immigrants to France).

Institutionalised Clergy

The trend towards creating an institutionalised clergy is recent and derives from the states and not from the clerics (except in Iran). This incomplete clericalisation starts at the top: the state controls the large *madrasa*, names a mufti or *shaykh ul-islam* and tries to give these authorities a monopoly on the nomination of mullahs (or mosque imams) and judges (who might issue *fatwa*). Official, bureaucratised clergy have emerged in Tunisia, Morocco, Egypt and in the Soviet Union (in 1941).

The primary demand of ulemas and mullahs is the complete and total implementation of the *sharia*, without regard to the character of the political system; this is fundamentalism *stricto sensu*, which as a corollary also entails a secular space: the place of power. Classical Islamic thought is overflowing with writings on governing, advice to sovereigns, and didactic tales. They do not reflect on the nature of politics, but on the nature of good ruler and of able government (advice, techniques, paradigms, anecdotes). The issue of ethics is at the heart of classical Muslim political philosophy. Obviously, within this body of thought there is no lack of overtone and controversy: Must one obey a sovereign who is himself a bad Muslim? Can one resign oneself to living in a state conquered by infidels? and many more. But the general framework remains the same. The fundamentalist clergy want the sovereign to apply the *sharia* and to defend the Muslim community. His genuineness lies therein. In the Sunni tradition, there is neither a transcendent source of political legitimacy nor a necessity that a particular type of state exists. The political demand of the fundamentalist clergy is that the law conform to the *sharia*; it claims the right to censure, not to exercise power. This traditional fundamentalism, which has been the base of much theoretical reflection by the ulemas, is the spontaneous ideology of most mullahs and other clerics.

The endurance of traditional religious teaching throughout the Muslim world, conveying this vision of the relationship to power, has often been obscured by the birth of Islamism. Not only does this teaching continue to perpetuate itself, but it is also expressed in what one might call not popular Islam — often mistaken with Sufism, magic and customs that are pre-Islamic in origin — but the "popular knowledge of Islam," which is to say the elements of an orthodox body of knowledge that whirl in nonclerical milieus. In the region in which I did field research (Afghanistan, Soviet Central Asia), this circulation is obvious: in the village mosques and among families (including urban families) I found a compilation composed of lithographed brochures (generally written in Persian, even among Turkish and Pashto speakers), the originals of which mostly date from the last century and contain both reports on religion (the pillars of faith, prayer rituals), moral advice (anecdotes, fables), and excerpts from classical works (Saadi), all put forward in rhymed prose or verse. Children learn these texts by heart under the guidance of their father or the mullah.

Even in Iran, until Khomeini the ulemas were content to have command over the laws voted by Parliament. It was Khomeini who first defined the conditions for the exercise of power by the clergy (theory of the *vilayat-i faqih*), a position that would finally be adopted by only a minority of the Iranian high clergy.

Although the ulamas and mullahs are potentially fundamentalist, they are never the ones who take power to implement a policy of "shariatisation," with the exception of Iran in 1979. There has never been a theocracy in Islam; clergy have never served as heads of state. From the Great Moghul Aurangzeb, the sovereign of India (1656-1707), to General Zia ul-Haq (the head of state of Pakistan from 1977 to 1988), by way of Saudi dynasty, all are secular figures — kings, generals or presidents — who undertook to realise the fundamentalist ulemas programme.

Two trends can be distinguished within this fundamentalism: one traditionalist, the other reformist. The traditionalist one accepts the interrelationship between the founding texts and their commentaries; it takes as its basic tenet imitation (*taqlid*), that is, refusal to innovate, while accepting what was said before; its admirers follow one of the great legal schools (Shafiism, Malikism, Hanafism, Hambalism); its vision of the *sharia* is essentially legalistic. It is sometimes connected to the popular sects of Sufism (hence the Barelvi school in Pakistan).

There also exists a reformist fundamentalism, which criticises the tradition, the commentaries, popular religious practices (maraboutism, the cult of saints), deviations and superstitions; it aims to come back to the founding texts (eighteenth century instances are Shah Wali Allah in India and Abd al-Wahhab in Arabian Peninsula). This reformism generally developed in response to an external threat (the influence of Hinduism on Islam, for example).

It is in keeping with this reformist trend that a fundamentalist current, the *salafiyya*, appeared in the nineteenth century, marking a period between fundamentalism and Islamism.

Salafist Reformism

In the nineteenth century, for the first time, the Muslim world felt structurally on the defensive, faced with a technical minded, conquering Europe. The evenness that had existed for centuries between Muslim and Christian crusaders, between Ottoman and imperial armies, had disappeared.

Why was Islam unable to compete with European colonialism? Outdatedness? Distraction? Divine punishment? The question arises with regard to the constant shrink of the Ottoman Empire, the arrival of the French in Algeria (1830), the disappearance of the Moghul Empire in India (1857), the Russian incursions into the Caucasus (1857) and Central Asia. Two means of resistance arose during the nineteenth century; the one of peasant and religious origin, the other urban and nationalist. On the one side charismatic leaders, generally ulemas or leaders of religious orders, launched the call for jihad and founded tribal coalitions. To unify the tribes, they imposed the *sharia* despite the local common laws; the fundamentalism of the mullahs emerged as a political force because the *sharia* was used against *asabiyya*, against tribal and ethnic segmentation, which in contrast was exploited by the colonisers. This group included Abd al-Qadir in Algeria, the Mahdi in Sudan, Shamil in the Caucasus, the Sanusis in Libya and in Chad, Mullah-i Lang in Afghanistan, the *akhund* of Swat in India, and later, Abd al-Karim in Morocco. These movements failed to advance further despite spectacular victories (destruction of the British Army in Afghanistan in 1842, the capture of Khartoum in 1885). The anti-imperialist banner was in turn raised, after the First World War, by movements that were more nationalistic than religious, even though the tradition of the fundamentalist jihad continues to our day (the Afghan *mujahidin*). The second mode of resistance lay in the constitution of modern states (Egypt, Iran, Turkey) by members of the urban, Westernised elite. The modernisation was authoritarian and ordered from above, following the model of the enlightened autocrat; it was obvious or opposed to Islam and shied away from democratisation (the dissolution of the Ottoman Parliament in 1878, the repression of the constitutionalist movement in Iran in 1907). Without any direct colonialisation, these regimes came under Europe's and particularly Britain's thumb, as a result of debt.

These historical background continue to haunt the Muslim, and in particular the Arab, imagination. The "backwardness" with respect to the West is now called underdevelopment, enlightened autocracy is called "ba'thism" and fundamentalism is re-emerging in all its forms (traditionalist in one part of the Afghan resistance, Islamist in the other, neofundamentalist in the Algerian FIS).

During the second half of the nineteenth century, a stream of thought within the framework of Islam attempted to address the backwardness of the Muslim world: it was the *salafiyya*, the "return to the ancestors," typified by its three canonical authors, Jamal al-Din al-Afghani (1838-1898), Muhammad Abduh (1849-1905), and Rashid Rida (1865-1935). Like all other fundamentalist reformist movements, it repudiated common law (*adat, urf*), maraboutism (belief in the powers of intervention of certain individuals blessed with *baraka*, or divine charisma), and alliance with other religion. But it went even further than its successors in rejecting the tradition of the ulemas (the textual commentary, *tafsir*, which is followed to the letter, *taqlid*), as well as the body of additions and expansions, whether relating to systematisation of the religion (the *madhahib* — the four legal schools), culture (philosophy), theology (religious beliefs and laws), or institutions (the clergy). Reform (*islah*) did not involve adopting modernity, but returning to the Tradition of the Prophet, which would enable one to conceptualise this modernity. Salafism pushed the logic of reformism to its extreme: it demanded the right to individual interpretation (*ijtihad*) of the founding texts (the Quran and the Sunna) without regard to earlier commentaries. The reopening of the right to *ijtihad* marked a prominent rupture with ten centuries of orthodoxy.

Al-Afghani

Al-Afghani was concerned less with developing a new corpus than with generating political and cultural activism, with wrenching Muslims away from the tyranny of a dead and ruining system of transmitting knowledge, with "bringing consciousness" to the people and the elite, to the point that others have wondered whether Islam was for him an end in itself or only a means of combating imperialism.

The demand for a resumption of *ijtihad* also aimed to destroy the ulemas' monopoly on the religious corpus. The Salafists, like the Islamists, did not belong to clerical origins. But their thought would touch a chord among certain reformist ulemas, such as Sheikh Ibn Badis in Algeria (1889-1940) who fought against maraboutism and the traditionalism of the great *madrasa*.

Politically, Salafist notion remained traditional. There was no extensive condemnation of existing Muslim governments. The state, as the political authority, was accorded little value: it was instrumental, distinct from the *umma*, whose domain was both smaller (civil society) and much larger (the community of all Muslims). Its only role was to apply the *sharia*. But Salafist thought was obsessed with the reconstitution of the Muslim *umma*, and particularly with the restoration of the caliphate. At the beginning of the twentieth century the Ottoman caliphate experienced a surge of popularity in Muslim non-Arab mulieus. In fact, the split between the Arab and non-Arab world was conspicuous on the issue of the caliphate: the Arabs, dreaming of the reconstitution of a vast Arab Empire, fought the Ottoman Empire, which all other Muslims unequivocally regarded as the best defense against imperialism and the starting point for a reconstruction of the *umma*. The suppression of the caliphate in 1924 forced the *salafiyya* to renounce the myth, especially since the personality of Ataturk and his role in the struggle against the West earned him the sympathy of ulemas — who were never suspected of secular complacency — such as Ibn Badis.

Although the *salafiyya* never became a political movement, it left its mark on all twentieth century fundamentalist reformists, precisely since Sheikh Abduh served as Grand Mufti of Egypt from 1899 until his death.

Index

ISLAMIC TERRORISM
Myth or Reality

ISLAMIC TERRORISM

MYTH OR REALITY

(In Two Volumes)

(Volume 2)

Editor

M.H. Syed

PUBLICATIONS

KALPAZ PUBLICATIONS

DELHI - 110052

ISLAMIC TERRORISM: Myth or Reality
[*Terrorism*]

Rs. 1800 (Set)
Rs. 900 each volume

ISBN: 81-7835-117-X (Set)
ISBN: 81-7835-140-4 (Vol. 2)

Published in 2002 in India by
Kalpaz Publications
C-30, Satyawati Nagar
Delhi-110052
e-mail: kalpaz@hotmail.com

Laser Typeset at: Alphabet, Delhi
Printed at: Chawla Offset Press, Delhi

Contents

Preface

Islam is not only a faith or religion. It is the philosophy, discipline and way of life. But, in spite of being a purely scientific and progressive religion, Islam is perhaps, the most misunderstood religion in the world. People talk of Islam but never make an attempt to know, what real Islam is. They simply do not bother to study *the religion, at all,* but always prefer to criticise. Indeed it has become a common practice. It appears that the whole West seems to be at war against Islam.

Recently, Islam has been attached to violence, coercion and terrorism, as incidentally or otherwise, many of the groups, engaged in struggle against various regimes, all over the world, are followers of Islam. But that does not necessarily mean, that all their acts are in accordance with the true spirit of Islam. And that's the prime difference, between the two things.

One should realise that Islam and Muslims are two different entities. Islam is what was preached by Prophet Mohammad (PBUH), Islam is not what is depicted by the action and behaviour of its followers—known as Muslims. Frankly speaking all the followers are not 'true followers' of the faith. Hence, there must be no confusion. If one desires to know the real Islam, then he or she should flip through the pages of Holy Quran, the Traditions and other scriptures and apply their mind to ascertain what the truth is. Only then, one may be able to know Islam—the real one.

Similarly, *Jehad* or holy war may be Islamic, but, the battles being fought in different parts of the world are not *Jehad*. This is really very dangerous to confuse some warring groups with Islamic *Jehadis* and their militant struggles with real *Jehad*.

This study, though a modest attempt, is a step in the direction of understanding Islam and eradicating the confusion and misunderstanding spread about Islam, as a faith.

Hopefully this humble endeavour should succeed in creating an awareness about the subject and erase the doubts resulted from half-baked publications in the west in particular and elsewhere in general. If this much happens, then the undersigned would feel honoured and rewarded in the academic world.

Editor

One

Worldwide Presence of Terrorism

The increasing tide of terrorism has considerably destabilised the present-day social structure. It remains an option chosen by a very small minority of the aggrieved throughout the world. One is therefore compelled to consider where and in what political circumstances it does emerge; from what kinds of grievance or cause; and how it proceeds from cause to action. Twenty years after the conclusion of the Second World War — with its distinctly arbitrary resolution of some troublesome border disputes and simple overruling of the claims of some national minorities — a generation of indignant, impatient and marginalised people composed one of the most intense and therefore dangerous elements of the peacetime world. They were undoubtedly more ready to take up their collective or individual battle because they had not been involved in war.

Terrorism is caused not least by the existing trend towards political agglomeration; as states form into groups for economic and military safety-in-numbers, so the interests of non-state minorities seem to be neglected and ignored. Even the small, less powerful Third World nations feel compelled to align themselves in a Non-Aligned Movement. A minority faction may be granted a special status — which may be no more than token — in such a forum, but it is unlikely to force itself on the attention of the group except by violence. The PLO achieved Observer status at the UN in the 1970s heyday of Arab power and clout; Kurds were allowed to participate in Non-Aligned events, as a reward for their years of bitter fighting against all the states in their claimed homeland.

The trend towards larger power coalitions has an echo in the trend towards the dominant images of fewer and fewer world political leaders. In a sense this makes terrorists more powerful, at least through the media, because pre-eminent leaders can no longer devolve security concerns to deputies and responsible ministers. Terrorists include not only those who have been disowned their homelands and national self-determination, but also the characteristic 1960s 'small is beautiful', anti-authoritarian factions and radical revolutionaries like the Red Army Faction; besides the clandestine agents of genuine states and powers. Old historical struggles like that between Britain and Ireland are one source of terrorism; peace treaties which end wars and settle new boundaries, like the Soviet-Turkish border in the 1920s, another; terrorism may be the chosen weapon to cure the fallouts of an unexpected war, as it was in part for the Palestinians after the Six Days' War of 1967; but equally terrorism can be the initiative of a small group of unrepresented yet unrepresentative radicals whose ideas could never gain currency in any larger arena than that of the faction itself — as one sees in most of the city or town — based revolutionary groups such as the Weather Underground, the United Freedom Front or the Red Guerrilla Resistance of the United States; the *Rote Armee Fraktion*/Baader-Meinhof Gang, and *Revolutionare Zellen* of West Germany; the *Brigate Rosse* or *Nuclei Armati* of Italy; and some more like the Angry Brigade through *Action Directe* of *Rode Hulp* of Holland.

In South America and some Far Eastern countries, where severe instability often alternates with severely dictatorial supremacy, terrorism tends to emerge in fairly traditional settings of popular revolt, and to be met by state terror exercised through the military apparatus. Out of power, the right rarely resorts to terrorism in such nations: control of the armed forces readily provides the tools for a takeover. In those European countries with a fascist past (notably Germany, Italy and Spain), however, the conventional remnants remain which in many ways apparently steal the cloths and the methods of the left, staging individual terrorist attacks to provoke a sense of crisis and instability — to which the absolute solution is a return to militaristic , authoritarian and nationalistic 'order'. Terrorism, for the faction which grows to using it, is an idea whose time has come. To some, like the Baader-

Meinhof Gang or the Red Brigades, it is a quick process: even though they may begin as fundamentalist pranksters more than political thinkers, the direction of their political development convinces them that traditional political channels, if they are considered at all, are closed to them, and violence overcomes exuberance. In Germany, the terrorists of the left were convinced that the state was beyond democratic transformation, imprisoned by bourgeois values and a stifling work-ethic, led by politicians who it was axiomatic — were corrupted by power.

The new right, in the then West Germany, had some surprisingly similar views to the leftist revolutionaries: both believed that the state had become an incompetent servant of the USA's strategic interests. Both left and right displayed a clear perception political urgency in the 1960s, one generation after the immense turmoil of Germany's national fate following the Second World War. The neo-fascists felt that German nationalism had been totally forgotten, that no one was fighting for re-unification of Germany any longer. The left wanted an end to American influence because they didn't like what America was doing in Vietnam. In 1968 and thereafter, students in Europe and the USA were demanding freedom for North Vietnam, freedom for the Palestinians, and freedom for themselves as well though what they wanted to do with theirs was never clear enough.

At different times (and occasionally at the same time) German 'trainee terrorists' of both left and right made their way to training camps or clandestine bases of the PLO, usually in Lebanon, in the late 1960s. The left were there partly for practical training, but more so out of a sense of 'solidarity' with the Palestinian struggle. The Baader-Meinhof revolutionaries, the self-appointed comrades of the Palestinians, were quite surprisingly, regarded as romantic and inefficient by their hosts, who never took them at all seriously; the militaristic neo-fascists, with their authoritarian and disciplined style, throughout appeared businesslike and serious.

Condition in Italy

In Italy, a similar diagnosis of the internal political situation again gave rise to varying terroristic responses by left and right. Italy was known for its inherent political base for mass political movements of the left — the strongest Communist Party in Europe, with its permanent dilemma of pursuing revolution through democracy. In the 1960s there took place a range of political movements of the left including *Autonomia Operaia,* CoCoRi and NAPAP — which wanted urgent social change in a state perceived as a non-functioning democracy: that is to say, the large number of political parties, frequent elections and acutely insubstantial governmental coalitions made the democratic business of political change through popular political action an impossibility. Activism through the existing political parties seemed to be impossible, they thought; new political parties would only make matters worse; nothing but terrorism could have presented the same challenge to established state powers, even though the terrorists were simply outnumbered by the non-violent radicals who attempted a form of extra-parliamentary politics which banded under the banner of Autonomia. What Autonomia meant was that the common masses would together decide — without reference to government — how they wanted their housing allocated, their schools run, their medical aid delivered; how much they would pay in the shops, how much they would be paid in the factories, and how many hours they would work. It was an example of organised anarchy, perfected into a political theory.

Terrorism somewhat inevitably accompanied the efforts of Autonomia — directed against the police who arrested and man handled demonstrators, against the bosses who resisted the workers' or unions' demands, against university professors who opposed them and against the politicians who tried to put an end to the whole thing. The left saw the whole state as discredited and obsolete, and terrorism would help to kill it off. The new right saw the same fragility of state institutions specifically as a reason to re-establish 'strong government' in the shape of military fascist regime. The fascists and Autonomists engaged in pitched battles in the streets of Italy's prominent cities in the early 1970s, and to amplify the sense of chaos, which they felt would provide their opportunity to seize power, the fascists staged occasional but gruesome bombings in which the death tolls were always far higher than any similar actions by the left. Substantial evidence emerged that members of the Italian police, secret service and armed forces plotted fascist attacks, and to throw the blame onto the left for some of them.

The example of Italy serves to illustrate a more general rule of terrorism: that the right has a distinct sense of scale; the more corpses, the greater thc impact and repercussions. The left tends to believe in selective resonant targeting, preserving at least nominally a sense that the mass support of their constituency (whether real or imagined) must not be frittered away.

If it is possible to reach some general conclusions about the political circumstances from which terrorism develops, is it possible to foretell in what settings it will occur, and what targets it will choose? Certainly terrorist incidents occur more frequently in democratic, free societies: partly because of opportunity of action and partly because of the potential advantage of publicity. While terrorism mostly takes place in the more controlled societies (and the very nature of such societies suggests that we may hear far less about their terrorism than might be justified by genuine events), the control of citizens' movements, work, political activities and media, limits both opportunity and effect. In a society which has officially banned unemployment it is an almost impossible proposition to live 'underground' and to disappear from daily life to wage a clandestine struggle.

Terrorism in pursuit of secessionist causes naturally occurs within the state in the case of a move towards regional independence: the only relevant place for the actions of Basque separatists is Spain. Confining the attacks to the disputed area is in part a propaganda strategy, in an effort to portray the struggle as — which it usually is not — a local territorial conflict between 'Popular Forces' and the distant state. However, these are nerely general trends and there are numerous and tactically appropriate exceptions. The terrorists of *Euskadi Ta Askatasuna* (Basque Homeland and Liberty), or

ETA, who have no boundaries to cross between Bilbao and Madrid, succeed in intermittent attacks against government targets on 'enemy' ground: their most significant success was the assassination of the Spanish Prime Minister, Luis Carrero Blanco, in 1973, which has become a legend of Arthurian proportions in Basque nationalistic congregations.

It is, thus, needless to say that separatist causes arise wherever power has changed hands; or where international conferences, convened by the powers of the age, have ruled that a number of distinct regional or national entities should be grouped into nations. The pre-eminent example is that of the Palestinians whose national refugee status and gradually increasing unrest gave rise directly to the PLO and its terrorism. While the PLO acts firstly against Israel — the disputed territory which was Palestine — its pervasive capacity to act, wherever targets are appropriate and available, against those whom it sees as obstructing national self-determination, gave rise to the very concept of 'international terrorism'. It is increasingly apparent , moreover, that international terrorism's relative efficacy in enticing public and political attention is having a 'copycat' effect upon a still wider variety of local and regional discontents. The Indian subcontinent, which for centuries has been an easy victim to the continuing resentments and rivalries of both a caste system and tribal competition, had only in the 1980s begun to see identifiable terrorism emerging as a medium for regional and racial separatism.

In Western Europe

Western Europe, with its preponderance of former colonial powers, consequently suffers far more direct terrorism than any other part of the world. (One excludes Lebanon, where terrorist strategies happen to be a prominent part of the format for a full-scale civil war). The United Kingdom, France, Spain, Portugal, the Netherlands, are all susceptible to angry or demonstrative attacks by dissatisfied subjects on their distant or former masters. The United States suffers its very substantial share of world terrorism for the same reasons not so much, perhaps, because it is genuine colonial power, but because it is very widely perceived as a nation which dominates many others through so-called 'economic imperialism'.

By definition, terrorists exaggerate: they usually subscribe to conspiracy theories which considerably over-estimate the powers of governments; in particular they take the exaggerated view that the US government can issue policy instructions to smaller, weaker and impoverished nations. It is as simplistic a view as the idea that multinational company operates without any kind of restriction or consultation: but the monster fits their myth, and the chosen ideological objectives are very accessible. Every city in the world has representatives of American and Western business corporations, essentially vulnerable to attack unless they decide that continuing political risks, dictate extreme security measures.

In some ways, international business is a more appropriate enemy for the terrorists than government: for like the terrorists, big business exerts actual power in a world set apart from the democratic, electoral process of voters and government. Arguably, business executives can have more genuine influence on individual lives than political executives. While terrorists envy the business community its non-governmental power, they attack it for the assumed purposes and purposes for which its power is used. For the majority of terrorists profess socialist or Marxist political tenets and theories and the embodiment of international capitalism makes a ready target.

Attacks on business are intended to cause a general sense of insecurity, and in this way to try to force a revaluation of the benefits of operating in the given territory. Attacks directed -- increasingly in Western Europe in the 1980s — at defence industries have the particular intention of dissuading the companies from operating in that sector of business. A very important secondary effect is the diverting of resources from the wealth-creating business of the corporate body into expensive and burdensome security measures, which in theory pushes the price of operating more impending to the level of unacceptability. No diplomatic mission wants to represent its country behind an inner-ring security sanctum of barbed wire, computer-coded entry systems and repeated body-checks: and no business wants to be transformed by its enemies' assaults into the stereotype that is their hostile caricature, of faceless, stateless and impersonal bureaucrats behind high walls. But the attacks are fast increasing, and the defences are becoming more and more necessary. The power of terrorism to alter outcomes — which is, to some extent, a function of the sophistication with which it is employed — changes dramatically according to the political situation in which it is used. Indeed, the strategy and efficacy of terrorist groups will vary according to the clandestine support they can rely on from their community, or their claimed constituency. In this respect it is useful to distinguish between 'grievance-terrorism' and 'ideological terrorism'.

Urban Revolutionaries

In the context of urban revolutionaries like the Red Army Faction or Action Directe there is little or no external constituency. But for nationalist/separatist factions, there is usually a substantial community. Catholics in Northern Ireland, Corsicans generally, Armenians scattered through the world — with a basic sympathy for the objectives of 'their' terrorists. The existence of this wider theoretical constituency often allows terrorists a (misplaced) sense of genuineness: that they are taking up the cudgels on behalf of others whom opportunity or lack of courage prevents from doing so. Not surprisingly, terrorists are of the belief they can find support for their actions from the community. Michael 'Bommi' Baumann, who was a member of the German Red Army Faction, argues in his book *Terror or Love* that the German terrorists were originally seen by German liberals as fundamentalist pranksters who had a salutary effect on stodgy German respectability, and thus gained a degree of amused approval. The French author Yann Moulier, who translated the prison/political memoir of Professor Toni Negri— a leader of Autonomia, sentenced terrorist, elected Radical Party Member of the Chamber of Deputies, and Dean of the Parisian political exiles' club — makes an even more emphatic statement.

It is hard to see anything but self-delusion or justification in such claims. On the other hand, there is enough evidence to suggest that in long-standing and hard-fought regional struggles such as those for Basque and Corsican independence, the fighters are so broadly supported — if only passively — that the efforts of police and security forces to suppress or eliminate them are in vain. In the case of the Basques in particular, there was a very deliberate effort to blur the lines between traditional celebration of folklore and festivals, political unrest, and full-scale participation. While the divisions are obscure to the outsider, however, it is obvious that community circles are very well aware who the fighters are. The *Euskaldunak* (Basques, in the Basque language of Euskara) had a specific campaign which employed their national traditions with the armed struggle. For both participants and spectators, the festive and cultural aspects help to make the military campaign acceptable.

Irish Catholic Republicans of Northern Ireland offer a considerable degree of at least passive support to the Provisional IRA. Here, too, the fighters have a degree of informal celebrity in the community, not least because the IRA seeks to enforce a local discipline on young offenders who misbehave, in order to establish its authority as an alternative to the (predominantly Protestant) police or the British Army. The position of the community, then, always plays a strikingly important role in the inevitable propaganda struggle which accompanies any substantial terrorist campaign. The government in question will definitely attempt to show that the terrorists represent no one by concentrating upon their violent, criminal procedures; while those who support their objectives will try to emphasise the large issue, aggrandising their role in pursuit of 'justice' while playing down the violent strategies.

Particularly during the period of the hunger strikes in 1980 and 1981, the British government and the IRA were waging a comprehensive propaganda war on both sides of the Atlantic. The target was the Irish community in the United States, where supporters of the Provisionals had been able to raise substantial sums of money for weapons over the years, and a wider Irish lobby has prevented tough action being taken against those who either fund arm or shelter terrorists within the USA. Both sides knew how much was under threat in winning the confidence of the community for whom the IRA claimed to be undergoing martyrdom. Nominally the hunger strikes were believed to be in support of five demands which Republican prisoners in the Maze prison wanted met; but it was actually a desperate tactical reaction to the belief, ludicrously articulated in public by British government sources, that the IRA was 'on the run'. The IRA found an issue on which to make the most potent possible protest, and exploited it with great skill to revive support from its own community. As the critic Denis Donoghue observed in the *New York Review of Books* of 22 October 1981, 'The declared conflict [between the British government and the IRA] is merely nominal'. His masterful reading-between-the-lines deserves quoting at length:

> The real conflict is between those Irish people who regard the IRA as perverts, corrupters of a great tradition. The Provisionals have only one aim at the moment: the compel the Irish people to acknowledge them as their true, legitimate sons.
>
> The IRA can hardly hope to achieve this aim by force of argument, definition and reason. They must transcend the terms of any such discourse. The only way to do that is by taking some mortally intimidating course of action, something that requires courage, passion and selflessness. Discourse can only be transcended by action: inside a prison, action can only take a symbolic form, all the more potent for being irrational and exorbitant. There is no gesture more compelling than the hunger strike, and ideally the hunger strike until death.

When Bobby Sands became the first to die, he gave the cause a martyr's image to sustain it. In a stroke of political genius he had been manoeuvred into the position of becoming an elected Member of Parliament for Fermanagh and South Tyrone. The Provos had their supporters painting murals throughout Republican West Belfast, to delineate the sacrifice of the hunger strikers. The most memorable and most photographed mural was a religiose portrait of a haggard, bearded hunger striker holding a rosary, captioned, 'Blessed Are Those Who Hunger For Justice'. As Denis Donoghue perceived, 'Bobby Sands's death by hunger has achieved what he could never have achieved by his outstanding skill with a gun. And it has been achieved not by reason or argument but by the primitive force of a symbolic act.'

During the hunger strikes, the BIS set about redressing the balance by issuing factual statements giving importance to the actual crimes of which the hunger strikers had been convicted.

Thus, a letter from one New York resident who described them as 'political prisoners' enraged the Press Officer of the BIS in New York to fire off a lengthy and lofty rebuttal, part of which read:

> These prisoners can by no stretch of the imagination be described as 'political prisoners', a term which is reserved for those imprisoned for their beliefs, not their actions. They have not been adopted as 'prisoners of conscience' by Amnesty International, which rejects the cases of those who have used or advocated violence: and the European Commission for Human Rights has stated that they are not entitled to political status.

Similarly, the BIS did not hesitate to circulate — with a strongly negative implication — the very comments of Danny Morrison, then Sinn Fein's publicity officer, which were to become a lasting rallying cry for the IRA's supporters. Examples of such propaganda contests demonstrate the importance for every terrorist group of a wider resource of support — from die-hard fundamentalists on the fringes of illegality themselves, or even from legal and legitimate political parties. Alongside any small group of genuine terrorists there will be found a wider faction which inhabits the margins between legal political activism and illegal terrorism. While revolutionary (ideological) terrorists can never rely on the active political support of publicly identified allies, nationalists and separatists, as it seems, always enjoy relationship with a legal, political front: the IRA has Sinn Fein; the Corsican FLNC has the *Conseil des Comites Nationalistes*; the Basque ETA has *Euskal Iraultzarako Alderdia* (Party for the Basque Revolution). France, pre-eminently, has a very wide range of Comites de Soutien or Support Committees for 'political prisoners' of every political colour: for Armenian political prisoners — that is, for Armenian terrorists imprisoned by the French courts for killing and holding hostage innocent persons in the Turkish Consulate in Paris; there is a *Comite de Soutien* for Basque political refugees in south-west France, and two Irish *Comites*.

Political Mechanics of Terrorism

These, then, are the political mechanics of terrorism, the places, political systems, causes and grievances which give rise to the happening that has marked a historical generation. They are focussed by two case histories of terrorist movements which stand at opposite ends of the spectrum of 'constituency support'. One of the most disturbing developments in terrorism in the 1980s is the New European alliance, involving French, German and Belgian factions, with intermittent parallel action from Portuguese, Spanish, Italian and Dutch comrades, apparently pledged to attack government, international agency, and business targets. The objectives are united by the anti-American, anti-business, anti-military, anti-nuclear, anti-NATO themes of the terrorists' scheme of things politics. The prime mover of this alliance had appeared to be the French revolutionary group Action Directe.

Action Directe is a second-generation European terrorist outfit. Its roots do not lie directly in the student *evenements* and movements of May 1968, which to a large extent gave rise to both Italian and German terrorism: but is politics lie in the same tradition. The political odyssey of Jean-Marc Rouillan shows an opportunistic willingness to espouse political cause or marginalised minorities, primarily to keep the outfit active. In this respect, Action Directe was unusual— no permanent, emphatic political objective animated all its actions, though since 1984 its ideology has crystallised into a jargon-ridden Marxism-Lenninism.

The activities of Action Directe have passed through five phases:

1. 1979-1980 — the group first became violently operational in firing machine-gun bursts at the facades of French government ministry buildings, the offices of gigantic companies, and the French National Police Headquarters. In 1980, a shell was fired from a rocket launcher at the offices of the Ministry of Transport — one of the twenty attacks in the same year in Paris and Toulouse.
2. 1981-2 — Action Directe took up pro-Palestinian, anti-Israeli operation, taking their cue not least from the Israeli invasion of Lebanon. They operated in tandem with an outfit named *Fractions armees revolutionnaires libanaises* (FARL), using the same weapons and issuing joint communiques. Together, they killed two diplomats — an American and an Israeli.

3. 1983 — the Italian period. Action Directe collaborated with Italian terrorists who had taken retreat in Paris. Members of Prima Linea and COLP (*Communisti Organisati per la Liberazione del Proletariat*) joint Action Directe terrorists in trouble to raise funds for both their purposes — in the case of the Italians, to establish a 'foreign front' for Red Brigade terrorism in Italy. In one setback, two French policemen were shot dead and one wanted Italian terrorist, Ciro Rizzato, was killed in the gun battle.
4. 1984 — Action Directe leaders took refuge in Belgium where the CCC (*Cellules Communistes Combattantes*) was very prominent as their counterpart. This was the beginning of a practical co-operation which brought Action Directe into the anti-American, anti-NATO Marxist camp of the erstwhile existing European terrorist outfits, including CCC, the Red Army Faction of Germany (by now in its third generation) and even the Portuguese faction, FP-25. A major theft of explosives in Belgium provided the means for more than thirty bombings in France, Belgium and West Germany.
5. 1985 — Action Directe returned to pursuing goals inside France, related for the first time to the internal politics of the country: noticeably with three bombs to protest the broadcasting airtime permitted to the ultra-rightwing National Front leader, Jean-Marie Le Pen, and with bombs disapproving French economic involvement in South Africa.

The leader of Action Directe, Jean-Marc Rouillan, was born in 1953 in Auch, the provincial capital of Gers. The French capacity for romanticising the menacing and daring criminals created a myth of an intelligent, cultivated art-lover, half-paranoid and half-megalomaniac, who never takes off his bullet-proof vest. As learnt, allegedly took part in cross-border 'missions' to strike at Spanish targets, besides many demonstrations and some physical atrocities on Spanish interest in France. In 1974 he joined a clandestine organisation, the *Groupes d'Action Revolutionnaire Internationalistes* (GARI), and like several students then and now, wore his radicalism around his neck in the shape of a Palestinian *keffiyeh* headdress.

His anti-Spanish stance got him arrested in 1974, and he was freed in 1977. He was re-arrested in July 1978 and spent half a year again in jail. At such a stage, that in 1979, Rouillan, Menigon and others (including Regis Schleicher, Frederic Oriach, and two French-Algerians, Mohand Hamami and Laouari Ben Shellal) founded Action Directe.

A former fundamentalist associate, 'Alain', analyses the political background to the establishment of Action Directe in terms of the larger political context of the radical left in France. A French counterpart of the Italian *Autonomia Operaia* (Workers' Autonomy) participated in the Paris demonstration by steel-workers from the moribund industrial town of Longwy, and were surprised by the violence which occurred in the mass march. "The problem was to find the capacity to widen these protests into a movement of mass support: with a repressive government, a mass movement is impossible, but a very radical part of the movement starts to consider "military organisation". The irony was that the French Autonomie worked assuming that the state was always repressive and, 'Alain' says, 'never entertained the notion that the Socialists would gain power by election — we thought it could only come by other means. Then the government stole the radicals' clothes, and cut the ground from under their feet, by taking up the themes that radicalise people — the Third World, South African apartheid and so on.

Terrorists and Military Groups

He even went on say: 'Terrorism always arises when there are no pre-eminent political issues to unite and maintain an organised public movement. And terrorists, people who support the militaristic groups, are much more efficient than radical activists — they are the other branch of the institutional form of politics'. So, according to 'Alain', the radicals who maintained legality and legitimacy had been stuck in a middle ground of impotence, while the 'real' politicians and the 'efficient' terrorists slug out the absolute battles. That was also the view of the founders of Action Directe: 'The concept of Action Directe, and the faction itself, developed from an absence of debate on the issues where they chose their targets', (i.e., defence, NATO, international monetary systems, American capitalism dominating the West). 'They were against the institutionalisation of the movement and criticised such a development as "mere words" - when they wanted strictly "Direct Action".

The political theory of direct action is mysterious: 'Alain' refers to a Maoist view that there need be no complicated political motive for a revolutionary action. 'First you act, then consider - was it well or badly done? How was it received by the people?' He makes the analogy that terrorism represents, more or less, the same approach to political problems — arbitrary, dramatic, and breathtaking — that the media employs in relation to 'facts', claiming that the real power lies not with the participants in events, but with the editor who has the power to emphasise coverage, put appropriate headlines and change meanings.

For ideologies of the extreme left, violence in itself is not an issue; the world is full of it, they say: state terror, wars devouring human cannon-fodder, hunger, natural calamities, disease. The only interesting question, they believe, which arises with the violence in political confrontation, is what effect it has. 'People in Autonomie used to say "we have committed an act of violence during a demonstration in order to avoid worse acts of violence occurring in isolation" — a kind of de-escalation,' says 'Alain'. Thus, it is thought-provoking to reflect on the purposes of Action Directe's leader Jean-Marc Rouillan, at least in the light of 'Alain's' description: 'He is very important, definitely the leader. He is un *baroudeur*, the kind of man who would have gone off to fight in the International Brigade in the Spanish Civil War. He was closely linked with the anti-Franco movement in the last years. He was absolutely not interested in intellectual matters, political theory, or anything like that. But he's not a mere gangster'.

Action Directe became operationally viable as a clandestine organisation of sheer force with a major robbery in the northern French town of Conde-sur-l'Escaut, on 29 August 1979. Around noon, five men and a woman burst into the main hall of the tax collection offices at 10 rue Notre-Dame, in the centre of the town. They were all fully armed and masked, some of them wearing welders' face-masks, some caps, and some ware bullet-proof vests. They rounded up the staff of the tax office, and cleared away 16 million francs from the safes and the piles of cash that were being counted when they arrived. They had walkie-talkie contact with their other colleagues outside in stolen cars, and their militarily specific operation was over as quickly as it had begun.

According to a woman member of Action Directe, interviewed by Radio France-Inter in 1981, 'The guys who did the robbery did it for the revolutionary movement in general. So the money was used for the whole revolutionary movement, not only the French movement, but certainly in part for international solidarity, for infrastructure, to get hold of papers, weapons, and to help comrades in jail'. It was widely believed, from the hallmarks of the raid, that the attack not only served to assist 'the international movement' but had been carried out with worldwide assistance. Both the Italian *Prima Linea* (Front Line) group and the Spanish GRAPO (Revolutionary Group of the First of October) were allegedly involved.

In France, the money raised by such robberies - 'proletarian expropriation' as Rouillan called them enabled Action Directe to go underground and procure the weapons used in twenty or more attacks on French government and business in 1979-80. Living a clandestine life is not easy at all, said Rouillan: 'We try to do these hold-ups as little as possible, only what is necessary. Stealing money from banks is justified, but we don't do it for fun. We do it out of need, in order to function, to buy apartments, cars, weapons, papers — false papers necessary for living underground'.

Like all terrorists, Action Directe depends greatly on fake papers — identity cards, passports, driving licences, social security numbers, car registration and insurance documents. Sometimes these can be bought, but more often legitimate, blank papers have to be stolen from the original source either the local government offices where they are issued, or the printers where they are first produced. On 5 August 1980, Action Directe launched attack the Mairie of the 14th *arrondissement in Paris*. One of the participants, a young woman, told Radio France-Inter what they were after: 'It was pretty simple: basically, we needed identity papers, in fact all the papers we could get from inside. We decided to go in to the Mairie, with some of the comrades, and help ourselves. We got the thing together very quickly, we had enough cars that we had stolen already. We made them open the safes, and we took away all the papers and rubber stamps that we thought were useful. Then we went out, got back in the cars and left. There was no violence because the people reacted very well and weren't unduly alarmed. They saw that we were calm and precise. Of course, we had our hoods up so that we could not be recognised, and the weapons were just to make an impression'. Just over a month later, on 13 September 1980, Rouillan's clandestine life came to a temporary end: at 6.15 p.m. in the rue Pergolese, Paris, a metallic coloured Peugeot 604 crawled along the street. Suddenly gunfire started and at the entry to an apartment building Rouillan was surrounded by police officers before he could reach for his Magnum .357. The die-hard leaders were tried and jailed and the round-up of Action Directe continued, with most of the principal figures imprisoned by the end of 1980.

Controversial Heads of States

But in May 1981, following a traditional but controversial practice of incoming presidents, Francois Mitterrand declared an amnesty for thousands of prisoners whose crimes supposedly had a political element: and to the amazement of many, by no means all counted among Mitterrand's political opponents, Rouillan and Menigon, along with other prominent Action Directe members were released from jail.

The imprisoned leaders gave secret interviews to Radio France-Inter; since their release Rouillan has given only one other interview, to the left wing newspaper *Liberation*, in August 1982. And in October the same year he supplied written replies to questions put by the communist newspaper *Le Matin*. But on neither occasion offered any guide to the overall intentions of Action Directe. Thus, Rouillan's somewhat hazy description of the political objectives of Action Directe — as outlined to France-Inter in 1981 — is of specific interest: 'We want a communist society, with every proletarian conscious of his class identity - that is to say the destruction of capitalist society based on the merchants reaping the benefit from the wage-earning class. And we think that the end of man's exploitation of man will come with the destruction of this capitalist society, full of unemployment, misery, exploitation, planned murder, accidents at work in the name of profit. We are true communists.'

In late 1981 and early 1982 Action Directe went underground, disappearing into the Arab ghettoes of the 18th and 20th *arrondissements* in Paris. There they made contact with, and recruited to their banner, radical Arabs, members of Turkish workers' groups who lived on the margins of legality, and people from the squatters' movement. At that stage Rouillan allegedly also pursued some contacts with the 'legitimate left'. One unconfirmed story suggests that when Rouillan was arrested, based on complaints from the owners of a 'squat' property which turned out to be sheltering seventeen outlawed Turkish workers, he was released within an hour after pressure on the investigating magistrate by a Socialist Party Deputy. Another rumour was regarding the fact that some of Rouillan's comrades had hijacked an official car belonging to Lionel Jospin, the Secretary of the Socialist Party, and stolen particulars 'important papers' which they quickly photocopied and scattered to a number of locations, some outside France. The interpretation was that any effort to prosecute Rouillan could be undermined by embarrassing revelations — of an unknown nature — about the government party.

In March 1982 Action Directe released its political manifesto entitled *Pour un Projet Communiste*. As a literary work it had no merit, consisting of indigestible Marxist-Leninist parlance. Its critique of world capitalism, and the particular examples that are singled out for vitriolic political abuse, do however suggest some of the targets of the following violence. One 'axis of intervention' is defined as 'French imperialism supreme arena of decadent capitalism'; and the document particularly attacks the International Monetary Fund, OPEC and American multinationals in these terms: 'America has systematically financed the invasion of the world by her multinationals and satisfied the hamburger-eaters of the world (MacDonalds - of course) thanks to the International Monetary System sustaining her power and the continuing domination of the developed world'. In terms of internal politics, the document bemoaned unemployment, empty housing and high rents, the difficulties of foreign workers, and the increasingly assuming international character of French industrial corporations.

During 1982 Palestinian terrorists (largely Syrian - supported) were particularly active, not only in the Middle East but in Europe as well. Paris had inherited London's former unenviable position as the battlefield for Middle Eastern terrorism, yet it was in London that Abu Nidal terrorists gunned down the erstwhile Israeli ambassador Shlomo Argov. Israel's response to this and an accumulation of other provocations was to mount 'Operation Peace for Galilee' - the invasion of Southern Lebanon which subsequently, transformed that country, drove the Palestinians out of Beirut, and lasted three years. But it was in Paris that most terrorist warfare against Israeli or Jewish interests took place. Even before the invasion, Action Directe's Arab connections had mounted an attack on the Israeli trade mission in April 1982. Within a few days, an Israeli diplomat was shot dead: this attack, too, was claimed by *Fractions armees revolutionnaires libanaises* as was the killing of the American attache Charles Ray. The FARL communique, after that discovered to have been printed by the same equipment as Action Directe material, was distributed in French, Arabic and Turkish. Over the following months a 'hot summer of terrorism' swept Paris, including the machine-gun attack on Goldenberg's restaurant in the Jewish Marais, thereby killing six people. Less publicised were three Action Directe bombings on Jewish targets, which Jean-Marc Rouillan justified to *Liberation* as 'a perfectly normal reply to the situation in Lebanon. This is international camaraderie. Action Directe actually claims the paternity of its attacks. The wave of terrorism that afflicted France was too much even for President Mitterrand whose amnesty of little more than a year earlier had been seen by many as at least partly responsible for the carnage.

At the same time, one such militant supporter of Action Directe was released from jail. Mme. Helyette Besse was one of Action Directe's most unexpected luminaries - fiftyish, swarthy and chubby lady anarchist who was the proprietor of one of Paris's most out-of-the-way backstreet 'alternative' bookshops, called 'Le Jargon Libre'. After that she announced the reactivation of *Defense Active*, a committee of support for 'French Political Prisoners'. The committee had first been instituted to protest at the omission of some names from President Mitterrand's amnesty

— some 'supposed' Action Directe members, some autonomist militants from NAPAP (*Noyaux Armes Pour l'Autonomic Populaire*), some anti-nuclear militants, some people arrested on suspicion of involvement in the Conde-sur-l'Escaut robbery. The revived committee, according to Besse, would 'regroup, in other forms, militants, ex-militants and sympathisers of Action Directe'. However, her personal freedom to campaign seemed unlikely by the fact that she was herself awaiting trial for possession of three blank Italian identity cards. (In August 1983 she was found guilty and fined 500 francs).

Despite the new illegality of the organisation, Action Directe continued to try to constitute, by involving disparate political minorities. It also plunged into the community of Italian 'political exiles' - ultimately becoming implicated in a gruesome shoot-out where two policemen died. This followed a robbery in May 1983, when a Parisian public relations consultant was ejected from behind the steering-wheel of his car as he left a smart restaurant in the 17th *arrondissement*. A few days later, in the avenue Trudaine, two policemen from the 9th *arrondissement* anti-robbery squad stopped the car and asked the occupants for their papers. Both officers were killed on the spot. At the end of the car chase that followed, a wanted Prima Linea terrorist, Ciro Rizzato, was shot dead by police, but his companion(s) managed to escape.

By the end of 1983 (when Helyette Besse was arrested by customs officials for occasional holding of foreign currency, in the shape of $10,030) Action Directe was beginning to look towards an international collaboration. A number of new radical leftist publications appeared in radical bookshops: *L'Internationale, Combattre Pour le Communisme, Ligne Rouge* (which specialised in the publication of terrorists' communiques, claiming responsibility for the attacks) and *Subversion* were among them. It was *Subversion* which published their political agenda. 'We must build a fighting Communist International, to destroy the party of war. This is the party of the capitalists, of multinationals dominated by American interests. The evolution of Western Europe is now the cornerstone of world struggle. So we must detach Italy from NATO, as that country is one of the weakest links. Elsewhere we must smash French social democracy, a traditional agent of imperialist wars'.

Subversion was the subject of an unprecedented police incident in Brussels. Its articles, identifying the USA, NATO, and the French arms industry as genuine targets for the class struggle, naturally provoked interest from the Belgian authorities. The first issue of *Subversion* carried two correspondence addresses, one (false) in Paris, the other a Brussels post office box a professional printer suspected of contacts with local terrorist outfits. The Brussels police sought a warrant from the authorities to open the postal box, but were refused permission; and although the second edition still carried the address (though not the one in Paris) no action was taken. From the beginning of 1984, the various component parts of the European terrorist alliance had started to turn their theories into actions, waging a really substantial campaign against the kind of targets identified in their political spheres. On 25 January 1984 a quantity of plastic explosives blew up at the Military Studies Bureau of the Aerospatiale Company at Chatillon; and on 29 January another bomb exploded at the Panhard-Levassor factory in Paris. Both attacks caused considerable damage. Action Directe's new Belgian headquarters was almost certainly in Brussels — where Rouillan and Menigon had helped to establish the CCC, and to set up the strong alliance with German outfits. The Belgian police were getting more alert to the dangers of their presence with every bomb that exploded in the name of the anti-NATO, anti-military coalition.

By some extraordinary mistake, a single officer — Jean Marie Arnould — was sent into the office, where he went to speak to a man whom he presumed to be an employee of the agency. It was Schleicher, who immediately grabbed Arnould's pistol, and with another man (presumed to be Rouillan) rushed to the car. The office manager, Christian Lemmens, told the press later: 'I thought they were trying to leave without paying, so I followed them into the street. The car was parked in front of our windows, with the motor running. Inside there was a woman with long hair, wearing a wool hat and a blouson jacket. She opened the door, pointed a pistol at me, and yelled "Get lost, fast!" At that point I realised that one of the three men was being held by the others. They all jumped into the Toyota and it disappeared.'

Inspector Arnould enjoyed only a short journey with his

abductors after a few minutes down the road to Waterloo they bundled him out of the car, having relieved him of his police identity card, his pistol (a GP7.65) and his radio set. But they let him keep his handcuffs, with his hands locked firmly in them. Despite roadblocks and a police hunt throughout Belgium, the leadership of Action Directe escaped *en masse*. And despite the type of the crimes for which the three were wanted by police across Europe, the French press relished their narrow escape.

There was no clear intention, except perhaps a sense of narrow escape, for Schleicher having left Belgium that day or the next. Possibly Rouillan ordered him back to France because his face was then well-known in Belgium — at least by Inspector Arnould. But two days later he was in France and to be more precise in police custody. Surveillance had revealed that the leadership of Action Directe was planning to reunite once again — either in Italy or in the Midi — and that Helyette Besse was handling the logistics of renting houses and raising funds.

If the arrest was a setback for Action Directe, it barely impeded the development of the 'European campaign'. Just as the big cash haul from Conde-sur-l'Escaut apparently sustained the European revolutionaries for many years, so another theft in Belgium provided the CCC-AD-RAF terrorists with the wherewithal for almost as many attacks as they had the will and the numbers to stage. If any confirmation was needed of the uses to which such a huge haul was to be put, it came with the first explosion — not in Belgium, but in France — on 23 August 1984. About twenty-three kilos of the explosive blew up in a car parked outside the Paris headquarters of the Western European Union, at 83 avenue du President Wilson. This attack, carried out by Action Directe, was closely followed by another on NATO oil pipelines in Belgium, by CCC; and a third, on a military training school in Bavaria, the then West Germany, by the Red Army Faction. There followed a further eight attacks on industrial, military and political targets in Belgium between October and the end of the year.

Between January and June 1985 there was a brief lull in Belgium: a pause in activity, however, which coincided with the rise in attacks in both Germany and France. With the turn of the year, Action Directe devoted itself to French political matters: that is, focusing on the specifically French element of the familiar target areas — defence contractors, industrial multinationals and so on — and carrying out attacks relating to French domestic and foreign policy.

In the erstwhile West Germany, on 7 January 1985, the Red Army Faction raided the explosives depot of a cement factory in Geisingen, Baden-Wuerttemburg. It was not a massive haul, but they got away with 35 rolls of fuse cord and 376 detonator caps. These materials were almost surely used in the first of a concentrated series of attacks on American military targets in the then West Germany on 7 August 1985, which was a model of terrorist tactics and rhetoric. A car bomb consisting of explosives and gas bottles killed two American nationals and injured more than twenty when it blew up at the United States Air Force's Rehin-Main base near Frankfurt. The responsibility of the attack was claimed jointly by the RAF and Action Directe: their Communique claimed the attack was a blow struck against imperialism. 'The USAF base is a centre for war against the Third World, used to transport American troops and military equipment for acts of intervention in the Middle East and Africa.'

The groups later admitted to the murder of a US serviceman whose identity card had enabled them to reach the base. The second-hand Volkswagen car which served to transport the bomb carried US military licence plates, and had been bought in Frankfurt ten days before that. West German police named the suspected purchaser of the car as Sigrid Sterneback, 'a veteran RAF hardliner' who had been on the wanted list since 1977.

Terrorists Attack

On 15 June 1985, an apparently new terrorist outfit attacked the American Forces Network Pomcus depot, in Monchengladbach. The responsibility of the attack was claimed by the 'Fighting Unit for the Creation of an Anti-Imperialist Front in Western Europe' — a title which neatly describes the collective objectives of the AD-RAF-CCC alliance. Their letter demanded the 'immediate release' of a jailed RAF outlaw, Gunter Sonnenberg, and the 'bringing together of the prisoners of the Red Army Faction and the anti-imperialist resistance in factions capable of interaction'.

Yet another new name — or possibly a new outfit emerged in late June. On Wednesday 19 June 1985 a parcel bomb exploded in a luggage locker at Frankfurt International Airport, killing three people. At first there was a stunning silence — breaking the normal pattern of terrorism, where the prime rule is to make a public claim. But three days after a bomb exploded in a letter box of the Bayer Pharmaceuticals Company in the heart of Brussels. A few minutes afterwards, an anonymous caller to the police claimed responsibility for the bombing, saying it was a response to pollution of the North Sea by toxic waste, and the seizure by Spain of the *Sirius* — one of the campaign ships of the environmental pressure group Greenpeace, who promptly denied having any connection with the terrorists. Later the same day, staff at Agence France Presse in Paris found a letter: written in English, it read 'Our brothers have just strike (*sic*) in Frankfurt Main. Congratulations'. The letter was handed, both in French and English, "The Peace Conquerors' the same name given earlier the same day to Belgian police, and never heard elsewhere. Neither claim did make mention of the other, but the letter opened by Agence France-Press in Paris went on to warn 'Stop Nuisance Stop Pollution Stop Airport' (most probably the airport extension at Frankfurt). The letter added: 'Before the end of the month we'll destroy a major Frankfurt Airport building, and a Jumbo Jet.' This warning certainly evoked a sudden, strong feeling of shock though little serious speculation of a line — when the very next day, an Air India jet went to the bottom of the Atlantic Ocean.

Attacks continued incessantly in Belgium throughout 1985. No individual names had yet emerged in connection with the CCC. No details about the organisation had been discovered. There are many examples in the past of terrorist groups inventing new names to distract and confuse the security forces pursuing them. It was tempting to speculate that the Belgian comrades-in-arms were a fiction, a Red herring to remove the attention from Action Directe and the RAF. The European police force were working on the assumption that the new terrorist coalition had four leaders: Jean-Marc Rouillan and Nathalie Menigon, of Action Directe; Inge Viett, a longstanding comrade of the Baader-Meinhof and Red Army Faction ranks; and a Belgian rebel (and former member of Action Directe itself), Pierre Carrette, aged thirty-three, the son of a policeman and a printer by trade, who had first come to the notice of the police when he championed the cause of confined terrorists in the then West Germany. (Late in 1985, however, the concrete reality of CCC's membership was confirmed with the arrest, following fourteen months of police investigation, of Pierre Carrette and three associates: Bertrand Sasoye, Didier Chevolet and Pascal Vandegeerde. The trio had been under surveillance, and when they met Carrette police blocked all the exists and moved in. All four were armed, but they did not resist arrest: subsequent searches of safe houses revealed incriminating documents relating to the CCC's twenty-seven bombing attacks, and police claimed they found Carrette's fingerprints on leaflets. All four had been filmed by police as they revisited the spot of their attacks).

By far the most dramatic and unexpected escalation of terrorist attacks, however, came in France. In January 1985, the first communique signed jointly by Action Directe and the Red Army Faction was delivered to AFP in Paris. It consulted 'the essential tasks facing communist guerrillas in Western Europe'.

We must construct a politico-military front in Western Europe, for the central project, in the present phase of imperialist strategy, is the attempt to unite European states into a homogeneous structure, into one hard block, which would be completely integrated in the noose of imperialist power NATO.

The new policy of NATO puts particular emphasis on the placing of Euromissiles, the revitalisation of the Western European Union, the creation in France of the Rapid Deployment Force, co-operation in weapons areas by NATO members, discussion of German participation in the French strike force, and its integration into NATO.

The production of this document has an interesting background. An Italian who was a member of Action Directe, before becoming a police informer, gave a back-door interview to *Liberation* in which he told of a meeting in Paris between French, Italian and German 'Euroterrorists' 'I went to a meeting-place on 6 January to take part in a meeting of the Committee of Support for the RAF hunger-strikers. We were very excited because we knew that a woman militant from the RAF would be there. She was actually there with another RAF woman, and there were people from Action Directe. Afterwards I was given this draft written by the Germans, reviewed by the French, it was agreed at another meeting the next day devoted to Franco-German links. To get this alliance, each side had made concessions: the Germans had distanced themselves from the Eastern bloc, and Action Directe was abandoning its libertarian side'.

On 25 January the US State Department — taking note of the new 'Euroterrorist' communique - predicted terrorist operations against 'targets related to NATO, and persons working in the defence area'. That same day Action Directe demonstrated what it meant to drop its, 'libertarian' attitude.

General Rene Andran, director of international affairs at the French Ministry of Defence, was one of the most senior figures of the French military-industrial complex and his murder sent shock waves throughout the French defence industry, which normally employs almost a million people. He had been in his post since 1983, after a long career in the arms industry, and was a technical expert of international stature; but he had no known political role.

Even though the German connection might have been a deliberate false lead, French police took the view that Action Directe almost surely did employ a German comrade to help in making the hit: not least because the German authorities were also pursuing enquiries into a nearly identical murder of Audran's close European aide and rough equal in the West German Defence Ministry, Ernst Zimmerman. Two terrorists had rung the doorbell of his suburban home early in the morning, on the semblance of delivering a parcel, tied up his wife, and shot Zimmerman dead in his bedroom.

About five months later, in the same year in yet another similar incident directed at a similar target, Spanish terrorists assassinated Rear-Admiral Fausto Escrigas Estrada, the then Director-General of Defence Policy. One or two men fired at the admiral's car with a sub-machine gun: the admiral died within minutes, and his driver was seriously wounded. The killers' getaway car was found in another area of Madrid, laden with explosives, and despite an attempt to defuse the devices, the car blew up. Witnesses later successfully identified one of the gunmen from police photographs as a member of the ETA-Militar 'Spain Squad'. Four months later, the death of yet another senior defence industry personnel in Belgium caused yet more speculation about the Euroterrorist campaign against the arms and defence industry. No clues to the killer's identity were apparent.

Action Directe attacks on military-industrial targets continued throughout the year in France: at 5.30 a.m., on 27 April 1985 they exploded a car-bomb at the Parisian headquarters of one of the Euroterrorist alliance's key enemies the International Monetary Fund. The car, a red Renault 11, had been hijacked earlier and loaded with explosives and gas bottles. The explosion caused every single window in the seven-storey building to shatter, besides many in neighbouring buildings.

It seems likely that a similar attack was plotted for the same weekend by Action Directe, who frequently grouped their attacks within hours or at most days of each other for greatest effect; but their plans were unsettled by the arrest of the delivery man, bringing the explosives for the job once again from the Ecaussines haul from Belgium.

Action Directe's attention was also directed to French domestic politics, where one of the most divisive developments had been the emergence of substantial support for the ultra-conservative and racist National Front Party, led by the supposedly charismatic personality in the shape of Jean-Marie Le Pen. The level of support for his party has given broadcasters little choice but to offer him opportunities to speak on their programmes — but it seemed too much for Action Directe. After he had appeared on Radio France-Inter's *Face Au Public*, and Antenne 2 television's *L'Heure de Verite*, Action Directe fired both barrels. The terrorists accused Le Pen of 'pushing the limits to see how far Capital can go in attacking the working class and dividing it with racism. While Le Pen was advocating Holy Capitalist War under the lights of radio and TV studios, the French military was carrying it out on various territories'. A third protest bomb exploded on the 17 October, at the High Authority for Broadcasting; Action Directe declared that the bomb was the work of the 'Commando Ahmed Mouley' - an Algerian 'martyr' (marking the racist context) who died in the Battle of Algiers on 3 March 1957.

Ultimately, Helyette Besse came to trial. Described variously as Action Directe's 'Hot Mama' and its 'Good Fairy', She had been imprisoned, charged with 'criminal association' since 17 March 1984. But the earlier charge of illegally holding foreign currency came to court on 30 September 1985. Her statement to the court summed up her plight properly: 'I am here because I am an anarchist, a Communist, and a militant member of Action Directe. This charge of illegal possession of currency is a side-issue.' She further claimed that France was a 'state which refuses to recognise political prisoners'. On 21 October the court found her guilty and ordered the confiscation of her illegal $ 10,000, a fine of 80,000 francs and a suspended prison sentence of one month.

Directions of Terrorism

In the case of terrorism directed towards regional self-determination or national liberation, it is usually the rule that a violent militant periphery has existed almost as long as the cause. In the Basque country, present-day fighters talk of a fight which has lasted 150 years, and frequently there is a family tradition — almost a vocation of 'the struggle'. The struggle to liberate Ireland from British influence belong to a history of seven centuries of intermittent violence.

The Armenian Secret Army for the Liberation of Armenia (ASALA), the preeminent terrorist outfit dedicated to recognition and independence for the Armenian people, surfaced in 1975, the diamond jubilee of what Armenian nationalists call 'the first genocide of the twentieth century', when Ottoman troops forcibly drove Armenians out of their homeland in north-eastern Turkey in 1915. In the 1980s, there were around two million Armenians in what they, like the Jews, call their 'diaspora'. They lived in Syria and Lebanon, France, the USA and Australia, among many other countries. One of the leaders of ASALA, who emerged as a public figure in violent Armenian circles, is Alec Yenicomechian, an accomplished linguist and former student of economics at the American University of Beirut. According to Yenicomechian, and indeed all Armenians, the Ottoman authorities forced nearly two million Armenians to leave the towns and villages where their people had lived for around thousand years: 'During this forced deportation, specially formed armed bands attacked the deportees' caravans, to deprive them of their minimum resources and massacre them, killing several hundred thousand Armenians.' Another several hundred thousand perished in the course of this long March of travail, from exhaustion or scarcity of food and water which was very often denied to them. And there were several hundred thousand more, who had survived the infernal deportation and armed attacks, who were literally exterminated by the Ottoman army in the Syrian desert. In total 1.5 million Armenians or more were massacred or driven to their death between 1915 and 1920.

Although historians argued on behalf of both sides to increase or diminish the figure, there is no doubt that a fearful death toll resulted from the forced marches. What was more significant in the light of the contemporary terrorist campaigns, was whether modern Turkey was to be held responsible for the actions of its predecessor power, the Ottoman Empire. Conscious of this historical lacuna in political responsibility, Yenicomechian was quick to add this to his accusation about the genocide: 'The scenario was completed a few years later by Kemal Ataturk, the father of present-day Turkey'. By 1975, according to him, the patience and hope of Armenian nationalists had been exhausted. 'For sixty years the Armenian masses had hoped that the world's conscience would awaken, and they would recover their rights. In 1965, the fiftieth anniversary of the carnages, we redoubled our peaceful efforts: in the next ten years, Armenians knocked harder on the doors of big and small countries, the United Nations; we sent memoranda, prepared documents and legal depositions; we organised peaceful demonstrations across the world, involving tens of thousands of people. All imaginable peaceful means had been attempted. 1975 was a year of reckoning, but there was nothing in credit'.

Therefore, in the words of Alec Yenicomechian, a sea-change occurred in Armenian thinking: 'After sixty years of waiting, sixty years of efforts and peaceful struggle, after so many years of humiliation, the Armenian people ultimately realised that nothing would be given to them freely, realised that if they wanted to regain their legitimate rights, it was imperative to pay with their blood. So Armenian fighting organisations saw the light day'.

The scheme of terrorist violence commenced in 1975; however, it was not the Armenians, but the modern Turks who paid with their blood. A highly efficient assassination campaign of Turkish diplomats started, conducted principally by two groups - the Armenian Secret Army for the Liberation of Armenia, and the Justice Commandos of the Armenian Genocide. ASALA, which had been the more active group, was based in Beirut, with significant links to pro-Syrian groups of the PLO. In that respect, they demonstrated that terrorists often benefit from the adage 'My enemy's enemy is my friend', Syrian-Turkish relations being characterised by mutual suspicion and continuing hostility.

Yet alongside the historical evolution of Armenian terrorism there was a chance catalyst which concentrated attention onto violent action and retaliation. The first Armenian terrorist was the most unlikely: Gurgen Yanikian, an Armenian engineer living in affluent retirement in California. The Californian courts were unmoved by Yanikian's defence, and at the age of 76 he was sentenced to life imprisonment. On his death in 1984 many members of Southern California's prosperous Armenian community assembled to pay their respects to this paradoxical emblem of the community. One Armenian newspaper editor told the mourners: 'We are gathered today to honour the memory of Gurgen Yanikian. There are those who think of him as a murderer, an assassin; there are others who think of him as a martyr. He could be both, or neither'.

In the underground Armenian press Yanikian celebrated as the first hero and martyr of the Armenian age of terrorism. His double murder in 1975 was a catalyst to militant young. Armenians to continue terrorist action against Turkey: in the course of the next seven years some fifty Turkish diplomats (and their unfortunate wives, children, or chauffeurs who happened to be in the line of fire at the wrong moment) were assassinated, mostly by ASALA. The carnage took place all over Western Europe, in the USA and Canada, and in Australia as well. Terrorist 'commandos', trained in Lebanon, took over embassies and consulates, demanding the release of imprisoned comrades. Bombs were planted, and grenades hurled, at Turkish Airlines (THY) and Turkish Government Tourist offices. As the death toll rose, the

Armenians were unable to detect any hint of flexibility or concession; therefore they enhanced the campaign to include bloodier, but suicidal attacks, inside Turkey.

On 7 August 1982 two terrorists, Levon Ekmekjian and Zahrab Sarkissian, took over a restaurant at Ankara's Esenboga International Airport. They hurled hand-grenades, and sprayed bullets into the crowded airport departures area; they made abortive attempts to negotiate with the Turkish authorities; and when Turkish troops burst into the restaurant, Sarkissian was gunned down and Ekmekjian captured, and later executed. Seven passengers had been killed. In honour of this action, three more Armenian members of ASALA calling themselves the Levon Ekmekjian Commando carried out a grenade and machine-gun attack in the covered market of Istanbul on 16 June 1983. According to *Hay Baykar*, the militant newspaper of the French Armenian community, the attack took place 'when a convoy of military jeeps was about to pass: the commando was trying to take three military hostages.' *Hay Baykar* said the death toll was 'three according to official Turkish sources, twenty-five, including seventeen Turkish soldiers, according to ASALA'. One of the commando, Meguerditch Madarian, seemingly blew himself to pieces with a grenade rather than be captured by Turkish soldiers, a gesture hailed by *Hay Baykar*: 'Meguerditch Madarian fell as a martyr in the flower of his youth, an image of Armenian youth which despair and cynicism about the success of our cause have led to the most awful, most insane sacrifice — Madarian, dead on the enemy's soil'.

This, then was the Armenian armed struggle, regarded by Alec Yenicomechian as the inexorable last resort for Armenian nationalist aspirations. 'Our experience and that of others have proved that the armed movement remains the principle means of regaining our legitimate rights: and we have opted for the armed struggle. Today we are accused of being terrorists but what does the world mean? We do not aim to sow terror. We are not terrorists. We are not fascists. We struggle for our cause and for our rights. We know who is our enemy and our struggle is directed against this enemy. Our enemy is the Turkish State — this state which has flouted the rights of Armenians, which has flouted and still flouts today the rights of the Turkish people, the Greek people, the Cypriot people, the rights of all minority people who live in Turkey. This state is the very incarnation of Terrorism.'

Armenian terrorists had become skilful at picking off the vulnerable, accessible diplomatic personnel of the hated Turkish enemy. In addition, ASALA began to think in a more political way and to confront one of the essential problems of their Utopian nationalistic dream which would be farcical in a less bloody context. While some Armenian revolutionary sentiment tends to consider the Soviet Socialist Republic of Armenia as 'already liberated', its population was secure and permanent. Turkish Armenia, on the other hand, has had a dwindling population for years and it is apparent that so many Armenians left the Middle East for more prosperous nations, with more opportunities (particularly the United States), that soon there would be no Armenians left for 'Armenia' to unite. Armenian radicals regarded this population-flow as a new form of the Ottoman forced-march strategy, and consequently began efforts to staunch the flow of their countrymen out of the homeland. Their prime target was Italy: they believed that a substantial exodus of Armenians was being aided by welfare and aid agencies in Rome, usually in liaison with United States agencies, as the USA was most of the time, the country of destination. In fact, by no means all of the migrants were coming from Turkey many were from Syria and Lebanon and some even from the then USSR. But ASALA decided to halt the exodus with relatively small-scale bombs and further threats to the aid agencies, including the World Council of Churches, as well as to the small Rome hotels where migrants stayed in transit.

The communique's irrelevant references to Zionism, in the extremist-Palestinian manner, bear witness to the kind of assistance that the Armenians' base in Beirut provided. The 'depressed people' finds an echo in Yenicomechian's words, in which he supported violence with enthusiasm: 'We are accused of using violence: I accept that accusation with pride, and I add that there are two sorts of violence - that of oppressors and that of the oppressed. The violence that we use is the violence of the oppressed and humiliated.'

Balance of Human Loss

At the time of the communique, the balance of death was highly favourable for ASALA. They had killed some thirty Turkish people without having any of their own number either arrested or killed. It was ironic, that Yenicomechian, the propagandist of Armenian terror, should have become the first such victim, blown up by the bomb he was preparing in a Geneva hotel suite in October 1980. In his own words — the words of a true believer — Yenicomechian can both justify and accept what happened: 'All peaceful ways were barred to use. Only the armed struggle cannot be barred. That is why the armed struggle saw the light of day. That is why I accepted the risk of this mission. Bad luck, or more likely my incompetence, meant that I was not able to accomplish this mission. As a result of the explosion of one of these devices in my hands, I lost my sight, I lost my left hand, I have problems with my ears and my balance, and I am very seriously handicapped, and very conscious of it. Perhaps I should be very demoralised, should regret having agreed to carry out this mission, and regret having become involved in the armed struggle. However, my morale is very high and I do not regret having chosen this duty. Because I know why I am fighting, I have a deep faith in the cause and the justice of the cause. I am still convinced that the armed struggle is the only way to regain our rights. The Armenian people has given thousands and thousands of martyrs during its history. I am not the first, and I shall not be the last.'

Terrorism heads to be a very short-term career, and Yenicomechian is an unusual case for his surprising survival to fight, or at least to propagandise, another day. But with or without him, the violence continued to increase over the next two years. Armenian terrorism's one of the worst atrocity occurred on 15 July 1982, when a large suitcase bomb exploded without prior warning by the Turkish Airlines check-in desk, Counter 61, in Orly-Sud Airport, Paris, killing four people instantly in the blast. The bomb consisted of only half a kilo of Semtex explosive, but it was connected to three portable gas bottles which explained the extensive burns among the fifty-six people injured, twenty-one of them with serious injuries of which three more died later.

Within barely more than an hour, an anonymous caller to the AFP bureau in Athens claimed the responsibility of the attack in the name of ASALA's Orly Group. 'ASALA takes full responsibility for the attack against passengers who were destined for Turkey. We will continue to attack Turkish interests and Turkish diplomats. We call upon the rest of the world to distance themselves from Turkish institutions, for Turkey and her interests are the target of the Armenians.'

The incident provided sufficient evidence of the strains imposed on a terrorist outfit that is getting nowhere, despite its adoption of the ultimate tactic of sheer, illegitimate violence. Orly was not just one more attack in the calendar of Armenian violence: it represented the first attack in a new, more hostile and more random policy of violence adopted by a faction of ASALA. The Secret Army had been under tremendous pressure since its valued advisers, the PLO, had been expelled from Beirut by the Israeli invasion in August 1982. ASALA moved back to the Bekaa Valley, then largely under Syrian control, in Eastern Lebanon. From there it was far harder to launch attacks into Europe than from Beirut, and tactics were under severe examination within the organisation.

In France, the selective violence was called *action ciblee* or marked action. *Hay Baykar*, the Armenian newspaper which openly supported *action ciblee*, claimed that the 'gangster' Hagopian had precipitated a split in the ranks of ASALA, and then launched an internal war in which members of the rival factions took to kidnapping, and in one instance, executing each other. The majority faction, sticking to the old 'targeted violence' tactic, appeared with a new name: ASALA/MR or Revolutionary Movement. It was to ASALA/MR that *Hay Baykar* gave its political backing: 'Every organisation has a moment of crisis sooner or later. It is a part of the way of life of revolutionary action. Nevertheless to break with a mistaken route often marks the beginning of great things in the future. This step backwards for ASALA may unveil two steps forward for ASALA-Revolutionary Movement ... Since 1975, young Armenians have experienced their nationalism through the rhythm of the armed struggle.

Armenian Terrorists

The activities of Armenian terrorists in France were abruptly restricted after the Orly operation, principally because the French police rounded up more than fifty Armenian extremists, lending credence to those critics of the government who had stated that Armenian terrorists were known but tolerated for domestic political reasons within France. Nevertheless, within a week of the Orly attack another incident took place which amplified fears of Armenian terrorism, and revealed the existence of a new terrorist group, or the fallouts of another split, this time within the Justice Commandos of the Armenian Genocide. Though the Justice Commandos had rarely operated within Europe, it was from Lisbon that the news emerged of an armed attack on the Turkish Embassy compound in the suburb of Restello. Around the middle of 1983, five gunmen attempted to storm the Embassy: a Portuguese armed guard shot one man dead and was wounded by the remaining gunmen, who made an abrupt change of plan and rushed into the Ambassador's residence. Half an hour later, an explosion rocked the building, and fire broke out: and when police penetrated the building they found the five charred bodies of the commando members. The wife of the Turkish charge d'affaires later died in hospital from multiple burns.

The first communique on behalf of the faction was received by AFP in Paris at 1 p.m. about the same time as the terrorists' bodies were found in the wreckage of the Ambassador's residence. It stated that the 'Armenian Revolutionary Army' claimed the responsibility for attack — a name which had been heard only once before, in the aftermath of the murder of a Turkish diplomat in Brussels two weeks earlier — though that assassination was first claimed by ASALA. Later in the day, a letter was sent to both Associated Press and United Press International, explaining that 'the operation was neither a suicide attack, nor a demonstration of fanaticism. By exploding a bomb in the Embassy, our comrades sacrificed themselves on the altar of liberty. In one of these communiques the ARA proclaimed that it was 'a new military organisation which is totally distinct from any existing Armenian organisation.' ARA claimed to speak 'in the name of third-generation Armenians' reflecting the sixty years, or two generations, which had passed since the killings, and the sense that the third generation was now taking up the cudgels for Armenian nationalism after years of neglect. And in a pointed reference to the extraneous political content — usually revolutionary Marxism which frequently penetrated nationalist sentiment, the ARA stated: 'Our battle against the Turkish government belongs strictly in the traditional Armenian cause, to the exclusion of all other interests. We strongly reaffirm our complete independence from any other powers, no matter who they may be'. Finally, the ARA revealed its probable origins by encouraging supporters of their parent faction to break away: 'We exhort other clandestine organisations, and in particular the Justice Commandos of the Armenian Genocide, to come and join us in order to proceed in united combat.'

Some interpret the whole practice as a smoke screen put up by ASALA to evade both their internal and external problems; but whoever the Armenian Revolutionary Army are, their existence does not represent a de-escalation in Armenian terrorist fervour or fire-power. Since 1983 fatal attacks have continued against diplomats and Turkish interests; the ARA was involved in attacks in Brussels and Vienna, and, on 12 March 1985, three ARA gunmen stormed the Turkish Embassy in Ottawa. Their cause apparently endures, however recondite the world beyond Armenian nationalist sentiment may regard it.

The Armenians once maintained a claim on an island which the tide of history has already swept away. Despite the fact that the Treaty of Sevres decided in 1929 that an Armenian State should be Formed, consisting of six provinces including Van and Trabizon (on the Black Sea), most political realists regard the continuing claims for Armenian nationhood as fanciful.

For Armenian militants, just as for the Palestinians on whom Armenian terrorists (among many others) had modelled themselves, there was no role for 'passive resistance'; there is no one for them, as it were, passively to resist. The Turks could be deliberately attacked, to provoke attention and the remote hope of 'justice' or the issue could be forgotten, and the Armenian communities of the world — in France, the USA, Australia and elsewhere — could confine ideas of their heritage to folkloric nostalgia. All Armenians in the world, as believed, are united by remembrance of the events of 1915, and it is a function of the militant outfits to remind their own people of the justifying power of the 'genocide' as they themselves act violently. One of the world's most prominent Armenians, the Governor of California George Deukmejian, had made a point of speaking at anniversary rallies to commemorate the massacres. On 24 April 1983, he told several thousand Armenian Americans who had assembled that they 'must not forget the killings of as many as 1.5 million people in 1915'. Most will continue to observe the traditional date of remembrance, but will also shun and deplore the militancy which answers injustice with improper justice and bloodshed. Yet there will remain a tiny minority unwilling to comply with the overwhelming weight of history, and prepared actively to resist. An elderly French Armenian declared, after the outrage at Orly Airport, that the existence of people ready to fight for Armenia meant that he could now die in peace: 'We have been given back our history,' he claimed. Well, even if we obtain nothing, we will slam the door on our way out and the world will have to remember us!' The Armenians are just one of many groups and movements, whose wishes and desires range from the comprehensible to the insupportable, who have learned to use terrorism by setting example. But the suitcase bomb left at an airline's check-in desk kill just the same number of innocent people if it explodes in the name of a just, or an unjust cause.

Two

Geostrategy of Islamism

The evolution of Islamism is not based only on ideological factors, but is also in keeping with the geostrategic context of the Muslim society. It is clear today that Islamism has not seriously modified this context, which is dominated by state strategies and not by ideological, transnational movements.

The failure of the Islamist model is chiefly the failure of the Iranian revolution. The war with Iraq identified the Iranian revolution with Shiism and Iranian nationalism: the Arab masses turned away from this version. The exportation of revolution has occurred only, and partially, within the Shiite ghettos of Lebanon, Iraq, and Afghanistan.

The Iranian revolution was apprehended as a threat by the conservative Arab states, which tried to develop a Sunni fundamentalist pole of attraction beyond their own borders in order to rift the momentum of the Islamic revolution: this effort accentuated the discontinue between Shiites and Sunnis and contributed to Islamism's drift toward a more conservative neo-fundamentalism.

But the Sunni Islamist movements were even less successful than the Iranian revolution in instituting a new political order. In Afghanistan, the 1989 Soviet retreat was followed not by the establishment of an Islamic State, but by an increase in infightings among Afghan *mujahidin*, based on issues that were more ethnic and tribal than ideological. The Arab regimes, whatever their ideological bar, have succeeded almost everywhere in dominating their Islamist opposition, while authorising a form of re-Islamisation that affects only mores and symbols.

Finally, the second Gulf War spread confusion in the entire Arab world by organising a conservative Arab and Western alliance against Iraq. Arab nationalists identified with Saddam Hussain, who is anything but an Islamist, while the principal backers of Islamists (Saudi Arabia and Kuwait) found themselves in the Western camp. Thus, Islam failed to play a consolidating role in Arab public opinion.

It is the strategy of states, and not the existence of a mythical Islamist International, that describes the placement and movements of Islamists on the Middle East checkerboard. With the exception of the Muslim Brotherhood, every attempt to create an international union (the Bureau of Islamic Propaganda in Qum, the World Muslim League of Jedda, and the Arab-Islamic People's Conference, established in 1991 in Khartoum) was primarily the product of a particular state whose main objective was to weaken rivals in the Muslim world itself, and the means of this end was the manoeuvering of ideological debates (Shiism, Wahhabism, and so on). The ideological struggle set Iran and Saudi Arabia against each other, and both attempted to operate Islamist groups to suit their foreign policies: the first played on revolutionary Islamism, the second on neo-fundamentalism. In the case of Iran, when the Muslim masses did not rise up in favour of the Islamic revolution, it supported and employed the terrorism of radical Shiite Islamist factions to resist the Western presence in the Middle East. By dint of petro-dollars, Saudi Arabia attempted to establish itself as the godfather of all Sunni Islamist movements, even of the extremist movements like the Afghan Hizb-i Islami, so long as they were hostile to Iran. This war gave a margin of autonomy to Islamist movements whatever their camp and internal direction.

Upon becoming mere instruments in the hands of existing state powers (Syria and Iran), the most radical groups were marginalised, leaving the way clear for mass movements such as the Algerian FIS, which lacked the ideological and organisational rigour of earlier Islamist parties. The Islamist movement split into two camps: a radical and isolated avant-garde that did not stop at terrorism, and a group of parties and movements that drifted toward a more or less depoliticised neo-fundamentalism.

Finally, it is appropriate to achieve a certain amount of distance from the vision of the 1980s as a decade of continuous conflict between Islamism and the West: one mustn't forget the dubious actions of the United States, which, like the Saudis, had attempted to use the Sunni Islamists as a tool against the then Soviet Union and Iran.

Islamist Family

We are concerned here with organisations and movements that claim kinship with the founding fathers of Islamism, Hasan al-Banna and Abul-Ala Maududi. Another Islamist centre is revolutionary Iran, which we will study later. As we have seen, these movements have always oscillated between a reformist tendency, aiming to re-Islamise the society, and a revolutionary tendency, aiming to achieve state power. With the exception of the Iranians, these organisations are not easily classified into one or the other tendency, since the leaders themselves have varied in their political status as circumstances have changed.

The Sunni Islamist community is characterised by the circulation of the themes and concepts analysed in Chapter I, based in the two centres: the Egyptian MB and the Pakistani Jamaat. These two centres have a very close and egalitarian relationship. In the rest of the Muslim world, the most politicised organisations have borrowed the themes, symbols and organisational model of the MB. The more conservative groups have generally drawn their influence more from books published under the auspices of the Pakistani Jamaat.

The networks are organised around cultural groupings: the Jamaat-i Islami for the Indian subcontinent and its diaspora (from Mauritius to the suburbs of London to South Africa), the MB for the Arab nations. Yet among Muslim immigrants to Western countries and in the countries of the periphery (Afghanistan), influences frequently overlap. Finally, as we shall see, by creating the World Muslim League, the Saudis have attempted to sponsor, unify, and manipulate the MB and Jamaat networks in their favour. The Turkish networks are autonomous, and Iran has real influence only over the Shiites.

Muslim Brotherhood

The centre with the greatest political weight today is that of the Arab Muslim Brotherhood, all of whose local branches are theoretically inferior to the Egyptian leader. Back in the 1940s, the Egyptian MB had organised a "Section of Liaison with the Islamic World," endowed with nine committees. This section dealt not only with propaganda but also with organising communication among other Islamic movements of the Muslim world. MB branches were soon established in countries like Jordan, Syria, Palestine, Kuwait, Sudan, and Yemen. The MB branch in Sudan, established in 1946, was transformed into the Islamic National Front in 1985 under the guidance of Hassan al-Turabi and participates actively in the military regime. The MB branch in Syria was founded in 1945 by Mustafa al-Siba'i, who took the title "general supervisor" (*muraqib amm*), thereby recognising the authority of the Egyptian leader. After the Islamist uprising was vanquished in 1982, the Syrian MB split: the most radical group, that of Adnan Sa'ad al-Din, took protection in Iraq, while his rival Ibrahim Abu Ghudda went to Saudi Arabia. The Jordanian MB includes numerous Palestinians in exile and is directed by Abd al-Rahman Khalifa; it maintains cordial relations with a segment of the entourage of King Husayn. In Kuwait, on the other hand, the MB is close to the leadership. The MB has never attempted to create a division in Saudi Arabia or among Shiites.

Outside its own branches, based solely in the Levant and in Yemen, the MB Society sponsors national organisations such as the Islamic Tendency Movement, led by the Tunisian Ghannouchi (which became the Nahda party in 1989), and Abd al-Salam Yasin's Moroccan faction "Justice and Charity" (*al-adl wal-ihsan*). The Algerian FIS was supported by the Saudis; the MB favoured the organisation of Sheikh Mahfud Nahna (who today leads a party called Hamas, separate from the FIS). Although the Islamic Renaissance Party, formed in the Soviet Union in 1990, is not part of the MB either, it shares its ideology. The MB has also had significant influence outside the Arab world proper. The founders of the Afghan Islamist movement (Niazi and Rabbani) adopted the notions of the MB during their studies at Al-Azhar University in the 1950s. Rabbani undertook the translation into Persian of Sayyid Qutb's *In the Shadow of the Quran*. The organisational blueprints of the Afghan groups and of the Arab MBs are similar, as are the seals and emblems, which generally describe the Quran between two swords. MB literature translated into Russian was distributed in the Soviet Union from the Afghan *mujahidin* centres in Peshawar (including books such as Muhammad Qutb's *Razvie bolsh'ie niet nieobkhodimostiv religii*? (Do we really no longer need religion?). Finally, in Malaysia, the Movement of Islamic Youth, created in 1971 and close to both the MB and the Jamaat, appointed Islamist cadres such as Anwar Ibrahim, who in 1983 rejoined the governmental coalition and was named minister of culture while maintaining his contacts with the MB and the Afghan Hizb-i Islami.

The MBs properly speaking thus exist only in the Arab countries of the Middle East and are theoretically inferior to the Egyptian leader, who since 1986 has been Muhammad Hamid Abu al-Nasr. As a general rule, the Egyptian centre is more moderate than the other Arab MBs or their sister organisations; these are influenced more by the radical theses of Sayyid Qutb, which have been condemned by the guide Hudaybi. Today an international agency assures the cooperation of the company of MBs. Its composition is not well known, but the Egyptians maintain a dominant position.

An Islamic International?

The Islamic International is in no way a Muslim Comintern, with local wings that follow a centrally defined strategy. First of all, there are several centres: the Egyptian MB, the Pakistani Jamaat, and the World Muslim League, based in Saudi Arabia. From there connections and collaborations are established around a network of personal relationships, riddled with disparities and divisions; their common denominator is not the MB ideology, but the simple desire to re-Islamise the society, a neo-fundamentalist desire. These networks are intermittently torn apart by conflicts that set the states of the Middle East against one another, as in the second Gulf War: MBs, Wahhabis, and Pakistanis side with their respective countries. The national structure still dominates everywhere: local organisations define themselves above all in relation to domestic politics. The supranational authorities serve as networks of financing and distribution rather than of command or organisation.

Cultural influence is facilitated by international networks

more than by political action. Saudi money has created numerous institutes and publication centres that finance and distribute works by many Islamist intellectuals, whose print-runs in their countries of origin are limited for political or simply financial reasons. This eclectic production generally carries apologies of Islam: they aim to show the good deeds of Islam or to present Islamisation projects in intellectual or scientific spheres, so as not to leave the West the monopoly on modernity. Seminars, colloquia, and conferences, at which MBs and Wahhabis, mullahs and university professors rub elbows, are held all over the world. The organisers include the World Muslim League and its subsidiaries, such as the Great Britain-based Islamic Council of Europe or the International Islamic Federation of Student Organisations (based in Kuwait).

A responsible role is played by the distribution of tracts, half-preaching, half-propaganda, destined for a very large and not very intellectual people, one that is therefore unable to distinguish among Islamist, fundamentalist, and traditionalist themes. Though distinct at the outset, the Islamist message grows hazy in the course of its diffusion, especially since there is no pyramidal organisation to ensure its transformation into a organised political practice from below, as was the case for Marxist movements. The Muslim Brotherhood, the Jamaat, Turkish organisations, and Shiite networks remain essentially headquarters and dispensaries for propaganda, and not structured, hierarchical militant networks suitable for repeating a political line and transforming it into a mass movement.

Small Extremist Groups

Operating at the periphery of the current MB are more radical organisations, many of whose members were and sometimes still are members of the MB or related groups. These are either parties close to the Leninist model, setup back in the 1940s and 1950s, such as al-Nabahani's Hizb al-Tahrir al-Islami (Islamic Liberation Party) in Syria, Jordan, Lebanon, and Palestine; or small radical Islamist groups motivated by the thought of Sayyid Qutb, such as the Egyptian factions. Takfir wal-Hijra and Jihad. It was in Afghanistan that the "Islamo-Leninist" model found its most perfect incarnation in Gulbadin Hikmatyar's Hizb-i Islami (to the point of aligning itself with the most extremist faction of the Communist Party, which had the same ethnic and tribal base). These two types of extremist organisations have often maintained ties to MB networks. Thus, Hikmatyar's Hizb-i Islami has an excellent relationship with the Jordanian MBs, while its mediocre rival, the Jamaat-i Islami, is closer to the Egyptians.

The other small radical groups were formed by former MBs, close to the theses of Sayyid Qutb and felt let down by the modernisation of the mother organisation, as for example the Palestinian Islamic Jihad, directed by Sheikh Abd al-Aziz Uda and the physician Fathi Shqaqi, or the "Army of Muhammad" created in Jordan in 1990. These small factions share the same ideology (that of Sayyid Qutb), are supporters of violent action, frequently use the same name (Islamic Jihad), but have not created a "radical union": they surface and disappear, reconstruct themselves, sometimes transforming themselves into simple signatures, a front for the actions of various secret services or of renowned political parties not in favour of openly claiming affiliation with a violent act. There is a constant back and forth between the "centrist" organisations, which constitute the bulk of the MBs, and these small extremist factions, sometimes raising doubt about the moderate nature of the MBs. Nonetheless, it seems that it is the MB's very framework as an "association", and not a party, that allows this uncontrolled circulation of members and sympathisers.

In addition, certain extremist Sunni groups seem to have mushroomed locally around charismatic personalities, such as the Saudi group of Juhayman al-Utaybi, responsible for seizing the Mosque in Mecca in November, 1979, or the supporters of Muhammad Marwa whose uprisings in December 1980, in the city of Kano, in northern Nigeria, left at least four thousand dead. These groups came out of the old millenarian tradition, which was violent and mystical, closer to a sect than to a political party.

The extremist sphere of the early 1980s was weakened and discredited by the more toward terrorism against state leaders and dignitaries in Sunni countries (Egypt) and by its transformation into an armed branch of secret services and splinter groups in Syria, Iran, Lebanon, and elsewhere. Thus, the faction of the

Tunisian Fuad Ali Salih, responsible for the 1986 attacks in Paris, is not a political organisation, but an operational network put together by the Iranian secret services. The ideological heritage of someone like Sayyid Qutb's extremism would find expression in a new radical cluster beginning in 1990, established by young "former combatants" of the war in Afghanistan. These youths, from every Arab country (but also including Turks, Iraqi Kurds, Sudanese, and ... African-Americans), had gone under the auspices of Saudi-sponsored MB networks to fight the Soviets alongside the *mujahidin*. They also wanted to lend and exclusively Muslim colour to the outside support for the Afghan resistance, which until 1985 had been essentially Western. Once back in their native countries, they often ended up disappointed by the moderation of the large Islamist organisations under whose auspices they had gone to war, such as the Algerian FIS. Now, they constitute the activist and militarist wing of these movements. Some have formed combat groups to move toward insurrection, like the Takfir wal-Hijra (no connection to its Egyptian homonym) of Tayyib "al-Afghani," an Algerian who organised on November 29, 1991, attack against the post of Guemar, on the Algerian-Tunisian border.

Terrorist Manipulation

Islamist terrorism until 1981 (the assassination of Sadat) was primarily an internal political affair. But beginning in 1981, these groups found "sponsors" in states, such as Iran, Syria, Libya, and Iraq. They were then used to promote the strategy of destabilising the conservative states and combating Western influence.

Iran and Syria used small terrorist groups issued most often from the Lebanese Shiite sphere. But is would be overly simplistic to undermine the foreign policy of these states to the simple manipulation of Islamic terrorism. Syria also brought perfectly secular terrorist groups into the action, such as the Palestinian group Abu Nidal, while Iran favoured non-terrorist political movements (such as Al-Da'wa in Iraq and the Hizb-i Wahada in Afghanistan). Other countries didn't mind to fish from the pool of terrorist groups, which turned mercenary for the purpose of specific attacks (Libya, Iraq). As for Islamist groups, the minority that moved toward terrorism did so either on the basis of an internal radicalisation during the 1970s (Egypt and Syria) and then no longer played a role on the international sphere, or on the basis of support for Iran after 1981. The latter fell rapidly under the influence of secret services and of Iranian and Syrian groups; nonetheless, the rivalries within the sponsoring countries gave them relative autonomy, which made them difficult to control, especially when Iran and Syria decided to reject terrorism and the taking of hostages as a method of foreign policy (domestic policy being another story). This manipulation also contributed to cutting these factions off from their popular roots, to transforming them into simple mercenaries and as a result depoliticising their partisans: only the Lebanese Hizbullah was able to continue both mass political activities (under the direction of Sheikh Fad-allah) and terrorist activity (the Islamic Jihad group).

Saudi Arabia Entering the Game

Confident in the legitimacy afforded by its control of the sacred sites, but hindered by its connection to Wahhabism, a doctrine rejected by a large section of Sunni ulemas, Saudi Arabia, thanks to petrodollars, has attempted to form a propaganda of strict religious fundamentalism that avoids the issue of political power. This was the purpose behind the creation, in 1962, of the Rabita, the World Muslim League, which prints Qurans and devotional books and subsidizes mosques and Islamic institutes throughout the world, paying the salaries of imams at many mosques in Europe, for instance. Certainly the Rabita is not openly Wahhabi, but the type of Islam it encourages is evidently conservative fundamentalist, based on a return to the Quran and the Sunna. Saudi Arabia also attempts, through publishing, grants and the organisation of colloquia and seminars, so influence Islamist production in a conservative manner. The Iranian revolution of 1979 immediately contested the very genuineness of the Saudi dynasty ("There is no king in Islam" said the slogans). So as not to leave Iran the monopoly on fundamentalist contestation, Saudi Arabia extended its activities beginning in 1980, encouraging in a more or less direct manner the formation of Sunni fundamentalist networks essentially directed toward non-Arab countries or toward European emigrant communities. In

1986 King Fahd adopted the title "Custodian of the Two Holy Sites" (Mecca and Medina) to highlight a religious legality that the Islamists denied him. Iran became the main adversary, but this antagonism was transformed in religious terms: true Islam versus Shiite heresy. The lines between MB reformism, which is very close to the Salafists, and Wahhabism tended to stain. Thus, the journal *Al-Jihad*, produced by Arab MBs supporting the Afghan *mujahidin*, denounces the "Wahhabi" qualifier applied to Arabs who support the resistance, seeing it as a stratagem by "the Western press, Radio Kaboul, the Sufi Marabouts, the Voice of America and Radio Free Iran."

For want of officers, but also because Wahhabi tenet often encounters stiff opposition among traditionalist Sunni mullahs, the Saudis relied on Sunni networks, which they financed on the basis of personal or even patronage relationships, rather than on a well thought-out strategy. Saudi Arabia thus experienced itself financing either fundamentalist networks that were indeed conservative, but also strongly anti-Western, or far more radical Islamist groups which demanded political powered but seemed more prone to prevent Iran from gaining ground (this is the case, for example, of the Hizb-i Islami in Afghanistan).

In the 1980s a kind of joint venture was formed between the Saudis and Arab Muslim Brothers. The Muslim Brothers agreed not to operate in Saudi Arabia itself, but served as a relay for contacts with foreign Islamist movements. Kuwait often acted as a revolving stage. The MBs also used as a relay in South Asia movements long established on an indigenous basis (Jamaat-i Islami). Thus, the MB played a major role in the choice of organisations and individuals likely to receive Saudi subsidies. On a doctrinal level, the differences are certainly striking between the MBs and the Wahhabis, but their common references to Hanbalism (the strictest of the four legal schools of the Sunni world), their refusal of the division into juridical schools, and their hostile opposition to Shiism and popular religious practices (the cult of "saints") furnished them with the common subject-matters of a reformist and puritanical preaching. This alliance carried in its wake older fundamentalist movements, non-Wahhabi but with firm local roots, such as the Pakistani Ahl-i Hadith or the Ikhwan of continental China.

War in Afghanistan

The war in Afghanistan furnishes the best example of this collaboration: the MBs organised "Islamic" humanitarian aid for the Afghan resistance and established an "Islamic legion," consisted of Arab volunteers who would head off to perform jihad in Afghanistan. The MB bureau in Peshawar was instructed by Abdullah Azzam (a Jordanian Palestinian, assassinated in November, 1989), who recognised Muhammad Abu al-Nasr, leader of the Egyptian MB, as his spiritual guide; a large share of the Saudi funds passed through him in Saudi Arabia, the key figure in the operation was Prince Turki, head of information services. The third partner in this joint venture was the secret service of the Pakistani army, ISI (Inter Services Intelligence). The MB and the Saudis did as per their potential to rally the Islamist sphere first around Sayyaf, then around Hikmatyar. The training camps of the Afghan mujahidin (including the Jaji camp in the Afghan province of Paktya, controlled by the Hizh-i Islami) also trained Islamist factions from Kashmir (including the Kashmiri Hizb-i Islami) and the Philippine Moros, as well, no doubt, as Palestinian Islamists. For the picture to be perfect, it should also be mentioned that Yasser Arafat, who was an MB in the youth, attempted to act as liaison between Hikmatyar and the communist rule in Kabul, from a base in ... Bagdad (in 1989 and 1990).

Thus, American and Saudi financing helped to arm radical Islamist networks that in 1990 would find themselves wholeheartedly allied with Saddam Hussain. Moderate Islamists, such as B. Rabbani, director of the Jamaat-i Islami, with personal ties to Sheikh al-Talmasani, the Egyptian MB guide prior to Abu al-Nasr, found themselves marginalised by the decision of the Jordanian MB and the Pakistani ISI to support Hikmaytar; Rabbani chose the Saudi camp in 1990.

This did not prevent other Saudi movements or personalities, such as Sheikh Ibn Baz, the highest authority of Wahhabism, from having their own networks. In Pakistan, the Saudi clergy bluntly supported certain fundamentalists organisations, such as Ahl-i Hadith, a movement founded in the nineteenth century and classified as "Wahhabi" by the British, falsely so at the time. They developed theological differences with the Hanafi school, in particular with respect to the manner of praying, which scandalised the Afghans, who are normally very orthodox Sunni Hanafis. In Pakistan, they transformed themselves into a political party. Curiously, they opposed the *sharia* bill (the law that would make the sharia state law), because they thought it was not for the state to legislate on the *sharia*. Their leader, Ihsan Illahi Zahir, was assassinated in 1987. The Ahl-i Hadith have been involved since the nineteenth century on the border between Pakistan and Afghanistan; they have *madrasa* in Attock, Akora, and in the Kunar (in the village of Panjpir). From the 1950s on, they trained many Afghan fundamentalists, especially in the provinces of Kunar and Badakhshan: though designated as Wahhabis by their adversaries, they prefer to call themselves "Salafis." During the war in Afghanistan, they founded small principalities (under Mawlawi Afzal in Nuristan, Mawlawi Shariqi in Badakhshan, Mawlawi Jamil al-Rahman in the Kunar).

The Wahhabis and Ahl-i Hadith, unlike the MB, have always favoured religious preaching over political action, and in particular the tussle against Sufism (destruction of "saints'" tombs) and Shiism. Their activities in Afghanistan, where Sufism and Hanafism are well rooted, led to religious conflicts among the population, which the MBs would have been happy to evade. The tensions between specifically MB networks and Wahhabi networks brought about conflicts that were all the more hard to understand as they were also related to tribal and ethnic differences. Thus, in the Afghan province of Kunar, the Wahhabi "principality," formed in 1985 and directed by Jamil al-Rahman, recruited from the Safi tribe of the Pech Valley and enjoyed direct Saudi and Ahl-i Hadith support. This faction formed an alliance with the local Hizb-i Islami, which was more established among the Meshwani and Shinwari tribes, until the second Gulf War and control of poppy fields pitted them against one another. The Saudis bribed the Salafis to chase away the Hizb, supported by the MB (May 1991). Jamil al-Rahman was assassinated by an Egyptian (named "Rumi" …the "Christian.") None of which prevented Prince Turki from coming in person to restart the dialogue with Hikmatyar in November 1991. Internal intrigues, corruption, personal accounts to settle, and tactical blows ended up, as always with the Saudis, replacing a long-term strategic vision.

The combination of competition and collaboration between the MB and the Saudis that preceded the Gulf War can be observed in other countries: Saudi Arabia funded movements without organisational ties to the MB, such as the Algerian FIS, while the MB tended to support the movement of Sheikh Nahna. For purely strategic reasons, Saudi Arabia also funded a fundamentalist movement in Yemen, mainly rooted in the northern tribes and out of keeping with the Islamist sociological pattern in that they are essentially tribalised peasants (Sheikh Abdallah al-Ahmar's "Alliance for Reform"). In addition, the Saudis financed networks of mosques in the countries of emigration, without concerning to learn more about the imams preaching there.

The Conjunction between Islamism and Conservative Fundamentalism

The fallouts of this rapprochement between Islamists (MB) and conservative fundamentalists (Wahhabis) were twofold: on the one hand, it helped confine Iran to the Shiite ghetto and to involve Sunni Islamists in the politics of their own countries and in international tie-ups (including with the United States in the case of Afghanistan). But the blurring of the borders between conservative fundamentalism and political Islamism also helped to give birth to neo-fundamentalism. Opposition to the West is increasingly expressed in religious terms: criticism of Christianity and Zionism, but also identified anti-Semitism. The neo-fundamentalists are leading a crusade for a return to a pure, Hanbal-style Islam, one ridded of ali syncretism as well as of all external values and influences, whether mystical or originating from Western "materialism". They oppose the assimilation of immigrants, favour the creation of "Islamised spaces" in Western countries, and are waging a relentless war against "renegades" like Salman Rushdie. It was neo-fundamentalist themes that radicalised circles that had previously rejected political action (in particular the Muslims of the Indian subcontinent), as is shown by the Rushdie episode.

Launched in the autumn in 1988 by Indian Muslims and Pakistani emigrants to Great Britain, all relatively close to Saudi Arabia, the mass condemnation of Salman Rushdie's novel *The*

Satanic Verses became an international issue on February 14, 1989, when Imam Khomeini issued a *fatwa* condemning the writer to death. While the crime with which Rushdie was charged, blasphemy and apostasy, comes out of a narrow and a political vision of the *sharia*, Khomeini's *fatwa* automatically lends it a political magnitude by calling for nothing less than terrorism.

The Gulf War Rift

Meanwhile, during the autumn in 1990, the Islamist and neofundamentalist networks abandoned Saudi Arabia en masse, accusing it of having allowed an infidel army to safeguard the sacred sites. The earliest to condemn the Saudis' appeal to the Americans were the Sudanese under Hassan al-Turabi, the Tunisians under Ghannouchi, the Jordanian MB, and the Islamic Jihad for the Liberation of Palestine (a Jordanian faction led by Sheikh Asad al-Tamimi), all of whom followed the leads of their respective governments in the process. In Egypt, Sheikh Umar Abd al-Rahman's Islamic Jihad and the MB group led by Ma'mun al-Hudaybi also condemned the Saudis. The Egyptian MB and the leader of the FIS, Abbasi Madani, attempted for a while to balance themselves between the Saudis and the Iraqis before choosing, under grassroots pressure, to support Saddam Hussain; while Hamas, dependent on Saudi money and opposed to a PLO tied to Bagdad, chose Riyadh. The anti-Saudi line was also adopted by the Sa'ad al-Din group, part of the Syrian MB, the Muslim Students' Association (a US based MB organisation financed by the Saudis), and the most fundamentalist of the Afghan Islamists (Hikmatyar, Sayyaf); the moderates (Rabbani) took a clear position in favour of Riyadh. Faced with this massive movement of the brotherhood into opposition to Saudi Arabia, the Kuwaiti MB, reorganised in the Islamic Constitutional Movement (Islah, directed by Ismail Shatti), quit the brotherhood's international agency in protest, followed by all MBs in the Gulf states, while the Saudis naturally cut off funds to the Islamist movements that had censured them, bringing about certain splits, such as the one in Tunisia that divided the Nahda party into moderates closer to Saudi Arabia (Abd al-Fatah Murro) and fundamentalists (Ghannouchi). But in the settling of accounts, the majority of Islamists passed into opposition to

Saudi Arabia. All these opponents gathered at the Islamic Popular Conference, called by Saddam Hussain in Bagdad on January 11, 1991; among the participants were the Jordanian minister of religious affairs, Ibrahim Zayd al-Kilani, an MB who had received his appointment a few months earlier; as well as the vice-president of the Algerian FIS, Benazzuz Zubda.

On the whole, then, the MB sphere was against Saudi Arabia, even though it remained under the contradictory influences of the moderates (still the Egyptians), who had been isolated by the departure of the MBs from the Gulf, and of the extremists, led by Turabi and Ghannouchi. But the rift between the MBs and Saudi Arabia left the MBs without sponsorship, especially since the pro-Iraqi regimes (Jordan and Tunisia), wishing their blunder to be forgotten, began marginalising or repressing the Islamists (in Jordan and Tunisia, respectively). Most Arab countries accepted, or at least paid lip service to accepting, the birth of the peace process, which the MB violently rejected.

An opposition front extending from the Islamists to the communists and united solely by its renunciation of the West and of the regimes in power then attempted to garner support throughout the Middle East. Iran came forward as a sponsor, thanks in particular to the work of Ghannouchi and Turabi. In 1991, Sudan helped by providing refuge and passports to Tunisian Islamists.

The Solidarity Conference with the Muslim peoples of Palestine, held in Tehran on October 19, 1991, and organised by the president of the Assembly, Karrubi, aimed to denounce the peace process and the PLO and to provide support for Palestinian Islamist movements. Iran cast a wide network for this conference, involving groups from Muslim Brothers to Ba'thists and communists (it achieved a rapprochement of all extremists, despite ideological differences: Georges Habache reached an agreement with Hamas: Ahmad Jibril grew closer to the Lebanese Hizbullah; and so on). For many, this new combat is only one chapter in the anti-imperialists struggle, which is occurring nowadays under the green banner instead of the red. Essentially, it is the Third World, anti-colonialist sensibility, always present in the history of Islamism, that is reappearing today in what is an undoubtedly temporary alliance with secular currents of the same sensibility.

The first reason for the about-face in Iran, which until then had been very prudent with respect to the American presence in the Gulf, was strategic: the only position Iran could occupy in the Middle East was that of collecting opponents to the peace process, even if it meant it later had to negotiate this role with the Americans. The acceptance of the peace process by all the large Sunni states (except Sudan) allows Iran to hope to succeed in its objective of the past ten years: to make headway in the Sunni Arab domain. Previously, it had to thwart Iraq, by developing its presence in Lebanon and Syria; now it has to get around Saudi Arabia, by establishing its presence in Yemen and Sudan.

To breakout of the Shiite ghetto, Iran needs Sunni relays. While it is still possible for Iran to use particular relay points, such as Turabi, it is unlikely that the MBs, which tend to be anti-Shiite and securely anchored in the Arab world, would develop a strategic and durable alliance with Iran. As is often the case, geostrategic alliances do not jibe with local alliances. Turabi, who is now teamed with Iran with regard to the Middle East, is close to Gulbadin Hikmatyar in Afghanistan, who himself condemns the peace process and I intimate to the Jordanian MB, but is also strongly opposed to Afghan Shiites and to Iran's potential role in that country. Deep antagonisms prevail over tactical alliances, even if the latter would be highly advantageous.

Shiites and Sunnis: Opposition or Alliance?

Islamism, both Sunni and Shiite, refutes the opposition between the two schools of Islam. It is characteristic of Islamism in general to put aside particularly theological questions in favour of political discourse. On a doctrinal level, Sunni Islamism even drew closer to Shiite thought by accepting the right to interpretation and by emphasising the charismatic leader, the amir. The year of the Iranian revolution was one of the great ecumenical discourse. Yet ten years of Iranian Islamic revolution has revealed that, despite Tehran's effort to make progress in Sunni milieus, the opposition between Shiites and Sunnis remains a key aspect of the contemporary Islamic world.

The tendency of Islamism toward neofundamentalism has brought a resurgence of Sunni fundamentalism's visceral anti-

Shiism. In Afghanistan, for example, the Wahhabis spread an anti-Shiite pamphlet titled *Tuhfa-i ithna ashariyya* (The gift of the twelve Shiites), republished in Turkey in 1988 and widely distributed in Peshawar; this book was written in the nineteenth century by the son of Shah Wali Allah, who was also the religious mentor of Sayyid Barelvi, founder of the Ahl-i Hadith movement. At the same time, a section of Iranian circles see the Wahhabis as a sect motivated by British imperialism.

Iran has succeeded only in rallying (or facilitating the creation of) small Sunni groups who emerge as token Sunnis at conferences but have little influence in their countries of origin. These include Sheikh Sah'ban's Movement of Islamic Unification (Tawhid) in Tripoli, Lebanon; the small Afghan factions led by Mawlawi Mansur and Qazi Amin; and the Jam'iyyat sect called Afzali in and around the city of Herat. Here and there, we also find Sunni Hizbullah (on the Afghan-Iranian border). In sponsoring Islamist groups renounced by Riyadh after the Gulf War (the FIS, Nahda), Iran will undoubtedly come up against the fact that these factions are in no way small and will not accept having their strategies dictated to them. The opposition between Shiites and Sunnis remains a decisive issue in the foreign relations and domestic policies of the Muslim states, where it corresponds to political, social, and (in Afghanistan) ethnic rifts. In Lebanon and Iraq, the Shiite community, though in the majority in terms of population, has generally been kept at a distance from national politics. In Iran, loyalty to the state is measured by one's religious, and not ethnic, affinity: Shiite Azeris and Arab-speakers feel more Iranian than do Sunni Kurds and Baluchis, who are nonetheless closer culturally to the Shiite, Persian majority. In all the petromonarchies, the Shiites are usually considered to be foreign agents.

The great ethnic, religious, and national rifts of the Muslim world are emerging to be stronger than all the calls to Islamic solidarity. Although this imaginary solidarity still has the power to mobilize mass support, it cannot provide the basis for an Islamist international union.

State Concessions to Islamisation

During the 1980s the Muslim states showed ambivalence toward domestic Islamist and fundamentalist movements. On the one hand, they overpowered radical Islamist factions that contested their legitimacy: the recapture of the Great Mosque in Mecca in 1979, the execution of the great Shiite Iraqi Ayatollah Baqir al-Sadr and his whole family in 1980, the execution of Sadat's assassins in Egypt in 1982, the bloody repression of the uprising in the city of Hama in Syria in 1982 and of the Shiites in southern Iraq in 1991, the inhibition of the Algerian FIS and the Tunisian Nahda in 1991 and 1992, and so on. In the countries that tend toward Sunnism but have strong Shiite minorities, the repression often takes an openly anti-Shiite turn (Iraq, Kuwait, Pakistan). But at the same time, almost all the regimes use for their own ends a form of re-Islamisation from the top both to take the sting out of Islamist contestation and to give themselves religious legitimacy. They thus attempt to create a division between small radical factions and centrist groups susceptible to being integrated into the political scene.

The collaboration between states and Islamist spheres has hardly anything to do with the nature of the regime. The same governments who used to refer to Arab socialism, nationalism, or secularism now lay claim to Islam. Islamisation from the top is not at all tied in with state clericalisation or the emergence of revolutionary regimes. Today, of the four countries that claim to have made the *sharia* the exclusive source of law, three are governed by nonclergy, who are utterly conservative besides: Pakistan, Sudan, Saudi Arabia, the exception, as always, being Iran. In fact, in the Sudan and in Pakistan during the tenure of General Zia (1977-1988), the policy of Islamisation resulted from an alliance between a putschist military and an Islamist-inspired minority party (the Pakistani Jamaat, the Sudanese Islamic National Front, whose cadres are secular) against large "Muslim" parties (the Umma party in the Sudan, the two Jam'iyyat al-Ulama parties in Pakistan).

The specific state strategies differ: either moderate Islamist parties are integrated into the political scene without any particular concessions being made to them (Jordan, Kuwait, Turkey), or integration is accompanied by a state-ordered re-Islamisation (Pakistan, Sudan, Egypt), or else ideological concessions are made toward re-Islamisation while Islamist political participation is blocked (the Maghreb), or, finally, no concessions are made, the contradiction being too massive between the founding values of the state and Islamism (secularism for Iraq and Syria, Qaddafi's philosophy for Libya).

In every case, the target is to control and claim Islam. To control it, the states attempt to set up an official clergy to whom they guarantee a monopoly on religious lines: they put Islam under state control by turning the mullahs into functionaries and creating centralised institutions. The state creates Islamic universities and state *madrasa*. In Afghanistan, the Faculty of Religious Sciences was established in 1951. In Tunisia the Zaytuna, a famous Islamic *madrasa*, was attached to the university in 1958, and a Grand Mufti of the Republic named; in April 1987 a Higher Islamic Council was setup. In Morocco the Qarawin, the equivalent of the Zaytuna, became a state university in 1960, and in 1980 King Hasan II founded a High Council of Ulamas. In Algeria in February 1966 a Higher Islamic Council was also setup and was granted the monopoly on *fatwa*; in 1984 the Islamic University Amir Abd al-Qadir was created and directed by Muhammad Ghazali, an Egyptian MB who was replaced in 1990 by another Egyptian. Occasionally, the state attempts to outlaw neighbourhood mosques in favour of large cathedral mosques, which are easier to control (Morocco).

We are witnessing a process of clericalisation of Islam by the states, which are aiming to counter Islamism, and the proliferation of new, uncontrolled, self-authorising clerics and mullahs. But in order to proceed with this clericalisation, they are striking a neofundamentalist chord (the reform of mores, the status of women, *sharia*, and so on) and offering important positions to the popularly moderate MBs such as the Egyptian Ghazali in Algeria and Zayd al-Kilani in Jordan.

The restoration of Islam also takes the form of a return to Islamic discourse in the official media and the re-Islamisation of law, even in "progressive" states such as Algeria, where Friday become an official holiday in 1976. The official radio stations and journals are being opened up to neofundamentalist advocating: *Al-Liwa al-islami*, an official Islamic journal in Egypt, has a higher circulation as compared to the famous *Al-Ahram*. In December,

1991 the Egyptian Security Court condemned the writer Ala'a Hamid to eight years in prison for blasphemy. Religious programmes are becoming more numerous on television everywhere, including in communist Afghanistan since 1986. In 1972 secular Turkey joined the Organisation of the Islamic Conference, and in 1982 it introduced mandatory religious instruction in primary and secondary schools. In Tunisia, President Ben Ali, who assumed office in 1987, made a point of promoting the country's Arab-Muslim identity while strongly repressing the Islamists: this translated into an increase in the number of religious programmes on television, the appointment of a minister of religious affairs, the regeneration of the Islamic University of Zaytuna, and so on.

In the realm of law, re-Islamisation is evident everywhere. It affects constitutions, personal status (the issue of women), and penal law. Even the two secular dictatorships, Syria and Iraq, have been forced to make concessions. Religious references are reintroduced into constitutions: Article 2 of the Egyptian constitution of 1971 specifies that the *sharia* is "the main source of legislation"; the Syrian constitutions of 1971 and 1973 reintroduce the demand that the president be a Muslim. The Afghan constitution of 1987 specified that Islam is the state religion.

States that had earlier legislated without taking the *sharia* into account (even if they mentioned it in their texts) began in 1979 conspicuously to claim it as their own. The law on personal status was promulgated by presidential decree in Egypt in 1979, although it was still criticised by the most fanatic fundamentalists. In 1983, Sudan proclaimed the shariatic penal code. In Pakistan General Zia introduced a system of shariatic tribunals to work parallel to the ordinary tribunals; new laws were put into effect (in 1979, shariatic penalties and authorised collection of the *zakat*, "the Islamic tax," on bank accounts; in 1984, the law of testimony); but the Sharia Bill, presented in 1985 to definitively replace Anglo-Saxon law, was never passed. The Algerian Family Code of 1984 reintroduced into divorce and child custody the Quranic dissymmetry between men and women. A new Family Code was promulgated in 1992 in reunified Yemen: polygamy was thus declared legal in South Yemen. In 1986, even the secular Indian parliament made the Islamic Code obligatory with respect to the personal status of Muslims. Turkey is a different case, since secularity is in its constitution, but without openly saying so the state made concessions to local forces: the veil is authorised in certain universities, forbidden in others; the obligatory teaching manuals for religion give solely the Muslim point of view.

The reclaiming of Islamism by states also occurred through politics, in which Islamist participation increased during the 1980s, even though this participation came to an abrupt (and temporary?) halt in 1991.

In Malaysia in 1982 the leader of the agitated Islamic Youth Movement, Anwar Ibrahim, joined the centrist coalition that governs the country, the United Malays National Organisation, and became successively minister of culture, of agriculture, and of education (in 1987). In 1984 and 1987 the Egyptian MBs, within the structure of an electoral coalition, obtained first twelve, then thirty-two seats in parliament, but boycotted the 1990 elections. In Jordan parliamentary elections were held in 1989 for the first time in twenty-two years; Islamist candidates (MBs and independents) secured thirty-four of forty-two seats (twenty-two of these thirty-four being MB). A Muslim Brother, Abd al-Latif Arabiyya, was elected president of the National Assembly, and the cabinet setup in January 1991 included several MBs. The MBs perished from the Jordanian cabinet during a ministerial shakeup in September 1991, but Arabiyya was reelected president of the National Assembly with the support of partisans of the king. In Morocco while repressing the Al-Adl wal-Ihsan party, the monarchy backed a neofundamentalist group, Abdellilah Benkirane's Jama'at al-Islamiyya. In Tunisia, the Islamic Tendency Movement, rebaptised Hizb al-Nahda, managed 14.5 per cent of the votes in the elections of April, 1989, but found itself outlawed in 1991. An identical sequence of events occurred in Algeria, where the FIS, after winning 54 per cent of the vote in municipal elections in June 1990, attempted a coup and saw its leaders arrested by the army a year later; it again carried the legislative elections in December, 1991, and found itself outlawed in new few weeks.

The last chapter in the states' reclaiming of Islam is related to diplomacy. Since independence, Algeria has directed the Grand

Mosque in Paris, whose rector, Sheikh Tijani Haddam, became a member of the Algerian High Committee in January 1992. The delegations from Al-Azhar University sent both to Central Asia and to Africa are resuming the general lines of Egyptian diplomacy: to thwart Iran, Libya, Sudan, and the fundamentalist MBs.

Islamist themes were thus bended together, reclaimed, watered down, but also distributed more widely. The enfeeblement of Islamism into neo-fundamentalism brought an end to the revolutionary dynamic but contributed to the popularisation and legalisation of re-Islamisation.

Vivacity of the Nation-States

The supranational networks (the MB, the World Muslim League) play a major role in the distribution of Islamist propaganda, but, as we have seen, they have never been able to shape an international policy that amounts to anything more than merely a reflection of the conflicts of interest among regional states. They therefore find themselves diminished to agreement on their smallest common denominator: pure neofundamentalist propaganda, isolated from its political dimension. It is true that this propaganda in favour of the re-Islamisation of society can have geostrategic consequences, relating essentially to the question of the integration of Muslim immigrants in Western society. For the rest, the position of the *sharia* in Saudi law bears no relationship to the question of Saudi Arabia's planned alliances, as we saw during the Gulf War. One could almost say the same for Iran, which is primarily following a policy of regional power. Thus, the nation-state fabric continues to be the determining one.

When Islamists participate in politics, it is on a national level and based on local standards. The positions taken by the MB have always been tied extremely closely to the situations in their respective countries-collaborationist in Kuwait and Jordan, pacific opposition in Egypt, armed hostility in Libya and Syria: it is the domestic situation and not the ideology of each branch that controls the positions adopted. Although the MB maintains a supranational agency the same cannot be commented for the Maghrebis, Afghans, former Soviet Muslims, and Turks, whose organisations are always adapted to the national structure. Despite its references to the

Muslim *umma*, the FIS is an Algerian nationalist movement as much as an Islamist movement. It is befitting to speak henceforth of Islamo-nationalism.

A significant case is that of the former Soviet Union: the decomposition of the empire prompted Islamist groups to organise on the basis of the new states and not to establish a supranational authority. Stalin had organised Soviet Islam into four geographic *muftiyya* (spiritual directorates) in 1941: Europe and Siberia, Northern Caucasus, Azerbaijan, Central Asia, and Kazakhstan. These four *muftiyya* are now further breaking apart with the creation of new national borders: the Turkmans, Tadzhikis, and Kazakhs have split off from the *muftiyya* of Central Asia, which is considered exclusively Uzbeki. The *muftiyya* of the Northern Caucasus split in 1991 into five entities, corresponding to administrative and political factions (four autonomous republics and one autonomous region, all included in the Russian Republic). The only running Islamist party in the entire former Soviet territory, the Islamic Renaissance Party, created in 1990, proved incapable of maintaining the *umma* of Soviet Muslims and split into national factions, the "Russian" section under Tartar and Northern Caucasian direction, while the Tadzhiki branch is autonomous.

The de-ideologisation of international relations is confirmed by the American attitude toward Islamism. The concept of a radical opposition between fundamentalism and the West is typically French, as is the association between Islamism and terrorism. The American attitude has been more inconclusive: Americans have never seen Islamism as an ideological enemy. They have favoured conservative fundamentalism (Saudi Arabia, Pakistan, General Numayri's Sudan), in order to take the wind out of the radicals' sails. They accepted as a minimum evil the cultural anti-Westernism of the MBs and of all the conservative radicals, since it seemed primarily a stumbling-block to Iranian and Soviet expansion. But they supported large sectors of radical Islamism until the Gulf War the Afghan Hizb-i Islami, which also had connections with the FIS in Algeria and Ghannouchi in Tunisia, was armed by the Americans until 1989). The Americans have subcontracted to their Muslim followers (Pakistan and Saudi Arabia) the management of certain Islamist groups: since 1982 the Saudi embassy in

Washington has housed a "Department of Islamic Affairs", directed by Prince Muhammad ibn Faysal ibn Abd al-Rahman, who is active in Islamisation programmes for black Americans and who maintains contact with American Islamic organisation (such as the Muslim Student's Association, founded in 1963, one of whose leaders during the 1970s was Muhammad Abu Sayyid, an Egyptian MB now established in Saudi Arabia).

Thus, the influence of Islamism, aside from the parentheses of the Iranian revolution and the war in Afghanistan, is essentially socio-cultural: it marks the streets and customs but has no power relationship in the Middle East. It does not control either state borders or interests. It has not created a "third force" in the world. It has not even been able to offer the Muslim masses a substantial political expression for their anticolonialism. Can it offer an economic alternative or deeply transform a society? The answer seems to be no.

Three

Terrorism in Central Asia

As in many global regional conflicts, it is possible to consider a conflict between the Turkish and Iranian populations which grew out of the Russian-British colonisation in the nineteenth century. The majority of the agricultural population in Central Asia at that time was composed of Tajiks, unprecedented in a region of Iranian people, who traditionally gravitated to Teheran. Before the intrusion of the Russians and British into Central Asia, the Tajiks were a cultural and political elite, the Tajik governors boldly resisted Russian expansion in Central Asia, and the Tajiks ruled in Bukhara, Khiva, Kokand, and their language was the official language of these states and the literary language of the elite. By creating the border with Afghanistan, Russia divided the Tajiks. It was the first displacement of the Tajiks. The preservation of a stable Pushtun Afghanistan guaranteed Moscow's dominance of the Tajik Pamirs from either sides of the border. Russia had an opportunity to promote a new Tajik and Turkish elite in Central Asia, which depended on Moscow, ensuring neutrality and support of this sub-region for the Russian mainland from threat from Iran. Prior to the October Revolution of 1917, the population of Central Asia identified itself as an integrated region and homeland.

Generally, the Afghan factor is present in the majority of conflict situations in the region. Historically, present-day Afghanistan and the states of post-Soviet Central Asia had a constant correlation. The significance of this factor increased after the Soviet-Afghan war and the consequent disintegration of the then USSR. The advent of the Soviet Army in Afghanistan coincided with the heyday of the Islamic revolution in Iran. The Tajiks always had social and cultural affinity with this country. During this period, Islamic clerics and Sufi fraternities in Tajikistan started becoming stronger, and the Afghan Tajik Islamists established contacts with the Tajiks serving in the Soviet 40th Army.

In Soviet Tajikistan, for want of sufficient information about Afghan events, the names of Burhanuddin Rabbani, Ahmed Shah Masoud and other leaders of the Afghan Jihad became considerably popular. In December 1987, the chairman of KSS of Tajik SSR, Mr. Petkel declared the presence of 'hostile foreign ideological centres and organisations'.

Tajikistan

The majority of the Muslims of the region are followers of the al-Hanafiya sect. The modern radicals take those ideas from al-Hanafiya philosophy which can be useful in political practice. The tradition of interference of spiritual leaders in politics was approved and admitted by the Tajik Sufis in the fifteenth century. Sheikh Hodja Akhror said, "To execute spiritual missions in the world, it.is necessary to use a political authority." This tradition in many ways defines the present process of the Islamic restoration in Tajikistan. The first stage of cooperation between religious radicals of Central Asia and Afghan talibs started in the 1990s. During the civil war, the Afghan factor considerably influenced the situation in Tajikistan, both in the political and military spheres.

The entry of the Islamic opposition into the state politics of Tajikistan was the first sign of the political revival of Islam in the region. In the fall of 1996 when the Taliban launched their northward blitzkrieg, the Tajik Islamic opposition had no other option but to choose between the ethnically kindred Rabbani-Masoud group or to side with the 'Taliban', whose radical opinions struck a chord in the hearts of many Islamic opposition leaders. Finally, they made contacts and relations with both sides: Davlat Usmon, the head of staff of the military detachments of the opposition, established contact with the Taliban leaders, while Hodji Akbar Turajonzoda announced that he would support President Rabbani. In September 1991, anti-Communist meetings started in Dushanbe and the so-called democratic-Islamic block took shape which was supported by the secular opposition also. On 26 October 1991, the first congress PIRT was organised. By the end of the year, the PIRT actively campaigned for the presidential nomination of Davlat Khudonazarov, a film director, who was renowned for his loyalty to the Islamic democratic movement. The Communist nominee, Rakhmon Nabiev, who was supported by regional clans - Khojent (Leninabad), Gissar and Kulob, and also Turkish (Uzbeks) and Russian populations won the Islamic-democratic coalition supported by the Badakshan and Kharategin regions. The ethno-regional factor thus became a defining factor in the political life of the republic; this had a decisive effect on the future development of events. So over decades the regional secession of the Tajiks became apparent in territorial-national politics.

The detailed sequence of events of the civil war in Tajikistan and the process of national reconsolidation is of specific importance. In this paper, it would be pertinent to reflect on the consequences of this war. Besides, it is necessary to highlight the connection between two nodal regional conflicts, as this correlation continues to remain a key factor in the developments of the regional situation and its effect on security. The connection between the Afghan and Tajik conflicts is not in doubt. It is also clear from the movement of weapons from Afghanistan to Tajikistan. Lack of monitoring and surveillance on the part of the state authorities on the borders resulted in Afghanistan becoming the main market for the purchase of weapons and ammunition for illegal activities in Tajikistan. For instance, in parallel with mass meetings which were taking place on the central squares of the capital, in 1992, there were heavily-armed participants, armed mainly with the weapons procured from Afghanistan. This has been one of the main reasons for political destabilisation and the civil war in Tajikistan.

Another important feature during the civil war was the direct or indirect participation of the Russian Army. On 10 May 1992, officers of the Committee of National Security attached to the Ministry of External Affairs, Dushanbe garrison (201 Russian Motorised Division) and frontier guards supported one another. They declared their neutrality, but the officers of the military garrison showed readiness to safeguard families of the officers from all departments. Participants of meetings were guarded by armoured troop carriers positioned around the building of the Committee of National Security, but for want of proper cover they were intercepted by an irate mob.

In this melee, about 8 persons were killed and nearly 10 wounded. The Commander 201 Division had given orders to protect the approaches to the building and the houses in which the families of the officers resided with five tanks and four armoured troop carriers. The fight was stopped and the opposition faction returned to central Shokhidon Square and the meeting then proceeded. In the evening, on a television channel, the leader of the Democratic Party, Shodmon Yusuf, stressed the fact that he did not exclude the possibility of asking for help from Iran and Afghanistan, if the arms of the Commonwealth of Independent States (CIS) were transferred to Tajikistan. He stated that the Russians in Dushanbe from that moment had become hostages.

The interference of Russia had a salutary effect: on 1 July 1992, the government of Tajikistan accepted the protection of all vital places in the republic. The protection of the hydroelectric station at Nurek and other installations and motorways on mountain posses along the boundary of the Kulob and Kuran-Tube areas was entrusted to 201 Russian Division as per an agreement with Russia. The protection provided by the Russian military prevented many catastrophes which would have had unpredictable consequences. After the events in May in Dushanbe, these developments acquired greater significance. Regular and large-scale attempts were made for transit of arms across the Tajik-Afghan borders, along with Tajik and Afghan instructors. Between May 1992 and the beginning of 1993, the Tajik frontier guards intercepted more than 1,000 infiltrators, including many Afghans, who then withdrew along with their weapons.

However, during the summer and autumn of 1992, nearly 500-600 Afghan mujahideen entered Tajikistan. A government delegation from Tajikistan led by Minister of Foreign Affairs Kh. Khaliknazarov reached an accord with Burhanuddin Rabbani and Ahmad Shah Masoud on various measures required for protection of the Afghan-Tajik borders. However, these measures did not change the ground situation in any way. The smuggling of weapons by some outfits and field commanders of Afghanistan continued in the area where battles raged with the forces of Rabbani-Masoud. Some of the weapons came to Tajikistan, in exchange for food, and industrial and economic goods.

During this period, mercenaries from the republics of the CIS (Russia, Baltic and Caucasus countries), groups of Afghans and Arabs took part in operations along with members of the Islamic opposition. The operations of the government forces (groups from the Kulob region) were directed by Russian military experts. In response, the opposition started an anti-Russian campaign: video materials were openly distributed which offered an award of 5 million roubles for the head of Gen. M. Ashuro (the new commander of 201 Division). During this period, the performance of the opposition varied qualitatively; because of some activities of leaders of the Democratic Front, it lost the majority of its supporters. Members of the 'Rastohez' movement rejected to participate in the war. A specialised group thus contributed to the Islamic revival in Tajikistan. By autumn 1992, an anti-Islamic coalition started shaping in two regions, Kulob and Khojent. Acting Prime Minister Abdulmalik Abdullojanov represented the Khojent area. The Khojent and Kulob regions started preparations, with the help of Uzbekistan, Russia, Kyrgyzstan and the forces of the National Front, which included Uzbeks (from Tajikistan and from Uzbekistan) and Tajiks from Kulob. In December, the troops of the National Front reached Dushanbe and let loose a reign of terror in the Pamir and Kharategin regions.

The policy of the new Tajik government in the first few months after assuming authority was to start oppressive methods against the opposition. In January-February 1993, practically all prominent leaders of the opposition movement in the north were arrested. In the south also, the government forces remained active against the opposition factions. Major armed operations were mounted in Kharategin (Garm, Romit) and Darvaz (Tavildara). Uzbek aircraft took an active part in these operations. The intervention of Russian and Uzbek forces decided the fallout of the war. By November 1992, a significant number of the armed United Tajik Opposition (UTO) left the republic for the northern provinces of Afghanistan. After regrouping of forces and other preparations, the UTO, however, started assaults on the outposts of the Russian frontier guards. In retaliation, Russian and Uzbek aircraft began bombardment of Afghan territories under the cover of the mandate of the collective peaceful force of the CIS.

By February 1994, the situation inside Tajikistan and on the Tajik-Afghan borders had deteriorated. The Council of Islamic Resistance of Tajikistan which was then in Taluqan (Afghanistan) protested against the use of the MFA of Tajikistan and armed groups of the Islamic resistance started firing from Afghan soil on the government forces. There were some armed clashes within the republic, and in a number of cases clashes also occurred between the government groups. The differences were not only regional but also ethnic. In this situation, Moscow could not find any means of effectively meeting the threat from Kabul because of the hand of certain political groups behind various developments. The armed underground forces in Dushanbe numbered 4,500 (2,000 in Kulob, 3,500 in Kargan-Tube) and 7,000 in Mountain Badakhshan (Pamir). These statistics testify to the ineffectiveness of the Russian policy in Tajikistan, and the inability or unwillingness of the Dushanbe government to initiate effective measures to terminate the conflict. However, from the beginning of March, Moscow was able to induce the government of Mr. Emomali Rakhmonov to negotiate with the opposition. Russian Deputy Minister of Foreign Affairs A. Adamishin paid a visit to Teheran with the purpose of establishing contact with the leaders of the Council of Islamic Resistance and other opposition groups. An agreement to hold further negotiations in Moscow was reached

Then the Russian Minister of Foreign Affairs F. Kozyrev conducted negotiations with the Tajik government in Dushanbe. After the visit, he declared that extensive contacts were made with the Tajik opposition. As a show of force, the Russian Army moved quickly to a place near Tiger's Beam on the banks of the Pyandj river on 24-26 March. The Armed Forces of Russia, Tajikistan and Uzbekistan comprised 950 personnel, 28 tanks, 104 machine guns and 20 combat aircraft. This was the first joint venture of the armies of the member states of the Agreement of Collective Security.

Unable to achieve their political goals through negotiations, the opposition started armed operations in the Tavildara river valley, in Darvaz, and some regions of Kharategin and Pyandj. After suffering a number of defeats and appreciable losses of its forces and installations, the government was forced to send a delegation to Teheran, and agreed to conditions imposed by the opposition. As an outcome of these talks, an agreement on blackout of lights was signed and the pre-election campaign started in the republic. Some militant groups from Kulob were moved to Khojent, the chiefs of militias were replaced by loyal and trusted person of Emomali Rakhmonov, and a media campaign to discredit Rakhmonov's main rival Abdulmalik A. Abdullodjonov began. In October, the first plenary meeting of the third round of the inter-Tajik negotiations was held at Islamabad. A stumbling block during the discussions was the request of the opposition for inclusion of a project in the joint document for creating a corridor on the borders for delivery of foodstuff, clothing and medicines for the supporters of the oppositions. The differences on this issue were so great, that it was possible only just prior to the close of negotiations to sign a communique on 1 November, agreeing to a three-month extension (till 6 February 1995) of the ceasefire and cessation of hostilities on the Tajik-Afghan borders.

Within a few weeks of the agreement of 1995, flare-ups and cross-border operations in the Pamir region resumed. The adversary parties consequently accused each other of violation of the cease-fire. The opposition particularly accused the Russian Frontier guards of starting the border flare-ups. Denying these charges, the Deputy Chief of the Russian frontier guards, Maj. Gen. A. Baranov said that the accusations were not only incorrect, but practically from day one of the ceasefire, it was violated by the opposition and it continued to infringe the agreement.

The fact was that small contingents of Russian, Kazakh and Kyrgyz frontier troops had opened fire with various kinds of weapons on several armed groups which made repeated attempts to cross the Tajik-Afghan borders. The situation in the region continued to remain tense, and now, it is known that armed cadres of the Movement of Islamic Revival of Tajikistan (from the area of Mountain Badakhshan) were responsible for armed retaliation against the Russian frontier guards. About 400 militants had also concentrated in the Kala-i-Humb region of Afghanistan. By the beginning of 1995, it was apparent that the economic and political situation in Tajikistan or the Tajik-Afghan borders had not changed for the better, only the deployment and high concentration of

Russian forces (with the mandate of the CPF) kept the situation under control. Attempts at penetration into Tajikistan by various armed factions and shelling of border posts from Afghanistan, however, continued. Giving details of various attempts of infiltration and cross-border incidents, the chief of the Russian frontier guards in Tajikistan, Lt. Gen. Pavel Tarasenko declared that 799 attempts at infiltration were made. On the Tajik-Afghan borders, 582 attempts to break through the defences were prevented, in 260 border incidents, the Russian frontier guards were subjected to firing 700 times. Attempts at smuggling huge quantities of weapons, including mortars, grenade-throwers, rifles and ammunition were also prevented.

The political situation continued to remain tense. A new round of inter-Tajik negotiations in Almaty, initiated by the special envoy of the UN, also did not lead to improvement of the situation. However, an agreement on extension of ceasefire was reached. Mr. Rakhmonov and Mr. Nuri met in Teheran in the middle of July, the negotiations between them having been arranged by the then minister of foreign affairs of Iran, Ali Akbar Velayati, who reminded the participants about '[the] negative consequences of instability for all Muslims; in the region. In response, Mr. Rakhmonov proclaimed that the 'Tajik government was determined to continue negotiations for removal of differences'. Nuri asserted that 'Consensus should take the interests of all sections of the population into account, and the national and religious aspirations of majority of Tajiks.' The problems of inclusion of the opposition in the constitutional process, termination of the armed opposition and return of the refugees from Afghanistan were also discussed in the conference. Attention was drawn to the roles of the forces of the CIS which protected the Tajik-Afghan border. On 17 August, as an outcome of the negotiations, a protocol was signed about the important principles of world and national consensus on Tajikistan.

The flow of events in 1997-98 was largely determined by the peace agreement signed on 23 December 1996 in Moscow between Rakhmonov and Nuri; despite key difficulties and failures, this agreement eventually worked. The Islamists continued to dictate terms in the areas of their influence (Kharategin and Darvaz), where they propagated a (so-called) Islamic way of life, which, according to them, prohibited watching movies with a frivolous content, partaking of alcoholic drinks, and enjoined traditional dress for women, etc. After the election, though the authority of the president, Rakhmonov, was well-established, nevertheless the situation continued to remain tense. The agricultural and industrial products which generated income were divided between the armed groups, mainly of Kulob origin, who had entered the National Front. These factions represented association of the natives of one district, or members of family-related groups. The income through sale of the greater part of the produce was appropriated by the chiefs of armed troops, and only a part of the proceeds was used for building of infrastructure. During distribution of the funds, there were frequent bloody clashes between various armed groups.

A matter of concern for the Russians and the world was that inhabitants of Khojent were accused of making an attempt to overthrow president Rakhmonov in May 1997. Among those nabbed was Abdulhafiz Abduloev, brother of the leader of a component of nationality and block National Revival and Abdulmalik Abdullodjanov, who was outside the country. Abdulhafiz Abduloev and others arrested in this connection were subjected to enormous pressure, however, they denied participation in any attempt to overthrow the president. The situation in Tajikistan caused serious concern in Uzbekistan. The representatives of Uzbekistan's law enforcement agencies contended that the local Islamists who were active in December 1977 in the Namangan area were supported by Tajik Islamist outfits of Jergetal district of Kharategin. Uzbek President I. Karimov in his book *Uzbekistan at the Threshold of the 21st Century,* indicated that the existing environment in Tajikistan poses a serious threat to the national security of Uzbekistan.

One of the main casualties of the civil war was the ongoing process of national reconciliation in Tajikistan and stabilisation of political infrastructure of the country as a single unit. The absence of a purely centralised authority and fragile balance of power between secular and religious-clerical components of the state created conditions for armed infiltration from Afghanistan into Central Asia. Possibly there was smuggling of large quantities of drugs, along with the infiltration of the armed groups. As brought out earlier, the Soviet ethnic-territorial delimitation of Tajikistan has been the key cause of upsetting the ethnic and regional balance. As a consequence of this arrangement, the mountain district in the valley of the river Sukhrobb-Vakhish, in north Kharategin then became a bastion of the Tajik Islamic opposition and a base for Islamic activists of Uzbekistan. The Islamic factor was clearly visible during the 'Batken events,' when armed rebel outfits established bases within the Tajik territory. In September 2000, Lt. Gen. Esen Topoex of the Kyrgyz ministry of defence, named the towns of Tajikistan, where bases and training camps of the Islamic Movement of Uzbekistan (IMU) existed in Kharategin zone, besides other areas like Pakshif, Demnora, Romit and Sangvor, Jirgital and Iskanderkul, Komsomolabad and Garm.

In a tete-e-tete with this author, Deputy Minister of National Security of Kyrgyzstan Gen. Valery Verchagin gave details of the routes taken by the armed groups. First form of Afghanistan's Qundiz province armed groups and extremists crossed the border into the districts of Kuluhtepa and Nijni Pyandj. Their supporters in the Tajik opposition helped them cross into Dushanbe through Kharategin. The second route appeared rather interesting, the insurgents crossed over into Afghanistan, from Pakistan (Chitral) over the Vakhan pass into the valley of the Vakhan river. In the small Pamir region, from Mountain Badakhshan, which is sparsely populated, they are transported to Kharategin along with their weapons. It is interesting to note that this route of infiltration had been denied both by the Tajik opposition, the Tajik government as also Pakistan and the Russian frontier guards. The infiltration of armed groups posed a great danger but it is always difficult to stop, because the relations between the government and Islamist opposition in Tajikistan are not very friendly.

Kyrgyzstan

A majority of people of Kyrgyzstan are of the view that the role of Islam in public life should increase as 80 per cent of the population of Kyrgyzstan are followers of traditional Islam. According to available information, there are about 1,100 functional mosques in different parts of Kyrgyzstan besides several madrassas and an Islamic institute run by the Spiritual Board of Muslims of Kyrgyzstan. A number of non-orthodox Islamic missionaries who belonged to organisations and sects of various Arab countries, Turkey and Pakistan were active in Kyrgyzstan. About half a dozen non-orthodox Islamic leaders (Imams), mainly from Garm region had settled in Chu valley. According to information available with the Ministry of Education, Science and Culture, many of these were trained in the religious/educational institutions of Saudi Arabia during 1992-96. Emissaries from many religious and political parties such as the Jamiat-e-Islami, Jamiat-ul-Ulema-i-Islam (Pakistan), Dawa-e-wal-Irshad, Sunni-Tehrik, Harkat-ul-Ansar and Islamic Jamiat-ul-Tuleba from Afghanistan, Taliban, etc., entered the republic illegally. In south Kyrgyzstan, jihad in its radical form was being exported from Afghanistan. It was given the name 'The Batken Events: 1999', 'Batken' being the name of the administrative region. The situation was earlier controlled through military and diplomatic means, but the conflict was renewed in the year 2000.

Batken Events: 1999

A silent invasion of the Islamists into Kyrgyzstan started from the Garm area of Tajikistan in 1999, which is also known as the 'Kharategin valley'. This sub-region was a traditional base of the Islamic radicals as the message of national reconciliation of Tajikistan was not heeded here. The presence of the Uzbeks in Kharategin was well known to the government in Dushanbe, but other countries were also informed that a huge number of so-called refugees were actually from a group of terrorists, headed by Jumah Namangoni. They took part in the Tajik civil war on the side of the Islamic opposition. About 1,500 members of these terrorist outfits who had intruded into Kyrgyzstan formed the main force. This factor has global ramifications as it aims to unite the Uzbek opposition with the Islamic fundamentalists of Afghanistan and some other countries.

In July 1999, a group of armed personnel were observed near Zardaly village in Batken. Mamataliev and the secret service officials tried to observe and follow the movements of the intruders, but the terrain complicated their task. These terrorists settled down in Jily-Suu district, which has not motorable roads and in certain areas the paths are so narrow and steep that it is not possible even to ride a horse: one can only walk leading a horse by the bridle. By August 1999, news about these terrorists had reached Bishkek and was publicised by the media. Mamataliev and three officers of the Osh Committee of National Security failed to return to Batken as they were taken hostage by the terrorists, who demanded that they should be allowed the use of the territory of Kyrgyzstan for intruding into Uzbekistan. While negotiations continued with the terrorists for the release of the hostages, the government took measures to locate the terrorists and mount an army operation to destruct their base. It was believed that the troops belonged to the Uzbek special forces and some commando experts of Dushanbe located in Batken. Authorities in both countries obviously understood that this was their common problem. On 13 August, following a negotiated settlement between the law enforcement agencies of Kyrgyzstan and leaders of the terrorists, all hostages were freed.

On 15 August, one flight of Sukhoi-24 light bombers of the air force of Uzbekistan bombed the terrorists' sites and the Kyrgyz troops started the second stage of their operations for liquidation of the terrorist groups. The secretary of the Council of Security of Kyrgyzstan, Esen Topoex, declared that as the terrorists had flouted the laws of Kyrgyzstan, they should be punished according to the laws of the republic. On 22 August, a group of 30 terrorists seized the villages of Zardaly and Kholja-Achkan, the campsite of the Japanese geologists' exploration. The terrorists took Kyrgyz Gen. Shamkeev, one soldier, and four Japanese geologists along with their interpreter as hostages. Leaders of the Kyrgyz law enforcement agency believed that it was the same terrorist outfit which had entered into Kyrgyzstan from Tajikistan on 31 July. Other sources revealed that another outfit of 200 insurgents had entered Kyrgyzstan from Tajikistan to support the terrorists at Zardaly.

On the night of 23-24 August as the fight began east of village Kan, terrorists retreated into deep gorges without suffering casualties, but there was information about the captives. About 200 terrorists of the radical Islamic opposition group headed by

Jumah Namangoni, who were based in the Kharategin zone, raised the strength of the Jumah Namangoni outfit to 350. According to Uzbek sources, the group comprised Uzbek, Tajik, Arab and Afghan Pushtuns, who had fought under Aizizkhan in Batken region. Kyrgyz President Askar Akaev discussed the progress of the combined operations with the erstwhile Tajik President Emomali Rakhmonov. The problems also came up for discussion at the summit of the Shanghai Five at Bishkek.

On the night of 24 August, terrorists blew up the bridge across the Sokh river which connects the canyon with Batken. The terrorists successfully the government troops and intelligence reports indicated that their strength in Batken and Chon-Alay regions had risen to about 1,000. On 28 August, Kyrgyzstan, Kazakhastan, Tajikistan and Uzbekistan confirmed the joint operations were being conducted against the terrorist groups in South Kyrgyzstan.

Joint Manifesto

The joint manifesto issued at the city of Osh at the meeting of Ministers of Foreign Affairs and Defence, along with chiefs of the national security services of the four Central Asian nations confirmed that terrorists were supported by external forces. At this meeting, modalities of joint action and the situation in South Kyrgyzstan were discussed. The meeting asserted that the terrorist groups include not only people from the Central Asian countries, but also nationals of many foreign countries. This indicated the pan-Islamic nature of terrorism and extremist organisations which posed a common threat to all states of the region. The participants of the meeting were convinced that the objective of the Islamic-international terrorist groups was to destabilise the Central Asian countries whose efforts were directed towards building of civilised, democratic and secular societies, it was apparent that the Islamic terrorists were trying to turn the clock back to the medieval age. All Central Asian countries are members of the UN, Organisation of Islamic Conference (OIC) and other international organisations and they are supported largely and unanimously by the world community in their struggle against international terrorism.

The participants appealed to the people of their respective

countries of stand united in giving a decisive rebuff to the provocative actions of the international brigands: they also declared that terrorists' violation of the state boundaries and violence towards the peaceful population will be stopped by hard and resolute means in accordance with international law. They expressed the hope that the world community would fully support the coordinated efforts of Kazakhstan, Kyrgyzstan, Tajikistan and Uzbekistan in quelling international terrorism. The document was signed by the ministers of foreign affairs of these countries. In an address to the people of the republic, Kyrgyz President Askar Akaev expressed his gratitude to the government of Russia for its willingness to help and assist Kyrgyzstan in liquidating the international terrorist gangs operating in south Kyrgyzstan. He said that the aim of the terrorists was to disturb peace and stability in the entire region and it was a well known fact that a section of terrorists belonged to Central Asian countries, but among them were a large number of mercenaries from various Islamic countries who were well-equipped and had experience of war in Afghanistan and Tajikistan. President Akaev also asserted that this activity was not just regional but global and Kyrgyzstan was being confronted with international religious terrorism and extremism. He expressed his sympathy for the families of those who had been killed and said that all efforts would be made for getting the release of the hostages. He stressed that the stability of the region was of key important. Adaev addressed his appeal to all segments of the people of the republic, not to permit any manifestations of inter-religious hostility.

New Offensive

A new offensive started on 8 August 2000, but the Kyrgyz Army was now ready, and in the first encounter near Touro pass in the Zerafshan range, atleast 42 attackers were killed. As the Kyrgyz line of defence extended to about 725 kilometres, the terrorists employed tactics of probing the weak spots in the defences. A marked attempt to infiltrate through the frontier was made on the night of 28 August and repeated the following night. A large group of Islamist terrorists tried to break into Batken area: Kyrgyz aircraft attacked them and these outfits suffered heavy losses. They retreated to the Tajik side and a small part managed to disappear in the mountain gorges of Kyrgyzia. The chairman of the security council of the country stated that an operational faction of government forces together with the Uzbek military had conducted operations in Jalalabad region in south Kyrgyzstan at the end of August to eliminate terrorists from frontier regions; in this operation many terrorists were killed and a clearing operation was conducted in the district. The Islamic terrorists, however, made many more attempts to infiltrate into Kyrgyzstan. The chairman of the security council also stated that as per the terms of the agreement of collective security within the framework of the CIS, Kyrgyzstan would receive military help from Kazakhstan in the form of combat aircraft. Besides technical aid, US$ 50,000 were contributed by Armenia, and large sums by Russia; Ukraine also declared its readiness to help.

At the end of August, the presence of a group of 40 outlaws was reported in the gorges of Large Chimghan about 80 kilometres from Tashkent because of the refusal of local inhabitants to cooperate with them. The level in the Charvak water reservoir was lowered before the action was undertaken against the insurgents to avoid disastrous fallouts to Tashkent in case the terrorists bombed and breached the reservoir. Special forces of Kyrgyzstan together with the Uzbek Army then completely dominated the frontier between Jalalabad area of Kyrgyzstan and Tashkent (Uzbekistan). After a clash, a number of extremists were killed, and large caches of weapons and ammunition were found. Simultaneously, there were several clashes in south Uzbekistan in Surkhan-Daria region. The extremists were ultimately liquidated by the end of September in this district.

In August, some Kyrgyz soldiers had managed to lay their hands on the offensive plans of the extremists; they were then confronted on the river Khodjia-Achkan and suffered heavy losses. On interrogation of the prisoners, it was revealed that they were supporters of Jumah Namangoni. According to the chairman of the Council of Security, Bolot Januzakov, extremists such as Ruslan Abdullin, a Bishkir, came from the village of Aznalino Kurgan region of Russia. Apparently he was trained for three months in a terrorist camp which was run by the citizens of Pakistan. After the interrogation, it became evident that in the Tajikistan Pamirs in the district of Talimgokh, there were many training camps for the extremists and this was a base for the instructors from Chechnya and Pakistan. Another prisoner, Ravshan Sharipov, a Tajik national belonged to Isfana town in Leninabad region of Tajikistan. He was recruited in Dushanbe. During the second session of the parliament of Kazakhstan, President Nursulatan Nazarbaev called for unity in the face of the developing security situation on the southern frontiers of the CIS. The president said that those events 'are forerunners of serious tests, which face the states of Central Asia as a whole'. He noted that in such conditions unity of the people and the political forces was necessary. The president briefed his deputies about the measures being taken to prevent a possible. Worsening of the situation in the country. Urgent measures were necessary in the south because of the infiltration of international terrorist groups in Kyrgyzstan and Uzbekistan. It was necessary to register religious associations to quell the extremist religious movement that wanted to destabilise the region and gain power under the garb of religious revivalism.

Problems Continue

By and large, problems continue in Tajikstan, Kyrgyz special services unearthed many underground cells of the Islamic movement of Tajikistan and discovered that there was intensive recruitment of youth and accumulation of sophisticated weapons. The Russian frontier guards while searching two mines warehouses in a gorge at Durg near the Afghan frontier found a large number of weapons. In the Kyrgyz city of Jalalabad, actions was taken against the supporters of Hizb-UT-Tahrir. The then acting chairman of OCSE Benita Ferrero-Valdenr expressed a hope that all the governments of the republics of Central Asia would take decisive measures to introduce democratic reforms and create an environment in which terrorism and extremism would not survive. Terrorist activities, however, continued unabated. Several attempts were made to infiltrate deep into Kyrgyzstan. Two groups of terrorists (about 50-60 strong) made attempts to attack the Jily-Suu post in Liauliak region by infiltration. Simultaneously, attacks were attempted from three different directions in the areas of saddle-points Jangiabad, Jily-Suu and Abramov glacier. Kyrgyz aircraft attacked spots of probable concentration of these terrorists. Radio intercepts revealed that they requested their commanders in Afghanistan for supply of medicines, weapons and ammunition.

In August alone, the terrorists received about US$ 2,000 from international terrorist centres of Afghanistan. According to the chief of the National Security Council, Bolot Januzakov, all movements of the terrorists and their future plans were being supervised by the government in Kyrgyzstan. The Armed Forces of Kyrgyzstan and Uzbekistan acting jointly have successfully countered various intruding terrorist groups in Tashkent area. However, the terrorist threats emerging from Afghanistan and Tajikistan, were considered as very serious by the Council of Security of Russian Federation. Minister of Defence lgor Sergeev stated that desperate attempts of the terrorists on the Tajik-Kyrgyz and Tajik-Uzbek frontiers emphasised the long-term objectives of Islamic extremists, to destroy logistics installations and attack military bases.

By the end of September, the Kyrgyz Army managed tc flush out terrorists from the glacier region on the Kyrgyz-Tajik frontier. Some terrorist units which stayed on in Kyrgyz territory, were destroyed.

Four

Traditional Afghan Society

The war in Afghanistan allowed Islamist militants to put into effect their notions of the organisation, since the main resistance parties (the Jamat-i Islami, the two Hizb-i Islami, but also the Shiite parties) are Islamist. It is true that the position of Afghanistan is particular in the sense that we are dealing mostly with rural guerrillas in a very orthodox society. But the weight of Islam is such that no other ideology, nationalist or secular, could have established itself in the resistance. Without attempting to tally up ten years Islamist practice, we will concentrate exclusively on the models of war in operation in the Afghan resistance, and examine the extent to which the ideological model of jihad allowed new forms of organisation to be imposed.

A war, especially a guerrilla war, does not occur in the hypothetical space of a chessboard. It presupposes primarily the existence of a society with its own cultural relationship to violence and conflict. It implies social mobilisation and is related to the political framework of the society. It brings into action individuals who think in terms of a strategy — defining objectives and the means of attaining them. In a guerrilla war, the objectives are chiefly political: What should be seized? What is a victory? The goal is to determine where the seat of power lies, which, when taken, will ensure victory. The exercise of war is formed by ideological models of collective violence (tribal war and jihad); these models presuppose a geographic space, a temporality, and an end result that are not those of modern guerrilla warfare as it was conceptualised by Mao Tse-tung, in which the goal is the seizing of state power through the organisation of "liberated zones" as counter societies.

The relationship to the state conventionally maintained by the various Afghan communities is one of externality and compromise, not of exclusion. That is, the violence that regularly characterises these relationships aims to re-establish an equilibrium, after measuring the balance of strength on which the necessary compromises will be based. Violence in general, whether it is against the state and communities, or individuals or even family members, is not an attempt to snap off relations or to destroy the adversary; rather, it aims to establish a intricate system of priority, which can be expressed through other symbolic relationships (one gives or takes a wife according to the rules). Tribal violence or even political violence (coups d'etat, fights for succession, and others) takes place in an essentially private arena, according to rules that are more anthropological than political. Ethnic conflicts, family feuds, the arrogance of a ruler or notable combine at the moment of crisis to define alliance networks, to which the state will be both judge and party. But everyone wants the state to exist, for it ensures functions that no one wants to take over, not out of deference, but out of disdain for these functions. Pillaging depends on the existence of some wealth; acquiring subsidies and arms depends on the existence and operation of a state that can implement strategies to receive them. To be chief of one's village, it is useful for a minister or a general (and, later, a humanitarian organisation or an information service) to give the nod of approval that marks the definitive distancing of the rival (this input can range from arresting the rival, to subsidising the official candidate, to transferring administrative duties to the loyal chief). Hence there finally develops a certain codification of violence within a determined space and temporality, according to tactical rules that are without a strategy: this codification makes coups d'etat closer to vendettas, tribal conflicts, or ethnic clashes than to the imposition of a new political model (the communist coup d'etat was perceived, in the days that followed, as the triumph of the Ghilzay Pakhtuns over the Durani Pakhtuns, although the ideological magnitude was quickly felt). This conflicting relationship between the state and groups is reconstituted regularly after each crisis. It was always a factor throughout the war, both in the resistance and in the regime.

Yet this war introduced extensively new elements without eliminating certain permanent situations. The first novelty was the idea of total war, that is, of a war that threatens the society at its roots instead of being one of its modes of operation (and no doubt regulation): modern war has no closed space unto itself, either geographic or social. There is no longer a battlefield, a division between public and private, a specific time for combat. Aviation, air-transported artillery and troops, brings combat everywhere. One leaves the closed space, the compartmentalisation inherent in Afghanistan, to enter an open space; since the old solidarities that defined the closed spaces had a tough time standing up to modern war, this open space was either empty a mass exodus or anarchic, or, finally, structured by previously unknown political institutions: the political parties of the resistance. The second unusual element is thus the politicisation of the Afghan resistance, perceptible in the establishment of political parties, which were formed according to three non-contradictory parameters: (1) the ideologisation of political life (faced with Marxism, Islam is thought of as a political ideology and not simply as a religion); (2) the necessity of adhering to a party in order to obtain arms (which involves new patronage relationships between chiefs of foreign-based parties and local commanders); and (3) the endurance of traditional solidarities (brotherhood, ethnicities, clans, families, patronage networks, and so on) beneath modern political forms (parties).

Behind the politicisation of the society, we therefore find networks of infra-political solidarities, as well as tribal and ethnic fragmentation. Very rapidly, in fact, the communist state began to play the traditional tribal game. The more the Afghan resistance endowed itself with political frameworks, the more the communist state went about ridding itself of all that qualified it as *communist* (abandoning the term "democratic" in the country's name in 1987. Acknowledging Islam as the official religion, establishing a multiparty system).

This de-ideologisation of the state brought about the quasi-disappearance of ideological Islamist references in the Afghan resistance, especially following the departure of Soviet troops in 1989: on the one hand, the parties functioned openly as simple networks of patronage and of ethnic or tribal camaraderie; on the other hand, the programme of the *mujahidin* became limited to neofundamenalist-type demands.

Does this suggest that Afghanistan is back to square one, that the traditional society has again come to the fore now that the superficial modernities have been exhausted? It is true that the candid discourse of political modernity is feeble in both camps: ethnic nationalism and neofundamentalism are the only ideologies that remain after the fall of Marxism and the crises in Islamism. But the war profoundly changed the society. The intermixing and displacement of factions of the population, as well as the rise in power of a new elite, changed the social structure of the country and led highly insular populations to assume new identities (ethnic, linguistic) beyond their connection to local solidarity groups. But rather than a return to the conventional society, it is more apt to speak of a transference of the solidarity networks and power of a traditional society into a modern and international context. The logic of modern war forced a remodelling of power relationships and of loyalty upon people who had earlier only two models of war, which were also traditional: tribal war and jihad.

Regardless of their political tendencies, all the military commanders of the resistance began by borrowing their strategies as well as their ploys from a traditional model of war that is from a model that presupposed a defined space and a massacred state. Thus, there was a contradiction between the emergence of parties and of modern political ideologies and an abiding traditional concept of war, a nonideological vision — even in jihad — in which one does not aim to annihilate the state. In fact, it seems that the true shift toward politics occurred through militarisation, and not through the implantation of parties or of modern ideological discourse. It was he necessity of manoeuvring one's troops in a strategic space that was no longer defined by solidarity factions, but by a desire to paralyse and thereby destroy the state apparatus, that in certain cases brought about the establishment of political structures that could rise above the split of solidarity groups, while on the other hand the absence of strategic imperatives, or more exactly of a strategic vision, brought about an appropriation of political frameworks by preexisting networks, even among the Islamist militants. Militarisation and a shift toward political involvement go hand in hand.

We will therefore examine the traditional forms of combat, the relationship to politics that they imply, their persistence in the Afghan resistance, and, ultimately, the type of societal structure that exists today: a new society, the old tradition maintained, or the transference of the traditional structure into a new sociological truth and discourse.

In the field, there is a wide diversity of cases: we go from the state-organised type of front (like Masud's) to the resurgence of medieval military traditions (the *ribat*, a fortress held by a fighting religious brotherhood that transcends tribal fragmentations), by way of the implosion of resistance fronts, in which the old cleavages have re-emerged in a climate of overarmament and exacerbation that renders ineffectual the traditional modes of intervention and arbitration.

Traditional Models of War

The Muslims insurgents who first opposed the communist regime, formed by a coup d'etat on April 27, 1978, and then opposed the Soviet invasion in December 1979 have two models of war: tribal war and jihad; each implies a defined space, strategy, and values and bestows priority to formal staging over any real strategy.

Tribal War

Whether or not it is a matter of tribal zones in the strict sense, we find throughout Afghan society solidarity groups called *qawm*, the sociological definition of which can differ (tribal clans, of course, but also endogamous professional factions, people from the same village or valley, an ethnic subgroup, an extended family, caste, or simply any network of patronage formed around an eminent citizen, the *khan*). These groups determine one's adherence network and constitute the basic identity of every Afghan. The tribal system *stricto sensu* rests on a far narrower definition of these groups, through genealogy, a group legend, a tribal custom (in every sense of word: definition of the ideal warrior, common law, value systems), and a group of institutions peculiar to the tribal world (the *jirga*, or council). The tribal system remains dominant within the Pakhtun ethnic community, particularly in the eastern part of the country. It is there that anthropologists studied the model of tribal war, which will serve in a broad fashion to define traditional war — one that does not integrate politics — and which may act as a paradigm for the spontaneous mode of waging war in operation within the Afghan resistance.

Tribal war is not a war; that is to say, the structure for violence remains that of ordinary society: the warrior is any adult man, the warlord is the civil chief, the "army" is the mass levy of warriors belonging to the group in question, which is normally struggling against the symmetrically similar group in the segmentary structure of tribal society. Tribal war is never total war and takes place in a specific space and at a specific time: fighting takes place among adult men, outside the village — except in the case of vendetta raids — and not during the harvest. The battles are more symbolic than real. The goal is plunder as an end in itself or as a retribution inflicted on the adversary, not the conquest of territory or the annihilation of a group. The adversary's very existence is not under threat. What is at stake is pre-eminence, made manifest in an economic advantage over the other (land or booty). The concepts of equilibrium and of the status quo are regular features of the tribal vision of violence and war.

Tribal war is in fact not very mobile; it occurs within the "solidarity space" as specified by the network of a solidarity group (except in tribal zones, it is rare for a *qawm* to take over a defined space exclusively). Tribal war occurs "in private". The stranger is safer than the native; the inferior is safer than the equal.

Precisely because it takes place at a private stage, tribal war is neither ideological nor political: the state being outside the tribal space, a group does not hesitate to form an alliance with it against a rival. The state's existence is not denied, but instrumentalised, on the condition, of course, that it not appear to desire a change in the rules of the game (by constructing a road or a military post, for example). But even in this case, the combat artistry against the state will be the same as in the war among clans, only more demonstrative: one mimics an attack against the post in order to improve one's negotiating position.

Jihad

Jihad, a concept considered to be the political imagination of Islam, is meant to introduce a radical break: it goes beyond tribal segmentation by appealing to the *umma* and transcends the values and the tribal code by calling on Islam and the *sharia*. It is pronounced by a religious leader, who is generally outside the tribal world; it does not occur at a private level, but opposes interior and exterior. It addresses each Muslim as an individual and not his group, his clan, or his ethnicity. By breaking up the *asabiyya* in favour of the *umma*, it therefore effects a rupture with the world of tribal warfare. The tribal obsession with symmetry and balance no longer applies.

Yet in the history of Afghanistan over the last two centuries, the tactics of jihad have been those of tribal war: temporal discontinuity, relative respect of civilians (although women can be booty), demonstration being more important than destruction, taste for plunder, and rivalry among *qawm* chiefs (the *khan*), which reappears the instant victory is in sight and is generally enough to prevent it. Victories are never exploited, and the ulemas have been able to impose *sharia* and discipline only momentarily. Jihad ignores the ABCs of war according to Clausewitz. Although the scale is larger than that of the vendetta or the revolt, jihad brings no innovation in tactics or in strategy, but only in the references of genuineness. Jihad in fact knows no political space, no state. Its space that of *umma*, of the community of Muslims; it is a symbolic space that one traces in an upward direction, toward conquest, or in a descending one, from the *hijra*. Jihad knows no borders; thus it too has only an instrumental vision of the state, which ends up being devalued. The state (*dawla*) is the temporary incarnation of the Muslim nation (*milla*); in reality, it exists only in crises and is not institutionalised. The ethical model that is at the heart of the notion of jihad prohibits political frameworks.

Modern War and Traditional Society

For the first time with the Soviet invasion of 1979, the Afghans were confronted with total war, that is, a war that knows no limits between war and space, either in time, or between categories of the population. Aerial bombardment can take place anywhere and at any moment of the day or year. More "civilians" are killed than combatants. The Soviet army waged a traditional war, which beginning in 1984 would just barely adapt to the realities of counter guerrilla warfare. The target of the Soviets was to transform Afghan society into one centred on the state. The Soviets' profoundly state-managed vision contrasted with the Afghans' indifference to the idea of the state.

Space of War

The 1978-79 anticommunist insurrection occurred on the lines of the model of jihad described above. Yet from the very beginning, the insurrection space was not a national space. One fights to liberate one's solidarity space, that is, the territory of a *qawm* or of a group of interdependent *qawm*. It is true that the solidarity space is not necessarily a homogeneous territory, confined by borders: it is above all an ensemble of networks (*qawms*, brotherhoods, ethnicities); but in any case this space produces its own borders (always in relation to the other *qawm* or other ethnic faction). The destruction of the state apparatus is closer to a purification and a symbolic reappropriation of the solidarity space than to a strategic aspiration for isolation and destruction of the state. One of the primary characteristics of the Afghan resistance is its strategic immobility.

The first level of politicisation is the establishment of political parties. Beginning in 1980, most of the Sunni fronts belonged to the so-called Peshawar parties. This membership should not be seen as merely a means of acquiring arms. Political affiliations remained relatively stable over ten years of war. The best equipped parties (Hikmatyar's Hizb, Sayyaf's Ittihad and Khali's Hizb) remained in the minority in relation to the Jamaat (moderate Islamist) and the Haraka (traditionalist fundamentalist), which would have been a different case if the commanders had joined only to stock up on weapons. The map of political affiliations in Afghanistan would be just as intricate as a Western electoral map. Thus, several political parties may be juxtaposed within a single space, with each one's front interwoven among those of its competitors, including identical administrations and headquarters. In a large part of the territory, the resistance groups constitute not a mosaic, but an interlinking of identical and competitive networks, each one founded on camaraderies that are ultimately expressed by affiliation to a political party.

Modern guerrilla warfare should occur within a geographic space defined in terms of military strategy, with ethnic issues becoming secondary (the typical example of this being Mao Tse-tung's Long March). Guerrilla warfare therefore requires an "open" space. But in Afghanistan, the primary space has remained that of the *qawm*. For an armed faction to leave this space, a psychological transformation must occur not only among the combatants, but also among the populations of the other spaces.

Tactics and Strategy

The definition of the objective (the Soviet-Afghan post situated along the border of the solidarity space) and the idea of the attack (demonstrating force without aiming to conquer or destroy the objective) are inherited from tribal war; this type of war is essentially defensive and not offensive, since it places little importance on capturing the only place whose conquest would end the aggression — the capital, thus the state — and since it rejects the only effective military strategy — the annihilation of the adversary's momentum. The warrior doesn't take power; he amasses it. The state in and of itself is not an aim: what is empty attracts the warrior, not what is occupied; you sack the bazaar when the king has left the palace. Similarly, the ideal tactic for most *mujahidin* is that of the surrender of the governmental post after arbitration or betrayal. Which explains a sensation that has generally gone unnoticed: during this entire war, the *mujahidin*, with the exception of Commander Masud, almost never attacked a government post, a *fortiori* a Soviet one, of a level higher than that of the company.

It is as if there were a desire (unconscious?) latent in the *mujahidin* behaviour to preserve an equilibrium between war and civil society, an equilibrium that would be thrown into question by the Vietnamese model of systematic assault. Hence no doubt the apparent immobility of many *mujahidin*, who safeguard themselves like lions but, when it comes to going on the offensive, are satisfied to call a vague *de facto* ceasefire that will protect the autonomy of the local community and the permanence of its way of life.

The way in which most of the *mujahidin* fronts have managed the Afghan campaign displays their renunciation of the establishment of a counterstate and the desire to maintain an equilibrium, in opposition to the concept of total war. There is none of the fiercely ideological aspect of our wars in Spain or Ireland, in which a man could have his brother shot. The networks not only survive the war, but become an integral part of it. The Soviet retaliation that inevitably followed a successful attack were thus perceived as particularly destabilising, resulting as they did in the flight of civilian populations and dishonour for the *mujahidin*, who had failed to safeguard the sacred family domain. The space and temporality of traditional war that they have attempted to protect has thereby been destroyed. Avoiding reprisals is a priority for the traditional fronts. The resistance of the civilian populations is tied to the maintenance of this equilibrium: in order to resist, it is more important for the society to survive in its frameworks and values than in its demography.

Yet jihad, which presupposes the absolute externality of the enemy, should have enabled the politicisation of tribal war by giving it the taking of the state as an objective. Two things should be mentioned here.

- Jihad really aimed only at Russia and left intact the interplay of hierarchies and competition within the "Muslim" camp, even if this favoured the introduction of Islamist parties. Within the government one found the same tribal game, that is, permanent negotiations. It is as if the Soviet invasion had displaced the notion of the infidel, from the local communist to the foreign soldier. This tendency was reinforced by the fact that beginning in 1980 the regime developed a "tribal policy" that obliterated any Marxist, or even revolutionary, references and reactivated a tribal mode of operation.
- Jihad, as is well illustrated by Jean-Paul Charnay, is an affair between the believer and God and not between the believer and his enemy. There is no obligation to obtain a result. Hence the demonstrative, even exhibitionist, aspect

of the attacks. It is an act of faith, the passion of penitents, who are satisfied with nocturnal fireworks *ad maiorem Dei gloriam*, Jihad is not political.

What is needed to create a strategy is predominantly a perception of the state as an objective of military strategy. Tribal strategy does not aim to take power, but to hinder its expansion. It is only with the target of taking control of the state that it is worth destroying the adversary or even simply taking over a post. One sometimes has the impression that this unwillingness to proceed with the "definitive" assault comes from the perception of the irreversible nature of this act: it would be the end of the closed and well-balanced world, the end of balance.

Refusal to Include the State into the Resistance

A true strategy of rupture with respect to the Central government would have meant a recognition of the society in terms of the state, and thus the creation of a counterstate in liberated zones. Similarly, a move toward truly effective combat tactics would have meant a militarisation of the resistance (professionalisation, centralisation, mobility), which would also imply the introduction of a state-run model in the resistance. But this militarisation would not occur automatically, for its presupposes a relationship with the society totally different from the traditional one.

Spontaneously, the majority of local resistance commanders endeavoured to avoid any professionalisation and militarisation that would call into question the frameworks of the traditional society. Rather, they attempted to translate into traditional terms the new state of affairs brought about by modern war. Not only combat tactics, as we have observed, but also the distribution of arms, the collection of taxes, the maintenance of justice, and the organisation of logistics were managed in accordance with traditional models. There was little or no organisation of a passive defence, enrolment of civilians, creation of an administration. Here are two common examples: women and the economy. There were no women fighters. The respect of the *haram* and of *purda* (confining women to the private space) was part of what the Afghans were endorsing against the Soviets. Integrating women into combat would have negated the reason for the combat. War's influence on the modernisation of the society reached its limits here: women are part of the private sphere. The private economy functioned without much mediation on the part of the *mujahidin*, who relied on it both for logistics and for provisions. There was no "*mujahidin* economy".

In the resistance we experience a regular feature of Islamic wars: the professional soldier (*asker*) is devalued not only with respect to *mujahidin*, who is a volunteer and a believer, but also with respect to the warrior and the merchant and artisan. The *asker* is viewed as a simple mercenary (*mazdur*, the salaried odd-job man), as a victim of forced enrolment, or as too stupid to have plied any other trade. From the Iranian Revolutionary Guard to the Lebanese Hizbullah militiamen, contempt for the professional military man goes hand in hand with the spirit of jihad.

The strategic and cultural immobility of jihad is elucidated by the role of the "military base" (*markaz*), a *mujahidin* camp protected by anti-aircraft and antimissile defence and heavy weaponry. Families never live there, and the mujahidin are formed for daily life, with bakeries, gardeners, stablemen, service boys, and so on. The *markaz* didn't exist in traditional tribal war, since the warrior lived at home between campaigns. Mobile groups leave from the *markaz* to search the solidarity space (considered to be identical with the "front," *jabha*) and mark out any governmental presence: the adversary's post will be indirectly besieged for years, and the roads occasionally ambushed.

We find two antecedents for the *markaz* in Muslim history: the refuge of the honourable bandit and the *ribat* of the fighting brotherhoods on the frontiers of the Muslim world. In Afghanistan we find some *markaz* that come close to banditry, such as Amir Rasul's, in the Baghlan, whose mastery over a mountain pass serves primarily for the collection of tax. But even for the authentic *mujahidin*, the "base" is less an element of military strategy than the sociopolitical restructuring of the space: it is a matter of reconstituting a camaraderie group (*qawm* or *asabiyya*) around a chief who comes from the new elite yet behaves like a traditional *khan*, even if he is of modest origins: he keeps open board and distributes munitions, money and small gifts. The social restructuring brought about by the war in no way implies the renunciation of the traditional conception of the exercise of authority: the newly risen embrace the way of life and behaviour of the former notables (significantly, the title *khan* is attached to the names of commanders, formerly students without prestige but now at the head of important fronts: Basir Khan, Ismail Khan, Bashir Khan...). The sociology of the chief has transformed with respect to the past, but not the behaviour of those who are perceived as the new *khans*. The chief is first and foremost the one who gives; arms and ammunition have replaced money and food.

This analysis explains the dramatic turn of events taken by the war in Afghanistan after the Soviets' departure in February 1989. The *mujahidin* failed to shift from a guerrilla war to a traditional war, less because they lacked arms than because such a shift would have presupposed the abandonment of age-old models of war, as well as the acceptance of the state by the guerrillas, and in particular the set-up of a single command and the circulation of combat units in a homogeneous space. The Pakistani armed forces who pushed the guerrillas to launch a conventional war in 1989 saw Afghanistan as merely a military map, about which one could move little blue, red, and green flags: the units were interchangeable, the objectives quantifiable. But the space as the Afghans observe it is sociocultural: it is one of tribes, ethnic groups, or influence zones of a particular chief.

The failure of the attacks against the cities of Jalalabad in March 1989 and Gardez in the autumn of 1991 illustrates the permanence of the models of traditional war. With Masud's capture of Kabul in April 1992, however, the question arises whether he has brought a new model of war to Afghanistan.

Masud's Example: A Settlement between Jihad and Modern Warfare

Of the few hundred Afghan *mujahidin* "commanders" active within the country, all employ a model of conventional war. Only one has attempted not only to launch an army but to employ a modern strategy.

In the beginning, Masud's front, situated in the northeast of Afghanistan, maintained a typical *qawm* framework. Masud, an Islamist militant and former student in engineering, took over the lower valley of Panjshir, of which he is a native, and which he conquered with few members of the Jamaat-i Islami party who came from Peshawar during the winter of 1979-80. The population joined the Jamaat because its supremo, Rabbani, was a fellow Sunni Persian-speaker, because it was the first party to bring in arms, and because the valley has an old tradition of radical opposition, transmitted by a network of traditionalist ulemas. The adjacent valleys (Shotol, Hazara) and upper valley (Paryans) immediately entered into the character, even though their inhabitants did not consider themselves Panjshiris. From the start, then, there was an enlargement of the solidarity space. There are many reasons for this. The foundation of Masud's operation is composed of Panjshiris either educated or working in Kabul, who are therefore less subject to the *qawm's* decisions. Although it is true that inhabitants of the Panjshir are peasants, they have been in the habit of emigrating to Kabul for some time, where they appoint a good number of the drivers, mechanics, and cooks for foreigners. Among these, "emigrants" Panjshiris a regional "Panjshiri" identity has developed that transcends one's village *qawm* association. For these people, the *qawm* is merely "Panjshiri" and no longer, for example, Nuruzkhayl (the name of the Masud family *qawm*, famous to have come from Central Asia), Sayyid, or other denominations. Masud's two assets are thus that he controls a homogeneous solidarity space (without tribal or other sub-divisions) and that, while remaining anchored to the traditional society, he has at his disposition urbanised, technically trained cadres. Very quickly, after having eliminated a few "Maoists" and Hizb-i Islami pockets and following his first triumph over the Soviet-governmental forces in the spring of 1980, Masud resigned in the name of the Jamaat over all Panjshiris. Up to this point, there is nothing new.

The personal Masud factor came into play from this moment onwards, in the establishment of an original military model, well before the matter of moving beyond the solidarity space arose. The Masud model consisted in militarising and specialising the troops. The military apparatus is no longer an armed duplication of civilian society, at least the farther one goes up the organisational chart. In fact it is the Vietnamese General Gap model. First, we have the base (*qararga*), where an unspecialised (*grup-e mahali*), locally recruited group ensures order and self-defence for several villages at a time, while continuing to attend by rotation to productive works. Then, on the district level, a "strik force" (*grup-e zarbati*) assembles local but permanent combatants, who are given uniforms and more sophisticated arms (antitank devises, machine guns); this faction participates only in the operations that occur within the structure of the district and furnishes the first level of defence in case of a surprise enemy attack. Up to this point, we are still within the conventional solidarity space. Next comes the "mobile group" (*mutaharrik*), which recruits locally and is stationed at a base, but circulates transcending the limits of the solidarity space, as military imperatives require. This is the first instance of a unit that goes beyond the bounds of the solidarity space. Beginning in 1985 "central units" (*qatiha-ye markazi*) were created, recruitment for which was totally independent of the *qawm* network. These elite units served as training centres for officers in a future army. All military operations against a post involved the participation of central units, mobile groups and local groups. Beginning in the autumn of 1986, Masud initiated a series of assaults against government bases held by battalion-level troops: the garrisons of Nahrin, Fakhar, Kalafgan, Kashm, Koranomunjan; finally, in August 1988, the first provincial capital, Taloqan, fell into Masud's trap. These operations took place in four different provinces.

The essential problem was thus to leave the Panjshiri solidarity space and to integrate others in order to move into a "national" space envisaged of in strategic terms. Masud's method consisted in bringing in local non-Panjshiri factions and leaders, generally on bad terms with the traditional leaders, training them and convincing them of the superiority of his model, then sending them back to their zones of origin with a few Panjshiri advisers to upgrade his system there. These new commanders, who generally belonged to this same educated and urbanised generation, found a form of social promotion in entering the Masud movement, which allowed them to get around local hierarchies that had become oppressive. It was by playing on a change in sociological structure (the rise of an "educated" class outside the powerful network of family relations) that Masud could hope to impose a military, and thus a political, mutation. The peasant population followed along insofar as this system normally enabled it to escape petty warlords. Beginning in 1982, factions who considered themselves ethnically different from the Panjshiris declares themselves of the Panjshiri *qawm*: these also included the Sunni Hazaras of the Hazara valley, and the people of Shotol, who, moreover, speak a different language (Parachi).

On the village level, Masud does not tamper at all with traditional frameworks. His system is imposed from above and through the military. To provide a political arm for his system, he created the "Northern Supervisory Council" (*shura-ye nazar*) in 1985, a collective structure meant to surpass solidarity space segmentation; it used the political framework of the Jamaat (although some party commanders remained reluctant to adopt a structure that once again denied them the status of *khan*, the traditional status acquired through war). The district leaders were named by the Council and, as far as possible, were recruited from outside the local *qawm*. Commissions (culture, health, finance, legal) formed the base of future ministries. Behind the military organisation, a model of state organisation was taking shape, even though it superposed, without eliminating, the traditional notables and the *qawm* system: any attempt to eradicate the traditional system would have thrown a part of the population into the arms of rival parties or the government. The traditional *qawm* and solidarity space rules have not disappeared. The local chief's rights are respected. At the same time, Masud does not touch either the economy or the society (except to build schools): this is where the foundation of the "civilian" identity resides. State control, in fact, touches only one very limited sector of the society: the political-military sector. Elsewhere the civil society has absolute autonomy, in particular with regard to logistics, which is surprising for such a militarised system: arms are carried by lapis lazuli drivers, who ride with empty saddle packs one way and are therefore happy to carry arms, but have no qualms about striking for a rate increase. Ethnicity is the limit of the process of modernisation, and might even be a consequence of this process. But Masud's army, at the peak of its efficiency, remained a Tadzhik ethnic army, with few Pakhtuns.

New Segmentations

The Masud model is unmatched in Afghanistan. Even an Islamo-Leninist type party like the Hizb-i Islami was unable to establish an instrument of modern war: the "professional armies" put together with Afghan refugees in Pakistan, then trained and endowed by the Pakistani army, turned out to be incapable of waging modern battles and found themselves rejected by the local populace, despite the fact that these populations had generally been won over by the *mujahidin*. This predicament brings to light the problems of the process of modernisation brought on by war.

This war brought about the decline of the traditional elite (the Pakhtun aristocracy of tribal origin) and the rise of a new elite: Islamist intellectuals, mullahs, small warlords within Afghanistan on the one hand, neofundamentalist "new intellectuals" among the emigrants to Pakistan on the other — all people who owe their emergence to the war and who, in certain cases have become "war entrepreneurs," living from and by the war. We have seen that the "new notable" status acquired by the resistance leaders is due mainly to their redistribution activity. But in order to distribute, one has to be plugged into the network of goods circulation; these goods cannot be the products of peasants, because then the leader would be viewed as exploitative and rejected. The goods that circulate — arms, subsidies, humanitarian assistance — come from abroad or from the government and are allocated for political reasons. Thus, this network originates with a state: either the local capital or foreign powers. The new powers are made more secure by the internationalisation of the war and of the distribution networks.

The protagonists, without always being aware of it and without ever gaining control of the process, have seen their activities inserted into a global geostrategy: between East and West, between radical and secular, between Shiite and Sunni, between the MB and Wahhabis, between producers and consumers of drugs, and others. This internationalisation brought with it an influx of international support (arms, money, humanitarian aid), which has profoundly modified and monetarised a rural and more or less autarkic economy. But the network for the circulation of goods and money became autonomous with respect to the state sponsors. Today, many chiefs manage their living through the production of drugs, which necessarily circulate through an international network, since they are not consumed in the country. Gun-running, drug production, and the corruption that arises free these new economic circuits from dependence on the decisions of foreign powers (the United States, Russia or Saudi Arabia) to support or not to support their allies in Afghanistan. The many power centres that manage this flow of goods were created by the war and are in direct contact with international networks: the domestic state and foreign states are short circuited by the growing autonomy of these networks for the circulation of "goods".

These new power centres are proving to be the nuclei of a new segmentation. The Islamists have used a modern political framework that of parties, to insert themselves into and attempt to transcend the traditional segmentation into *qawm*, clans, tribes, and ethnic groups, in which the traditional power of notables was grounded. The result is not so much the imposition of political modernity as a transferring of traditional forms of division and power into a new system.

In a first phase, the Afghan resistance, although it did often topple the usual notables, developed around the society's traditional structure of segmentation into *qawm*: a growing number of "local commanders," who were at times in charge of only a few dozen combatants, safeguarded their independence with respect to the more important commanders by adhering to a rival party from which they drew sufficient subsidies to maintain their status. We have noted the link between the military crippleness of the *mujahidin* and the fact that the protagonists considered the geography of the networks and territories as natural: a "commander" rarely seeks to exterminate or chase away a *qawm* that has given itself a political identity by adhering to a party opposed to his own.

In a second phase, the new chiefs that appeared from the war assumed the same manner of exerting power as the notables: they established a patronage network, this time made possible because they could redistribute goods by promoting an international network (of inputs: arms, subsidies; of output: drugs and ... arms). By acting as distributors, they could avoid leeching off their own society. Political groups tend to structure themselves on the operational model of the *qawm*, through matrimonial alliances, exchange of benefits, nepotism, and so on. Thus, we see new *qawm* emerging, created around a pole of power and the distribution of goods, and no longer representative of the old *qawm*. The former segmentation, including that of ethnic identity, tends to be rearranged around new poles of power. But these new poles are perpetuated only through the internationalisation of the conflict. Essentially, the attainment of any power within a political party gives access to a new commodity — weapons — at times accompanied, for the most powerful commanders or those most gifted at public relations, by the arrival of humanitarian and financial assistance from abroad. Often a right-hand man jealous of his chief will open a front the way one opens a shop; to attract a clientele, one has to give something (guns, but also humanitarian aid: "French doctors," for instance, became political money); one just promise to take the civilian population under one's wing. It is like a true small time electoral campaign in which the "constituent" is king.

Transfer of Traditional Segmentations

Thus, the politicisation of traditional society in Afghanistan both by war and by Islamism has produced only one form of relatively modern politico-military organisation: the Masud system. Should the Afghan case be interpreted as a concrete illustration of Islamism's inability to produce an effective political model? It would be premature to generalise and to conclude that Islamist discourse generally is a mere cover not for the permanence, but for the rewriting in modern terms of traditional modes of division, patronage, and the exercise of power. A more probing study remains to be done. But other field inquiries tend in this direction. There structuring of politics in the type of a new segmentation is not unique to the Afghan Islamists; the same case is noticed in the ex-Soviet Tadzhikistan.

It is significant that the militia war in Lebanon from 1975 to 1991 offered an urban version of the Afghan model. There is, first of all, a surprising correlation between the two guerrilla wars: according to Michel Seurat, the armed groups did not trespass on enemy territory or seek to destroy the enemy. It was primarily a matter of marking a territory in order to capitalise this advantage later in terms of profits and redistribution to one's group. This guerrilla warfare is also demonstrative and symbolic; hence the role played by the taking of hostages. We have here a transference of conventional war to an urban model.

The Lebanese militia, like the Afghan guerrillas, also perpetuated themselves by plugging into a globalised system for the circulation of goods: arms, drugs, subsidies, and then, in peacetime, real estate speculation (the reconstruction of Beirut with Saudi capital).

But what about jihad? In Lebanon, the Islamist militia's types of combat did not seem basically different from those of the other militias, whether Christian, Druze, or "progressive." Lebanon offers an excellent field for comparative studies, since it presents the entire range of ideological motivation: communalist, jihad, mercenary, mafia, and so on. The "progressive" groups were the first to lose their ideological essence and transform themselves into purely communal groups, but the Islamists did not follow suit.

Jihad furnishes a discourse of legitimation for the new elite, but neither an organisational model nor a new political structure for the combatant society. It remains to be seen what will happen to the model created by Masud, particularly since it will be called on to play a role in the vacuum created by the disappearance of the Soviet Union, provided that it doesn't fall into this void itself.

Five

Iranian Revolution

Iran is the only country in which Shiism is the state religion, and the only one in which a true Islamic revolution occurred. The Iranian revolution is very intrinsically linked to Shiism, conceived of not as a corpus, but as a history. The identification of Shiism with Iran reflects a historical process that occurred in two stages: first, Iran's conversion to Shiism under the Safavids during our sixteenth century, then the unfinished Iranianisation of foreign Shiite minorities through the progressive establishment of a predominantly Iranian, hierarchised, and centralised clergy, a considerable innovation with respect to Sunnism.

Nothing in Shiite thought, however, predisposes the clergy to play a contestant political role. Shiism even evolved a remarkable quietist and Sufi current (first made known to the West by Henry Corbin). It was the historical course of the Shiite clergy's evolution into a self-perpetuating hierarchical body that is autonomous both financially (followers pay dues directly) and politically (the hierarchy is formed in a territory that eludes control by the Iranian state), that in the twentieth century enabled it to become a tool for taking power. On the fringes of the Shiite corpus, a blend of traditionalist fundamentalism and Marxist-leaning ideology was developed.

The Iranian revolution is the only Islamist movement in which the clergy played a decisive role, but it was also the most apparently ideological one: a Third World revolutionary movement generated by an extraordinary alliance between a radical intelligentsia and a fundamentalist clergy. The Islamisation that followed victory therefore did not take on the conservative cast which marked the process of state Islamisation in countries like Pakistan, Saudi Arabia, or Sudan, and which we may still see in

Algeria. Nevertheless, there was an anticlerical trend in Iranian Islamism that contested the clergy's religious monopoly; this tendency was embodied in the thinker Ali Shariati and in extremist factions such as the People's Mujahidin (Mujahidin-e Khalq), but was rejected by the opposition as soon as revolutionary institutions were setup.

Conversion to Shiism

Shiism is historically an Arab phenomenon: it is based on belief in the genuineness of the Prophet's family, which is Arab par excellence; the language of the imams, direct descendants of Ali, as well as of the theological literature, is Arabic; most of the holy sites of Shiism are on Arab territory, most of the great ayatollahs have been sayyid, a title bestowed on descendants of the Prophet; many are of Arab ancestry, and all are perfectly fluent in the Arabic language.

In the early sixteenth century, the devotional guide of a sect combining Shiism with shamanism that had become established among Turkoman tribes (the Qizilbash) took control of the territory that is now Iran and instituted the Safavid dynasty. The new sovereigns, who spoke Turkish, had to rid themselves of their purely tribal and sectarian origins in order to build a enduring state. Shiism was so foreign to Iran at the time that in order to create a state clergy the Safavids had to meet Arab theologians from what is now south Lebanon (the region of Jabal Amil) and from the Persian Gulf (Bahrain). The Shiitisation of Iran was part of the process of constructing a territorialised state apparatus. The religious leader of the Iranian clergy (the *sadr*) was a functionary at the court. In its framework, the Shiite clergy of that era differed letter from its Sunni counterpart: on the one hand were the court ulemas; on the other, the village mullahs. The establishment of an autonomous clergy was made all the less likely by the fact that the Safavid dynasty itself was invested with religious legitimacy.

Iran's conversion to Shiism did not happen without the resistance and massacre of Sunni clerics, as witnessed in Herat; Shiism did not become totally established until the region of King Abbas (1587-1629). The current boundaries between Iran, on the one hand, and Afghanistan and Turkey on the other, date from this time and are not ethnic but religious, opposing Shiites and Sunnis.

Creation of Transnational Shiite Clergy

The eighteenth century brought a series of fundamental changes. First, the Zand and later the Qajar dynasties (the latter also Turkish-speaking) no longer held religious legitimacy and were considered as purely secular. Then the Persian ulemas, feeling threatened in Iran (following the Afghan invasion of 1722, Nadir Shah attempted to revive Sunnism), developed a pattern of settling in Najaf and Karbala, holy Shiite sites in Iraq. These two cities had been under Ottoman command since 1638. The move posed no obstacle to the freedom of the Shiite clergy; on the contrary: since the Ottoman empire was not a "nation," it was far more receptive than Iran to bestowing extraterritoriality to exogenous religious groups; the Shiites were persecuted only insofar as they emerged to challenge the cardinal power (in south Lebanon), and not as a region. The first Iranian spiritual leader to settle permanently at Najaf was Muhammad Baqir Akmal Vahid Bahbahani (1705-1791).

This movement was accompanying a theological debate that rocked through the Shiite clergy; it had to do with the reopening of the right to interpretation (*ijtihad*). The *akhbari* ("traditionalists") were of the belief that this right had been closed since the disappearance of the twelfth imam; their position was close to that of the Sunnis. This *usuli* ("fundamentalists") believed that this right resided with the high ulemas. The triumph of the second group (generally Iranians marked a fundamental breach with Sunnism and paved the way of the creation of the modern Shiite clergy. The right to *ijtihad* is recognised only for high ulemas, who form a collegial body and who are referred to as mujtahid or ayatollah ("sign of God"). As a result, each believer must obey the interpretation of an ulema, whom the chooses from among the college of grand ayatollahs, in general by intermediary of the local mullahs, who have received their coronation either directly or indirectly from a grand ayatollah. Clericalisation (the formation of an autonomous body of clerics separate from the state) is a consequence of the victory of the *usuli*.

This evolution also exalted the financial autonomy of the

clergy, which is still in effect, with followers paying the Islamic tax directly to their *mujatahid's* representative rather than to the state. The money is gathered by the clergy, then redistributed into spiritual works, many of which have a social component. Since the eighteenth century, then, the Shiite clergy has played a social and educational role with no parallel among the Sunni clergy.

The nineteenth century witnessed the establishment of an internal hierarchy within the clergy, approved by co-optation, as a function of the level and prestige of one's diploma: *hujjat al-islam* ("proof of Islam"), *ayat allah* ("sign of God"), *ayat allah al-'uzma* ("grand ayatollah" or *mujtahid*); only the last can be origins of imitation (*marja'al-taqlid*). Financial and geographic independence (Najaf and Karbala were outside the frontiers of the Iranian empire); the right to interpretation, even to innovation, on all questions, delegitimation of the state (this was new since the time of the Safavids); strong hierarchy and frameworks: all operated to make the clergy a political force. The Shiite clergy first turned political at the end of the nineteenth century, when the weakness of the Qajar rule in the face of British and Russian encroachment made it the only protest force. From this period on, the defence of the Iranian nation has been intertwined with that of Islam and Shiism. The clergy's passage into politics began with Ayatollah Shirazi's *fatwa*, which in 1891 prohibited the use of tobacco as long as the monopoly that had been granted to a British company the previous year was not rescinded. In 1906 the majority of the high clergy advocated the Iranian constitutionalist movement. In 1920 the Shiite clergy was the soul of the resistance against the English in southern Iraq. Even though the clergy raised demand of a traditionalist-fundamentalist nature (that the state apply the *sharia*), it would regularly serve as a limit of contestation, especially during crises in power (1890-1921, 1950-1953, 1978).

The concept of *vilayat-i faqih*, elaborated by Imam Khomeini, was the culmination of this politicisation and would serve to mobilise Shiite communities beyond nationalist references and state gadgets.

Alliance of Clerics and Intellectuals

We notice in Iran the same factors that feed Islamism throughout the Muslim world (Islamist intellectuals, urban masses who have experienced a loss of social status). The originality of the Iranian revolution lies in the coalition between the Islamist intelligentsia and a part of the clergy, which was able to bring with it the entire corporation, out of esprit de corps as much as confidence and firmness.

The Shiite clergy is incontestably more open to the non-Islamic corpus that the Sunni ulemas. The ayatollahs are great readers (including Marx and Feuerbach): there is something of the Jesuit or Dominican in them. Hence, they combine clear philosophical syncretism with an ardous casuistic legalism. The opening of the Shiite *madrasa* to a non-Islamic corpus dates from far earlier than that of the Sunni *madrasa*. The two-fold culture of the Shiite clergy is significant: highly traditionalist (one need only read the Imam Khomeini's *Tawzih al-masa'il*) and yet very open to the present-day world; behind the legalism lies philosophical thought.

Nonetheless, it was not until Khomeini that the logic of the clergy's politicisation, pushed to the extreme, came to require that clerics exercise power. During his courses in Najaf in the 1960s, Ayatollah Khomeini developed the notion of *vilayat-i faqih* (government of the doctor of law). This concept is the Shiite version of the Islamist state: it is not sufficient that the laws promulgated be in conformity with the *sharia*; the state must be Islamic in its essence. But while Sunni theoreticians have had difficulty defining the form of such a state, as we have observed Khomeini had an answer, for unlike the Sunnis, the Shiites have an institution that can determine who is the most learned, the best Muslim, the guide. Since there is a supreme religious supremacy in Shiish, this authority should hold supreme state power. Thus, the exercise of power should fall to the supreme clerical authority. This does not mean that the clergy governs directly as a confederation: although the guide is a cleric, he does not represent the clergy; he is above all institution. Khomeini never favoured the clergy as an institution: on the contrary, he sought the support of the Islamists and the *hujjat al-iṣlam*, younger clergy of lower status, rather than that of the high clergy, guardians of the century-old tradition of clerical "corporatism".

It is thus not surprising that the *vilayat-i faqih* thesis was renounced by almost the entire dozen grand ayatollahs living in 1981: they either unreservedly opposed Khomeini, as did Abu al-Qasim al-Khu'i and Shariat Madari (who died in 1986), or they maintained a diplomatic distance, refusing official posts, as did Gulpaygani, al-Qummi, al-Shirazi and al-Najafi al-Mar'ashi. In fact, the high clergy maintained its distance from the revolution. Only one grand ayatollah, Muntazari, a former student and the designated successor of Khomeini before being rejected in 1989, approved the idea. Moreover, Khomeini was not the most influential ayatollah during the Islamic revolution. The one who had the most developed network of disciples and former students was the very old Ayatollah al-Khu'i (born in 1899), an Iranian Azeri whose enormous influence reached from Lebanon (the spiritual leader of the Hizbullah, Sheikh Fadlallah, is one of his disciples) to Afghanistan, by way of the Iran's Khorasan province and the former Soviet Azerbaijan. Al Khu'i did not leave Najaf during the war between Iran and Iraq and always renounced the concept of *vilayat-i faqih*; certain religious chiefs, such as Fadlallah, would support him in this theological opposition while politically supporting the Islamic revolution. There is still no direct relation between dogma and political action.

Thus, the Iranian revolution was not a revolution of ayatollahs, but of the *hujjat al-islam*, many of them former students of Khomeini, who favoured political activism than studies in the press of movements against the Shah in 1963. Imam Khomeini relied on this network of former students, supported by young Islamists of secular origin, who saw in him the synthesis they were seeking between political radicalism and religious conviction, and which they apparently were unable to find either among the more prestigious ayatollahs, such as al-Khu'i, or among the groups of the extreme left, which though very active were also highly authoritative.

These two networks, clerical and Islamist, became interpenetrated because there was an environment of cultural flexibility in Iran; clerical families were not against giving their children perfectly Western educations, while many of the youth educated in the West followed courses part-time at religious institutions for the "secular" (the *husayniyya*). The distinction between mullahs and intellectuals was not as distinct in Iran as in the Sunni world.

Ideologisation

Even though one can read Shiism both as a quietist and mystical religion and as a political one, as did Ali Shariati there is unequivocally a thematic in the "Shiite imagination" that is more easily adaptable to the notion of revolution: a sense of history, millenarianism, the concept of social justice, the devaluation of temporal power, martyrdom. These themes are illustrated by the founding paradigms: the martyrdom of the "just" Husayn, son of Ali, and of his hangers-on in Karbala at the sword of an illegitimate tyrant; the figure of the politicised woman (Zaynab, Hussain's sister), and so on.

For the Sunnis the Islamic revolution is a negation of History, while on the contrary for the Shiites it is an advent, a Parousia, the realisation of a promise that is made possible only by the practice of occultation of the mystical Imam, the one who will return to earth to ensure the reign of justice.

Contemporary Iran has also had a more extensive development of syncretist ideologies (Hegelian-Islamic, Islamo-Marxist) than the Sunni world, as elucidated by an author like Ali Shariati and by the organisation, half sect, half political party, of the People's Mujahidin. Even though the clergy may have endeavoured to reject this syncretism, it has rubbed off on the secular Islamists. One of the reasons for this syncretism is unmistakably the influence of Marxism in Iran, an influence that is unprecedented in the Arab countries: Iran has one of the oldest communist parties in the world, the Tudeh, whose membership includes distinguished intellectuals.

Sympathy for the Third World was a constant of the Islamic revolution. The Iranian press, during the ten years when revolution was the essence (until the death of Khomeini in 1989), devoted extensive coverage to non-Muslim revolutionary movements (from the Sandinistas to the African National Congress and the Irish Republican Army) and disregarding the role of the Islamic movements considered conservative, such as the Afghan *mujahidin*. During this period Third World camaraderie took precedence over Muslim fraternity, in absolute departure from all other Islamist movements.

Yet a schism emerged when ideologisation found itself in contradiction with the sharia. For most of the members of the clergy, Islamisation had to take precedence over revolutionary logic, which meant, for instance, that private property took pre-eminence over state control, respect of the private home over police investigations, repudiation over divorce proceedings, and so on. For the fundamentalists on the contrary, revolutionary logic was more significant than legalism, even the legalism imposed by the *sharia*.

State and the Institutionalisation

The Iranian revolution had a national, state-controlled, and institutional structure. It endowed itself with institutions and never had a single party (the Islamic Republican Party was dissolved in 1986 at Khomeini's request). The Iranian nation-state, despite a pan-Islamist rhetoric, was never suspected by the Islamic revolution. True, the constitution does specify that the guide need not be Iranian, but the nationality code is extremely stern: it is as difficult for a Persian-speaking Shiite from Afghanistan to marry an Iranian as it is for a Frenchman to do so. One of Khomeini's close colleagues, Jalal al-Din Farsi, could not run for president because his father was born an Afghan.

It is no doubt the amalgamation of a clerical institution and a state tradition that spared the Iranian Islamic revolution the never-ending logistical questions of political Islam: Who should be the supreme guide? Who is authorised to legislate in matters of religion? Why form a positive law when we have the *sharia*? Without worrying too much about its conformity with the *sharia*, Iran essentially endowed itself with a bonafide constitution, not a mere slogan but one that truly organises the functioning of an ensemble of institutions; significantly, the legitimacy of the constitution is clearly founded in its first article on popular will, and not only an the *sharia*. Thus, the problem of the amir is settled. The procedures for choosing a guide are properly defined: the Council of Experts, elected by universal suffrage, designates him. If at a given moment a guide exists, then he is *index sui*, his own evidence, and the people will merely endorse this by voting, conceived of in this case as a show of allegiance (*bay'a*). If no guide is in evidence, then institutions exist to deal with this absence, just as the Shiite clergy have been dealing since the ninth century with the desertion of the twelfth imam; in this case popular suffrage is a mode of legitimation.

We see then that, aside from periods when a guide recommends himself to popular adherence, the constitution is what organises power and its legitimacy. There is a political order, which does not ruin itself before the implementation of the *sharia*. This is where the Iranian revolution differs from Sunni Islamism.

Islamic Constitution or a New Secularity?

By adopting a constitutionalist model (even certain strategic safeguards ensure the precedence of those who fought the revolution), by affirming the genuineness of universal suffrage, by transforming what should be a theocracy into a presidential system (what I call a "constitutionalist theocracy"), Iran has been able to find a political space, beyond Islamist and revolutionary hyperbole, that does not depend on the unachievable virtue of its members, but rather functions on the basis of institutions that survive in the non-existence of the divine word. A space, in short, that is secular.

In Iran, in fact, the constitution sets the place of the *sharia*, and not vice versa; more minutely, the authorities responsible for reporting on Islamic law exercise their duties in the same way that the French Council of State and Constitutional Council do, that is, within an institutional structure defined by the constitution. The new Islamic state developed a positive law that became "Islamic" by virtue of the single fact that the state was Islamic: it thus marked the end of the *sharia* as the only foundation for the judicial norm, an idea what is unacceptable to Sunni neofundamentalists. The Iranian model is in fact a "secular" model, in the sense that it is the state that defines the place of the clergy and not the clergy who define the place of politics. Thus, when Khamanei, erstwhile president of the republic, announced the supreme importance of the *sharia* over other laws in the sermon on December 31, 1988, Ayatollah Khomeini issued a public letter of reply, on January 7,

1989, in which he clearly affirmed the prominence of the revolutionary logic and the laws of the Islamic state over the *sharia*.

It is true that the *sharia* is supposed to be the supreme law and that the parliament assimilated in legislation the most symbolic of the punishments provided for in the *sharia* (*qisas*, retaliation; *diyat*, bloodletting; *hudud*, capital punishment for an wrongdoing against God); but the parliament legislates, and judges must refer to the promulgated law and not directly to the *sharia*.

On vital questions, Iranian law has remained fairly un-Islamic. The constitution grants equality of rights among men and women (Article 20). The discretionary law of repudiation is not recognised for men. There is no legal favouritism on the basis of personal status against Christians, Jews, and Zoroastrians, all of whom perform military service, pay no special taxes, and hold full citizenship; nevertheless, they are debarred from assuming leadership posts and vote in separate colleges. Similarly, a Muslim foreigner has the same status as a Christian foreigner. In brief, Iranian citizenship is not an Islamic concept. Finally, Iran kept the solar calendar and celebrates the new year on March 21.

The establishment of institutions to ensure that laws passed by the parliament are in conformity with Islam reflects an absolute recognition of a nonshariatic judicial space: the Council of Guardians of the Constitution consists of six ulemas named by the guide and six (secular) "jurists" selected by parliament from a list provided by the chief judicial authority (Article 91, an amendment to the constitution). The Council must authenticate that the laws voted by parliament are in conformity with Islam (by the majority of the doctors of law) and with the constitution (by a group majority): thus there is a recognition of a constitutional logic that cannot be degraded to the *sharia*.

In fact the Iranian constitution could work in an almost secular manner, insofar as power resides ultimately with universal suffrage and with parliament. The authorities who supervise the conformity of laws with the *sharia* are chosen not by the clergy, but by the political authority. Although the mullahs play an important role, no positions of authority, barring those of guide and half the Council of Guardian, are exclusively reserved for them. Mullahs are named to high administrative functions through political channels. Even the Council of Experts, which is responsible for nominating the guide, is elected by the people.

End of Religious Transcendence

The personal role played by Imam Khomeini muddled matters and drew the high clergy into a political revolution for which it was not prepared. Khomeini was both a traditional fundamentalist and a Third World revolutionary; he was able to mobilise a large portion of young Islamists to the clergy, yet at the same time he flouted the rules that had been established among the clergy over two centuries.

The death of Imam Khomeini, on June 3, 1989, brought an end to the logic of the Islamic revolution, according to which the highest authority of the clerical institution tallied with that of the state. Indeed, his successor, Ali Khamanei, former president of the Islamic Republic and hastily designated the new guide by the Council of Experts (which had itself dismissed its only real dauphin, Ayatollah Muntazari), does not posses the mandatory theological qualifications to be the supreme religious leader, a grand ayatollah, a "source of imitation." Khamanei is only a *hujjat al-islam*, who, although he was elevated to the rank of ayatollah the day of Khomeini's death, had neither the seniority nor the diplomas required to compel the recognition of his counterparts. There is thus a divorce between the supreme religious function (held today by an aged, little-known ayatollah who is not politically active) and the highest political function. The *vilayat-i faqih* is non-existent, but it is too late to go back to the old system.

The paradox is that Khomeiniism undermined the Shiite clerical system that had developed over the course of three centuries. Khomeini made the *sharia* subsidiary to the revolution; he affirmed, against the tradition, that the *fatwa* pronounced by a grand ayatollah survived that ayatollah (as in the case of the infamous *fatwa* against the writer Salman Rushdie). To his own interest, Khomeini put an end to the collegiality among grand ayatollahs, whose legitimacy he doubted by "defrocking" Shariat Madari (who died in 1982) and by promoting clerics as a function of their political allegiance and not of their religious status. The most brilliant clerics gave up their studies to get involved in political activism, and today there are no successors to the surviving grand ayatollahs. Since Saddam Hussain's execution of the Ayatollah Baqir al-Sadr, all the grand ayatollahs are Iranian: this marks the end of the end of Shiite universalism. The Shiite clergy's system of self-perpetuation and co-optation is worn-out.

Khomeini eliminated the transcendent, autonomous space from which the clergy spoke: the clergy was brought down to the level of the state, yet without properly controlling it, since the political hierarchy is not the religious hierarchy. Today there is not a single grand ayatollah in power. The "Republic of Ayatollahs" is a journalistic coinage. But the end of the preeminence of the grand ayatollahs, socially committed scholars who were careful not to compromise themselves in politics, means the end of a certain Shiism.

The dilapidation of Shiite legitimacy may have dramatic ramifications for Iran. A general rule, valid since the sixteenth century, has it that loyalty to the central state is based on Shiism and not on ethnicity: the Shiites of Iran perceive Iranian no matter what their ethnic category (Persian, Arab, or Azeri), whereas the Sunnis do not feel Iranian even if they are of Iranian culture (Kurds and Baluchis). But Shiite camaraderie has been badly hurt since the end of the war with Iraq. Tehran's passivity during Saddam Hussain's attack against Najaf and Karbala in March 1991 marked the ascendancy of the concerns of the Iranian state over Shiite camaraderie, and thus an end to the legitimation of the Iranian state by Shiism, which alone guaranteed its maintenance as a multiethnic nation.

To make matters worse, since the split of the Soviet Union there are national poles of identity for Azeris and Turkomans, something that has not been the case since the formation of modern Iran in the sixteenth century. At the same time, Iran's Sunni population is gradually increasing as a result of the influx of Kurdish and Afghan refugees. Iran's largest province, Khorasan, now has a Sunni majority. The Afghan refugees, although they are Persian speakers, do not assimilate; they have their own educational networks (often funded by Saudi Arabia).

There is risk that the failure of the Islamic revolution and the crisis in Shiite legitimacy will mark the return of ethnic nationalism.

Radicalism and Nostalgia

The weakening of political Islam is bringing about a detachment from religion. The fact that the revolution took place means that the flow can run only in the direction of secularisation, which has touched its limit with the existing administration; how can a government that is not sure of winning free elections doubt the very element that gives it legitimacy, Islamic symbolism? This is why the issue of the chador is more prominent in Iran than elsewhere: the obligation to wear the veil is difficult to accept in the post-revolutionary era; it is better tolerated in fundamentalist countries like Saudi Arabia. Indeed, daily life is less "Islamic" in Iran than in many Muslim countries. The revolution created a middle ground between certain modern activities and Islamic benchmarks: in sports, for example (Ping-Pong in a chador); in women's right to work (and they do work); in the Islamic wardrobe, which permits denim and raincoats; on television, which shows Islamic female announcers; and in martial music, which is composed in Western fashion.

These areas of compromise are contested neither by the fundamentalists nor by the majority of the clergy. Cultural anti-Westernism is no characterised by hypersensitivity found in some Sunni neofundamentalist milieus.

But some are nostalgic for this revolutionary legacy — they are the ones who are referred to as "radicals," who seek to retain the gains and symbolism of a revolution that brought them to power, rather than to export an Islamic fundamentalism whose failure has been evident for years. Having been unable, in ten years of revolution either to impose or even to conceive of a systematic model for an Islamic economy or society, torn between the strict "fundamentalists," concerned predominantly with preserving Islamic laws, and the "progressives," preoccupied with developing a state-run, revolutionary model that would break with the previous order, the radicals can only fight a rearguard action. Their chink lies in the fact that they are in a "conservative" position, guardians of a heritage that is more symbolic than real, and not representatives of economic interests or of organised political forces. They are "against": against opening up to the West, against abandoning the notion of exporting the revolution, against softening the control on mores. The radicals are powerful in institutions produced by the revolution, like the "foundations" — kinds of holding companies that manage abundant funds. These foundations have privileged access to currency at the official rate, which allows them to distribute among their "clientele" consumer goods (refrigerators, mopeds, air conditioner, and many more) acquired at the official rate. We thus find behind the apparatus of the Iranian state the same solidarity and clientele networks as elsewhere, except that the weight of the state in Iran compels them to define themselves through political projects and to work through institutions, even if it means turning the ministries into fiefdoms.

This opposition has little of the die-hard neofundamentalism one observes in Sunni countries: its point of contention are neither the *sharia* nor the status of women, but symbols like the *fatwa* against Salman Rushdie, or already age-old strategies, like the refusal to open up to the West, whether in the form of loans or of diplomatic relations.

All that would be required for the constitution of the Islamic Republic to work in a secular fashion would be a political overture allowing truly different parties to run in elections, the guide becoming a kind of "constitutional theocrat."

Six

Abu Sayyaf: Fundamentalists or Mercenaries?

Dagmar Hellmann-Rajanayagam

In early December 2000, the Malaysian Armed Forces conducted operations aimed at guarding the coastal waters off the coast of the east Malaysian state of Sabah and the outlying islands. This was a somewhat belated reaction to the abduction and eventual release for ransom of 21 foreign tourists and Malaysian employees of the exclusive island diving resort of Sipadan.

The incident had been the action of a nebulous armed outfit called Abu Sayyaf ('Bearer of the Sword'), active on the Philippines island of Jolo in the province of Sulu. The existence of the group came to light in 1991, but its numbers, leaders and ideology remained somewhat unclear, though it was considered that it fought, like comparable groups in Mindanao and Basilan, for an independent or at least autonomous Muslim state in the Southern Philippines. Before Easter Sunday, Abu Sayyaf had become known for its abductions and extremely brutal attacks on Christian in the Southern Philippines, but which had until now refrained from attacking foreigners, particularly those from neighbouring nations. The piquancy of the situation consisted in the fact that the neighbouring country was Malaysia which had long been known to assist the independence movement in the Southern Philippines with more than just moral assistance. Indeed, Sabah had at one time been a vital training ground and retreat base for the Moro National Liberation Front (MNLF) and a refuge for Muslims from Mindanao who had fled the fighting of the 1970s. The piquancy was not escalated by the fact that the island of Sipadan is disputed between Indonesia and Malaysia. The incident, thus, had all the hallmarks of an international conundrum, though Malaysia immediately announced that since the hostages had been taken to Jolo, the case was the responsibility of the Philippines government.

To properly understand the situation behind both the kidnapping and that in the Southern Philippines generally, a brief look at the history of the Muslim independence movement in the area is indicated.

Factual Background of the Muslim Upsurge

Shortly after the abduction of the island of Sipadan, on 14 May 2000, one of the leaders of the movement, a self-styled head of politics named Radulan Sujirom (Raddulan Sahirun) published a proclamation aimed at explaining and justifying the action. The much confused writing mentioned that the Moros had been Muslims centuries before the Spaniards had conquered the region, had never come under foreign rule, but had always been ruled by their own sultans, and had never been part of the Philippines. In this declaration, only the statement that Sulu and Mindanao could be brought under foreign rule only with hardships, and were never converted to Catholicism like the rest of the Philippines, is correct. In fact, the region had converted to Islam only a short while prior to the arrival of the Spaniards, namely, when in 1451 the Sultanates of Sulu and shortly after that of Jolo were established. In time, they also acquired control over Mindanao, Basilan, Tawi-Tawi and other islands.

Though the Spanish were unable to suppress the Moros (as they were called in a modified version of the term 'Moors' for Muslims in North Africa), they did not give up and managed to extract several treaties concerning tribute and vassalage from the sultans. In 1878, the Sultan of Sulu, exhausted of the pressure, signed over some of his territory, North Borneo, to the British, against payment of a lumpsum. Other sultans signed their territories over alternately to the Spanish, the British or even the Americans for monetary considerations. The problem with these treaties was that those were written in different languages and thus subject to differing interpretations. This eventually led to tension between the Philippines and Malaysia over who had the right to claim Sabah. After the USA trounced Spain in the war of 1898 and took over the Philippines, they began to 'pacify' the southern islands and bring them under some sort of control.

The Bates Treaty of 1899, however, granted the Muslim areas internal autonomy against recognition of American suzerainty, and this autonomy remained until the Philippines attained independence in 1946. At that time, the Muslim-majority areas in fact demanded to remain under American rule in order not to be ruled by the Christian Filipinos. America rejected this request and Mindanao and Sulu became part of the Philippines. As is the case in many similar situations, the southern Philippines was one of the most impoverished, least developed, least literate areas of the whole country, and has been unable to catch up until today. The attempts of the Americans at educating and training the native population had met with stiff resistance, unlike in the rest of the Philippines. The region was, moreover, thinly populated, and the Muslims could not show written title to their land, which made matters worse when new settlers were brought into the area. During the early years of independence, the Philippines were preoccupied with the conflict against the Communist insurgents of the Hukbalahap. These were defeated by 1954 through a skilful blend of carrot and stick by then president Macapagal. The surrendered Communists were settled on Mindanao which was considered 'empty'. The new settlers received preferential land grants and support, which did not go down well with the Muslims and the native inhabitants. In time, the demographic profile of the islands changed. The percentage of Muslims in the region lessened from 76 per cent to 23 per cent today.

The situation was fouled up in the early 1960s when the Philippines' claims to Sabah became entangled with the demands of the Muslims in Mindanao and Sulu. Sabah (British North Borneo) was set to become, along with Sarawak, a part of Malaysia in 1963. Against this plan, the Philippines supported their claim to Sabah on the strength of the fact that the Sultan of Sulu had held suzerainty over Subah before the British entered the area. Both Britain and Malaysia denied this claim. In retaliation, the Philippines army created a covert force made up of Muslims from Mindanao for infiltration in Sabah. For the Philippines government, this was much like killing two birds with one stone: on the one hand, the inconvenient young militants in the Muslim areas could be tamed and their interests diverted, and Malaysia could be kept on tenterhooks. Resistance against the government had never totally perished, but the elite and established aristocracy in Mindanao and Sulu had been co-opted through civil service or government positions, preferential treaties and similar methods.

In 1968, an incident occurred which became known as the 'Jabidah Massacre'. Apparently, the Muslim trainees rebelled because they were not paid, and refused to intrude into Sabah, and 50 were allegedly shot. Azurin claimed this massacre never took place and was merely a founding myth for the MNLF; most scholars, however, still agree that some sort of incident occurred, but interpretations differ as to what actually happened. The incident led to outrage in Malaysia, both because of the killing of Muslims, and because of the planned intrusion of Sabah. Prime Minister Tungku Abdul Rahman termed the incident as genocide.

Massacre of Manili

In 1971, another incident occurred, the so-called 'Massacre of Manili', where some people were killed inside a mosque. Malaysia again expressed its outrage. Whatever the truth behind the carnage, in 1968 the first Muslim Independence Movement (MIM) was founded under the leadership of Udtong Matalam, and in 1971 the MNLF as an active fighting outfit under Nur Misuari, a graduate of the University of the Philippines with mildly socialist and leftist leanings. The Bangsamoro Liberation Organisation under the conservative Rashid Lucman acted like umbrella organisation. The MNLF openly demanded an independent Muslim State in Mindanao. This led to a period of fierce clashes in the early 1970s between MNLF and government troops and their respective warloads and private armies: Ilagas (rats) for the Christians and Barracudas and Blackshirts for the Muslims. The fighting caused massive casualties and created a stream of Muslim refugees to Sabah. The chief minister of Sabah at the time, Tun Mustapha Harun, himself an ethnic Tausug (like Nur Misuari) and related to the Sultan of Sulu, supported both these refugees and the rebels for an independent Muslim state, though the majority Kadazan-Dusun population in Sabah — mostly Christian — resented the influx of Muslims.

Tun Mustapha actively supported the MNLF and was backed

in his endeavour by the Malaysian government which provided training camps in Sabah, and rendered assistance to Nur Misuari in the form of finance, weapons, safe conduct and safe houses in Malaysia throughout the early 1970s. Nur Misuari ultimately went into exile in the Middle East (Saudi Arabia and Libya) where he propagated the Moro cause for recognition by the Organisation of Islamic Conference (OIC). When Tungku Abdul Rahman became the secretary general of the OIC in the 1970s, he defended Nur Misuari's request for recognition by the organisation, and the OIC got actively involved in finding a solution to the problem.

These efforts finally led to an agreement brokered by Libya in 1976: the Tripoli Agreement between the MNLF and the Marcos government, settled by Imelda Marcos. The agreement envisaged autonomy for the Muslim provinces, subject to a referendum. It formed an autonomous Muslim region in Mindanao, but the referendum led to two autonomous regions and not one, because the Christians refused to submit to a Muslim autonomous government. One region (Region IX) comprised Zamboanga del Norte, Zamboanga del Sur, Basilan, Sulu and Tawi-Tawi; while the other (Region XII) comprised Lanao del Norte, Lanao del Sur, North Cotabato, Sultan Kudarat and Maguindanao. The agreement ultimately broke down over these stipulations, because the MNLF was not prepared to acknowledge two autonomous regions. The government claimed that Muslim factionalism had led to the split into two regions instead of one. These claims were not entirely unfounded, because in 1978, a new movement had split from the MNLF, the Moro Islamic Liberation Front (MILF) under Hashim Salamat. The split had ideological and ethnic causes: the MILF opposed the Tripoli Agreement and blamed Nur Misuari for being too leftist and not Islamic enough. Hashim Salamat emphasised the Islamic character of the movement and endeavoured to create a purely Islamic state in miniature in the organisation's headquarters in Camp Abu Bakar on Mindanao. What some scholars consider equally significant, however, is the fact that Nur Misuari is an ethnic Tausug, and so are the members of the movement, whereas Hashim Salamat was a Maranao and the MILF was dominated by Maranaos. Alongside these two factions was an MNLF Reformist Group under Dimas Pindato since 1982 which was close to the government and was considered collaborationist by the other groups. The New People's Army (NPA), a resurrected Communist guerrilla outfit which established itself due to the repressive character of the Marcos regime, alternately supported the MNLF and the MILF.

Inspite of the Tripoli Agreement, no real solution was found and implemented, and the sporadic war went on, while Nur Misuari remained in exile in the Middle East. Money and weapons flowed to the MNLF from Saudi Arabia, Libya, Sudan, Pakistan, Iraq and Syria to Mindanao, with Malaysia acting as middleman. The OIC remained committed to assisting find a solution for the Moros, though it had rejected the MNLF's secessionist claims and pleaded for a solution envisaging autonomy.

In 1986, President Marcos was forced to step down and the widow of his assassinated opponent Benigno (Ninoy) Aquino, Corazon Cojuangco Aquino, became president. She endeavoured to restore democracy to the Philippines, drafted a new Constitution and circumscribed the powers of the president. She also promised to be more open and generous to Muslim demands. Negotiations consequently arose again in 1986/87, which led to a new agreement based on the Tripoli Agreement and covered 23 provinces. This agreement envisaged autonomy, again subject to a referendum, but also emphasised support for economic development. The MILF again opposed the agreement because of the planned referendum, and eventually even Nur Misuari withdrew his consent because the implementation of the agreement proved inadequate. Nevertheless, an Autonomous Region of Muslim Mindanao (ARMM) had by that time been established, without, however, the Muslims having a decisive say in it, and divided into four zones or provinces.

The MNLF was at a comparative disadvantage. Though help continued to flow in from sympathetic Muslim countries, this decreased after the OIC pronounced in favour of autonomy. Once Chief Minister Tun Mustapha Harun of Sabah had been removed in mid-1970, the new chief minister, Harris Salleh, denied to give the decisive support which his predecessor had granted to the rebels. Malaysia always officially denied support for the movement, though clan destinely, it always admitted to it. The fact that different factions strove for predominance among the Moros proved damaging for the movement, because it enabled the government forces to gradually decimate its strength and weaken it to the point of extinction. At the same time, the government declared that it only recognised the MNLF as a partner for negotiations. Even so, it took almost 10 years until another agreement could be framed. In 1993, Nur Misuari declared himself ready for renewed negotiations with the government of Fidel Ramos. These lasted — with Indonesia now as a mediator — nearly three years, until another agreement was arrived at in 1996. In exchange for its services as mediator. Indonesia hoped for Philippines' understanding for and non-intervention in, its stance in East Timor which was duly granted. Negotiations were conducted mainly in Java. The 1996 Organic Act more or less kept to the lines of the earlier agreements about autonomy. This time, Nur Misuari explicitly discarded independence and accepted autonomy for the region, while at the same time pushed into the position of governor of the Autonomous Region of Muslim Mindanao. The ARMM was extended and its powers increased, but again subject to a referendum planned for 2000. The referendum could not be conducted because of the upheaval in the region. For a period of three years, a Special Zone Of Peace And Development (SZOPAD) was to be established, in which the economic advancement of the region would be accelerated. Responsible for these efforts would be a South Philippines Council for Peace and Development (SPCPD), in which all native and religious as well as pressure groups and NGOs would be represented. The majority of seats (44), however, would be given to the MNLF, and Nur Misuari was to be made chairman of the council. In contrast to widespread feeling, the council would not have any governmental powers, but would act more on the lines of a presidential commission implementing and observing development projects and the wooing of foreign investment. Simultaneously, five billion Philippine pesos were dedicated for the development of the hitherto underdeveloped and utterly poor region, for the allotment of which Nur Misuari would be responsible.

With regard to the armed fighters of the MNLF, a new regulation was worked out. They were trained be integrated into the Armed Forces of the Philippines and into the police force (Special Regional Force) for the ARMM according to a formula which recruited about 5,000 fighters into the army and the rest into the police forces. For a start, the Muslim fighters would be organised in separate regiments. These fighters took part in actions against the Abu Sayyaf towards the end of 2000. While the MNLF fighters in due course surrendered their weapons, the MILF refused to either honour the agreement, or to lay down its arms. Several ceasefire attempts were undertaken, but after Josef Estrada became president in 1998, the fight started again and raged until early 2000 when the AFP seemed to gain the upper hand. On 9 July, after the kidnapping, the troops finally captured and destroyed Camp Abu Bakar. The guerrillas took shelter into the surrounding towns and villages, and Estrada offered a ceasefire and negotiations, but Hashim Salamat called for a Jihad.

Emergence of Abu Sayyaf

Until 1995, when the Abu Sayyaf committed the outrage at Ipil, hardly anybody had heard about the organisation. They are supposed to have been founded in 1991 as an even more radical offshoot of the MILF. In that very year, a radical Muslim preacher with the pseudonym 'Abu Sayyaf' is said to have called for a holy war, or more precisely a 'Jihad', against the government and the Christians in Mindanao. The movement was then known as 'Al Harakatul Islamia'. According to other accounts, the movement had already split from the MNLF in the 1980s, under Abdur Rajak Janjalani, about whose background very little is known, except that he was born in 1963 on Basilan (according to other sources in Lumut/Malaysia) and trained in Lumut as well as Palestine and Libya. He was apparently shot and killed by the Armed Forces in 1998, and his brother Khaddafi Jan Jalani ultimately took over as leader. Khaddafi never put in an appearance during the kidnapping, which was masterminded by yet another leader, Cdr Robot (so called because of his jerky movements; his real name seems to be Ghalib Andang) with the assistance of Radulan Sujirom. 'Abu Sayyaf' translates either as 'Bearer of the Sword' or as the initial letters of the names of the leaders.

The group endeavoured to follow an even stricter form of

Islam than the MILF. Both groups were, however, said to have granted each other refuge and military support. Group membership seemed to be quite small: estimates ranged from 100 to 500 active fighters. The hallmark of the group seemed to be a burning hatred of Christians and non-Muslims: for example, it demanded the removal or conversion of all Christians from Muslim areas, the prohibition of missionary work and the demolition of churches. The mentioned manifesto by Radulan Sujirom even declared that the fight of Abu Sayyaf is a 'continuation of the crusades and the Moro wars'. Abu Sayyaf's actions support this ideology: they got known with bombing of churches, attacks on missionaries and church dignitaries, kidnapping of affluent businessmen (preferably Christians) for ransom and so on. A gruesome action occurred in early 1995 in the largely Christian town of Ipil on Basilan where Abu Sayyaf descended on a crowded marketplace, randomly shooting everybody in sight. Nearly 50 people lay dead after it was all over. Abu Sayyaf reportedly had the habit of mutilating the bodies of the slain in a horrendous manner. According to Cdr. Robot, one of the leaders in the abduction of the foreign tourists, this had been done so that these people could not be resurrected on Judgement Day, where only whole bodies could rise.

The demands of Abu Sayyaf are a blend of religious, economic and political issues. After the abductions of 31 hostages on the island of Basilan in March 2000, mainly school children, teachers and a Roman Catholic priest, they put up four genuine demands.

- rice (200 sacks), gasoline, crude oil and canned food;
- the release of the blind Muslim cleric Abdul Omar and of Ramzi Yussef who had been jailed for life in America for the bombing of the World Trade Centre in New York in 1993;
- the introduction of an Islamic state in Mindanao and the interdiction of putting up crosses in churches, chapels and cemeteries on Basilan;
- the eviction of foreign trawlers and fishing boats which poach in Philippine waters and thus destabilise the local fishing industry.

The government rejected all demands, though government negotiators handed over 15 sacks of rice. Instead they tried to free the hostages by military action, which turned out to be a moderate success. The government took the threat presented by Abu Sayyaf seriously, and it is even claimed that double agents had infiltrated the outfit and knew many of its moves. But this could not prevent the abduction of the 31 on Basilan, nor could it prevent (or foresee) the kidnapping of the foreign tourists on Sipadan, though the German intelligence service had already exhausted one year earlier that Abu Sayyaf was planning something along these lines.

Transnational Moorings

Before we discuss the kidnapping in a precise manner, we should look at the relations between Abu Sayyaf and other Moro organisations and at the extremely interesting external ramifications of the outfit. As mentioned, the MILF granted refuge to fleeing or retreating Abu Sayyaf members at least until the beginning of 2000. The MNLF, however, rejected both the programme and the methods of the Abu Sayyaf, and former MNLF fighters participated in the pursuit of the kidnappers in September. This might have helped their eventual success, because, like Abu Sayyaf, they know the terrain, but were much better fighters than the latter. Much more interesting are the connections of Abu Sayyaf to foreign Muslim organisations, often with allegedly terrorist backgrounds. These contacts have a far-reaching tradition, because both the MNLF and MILF, as we saw, had contacts with and help from the Muslim world, particularly the Middle East and Malaysia. Some of their fighters trained with the PLO and had contacts with other fundamentalist Islamic Organisations in the Middle East. Since Abu Sayyaf is said to be an offshot of the MILF, these contacts would have applied to them as well. Members of all Moro factions, among them Abdur Rajak and Abubakar Jan Jalani participated in the Islamic contingent which fought against the Russians in Afghanistan. There, they learnt military skills as well as a fundamentalist variant of Islam. Contacts once established were maintained after the Russians left Afghanistan and the brigade returned home.

In this way, it is said, connections were also formed with Osama bin Laden and with the two men responsible for the

World Trade Center bombing. Ironically, the activities in Afghanistan were funded and sponsored by the USA, which would have employed any means to defeat the Russians in Afghanistan. This has led to allegations that, in reality, the CIA was involved in the kidnapping in Sipadan because it wanted to distract attention and discredit the Islamic movement. The well-trained veterans eventually joined the Abu Sayyaf. Support came from the countries which had earlier supported the MNLF as well: Pakistan, Afghanistan, Sudan, Syria, Egypt and Saudi Arabia. In fact, intelligence sources were of the view that the Philippines was intended to become a clandestine headquarters for an Islamic fundamentalist armed struggle world wide, a conclusion which is supported by a number of actual or planned actions, among them kidnapping of foreigners, bombing of aircrafts, murder of missionaries, etc. The Philippines was also intended to become a conduit for funds and a money laundering centre. Muslim fundamentalists in the guise of teachers, academics, NGOs, etc., were already there or would be infiltrated into the country. The Philippines was considered a convenient country since it was free politically and entry was much easy and unhindered. It would then be possible to construct a crescent of Muslim fundamentalism and terrorism from Aceh in Indonesia through Malaysia (where an allegedly fundamentalist militant movement, Al Ma'lunah was eliminated), to the southern Philippines. It is not clear to what extent these plans have come to fruition or how strong these connections really are, but they were already known or suspected in 1995. But it is apparent that they are disturbing for the governments of all three countries. Malaysia's casual support of the separatist movement in Mindanao ceased after the 1996 agreement, possibly even earlier, and after the abduction, the Abu Sayyaf is anathema, because it touches Malaysia's own security concerns and interests. This is demonstrated in an utterly heart-rending manner by the security exercises.

What has to be determined, however, is whether Abu Sayyaf is really a fundamentalist Islamic outfit with a coherent programme, or whether it is something altogether different. Too look into this, we now have to discuss the kidnapping of Easter Sunday.

Abduction: The Instrument of Terror

World interest in the situation in Mindanao earlier was more or less moderate because the problem was considered a domestic Philippines one. Only in April 2000 did it become an international drama. On Easter Sunday, 23 April 2000, 21 people, comprising 11 tourists and 10 employees, were kidnapped from the diving resort of Sipadan, off the Malaysian state of Sabah. According to reports of the released abductees (and an American couple which was left behind on the plea that they could not swim), they were forced to swim to some motorboats and then subjected to an arduous and uncomfortable journey across the sea to Talipao on the island of Jolo. There, they were put in temporary shelters with even basic necessities lacking. Among the hostages were 3 Germans, 2 Finns, 2 South Africans, 3 French, and 1 Lebanese. The other hostages comprised 9 Malaysians and 1 Filipino.

The abduction generated mass outrage as well as confusion. Initially, it was not even clear whether the abductors were really members of the Abu Sayyaf, until Cdr. Robot not only confirmed this, but also presented the hostages to the international media in all their misery. He positively invited the media to visit the hostages and to publicise his demands. What they wanted above all, apparently, was publicity. They were satisfied to be photographed with the hostages, brandishing their weapons, and the media were only too happy to oblige. It turned out that most of the members were not only young, inexperienced and unstable, but also extremely well armed and very dangerous as well. Yet for a number of days, the kidnappers did not make their demands public until the request to release the men responsible for the World Trade Centre bombing came out. Since no Americans were among the hostages, the USA turned a deaf ear to the request. In the following weeks, it became clear that the organisation and chain of command in Abu Sayyaf were obviously confused, at best. At one stage, it was not even clear who was in charge and with whom one should arbitrate, since, according to the Philippines government, Abu Sayyaf was split into at least five minor groups. Cdr. Robot's deputy was Radulan Sujirom (Raddulan Sahirun), but the mythical Jan Jalani did not appear anywhere.

In the meantime, the AFP had stormed the hideout where

the Basilan hostages were kept, freed 15, but 4 were killed, and some remained in the possession of the Abu Sayyaf. The government also attempted a military operation to free the hostages, but this was unsuccessful because of the elusiveness of the rebels and because they used the hostages as human shields. Pictures on prime-time TV of hostages fleeing the hostilities of the Philippines Armed Forces led to strong representations by the governments concerned to President Estrada to desist from military action.

Nur Misuari was originally appointed as chief negotiator, but lost this position after less than a week because both sides got dissatisfied with him-the government because of his inadequate efficiency, the Abu Sayyaf because they considered him a traitor. Instead, Robert Aventajado was appointed chief negotiator by President Estrada. The crisis dragged on for several weeks without any indication of solution, since the Philippines government refused to even talk about possible ransom payments. It was obvious that some of the hostages were in bad condition. One young woman who was pregnant eventually had a miscarriage. But it was the elderly German hostage who enjoyed most attention - at least in Germany, because she seemed to be close to a complete nervous and physical breakdown most of the time. A Filipino doctor who was eventually allowed to examine her, confirmed that her health was fragile. The hostages had been told at the beginning that their captivity would last for a period of three months at least, and the Philippines government seemed to concur with this estimate in the light of the experience of other kidnappings. This was simultaneously a hint that someone would pay in the end.

After over a month of non-activity during which the world media handed each other the door knob to the jungle hut so to speak, former Libyan ambassador to the Philippines Abdul Rajab Azzarouk was made a participant to the discussion, which had been one of the rebels' demands. The foreign governments, specially Malaysia, became increasingly impatient and nervous. Malaysia had left the solution of the crisis in the hands of the Philippines government because the centre of action had moved into their territory. However, it had to be seen to be concerned and eventually sent its ambassador, Arshad Hussein, to Jolo. He contacted the 'Mindanao sea weed king', Lee Peng Wee, a Chinese businessman from Zamboanga, and with his help made contact with the kidnappers. With Lee Peng Wee as a conduit, Malaysian businessmen eventually paid US$5 million ransom for the Malaysian hostages, who were then freed in batches from 24 June onwards until 20 August.

The Philippines government was in an impossible position: the governments concerned argued staunchly against military action, supported by appeals by the hostages who did not enjoy being used as human shields. At the same time it could not be expected, and was not willing, to pay ransom of that amount, because it argued — rightly, as it turned out — that giving in to ransom demands would engender further kidnappings and higher payment demands. Finally, it declared that it would not pay anything, but that other governments and agencies would be free to do so. In the meantime, the whole affair became more and more bizarre. The AFP achieved further success against the MILF in Mindanao, but nothing moved in Jolo. The presence of the press turned out to be self-defeating, because in a bizarre turn of events, several of them got kidnapped in turn: three French journalists, and the German Der Spiegel correspondent Andreas Lorenz (who was abducted on 2 July) while trying to establish contact with the kidnappers through a mediator called Ghazali. Lorenz obviously got abducted by a different faction of Abu Sayyaf (led by somebody with the war name Jerome and one Nakora, also called Cdr. Daya, 'the rat who eats cats') which generated considerable confusion initially, since nobody had any idea of with whom to negotiate, and was released after 26 days of captivity, on 27 July, against a payment of US$ 300,000 paid by *Der Spiegel* and effected with the good offices of the Libyan ambassador to the Philippines.

The going rate for the other hostages was quoted as US$1 million per hostage. Several ever stranger hostages were added on to the group even while others were released: a group of evangelists who entered the camp to pray and meditate; 10 Malaysians from the island of Pandanan, on 10 September; a Filipino media person, Roland Ullah; and finally an African-American, Carl Shilling, whose wife was allegedly related to Cdr. Robot. By that time, Abu Sayyaf had lost any political or religious credibility it might once have had. It was clear that kidnapping had become a lucrative business on Jolo, and that even more factions wanted to get in on the action. At that point, the German government also decided to act on its own. It bypassed the Philippines government which it considered inefficient and corrupt and mobilised the very good contacts the German intelligence service had with Libya. The director of the Bundesnachrichtendienst (BND), Hanning, personally flew to Tripoli several times to confer with Gaddafi and his son, about possible mediation on their behalf. Libya was only too glad to be of assistance. Germany strongly supported the efforts of Abdul Rajab Azzarouk. Against the promise of 'development aid' and 'reimbursement for board and lodging' from Libya eventually the hostages were released. First Renate Wallert was freed on 17 July 2000 and recovered miraculously, but her husband and son had to stay behind for a few more weeks. The remaining hostages were freed in batches until 17 September. The US voiced strong objections about letting the Libyans act as mediators, though no American hostages had been involved in the drama at all, but merely on the strength of an American perception that Libya was a 'terrorist state'. Eventually, France also began to talk to the kidnappers through Libya, while the UK regarded the German success with a rather beady eye. By 17 September, all the hostages taken from Sipadan had been freed, and Jolo was flush with money.

This was an indication for the Philippines to act. When most of the Western hostages were out of the centre of attention, on 16 September it started what it probably had wanted to do all along: make an organised military effort against Abu Sayyaf to free the remaining old and new hostages. The build up of the military in Jolo had begun in August, and by September, 4,000 troops were ready to act. While one French woman scribe had been freed, two men were still captive. The army was less swift than announced, but it acquitted itself well nevertheless: first, the French hostages were left to fend for themselves when Abu Sayyaf started to retreat before the army, and a few days later the army managed to release the remaining Malaysian hostages. The hostile noises from France and Malaysia turned into congratulatory apologies (or apologetic congratulations). The only remaining hostage was Carl

Shilling, the American who repeatedly protested against violence and pleaded for help because Abu Sayyaf were ill treating him and planned to kill him. Even the evangelists were let off.

Conclusions and Fallouts

After the first amount had been paid, Jolo was, as mentioned, awash with dollars. Two go-betweens for the Abu Sayyaf were caught in a bank in Jolo town when they tried to exchange US$240,000 for pesos. They simply had no idea as what to do with that amount of cash. The price of small arms on Jolo tripled, and the Abu Sayyaf provided itself with arms, ammunition and other security measures against the inevitable onslaught by the Philippines Armed Forces.

It seems, however, that the vast amount of money paid had been the final undoing of Abu Sayyaf. Even while negotiations were going on, it became obvious that the new abductions were performed by splinter groups which considered that they had been treated with neglect and not given their due share. Andreas Lorenz, for instance, was abducted by a splinter group calling itself the 'Lost Command', and the action on Pandanan is said to have been plotted by Radulan Sujirom, who felt himself being cheated out of the money due to him by Cdr. Robot. Abu Sayyaf fragmented into ethnic and lineage factions squabbling over the spoils, which facilitated the task of the AFP. The significance of the episode must be seen at several degrees; it does not only concern Abu Sayyaf or even the Moro movement alone. In the eyes of many Western governments, it also exposed the corruption perpetrated by the Philippines government: on 9 December 2000, *Der Spiegel* carried an article accusing Estrada and Aventajado of pushing up the ransom demands in their own interest and taking a cut of over 50 per cent for themselves. This was strongly denied by Estrada, but the suspicions have not been finally cleared. Questions too were, raised about the role of the MNLF soldiers and Nur Misuari in the matter.

What remains most doubtful and most debated, however, are the aims and character of Abu Sayyaf. These have been subject to very wide-ranging interpretations. One school considers them little better than mere gangsters and criminals, not even deserving the name 'terrorists', at best 'pirates' in the time-honoured fashion of the South Seas. Kidnapping people as slaves or for ransom has, according to this school, quite a long tradition in these parts and has no relation with political or religious ideology. After the money began to roll, PP 3,500 were offered to any young man in Jolo to join Abu Sayyaf, a method which is said to have increased membership of the outfit to nearly 1,000. This might show two things: one, they are a mercenary outfits; and two, they are short of manpower because of factional squabbles. It also hints at utter poverty in the area. The fact that in the Basilan case they mainly demanded sacks of rice and petrol testifies to the poverty and the basic demands of these people. They needed modes for survival, not political fancies.

There is, however, another, and potentially more sinister side to Abu Sayyaf to consider. Some commentators attribute high-flown political and religious objectives to the Abu Sayyaf and its founder-leader Jan Jalani. According to these interpretations, he was a brilliant head and fighter who wanted only what was due him, as well as a pious Muslim to boot. If this interpretation, that puts Abu Sayyaf in the radical wing of the MILF, is correct, then the violence is not merely criminal or purpose-bound, but is religiously influenced, rationalised and justified and employed knowingly against selected targets. These targets are preferably Christians, Catholic priests or missionaries and churches or church institutions. While one might ascribe economic motives to these actions as well, since Christians are seen as rich and powerful, they nevertheless seem, according to Abu Sayyaf's own pronouncements, chiefly informed by religious antagonism. Even well-to-do Muslims on Mindanao and Basilan islands are now getting apprehensive of Abu Sayyaf and its radical brand of Islam. The question is how well informed Abu Sayyaf are about Islam and the Quran, and here they definitely seem to have been influenced by the fundamentalist school represented by the Taliban in Afghanistan and similar movements. If this interpretation is true, then it would make a solution to the conflict extremely difficult, because in such a case, economic development might just not be enough. The demands of Abu Sayyaf and the other Moro organisations are a mixture of quite reasonable economic requests, e.g., termination of poaching by foreign trawlers, or the protests (in this case by the MILF) against a dam project in Cotabato which would have destroyed the livelihood of the native people, and rather disquieting religious and political demands, for instance, freeing the men convicted in the World Trade Centre bombing. The later was disquieting because it hints at international ramifications beyond the Philippines. Nevertheless, most disturbing are the radical religious demands, because they aim at the interdiction and elimination of expressing religious beliefs and adherences on Basilan and Mindanao, other than a form of Islam defined and approved by Abu Sayyaf alone. This not only goes against Muslim tenets adhered to by a majority of believers, but also against the character of the Philippines Constitution and the terms of the agreement of 1996. While fundamentalism and violence cannot and should not necessarily be tallied in all cases, in Abu Sayyaf they might have entered into a symbiosis.

Yet again, it cannot be excluded that even in the case of Abu Sayyaf, the religious argument is just a convenient tool to embellish and make more respectable, centuries old criminal practices of abduction, piracy and blackmail. If in the process, the religious card provides global attention and support, so much the better. Whatever the truth of the matter, for the time being, instead of the 'development' promised by the payment of millions of US dollars, the money seems to have disappeared into the pockets of splinter groups which provide themselves with the latest weapons to combat the Philippines Armed Forces, and preferably among themselves. Moreover, international support seems to have faded out in the light of the revelations about the group's modus operandi and brutality: no Islamic nation wants to be associated with Abu Sayyaf at the moment, since their Islamic credentials have turned out to be extremely unyielding. While in many cases, spectacular actions can and have served to draw world attention to a particular problem, as with the Palestinians when they started hijacking planes in the 1970s, the net effect of these actions has chiefly been to discredit even otherwise justifiable causes: when people were kidnapped in Lebanon and held for years, this did nothing for the reputation of the respective groups nor their ideology. Reports about the women hostages being molested and even raped, though eventually retracted, have been received with dismay. Malaysia, which has to deal with its own brand of fanaticism in the shape of the Al Ma'unah movement, has denounced Abu Sayyaf decisively, though rumours persisted that it had helped arm the group, and even that security personnel and electronic surveillance on Sipadan had been withdrawn before the abduction in order to facilitate the action, accusations hotly denied by the Malaysian government. But it only secured the coastline after 138 days when it conducted the mentioned exercises off Sempoerna, and started to deport the hitherto tolerated 'illegal Philippine immigrants'. Piracy has been a problem in the waters of the South China Sea for a considerable time and has enhanced in recent years independently from any ideological content. So increased security probably does not come amiss. For Malaysian tourism, the affair has been disastrous, particularly for luxury diving holidays on unmanned islands.

The affair has, on the other hand, enabled Libya to join the club of 'respectable countries' again, an European businessmen are already raring to get active there. The Philippines government has finally come out of the affair tolerably vindicated, though criticism of its inefficient and even corrupt handling of the crisis has not totally died down. It is anyway now convulsed with Estrada's impeachment and cannot give enough attention to affairs in Mindanao. Nur Misuari, however, has lost standing and credibility by his inefficient handling of the negotiations. Is Abu Sayyaf then a spent force? One might come to this conclusion, since even the MILF has entered into a tentative ceasefire after being weakened by constant attacks. Military action appears to have put at least a temporary stop to the kidnapping enterprise. But the Philippines have not been able to prevent other kinds of retaliatory actions which Abu Sayyaf had threatened during the kidnap crisis and even earlier: Nobody knows yet who is responsible for the bombings in Manila on Christmas Day, but it might be a taste of things to come. Mark Turner stated as early as in 1996 that Abu Sayyaf, together with other allies, had planned and conducted terrorist attacks in Metromanila and beyond: attacks on churches, bombs in planes, attacks on embassies. When pursued, the Abu Sayyaf tends to splinter into smaller units and later regroup, which is facilitated by its inaccurate organisational structure. It remains to be seen whether they can achieve this yet again. Unless the Philippines government finds a way to deal with the economic problems, the social inequality and the concerns of religion and identity on the southern islands simultaneously, actions like those of Abu Sayyaf cannot, ultimately, be checked. They might continue even without any political, ideological or religious content, simply as forms of business enterprise and redistribution.

Seven

Defiance in Algeria

Unlike Egypt, Algeria has no tradition of early Islamic revivalism. Nor does it have a deeply rooted history as a political entity or a well-defined national identity. The country was molded largely by France in the nineteenth century to suit its colonial purposes. The colonisation of Algeria was both long (1831-1962) and intense, seeking the assimilation and incorporation of the country as an integral part of France: not a colony in the traditional concept, but a department or province. The aim was to Frenchify—to cast Algeria in the image of France culturally, linguistically, and even demographically—through the proliferation of the French *colones* (colonial settlements) and the associated displacement and remodelling of the native population. French influences were thoroughly woven into the fabric of the society, diluting indigenous culture and identity. This powerful colonial legacy would leave an indelible impression on Algeria's quest for national community—one that persisted even when independence was achieved; the country continues to grapple with the deep Francophone -Arabist schism and the generally overlapping prevalent Berber-Arab cleavage.

French Influence

The pervasive French cultural and educational influences were ascendant throughout much of Algeria's colonial existence. A European-like secular culture developed and assumed importance, especially in the urban centres. In the absence of a counterbalancing Islamic reform movement, Islam remained essentially marginal in the public life, confined to the rural Sufi orders (the *marabout*, or cult of the holy men), with their age-old ritualism, and to the few urban-based networks of the *ulema* (religious scholars) dealing primarily with religious and social issues and morals. Islam was largely devoid of a dynamic, activist spirit. Certainly the French would not have tolerated any pattern of Islamic revivalism that might have threatened their rule. Nor were the French-educated Algerians susceptible to a revivalist call in light of the fact that many of them associated religion with the rituals and backward practices of the *marabouts*. The only exception to Islamic dormancy was the founding in 1931 by Sheikh Abdul Hamid Ben Badis (1889-1940) of the Association of the Algerian Muslim Ulema. Basically reformist, its objective was to deliver Islam from the polluted and corrupt innovations of the Sufis through a cultural and educational revival, with emphasis on the original sources and the ways of *alsalaf* (the ancestors of early Islam). The movement championed a reformed, *salafi* (invoking ancestral heritage) Islam against the rural traditional Islam of the "holy" men. It also sought to renew interest in the Arabic language, which was falling into disuse, and to improve the standard of education among native Algerians through religious Qur'anic schools.

The movement soon became more involved in the initial nationalist demands for equal rights and preservation of a distinctive Muslim identity. While rejecting the concept that Algerian Muslims could become Frenchmen, the movement stopped short of challenging French rule. It remained essentially a reformist religious association, with no tradition of political activism. This was implied in Ben Badis's slogan, "Islam is my religion, Arabic is my language, Algeria is my homeland," the enunciation of a stance counter to Europeanisation. The message of the reformers laid the foundation of an Algerian national Muslim consciousness and identity that would give necessary stimulus to the revolution in 1954, which initiated the war of independence (1954-1962). As the revolutionary momentum swept the country, the Islamic reform movement became an integral part of the wartime FLN (National Liberation Front), and by 1956, it was completely subsumed. The paramount position of the FLN, with its predominantly secularist-modernist orientation, established the supremacy of the mostly French- educated secular leaders and the subordination of the *ulema*. The FLN viewed Islam simply as one important element of national and cultural identity. Its stance was far from a commitment to religion.

Rise to Prominence

Thus, when Islam rose to prominence during the struggle for independence in the 1950s, it was more as a Third World nationalist force than as a religious revivalist force. The emergent nationalist movement was a militant anticolonial movement that utilised Islamic sentiments to bring about the mobilisation of the populace in the battle for liberation. Colonial France was rejected by the assertion of native Islamic culture and identity; religion was honoured more for form than for substance. Hence, the initial declaration of the Algerian revolution in November 1954, calling for the establishment of an independent sovereign state "within the framework of Islamic principles," was an appealing linguistic construct that failed to materialise in Algerian public life. The wordly FLN took control of the future Algerian state and shaped it in accord with its own secularist vision—in the French, not Islamic mold. Accordingly, the tradition of secularism continued after independence in 1962. Over roughly the following thirty years, the National Liberation Front, which became Algeria's sole ruling political party, steered the country in a modern socialist direction, depriving Islam of a public role lowering it to the status of a cultural element in the makeup of Algerian nationhood and identity, with no legal or political implications.

The FLN-run state followed the logic of its own nationalist *raison d'etat*, not Islamic doctrine. At best, it paid lip service to Islam, while accurately controlling the religious establishment and the interpretation of Islam. Thus, in 1966, the state constituted the Higher Islamic Council as the sole authoritative body to render *fatwa* (religious-legal opinion). In fact, official Islam became an integral part of the state bureaucracy under the supervision of the Ministry of Religious Affairs. In the end, neither Islam nor Arabic — the language of Islam—enjoyed much esteem or status. Islam was used to justify state socialism, and Arabic (despite a crash programme of Arabisation in the 1970s) remained the language of the half-educated young urban poor—the disenfranchised—secondary to French for purposes of social mobility. Ironically,

French became more widespread, due to the large-scale expansion of education and the continued use of French in the growing state bureaucracy, even after more than thirty years of independence. Arabo-Islamic education was cast as inferior and therefore undesirable. Throughout much of the 1960s and 1970s, the Algerian state, under the European- moulded party-miliary-bureaucratic elite, remained largely unaffected by the pull of Islam felt elsewhere.

Although Islam was generally dormant during these two decades, it went through occasional revivifying moments before the rise of the Islamic Salvation Front (FIS) thrust Algeria into the throes of Islamic fundamentalism—political Islam. Early manifestations of Islamic dissatisfaction with the secularist course appeared shortly after independence, with the rise of the first autonomous Islamic movement: Jam'iyat al-Qiyam al-Islamiyya (the Association for Islamic Values). Founded in 1964 by Sheikh Ahmed Sahnoun—a disciple of Ben Badis's reform movement—along with Muhammad Khider, a revolutionary war hero, al-Qiyam advocated revival of Islamic values and ethos and adherence to Islamic principles in social life generally. It was critical of destructive foreign cultural influences on the moral fiber of Islamic society. Though emphasising mainly the societal-ethical dimension, its message was laced with antimodernism and antisecularism. Hence, despite its ostensibly apolitical nature, the movement was quelled by President Houari Boumedienne in 1966, and its leading figure, Muhammad Khider, was assassinated the following year. The movement was formally banned in 1970, but its ideas did not wither away.

Islamic revivalism surfaced again toward the end of the 1970s and in the early 1980s, the consequence, not surprisingly, of President Boumedienne's leftward socialist-Marxist revolution, state bureaucratic elitism, and cultural revolution. His nationalisation policies extended to seizure of private small businesses and expropriation of farmland, and the consequent disaffection of great numbers of Algerians took an Islamic form against alien Marxist state socialism. The socialist state-run economy endorsed a new class of modernists, French-educated technocrats with special privileges and status that set them apart.

A new caste of overlords—the terminology—ran the country as its fiefdom, singing the promises of socialism and living the lives of capitalism. The common people's resentment was increasingly expressed in terms of Islamic egalitarianism, advocating the values of social equality and justice.

Meanwhile, Boumedienne's cultural revolution—the Arabisation programme which he pursued in earnest as a means to confirm the regime's Arab revolutionary credentials and to link with the populace at the cultural-emotive level, meant that many Algerians found themselves at a standstill. The Arabisants (Arabic-educated), with their Arabic centred mediocre schooling, were at a distinct disadvantage when it came to social mobility in a system that continued—despite its Arabist rhetoric—to value French.

The new urban migrants felt betrayed by a self-proclaimed socialist regime whose Islam was all pretence and who had little use for the Arabic tongue. It was those multitudes of disillusioned — the underclass—who provided the legions of recruits for the Islamic movement in the late 1980s. Although some of the regime's policies would foment, albeit indirectly, a future Islamic revival, no significant Islamic challenge was posed to the regime. Throughout most part of the 1970s, state authoritarianism coupled with state welfarism — both fully developed and institutionalised under Boumedienne — served to stifle all opposition, Islamic and otherwise. The authoritarian state, resting on single-party (FLN) rule and supported by the military and the security apparatus, built and operated a comprehensive network of controls over all aspects of the nation's life. The state kept a tight control on Islamic spaces — places of worship, religious education, and religious foundations — thereby effectively nationalising Islam. Further, it turned official Islam into a "government mouthpiece." Thereby monopolising religion.

On the distribution level, the state welfare system was still solvent — thanks to substantial oil and gas revenues — and thereby able to meet the primary demands of the people. Welfare services ranged from foodstuffs, education, and job opportunities to medical care. The promised development and prosperity were the substitute for political participation: a condition akin to the Stalinist model of development at the expense of freedom. Thus, the regime was able to maintain a semblance of genuineness based upon an implicit social contract — "We take care of you, we rule over you" — and arrangement common to all other Arab authoritarian systems.

In addition, despite rampant official corruption and economic mismanagement, it still could invoke the heroic revolutionary war — the liberation struggle and the role of the "historic chiefs" who started it in 1954 — to buttress its standing. The legitimacy formula anchored to oil, state welfare, and revolutionary mythology remained operational during the Boumedienne years and helped to halt Islamism. Only after the death of Boumedienne in 1978 was there a sign of Islamic opposition, with the emergence of Rabitat al-Da'wa al-Islamiyya (the League of the Islamic Call) in the early 1980s. In fact, the Islamic movement in Algeria is a product of the worsening conditions in the 1980s. The effects of years of socialist economics mismanagement, rampant official corruption, and bureaucratic fiat came home to roost during the successor regime of Chadli Benjedid: high unemployment, educational decline, agricultural failure and food dependency, overpopulation, rural migration and the attendant urban bloat and decline, and exorbitant foreign debt — and the list goes on. These crises were compounded by the precipitous tumble in oil prices, inducing mounting deficits, general economic stagnation, and worsening social services. Once the exemplar of Third World development, Algeria was becoming more and more like Egypt.

With the country seemingly near the nadir, the old legitimacy formula began to unravel. Neither the authoritarian state nor the welfare system was able to hold on under the heavy weight of hard times. The authoritarian structure was cracking. Further, the mystique of the revolutionary war had virtually dispersed as people were being swamped by the harsh realities of daily existence. State dictatorship gave way to Benjedid's economic liberalisation and political relaxation. One can conjecture that Benjedid, who had been the compromise presidential candidate of the ruling political-military establishment, lacked his predecessor's power and charisma. A colourless colonel, he had been chosen more for his neutrality and malleability than for his audacity and assertiveness. The regime's change in direction was reflective of his leadership style: less command and coercion and more conspicuousness and concession.

The shift did not alleviate, but instead aggravated the economic difficulties. Like Sadat's *infitah* (openness), Benjedid's moves promoted a "new class" of entrepreneurs and middlemen made fat by the opportunities afforded by the liberal domestic economy, by international companies, or by connections to the ruling elite. And the lives of the overwhelming majority of Algerians continued to deteriorate; disparities between the haves and the have-nots grew ever wider. To those who hurt most, the new liberalism seemed directed more toward meeting the needs and requirements of integration into the global economy — as stipulated by the international financial agencies, such as the International Monetary Fund (IMF), or the foreign lending governments, the Western powers and Japan — than toward ameliorating the economic distress of Algerians.

These circumstances were fertile ground for the Islamic movement. Its growth corresponded with the revelations of a tired and confused state socialism and corrupt authoritarianism. The Islamists came to public prominence in the 1980s as a fallout of government failure and public discontent, not of a burst of pietism. The emergence of the League of the Islamic Call early in the decade set the stage for the challenge to the state by Islamic outfits: this opposition would reach its zenith late in that same decade with the birth of the FIS. Under the League, the Islamic movement was largely amorphous: it had no organised structure, coherent programme, or Central leadership. And, most of all it was not a mass movement. It revolved primarily around a number of diverse leaders such as Sheikh Ahmad Sahnoun, Sheikh Abdullatif Sultani, Abbas Madani, Mahfouz Nahnah, and Abdullah Jab, all of whom advocated a moral and social overhaul in accordance with Islamic tenets. Therefore, adoption of these principles was a requisite to stem the detested modern *jahiliyya* (pagan) conditions - brought into being Western values - and to achieve the nation's salvation. Though the message was not clearly political, it pointed toward the exercise of political power to bring about the desired transformation.

Still, at that early stage, the Islamic movement did not overtly represent a national front with open political ambition. Instead, it was more in the mold of Muslim conservatism — demanding thorough Arabisation, the implementation of Islamic personal status laws, a ban on alcoholic beverages, and enforcement of public morals — than an organised political movement. Thus, the Benjedid government did not see it as imminent threat and even implicitly acquiesced in the proliferation of its activities: mosques, universities, charitable organisations, neighbourhood social welfare services, and religious and moral propagation as enjoined in the Muslim dictum "to command that which is righteous and to forbid that which is reprehensible." Throughout the 1980s, the Islamists managed to build a network of independent mosques and religious centres, especially in city slums, small towns, and depressed rural areas — all outside the control of the government. In fact, Benjedid quietly abetted the Islamists early on so as to check the power of other contenders, mainly leftist students, hard-line Boumediennist socialists, Berberist (the Kabyle) forces, and feminist factions, in an effort to consolidate his position and to carry out his reforms.

Despite the Islamic movement's growing power, throughout much of the decade it remained largely limited as a national force and rather manageable by the government. It was not yet a mass movement. Thus, when clashes between Islamists and leftist factions on campuses in the early 1980s escalated into violent confrontations, the government moved to control the Islamists. Some of their leaders were arrested and later released, and a few members were brought to trial — measures that fell short of completely silencing the movement. The government's indecisiveness and irresolution in dealing with the Islamists were a manifestation of its equivocal stance and the lax and fluid political context under Benjedid.

However, things changed when a militant faction led by Mustafa Bouyali — a former *mujahid* (holy warrior) in the war of independence — took up armed struggle in the mid-1980s. In this first open Islamic rebellion against the state, the government acted decisively to crush the outfit, killing its leader and many of his supporters and giving long prison terms to others. For most of the decade, the government generally kept the Islamic movement within bounds. What marked the metamorphosis of the Islamic movement into a people's movement and catapulted it centre stage were the October 1988 riots, which swept the principal cities and gave rise to the FIS. The upheaval revealed the dismal failure of Benjedid's policies and the overwhelming popular rejection of the degenerate FLN-run state, demonstrating the difference between state and society.

To many of those born following independence in 1962 (over 70 per cent of the populace), it was apparent that the post-colonial state had failed them and was no longer legitimate. Calling in the army to restore order, which exacted a toll of 200 to 500 lives, was no solution. A new social consensus was an imperative. Its achievement was Algeria's predicament. The course and pace of change that followed - full and immediate democratisation — soon plunged the country into chaos. A new constitution adopted in February 1989 terminated the power monopoly of the FLN and established a multiparty parliamentary democracy. Within a year, more that fifty parties materialised. Still, the appeal of democratisation and political openness was short-lived. A civil polity under a new social contract remains elusive.

The FIS arose from the massive civil disturbances and crystallised, under the new constitutional changes, as the principal Islamist movement when Abbas Madani and a group of radical, Islamists, such as Ali Belhaj, separated from the League of the Islamic Call and formed their own organisation in February 1989. It was officially recognised as a legal party in August 1989, despite the legal prohibition on religious, regional, or ethnic political parties — a status that most Arab countries have resisted granting. Unlike the new secular parties, the FIS's popular-protest origins and its fundamentalist Islamic theories put it on a collision course with the post-independence, secularist-nationalist structures and culture that had prospered under the military-political establishment. Although the FIS is an amalgam of divergent tendencies, especially moderate and radical faction, the movement in general is against the secular nation-state, calling for an Islamic system based on *Shari'a* (Islamic law). In its consideration, the Algerian state is not an Islamic state: it does not follow the commandments of God or the ethics of Islam.

The FIS mission therefore is to bring about the re-Islamisation of society, using the movement's extensive network of neighbourhood mosques, social services centres, religious study groups, and health clinic to work its way into local and national governments. Accordingly, with two diametrically opposed visions of society — secular versus Islamic — the fault lines in the Algerian struggle are deeper by far and more potentially detabilising than their equivalent in Egypt. The opening of the political process following the 1988 upheaval thrust the Islamic Salvation Front to the forefront in the struggle against the status quo. Its stunning triumphs in the June 1990 municipal elections (the first free elections in twenty-eight years) and subsequently in the December 1991 national election showed up the stark contrast of opposites: a losing ruling elitist party and a triumphant oppositional popularist party.

At the local level, the FIS captured more than 55 per cent of the municipal councils and about two-thirds of the provincial assemblies. In the first round of the national election, which included more than fifty parties, it came in first with 188 seats, only 28 seats short of a majority in the 430-seat National Assembly; the FLN was third (15 seats), trailing the Socialist Forces Front (25 seats). It is ironic that the two top-notch parties were Islamist and Berberist — testimony to the lack of a rallying national movement to substitute for the pulverised FLN. Indeed, many of the new political parties were composed merely of personal followers of those leaders who were old FLN members, imbued with the same authoritarian political culture. The magnitude of the victory gave the FIS a sense of empowerment in fulfilling its mission to deliver state and society from the decadent state. It stood as the only possible successor to the FLN and the secular elite and offered a coherent and appealing alternative. The general motto "Islam is the solution," in reference to the severe economic adversities—but carrying little by way of specific remedies—is reflective of the notion of religious deliverance, something that many of the desperate and despondent young were ready to accept. That belief was shared by most other radicals throughout the Arab world, who hailed the Algerian Islamists' victories as harbingers.

Indeed, the elections, which Abbas Madani, leader of the Islamic Salvation Front, was willing to try, only confirmed what he had always asserted: his party had a "mandate from God." This was in concert with the party slogan: "To vote against the FIS is to vote against God." Thus, the FIS, unlike any other party, presented itself as a divine expression of the popular will (the Muslim *umma*). Therefore, once in power, it would be inconceivable to dislodge it by voting it out. Surely this is far from a commitment to democracy; it runs contrary to the democratic assumption of the right of an electorate to vote for change in periodic elections. The fact is that many votes were cast for the Muslim fundamentalists in protest against the corrupt rule of the National Liberation Front rather than in support of an Islamic state. The FIS was the vehicle of nay saying. Its two largest allies were the believers who heeded the Islamic call and the host of Algerians disenchanted with thirty years of mismanagement, malfeasance, and impropriety.

The overwhelming fundamentalist victory nevertheless aroused the anxiety of many Algerians who feared the changes it portended. The Islamic Salvation Front's generally theocratic theories were inimical to secular traditions and institutions. Its assured hegemony in parliament and its coveting of the presidency-Abbas Madani repeatedly demanded a presidential election, hoping to become Algeria's first Islamist president-augured an altered constitution and the establishment of Islamic law. Surely these prospects would have derailed the infant democratic process, but the army was quick to step in and stymie the process in order to preempt the fundamentalists. The emergent fundamentalist-secularist dichotomy as to the vision of Algeria and the mediation of the military — the bastion of secularism — would ultimately plunge the country into its worst political violence since the war of independence.

Unlike Egypt's military, the Algerian military—the real power centre of the state and the sole "kingmaker" of presidents since independence—had taken the lead in the fight against the fundamentalists. In fact, the top echelon had been tepid, at best, to Benjedid's opening of the system, fearing that liberalisation would divest the military establishment of its role. Rooted in a bloody and prolonged liberation struggle, the army has always had strong political proclivities and perceived itself to be the guardian of the Algerian national state. But, above all, its equally strong secularist orientation made it particularly wary of the FIS and deeply doubtful of the merits of sanctioning the Islamic party, a legally questionable move. The military felt extremely threatened by the sudden surge of the Islamists, and, unlike Benjedid, who showed a willingness to deal with them and to work out "a framework for cohabitation," it was not amendable to sharing power, was staunchly opposed to the notion of Islamic rule, and was determined to stop it.

The first showdown occurred in May-June 1991, a year after the FIS won its impressive victories in the local elections; demonstrations and strikes protested changes in the election laws, introduced just before the national election (scheduled for late June 1991), that presumably would favour FLN candidates." With thousands of jobless youths on the streets of Algiers "on the barricades," clashes with the military resulted in carriage and the arrest of about 3,000, including the leader, Abbas Madani, and his top lieutenant, Ali Belhaj; the imposition of martial law for four months; and the suspension of the scheduled national election. For the second time in three years, intervention demonstrated the army's pivotal role as the protector of state security. The army crackdown and the absence of leadership put the movement increasingly under the influence of the extremists, who sought to radicalise it. At the same time, moderate Islamic organisations, such as Hamas (the Movement for Islamic Society), under Sheikh Mahfouz Nahnah, and al-Nahda al-Islamiyya (the Islamic Renaissance), under Sheikh Abdullah Jab, announced a break with the FIS leadership, but — contrary to the military's expectations of a weakening Islamic challenge — the ensuing divisions contributed to the proliferation of militant outfits, and the situation worsened.

This was especially so after the army coup of Defense Minister Khalid Nizar on January 11, 1992, which forced Benjedid's resignation (two years before the conclusion of his third term), set aside the results of the December national election, and cancelled the upcoming second round. Many radical elements subsequently left the FIS to form the rebellious groups that have since been combating the security forces. Chief among them were the Islamic Guards (former followers of Bouyali's insurgency); the Algerian Afghans (veterans of the Afghan *mujahideen* struggle against the Soviet occupation); the Apostasy and Flight Organisation (a radical ideological group, with no relationship to its Egyptian namesake, that accused those who follow the democratic path of apostasy); and the Algerianised faction, al-Jaz'ara (a group that started out as moderate, but that became radicalised in the wake of government repression). These groups later coalesced to form two prime militant clusters: the Armed Islamic Group (GIA) and the Islamic Salvation Army (the FIS military wing).

Muslim Insurgents

The Muslim insurgents, especially the GIA, strongly opposed Abbas Madani's moderate stance and vowed to bring down the government by force and install an Islamic state. They pursued a violent and bloody course, denouncing their opponents as *kuffar* (apostates). Today it is clearly evident that the imprisoned FIS leadership is in charge of neither the GIA nor the Islamic Salvation Army, which together spearhead the relentless Islamic *jihad* (holy war) against the state. Under the pretext of order and stability, the military suspended the nascent democratic process altogether. The newly-instituted democratic procedures - elections, voting, parties, assemblies, and so on - could not assuage the intense apprehensions evoked by the prospects of a fundamentalist parliament, with an agenda akin to that of some of the fundamentalist-controlled town councils. This was especially true in light of the excessive social code agenda some of the Muslim municipalities imposed: closing down movie theatres, segregating coeducational schools, prohibiting alcohol production and consumption, and harassing women in Western dress. The problem was that Algerian democracy was introduced at a time of social upheaval and the simultaneous brewing up of a potent Islamic movement whose ideology raised the spectre of social and political regimentation.

The question that arises, then, is: should democracy be equated with the formal act of free elections and majority rule regardless of the fallout? More than a century and a half ago Alexis de Tocqueville, in the classic *Democracy in America*, grappled with the issue of majority rule deteriorating into tyranny. The Algerian elections presented the Arab world with a similar quandary: how to implement democracy without risking a fundamentalist victory that could conceivably turn state and society topsy-turvy and even vitiate the very notion of democracy. This is especially vexatious in view of the Islamic Salvation Front's vague and inconsistent pronouncements in regard to democracy, which cause anxiety as to its actual intentions.

It is evident that, in the absence of rooted democratic traditions and values and in the presence of a lingering authoritarian subculture, the attempted transition to democracy was hazardous and tenuous. Democracy easily gave way to apprehension and was undone by the spectre of a fundamentalist sweep. Shortly after the military takeover, a five-man High State Council (presidential council) was formed to fill the presidency, and Muhammad Boudiaf — a rebel war hero in exile in Morocco since 1965 — was called upon to be its head. Essentially, the council was the handmaiden of the military, formed to provide a semblance of legitimacy for indirect army rule — Boudiaf and successor presidents were powerless figureheads appointed by the military.

The government, acting under a declared state of emergency, then arrested more of the FIS leaders and detained thousands of its supporters in desert camps, banned the party as illegal, annulled both the national as well as the local elections, and dissolved the assemblies. The new regime also undertook drastic steps against the Islamists' autonomous networks centred mainly around their independent mosques, replacing thousands of imams (religious preachers) and closing down many private mosques. (In Algeria, the FIS local power is centred around the neighbourhood mosque: the command and operation centre.) Meanwhile, entire neighbourhoods in Algiers, mostly poor and pro-Islamist, were put under virtual siege by heavily armed security forces. The military rejected out of hand coexistence with or accommodation to fundamentalism. The strategy was confrontation and repression.

Radical Elements

A countercampaign of vicious violence by radical elements of the FIS and armed Islamist factions was the result. A holy war was proclaimed; senior government officials, army and security officers, and political figures were the first targets. Boudiaf was assassinated in June 1992, a killing shrouded with suspicion which is still unresolved. Later came a terroristic drive against intellectuals, judges, journalist, and academicians. Resort to violence led only to more repression and further fragmentation of the Islamic movement. The die-hard militant elements, thrust into the lead as "holy worries," committed ever more horrific acts. Since 1993, Muslim militants, especially the Armed Islamic Group, have intensified the terror, bringing the country close to implosion. The increasing violence has targeted civilian professionals in all fields: artists and actors, popular singers and media personalities, school teachers and school girls, university professors and students, leading women, managers of state enterprises and public employees, policemen and soldiers, and foreign nationals. In addition, indiscriminate car bombings and explosions in city streets and residential centres have wreaked havoc. Even the infrastructure — bridges, central warehouses, public buildings, power stations, and schools and institutions of higher education — has not escaped the ravages of the fundamentalists.

The climate of fear has provoked the flight of thousands upon thousands of Algerian intellectuals and professionals who found themselves at risk of assassination, as well as the exodus of the foreign community — thereby sapping significant societal resources and damaging the economy. The objective of the Muslim militants is to break the government's resolve and bring it down, but the government has responded as before — with repression. It hunts down armed fanatics with special forces (commonly called "Ninjas" because of their masks); convenes special antiterrorist courts, which hand down death sentences and long prison terms; conducts sweeping raids of pro-Islamic, poor sections of Algiers; and wantonly violates human rights and liberties under the guise of state security. The bloody conflict does not seem to be something foreign to the Algerian character; rather, it somewhat mirrors the revolutionary war. It is as if the country is caught in the grip of violence. The struggle now is between two polarised indigenous forces battling for the future of post-colonial Algeria. For the Muslim fighters, it is an extension of the revolution; they seek to implement its Islamic tenets, which were betrayed by the Francophile elite. For the eradicationists in the military it is a matter of rooting out the fundamentalists.

Most significant, the fundamentalists have singularly failed to ignite a popular revolution a la Ayatollah Komeini's against the Shah of Iran. This is largely because notable coalition of Algerians, although not supportive of the coup or the FLN, are adamantly opposed to a fundamentalist takeover, especially in light of the Iranian example. They include professional and business groups; a large number of intellectuals, academics, and journalists; civil administrators; women's organisations; the Algerian trade union movement (UGTA); leftist syndicates; and the various socialist-secularist parties. Such liberal and predominantly middle-class cohorts remain committed to a secular vision of the state as opposed to the fundamentalist religious vision - these two perspectives are in conflict over the very nucleus of Algeria's national life. Although the antifundamentalists equally wanted to change three decades and more of the closed power structure, they did not see the Islamists as the change agent. Equally relevant, they have been completely repulsed by the Muslim extremist's violence and nihilist strategies; they maintain that the fundamentalists simply cannot be entrusted with the reins.

Added to this cauldron is the all-important ethnic factor in the sociocultural configuration of Algeria. The Berber areas, containing 20 per cent of the population and concentrated mainly in the Kabyle region near Algiers, are the strongholds of the top-notch secularist and socialist parties such as the Berber-led Socialist Forces Front (FFS), headed by Huceine Ait Ahmad (a revolutionary war leader), and the Rally for Culture and Democracy (RCD), led by Said Sadi. They advocate a society that is a secular, democratic, pluralist, and multicultural — the antithesis of the fundamentalist agenda.

Against Arabisation

Culturally, the Berbers, although Muslims, are generally against Arabisation, preferring French over Arabic - a legacy of colonial policy. They are similarly against the imposition of *Shari'a*, aspects of which contravene traditional Berber tribal customs. Indeed, some Berbers have found themselves in a rather ironic position of having to acquiesce to the very state power they have opposed in order to escape the Islamic alternative. Others have taken up arms as part of the antiterrorist local militias, advocated and supported by the government. Additionally, the FIS did not actually muster the mass support that it asserted. This is evident in the number of votes cast for each of the three leading parties in the December 1991 national election. The number of seats won (FIS, 188; FFS, 25; FLN, 15) is disproportionate to the number of votes cast - primarily because of the winner-takes-all or absolute majority rule. To illustrate, the FLN received 1.5 million votes and the FFS 0.5 million; yet, the two combined got only forty seats, slightly more than one-fifth of the seats accorded the FIS, which received about 3 million votes.

Moreover, seeing the election largely as a contest between two undesirable choice, FLN versus FIS, almost 5 million people, or more than 40 per cent of the 13.2 million registered voters, did not cast ballots. With this low turnout, the three million voters for the FIS accounted for less than 25 per cent of the total electorate, surely much less than a popular mandate. And, undoubtedly, many of these 3 million votes were cast more for change and reform than as expressions of party loyalty. Regardless of these limitations, how to bridge the gap to the 3 million who voted for the FIS remains the greatest challenge facing the Algerian government in the long term as it gropes for a way out of its crisis of authority. This can be managed only by addressing the grievances that led to the vote for the Islamic movement. Since assuming office in February 1994, President Liamine Zeroual, a reputed moderate in the power structure; has pursued a two pronged strategy: economic reform and recovery, and political dialogue coupled with repression.

On the economic front, the cabinet — mostly technocratic-professional figures — under former Prime Minister Mokdad Sifi (April 1994 - December 1995), an able administrator, who replaced the hard-liner Reda Malik, gave maximum priority to the ailing economy. Making internal reforms and seeking financial help from international institutions and foreign countries, it was hoped, would undercut the extremists' contention that the regime was doing nothing. The government took a series of radical steps to meet the conditions set by the IMF. It cut the budget deficit from 9.3 to 5.4 per cent of gross national product by eliminating state subsidies on a wide range of food items and by lessening social welfare expenditures, devalued the currency (the dinar) by more than 40 per cent, freed prices in accordance with a market economy, and liberalised trade and investment codes. The government also sought to streamline, and possibly even privatise, the inefficient state-owned industries — a major undertaking given the political instability. All of this prompted the French director-general of the IMF, Michel Camdessus, to describe Algeria's performance as a "model for developing countries."

Algeria Receives INF Loans

In recognition of its efforts, Algeria received additional IMF loans and extended fund arrangements, as well as a rescheduling by the Paris Club of official lenders of the staggering $14.5 billion owed to Western governments — almost half of the total foreign debt — thereby reducing annual debt service from $9 to $4.5 billion. The government also held talks with the Export-Import Bank of Japan and other agencies to secure export credits for new major projects to expand its gas and oil export capacity. So far, the gas and oil industries have been broadly protected from any violence. Surely the receptivity of the Western powers, especially France, to Algeria's economic plight is evidence that, despite assertions to the contrary, they do not want to see Algeria go under and thereby become susceptible to a fundamentalist takeover."

Such economic methods are directed more toward long-term improvement than short-term relief. In fact, they may exacerbate immediate distress — unemployment, inflation, and quality of life — enhancing the potential for further social dislocations and unrest. Therefore, a parallel strategy to bring about national equanimity is more imperative for the success of the reforms. Economic and civic health are inextricably linked.

The standoff in the protracted and vicious conflict among Algerians (despite some lowering of the level of violence), the escalating powers exercised by a band of senior army officers, and the dimming prospects for democracy widened the chasm between the major secular political parties (including the FLN) and the regime. Such realities precipitated calls for a broadening of political participation to involve all Islamist outfits that denounce violence. President Zeroual moved cautiously in search of a settlement. Thus, in addition to using force against the militants to placate the hard-liners in the military, he initiated dialogue with the opposition forces. Most important, he opened direct contacts with jailed FIS leaders in an attempt to defuse the crisis. Senior government officials held repeated talks with Abbas Madani and Ali Belhaj in the late summer of 1994, after having released two prominent FIS personalities, Sheikh Ali Jeddi and Sheikh Abdul Kader Boukhamkham, earlier in the year. These preliminary approaches came to an end in October, with no apparent outcome. The two sides remained far apart on the major issues: ending the Islamic armed rebellion, releasing the FIS leadership and members in detention camps, and lifting the ban on the party.

The initial hitch notwithstanding, the Zeroual government kept the lines of communication open. Beginning in mid-January 1995, the Rome meeting of the Algerian opposition parties, under the auspices of the Sant' Edigio Catholic Community, rekindled the prospects for a negotiated settlement. The eight political parties — the leading among them being the FLN, the FIS, and the FFS, which together won about 85 per cent of the vote in the December 1991 parliamentary election — agreed on a programme called al-Aqd al-Watani, or the National Pact. Its agenda sought the restoration of a democratic civil society under the rule of law and rejection of "all forms of dictatorship regardless of its nature or form"; adherence to constitutional theories and procedures, and state institutions based on the sovereign will of the people; respect for human rights and individual freedoms regardless of ethnic, religious, or linguistic differences; rejection of violence and gruesome killing of civilians and foreign nationals; and recognition of pluralism and multiculturalism in political and social life. It also asked for a lifting of the ban on the FIS and the release of all political prisoners, an end to the military's intervention in politics, and the convening of a national conference at which representatives of the government and of opposition parties would be empowered to prepare the groundwork for "free and pluralist" elections.

Rome Agreement

The Rome agreement was a triumph of sorts for the FIS. It gained legitimacy on a par with all other opposition parties and secured the adoption of demands it had made earlier as the basis for any future negotiations, thus consolidating its position. At the same time, it did not have to renounce its goal of an Islamic state or call for an end to *jihad*, or armed opposition. On the other hand, the document marked a clear pledge, though on paper only, to tolerate political pluralism and power sharing, social and cultural diversity, and constitutional and legal norms. This was a significant transition in the Islamic movement's stance and could help promote future compromise. Equally, the new association between the FIS and the secularist opposition parties could facilitate further dialogue with the state as the FIS moves more toward mainstream opposition politics and away from the Islamic terrorists. The latter, especially the notorious GIA, came out openly against the Rome accord, decried the FIS role, and vowed to continue the armed resistance against the government.

Although the government's initial response was to reject the Rome accord "totally and in [every] detail," it revealed some flexibility and moderation in dealing with the opposition parties that endorsed it. The government did not clamp down on their activities, for instance, when their representatives, including the FIS, met in Algiers in late January 1995 to refine the proposals — a meeting that could not have taken place without government acquiescence. Another indication of a shift was the government's allowing, for the first time in almost four years, a public rally by the opposition in early June 1995 in Algiers, with FIS participation. About 10,000 people called for an end to emergency rule and a return to democracy.

The government even established contacts with the opposition that culminated in renewed direct talks with FIS leaders in the summer of 1995, but to no avail. Consensus proved to be elusive; differences were deep and contentious. Most contentious of all, political Islam — a religion-based ideology for sociopolitical change — is predicated on challenging the secular system, not coexisting. And the ruling establishment was determined to uphold the secular state. Meanwhile, the government pressed ahead with plans for an early presidential election on November 16, 1995. President Zeroual described the presidential vote as the proper means to conduct a "direct dialogue with the people" and to establish a measure of legitimacy that would lead the way to normalcy. But such a vote falls short of the overall political settlement demanded by the National Pact parties, and they withheld their support.

They were also against the process of elections supervised by the military-controlled government, which continues to ban the FIS. Absent participation by the major opposition parties, the presidential election alone could neither bestow legitimacy nor restore political stability. The 1995 presidential election did not induce a reconfiguration of the Algerian political elite. Rather, it confirmed the prevailing power structure, sustained by the military-technocratic-administrative alliance. In fact, the landslide victory of President Zeroual, the regime-backed candidate (winning over 61 per cent of the vote), over the three minor contenders — Mahfouz Nahnah of Hamas, Said Sadi of the RCD, and Noureddine Boukrouh, a Muslim moderate and leader of the Algerian Renewal Party — probably strengthened the regime's determination to maintain the political framework and to exclude the outlawed FIS. President Zeroual ran on a platform of reaching out to the secular and moderate Islamist opposition and quelling the hard-line fundamentalists. And people voted more for peace, security, and order than for candidates in a levelled election field.

It appears, then, that the chance of finding a solution to the political crisis through dialogue appeared to be slim. Although the FIS, in an about-face, admitted the legality of the election results and the legitimacy of the newly — elected president and appeared to concede to the regime by calling for a unilateral ceasefire and renewed talks with the government, its seemingly conciliatory gestures were out-and-out ignored. In his inaugural speech, President Zeroual omitted any mention of the fundamentalists in any future negotiations. He seemed more inclined to look at Muslim moderates, such as Hamas and the

Algerian Renewal Party, who together won approximately 30 per cent of the vote, as the only legitimate Islamic political movements on the national scene. In fact, the cabinet formed in early January 1996 under Prime Minister Ahmad Ouyahya — President Zeroual's former office director — included members of both groups. Although the new cabinet is mostly a holdover from the previous technocratic one, with considerable emphasis on continuing economic reforms and establishing social peace, the Prime Minister is considered close to Said Sadi — leader of the RCD — and his secular, anti-Islamist orientation.

Rift between Military and Islamists

Further, the rift between the military and the Islamists is as wide as ever, and intense suspicions linger. Many in the army command, particularly the hard-liners, dislike the Islamists in the extreme and see them as a dangerous religio-political force bent on nothing less than total victory. If the application of *Shari'a* is an immutable theories and beliefs in the projected Islamic state, then it is doubtful that the FIS will abide by constitutional rules, the Rome platform notwithstanding. Also, mindful of what befell the Iranian officers under Khomeini, Algerian officers were likely to continue to oppose lifting the ban on the FIS. Equally, they felt bolstered by the high voter turnout (almost 75 per cent) in the presidential election and the perceived popular mandate given to the military-appointed candidate, which they viewed as an endorsement of eliminating the FIS as a political force.

Others in the military hierarchy, especially the proponents of dialogue, were ready to live with a less dominant, less ideological, and more moderate FIS - one that did not seek hegemony or impose Islamic rule. Although the FIS had of late, dissociated itself politically from the Armed Islamic Group, it is yet to stand against violence generally and call for an end to *jihad*. It seems doubtful that the FIS is willing to go that far to reconcile itself with the secular institutions and to accept the secular premises of the Algerian state in order to be integrated into the political life like any other party. Indeed, such a course would be equivalent to an abandonment of its core Islamic ideology and therefore the loss of its *raison d'etre*. A reformed liberal FIS would not be the FIS. But, above all, both factions in the military seem to agree on the necessity of preserving the state's institutions and its secularist structure. They also agree on the need to separate religion from politics, although the latter faction is willing to use religious vocabulary in public discourse. Further, they are emphatic about not repeating Benjedid's mistake of legalising the fundamentalist FIS, which led to Algeria's political morass.

Finally, regardless of the outcome of dialogue with the opposition, the army was not apt to relinquish, of its own accord, its power "behind the throne." Probably it would continue in its customary role as supreme arbiter of national politics and protector of the secular state. The military-bureaucratic-secularist power elites seemed determined to prevail against the fundamentalist challenge. This was especially so in the post-presidential election period, as the worst seems to be over for Algeria. In a show of self-confidence about the future, the government has announced a general amnesty for political prisoners and has called on Muslim rebels to put down their arms in exchange for pardon and rehabilitation. Also, in an attempt to destabilise the opposition parties, it abetted and supported a change in the FLN leadership, which moved the party away from the National Pact alliance and closer toward the government — thereby fracturing the opposition and nullifying the pact.

Given the inability of the fundamentalists to tear down the prevailing power structure, the regime will doubtless continue to keep its hold on power, tolerate a measure of opposition and even allow some limited participation by secularist and Islamic moderate faction, and strike against Islamist violence. Meanwhile, as Muslim extremists intensify their terrorism and split into even more factions, they may weaken the Islamic appeal and ultimately diminish the FIS role in society and politics. In fact, the FIS influence seems to have eroded considerably due to the heavy toll of the struggle, mounting internal divisions, and rival armed factions. The extremists' sanguinary cycle of violence, which is turning the Islamic dream into a living nightmare, could prove to be the antidote to Islamism. Indeed, some Algerian secularists saw in the high turnout for the November 1995 presidential election an indication of the retreat of fundamentalism. In the end, Algeria will not be North Africa's Islamic republic. Nor will it be the model democratic "civitas" on the Southern Mediterranean. With its polarised society and politics, Algeria seems unlikely to break away from its authoritarian past, based upon the belief that the state has primacy over the civil society.

Eight

Journey of Neofundamentalism

The Enclosure of Islamist thought within its own premises goes hand in hand with the weakening of Islamist specificity in connection with the strictly fundamentalist movement. During the 1980s, there was a noticeable drift of political Islamism toward a "neofundamentalism". Militants who were previously striving for the Islamic revolution are becoming involved in a process of re-Islamisation from below; they advocate an individual return to the practices of Islam and, with their pro-*sharia* campaign, resemble the traditional radical mullahs from whom they are now differentiated only by their intellectual origins, professional insertion in modern society, and involvement in politics. I speak of a drift because there is no rift between Islamism and neofundamentalism; it is the entire Islamist movement, with the exception of a few tiny often Shiite, revolutionary groups, that is changing strategy little by little, rediscovering the puritanical and formalist inspiration that was always present among the founders, such as Hasan al-Banna. Islamism was a moment, a fragile blend between Islam and political modernity, which ultimately never took root.

The populist theme of the "return to Islam" is still just as powerful a motivator, but it is assuming a new conservative, polymorphous stature and it is more socio-educational than political, while playing the card of political integration, this neofundamentalism works its way deeply into the society before questioning the state. It turns out to be, perhaps, even more distant from Western values than political Islamism, fascinated as the latter has been by modernity.

It is true that the goal of assuming power has not been

abandoned, as is shown by the activities of the Algerian FIS (Islamic Salvation Front) or the Hizb-i Islami in Afghanistan, but the revolutionary project of ideologically remodelling the society is being substituted by a plan to implement the *sharia* and to purify mores, while the political, economic, and social realms are challenged only in words. Women are denied participation in political field. The right to individual interpretation (*ijtihad*) has been surrendered. Present-day Islamism, from which both political reflection and ascetic elitism have disappeared, focuses all its actions on filling daily life with morality and establishing the *sharia*. It substitutes a discourse on the state with a discourse on society. This is the model of the Algerian FIS, which, if it assumes power, will alter mores, but not the economy or the functioning of politics.

This evolution was determined by internal and external factors: (1) the subordination, within Islamism itself, of strictly political action in favour of the reformation of morality; (2) the loss of the Iranian model; (3) the failure of terrorist or revolutionary efforts; (4) the adoption by states of Islamic symbols, while traditional countries such as Saudi Arabia have set out the finance and thereby lead Islamist networks, attempting to influence their activities and ideology in the direction of a more conservative neofundamentalism.

The "neofundamentalist" movements have maintained the idealism of Islamism, the millenarianism, and the demand for social justice: the inkling that the integral application of Islam will guarantee the reign of justice and emergence of a perfect society still bears the imprint of a revolutionary mindset, which cannot be found in the legalism and casuistics of fundamentalist mullahs. When conditions allow, they make headway under their own banner onto the political scene, forming parties and running for office, unlike the extremely fundamentalist or quietist movements such as the associations of ulemas or the Tablighi Jamaat.

New Strategies

Three strategies, which are not necessarily complementarily exclusive, can be detected: entry into official political life; reinvestment in the social sphere, either on the level of mores and customs, or on the level of the economy; and the formation of tiny groups—either ultra-orthodox religious movements or terrorist groups. Thus, we find a series of manifold practices, many of which hark back to the activities of the Egyptian Muslim Brotherhood during the time of al-Banna, that is, before the political radicalisation of the entire Muslim world that we began witnessing in the 1960s.

In the 1980s, the Egyptian Muslim Brotherhood entered electoral politics and observed a few of its deputies voted into office; we find Muslim Brothers in circles close to power in Jordan and Kuwait, the team of technocrats that surrounded Turkish president Turgut Ozal was composed mostly of former Islamist militants from the National Salvation Party (rechristened the Prosperity Party in 1983), an Islamist movement that is engaged in parliamentary elections and participates in government. The Algerian FIS ran candidates in the 1990 and 1991 elections. In Tunisia, the Islamic Tendency Movement, which changed into the Nahda party in 1989, attempted to redeploy itself within the legal political system, despite fiendish opposition in governmental circles. Significantly, these groups are now demanding to head ministries simulating culture and ideology, including that of education: thus in 1990, in the Jordanian cabinet directed by Mudar Badran, the MB grasped the ministries of education, of higher education, of social development, and of information.

Yet, this strategy of insertion into political life underwent a series of turnabouts in 1991: the repression of the FIS in Algeria and of the Nahda party in Tunisia, the setting up of cabinets in Jordan that did not include the MB. This reversal is also a fallout of the Gulf War, in which the Islamists generally supported Saddam Hussain and condemned the peace process with Israel.

On the other hand, the spread of Islamist and neofundamentalist themes in modern professional circles is phenomenal. The social base of neofundamentalism combines that of Islamism (intellectuals with modern education who have experienced a loss of social status, the recently urbanised masses) and that of age-old fundamentalism (merchants, the urban lower middle classes). From the Islamists' ideology, the neofundamentalists have retained the concept addressing all of society; their actions extend to all levels—canvassing preachers, organisers of various associations, union or grassroots organisers. We are talking about militants of every stripe, and not mosque keepers or practitioners of religious practices. As a group their objective is society and not the state. Their policy is to reconquer society adopting social action, a little like the old Western leftists who became grassroots militants in the 1970s.

Many former Muslim Brothers are abandoning politics to commit themselves to advocating the transformation of daily mores, the return to strict religious practice, and lobbying for the implementation of the *sharia*, thus also returning, after a period of political activism, to a typically radical approach. The revival of the *sharia* is becoming the cardinal theme in neofundamentalist demands.

But in Egypt as in Turkey, the Islamists are also assuming status in professional associations (lawyers, engineers), even in finance (Islamic banking institutions, which, despite their rejection of interest, turn out to be very profitable). In brief, far from being the revolutionary, political pioneer, the Islamists have branched out into both civil society and the political class. Although the spectre of Islamic revolution is fading fast Islamic symbols are penetrating the society and the political discourse of the Muslim world more than ever. The evacuation of political Islamism has been accompanied by the headway of Islam as a social phenomenon.

The formation of small groups concerns the most radical of movements. This was underlying, as we saw, in the notion of the party as a sect more than as a tool for attaining power. It is in the most extremist Egyptian group, Takfir wal-Hijra, which takes the Islamist concepts of Sayyid Qutb to their full extension, that the abandonment of politics can be seen in the idea of the hegira, retreat from the world, *hijra* (even though the group didn't give itself this name). The group is openly fundamentalist and at the same time renounces the notion of taking power; it is as if radical Islamism's inherent pessimism has pushed it to no longer believe in its own actions: without the purification of souls, what's the point of political success?

People-friendly and Puritan

The neofundamentalists try to re-Islamise society on a grassroots level, and no longer through state power. This is consistent with what we have noted about Islamism: if the Islamic society is largely based on the virtue of its members, then individuals and practices must be reformed. The spread of this Islamisation will necessarily lead to an Islamic society.

Advocating aims to encourage individuals to agree to return to the practice of Islam in daily life (prayer, fasting, but also exclusive consumption of religiously approved food—*halal*—and the wearing of veils for women), while supplemented by local social activities: meeting spaces, clubs, lending libraries, classes for children, as well as cooperatives, the establishment of alternative (segregated) mass transportation, and so on. Re-Islamisation thus takes place along two axes: individual reform through preaching (*da'wa*) and the establishment of Islamised spaces, either in purely spatial terms (cities, neighbourhoods) or in terms of practical considerations and networks (Islamic banks). One can prepare for the Islamic society through local militancy, associations, cooperatives, and other institutions: in this way neofundamentalism is to Islamism what social democracy was to Marxism.

The reform of mores centres on the return to individual religious practice. Here neofundamentalism coincides with much older movements, such as the Tablighi Jamaat. The preachers go door to door in city entryways; they "sermonise" and reprimand Muslims who have forgotten their practices, touching on a sense of guilt and respectful nostalgia that the "sociological" Muslim (non-practicing, but to whom being a Muslim is still important) asserts with respect to Quranic references and the *sharia*. They also touch on the uneasiness of those who find their values and families falling to pieces, tracing a parallel between this demise or loss of status and the misleading temptations of Western society (alcohol, licentious films, permissiveness for girls).

"Puritanism" is characterised by the rejection of all distraction, of music, theatre, and all diversion in the Pascalian sense of the word, and the desire to wipe out places of pleasure and leisure (cafes, video and dance clubs, cinemas, certain sports clubs). Preaching focuses on a return to the needfuls: religious practice and fear of God. There is a kind of millenarian pessimism, which is actually rather far from traditional Islam, in which pleasure is legitimate as long as it does not surpass either the *sharia* or the superior goals of man.

But beyond individual conversions, this preaching aims to create "Islamised spaces," the equivalent of the "liberated zones" of the liberation movements of yesteryear, that is, space already ruled by the ideals of the future society; yet unlike liberated zones, no counter-power is formed, no counter-state. Here again, we find a significant parallel with the "alternative" spaces and networks of the post-1968 movements, especially in Germany. Once such a space is formed, as much through persuasion as through intimidation, one endeavours to force the state to confirm its existence, with the idea of later spreading the principles on which it is founded to the whole of society. This strategy is interpreted by the Algerian FIS, whose prime concern was to win over municipalities (the elections of June 1990) and establish Islamic principles there (the Algerian motto and flag have been replaced with the inscription "Islamic Municipality"). But at the same time we find similar efforts in such disparate places as the Muslim areas of Great Britain, certain neighbourhoods or cities in Egypt (Asyut), Turkey, Soviet Tadzhikistan, and so on. In Great Britain, for instance, Kalim Siddiqui, president of the Muslim Institute of London, is attempting to obtain from the British government the legalisation of a certain number of *sharia* principles, to be applied to the entire Muslim community, considered to be a kind of "separate society". As in the case of Islamism, the movement is an essentially urban one, except, once again, in Afghanistan, where the liberated zones were like Islamised spaces, usually devoid of proper political structures.

In these spaces, women are compelled to wear veils, alcohol is prohibited, coeducation is condemned, and attempts are made to promote the moralisation of the society by fighting (just as fundamentalist Christians or Jews might do) against "pornography," gambling, cafes, and sometimes music, drugs, and crimes. On another front, there is the demand that daily life be adapted to the practice of Islam (free schedule for prayers, the consumption of *halal* food, special hours for Ramadan). Finally, one of the highest priorities is the adaptation of the school system to Islam (Arabisation, censoring impious materials, banning coeducation). In short, the goal is to create a genuinely Muslim micro-society within the society at large, which is no longer in, or has not yet attained, such a state. These methods can be adapted, to varying degrees, to European societies, where Muslims can live as more or less ghettoised minorities: the ghetto is thereby naturally reinforced.

These Islamised spaces thus form their own territories, hence the importance of strategies for triumph in local elections. At the municipal elections of June 1990 in Algeria, the FIS seized most of the large mayoralties: it immediately banned *rai* (a synthesis of traditional music and rock), had nightclubs closed, forbade the serving of alcohol, stopped subsidising athletic activities, organised "Islamic markets" (where back-to-school supplies at the start of the school year and foodstuff during Ramadan were available, in contrast to shortages in the official markets and the higher prices on the black markets), and issued a municipal order making "Islamic attire" (a code of modest dress) obligatory. Thus, a neofundamentalist social space serves as heir to Islamism. The strategy for the creation of Islamised spaces has sometimes been attempted in Europe, among immigrants, with limited success (the 1989 "affaire des foulards" in France, in which two Muslim schoolgirls tried in vain to get permission to wear a veil in the schoolroom).

But although the issue of morals is key, it is not the sole objective. The Islamised spaces are also filled with networks of mutual social and economic aid. The insufficiency of the state is justified by the establishment of mutual help networks (in Egypt and Algeria, separate buses for male and female students, lending of photocopies; in Algeria, the municipal social activity described above). The mosque is again becoming central as a social space.

The results vary to a large extent. In fact, one may observe the establishment of "fundamentalist pockets" much more along the lines of social strata and region than of country. Where the social context and tradition are favourable to neofundamentalists, their demands are imposed without state mediation. The bastions are sometimes regional (Upper Egypt, Erzurum in Turkey, the Muslim immigrants in Great Britain), but generally the popular sections of the large metropolises are the most fertile grounds for neofundamentalism.

Cultural Compromise

Neofundamentalists are obsessed with the corrupting influence of Western culture. Unlike the Islamists, they are not fascinated by modernity or by Western ideals in politics or economics. The break they want to effect with the Western model occurs within the very body of the follower and in the very forms of conviviality. It takes on a "cultural" aspect in the anthropological sense of the term. Body language and clothing are recast: while Islamists didn't hesitate to dress in a European pattern, so long as they Islamised them (scarves and raincoats for women), neofundamentalists accept traditional clothing. The Islamists attempted to create a synthesis, a compromise in fact, between modernity and Islam, which the neofundamentalists deny. Compromise with the West is prohibited: neckties, laughter, the use of Western forms of salutation, handshakes, applause. The difference is marked by avoidance. Non-Muslims are disfavoured from participating in rituals or using expressions considered to be exclusively Muslim: the foreigner who risks using the term *salaam alaykum* as a salutation is humiliated. Certain social practices are avoided even if they are not explicitly condemned, such as participation in sports. The believer is confronted with a sort of obligation to prove he is a true Muslim, which would be irrational in the context of popular religious practice or of the Islam of ulemas, but which makes sense for someone who lives in a society that functions in a largely Western manner, whether he be immigrant or city-dweller. Neofundamentalism entails a shrinking of the public space to the family and the mosque.

Women

One of the most noticeable differences between Islamism and neofundamentalism is the status of women. As we saw, Islamist politicisation allowed women access to the public domain, which the neofundamentalists are now taking away. Whereas there were female Islamist militants, there are no neofundamentalist militant women: the women's organisations of the FIS are singularly silent; only men appear at protest rallies and mosques. The FIS is against women's right to work, a right that Khomeini considered self-evident. Here, the conservatism is obvious. Many foreign women, doctors or journalists, who were accepted by Afghan and Iranian Islamists, have become *personae non gratae*. The neofundamentalists are exerting pressure to restrict women's right to vote (they found unexpected allies in Algeria among the chiefs of the FLN during the 1991 electoral debates). It is noteworthy that the 1990 agreements between the Afghan Shiite *mujahidin* backed by Iran and the Sunnis supported by Saudi Arabia failed, among other things, on the issue of women: the Shiites demanded women's right to vote; the Sunnis denied it. The question of personal status (wives, family, divorce) is becoming the main area of neofundamentalist assertions, which brutally re-establish the letter of the *sharia* without the social and educational measures that the Iranian or Egyptian Islamists supported.

"Lumpenisation"

As the strategy of Islamising spaces tends to become the neofundamentalist priority, we are witnessing a profound decline in the Islamist political apparatus. The elitist notion of the Islamist party, as an assembly of the pure, is tending inevitably to assume the status of a mass movement, a danger of which Maududi was well aware, concerned as he was with making the Jamaat-i Islami as well as the Muslim Brotherhood parties of elite, harping on the personal formation of the militant. The drift of the these elitist parties, of strong mystical inspiration, toward populist parties of the masses, on the order of the Algerian FIS, has brought a drastic downturn in the formation of militants. These new parties seek mainly to organise the popular masses for immediate political action; since they are recent creations, they are not deeply implanted. The rhetoric of virtue is a poor cover for the purely demagogic and people-friendly nature of such organisations. The Algerian FIS, for example, is more a "front", a movement, than a genuine party: it groups together different tendencies, some of MB inspiration, others, on the contrary, more nationalistic, the union of which lies mostly in a vulnerable consensus (to participate or not to participate in elections) that will not hold together when faced with the proper management of power.

How can one combine neofundamentalism and the expression of popular demands? How can one enter into politics on the basis of a programme that devalues the process? How can one act within a democracy one disdains? The transformation of Islamist movements into neofundamentalist, populist, and contestant movements weakens their originality, but also the model of virtue they put forward, in favour of formalism and appearances, in favour, in other words, of hypocrisy.

Intellectual research, which was already deficient in the Islamist movement, is missing from neofundamentalism and has been replaced by fideism, a reliance on faith: everything Islam says is genuine and rational. It is pointless to seek an accommodation or a compromise with modernity. The literature in Islamic libraries is a collection of defensive brochures, hitting the reader repeatedly over the head with the simple axioms necessary for the believer in a preaching, admonishing tone. The neofundamentalists no longer even demand the right to *ijtihad* or the renewal of thought.

Since Islam has an answer to everything, the distress from which Muslim society is suffering is due to nonbelievers and to plots, whether Zionist or Christian. Attacks against Jews and Christians appear regularly in neofundamentalist articles. In Afghanistan, the presence of Western humanitarians, who are associated with Christian missionaries (which makes one smile, given the secular and often leftist backgrounds of most "French doctors" — those serving in the organisation Medecins sans Frontieres, (Doctors without Borders) is denounced. This obsession with the internal rift and the homogeneity of the Muslim community is more reminiscent of a sect with its concern for purity than of a society confident in its identity. It, thus, becomes imperative either to convert or to expel, which goes against the traditional vision of the ulemas, who, whatever their ideological position, all recognise the legality of the presence of Christian or Jewish communities on Islamic soil in conformity with the *sharia*. Compare, for instance, the Egyptian neofundamentalists' hatred toward Copts to the tolerance Maududi showed with Hindus and Khomeini, Armenians.

Another sign of the regression of the neofundamentalists with respect to the Islamists is their analysis of the perverse effects of modern technology. The Algerian FIS has declared war on satellite antennas, which facilitate the reception of Western television. The neofundamentalists do not partake the Islamist fascination with science and technology. They advocate a retreat from modernity and not its adoption.

New Clergy

The spread of Islamist themes through a variety of social milieus has diversified the profile of neofundamentalist militants. Two categories play important roles: graduates and what I will call the "lumpen-intelligentsia". Graduates generally play a role in professional associations (engineers, doctors, lawyers) striving for a re-Islamisation of society. But some find themselves involved in religious preaching, like Zuhayr Mahmud, an Iraqi with a doctoral degree in electronics who is director of the Institute of Islamic Studies at Saint-Leger du Fougeret in France. Yet, most militants active in preaching today are from a lumpen-intelligentsia that is poorly educated and quickly cast out of an overpopulated educational system in deep crisis. It is significant that in the 1980s the recruitment of Islamist "intellectuals' shifted from the universities to the secondary schools; thus, in Pakistan, for the first time in 1983 the student branch of the Jamaat, the *Jam'iyyat-i Tulaba*, counted more militants from secondary schools than that from institutes of higher learning.

Aside from this distinctly more mediocre education, what is new about neofundamentalists as compared to Islamist militants is that they try to pass for mullahs. While both share the same distress for the official ulemas, the same anticlericalism does not obtain. Political militants have given way to a new category of mullahs, imams, and other sheikhs, this time self-proclaimed. They have abandoned the political discourse of the Islamists in favour of a self-authorised form of preaching. The figure of the mullah is taking on positive connotations again, even though the official training centres are disowned. The new mullah dons

"Islamic" attire, white skullcap and robe. The neighbourhood mosque, managed by such a mullah, is again becoming a centre of activism, a base for the reconquest of the neighbourhood, which begins with loudspeakers: the Islamised space is wired for sound. These mosques are becoming disputed territories in political conflicts between neofundamentalists and the state, but also between the different associations themselves. Thus, it was due to the conquest of the mosques that the Algerian FIS was able to ensure its local power, which was not the case of the Arab MBs.

Since the 1980s, this new tier of mullahs has been courted for training by Islamic centres that are separate from the *madrasa* and the religious universities, which have been taken over by the state. These Islamic centres and institutes are financed by essentially private organisations close to the Saudis, most often by the intermediary of the World Muslim League, but often also by the Tablighi Jamaat and groups attached to the MB. The students at these institutes are generally Islamist militants or neofundamentalists who have already completed some studies (high school, even university) and have decided to become mullahs. They are blending between Islamist militants and traditional mullahs, since, on the one hand, these students come out of Westernised educational systems, but on the other, they aspire to become "religious professionals" who will then be in charge of mosques in areas of re-Islamisation (suburbs, immigrant communities), sometimes far from their country of origin: hence the Iraqi imams found in France. The Islamic Institute of Saint-Leger de Fougeret was setup by the French Union of Islamic Organisations in January 1992 to provide cadres for Muslims living in France.

In Afghanistan, for example, religious schools or centre of Islamic education sponsored by the Saudis take in young educated Afghans who are living as refugees in Pakistan; they at times do prolonged internships in Saudi Arabia. Once they are back among the refugees, they gradually supplant the older generation of Islamist militants, such as Masud, who have been present in the area since the outbreak of the war, or the generation of ulemas educated in traditional *madrasa* but now have started becoming extinct.

In the following chapter on the "new intellectuals," we will examine the cognitive conditions of these militants as well as the activities of the institutes.

A New Popular Islam

The degeneration of Islamism into neofundamentalism has allowed it to penetrate milieus that were earlier unwilling to accept its approach, in particular those of popular Islam and Sufi brotherhoods. The areas of "popular Islam," generally composed of peasants strictly imbued with Sufism, like the Barelvis on the Indian subcontinent, have long been the target of both Islamists and reforming fundamentalists, particularly the Wahhabis, who are virulent detractors of all forms of Sufism. But these "popular Islams" were radicalised by contemporary conflicts (the struggle against communism in Afghanistan, the second Gulf War) and the sociological changes of the modern world: urbanisation and emigration. The sensational Rushdie episode is a good example of this radicalisation of popular Islam: it was launched by Pakistani immigrant milieus in Great Britain, which are generally very conservative, and only later picked up by Iran. In Pakistan, there has been an apparent penetration of neofundamentalist concepts in more or less conservative and Sufi circles. Islam in Pakistan is divided into three tendencies: the *Jamaat*, which is the Islamist party and which, although it does not have extensive popular roots, has sufficient political influence; the *deobandi*, administered by fundamentalists and reformist ulemas; and the *Barelvi*, which recruits from popular and Sufi Islamic circles. These three currents were amalgamated in the Rushdie affair, as well as in the criticism of the alliance between Saudi Arabia and the United States during the second Gulf War. Thus, we are seeing Sufi milieus, generally fairly lenient with respect to the strict application of the *sharia*, move toward neofundamentalism, despite the age-old hostility that sets them against Wahhabism. In fact, we are also witnessing a reformation of Sufism: the brotherhoods were either of marabout variety, implying the adherence of the whole segments of the population, which is often clannish and tied to guilds, to a "saint" supposedly gifted with quasi-supernatural powers, or of a *sharia* type, corresponding to "meditation clubs' that associated educated people around a master who, among other things, had all the qualities demanded of *ulema*. The desolation of old solidarities, induced by the modernisation of Middle Eastern societies, has increased the fragility of these traditional brotherhoods. As a result, the brotherhoods are becoming less mystical and more fundamentalist. The phenomenon is particularly apparent in Turkey, where modern, recently-established brotherhoods like the *suleymanci* and *nurcu* are displaying a willingness to reconcile Islam and modern science. In Senegal, Abdou Lahat M'Backe, who assumed charges of the Murid Brotherhood in 1969, imposed stricter rules, banned dancing, games of chance, and the consumption of alcohol. This tendency can also be found in immigrant surroundings such as the Pakistani Barelvis in Great Britain.

Nine

Emergence and Evolution

Muslim Brotherhood before 1967

The mother organisation of the Muslim Brotherhood society was established in March 1928 in Isma'iliyya, Egypt, by Hasan al-Banna and a small group of his compatriots. The target of this organisation, which later became one of the largest political parties in Egypt and the Arab East, was to build an Islamic society by applying Islamic law (*shari'a*). Since its establishment, the Muslim Brotherhood has called and worked for achieving that target.

The relationship of the Muslim Brotherhood Society with Palestine began in 1935, when 'Abd-al-Rahman al-Banna, Hasan al-Banna's brother, paid a visit to Palestine and met with Hajj Amin al-Huseini, who was the Mufti of Jerusalem and head of the Higher Islamic Council at that time. During the Palestinian revolt of 1936, the Egyptian Muslim Brotherhood undertook propaganda activities on behalf of the Palestinians. They formed a committee (the General Central Committee to Aid Palestine), headed by Hasan al-Banna, the Muslim Brotherhood's general guide, to stage protest against Britain and to defend the Palestinian cause. The society established a students' committee to explain the Palestinian issue to Egyptian students. In addition, a small faction of Muslim Brotherhood members took part in armed attacks on Jewish installations in Palestine during the 1936 revolt.

In the aftermath of World War II, the Muslim Brotherhood sent representatives to Palestine, not only to advocate the *da'wa* [call to Islam] and invite opposition to Zionism, but also to assist in the training of Palestinian scouts. The most celebrated of these representatives was a retired officer named Mahmud Labib, who supervised the Brotherhood's volunteer movement and also led its military units. Labib, who later became deputy general guide for military affairs, was sent to Palestine to assist in the military training of civilian groups and to render co-operation to Palestinian paramilitary organisations, such as al-Najjada and al-Futuwa, unify ranks.

The Brotherhood's position on Palestine increased the society's popularity, mostly after its active participation in the Palestine war of 1948, in which many Muslim Brotherhood volunteers joined. In April 1948, before the end of the British mandate over Palestine and some weeks before the outbreak of the war, the Muslim Brotherhood in Egypt sent three battalions of volunteers. The majority of the volunteers were members of the Muslim Brotherhood. The three battalions were steered by Lieutenant Colonel Ahmad 'Abd-al-'Aziz, Lieutenant Colonel 'Adb-al-Jawwad Tabbala, and Captain Mahmud 'Abdu. Moreover, the Muslim Brotherhood in Jordan sent a force guided by 'Abd-al-Latif Abu-Qura, head of the Muslim Brotherhood in Amman. A force was also sent from Syria, under Mustafa al-Siba'i, the Muslim Brotherhood leader in Damascus. The total number of Muslim Brotherhood volunteers sent from Egypt, Syria, Jordan, Palestine and other countries was 471. Ahmad 'Abd-al-Aziz, the leader of one of the volunteer battalions, asserted that he had 804 volunteers under his command, including 344 Egyptians. The remainder were members of the regular Egyptian army with some volunteers from other Arab countries. In March 1948, Hasan al-Banna declared that he had 1,500 volunteers inside Palestine.

Despite its limited scope, the role of the Muslim Brotherhood in the war was highly publicised. No other political faction had involved in such an activity. The size of Muslim Brotherhood participation in the volunteer efforts in Palestine was not commensurate with the size of the society's membership, which at that stage was in the hundreds of thousands and perhaps surpassed a million. One of the reasons for this discrepancy could have been the Egyptian government's unwillingness to assist the Muslim Brotherhood. The government feared that the group would exploit the situation, procure arms and ammunition and training, and then try to overthrow the ruling regime in Egypt. Nevertheless, the Muslim Brotherhood continued to smuggle in volunteers on a smaller scale. The society disguised this endeavour by forming " scientific missions" whose declared task was to conduct explorations in the Sinai desert. Other volunteers went to Syria, en route to Palestine, by sea.

The Egyptian government later changed its position. In March 1948, it announced its desire to train volunteers and to arm them for the *jihad* in Palestine. In fact, it opened two military training camps, the first one in Hakstab, near the Suez Canal, and the second one in the Marsa Matruh area, near the Libyan border. Officers of the Egyptian army were asked to supervise the camps and the training. The Muslim Brotherhood's officer in charge of military affairs, Mahmud Labib, co-operated in this effort. Despite the fact that Brotherhood members were unable to continue their *jihad* in Palestine, according to one source they were successful in dragging Egypt into taking part in the Palestine War.

With the co-operation of the Muslim Brotherhood Society in Egypt, another Brotherhood branch was founded in Palestine. Sa'id Ramadan, a Muslim Brotherhood leader, opened the society's first branch in Jerusalem on October 26, 1945. In 1947, there were about twenty-five Brotherhood units in the country with a membership that ranged from twelve thousand to twenty thousand working members. These branches were under the supervision of Muslim Brotherhood leaders in Cairo. Hajj Amin al-Huseini was designated a local Brotherhood leader in Palestine. The application of the Mufti's name helped the society to spread its influence in Palestine.

The physical presence of the Muslim Brotherhood volunteers in Palestine and along the border with Egypt, in the areas of Rafah and al-'Arish, and the existence of Muslim Brotherhood officers and troops in the ranks of the regular Egyptian forces deployed in those areas, increased opportunities for contact between the Muslim Brotherhood and Palestinians, especially in the Gaza area. At the end of 1949, Brotherhood members who had fought the war with Egyptian troops in Palestine went to the Hebron area to establish units in several towns and villages, such as Jenin, Qalqiliya, 'Anabta, Dura, Surif, Sur Bahir, Tubas, Kafr Burqa, Jericho, and some refugee camps, including 'Aqabat Jabr nerar Jericho, and al-'Arrub in Bethlehem.

The West Bank

The situation of the Muslim Brothers in the West Bank before 1967 was different from their situation in the Gaza Strip. After the West Bank was annexed to Jordan in 1950, its inhabitants embraced Jordanian citizenship. The West Bank Muslim Brothers were not subjected to the same inhuman treatment their counterparts received in Gaza under the Egyptian administration. The Muslim Brotherhood in the West Bank was permitted to continue its activities openly, after the Jordanian government had recognized them as a legal, non-political organisation. The society had established branches in different areas of the West Bank. The government's relative tolerance of the Muslim Brotherhood was attributed to the character of the society's activities, which were basically confined to the publication and distribution of Islamic literature, as well as to the conduct of social activities. It was also the fallout of the nonantagonistic relationship that existed between the government and the society. The Jordanian government desired to use the Muslim Brotherhood to counter the influence of other political parties in the country that were prohibited by law. Despite the fact that the regime granted the society some encouragement and support, the Muslim Brotherhood was not given total freedom to pursue its objectives.

For its part, the Muslim Brotherhood did not hesitate to criticise the regime and even to occasionally clash with it over particular issues. The society opposed the regime's strong ties with the West, especially Britain. In 1954, the Brotherhood staged protests against the presence of British officers in the Jordanian army and demanded their ouster. Sources state that the Muslim Brotherhood Society in Jordan was anti-West ever since its inception and had publicly and vehemently attacked colonialism. Moreover, the society opposed certain domestic Jordanian policies, such as permissiveness toward the use of alcoholic drinks, the visible disregard of Islamic *shari'a* principles, and the nonobservance of the moral values that Islam proclaims. This opposition led to the arrest of the society's general guide on several occasions in the early 1950s. The Brotherhood supported Jamal 'Abd-al-Nasir in his anti-Western positions. Such attitudes ignited the resentment of the Jordanian government and created a climate of mutual suspicion between the regime and the Brotherhood.

As a result of its stance, the Brotherhood was placed under supervision and restrictions, and some of its leaders were arrested. However, these measures were not as rigid as those imposed on other political parties in the country. Because the Muslim Brotherhood Society was a legal organisation, its activities and the regime's reaction to them differed from the experience of other political parties. The Brotherhood's meetings were organised openly, and at times government officials, army officers, and prominent religious leaders attended them.

The relationship between the Muslim Brotherhood and the Jordanian regime changed over time. It was characterised by tension and frequent disputes, although interests coincided on some occasions. The Brotherhood gave its support to King Hussein in the showdown that occurred between him and other local political forces, such as the communists, the Arab nationalists, and the pro-Nasire elements, in 1957, during a conflict between the kiny and his prime minister, Suleiman al-Nabulsi, who had enjoyed the blessings of nationalist forces, the Brotherhood held several mass rallies in support of the king, praising his role as a "supporter of Islam".

Some Muslim Brotherhood Society leaders attribute their non-confrontational stance toward the Jordanian regime in the 1950s to King Hussein's tolerance of them and to the fact that he did not treat them harshly, as Nasir treated the Brotherhood in Egypt. Yusuf al-'Azam, one of the Muslim Brotherhood leaders in Jordan, asserts "The Muslim Brotherhood did not provoke the king. We had a truce with him, because we were unable to open fronts with all sides at one time ... We agreed with the king because Nasir was irrational in his attacks against him. We were skeptical about Nasir's relations with America ... We stood with the king in order to protect ourselves, because if Nasir's followers had risen to power, or a pro-Nasir government had been established in Jordan, the Muslim Brotherhood would have liquidated, as they were liquidated in Egypt.

The Muslim Brotherhood Society in Jordan entered all parliamentary polls, even those boycotted by nationalist political parties. The society, in both the West and East banks of the river Jordan, was able to secure four seats in one of these elections. Of the thirty seats allocated to the West Bank, the Brotherhood won one seat. However, during several election sessions, the number of Muslim Brotherhood members in parliament differed between two and four. Muslim Brotherhood candidates ran for elections, though as individuals, when other political parties were debarred from participation. The Muslim Brotherhood's relationship with the Jordanian rule during the period before 1967 could be described as "loyal opposition."

It is difficult to ascertain the exact size of Muslim Brotherhood membership in the West Bank just before 1967, but this membership is estimated at between seven hundred and one thousand. Obviously such an estimate reflects a sharp fall from the society's membership in 1947. The loss of Palestine and the annexation of the West Bank to Jordan, together with some other mediating circumstances, may account for the weakening of the Brotherhood Society and this decline in its membership. Members came from all social and economic strata. About 25 per cent of the members were merchants and property owners of different kinds, while 13 per cent were from the intelligentsia, 13 per cent were workers, and an equal percentage were engaged in farming.

In contrast to the post-1967 situation, the Muslim Brotherhood did not, prior to this date, gain widespread student support. They had not achieved any tangible success in terms of recruitment among this division of the population. In the 1957 elections of a student committee, which represented the student body in the West Bank, the Communists won five seats, the Ba'thists won four, while the Muslim Brotherhood failed to win a single seat. However, the branches that the society had opened in the main refugee camps did have some following. In the 'Aqabat Jabr refugee camp in Jericho the society tussled with the Islamic Liberation party to win the allegiance of teachers and students.

The Gaza Strip

In the Gaza Strip the Muslim Brotherhood Society was popular because of its participation in the 1948 Palestine war. Consequently many Palestinian youths in the Strip joined the society's volunteer battalions. A number of Gazans who worked in Egyptian army camps in the neighbouring areas of Rafah and al-'Arish were exposed to the influence of Egyptian officers and troops who were members of the society. The Egyptian officers were guided by 'Abd-al-Mun'im 'Abd-al-Ra'uf, a member of the Muslim Brotherhood leadership. These officers and troops tried to constitute Brotherhood cells among the Palestinian workers. The circumstances were propitious for such an endeavour, considering the sympathy and admiration the Muslim Brothers enjoyed. The first Brotherhood recruits in Gaza included Muhammad Abu-Seidu, 'Uthman Abu-Seidu, Musa Subeita, Faheem Saqr, and 'Ayish 'Amira."

With the spread of the Muslim Brotherhood's concepts and the growth of its membership among the various divisions of the population, the Brotherhood's presence in the Gaza Strip began to take on a defined organisational status, and the society's first branch was formed in Gaza by 'Ayish 'Amira. This branch was similar to the Brotherhood units in Haifa and Jerusalem, which were established in the 1930s. When the Brotherhood was banned by the Egyptian government in 1949, the society in Gaza turned its branch into a religious educational centre. The *Jam'iyat-al-Tawhid* [Unification Society] was founded as a front organisation for the Muslim Brotherhood.

The revolution of July 23, 1952, in Egypt marked a turning point in Muslim Brotherhood relations with the masses. Relations between Brotherhood leaders and the Free Officers who deposed King Farouq and marked an end to monarchical rule in Egypt were good. These relations increasingly improved to a point where the Muslim Brotherhood was considered as the "party of the government."

In the outcome of the revolution, an official religious mission, *Ba'that al-Wa'dh wal-Irshad* [the Mission of Admonition and Guidance], was sent from Cairo to the Gaza Strip. Distinguished members in the society were part of this mission. The first group included Sheikh Muhammad al-Ghazali and Sheikh Muhammad al-Abasiri. In addition to their work as religious advocates, members of this missions functioned as liaison officers between the Muslim Brotherhood Societies in Egypt and the Gaza Strip.

The relationship between the Muslim Brotherhood leadership in Egypt and the revolutionary government of Nasir went downhill in 1954 following the government's endorsement of the Evacuation Treaty between Britain and Egypt. The Brotherhood opposed the treaty because it thought that its terms were unjust to the Egyptians. An attempt was then made on the life of Nasir, and the Muslim Brothers were accused of being accomplices. The Brotherhood organisation was consequently banned in Egypt as well as in Gaza. Following the ban, the activities of the Brotherhood became secretive or discrete. This change in circumstances greatly affected the position of the Muslim Brotherhood in the Gaza Strip. After being a party that enjoyed the sympathy of the government as well as freedom of movement and organisation, the Muslim Brothers were chased down and the development of their organisations was hampered due to the restrictions imposed on them.

Before the ban, the Muslim Brotherhood in the Gaza Strip was one of the largest organisations. In 1954, membership reached the figure of more than one thousand in eleven society branches. Most of the members were school students in the refugee camps because the Muslim Brotherhood was in operation in the schools for Palestinian refugees operated by the United Nations Relief and Works Agency (UNRWA). Students who were studying in Egyptian universities also joined. The League of Palestinian Students was set up in Cairo and was controlled by students who belonged to or sympathised with the Muslim Brotherhood. One of the most prominent of these sympathisers was Yasir Arafat (who was even thought of as a member of the society). A few members of the society later became founders of the Fatah movement as well. Those included Salim al-Za'nun, Salah Khalaf, and 'Abd-al-Fattah al-Hmoud. Most of the leaders of the society's administrative centre in Gaza, *al-Markaz al-Idari al-'Am*, were civil servants and included Sheikh 'Umar Suwwaan, Zaki al-Susi, Kamal Thabit, Hasan al-Nakhal, Zuhdi Abu-Sha'ban, and 'Ali Hashim Rashid.

Compared to other factions, the Muslim Brotherhood had more financial resources. Because of the poor economic status in the Gaza Strip, the Muslim Brothers received support from the mother organisation in Egypt. Support also came from certain Brotherhood members and sympathisers working in Saudi Arabia and the Gulf region and from donations by specific wealthy people in those countries. The Brotherhood always had cordial relations with individuals of the Saudi royal family who gave material support to the Muslim Brotherhood Society in Egypt and the Gaza Strip. Muslim Brotherhood contacts in the Gaza Strip were circumscribed to Saudi Arabia and to the mother organisation in Egypt.

The most visible political activities of the Brotherhood in Gaza started in 1955. In the same year, the Brotherhood participated with other political groups in mass demonstrations protesting a proposed plan to resettle Palestinian refugees from the Gaza Strip in the Sinai desert in Egypt. The Egyptian government, which corroborated the plan, had to abandon it under popular pressure. In 1956 the Brotherhood participated in the opposition to the Israeli occupation of the Gaza Strip. And in 1957 the Muslim Brothers participated in nationalist demonstrations rejecting a plan to internationalise the Gaza Strip.

The Egyptian administration in the Gaza Strip and the Muslim Brotherhood continued to have cold relations up to the 1967 war. Every time the mother organisation in Egypt was persecuted, members of the Gaza organisation would also suffer. After an attempt by the Brotherhood to seize power in Egypt in 1965, members of the society in Gaza were subjected to far-reaching arrests, which resulted in the detention of several of the society's known leaders such as Sadiq al-Muzeini, 'Abd-al-Rahman Barud, Riyad al-Za'nun, and Shakir Shubair. Among the members who were arrested was Ahmad Yasin, who later became the leader of the Islamic Resistance Movement (Hamas).

Despite sympathy for the Muslim Brotherhood, detrimental conditions and difficulties of underground work reduced the society's following and membership. When the cadres in the faction found themselves chased and under siege, they began to search for a refuge. Some of these cadres emigrated to Saudia Arabia and the Gulf region. As a result, since the late 1950s until 1967, the Muslim Brotherhood organisation was weakened and reduced to a small number of senior members, who had been part of the society from the inception, in addition to a small number of high-school students. The structural foundation of the Brotherhood had crumbled and only ideological loyalty remained. However, some traditional dignitaries continued to represent the Muslim Brotherhood Society including Sheikh Hashim al-Khuzundar, Sadiq al-Muzeini, and As'ad Hasaniyya.

Between 1948 and 1967 new political organisations had emerged in the Gaza Strip. In addition to the Gaza Communist and Brotherhood organisations, two pan-Arab nationalist organisations, the Ba'th party and the Arab Nationalist Movement, were started in 1953 and 1958 respectively. These two organisations enjoyed at varying times the support of the Nasir regime in Cairo and the Egyptian administration in Gaza. In the second half of the 1950s, the Fatah movement also began to appear. With the advent of these political organisations, popular support was no longer limited to the Brotherhood or the Communists. Availability of alternative choices had massed some of the support that could have been accorded to the Brotherhood.

Between 1958 and 1967, the Brotherhood in the West Bank and in the Gaza Strip suffered a serious setback by a high tide of Arab nationalism. It was a time when anti-imperialist ideas and slogans predominated, and when the Arab people tried to consolidate national independence and achieve development and social justice. During that period the issues of nationalism, Arab unity, socialism, and the liberation of Palestine dominated the attention of both the governments and the masses of the Arab world. Such issues, with the exception of Palestine, did not greatly concern the Muslim Brotherhood, which focussed on Islam as a frame of reference and as an identity.

Muslim Brotherhood after 1967

After the Israeli occupation of the West Bank and Gaza in 1967, the Muslim Brotherhood Society remained weak. The advent of Palestinian armed resistance immediately after the occupation and the Brotherhood's reluctance to participate in this resistance thwarted the emergence of the society as an active political power. Unlike the Palestinian resistance movement, the Muslim Brotherhood in the Occupied Territories was not willing or ready politically, ideologically, or militarily to undertake direct and organised military action against the Israeli occupation. Some Brotherhood elements, however, merged in the Fatah movement in Jordan until the resistance movement was expelled from there in 1970/1971. Nevertheless, the society remained a sluggish political power which was to emerge a few years later in the late 1970s.

In the mid-1970s, the leadership of the Muslim Brotherhood was reorganised. The Muslim Brotherhood Societies of the Gaza Strip, the West Bank, and Jordan formed one organisation called "The Muslim Brotherhood Society in Jordan and Palestine." The Gaza Muslim Brotherhood became part of the society in Jordan and no longer remained a part of the society in Egypt. The new relationship affected the positions and policies of the Muslim Brothers in the West Bank and the Gaza Strip, who began to receive counselling from the society's leadership in Jordan and from the International Organisation of the Muslim Brotherhood, represented by the General Guidance Bureau. Reliance on external Brotherhood guidance did not, however, suggest complete compliance or coincidence of views. The Muslim Brotherhood believed that each Islamic movement must enjoy some freedom in its own country in order to satisfy its own needs and to address its peculiar circumstances.

From the very beginning, the emergence of the Muslim Brotherhood's influence and the advent of the Palestinian Islamic groups in general were linked to a number of outside domestic factors. One of the most important external factors was the Arab defeat of 1967, which the Islamic movement regarded as a considered for secular, nationalist, and socialist thinking in the Arab world. This defeat also led to an increase in the influence of the conservative Arab camp, which had an Islamic adaptation, in contrast to the nationalist camp, which tended to be socialist, especially in the case of Nasir's Egypt and the Ba'thist regime in Syria.

The wars of 1967 and 1973 were used by Islamic groups to raise Islamic awareness in the region. The Muslim Brothers in Egypt, for example, considered the 1967 defeat a "divine revenge" against the regime for what had befallen them and the inhuman treatment they were subjected to in government prisons. The society tried to use the humiliation for its own purposes. It argued that the state's lack of religious faith and its failure to follow divine laws were the basic causes of the disaster.

The 1973 war, on the other hand, served to strengthen the religious climate in Egypt. The Egyptian "victory" in the war was attributed to the faith of the troops and the power of tenet. It was reported that Egyptian troops shouted *allahu akbar* [God is great] while crossing the Suez Canal, proving that religious sentiment was an impressive motivation for liberation and resistance. Furthermore, Islam and the 1973 war were related in other ways. The war occurred in the holy month of Ramadan, during which Muslims fast. In addition, the code name bestowed to the war was "Badr", which is a reference to the historical battle of Badr in which the Muslims, led by Prophet Muhammad, fought against idolaters in the Islamic year of 623 and in which they achieved victory.

Another factor contributing to the growth of the Islamic Movement was the oil revolution. The oil wealth enhanced the influence of the oil-producing states in the Arab world, particularly Saudi Arabia and the Gulf states. These states had a strong Islamic orientation, which other Arab countries could hardly ignore. Islamic movements within and outside the oil states benefited from the new found wealth and power.

Fundamental Islamic Groups

The rise of fundamentalist Islamic groups in Egypt such as the Saleh Sirriyya Group, the Atonement and Holy Flight, and the Jihad Organisation, and the acts of violence these organisations undertook, were not only a challenge to the ruling regime in Egypt, but also to the Muslim Brotherhood, both in Egypt and in neighbouring countries. The formation of these militant Islamic outfits had increased public awareness of Islamic issues and organisations. A few years later, these factions became relevant to the Palestinian context since they provided a source of inspiration for a splinter faction, the Islamic Jihad, to break away from the Muslim Brotherhood Society in Gaza.

The Islamic revolution in Iran had a considerable impact on Islamic groups in other countries, including the Islamic movement in the Occupied Territories. This revolution offered evidence that an Islamic state could be established, and it offered hope that the Islamic movement could triumph over tyranny and repression.

The Islamic revolution in Iran gave other Islamic movements an example to emulate.

Finally, one can look at the rise of the Islamic movement in the West Bank and the Gaza Strip as a part of the phenomenon of Islamic reformation in the region and the world in reaction to what is considered as Western challenge and hegemony. This Islamic revival sought to rid the Islamic societies of subjugation, to confront westernisation, to desist decline in traditional Islamic values, and to revive Islamic character to these societies.

Palestinians were motivated to join Islamic groups by the continuing Israeli occupation. This occupation threatened Palestinian Arab and Islamic identity. It was perceived as having twisted and foreign values. The rise of fanatical rightist and Zionist tendencies within Israel itself was a catalyst for the expansion of Islamic influence. The Islamic factions also grew because supporters of these groups spread the argument that Israel's victory was a result of the adherence of the Jews to their religion, and that the Arabs' defeat was a result of their failure to cling to Islam.

The Israeli occupation of the West Bank and the Gaza Strip provided both access and opportunity for communication and co-operation among Islamic outfits in Palestine. Under the occupation, these Islamic groups acquired a new demographic and geographic depth, which made it possible for the groups in the West Bank, Gaza, and Israel itself to exchange visits, viewpoints, and publications.

The PLO

Although the influence of the Islamic groups grew as the influence of the PLO came downhill, neither the growth nor the decline was directly caused by the relationships between the two sides. The change in the balance of power was the result of local and regional political factors. One such factor was the expulsion of the Palestinian resistance movement from Jordan in 1970-1971, which resulted in the weakening of the movement and of its relationship to the Occupied Territories. The ouster of the PLO forces from Lebanon in 1982, in the aftermath of the Israeli invasion of that country, further mitigated the movement and brought into question its conduct, its efficacy, the quality of its leadership, and the soundness of its strategy, tactics, and political programme as a whole.

Another factor was the October 1973 war which refocused attention on the importance of Arab armies and paved the way for a political settlement with Israel. In the aftermath of that war, the PLO entertained political and diplomatic solutions instead of armed struggle. The organisation began to consider the concept of establishing a national authority on any piece of land freed from Israeli occupation. This is the notion that later evolved into the idea of the Palestinian state in part of Palestine, instead of slogans of complete liberation of Palestinian soil or the formation of a secular democratic state in Palestine. The Islamic groups in the West Bank and Gaza depicted such evolution of PLO stands as concessions that were not corresponded by Israel.

The failure of the PLO to deliver on its declared objectives, the problems that the organisation faced in Jordan and Lebanon, the continual changes of its political positions, and the corruption and inefficiency attributed to its institutions and leaders affected the icon of the PLO in the minds of the masses in a negative way. The PLO's problems and changing positions created a state of anxiety, uncertainty, and a bit of despair. After more than twenty-five years since its inception, the PLO seemed to be going nowhere. As a result, trying an alternative to the PLO was no longer unthinkable. Islam, which is an integral component of Palestinian society, was to provide that alternative.

The Islamic movement managed to capitalise on the differences and divisions within the PLO and its following. These differences and segmentations decreased public trust in the PLO and in the soundness of its policies and turned attention to the Islamic alternative. The Palestinian Muslim Brotherhood raised political slogans and offered theoretical alternative solutions to critical issues without having to put them to the test. The fact that the Muslim Brotherhood did capitalise on the weakness of the PLO was recognised by the pro-PLO nationalists themselves. One such nationalist writer attributed the growth in the Islamic movement's influence to the problems the PLO was facing inside and outside the Occupied Territories:

> It is evident that the organisational and political problems

> inside and outside the Occupied Territories have been one of the main factors for the growth of the irrational religious trends which now threaten to divide the people in these territories. The growth of these trends began after the mid-seventies, exactly when the bureaucratic apparatus of the PLO was formed and completed.

The PLO factions that engaged in direct conflicts with the Israeli occupation (either through armed resistance or nationalist and political work) suffered from Israeli repression. The Muslim Brotherhood was not subjected to the similar treatment because it was not involved in armed resistance. Therefore, the Brotherhood was able to build an organisational framework, to reach the masses and subsequently to organise them with less Israeli intervention.

The PLO supporters claim that Jordan played a role in strengthening the influence of the Islamic factions. When the influence of its supporters in the West Bank was weakened, Jordan began to mobilise support and to seek new allies, the motive being to counter balance the influence of the PLO, whose followers seized a number of local institutions. Jordan offered political support and money to certain Islamic outfits, including the clergy and the Islamic Waqf Office, which supervised the mosques and endowment property. Aid was also granted to Islamic colleges. Saudi Arabia, for its part, gave assistance to Islamic institutions in the West Bank and the Gaza Strip.

Beginning in 1967, the Muslim Brotherhood started to establish mechanisms to spread its principles and increase its influence. The society founded Islamic charity associations, which supervised religious schools. It also governed nursery schools and kindergartens, which were normally attached to mosques. The Brotherhood also established neighbourhood libraries and sports clubs. In subsequent years, the Muslim Brotherhood and other Islamic elements founded several Islamic societies and organisations in Hebron, Nablus, Jenin, Jerusalem, the Gaza Strip, and other Palestinian towns.

These organisations helped to spread religious ideas and mobilise support for the Islamic movement. The Muslim Brotherhood used alms money *zakat* to help thousands of needy families. And thousands of students and children were admitted in schools and kindergartens run by the Islamic movement. Loans were also granted to students in Palestinian and Arab universities. The Islamic movement also benefited from traditional Islamic institutions. The Muslim Brotherhood was able to stay close to with the masses and to influence them through charitable, social, and religious activities and celebrations. *Waqf* (religious endowments) and mosques provided useful methods for the spread of Islamic influence.

The religious institution of *waqf* controls an extensive network of property that it leases to the local inhabitants. In the Gaza Strip, for example, the *waqf* constitutes "10 per cent of all real estate....hundreds of shops, apartments, garages, public buildings, and about 2,000 acres of agricultural land belonged to its trusts, and the *waqf* employed scores of people, from preachers and other clerics to grave diggers". Since Muslim Brothers or sympathisers are among these employees, the Brotherhood achieves significant access to the population and thereby gains an unofficial influence, because the people will credit the Brotherhood for the variety of services provided.

The mosque has been one of the most effective means of expanding Islamic influence. Unlike other institutions, the mosque remains open all the time. Being a sanctuary, the mosque could be used as a place for political work and organisation, away from the eyes or intervention of the Israeli authorities. Religious functions and activities are not subject to the same restrictions to which the nationalist or political activities are subjected. The Muslim Brotherhood has used mosques to enroll followers.

Increase in Number of Mosques

The increase in the number of mosques in the West Bank and Gaza is also an evidence of the rise in Islamic influence. In the period between 1967 and 1987, this number nearly doubled in the West Bank, increasing from 400 to 750. During the same period of time, the number of mosques in the Gaza Strip had increased threefold, rising from 200 to 600. This increase, which helped raise Islamic political influence and consciousness, was the outcome of political, religious and charitable considerations. The Islamists have been aware of the importance of the mosque as a mechanism for spreading and consolidating political influence vis-à-vis secular and nationalist forces. For this reason, they turned to building more mosques. Mosques are also needed for their religious implication as places of worship. As the population of worshippers increased, more mosques would be needed. Charity directed at building new mosques is most alluring to wealthy believers who wish to be remembered on earth and later rewarded by God in heaven.

In 1973, *al-Mujamma' al-Islami* [the Islamic Centre], a frontline organisation for the Muslim Brotherhood Society in Gaza, was established. The centre provided an umbrella for Muslim Brotherhood activities in the Gaza Strip. The Brotherhood pursued most of its activities through this centre. From a practical standpoint, all religious organisations and institutions belonging to the Brotherhood, including the Islamic University in Gaza, were subject to the authority of the centre and its leadership.

The centre was primarily set up as a mosque, but attached to it were a medical clinic, a youth sports club, a nursing school, an Islamic festival hall, a *zakat* committee, and a centre for women's activities and for training young girls. The founders of the centre included Sheikh Ahmad Yasin (the leader of the Muslim Brotherhood in the Gaza Strip), Salim Shurrab, Ahmad Ibrahim Dalloul, Isma'il Abu-al-'Awf, As'ad Hasaniyya, Mustafa 'Abd-al-'Al, 'Umar 'Abd-al-'Al, Abd-al-Hai, 'Abd-al-'Al, Lutfi Shubair, Ya'qub Abu-Kuwayk, and Ahmad Abu-al-Kas. The most prominent leaders of the centre, in addition to Yasin, include pharmacist Ibrahim al-Yazuri, the centre's executive director, Dr. 'Abd-al-'Aziz al-Rantisi and Dr. Mahmud al-Zahhar.

The centre extended its influence over a large number of the mosques in the Gaza Strip. Currently the centre controls about 40 per cent of these mosques. The centre has also opened branches in other parts of the Gaza Strip. Since its establishment its membership has increased to more than two thousand. In 1979, six years after it was founded, the Israeli authorities granted the centre a legal licence. Ahmad Yasin is considered the leading figure in the Islamic centre.

Islamic influence has also found its way to educational institutions in the Occupied Territories. The Palestinian universities in the West Bank and Gaza have been a significant field for Muslim Brotherhood activity and a platform for the dissemination of concepts and for gaining influence. In the aftermath of the Iranian revolution of 1979, local Muslim leaders and activists visited these universities and asked the youth to pay attention to political questions. Such appeals were not common before the revolution. Islamic student bodies started to complete successfully with nationalist student groups, and the influence of Islamic student bodies steadily increased in subsequent years. In 1979 elections of the student council of Najah University in the West Bank, for instance, the Islamic Bloc won ten out of eleven seats. In 1980, this group had five seats, while the National Unity Bloc, representing PLO factions, had six. In the 1981 elections, the Islamic Bloc won all student council seats. One of the key reasons for this victory was the failure of the nationalist rivals to unite in order to counter the Islamic Bloc. In the student council elections of 1986, the Islamic Bloc managed to win 1,160 votes, compared to 1,480 votes for the Student Youth Movement, which supports the Fatah movement.

The Muslim Brotherhood enjoys massive support in the universities of the West Bank ands Gaza. The votes of the society's supporters fluctuate between 30 and 50 per cent. Even in Birzeit University, which has been known for its strong nationalist, leftist, and liberal tendencies, the Islamists mobilise considerable support in the student body. Muslim students have always controlled the student council in the Islamic University in Gaza. Currently, they also govern the student council in the University of Hebron.

The Islamic University in Gaza, founded in 1978, is perceived the principal Muslim Brotherhood stronghold. The university's administration, most of the employees who work there, and the majority of students are Brotherhood adherents. Current student enrollment in the university is estimated at five thousand. This university, along with other Palestinian universities, supplies the mosques in the West Bank and Gaza with young preachers. More importantly, these universities graduate a new breed of educated Muslim leaders who can hold key positions in society. But the Muslim Brotherhood's stronghold in the Palestinian universities, including the Islamic University in Gaza, especially on the student level, has not been unchallenged. In the student council elections of 1987, the Islamic Bloc secured nearly 800 votes while the Fatah supporters managed to win 650. The Islamic Jihad movement won 200 votes, while supporters of the Popular Front for the Liberation of Palestine (PFLP) won 150 votes. In a previous year, the Islamic Jihad was able to win 400 votes. Islamic student bodies control student councils in several high schools and community colleges across the West Bank and Gaza.

The society particularly aims youth in the villages and refugee camps, school students, teachers, civil servants, and low income groups in general. To date, however, the Brotherhood has not actively sought to recruit workers or women in trade unions or professional organisations.

Financial Resources

Availability of financial resources has helped the Muslim Brotherhood to spread its notions and influence. Money comes from membership dues, from donations from abroad, and from within the Occupied Territories. As part of a regional and worldwide Islamic movement, the Muslim Brotherhood could rely on its brotherly links with other Islamic factions to ensure not only moral and political support, but also financial and material assistance. Muslim institutions and individuals from all corners of the world could send *zakat* money to the "Muslim *mujahidin* [Islamic fighters] in Palestine." Members of the Muslim Brotherhood inside the Occupied Territories are known for their proper conduct, benevolence, and anticorruption stands. The religious assimilation of the Islamic groups solicits sympathy from a society that is essentially Muslim. This sympathy can be expressed in financial aids that are given for the religious and moral purpose of assisting the poor and the political purpose of strengthening Muslims vis-à-vis their enemies.

To spread their notions and to expand their influence, the Muslim Brotherhood has distributed religious books published by well known Islamic leaders. The shelves of Islamic libraries and associations are filled with a huge collection of these books and other relevant writings. More than half the publications found in West Bank libraries and bookstores are of a religious nature. Some of these publications have been imported from abroad. At home, several magazines are published, either regularly or intermittently, by Islamic institutions or student bodies in Palestinian universities or community colleges. The contents of these publications concentrate on individual behaviour and suggest that the Islamic culture has been hampered by Western influence. Anti-Israeli rhetoric was tolerated because of the religious stance of these publications. But since the eruption of the *intifada*, these publications have contained strong political messages. In addition to a repeated call for a return to Islam, strong criticism is directed at local nationalism and secularism. Israeli occupation is described as a condemnation or punishment from God because the Palestinians have left the true path of Islam. Israel, the United States, the West and Arab governments are also targets for attacks. Together with published material, the Muslim Brotherhood circulates recorded sermons and speeches of frontline Islamic leaders and preachers. Tapes containing such sermons and messages are found in street stands or shops in all locations of the West Bank and Gaza.

On numerous occasions supporters of the Islamic movement attacked shops that sold alcoholic beverages, and on a few other occasions they attacked women who were not covering their heads or wearing sufficiently decent clothing. They also attacked wedding ceremonies that were not being conducted in traditional ways. Such actions gave rise to negative feelings and caused anxiety and fear among many people. The Islamists were criticised for using intimidation to force conformity and obedience.

The overall conditions in the Occupied Territories appeared to have been conducive to a rise in Islamic influence. While Islam has been an indispensable part of Palestinian society, all the factors that have been discussed above are contributing dynamics. A field survey of a group of entrepreneurs conducted between 1971 and 1973 indicated that 55 per cent of those who responded preferred to have religion incorporated into social life. The study also indicated that Islam was the frame of reference for 76 per cent of those who responded.

An opinion poll conducted on people randomly selected from towns, villages, and refugee camps in the West Bank and the Gaza Strip showed that approximately 26.5 per cent of the respondents preferred a system of government based on the Islamic *shari'a* in the event an independent Palestinian state was established; 29.6 per cent said that they would choose an Islamic Arab Palestinian state; 10.4 per cent signified that they would want a democratic secular Palestinian state; and 12.2 per cent said that they wanted a democratic Palestinian state.

The Survey

Another survey conducted in 1982 among 150 Muslim college students who were predominantly from villages and refugee camps in the West Bank and the Gaza Strip, found that 54 per cent of the respondents came from families all of whose members prayed regularly and observed fast during the month of Ramadan, with the females dressed in traditional Islamic ways. Twelve per cent of these students came from families in which only the father performed Islamic duties, 16 per cent from families where the mother executed these duties, 14 per cent from families where brothers or sisters performed these duties, and only 4 per cent from families where no one practiced these duties. Fifty-four per cent of the fathers were workers, 30 per cent were farmers, while 16 per cent worked in service occupations.

Sixty-four per cent of the 150 Muslim students who were polled said that they strongly supported the Muslim Brotherhood Society and 32 per cent said that they moderately supported the society. Only 4 per cent said that they vehemently opposed the society and accused it of furthering the interests of Israel and the United States. These polls signify a strong leaning toward religion, especially in villages and refugee camps, where the largest number of Palestinians live. The Muslim Brotherhood is not the only beneficiary of the support of religious minded individuals. Nationalist organisations, such as the Fatah movement, are also endorsed by people who want an Islamic Palestinian state.

Although the Muslim Brotherhood Society, according to one Muslim leader on the West Bank, is still more vulnerable than the PLO in terms of following, the strength and influence of the Brotherhood cannot be underestimated. The society has an excellent organisation and a potential to bring about strong sympathetic feelings and loyalty in a community that is generally religiously inclined.

The Muslim Brotherhood seems to enjoy stronger influence in the Gaza Strip compared to the West Bank. This is attributed to historic and socioeconomic reasons. The Muslim Brotherhood connection in the Gaza Strip dates back to the 1930s. Moreover, the nearness of the Gaza Strip to Egypt provided the Brotherhood with means of communication with the mother organisation. Palestinian students studying in Egyptian universities were exposed to, and influenced by, Islamic concepts and trends. Society in the Gaza Strip is more socially conservative and less susceptible to outside influences than the Palestinian society in the West Bank. The West Bank Palestinians have been more energetic than the Gaza inhabitants. The dense population, poverty, and harsh economic conditions, together with conventional social relationships, have provided a propitious climate for the followers of the Islamic movement to gain influence.

Although the period from 1975 to 1985 witnessed a continual increase in the Muslim Brotherhood's influence, the PLO's gradual recovery from the setback it suffered in Lebanon in 1982 restored a political balance in favour of the PLO. Another intervening factor mitigating the Brotherhood's influence has been the rise of the Islamic Jihad movement in the early 1980s which came to challenge the moderate nonmilitant line of the Muslim Brotherhood. A downturn in the Muslim Brotherhood's influence in the Gaza Strip was reflected in the elections of Arab Medical Association. In 1985 the Muslim Brotherhood won three seats, Fatah four, and the leftist factions won the other four seats. In the association's polls of 1987, the PLO factions won nine seats, while the Muslim Brotherhood won only two. In the Engineers Association the Muslim Brotherhood won only one seat in the 1987 elections, after having won the bulk of seats in 1981. But in the elections of 1989, the Brotherhood (Hamas) won five out of nine seats in the association, which reflected a downward trend in the PLO's influence.

Regarding the relative strength of the Brotherhood vis-á-vis the PLO in Gaza, it was suggested that if elections had been held before the *intifada*, the PLO supporters would have secured the majority of votes, and the Islamic trend would not have won more than 10 per cent of the vote. In the West Bank the number of committed Muslim Brotherhood members in the early 1980s was estimated at no more than a few thousand, although the number of supporters was much higher than that. But the ability of the Muslim Brotherhood to mobilise the masses greatly crossed its numerical size. The society has always enjoyed the sympathy of landowners, merchants, and shopkeepers. During the 1980s, the Brotherhood has found its way into student bodies and elite companies, including intellectuals and university professors in Gaza, Nablus, and Hebron.

Geographically, the Muslim Brotherhood's following in the West Bank has traditionally been engrossed chiefly in the northern and southern towns, which are predominantly conservative. After 1948, the northern towns had maintained some links with the Palestinian Muslim in Israel. The southern towns were specifically influenced by the Muslim Brotherhood volunteers in 1948.

In the Gaza Strip, the Brotherhood following was concentrated in Gaza City and in the southern area of the Strip. But over the years, the society broadened in all parts of Gaza, as well as among the refugee camp population.

In the central part of the West Bank, where the cities of Jerusalem, Ramallah and Bethlehem lie, there is a sizeable Christian minority. These cities have also been centres of secular influence. Jerusalem and Bethlehem are sites for Christian holy places and are therefore exposed to foreign visitors and their influence. Ramallah has traditionally been a centre for Arab nationalist and Communist political factions, and a large segment of the city's population live or work in North or South America but keep returning to Ramallah.

Open coordination between the Islamic outfits of the West Bank and Gaza and their counterparts inside Israel is forbidden by Israeli law. Yet several Muslim leaders in Israel have received their training in the West Bank. For example, Sheikh 'Abdallah Darwish, one of the most front ranking of these leaders, received his religious education at the Islamic Institute in Nablus. During his study, Darwish had the opportunity to establish relationships and communications between the Islamic outfits in Israel and those in the Occupied Territories. Religious leaders in both communities exchange visits and participate in joint activities.

Other forms of cooperation may be occurring, perhaps secretly. Islamic leaders in the West Bank and the Gaza Strip are usually reluctant to talk openly about their relationship with the Islamic groups in Israel, but these leaders argue that Islam calls for cooperation with Muslim both inside and outside of Palestine.

Ten

The Intifada

In December 1987 a Palestinian popular rebellion, an *intifada*, broke out in the Occupied West Bank and Gaza Strip.

The eruption of the *intifada* was a function of a blend of root and immediate causes as well as catalysts.

Causes and Catalysts

The root causes of the unrest were embedded in twenty years of Israeli occupation and Israeli policies aimed undermining the material and national existence of the Palestinians in their own land. The Palestinians perceived that under the guise of maintaining its security, Israel had pursued a host of policies harmful to Palestinian society. Israel had confiscated Arab land and launched an aggressive settlement policy that had left the West Bank and Gaza splintered both geographically and demographically. Israeli "iron fist" policies—marked by repressive measures and human rights violations—had resulted in loss of life, imprisonment, detention, house or town arrest, razing of dwellings, deportation, fines, interrogation, travel restrictions, curfews, closures of educational institutions, unjust taxes, economic hardships, and the like. Hardly a single Palestinian household had been left unaffected.

Unlike classical patterns of colonialism, the Israeli occupation failed to win over the confidence of any meaningful sector of the occupied population. Even those social classes that have traditionally allied themselves to foreign occupation in other colonial settings found themselves in the Palestinian context at loggerheads with the Israeli occupation. Under an active policy of land confiscation and Jewish settlement, major Palestinian landholders were the worse sufferers. Even the leading Palestinian merchants were restricted and had to contend with discriminatory competition from their Israeli counterparts, who enjoyed differential treatment from their government.

Such attempts to undermine the material existence of the Palestinian people were augmented by continuous Israeli denial of Palestinian national aspirations, which included self-determination and an independent Palestinian state in the West Bank and Gaza. Israeli denial was considered by the Palestinians as a deliberate attitude that blatantly ignored international recognition of legitimate Palestinian rights.

National and political awareness among the Palestinians had gradually descended throughout the twenty years of Israeli occupation. The Palestinian national movement and the process of Palestinian nation-building had contributed to the growth of this awareness. When harsh Israeli occupation policies entered a collision course with this exacted state of national awareness among the Palestinians, twenty years of seething discontent ripened into an uprising.

The uprising did not happen in a vacuum. It was dormant, awaiting the appropriate historical occasion to erupt. In fact its manifestations and attributes were already somewhat visible and indicated that the uprising itself was very much on the anvil. Those who observed the situation in the Occupied Territories closely and saw events in continuum were bound to come to this conclusion.

In the three years preceding the rebellion, forms of popular resistance to the Israeli occupation were enforced. The setting for the December uprising was being staged. One can even venture to suggest that the uprising had actually started, though partially, long before December 1987. The tactics and forms of conflict employed by the Palestinians in the uprising and Israeli retaliatory measures were in fact in place before the eruption of the uprising. One can find substantial evidence in both Israeli and Palestinian sources.

In his 1987 report, Israeli researcher Meron Benvenisti, director of the West Bank Data Project, indicated that in the period between April 1986 and May 1987, 3,150 violent protest rallies had taken place. Palestinian sources indicate that between 1985 and 1987, 115 Palestinians were killed and 828 were injured while confronting against Israeli occupation. These figures seem to include Palestinian casualties inside and outside the Occupied Territories.

The objective conditions for the outbreak of an uprising within the Palestinian society were ripe. The language and discourse of the uprising were in use before the rebellion itself began.

Twenty years of occupation produced a state of deep remorse and frustration among the Palestinians. Though initially internalised, these pent-up emotions sought an outlet through which to explode. The scope, magnitude, and endurance of the uprising attests to the depth and intensity of that anger and frustration. A number of developments in the Palestinian, Arab, and Israeli arenas found their way into the awareness of the Palestinian people under occupation. These developments came to provide the immediate cause for the *intifada*.

In the Palestinian sphere, the PLO and its leadership were unable to deliver on their promises. Just prior to the uprising, the PLO had reached its lowest ebb. Armed resistance was reduced to an empty slogan. The evacuation of the PLO's military forces from Lebanon highlighted an unimaginable degree of weakness. Splits and lack of meaningful national unity among the PLO factions only aggravated this weakness. The Palestinians in the West Bank and Gaza gradually began to realise that they could no longer count on the Palestinian "exterior" alone for their salvation, and that they had to be more self-reliant.

Apart from their growing apprehension at the PLO's increasingly obvious military weakness, the Palestinians in the West Bank and Gaza were further diverted by the PLO's persistent attempts to bypass them politically and to abort whatever national gains they had achieved over the last twenty years. American notions of "improving the quality of life" for Palestinians in the West Bank and Gaza and the "Jordanian Development Plan" were viewed in this connection and therefore rejected.

In the Arab arena, the Palestine problem sank for a number of reasons to a position of less importance. Among these reasons were the weakness of the PLO itself, the problem of Lebanon, the

Iran-Iraq war and the Arab preoccupation with it, and a variety of specific problems facing each Arab nation-state.

In the Israeli arena, Israeli intentions regarding the future of the Occupied Territories had become crystal clear, as indicated in the active Jewish settlement of the West Bank and the Gaza Strip. Palestinian frustrations, doubts, and apprehensions were perpetuated and reinforced by the clear and significant Israeli voices calling for the "transfer" of Palestinians in the Occupied Territories to the East Bank of Jordan or for the formation of an "alternative homeland"(*watan badil*) for them in Jordan. The transfer and the "alternative homeland" were considered as Israeli attempts to confront the Palestinian demographic issue that threatened the homogeneity of the Jewish state and its Zionist nature should Israel decide to include the West Bank and Gaza. According to Benvenisti, Palestinians and Jews in "Eretz Yisrael" would reach demographic parity in the year 2010.

Israeli voices calling for the "transfer" were not considered lightly by the Palestinians, since they were no longer isolated voices. When Meir Kahane first demanded the expulsion of the Arabs from "Eretz Yisrael," apologists claimed that Kahane represented only himself. Just a few years later, important personalities, political parties, and a large segment of the Israeli society in fact came to accept Kahane's views. References can be made in this regard to former minister without portfolio Yosef Shapira, former deputy minister of defence, Michael Dakel, and most important, former defence minister Ariel Sharon, a leading figure in the Likud party. The Tehiya party, Gush Emunim, the majority of settlers, and over thirty per cent of the Israeli population simply did not object to the idea of "transfer."

Furthermore, Israeli intransigence had appeared to increase over time, despite what the Palestinians perceived as Palestinian and Arab concessions, represented, for example, in the 1982 Fez Peace Plan. The Fez Plan speaks of Arab willingness to recognise Israel as part of a comprehensive peace settlement in the region. What is especially significant about the plan, which accepts Israel's right to exist within secure borders, is the fact that it was instituted by the Arabs themselves and not by a third party, as had been the case with previous peace plans.

The Palestinian-Jordanian Accord of February 1985 was perceived by Palestinians in the same conciliatory light. The accord made no umambiguous reference to an independent Palestinian state. It also spoke of Palestinian self-determination only within the framework of a Jordanian-Palestinian confederation. Yet Israel adamantly refused to recognise any fundamental change in the Arab/Palestinian position. The net effect was growing Palestinian certainty that Israel was not interested in a meaningful peaceful settlement to the conflict.

Apart from the causes—both fundamental and immediate — a number of developments acted as catalysts in precipitating the outbreak of the *intifada*. Immediately prior to the uprising, a state of anxiety and psychological mobilisation prevailed in the Gaza strip, where the uprising initially erupted. This state of anxiety and mobilisation emerged in the wake of the successful escape of six members of the Islamic *Jihad* movement from the Gaza central prison. This escape incited nationalist sentiments and created a sense of mobilisation and awareness among the population.

A short while later it was realised that members of this group were not only still in Gaza but were also responsible for a number of daring campaigns launched against the Israeli occupation. One such operation was the assassination of Captain Ron Tal, head of the Israeli military police in Gaza. After this incident, for which the Islamic *Jihad* claimed responsibility, a situation of tension and anxiety prevailed until the outbreak of the uprising.

Just prior to the uprising, a bloody encounter between the Israeli security forces and a group of Islamic *Jihad* members, which resulted in the death of four Palestinians and one Israeli intelligence officer, provoked an unimaginable display of highly charged nationalist sentiments. Demonstrators took to the streets in a number of areas in the strip, and in a show of solidarity thousands of people visited the homes of the deceased to offer condolences and express support.

Muslim Brotherhood Society and the Intifada

Despite claims to the contrary, the eruption of the *intifada* caught the Muslim Brotherhood Society by surprise, the way it caught the wings of the PLO in the Occupied Territories. Although the Muslim Brotherhood and the PLO each claim that it was behind the eruption of the *intifada*, the fact of the matter is that the *intifada* broke out without any political decision by any organised group.

The *intifada* marked the beginning of a new phase in the evolution of the Muslim Brotherhood Society in the West Bank and Gaza. This phase, characterised by proper resistance to the Israeli occupation, may be seen as a beginning of the actual *jihad* by the society. One of the leaflets issued by the Islamic Resistance Movement (Hamas) expressed this new direction: "What is happening today in this blessed land is but a new creation of the Islamic *umma* and of the Muslim generation that carries the banner of Islam."

The leaders of the Brotherhood in the Occupied Territories accepted the notion of transition into a new stage with some variation of opinion. Sheikh Ibrahim al-Quqa, a deported Hamas leader, stated that the *intifada* was "a phase, and a prelude to a more serious process of getting rid of the nightmare of the Zionist presence on that land." Some Muslim youth leaders in the Occupied Territories think that Muslim Brotherhood participation in the *intifada* is an indicator of a new stage, and that the *intifada* is a mechanism to mobilise the masses, in order to create a generation of *jihad* to fight Israel. They also suggest that the *intifada* is one form of *jihad* and a prelude to armed *jihad* action and, accordingly, is perceived a part of a new phase. Yusuf al-'Azm, a Muslim Brotherhood leader in Jordan, says that the *intifada*, has moved the Brotherhood from one phase to a new one in "a natural childbirth and not a Caesarean."

The Muslim Brotherhood claims that it laid the groundwork for the *intifada* and is directly responsible for its outbreak. In this connection, the society points to the participation of the Islamic student blocs in the violent demonstrations which broke out against the occupation in the Palestinian universities prior to the *intifada*, and especially to the role of the Islamic University in Gaza. The society emphasises the importance of this appeal in the preparation for the *intifada*. Furthermore, the Brotherhood claims that the *intifada* started as a result of a decision made by the society. Sheikh Yasin says that the Brotherhood was the party which unleashed the *intifada*, and it is the party which leads it.

Regarding the role of the Brotherhood in the *intifada*, Hamas leader Dr. 'Abd-al-'Aziz al-Rantisi intimates that the *intifada* began "with one fixed outcry, *allahu akbar* [God is great], and took off from the mosques, where the Koran was being recited, and the Islamic songs sung, and the people provided with guidance. The [Israeli] detention camps have been filled with Muslim youth who had converted them into mosques. The streets and mosques were filled with the pamphlets of the Islamic Resistance Movement, to which the people reacted noticeably. Those who will monitor the various political and press statements will note that these statements indicate the fact that the Islamists are behind the *intifada*."

Egyptian Islamic writer Dr. Hilmi Muhammad Qa'ud, attributes the outbreak of the *intifada* to the frustration of the Palestinian people in their outside organisations, after they had been disappointed in an effective support from other Arab nations. The Palestinian people had to take the initiative on their own after everyone else had backed away, and they had to "declare their true identity without shame, and to say to the whole world: we are Muslim people...and Palestine is Muslim."

There are some Islamic writers who cast the *intifada* and its continuation, and the Islamic Resistance Movement (Hamas) in a divine perspective. One of these writers says: "The will of God hurled the stone in order to destabilise the balance of international peace in accordance with a precise divine order. The continuation of the *intifada* is divine destiny reflected in the will of the Palestinian Muslim masses who know that stopping the *intifada* is the trap that God's enemies at home and abroad have planned, in order to besiege this people, and then to annihilate and exterminate it.

With reference to the rise of Hamas, the same writer continues: "Perhaps the most important event in this century is that the Islamic Resistance Movement emerged in this place, at this time...in the heart of Palestine, Jerusalem, the Aqsa mosque....Jerusalem was the first *qiblah* [direction for prayer] for Muslims. Why is it not also the first *Jihad qiblah* in this era, so that it can be the first shearhead of the establishment of the Islamic state?" This writer also suggests that Hamas "has appeared by divine will and timing and, therefore, God will protect it from all its enemies, defend it and make it victorious."

Regarding the targets of the *intifada*, Ibrahim al-Quqa sees them as follows: "The *intifada* is not aimed at toying with the Palestinian issue in the circles of politics, or promoting and discussing this issue in conferences or organisations, but is aimed at liberating the land, all the land, and the honour and creed. It is aimed at the comprehensive and far-reaching liberation [of Palestine] from the hands of the imperialist oppressors and at restoring the cause to its free and independent Islamic framework."

Concerning the significance of the *intifada*, an Islamic writer says that it "exposes the opportunistic regimes and organisations, which made capitulation a strategy and concessions a tactic, and which aimed from the initial at using the *intifada* to polish the fading faces of some Palestinians at home, so that they can be the nucleus of the unilateral Jewish-Palestinian solution, which is based on autonomy as it is considered by Shamir and his colleagues, and to pave the way for the international conference....The Palestinian Muslim people know that the PLO will ride the wave of the *intifada*, as is its practice, in an attempt to turn it to its advantage politically and for propaganda purposes, while it has no genuine claim to it. Let the *intifada*, God willing, be the death of every defeated coward."

Founding of Hamas

As a response to the outbreak of the *intifada*, the Brotherhood in Gaza began to draw up contingency plans to deal with the new and sudden development. These contingency plans began with a meeting held in the house of Ahmad Yasin on December 9, 1987. Present at the meeting were the most leaders of the Islamic Center in the Gaza Strip. In addition to Yasin, six other figures were also present. Those were 'Abd-al-'Aziz al-Rantisi (a physician), Ibrahim al-Yazuri (a pharmacist), Sheikh Salah Shihada (a staff member of the Islamic University of Gaza), 'Issa al-Nashshar (an engineer), Muhammad Sham'a (a teacher), and 'Abd-al-Fattah Dukhan (a schoolmaster). This faction comprised of the first Hamas leadership that had established leadership wings or committees in the political, security, military and information spheres.

The launching of the Islamic Resistance Movement (Hamas) was not a precise conscious decision, but rather a decision that evolved over time. The purpose of the December 9, 1987, meeting was to discuss ways to manipulate an incident that took place on December 8 of the same year, one day prior to the meeting.

A few days later, the Brotherhood leaders issued a statement calling on the people to stand up to the Israeli possession. Hamas retrospectively considered this statement the first of Hamas's serialised leaflets. As the disturbances in Gaza and the West Bank continued and compounded, Yasin and his colleagues continued to meet. In the meantime, Sheikh Yasin established contact with Sheikh Jamil Hamami, on of the young preachers of Al-Aqsa Mosque in Jerusalem. Hamami, who coordinated very intimately with Yasin and acted as a liaison between the West Bank and Gaza Brothers, formed a parallel leadership body for Hamas in the West Bank. He also acted as a liaison between Yasin and the leadership of the Muslim Brotherhood in Jordan.

Role of Sheikh Ahmad Yasin

Sheikh Ahmad Yasin, the leader of the Muslim Brotherhood and founder of the Islamic Center in Gaza, is also the leader and main founder of Hamas. He came from a relatively prosperous middle-class land-owning family. But when Yasin's family left Palestine in 1948, it settled in a refugee camp in Gaza. The disorientation of his family would have a lasting impression on young Yasin, and later on his adult life as well as on his thinking and fundamentalist views.

Yasin continued to act as the leader of the Muslim Brotherhood Society in Gaza. But as it later became apparent, Yasin was not deterred by the Israeli authorities. During this *intifada* he was implicated in the kidnapping and killing of two Israeli soldiers and other violent deeds against Israelis and Palestinians collaborating with them. In May 1989, Yasin was arrested and was later sentenced to fifteen years in jail.

Although Yasin had assumed the status of the most prominent Islamic figure in the Gaza Strip and perhaps in the West Bank as well, the underlying reasons for his importance are political. The emergence of his Brotherhood movement as a rival to the uncontested secular PLO brought him attention and high visibility. His decision to take part in the *intifada* at a later stage and to engage the Israeli occupation increased that attention and visibility. But Yasin is essentially the product of this political setting. His importance cannot be attributed to any significant theological or doctrinal contributions. He is not a Khomeini, a Shari'ati, or a Fadlullah. He is neither a Banna nor a Qutb. Yasin should be seen in the political context of the Palestine issue, and not in any regional or global context.

From time to time, Hamas would reorganise its leadership bodies because of the frequent arrests of its leaders. After the arrest of Sheikh Yasin in May 1989, Dr. 'Abd al-'Aziz al-Rantisi became the most outstanding Hamas leader in the Occupied Territories. But part of Hamas's influential leadership resides outside the Occupied Territories. Some of the known leaders are Dr. Musa Abu-Marzuq, the chief of the Politburo of the movement, Ibrahim Ghusha, the official spokesman of the movement, Muhammad Nazzal, Hamas's representitive in Jordan, and Emad al-'Alami, the representative of the movement in Iran. There are other distinguished leaders of Hamas whose names are not publicised and who reside in a number of Arab countries.

Hamas is virtually led by a consultative council (*majlis shura*), whose members reside inside and outside the Occupied Territories. And since the Muslim Brotherhood Society in Palestine belongs to the society in Jordan organisationally and otherwise, the Jordanian Muslim Brothers play an influential role in the leadership of Hamas. The Jordanian Brotherhood is the ultimate frame of reference for Hamas, although the attitudes and politics of the two movements may not be similar.

After more than five years of effective participation in the *intifada*, Hamas managed to form several echelons of cadres or leading activists who had gained experience in the field or in Israeli jails and detention camps. Therefore, while the Israeli December 1992 collective expatriations of the Hamas leaders and activists have emptied the Occupied Territories of the first, second, and perhaps third echelons of leadership, the movement has the manpower to produce, over time, a younger breed of leaders to fill the vacuum. This breed may be more militant than the politically seasoned older generation of leadership.

Hamas, which suggests "enthusiasm" or "zeal" and which is the acronym for *Harakat al-Muqawama al-'Islamiyya* [the Islamic Resistance Movement], was therefore established as a response to the eruption and prolongation of the *intifada*. Hamas emerged in a context of disillusionment with the Palestinian secular political movements and with the frustrated expectation of achieving salvation from the Israeli occupation through them. In addition to that, the popular turn to Hamas was motivated by the search for psychological comfort, strength, and endurance which a religious ideology normally provides. According to Yasin, "when all doors are sealed, Allah opens a gate."

Furthermore, Yasin and Hamas offered the population a more enticing combination than that of the PLO: "[T]he fundamentalist groups offered a special category of activism that combined patriotism with moral purity and social action with the promise of divine grace. Sheikh Yasin offered the young Palestinian something far beyond Arafat's ken: not just the reclamation of the homeland, but the salvation of his own troubled soul."

The Muslim Brotherhood had more than one reason to form Hamas. Yasin's stated reasons for the formation of Hamas are consistent with the message of his movement. In his reply to the charge of having established the Islamic Resistance Movement, Yasin asserted that the establishment of Hamas was not only his basic and natural right, but also his main duty as a human being, as a Muslim, as an Arab, and as a Palestinian, since he and large segments of his people have for long been struggling under the yoke of an intruding and oppressive occupation. Yasin argues that Hamas is basically a political movement and its primary goal is to secure the genuine and natural rights of the Palestinian people by ensuring them safe and peaceful existence on the land of Palestine.

Yasin was initially cautious and unwilling in endorsing an all-out and full-fledged Brotherhood participation in the *intifada*. He was not very interested on dragging the Islamic Center and the Brotherhood as a whole into an uncertain confrontation with the Israeli occupation. But he could not, even if he desired, sit on the side and ignore the internal pressures within his movement and the unprecedented events taking place around him. He was forced to make serious and risky decisions.

Like the other PLO outfits, Hamas participated in the various activities of the *intifada*. But since it is larger in size, in terms of following, than any single PLO faction barring the Fatah movement, Hamas's participation in the *intifada* has been characterised by regularity, extensiveness, and diversity of forms. Hamas has relied on its substantial presence in the various areas of the West Bank and Gaza to ensure the continuation of the *intifada*. This kind of presence helped the movement to absorb repeated Israeli strikes or arrests of its leaders and members without impeding its ability to continue its activities in the *intifada*. Furthermore, Hamas had not been concerned with participation in the peace process and could as such dedicate its efforts to the *intifada* and avoid the internal differences and change of strategies and tactics which other PLO factions had to go through in order to harmonise their involvement in the negotiations with Israel.

In addition to the regular activities of the *intifada* (demonstrations, strikes, stone-throwing, etc.) Hamas's resort to violent tactics against Israeli targets, including the use of firearms, had compounded over time and exceeded in volume similar tactics undertaken by other groups. Hamas has established for this purpose a special militant body called Kata'ib 'Izz-al-Din al-Qassam (Regiments of 'Izz-al-Din al-Qassam). These regiments have targeted Israelis as well as Palestinians collaborating with the Israeli possession.

Yasin, the calculating and astute politician, has his own way of doing things. He and his close associates in the Brotherhood had to find a way to join the *intifada* without putting their future and the future of the movement in crisis. It was Sheikh Yasin's idea to create a special organisation from the Muslim Brotherhood in Gaza to take responsibility for the participation of the society in the *intifada*. Yasin's main concern was to safeguard the Brotherhood and the Islamic Center which he "had built with such effort and care."

The Muslim Brotherhood probably thought that in case the *intifada* failed, Hamas would take the responsibility. But Yasin was mindful of other considerations. Like the PLO, the Brotherhood needed a parallel resistance body. And in the immediate sense, Hamas was the Brotherhood's parallel to the PLO's newly formed Unified National Leadership of the *intifada* (UNL).

Furthermore, the participation in the *intifada* confronted the Brotherhood with an ideological dilemma. Until the day the *intifada* broke out, Yasin was arguing that the Brotherhood was still going through the stage of Islamic upbringing and preparation and that the time had not yet come for the actual *jihad*. A seemingly new framework such as Hamas was therefore imperative to justify the ideological shift by Yasin and the Brotherhood and the new direction they were taking. But owing to the success and popularity of Hamas, the Muslim Brotherhood Society in the West Bank and Gaza would become gradually submerged in it. Hamas has become a dependable and convenient name for a rehabilitated Muslim Brotherhood Society. The "new" organisation has attracted followers and supporters who were not members of the Muslim Brotherhood.

The Brotherhood's participation in the *intifada* through Hamas was also politically instigated. Yasin sought to maintain his movement's position vis-à-vis other political factions in the Occupied Territories. Perhaps the Brotherhood has also intended by its participation in the *intifada* to set a claim in any future political negotiations or settlement.

The establishment and consolidation of Hamas was a turning point for both Yasin and his movement. Contrary to PLO nationalists' assertion that the Brotherhood had joined the *intifada* late and under pressure, the Brotherhood's participation has been both far-reaching and effective. Yasin himself claims that his movement was responsible for the eruption of the *intifada* and its leadership. When asked if the *intifada* was unprompted, he replied: "I believe it happened as something destined by God. There is nothing called spontaneous in Islam."

Because of its ideological and political beliefs, the Brotherhood's participation in the *intifada* was not suggested to support the political programme and goals of the PLO. This participation was intended to serve the political aims of the Muslim Brotherhood. The main point of convergence between the

Brotherhood and the PLO was the common goal of putting an end to the Israeli occupation of the West Bank and Gaza. The views of the Brotherhood and the PLO diverged on most other issues.

The participation in the *intifada* publicised Yasin and the Brotherhood and strengthened their political clout. Yasin and his movement became more vocal and less discrete in terms of political visibility and stands. Because of this participation and the establishment of Hamas, Yasin could, with almost no negative political consequences for his movement, challenge the PLO and its leadership, the organisation which thus far has been accorded the genuine representation of the Palestinian people. Yasin and the Brotherhood began to clash with the PLO for the representation of the Palestinians in the Occupied Territories and managed over a relatively short period of time to become a force to reckoned with and to become a serious challenge to the secular forces led by the PLO.

Since the beginning of the *intifada*, Hamas struggled to assert itself and achieve honour as a major counterpart to the PLO's UNL of the *intifada*. Even after this concession was made by the UNL, Hamas continued to insist on distinguishing itself from the UNL. While Hamas and the UNL generally honoured what was included in their respective *intifada* leaflets and bulletins, such as the demonstrations and other activities, Hamas arrested every opportunity to demonstrate its independence and authority. All through the *intifada*, it called for total strikes on days that the UNL had not specified as general strike days. These days often coincided with religious anniversaries or other historical events celebrated by Muslims.

The appeals of Hamas for strikes, especially in the Gaza Strip, were met with far-reaching popular response. The Brotherhood enjoyed greater influence in Gaza than in the West Bank. The prevailing conditions in the Gaza Strip were readily conducive to militancy. Pressure was already building up in Gaza before the *intifada*, and a number of dramatic incidents that took place in the preceding weeks created a condition of tense anxiety and high mobilisation among the population.

Another indication of the great practical and moral authority of Hamas and the Muslim Brotherhood in the Gaza Strip was the large number of people who repeatedly visited the leaders of the movement soliciting assistance for their various problems. Since June 1988, scores of people from various walks of life (religious and non-religious, poor, well-to-do, educated and noneducated alike, merchants, businessmen, and even some Christians) visited the home of Sheikh Ahmad Yasin, the leader of Hamas, seeking his good officers on a daily basis. People resorted to such informal intervention because of the absence of authority structures that are usually entrusted with this role, or because of the lack of credibility on the part of these frameworks. During the *intifada*, most of the Israeli controlled government structures and institutions, including courts, were practically shut down. The secrecy of the PLO factions and the fact that they do not enjoy spiritual authority augmented the demand for the arbitration of the Hamas leaders. While the resort to Hamas undermined the authority of the Israeli occupation, it also undermined the authority of the PLO and nationalist institutions.

It is worth mentioning that those who visited the Hamas leaders believed that these leaders were able to judge issues and make judgments and that they had the capability to implement them. In addition, the Hamas leaders settled disputes without receiving personal payment.

Attempts have been made by the Hamas leadership and the Unified National Leadership to resolve their disputes and to contain the imbroglio and the negative effects that could emanate from it.

However, Hamas has continued to call for its own strikes without synchronising with the Unified National Leadership. Clearly the *intifada* had upset the old balance of power and the Islamic movement had become a political force to reckon with. Hamas has become a formidable rival to the PLO factions in the Occupied Territories. On a few instances, violent clashes took place between the supporters of Hamas and those of the UNL.

Hamas demands that the PLO commit itself to an Islamic programme as a precondition for serious alliance and cooperation. SheikhYasin says: "There must be a mutual common ground, based on commitment to Islamic values and principles, without violating them in times of resistance. There must also be prior agreement that after liberation, the state will be Islamic. We opposed the Palestine National Charter because if we had accepted the establishment of a secular state, we would have violated Islam. The Palestinian organizations were established for political and nationalist goals, the Muslim Brotherhood has political and nationalist goals, but they fall within a broader Islamic framework."

In response to the Unified National Leadership's leaflet number twenty-eight entitled "Proclamation of Independence," in which the UNL asked the inhabitants of the West Bank and the Gaza Strip to hold mass rallies and celebrations to mark the convening of the PNC session and the declaration of independence," Hamas appealed to the masses to turn the days in which the PNC was in session into "days of confrontation, opposition, and rejection of peace with the murderers....Let us tear down all appeals for capitulation and let us put an end to toying with the cause by weaklings and those who are betting on the enemy's elections."

In response, the UNL urged the Islamic Resistance Movement to stop opposing the PLO decisions: "The Unified National Leadership calls on specific fundamentalist quarters to put the national interest of our people over their partisan principles and interests, and to abstain from casting negative positions, which by necessity serve the enemy." Muslim Brotherhood sources indicated that Yasser Arafat asked the general guide of the Muslim Brotherhood in Egypt, just before the convening of the PNC's nineteenth session, to support the resolutions that the PLO leadership was intending to adopt, to mediate with the Muslim Brotherhood leaders in Jordan and the Occupied Territories in order to narrow differences between Hamas and the UNL, and to avert any conflict between the two sides.

The appeal, however, fell on deaf ears. Hamas considered the declaration of the Palestinian state to be premature. Sheikh Yasin argued: "We have not liberated any part of our country upon which we could found our state. We are still under occupation, and we have not yet put an end to it. In what place would we establish the state?...We must have land upon which we can stand in freedom and establish our state without prior conditions and without concessions." Hamas's leaflets that were issued after the PNC session expressed a similar position.

On November 15, 1988, the PNC announced the establishment of the state of Palestine. The declaration was based on the UN Partition Plan of 1947, which segmented Palestine into two states, UN resolutions 242 and 338, and the need to ensure the legitimate national rights of the Palestinian people, including the right to self-determination. Following the PNC session, Arafat held a press conference in Geneva in which he recognised the existence of Israel, accepted UN resolutions 242 and 338, and rejected terrorism. By doing that, Arafat fulfilled the United States's requirements to open a dialogue with the PLO. Like the PNC resolutions, Arafat's "concessions" were attacked by Hamas.

When dialogue between the PLO leadership and the American government was instituted, Hamas demanded an end to this dialogue with "the American enemy who has proved to us that it is manoeuvering for time to benefit the Zionists, so that they can defeat the will of our people in the Occupied Territories, tranquilise the Muslim Arab masses around us, and remove them from the scene of the battle."

Hamas also repudiated the April 1989 proposal of Israeli Prime Minister Yitzhaq Shamir for elections in the Occupied Territories. It considered the proposal a trick to cripple the *intifada* and to gain a public relations victory.

Hamas repeated appeals urged the PLO leadership not to depend on America or on attempts to negotiate with Israel and to stop making relaxations: "They must reconsider their stance while they are in the middle of the unknown road to concessions, and ask themselves frankly about where they are heading. Not a single day goes by without hearing about a Palestinian step by which we concede part of our right...while our enemy does not falter. For how long are the concessions going to continue? What will we gain from them?"

Significance of Intifada

The Muslim Brotherhood stresses the importance of the continuation of the *intifada* until its causes, represented in the Israeli occupation itself, disappear. The appeals of Hamas and the statements of its leaders in this regard point an accusing finger at PLO leaders: "The *intifada* will go straight ahead until the usurper is ousted and the land of prophets is freed from the defile of the occupier. This is the voice of the entrenched and no attention will be paid to the unyielding talk which aims at burying the stone and the will for a mirage of futile promises from the protectors of Israel in the East and the West....It is rumoured that our people have given enough, and that the time of harvest has come." Sheikh Yasin states that Hamas is responsible for the eruption of the *intifada* and its continuation, even if the other outfits decide to end their participation in it. It is not, however, certain that Hamas can sustain the *intifada* without the involvement of other Palestinian factions.

After the PLO's decision to sanction Palestinian participation in the Madrid Peace Conference of October 29, 1991, and the subsequent Palestinian-Israeli diplomacy in Washington, the prospects for direct clash between Hamas and the Fatah movement, the largest of the PLO factions, loomed on the horizon. In July 1992, Fatah and Hamas supporters grappled with each other in several areas of the Gaza Strip, where scores of people were injured. Clashes between the two sides lasted quite a number of days but were finally contained through the intervention of prominent Palestinians in the Occupied Territories.

Hamas's influence and popularity had also increased manifold since the beginning of the peace process. Fatah and its following could not reconcile themselves to the rise of a rival force that could challenge the mainstream faction. Fatah's high perception of itself and its influence clashed with the new emerging reality of Hamas. The clashes that broke out between the two movements came against this background. In this test of wills, Hamas emerged as an equal counterpart to the Fatah movement.

The leaders of the Muslim Brotherhood inside and outside the Occupied Territories said that their opposition to the PLO would be democratic. This position came against the backdrop of the Brotherhood's realisation that the balance of power at the present time was still in favour of the PLO. However, the Islamists, according to Saqr, would be bound by the rules of the political game and will oppose in a civilised fashion. This Palestinian attitude is similar to the positions of the Muslim Brotherhood Societies in Egypt and Jordan toward their respective governments, which are characterised by coexistence.

During the *intifada* a group of Hamas leaders had occasionally voiced ideas that reflect moderation. For example, one Hamas leader once outlined the possibilities and means for resolving the conflict with Israel. Dr. Mahmud al-Zahhar, from the Gaza Strip, authored a scenario as to how and by what steps the Palestinian-Israeli conflict could be settled.

Sheikh Yasin himself made a statement in which he indicated for the first time the willingness of the Brotherhood to negotiate with Israel, but under specific conditions. These conditions stipulated that Israel must "first acknowledge the Palestinian citizens right to self-determination and right of return to their land." On a different occasion, when Yasin was questioned about negotiating with Israel, he quipped: "Yes, if Israel acknowledges our full rights and recognises the Palestinian people's right to live in its homeland in freedom and independence. But the Islamic movement will not negotiate as an alternative to the PLO. We want to negotiate with Israel so the Palestinian people inside and outside Palestine can live in Palestine." These utterances of Yasin, and similar utterances by other Brotherhood leaders, might only be tactical.

Such ideas and positions contradict the traditional Islamic position with regard to ending the conflict with Israel. Perhaps the *intifada* was the reason that impelled some Hamas leaders to reflect on "realistic" positions, such as the positions the PLO leaders adopted in the nineteenth PNC session in Algiers in 1988.

In the course of the *intifada,* Hamas relied on a number of mechanisms and methods to mobilise mass support and participation in the various activities of the *intifada* and vis-à-vis the Israeli occupation. The mosque in particular played a key role as a rallying point and as a place for launching demonstrations and other *intifada* activities. Hamas used the mosque as a platform and turned it from a place of worship into a hub of learning, and later on a place for political organisation. The pro-PLO nationalists did not possess a parallel mechanism or equal function and significance.

The Islamic movement had also relied on leaflets and graffiti. The leaflets are statements or bulletins that contain an agenda for the *intifada* activities for a period of time ranging from one to two weeks. In the development of the *intifada*, the Islamic Resistance Movement has issued scores of these leaflets. Hamas leaflets differ in content from those of the UNL. They reiterate the political targets and positions of the Muslim Brotherhood that are at odds with those of the UNL, especially Hamas's opposition to the concept of establishing a Palestinian state on a part of Palestine and concluding peace with Israel or recognising it. On the other hand, most of Hamas leaflets, in contrast to the leaflets of the UNL, have lacked an integrated scheme for a specific timeframe in terms of activities and appeals to escalate the *intifada*, especially during the initial stages of the uprising.

Hamas's leaflets usually begin with and contain several Koranic verses and are full of Islamic historical and religious practices. They call for standing up against the Israeli occupation and its policies and criticise Arab rulers, referring to their responsibility for Arab defeats and the loss of Palestine. The Hamas leaflets had lambasted political initiatives and plans which sought to find a solution to the Palestinian Israeli conflict: "Today, the American plot seems once more in order to abort your Muslim *intifada* through the Arab kings, presidents, and rulers under baseless slogans such as the exchange of land for peace and the umbrella of the international conference. This is only a mirage and delusion, and a containment to your *intifada* and your emotions." But as the *intifada* had advanced, the Hamas leaflets which by mid-1993 numbered about a hundred, became more militant in content and in the tactics they prescribed, especially with regard to armed strikes against Israeli targets and opposition to the peace process.

During the *intifada*, Hamas has also resorted to the use of violence and firearms. As its involvement in the *intifada* intensified, Hamas was being steadily radicalised. Harsh Israeli measures to suppress Hamas contributed to this radicalisation. Hundreds of Hamas activists have been detained, and many of its leaders have been exiled. With the decline of mass demonstrations and other peaceful activities of the *intifada*, the tendency within Hamas toward violent tactics has increased. Some of the Hamas leaders were charged in Israeli military courts for forming a military wing of the Hamas movement. This evolution in orientation was also inspired by a conscious decision on the part of the Hamas leaders.

If the Hamas activists were expecting religious or political reference to engage in violence, they could readily find the justification they need in the utterances of their leader, Sheikh Ahmad Yasin.

Yasin always questioned that the way to regain Palestine is through the exercise of *jihad*. When asked about his willingness to resort to *jihad* as a means to realise his aspirations, Yasin replied: "What is the other alternative available to those who cannot regain their rights by peaceful and non-violent means?" Yasin argued that the Palestinian people preferred, and still prefer, the pursuit of peace and not violence in order to fulfil their objectives. But he also added that if the Palestinians resort to violence, then it is forced on them for self-defence and because the Israelite occupier understands the language of violence and force only. Under such circumstances, "the gun is the only means that should be used in addressing the enemy." As a people under occupation, the Palestinians, according to Yasin, chose the course of resistance that were available to them. This may account for the various tactics, violent and nonviolent, used by Yasin's Islamic Resistance Movement during the *intifada*.

According to Yasin, the resort to war and violence has only one objective, which is the removal of oppression and corruption and the establishment of justice, and not the extermination of human beings who engage in them. Those who defend oppression and try to sustain it are equal in the eyes of Islam, irrespective of their religion or beliefs. Based on that, when Yasin and the brotherhood resorted to firearms, they used them against the Israeli authorities who defended oppression (the occupation) and tried to sustain it by the force of arms.

The articulations of Yasin and the Brotherhood on the issue of *jihad* differ and were sometimes contradictory. While Yasin argued that *jihad* should start following the completion of Islamic transformation of the Palestinian society, he and the Brotherhood believed that the Muslim who are reticent about the occupation of Palestine are committing a sin because Islam requires them to engage in holy war.

The publication of the Hamas Charter is considered an important and fundamental manifestation of the establishment of Hamas as the resistance wing of the Muslim Brotherhood Society.

With the foundation of a resistance wing the Brotherhood became, in a way, akin to the nationalist factions comprising the PLO. Despite the fact that this charter does not represent a coherent and sophisticated political or ideological programme, compared to programmes of other political parties, or even the ones of the PLO factions, its publication does define once more the ideological and political positions of the Muslim Brotherhood Society in the Occupied Territories.

According to the charter, the "Islamic Resistance Movement is a faction of the Muslim brotherhood in Palestine, and the Muslim brotherhood movement is a world organisation." The charter also informs that the "Islamic Resistance Movement is a distinct Palestinian movement that gives devotion to God, takes Islam as a way of life, and works to raise the banner of God over every inch of Palestine." The charter reiterates the Brotherhood's well-known motto: "God is the goal, the Prophet is the model, the Koran is the constitution, the *jihad* is the path, and death on God's path is our most sublime aspiration."

Islamic Resistance Movement

With regard to the Islamic Resistance Movement's attitude toward Palestine, Hamas believes, as the charter states, that "the land of Palestine is an Islamic *waqf* for Muslim generations until the day of judgement. No Arab state or all Arab states, or a king or president, or all the kings and presidents, have that right. No organisation or all the organisations, whether Palestinian or Arab, have that right either, because Palestine is an Islamic *waqf* for the Muslim generations until the day of judgement."

About peaceful solutions, initiatives, and the international conference, the charter narrates: "Initiatives, so-called peaceful solutions, and international conferences to solve the Palestinian issue are at variance with the principle of the Islamic Resistance Movement. Abandoning any part of Palestine is an abandonment of a part of religion. The patriotism of the Islamic Resistance Movement is a part of its religion. Initiatives, proposals, and international conferences are a waste of time and an exercise in futility. The Palestinian masses are too precious for anyone to play with their future, their rights, and their destiny."

The charter of the Islamic Resistance Movement highlights three factors related to the liberation of Palestine: the Palestinian factor, the Arab factor, and the Islamic factor. Each of these three factors has its role in the struggle with Zionism. The charter also refers to Hamas's position regarding other Islamic and nationalist factions on the Palestinian scene: "The Islamic Resistance Movement looks at the other Islamic groups with respect and esteem. If it differs with them in a given aspect or notion, it agrees with them in general aspects and ideas. It looks at those movements as being covered by the principle of *ijtihad* [Islamic legal judgment], as long as they are sincere and well-intended, and as long as their deeds remained within the limits of the Islamic framework.

As for the nationalist outfits, the charter states that Hamas "exchanges respect with them and appreciates their circumstances, the factors surrounding them, and the impact of these factors. Hamas presses on their hands, so long as they do not give their adherence to the communist East or the crusader West." Hamas "assures all nationalist trends functioning in Palestine that they have its support and assistance for the purpose of liberating Palestine. Hamas will do nothing other than that, in word and action, and in the present and the future. It will unite and not divide, preserve and not dissipate, consolidate and not fragment, value every good word, sincere effort, and good offices, close the door to side disputes, and adherence rumours and ill-intended words, with the understanding that it has the right to self-defence." Hamas, according to the charter, is prepared to discuss "objectively the new developments on the local and international scenes concerning the Palestinian issue, in order to determine the extent to which these developments fulfil or hamper our interest from an Islamic perspective."

As regards the PLO's positions, the charter reflects some kind of evolution in the Muslim Brotherhood standpoint. It says that Hamas "considers the PLO to be the closest to the Islamic Resistance Movement and regards it as a companion and guide alike. Can the Muslim be separated from his father, brother, relative or friend? Our nation is one, our misfortune is one, our destiny is one, and our enemy is one." But the charter also reiterates the existing Brotherhood reservations vis-à-vis the PLO: "The PLO endorses secular ideas....Secular thought is incompatible with religious thought, completely incompatible. Accordingly, and with our esteem for the PLO...and what it may evolve into, and without underrating its role in the Arab-Israeli struggle, we cannot abandon the present and future Islamism of Palestine, so that we can advocate secular thought. The Islamism of Palestine is a part of our religion, and those who abandon their religion, will lose....the day the PLO adopts Islam as its way of life, we will be its troops and the force behind destructing the enemy."

Position of Hamas

Finally, with regard to the position of Hamas in relation to the Arab and Islamic states, the charter says: "The Arab states around Israel are asked to open their borders for the *mujahidin* of the Arab and Muslim peoples, so that they play their role and add their efforts to the efforts of their fellows, the Muslim Brotherhood in Palestine....As for the other Arab and Islamic nations, they are asked to facilitate the *mujahidin's* movement. This is the very least to be done."

A thorough reading of Hamas's charter reveals that some of its sections and ideas were written cleverly and can be interpreted in various ways. Perhaps the motives behind that were political, taking into account the circumstances under which the charter was formulated and published, illustrated by the absence of certainty and lack of conclusive knowledge of an unfolding situation as well as by the circumstances of the continuing Israeli occupation of the West Bank and the Gaza Strip. It is also apparent that the charter is loaded with rhetoric and idealism. The subsequent conduct of Hamas following the issuance of the charter has not perfectly reflected what was articulated in the charter, especially with regard to the PLO.

The *intifada* has been a change behind a process of differentiation and debate within the Muslim Brotherhood Society in the Occupied Territories. The Brotherhood's decision to participate in the *intifada* was made against the backdrop of a debate that was taking place within the leadership of the movement. The question argued was whether it was incumbent upon the society to delay the *jihad* against the Israeli occupation until an Islamic society is established, or whether it was the Brotherhood's duty to enter into the conflict immediately. Traditional Brotherhood leaders were not enthusiastic about an early participation in the *intifada,* but the young leaders were able to impose their desire and vision in this regard. On the leadership level, the *intifada* had broadened the differences between the traditional Brotherhood leaders, who are linked to Jordan by virtue of being *waqf* employees receiving their salaries from the Jordanian government, and the young Muslim leaders, who started to emerge after 1967. The *intifada* has also compelled the Brotherhood to define more clearly than ever its position toward the Israeli occupation and the way to deal with it, as well as the means and strategies that should be employed in opposing it.

The differentiation process and the debate can, in fact, be traced back to the second half of the 1970s. After the Islamic restoration that began during that time, especially in the universities of the Occupied Territories, scores of the graduates of these universities were either Brotherhood members or sympathizers. Many of them occupied functional positions in society. These young leaders gradually began to hold the centre stage in the actual leadership of the Brotherhood. They adopted positions that were popular and nationalistically appealing. Unlike the traditional leaders, they demanded that the issue of nationalism be given more significance by the society, in terms of thought and practice, and that the nationalist issue be considered a matter of priority. They also endorsed the idea of cooperation and coordination with the factions of the nationalist movement instead of an antagonistic relationship. The young leaders argued that failure to reevaluate all positions, especially those pertaining to the Palestinian issue, could stimulate differentiation within the ranks of the Brotherhood. The emergence of the Islamic *Jihad* movement, which is a breakaway group from the Muslim Brotherhood, can be viewed as one form of this differentiation. The Brotherhood will find itself facing the same position it encountered after the emergence of the Islamic *Jihad,* where the society was disorganised and had lost part of itself, if it fails to devise ideological and political views on Palestine that are acceptable to the rank and file of the society.

One major example of the differentiation process in the ranks of the Muslim Brotherhood leadership was related to the position the Muslim Brotherhood had to take in relation to the *intifada*. Some traditional Brotherhood leaders were distrustful and questioned the wisdom of taking part in the *intifada*, on the grounds that non-Islamic parties could be the ones to reap the fruit of the *intifada* and use it for political targets that are not acceptable to the Muslim Brotherhood agenda. The traditional leaders also argued that the Brotherhood would not be able to guide the *intifada* in a direction that was congenial with its positions. In contrast to this position, the society's young leaders saw that it was the Brotherhood's responsibility to participate in the *intifada* and to strive to guide it in the line that the Islamic movement desired, without consideration for the goals of other groups, or for the fact that the *intifada* could be used for specific political purposes.

The *intifada* and Hanas provided the Muslim Brotherhood with renewed doctrinal conviction and credibility. Putting the Islamic principle of *Jihad* into practice, through in a modest manner, had a reviving effect on the followers of the Brotherhood. It also had a similar effect on other Islamic movements outside the domain of Occupied Territories. Through the *intifada*, the Brotherhood as well as the Islamic *Jihad* have been transforming Islam into a liberation theology. By becoming popular itself, Hamas has increased the popularity of political Islam in the Occupied Territories. But no conclusive estimate of this popularity or of the actual significance of Hamas vis-à-vis that of the PLO can be given without conducting free and democratic elections for the mass of the Palestinian population in the West Bank and Gaza.

The rise in Hamas influence and popularity has also been related to an extensive network of foreign contacts, which provide the movement with all forms of doctrinal, political, moral, and material support. Hamas enjoys the support of movements in countries like Jordan, Egypt, Saudi Arabia, the Gulf states, Sudan, Algeria, Tunisia, and elsewhere. Even Muslim communities and organisations in the United States and Europe extend support to Hamas.

After the eruption of the *intifada* and the formation of Hamas, the relationship of the Palestinian Muslim Brothers with Iran improved. Iran viewed favourably the Brothers' engagement in defying the Israeli occupation. But this improvement also came against the background of a rapprochement between Iran and the Muslim Brotherhood Society in Jordan. During the Gulf imbroglios and the Gulf War of 1991, Hamas relationship with Saudi Arabia and the Gulf states worsened. It appears that Hamas was keen to find new allies, hence the improvement in relation with Iran and its appointment of a permanent representative for the movement in Tehran.

Unlike the PLO, Hamas does not posses a complicated or extensive bureaucracy. Therefore, its financial responsibilities are less than those of the PLO. It also known that Hamas style of spending is simple and far from being extravagant or corrupt. Hamas popularity among the Palestinians of the Occupied Territories cannot be attributed to the movement's financial capabilities, since those potentialities cannot be compared to the relatively huge resources the PLO musters and the organisation's extensive financial penetration of the Palestinian society.

The political gains accrued as a result of participating in the *intifada* and the footing of Hamas have been an eye-opener, especially for the Muslim Brotherhood in the Occupied Territories. The society has realised that it did not require much to establish itself as a strong contender and rival to the PLO and as a source of trouble to the Israeli occupation. It is true that the leaders and followers of the Islamic movement have been subjected to incarceration, death, and other forms of punishment from the Israeli authorities but considering the political gains achieved, this price can be tolerated. The Muslim Brotherhood has overcome fear vis-à-vis Israel and has emerged as a major challenger to the PLO. With Hamas in the forefront, the Brotherhood could achieve, in less than four years, the kind of plausibility, popularity and legitimacy the PLO has earned over two decades. Through its participation in the *intifada* and the sacrifices that participation entailed the Muslim Brotherhood, together with the Islamic *Jihad*, have setup a record of Islamic resistance that can be claimed and drawn upon, and have built a tradition that can be used as a source of inspiration for future generations.

Eleven

Arab and Islamic Terrorism

Place names often strike a resonance, create images, form expectations. Sallynoggin, a part of Greater Dublin, for examples, seems to be such a name — a romantic and intriguing Irish name, suggesting at the least an attractive old Dublin community with pubs and old shop fronts, full of 'characters' who entertain with quick witticism and jokes over a Guinness in the bar. The reality of Sallynoggin is, albeit, very different. It is an area of low price and public housing to the South of Dublin.

In a quiet close in an area of run down council property live a family of mother and daughter. Their lower maisonette is of undistinguished appearance, poorly maintained, with red paint peeling from the window frames. Its front door is battered, and the garden neglected. This is not a particularly bad house to live in, and many single parents live in similar or worse conditions. The mother is pretty; dark-haired, sunburnt with freckles, but not very well dressed. But neither she nor her daughter are ordinary. Their story captured the world's headlines, and takes us to the very heart of one of the most thrilling ever terrorist exploits.

Ann-Marie Murphy and her daughter Caoimhe lived with the appalling knowledge that Caoimhe's father deliberately conspired to kill them both with a bomb which Ann, unknowingly, attempted to carry on board an aircraft whilst she was pregnant. In her words: 'I was so in love with him. I'd never had a boyfriend before and when he said he loved me I believed him. Her boyfriend, the father of Caoimhe, and the man who attempted to kill Ann-Marie Murphy, his unborn daughter and some 375 passengers of an El Al Jumbo Jet was Nezar Hindawi.

A Family Plot

Nezar Hindawi was born in 1954, the son of a Jordanian family who had been forced to flee to Jordan from a relatively prosperous farm during the troubles that accompanied the formation of the State of Israel. The family was regarded as once being prosperous, having moved in 1922 to the Trans-Jordan from Libya. Their social status appears to have remained high, and indeed in the 1960s and 70s, two uncles were members of the Jordanian Cabinet.

Whilst Hindawi's mother, some brothers and sisters continued to live in Jordan, one brother and his father eventually moved to the United Kingdom, where they built up permanent residence. When he was 26, Nezar visited England. He enrolled on various English language courses in London, and even became the London correspondent for a number of Arab journals. Whilst attending English language classes in Kensington in 1980, he met and later married in December, Barbara, the daughter of a Polish farmer, who was also attending the language classes. After a brief stay in London, they left for Poland, where Natasha, their daughter, was born in 1981. It seems that Nezar continued this relationship. Interviewed once in 1986, Barbara claimed that her relationship with Hindawi had continued, but that Hindawi would disappear for long periods on his journalistic assignments, returning all of a sudden and often without warning.

The fateful first meeting between Ann-Marie Murphy and Nezar Hindawi happened in late 1984. Ann-Marie Murphy was 29 when she first arrived in London from Dublin in October 1984. She lived with a friend, Theresa Leonard in Earls Court, and managed a job as a chamber maid at the London Hilton Hotel. Ann-Marie was introduced to Nezar Hindawi by Theresa, who was friendly with a Jordanian who shared a flat with him. Nezar was narrated by people who knew him at that time as an arrogant and flamboyant man, who enjoyed good living. For a girl like Ann-Marie Murphy, whose experience of life extended hardly beyond the factory in Dublin where she had worked, Hindawi must appeared as a dashing and irresistible figure. Her brief relationship with him lasted until Christmas, 1984, when Hindawi abruptly disappeared. By this time, Ann-Marie was pregnant, but by the time Hindawi re-appeared in February 1985, she had miscarried. He seems to have had proposed marriage to her around this time, telling her that he was divorcing his wife in Poland. He also seemingly asked her if she could put him in touch with the Provisional IRA for what he described as a journalistic interview. In the light of what we now know of Hindawi's activities at that time, this may be a revealing insight into his thinking. During this period, Hindawi was frequently absent, but shortly after he re-appeared from a long absence in November, Ann-Marie found she was pregnant again.

On the other hand, Nezar seemed to have been anxious to make the arrangements for marriage as quickly as possible. To Ann-Marie it must have seemed that her troubles were over. But her naivety seemed with hindsight alarming — she seemed to have given little thought to the practical issues involved, and Nezar seems to have given her little encouragement to explore them. This offer of marriage took place in April 1986.

We now know from immigration stamps in Hindawi's Jordanian passport which we found in his brother's flat after his arrest, that during the period 1985 and 1986 Nezar Hindawi undertook long journeys across Europe and the Middle East, visiting Poland (where his wife and daughter lived), East and West Berlin, Egypt, Syria, Italy, Bulgaria, and Rumania. It seems that these journeys were related to Hindawi's attempts, with his brother Hasi, to generate support and funding for terrorist attacks on Israel.

Amongst other places, this effort to garner support took the brothers to Libya in late 1985, using the contacts with the Libyans that Hindawi had already established in London. They received some ideological instruction, but their apparent inexperience seems to have had deterred the Libyan authorities from trusting them, and all they received was a very modest handout of US$5000, with no particular mission but a suggestion that they return when they had proved themselves.

The organisation that Nezar Hindawi claimed to represent was the Jordanian Revolutionary Movement. It seems that this organisation was established by Nezar, his brother Hasi and Farouk Salameh, during discussions in Hasi's Berlin flat in March 1985.

Nezar's cousin, Awni, was also probably involved. Nezar seems to have claimed before them that he was already a member of a terrorist organisation, and also seems to have had used his modest relationship as an informer with the Libyans in London to support this claim and impress Hasi and Farouk. Both Hasi and Farouk had previous criminal records, but no known substantial terrorist associations, and they appear to have believed that Nezar was mobilising them into what they thought was the well established Jordanian Revolutionary Movement. There is no independent evidence that this organisation had existed outside Nezar's imagination and it seems likely that Nezar, up to this time, had operated only on the fringes of Arab terrorism. The first target Hasi and Farouk were 'recruited' to attack was the German-Arab Friendship Society in Berlin. Nezar was confirmed that this organisation was thoroughly infiltrated by Israeli agents. It seems to have been this plan to attack the German-Arab Friendship Society that Hindawi had proposed to the Libyan authorities, and later more productively to Damascus.

In November, the same year, Hasi Hindawi and Farouk Salameh were both tried and convicted in a West Berlin court for his bomb attack. Hasi was given a 14 years prison sentence, while Salameh received 13 years. The court also issued a worldwide arrest warrant for a man described as a Syrian military intelligence officer, Colonel Haitham Said, who had brought the bomb into West Germany from Syria. Both Hasi and Salameh confessed to the attack, and they implicated Said as the Syrian agent responsible for the provision of the bomb. They also implicated Nezar Hindawi as the man who both masterminded and organised the attack.

The creation and initiation of the Jordanian Revolutionary Movement through the bombing of the German-Arab Friendship Society, all coincide with the time of Ann-Marie Murphy's second pregnancy and Nezar's offer of marriage to her. Given Nezar's central role in the bombing attack in Berlin, as events unfolded after the bombing of the German-Arab Friendship Society it becomes increasingly difficult not to perceive a malign and cynical manipulation of Ann-Marie Murphy into Nezar Hindawi's terrorist plans. In particular, Nezar Hindawi's hurried plans to marry Ann-Marie in '*the Holy Land* assumed new and dreadful significance, suggesting a degree of forethought and sceptical manipulation of Ann-Marie.

Bomb Explosion in Berlin

We now know that in February, before the bomb successfully exploded in Berlin, Nezar Hindawi had made a further visit to Damascus to meet Colonel Said, this time accompanied by his cousin. Awni is thought to have had existing links with the terrorist outfit of Abu Nidal, but although he was arrested on several occasions by the Italian authorities in 1986 and 1987, he was never charged with terrorist offences. What does appear clear, however, is that he had contact with a number of prominent Syrian officials and others with connections to terrorist organisations. This visit to Damascus appears to have concerned Nezar's plan to bomb an El Al aircraft, using Ann-Marie Murphy as his unwitting associate to place the bomb on board in a bag. It seems likely that the target selection, and possibly the means of passing the bomb on to the aircraft, were settled by the Syrians; in any event, the target was confirmed at this meeting, and Nezar was shown the sophisticated timing device and the bomb, located in the false bottom of a bag, which was planned to destroy the aircraft.

At this time, Nezar was also given by Said a fake Syrian passport which he used to return to the United Kingdom. This passport had in it a legitimate visitor's visa to the UK issued by the British Embassy in Damascus on 11 February. Using this passport, Nezar travelled to London. On arrival at Heathrow, Nezar Hindawi, as Izzam Shara, was passed through immigration and was also given a stamp in the passport authorising him to stay in the United Kingdom for six months. The value of this passport to Hindawi was that it was assumed that he would use it to escape from the country after the bomb had been placed on the El Al aircraft, given that his real identity might become compromised in the following investigations. Soon after his return, Nezar Hindawi made a practice run to collect the aircraft bomb in London.

Nezar made a second trip to Syria from London and apparently received further training in the priming and use of the bag bomb. This training reportedly took place in the Bekaa Valley in Lebanon, and was conducted by three Syrian security officials, including Said. In particular, he was instructed how the priming device for the bomb was located in a pocket calculator, which was activated by the insertion of the calculator batteries. The bomb arrangement was innovative and creative; the detonator and timer disguised by the calculator were located in the body of the bag, whilst the explosives were hidden in the bag's false bottom. The detonator needed only to be placed near the main charge to result in an explosion. This made detection of the bomb by airport X-ray machines much more difficult. Raw explosive is hard to detect on X-ray and may not even be discovered in security screening, but the tell-tale wires and batteries of the detonator are the usual sign of the presence of a bomb.

As events subsequently developed, major weaknesses in the way the British Embassy worked in Damascus emanated, particularly in the management and control of the issuing of visas. It seems likely that the processing of the visa applications for the passport in the name of Izzam Shara was welcomed by a member of the Embassy's local staff who was himself a Syrian Agent. He seems to have had manipulated procedures to avoid the kind of cross-checking which might have been expected to take place. After Nezar's planned arrest, this member of the Embassy staff disappeared, taking with him records which included the visa applications and also accompanying photographs for Izzam Shara. He also took a number of other records which presumably relate to people who have received visas to the United Kingdom on fake passports.

Nezar's second visit to Syria ended on 5 April, when he returned to London. On his arrival, he booked into the Royal Garden Hotel with Colonel Said's brother, Ghassim Said. Both impersonated as crew members of Syrian Arab Airlines. The following day, 6 April, Nezar was met by another Syrian agent, Adnam Habib, who gave him the bag containing the concealed explosives and the calculator detonator. The bag contained about three and a half pounds of Semtex explosive.

At the time Nezar Hindawi was engaged in the development of his planned attack using Ann-Marie Murphy, there was a second terrorist strike in Berlin which may also have had links to Hasi Hindawi. On 5 April 1986, a bomb was detonated in the La Belle discotheque in West Berlin which killed a US serviceman and a Turkish woman, and injured some 230 people. Incriminating documents were eventually found in Hasi's flat when searched by the police, and there were similarities to the other bombs used by the Hindawi's, in terms of the types of explosives used. Hasi, however, denies involvement in this bombing.

Ann-Marie Murphy had no knowledge of all of these events. After he returned from Damascus, Nezar Hindawi suddenly re-appeared in Ann-Marie's life, and not only proposed to marry her but that he should do so immediately, and that the marriage and honeymoon should take place in Israel. Ann-Marie ultimately agreed to travel to her wedding in Israel on her own, as Nezar already had a ticket to Jordan because of his journalistic assignments.

Ann-Marie Murphy started to plan her pregnancy and her marriage in Israel to Nezar Hindawi in the short time she had left before her departure. He gave me £100 to go and buy a wedding dress and he wanted me to wear black shoes and black tights. I went to a chain store first but I couldn't find anything. Then I saw this dress in another shop. It was perfect. It was pale blue silky with a drop waist....I was really excited. I thought it was beautiful.

'My passport had run out so I had to go and get another one. I remember it was the same day that I had first seen my baby on a scan at the hospital. '....He gave me another £100 to buy some more dresses and underwear and then he came with a new bag for me. I remember being a bit puzzled about him buying a new one because I had a suitcase already — but he insisted. He wanted to pack it for me so that I wouldn't have to keep bending down and I was pleased he cared. He insisted so I let him. He packed the bag and told me not to touch it or go near it.

'He didn't stay with me that night — our last night in London. I was a bit surprised but he said he had to see someone and would stay in a hotel.

'When he came for me the next morning I was ready. I'd decided to wear my wedding dress so I'd look nice for his family when I arrived. He'd told me he wouldn't be able to travel with me because he had to go to Jordan to do something for the newspaper he worked for as a journalist. Nezar insisted on carrying the bag downstairs to the taxi because he thought it would be too heavy. And he'd bought me a little set of wheels so I wouldn't have to carry it at the airport.

'When we were in the taxi he seemed a bit nervous. He was smoking and it made me feel sick. But I didn't want to say anything to spoil the day. He took out a calculator which he said he'd had repaired for a friend of his over there and I was to take it with me. He put batteries in and placed it back in the bag, I think towards the bottom.'

Unknown to Ann-Marie, but well known by Nezar, by putting the batteries into the calculator he had set the timer on the detonator. It was scheduled to explode exactly 5 hours, 1 minute and 1 second later, triggering the explosives hidden in the fake bottom of the bag, by which time, if everything had gone to plan, Ann-Marie's flight, El Al 016 on 17 April, should have been at its cruising height of 39,000 feet somewhere over Southern Europe. The impact of an explosion at such a height would have been similar in its effect to that which destroyed Pan Am flight 103 over Lockerbie in Scotland in December 1988. The 375 passengers on board El Al flight 016, including Ann-Marie Murphy and her unborn child, would have been killed.

'Then we got to the airport and he put the bag on a trolley. I wanted to go to the toilet and he was annoyed. I asked someone where the Ladies' was. It was just at the top of the escalator. I said I would only be a minute but when I suddenly turned round on the stairs he was right behind me carrying the bag. I thought he was being really nice and attentive.

'When I came out we got onto one of those moving walkways and Nezar was in front of me. When we got to the end of the walkway, he kissed me on both cheeks and said "Good Bye."

'But after he left me, I realised I was in the wrong place....I didn't want to take the bag with me on the place - I wanted to put it through the luggage desk. But I went by accident through the place where you show your passports and put the bag on the security belt thing. It went right through all right but then I had to go to the El Al Security desk.'

El Al security staff decided to subject the luggage to a thorough search. It seems likely that they were in a sublime state of alertness at this time as a result of a warning they had received of an attempt to blow up an El Al civilian aircraft. All the contents of the bag were removed in her presence, including the calculator, but nothing sceptical was found. A member of the El Al staff even made a simple calculation on the calculator to check that it worked, which it did. It was only when a member of staff picked up the bag to repack it that he felt it was unusually heavy for an empty piece of baggage. The bag was then taken to a nearby office, and was taken apart. Underneath the interior cardboard base a flat blue plastic package measuring 16 inches by 9 inches by 3/8 inch which was shaped to the contours of the bag. On unravelling, this proved to be 3 lbs 4 oz of the Czech made high explosive Semtex. Initially, the find created some surprise to the Security Officers because there were no detonators attached to the explosives. The role of the calculator as the timer and detonator was ultimately discovered by the bomb disposal expert called to the scene. Ann-Marie was detained by Heathrow police, and subsequently handed over to Anti-Terrorist squad police officers. It was very soon established that she was the innocent dupe of Nezar Hindawi.

'The man looked in my bag then took it away. I waited about 20 to 30 minutes, then he came and took me to a room. Two British policemen with guns and tracker dogs came in. I kept thinking "Oh my God what is it?" then one of them showed me a brown taped parcel and asked if I knew what it was. I said I'd never seen it before. I was sobbing. One of them told me the parcel contained....explosive. My world fell apart.

'I thought: "Oh my god, he wanted to kill me and the baby. He wanted to get rid of us."

'It didn't enter my head at that time that all those other people would have died. The officers took me to another room and told me to take everything off. It was terrible, awful...They cut a piece of my hair and scraped under my nails. They gave me a white paper boiler suit to put on. Then they handcuffed me and led me through Heathrow to a police car and took me to Paddington Green Police Station.

'They put me in a cell and kept asking what I knew about politics and where I'd met Nezar ...I'll never get over what he tried to do.'

Whilst this was happening to Ann-Marie, Nezar Hindawi following a pre-defined plan, returned to the Palace Hotel, collected his luggage and went back to the Royal Garden Hotel to get a lift back to Heathrow with Syrian aircrew in order to catch the 1400 hours Syrian Arab Airline flight to Damascus. But shortly after 0900 hours, the discovery of the bomb was made public through the media, and a person called Mohammed Raja Zidan, a Syrian agent, who was travelling with the aircrew, gave Nezar an unaddressed envelop and asked him to go straight to the Syrian Embassy at 8 Belgrave Square.

When he arrived at Embassy, Nezar presented the letter, and was greeted by a Syrian diplomat. He later was more formally and warmly received by the Syrian ambassador, who in Nezar's presence telephoned Damascus to know about further developments. The Ambassador told Nezar that Damascus was very pleased with his actions, but that it had been decided to hide him in a safe place in England for a few days, before helping him to leave the country. Nezar was then given over to the charge of two Syrian Embassy diplomats, Mounir Mouna and Ahmed Abdul Latif, who took Nezar to Mouna's flat at 19 Stonor Road, West Kensington. Whilst in the flat, Nezar's hair was cut and dyed.

At around 05.30 hours on the next morning, Mouna and another man, Zaki Oud, arrived at the flat, and told Nezar that he was to be taken away back to the Syrian Embassy. Nezar became suspicious of this, and declined to go. Oud then attempted to force Nezar into the car, but after a brief scuffle, Nezar broke free and ran away. Nezar's suspicions appear to be well founded, and it seems likely that he was being taken on orders from Damascus to be killed. He roamed around Kensington for a while, and eventually went to the Visitors Hotel which lies between Notting Hill and Earls Court. This hotel was owned by a Jordanian whom Nezar knew, Niam Al-Oran.

By this time, Nezar's role in the attempted bombing was well understood by the police and his picture had appeared on television as well as in the press. As part of their investigation, the police had also sought the intervention of Nezar's family to capture him. The staff of the Visitors Hotel smelt danger when Nezar tried to book in using a Syrian passport in the name of Izzam Shara and the hotel manager telephoned the owner. Al-Oran perceived this must be Hindawi, and in turn contacted Nezar's brother Mahmood; who had already been approached by the police. Both Al-Oran and Mahmood rushed to the hotel and tried to persuade Nezar that he should surrender himself to the police, promising him that they would seek assurances from the British police that they would not hand Nezar to Mossad, the Israeli security service. Ultimately, he was arrested at the Visitors hotel, and was taken into custody. He made no attempt to resist arrest, and onlookers reported that he was led unhandcuffed from the hotel to a waiting police car.

'I was so in love with him. I had never had a boy friend before and when he said he loved me I believed him.' There is little doubt that Ann-Marie Murphy was innocent of any involvement in Nezar Hindawi's calculative attempt to blow up the El Al aircraft on 17 April. Ann-Marie Murphy had been used in a way which was almost unimaginably evil and barbaric, and the inescapable conclusion is that she was an innocent abroad in a world which she simply did not understand. This combined with her openness and naivety, and perhaps her anxiety and despair on finding herself pregnant again and the release Nezar Hindawi appeared to offer her through marriage, allowed her to be utilised in a plot involving herself and her unborn child as a human time bomb.

At his trial, Nezar Hindawi showed no self-reproach or remorse at what he had done. During the trial, when Ann-Marie was giving evidence, she broke down in the witness box and shouted across the court at him 'You bastard you. How could you do this to me. I hate you, I hate you....' Throughout Ann-Marie's outburst, as in most of the trial, Hindawi remained impassive, showing no emotion. After the jury returned a verdict of guilty, he was sentenced to 45 years imprisonment.

The Hindawi trial brought to the light what must be one of the most callous acts of attempted terrorism ever undertaken. Given the general ruthlessness of terrorist behaviour, this is a quite significant comment. It is not clear, however, whether Nezar Hindawi's terrorist career was confined to the series of events described above, or whether it went further. Some comments at his trial indicated that he had a broader background in terrorism than emerged at the trial, and there was some press speculation of links with a range of Arab and European terrorist outfits, including the Red Brigades and even the Provisional IRA. Certainly his family involvement enabled contact with a range of terrorist outfits, and it seems, in particular, that his cousin Awni was a significant point of contact, if not anything more. Hindawi's acknowledgement of the importance of Awni's role can be seen in a letter published in the British Press and reproduced below which was smuggled out of Brixton prison, written by Hindawi to Awni during the trial.

Dear Brother, many greetings, it is time to act. This is your time. I write to you hoping you won't disappoint me.

Go to Damascus and talk to brother Abu and Ahmed-Haithan of the following: Ahmed Gebril has two Israeli prisoners. Haithan has his word. Thatcher will be visiting Israel next Saturday. He has two Israeli prisoners. Abu has their word as well.

A prisoner exchange should be organised which must include my brother Hasi. If necessary this can be accomplished in Thatcher's visit. Tell Haithan if necessary to include some foreigners from Beirut in the exchange. Have them give you 15,000 Deutschmarks for my brother's lawyer and the same amount for my family.

You are authorised to study any solution. Time is running out quickly.'

This letter was intercepted before reaching Awni, but it seems clear that Nezar saw Awni as someone with contacts that could prove helpful for him. Clues to these contacts can be seen from the world in which Awni Hindawi lived. Awni lived in Genoa, which at that time was a major base for Arab and Palestinian terrorism. There seem to have been two major Palestinian factions operating Genoa, one centred on Abu Abbas, the other related to a splinter group from George Habash's Popular Front for the Liberation of Palestine', the 'Abu Ibrahim' faction. It appears likely that the Hindawi's were associated with this latter grouping. A member of the Abu Ibrahim faction arrested at around the same time (but for reasons unrelated to Hindawi's) was considered to also have close links with Abu Nidal's 30th June Group', for whom he acted as an arms supplier for strikes in Europe. Specifically, this person has been implicated as the supplier of arms for attacks in Italy. These links give a fresh connection with Syria. Awni was known to have been in contact with someone close to the Abu Nidal group that carried out the Fiumicino attack in Italy in 1985.

Suspicions regarding Awni appeared to be confirmed when Nezar's letter to him was intercepted as it was being smuggled out of Brixton Prison in London. This letter suggests a prisoner exchange, drawing on two captives held by Ahmed Jibril and on two other captives held by someone else of importance. Of some implications, omitted from the translation above, is the sentence "You have the capacity to do all this and your word will carry weight with the others.' The Italian police arrested Awni, but later released him because of lack of evidence. Awni was subsequently re-arrested twice in 1987 on charges related to involvement with terrorism, but released later on both occasions. The conditions of his release required him to report to the Carabiniere twice a week, but in June 1987 just as a decision regarding his future liberty was to be taken, he got on a flight from Genoa to Rome and, despite the fact that his passport was not valid for leaving Italy, he did so. It is only possible to guess about the role Nezar Hindawi might have played with Awni's contacts.

A Top Notch Terrorist?

Whilst the precise details of the Hindawi family's involvement with terrorism might be ambiguous, the events surrounding Nezar Hindawi do show us how terrorist networks can be formed, especially within the Arab or Palestinian context. Under the impetus of an initiator, a small faction is formed which is relatively isolated from other similar groups, but connected to a central 'core' of terrorism through the initiator. A remarkable strength of the group often lies in clan, family or long standing friendship. Close ties of this kind both bind people together, intensifying a sense of loyalty, and also protect against the insertion of informers. Such groups present themselves to embassies seeking sponsorship, and through the diplomatic intelligence connections of an embassy which is attracted to what they can offer, the group finds itself related to the mainstream of what is essentially State sponsored terrorism. The group may be used for courier work, information gathering, or action, but it may also be allowed to 'sleep' until the proper opportunity comes along. Such groups may even be 'traded' between friendly embassies as needs for political violence break out or change. The Hindawi's were attractive to the Syrians because they were urbane and westernised, and had roots in Western countries that facilitated their residence there. They also came along at a time when the Syrians were actively seeking a medium of retribution against the Israelis, after the Israeli Air Force had intercepted a Libyan executive jet in February 1986 and force landed it at Tel Aviv airport. The jet was en route from Tripoli to Damascus, and was thought by the Israelis to check Dr. George Habash, leader of the Popular Front for the Liberation of Palestine. Instead, travelling the plane was Mr. Abdullah Ahmar, Assistant Secretary-General of Syria's ruling Ba'ath Socialist Party, who was arguably the most important person in the Syrian Government hierarchy after President Assad. This was taken by the Syrians as a great affront, and demands for retribution against the Israelis were vociferously made.

But was Nezar Hindawi a 'top grade terrorist' as was stated at his trial? He certainly had links with high-ups in the Palestinian terrorist world, and his actions and those of his family placed large numbers of people at risk. He acquired noticeable support from a major sponsor of State terrorism, Syria, whose officials undoubtedly provided the inspiration, guidance and material aid for both Hasi's and Nezar's terrorist activities.

But Hindawi's behaviour does not seem to be that of a cool calculating top notch activist. He certainly had little regard for his victims, as evidenced by his treatment of Ann-Marie Murphy and his unborn daughter. But his actions do not give the impression of a man commanding an outfit that followed his plan or strategy. He appears to have had worked to a script devised for him which gave little room for improvisation, and when things had started going wrong, he showed little ability to take charge of events himself and effect his escape. Indeed, he seems to have made a number of rash decisions that led him back to familiar locations and people, which inevitably made him accessible to the police. His flight to the Syrian Embassy betrays an unprecedented measure of naivety and seems at best to have been an ill-judged feedback from the point of view of his own safety. Subsequent events early in the morning of 18 April may well have had confirmed this. From the perspective of his Syrian supporters, as things had started to go wrong, Hindawi must have appeared to be a major liability, leading them into a diplomatic crises of major proportions.

The weaknesses exposed by Nezar seem to have been shared by Hasi Hindawi, who also showed little capacity for 'creative' terrorism. Both seemed to have had a limited capacity to endure interrogation. Indeed, only Awni seems to have shown much talent for escape from justice, but there is, in any case, no public evidence directly relating him to any specific acts of violence. Reports at the time emphasised Nezar's mercenary motivations, rather than political, and this seems to be much more in accord with his behaviour, despite his conspicuous hatred of Israel. People who knew him in London give the impression of an avaricious, boastful and deceitful man. Despite his apparent certainty and confidence that a deal would be done to arrange his early release, so far he remains imprisoned, emotionally volatile and showing a degree of deep suspicion of those around him, verging on the paranoid.

Yet Nezar Hindawi kept returning to the surface of public consciousness. In 1992, he claimed that the British Government had failed to keep promise on a deal to release him and three others in return for the release of Terry Waite and other hostages held in Lebanon.

As an act of terrorism, what Nezar Hindawi did was not specifically unique. Other terrorist outfits have from time to time deliberately used people as 'human bombs', creating conditions in which the person carrying the bomb would almost undoubtedly be killed as the bomb reached its target. The Provisional IRA, for example, have from time to time used this tactic. Vehicles and drivers had been hijacked, and with the driver tied into the vehicle carrying a remote-controlled bomb, the driver has been ordered to drive to some sensitive location, where the bomb has been detonated. Ironically, given the circumstances of the Hindawi affair, the Syrians were the target of identical attacks by Christian Militia Forces in Lebanon. In November 1987, a young woman was used to carry a booby-trapped suitcase bomb into Beirut

Airport, which was then controlled by the Syrians. The suitcase blew up just inside the main terminal, killing her on the spot. At about the same time of the day, another woman carrying a booby-trapped box of chocolates was killed just inside the American University of Beirut. Reports at the time suggest that both young women were drugged, although that would be baffling to establish in the circumstances. In a similar incident in 1982, the influence of drugs can be more authentically established. A young woman, under the influence of drugs parked a car filled with powerful explosives in an underground car park beneath the Ministry of Information in West Beirut; but she was nabbed and the bomb was also defused.

What is unusual in the case of Nezar Hindawi is not so much about the use of a woman to carry a bomb, but the abuse of what Ann-Marie Murphy thought was a personal relationship to deceive her into carrying it. His contemptuous use of Ann-Marie from his own perspective and that of his Syrian paymasters had many positive aspects. Women are often used by terrorist outfits to move bombs, or gun parts around. They are frequently (but wrongly) seen as non-threatening, and able therefore to carry weapons more readily; they tend to arouse less suspicion when entering shops for example. Women accompanied by children, or pushing prams, or pregnant, are often perceived by police officers or soldiers as unlikely assassins, and are therefore even more attractive in their capacity to smuggle explosives. Experience in Northern Ireland, for instance, shows how misplaced is this view. From the point of view of delivering a bomb, a pregnant woman offers many attractions. Even more attractive is someone who does not know they are doing so, and who when the event breaks out, will be killed, thereby effectively destroying any evidence that might lead to the terrorist. Regrettably, Ann-Marie Murphy met all of these conditions.

Terrorism and Al-Jihad

Nezar Hindawi attacked a target that was tempting to Arab and Palestinian terrorists. He himself was an Arab, and there is no doubt that Syrian funding of his activities were related to broader Syrian efforts to attack and sabotage the State of Israel, whatever the immediate context of Hindawi's actions might have been. In the public imagination, his attempted bombing of the El Al aircraft probably embodies many of the qualities of Islamic and Arab terrorism. It fits into other radical and extreme forms of terrorism that have had been associated with Islam, such as the suicide bombings of American and French forces in the Lebanon in 1985 and 1986. Like the instigators of those attacks, Hindawi displayed an extreme lack of regard for human life, and like them showed a determination to attain the target regardless of the fallouts.

But Hindawi's actions strike little sympathy with Islamic extremists, and they show minimum regard for what he did. What he did to Ann-Marie Murphy is not typical of Islamic political violence, and many Islamic activists find the moral foundation of Hindawi's actions offensive.

'We value human life, as the Prophet taught us....Relationships matter in Islam, and knowledge and choice in what we do are gifts from Allah to his people. Death in *Jihad* is appropriate, even necessary, but not in this way....'

'His actions desecrate the name of Islam. Yes, we have a philosophy of confrontation...it is a political and Islamic analysis....it gives us an Islamic base to confront the secular government....political violence is a reaction. We are committed...to the benefit of our religion...'

Over the past few years, Cairo seems to have had changed very little, at least at a superficial level. The traffic is as bad as ever, the fumes and smoke and dust as prevalent as ever. In poorer parts of the City, like Imbaba, the degree of poverty is as striking as ever, and the contrasts between rich and poor remain as striking as ever; but above all, it is the sheer press of people that strikes the Western visitor. The bustle and movement of people in the *souks* seems to come from an apparently endless flow of people, and even away from the primary areas, people are everywhere. This weight of people serves to emphasise the fact that Cairo remains the nucleus of the Islamic world in the Middle East. It is still the largest and most populous city in the Arab world, and Egypt continues to provide the impetus that mould the Arab thinking.

But there are changes in the city. Disorganised and complex

as it is, there is a discernible change in the moral and political milieu affecting the lives of its people. This change relates more than anything to the growing influence of Islam, and perhaps the most significant visible indicator of that is the growing number women wearing Islamic style dresses and head dress. Whilst the majority of the population of Cairo adhere to Islam, its observance has always been less than strict. Cairo has always been considered a city where the influence of the West was apparent, but the modernisation of Egypt in the 1950s and 60's seemed to accelerate the degree of Western influence to a much greater extent than ever before. The middle classes had greater access to wealth, and the influence of Western industry, foreign travel and foreign media seemed to be producing far-reaching changes in Egyptian society.

Clear indications that this process of Westernisation was neither inexorable nor particularly welcomed by significant sections of the Egyptian community were seen in October, 1981, when President Sadat was assassinated by a group of army officers. The group that assassinated Sadat, known as *al-Jihad* (sacred combat), were hardly known at the time, and the Egyptian security services initially made determined efforts to ensure that little emerged of the group's political and ideological agenda. But it is quite apparent that the conspirators were motivated chiefly by a kind of belief in Islam that reflected a major strand of contemporary Islamic thinking. The assassins of Sadat were undoubtedly Egyptian nationalists in one sense, concerned about the present-day state of Egypt; but their concern was drawn from a broader Islamic perspective which offered a critique of the evils of modern society not only as they occurred in Egypt, but throughout the entire Islamic world.

We know something of the beliefs of the *al-Jihad* Group, however, from the work of the chief ideologue of the outfit, Mohammed Abd al-Salam Faraj, who produced a pamphlet describing the aims and objectives of the group. Faraj was executed, along with four of the key plotters of the assassination of Sadat on 15 April 1982, but his work, *The Neglected Duty* (*Al-Faridah al-Gha'ibah*), survived him. In the West, these people are described as 'fundamentalists', but as in the case of the term 'terrorism', people are often confused and unclear about what they mean. A clearer understanding of the aspirations of organisations such as *al-Jihad* as Islamic fundamentalists will help us understand better what is often seen in the contemporary world as one of the major sources of political violence, and which presents itself as a threat to the West.

The assassination of Anwar Sadat was in one sense a failure as far as *al-Jihad* Group was concerned. It did not prompt a mass agitation nor a return to the *Shari'a* (Islamic law), and the Egyptian State has continued along broadly similar paths under the present leadership. On the other hand, there have had been conspicuous concessions towards Islamic thinking in the area of criminal justice, and perhaps more importantly, there had been a discernible shift in the Egyptian public's view on the implementation of the Shari'a and the general processes of Islamisation. Empirical testimony on this is difficult to find, but in 1985, the Egyptian National Centre for Social and Criminal Research conducted a survey on public views on the implementation of Islamic law. This showed very large percentages of respondents (in excess of 95 per cent) to be in favour of '....the implementation of Moslem law (*al Shari'a*) vis-à-vis crimes against the bounds set by Allah (adultery, false accusation, drinking alcohol, theft, brigandage, apostasy)'.

However, when the respondents are broken down by religion, some 33 per cent of Christians included in the survey expressed dissent at the implementation of Shari'a. As can be seen in Sudan where the process of Islamisation has made considerably more progress than in Egypt, the position of a dissenting Christian minority ominously deteriorating as Islamisation progresses, and is a source of major social strains.

Those four members of *al-Jihad* directly involved in the assassination of Anwar Sadat, in addition to it Mohammed Abd al-Salam Faraj, were eventually executed. In retrospect, none of them appear to have been politically sophisticated. Khalid al-Islambuli was the leader of the assassination team, and he appeared to have had made the decision to assassinate Sadat. He was a lieutenant in the Egyptian Army artillery, and was 24 years old at the time of the assassination. Khalid appears to have had planned the attack. He had been placed in command of an armoured transport vehicle which was set to take part in a military parade reviewed by Sadat to commemorate the eighth anniversary of the launching of the October War against Israel. In the middle of the parade, in full view of television cameras, the four conspirators left their vehicle in front of the reviewing stand, and sprayed bullets indiscriminately.

But the execution of the assassins did not end the *al-Jihad* outfit. The group continued in Egypt, but took two different forms. One group continued under the leadership of the mufti of the original group, Sheik Umar Abd al-Rahman. The other faction continued under the leadership of one of the original intrigues who escaped the death sentence, but remained in prison, Colonel Abbud al-Zumur.

Sheik Umar Abd al-Rahmad was a blind professor in the Azhar Faculty in Asyut. He had long established contacts with radical Islamic groups in Egypt, and had developed his own distinctive following amongst Islamic students. He could aptly be described as a fundamentalist in the sense used here, in that he translated into behaviour the ideological and theological priorities of Islam as he understood them. After the assassination of Sadat, Sheik Umar Abd al-Rahman left Cairo and moved to the United States, where he established himself and a small group of followers in New York. He continued to develop the fanatical and violent agenda described by Faraj, and it was his group that was probably responsible for the attack on the World Trade Centre in New York in 1992.

The group that continued around Colonel Abbud al-Zamur are probably the more marked inheritors of Faraj in terms of political sophistication and opportunity to influence the Islamic movement. In particular, Abbud al-Zumur seems to have had a political stature that distinguishes him from other fanatical fundamentalist leaders. Whilst Abbud was involved in the discussions with Khalid al-Islambuli about the attack on Sadat, he seems to have had considerable reservations about the effectiveness of the assassination, in terms of the preparedness of the organisation to mobilise and endure a general uprising. Abbud was 35 at the time of the assassination, and showed a much more mature approach to the political analysis of their actions. There is no doubting Abbuds' Islamic fervour, but his realistic recognition of the realities of revolution place him in a different category to the other conspirators.

Whilst Abbud al-Zamur had remained in prison since the assassination of Sadat, a group of radicals had had emerged around him. This group, adopting the name of Islamic *Jihad*, seems to represent a significant element in the current terrorist violence in Egypt aimed at both the Egyptian Government and at Westernising influences, for instance, tourism.

'...political violence is a reaction. It is not an action against some other incident ... Abbud al-Zumur and his followers are committed to debate for the good of the country, and to prevent bloody violence. But oppression is the main policy of the (Egyptian) Government. These violent actions are a reaction.

These are the words of an Islamic activist and leader of the *al-Jihad* outfit in Cairo who is closely connected to Abbud al-Zumur. We met on a number of occasions, in Cairo and elsewhere. For many hours, we discussed, in a detailed manner, the issue of terrorism and political violence within the Islamic movement in Egypt. For reasons of his own security, it is not appropriate to give any further personal details of him, other than to note that he was relatively young and had been from a professional background. But the abiding impression he gave after long discussion was of integrity and dignity. He, and others like him, are apparently motivated by a cause that they believe in. Their struggle is as much a moral as a political struggle, and they take religion seriously, in the sense that they struggle to put in place in society what their religious beliefs dictate. In this sense they are fundamentalists. But to suggest that their fundamentalism narrows their view of the world is too simplistic. The sincerity with which he expressed his views leaves us impressed, not so much by the views themselves, but by the unassailable strength and confidence of commitment.

'..*al-Jihad* have a military plan, which we will implement when the time is right. We are powerful in the military, we still have the roots of our support there... The military wing are informed by the political structures... We see the organisation from three sides; the military, the political and the media.

'The attacks on tourists are unnecessary. They are carried

out by Umar abd al-Rahman's group ....we reject that, but now we are starting to hit and bomb the Government, not the people, not the tourists. We now confront the police and the Government... we seek a political change that will bring Islam to our country... ours is a continuation of Islamic revolutionary activity, this is how the Islamic revolution continues. We develop our military strategy from the Qu'ran.'

The recent changes in Sudanese society have had a far-reaching effect on the Islamic world, both by way of moral and political example and as a channel through which more significant assistance to Islamic movements can be developed.

'...We do not have any links with the Sudanese. We see them as brothers, but their fight is not our at this moment. Indeed, we believe that the analysis of Turabi (the principal architect of the Sudanese Islamic State) is wrong in important ways... it is not an Egyptian way...

'The Government does not have a mature view of political change... Yes, *al-Jihad* has some problems because of the Government's security actions which depend upon the violation of human rights, on torture ... but we work within the Islamic movement, within Islam... the military courts will pass...'

Islamic *Jihad* perceive their relationship with Umar abd al-Rahman's faction in the United States, but from the following it is quite apparent that they see themselves as having developed a clearer and more sophisticated political and ideological base for their activities.

'The two groups (Umar abd al-Rahman's and Abbud al-Zumur's) grew from one base, from one source. The difference between them concentrated on how to change the social and political government in Egypt. In detailed ideology, there is no difference between them... there is a common thinking in relation to principles, there is complete agreement between the two groups. There are differences in membership of the two groups, and because of these differences they have some differences in implementing their policies... only differences in implementing... It is very hard to prove that Umar abd al-Rahman was responsible for the bombing in the World Trade Centre in New York, but what if he did. It was in my opinion a nonsense and useless act... it lacks the strategic thinking, the broader view of the political situation from the military side...'

In discussions, what appears is a sense of the inevitability of the outcome of achieving an Islamic State, and a sense of desperation in that violence seems now to be the only way in which that could be achieved.

A further document discusses and elaborates on 'The General Principles of our Ideological Programme'. This document, dated 1993, bears several similarities to the discussion by Mohammed Abd al-Salam Faraj in 'The Neglected Duty'. It discusses the need for struggle within the context of the debilitated state of Islam, and the power of Western secularism. It quite clearly and formally establishes the Qur'an and the Sunna as the basis of the programme, offering a logical and compelling (if the assumptions are accepted) account of the inexorability of violent confrontation.

Arab Terrorism and Islamic Political Violence

The discussion in this chapter illustrates two quite opposite aspects of Middle Eastern terrorism. The Islamic movements, of which the *al-Jihad* organisation is an example, belong to a refined and well established tradition. But the violence is not in itself of primary significance to the analysis. It is firmly located within an ideological context that ignores extreme violence both to others and to the activists themselves as a means to a greater achievable but above all necessarily better state. The ready acceptance of martydom by Islamic militants should not be corresponded to the desperation of the suicidal; rather it is the acceptance of the religious logic that necessitates and pardons violence both against others and sometimes against one's self. Words like 'integrity' and 'morality' spring to mind when thinking of the individuals involved.

In psychological expression, this results in extreme control over behaviour by ideology, a control augmented by millenarian influences. There was an intensity about the activist whose account is stated above that conforms to this view. On one occasion whilst with him on a visit to the West, dietary restrictions presented something of a problem in eating out in an environment not suited to cater for Islamic dietary practices. His response to problems -

'Man does not live by food alone, there are other more important sustainers' - was not simply a way of overlooking a potentially embarrassing social problem when food proved to be unacceptable; it properly reflected an approach to life which was in a large measure 'other worldly'. But what is surprising to the cynical Western vista is that this does not occur in any sanctimonious context. The strength of feeling was a natural part of life, which both challenged and enriched it.

This does not appear to be the world of Nezar Hindawi and the Jordanian Revolutionary Movement. The actions of Hindawi gained little sympathy from Islamic activists who used the term 'terrorist' in a pejorative sense to describe his nature. It has to be said, however, that the irony of their use of 'terrorist', when we would undoubtedly also regard them as terrorists, was to a large extent lost on them!

What Hindawi had done seems to have little place within an Islamic analysis, nor does his behaviour conform to that of the Islamic activist. Hindawi used to drink alcohol, he clearly had little regard for Islamic restrictions on sexual behaviour, and seemed to regard his responsibilities towards Ann-Marie Murphy in a very un-Islamic way. At one level, Hindawi was undoubtedly calculating and manipulative, but it appears that this was largely for his own ends, rather than some greater ideological design. Hindawi's actions seem to belong more to the realm of criminal behaviour, rather than political terrorism, although his behaviour was used within a political context. The Islamic activist may well merit the term fanatic, in the sense of an individual stimulated with religious enthusiasm. Such people may well make uncomfortable allies, and they no doubt view the West with suspicion and utter disdain. But however misplaced it may appear, they do have a sense of righteousness which misplaced it may appear, they do have a sense of righteousness which allows a measure of regard. This cannot be said of Nezar Hindawi.

It would be wrong to characterise Palestinian political violence as essentially being like that practised by Hindawi. For many Palestinians, the spartan ideology of nationalism finds many parallels with the Islamic Movement, and indeed there are many areas of common cause between them. The vision of Islam which lies behind the Islamis also lies for many behind the aspiration to a Palestinian State, and this is, of course, highlighted by the historical basis of conflict between Jew and Arab. It seems likely that Hindawi to a large extent, stands aside from the broader Palestinian movement. His marginality in this sense seems reasonable to be confirmed as changes in the relationships between Israel and the Arab States occur.

Twelve

Muslim Brotherhood and Palestine Issue

Brotherhood Strategy toward Palestine

Since the establishment of the state of Israel in 1948, the ideological and theoretical perspective of the Muslim Brotherhood Society toward Palestine has not changed. The society considers all of Palestine to be Muslim land and holds that Israel has no right to exist. The society also believes that no one has the right to relinquish any part of Palestine and considers any political settlement that leaves Israel intact a matter of treason. The Brotherhood rejects the formation of a Palestinian state in the West Bank and Gaza, or on any part of Palestine, if that entails conceding the rest of Palestine to Israel. Recognising Israel, from the Muslim Brotherhood's point of view, is an acknowledgement of the legitimacy of occupying Muslim land.

According to the society, the *jihad* for Palestine will start after the completion of the Islamic transformation of Palestinian society, the completion of the process of Islamic reformation, and the return to Islam in the region. Only then can the call for *jihad* be relevant because the Palestinians cannot alone liberate Palestine without the intervention of other Muslims. The Palestinians are only the spearhead in the battle for liberation, and the Muslims in Palestine are the vanguard of fighters.

Unlike nationalist factions, the Muslim Brotherhood does not make its claim to Palestine, or define its attitude toward it on nationalist or geographic bases alone. The notion of nationalism, according to the society, has geographic boundaries. Commitment to land alone is a glaring mistake, since one piece of land can be replaced by another. From an Islamic point of view, Palestine is a religious matter. But on the other hand, Palestinian Islamists cannot restrict their message to Palestine only. In the words of one Brotherhood leader in the West Bank, Islam was not exposed to solve the Palestinian problem.

In this regard, one Islamic writer goes as far as rejecting the idea of making Palestine the primary and core issue for Muslims. Muhammad 'Ali Qutb says: " It is a matter of obscured vision or shortsightedness or treason for Arabs and Muslims to be preoccupied with the Palestinian issue and to make it the pivotal point of the struggle between them and the Zionists, who are supported by Western imperialist capitalism, and to forget, or pretend to forget, that the toppling of the Ottoman State ...with all its political, military and geographic, and even regional realities, was the major step toward the breaking down of the gateway to the East and the onslaught on the Islamic world. They also forget, or pretend to forget, the disputes that have occurred, and are occurring, in Kashmir, Cyprus, Afghanistan, Somalia, Eritrea, and the Moroccan (Spanish) Sahara." But perhaps Qutb is trying to alert the Arabs and the Muslims to what he presumes to be a foreign onslaught whose magnitude goes beyond Palestine.

The Muslim Brotherhood views Israel as a spearhead of Western influence and the tool that escalates Western corruption, with its plots against Islam. Failure to make Palestine part of the broader Muslim concern amounts to treason, since that would exclude millions of Muslims from the revolt against Israel and its allies. The Muslim Brotherhood invokes history to prove the genuineness of such an argument. Palestine, they recall, was freed from the crusaders under the banner of Islam. The society, therefore, calls for the abandonment of secular ideas and adoption of Islam as a way to liberate Palestine.

The society renounces the secular nationalist programme of the PLO and the programmes of its various factions. It also rejects the notion of "liberation first, then ideological commitment," which was raised initially by the Fatah movement. Liberation, according to the Muslim Brotherhood, cannot be attained without commitment to the Islamic religion, which provides the Palestinians with the necessary ideological, spiritual, and psychological preparedness they require.

The Muslim Brotherhood accuses the Arab governments for

the loss of Palestine in 1948 because these governments "handed Palestine over to Israel in a theatrical battle which lacked planning, military training, and the amassing of arms." The society believes that the way to Palestine and the holy struggle for it cannot be realised without "returning to Islamic principles and containing the existing non-Islamic reality," in order to "liberate all the land and return it to Islam and for the sake of Islam."

The society considers any position that contradicts this idea to be false and too concessionary. The Brotherhood argues that the Muslims' right in Palestine is a historical and religious right that cannot be removed or deleted. This right is derived from belonging to Islam, the revealed religion, which displaces all preceding heavenly monotheistic religions. The society also argues that the Muslims' right in Palestine are strongly embedded in history, in the recognised beliefs of human rights, and in the modern concepts of international law.

The Muslim Brotherhood argues that Muslims who are tight-lipped about the occupation of Palestine are committing a sin because Islam requires them to involve in a holy war.

The Muslim Brotherhood tends to consider the loss of Palestine to the Jews as both a curse and a blessing. It is a curse because the Jews, who are "the dirtiest and meanest of all races, are defiling the most sanctified and hallowed spot on earth, a spot to which Allah sent a herald angel, and where the Prophet Muhammad made his midnight journey." And it is a blessing because the Jewish conquerors provide sheer motivation to the people to recommit themselves to Islam and "to remove the vagueness of humiliation and the veils of submission from Muslim souls, and to guide the people to the pleasure, beauty, glory, and reward inherent in the craft of death." Unlike the nationalist groups of the PLO, the Muslim Brotherhood makes no discrimination between Jews, Zionists, and Israelis. Insistence on using the term "Jews" reflect the underlying religious nature of the conflict as defined by the Brotherhood.

The Muslim Brotherhood considers itself as the only party capable of "extracting the fate of the [Palestinian] cause from the hands of the negligent and the weak." It assumes itself as the only party "capable of the steadfastness and *jihad*, and of sincere giving and persistence, that will enable future Islamic generations to build a prosperous future under the supreme word of God." The society believes that the way to Palestine is an Islamic way: " The contemporary Islamic movement everywhere in the world has proven to the whole world that there is only one way to Palestine, and that is Islam, as a doctrine, movement, and holy war." The reference here is to the approaches embraced by the PLO units and the secular and pan-Arab nationalist regimes. The Brotherhood attributes the setback which the Arabs and the Palestinians have suffered to the fact that those who are in power did not raise the banner of Islam.

The Muslim Brotherhood has an alternative strategy toward Palestine. The strategy of the society seeks the formation of an Islamic state, society, and regime in one of the Arab countries neighbouring Israel, such as Syria, Egypt, or Jordan. This Islamic entity will function as a foundation for the Islamic movement in Palestine, and as a basic prerequisite to realise the general goal embodied in the victory of the Islamic call. This state should be ruled by an Islamic elite that is dedicated to Islam as a constitution and a way of life. This elite should be elected by a people which is also considerably committed to Islam. The ruler of this state will, during a period of a decade, consolidate and prepare the *umma* [the Muslim nation] for the "decisive battle with the Jews."

One Islamic writer narrates the Brotherhood's strategy in the following manner: "We must effect a broad popular change. If we manage to do that, we can establish an Islamic bloc or state which we can use as a springboard. Then we could invite battalions of *mujahidin* from all parts of the world." It appears that this Islamic writer was alluding to Syria, where the Syrian Muslim Brotherhood was involved during the 1980s in a fierce and violent struggle with the regime of President Hafiz al-Asad: "The Muslims who are engaged in a holy war in our beloved Syria will provide the demographic and strategic depth for our fighting brothers in Palestine. If the Islamic revolution in Syria succeeds, this will provide the faithful of the Aqsa Mosque and the Palestinians everywhere with the best of news, that the time of their salvation is near. They will be inspired in their holy war against their enemy and will be relieved of all those forces which oppress them."

During times of material weakness, the Muslim Brotherhood emphasises the importance of upholding the will of doctrinal change through steadfastness and resisting attempts to kill this will "by those who are apparently hostile to Islam, or by those who indirectly are trying to do the same by raising the slogan of Islam and Islamic restoration, while taking a contradictory path to Islam, and stabbing Islamic revival in the chest and back."

The steadfastness that the Brotherhood calls for "is not simply a negative renunciation as has been practiced, but is rather a positive and active initiative which cannot be confined to the Palestinian issue or to the sons of Palestine and their Muslim brothers in other countries. It is an initiative that rejects everything that is in contradiction with the truth in the context of Palestine, and in the case of every other issue and aspect of our lives, our world, and our era."

Muslim Brotherhood and the PLO

Ideological and political differences between the Muslim Brotherhood Society and the PLO have resulted in suspicion, tension, and even conflicts. Suspicion has been nourished by past experience dating back to the 1950s when the Muslim Brotherhood in the West Bank sided with the regime in Jordan against the nationalist and secular political parties.

The Muslim Brotherhood ensures the PLO for its stance toward the Palestinian issue. The society is especially critical of leftist factions, which the Brotherhood fears might gain too much influence or even dominate within the PLO. The Muslim Brotherhood believes that leftist groups, such as the Popular Front for the Liberation of Palestine (PFLP) and the Democratic Front for the Liberation of Palestine (DFLP) have been trying to undermine the hold of the Fatah movement over the PLO.

The Muslim Brotherhood has always been especially hostile toward the Communists. A local publication of the Brotherhood asserts: "Communism has caused setbacks for our society in the areas of doctrine and politics. It is a mercenary party working on behalf of super powers. Communism serves its own interests and the interests of Israel. This is in addition to the actual profanity that is contained in communist books, pamphlets, and festivities.

Furthermore, communist miss all Islamic moral values and obligations...in their private lives, and in their relationship with our beloved society."

Despite the fact that Fatah went on to be ideologically the closest of the PLO factions to the Brotherhood, disputes between the two sides continued. On certain occasions, confrontations between the two sides took place and were more violent than any confrontations between the Brotherhood and leftist factions. The relationship between the Muslim Brotherhood and Fatah could best be described as a love-hate relationship. In a way, the Muslim Brotherhood sees in Fatah a legitimate son, but it feels dismayed by Fatah's gradual abandonment of its Islamic Learnings. The Fatah movement is also considered as the society's most serious rival in terms of popularity and influence. Several of the Fatah founders were former Brotherhood members who have maintained over the years friendly ties with the society.

The Muslim Brotherhood believes that the Palestinian issue has gradually worsened because of the PLO's efforts to separate the religious beliefs of the Palestinian people from the rifle: "It is the Occupied Territories these days that are seeing an increase in the fruits of the *Jihad* of the youths of the Islamic movement...on all levels, while the Palestinians locally and abroad are seeing a clear decline in the numbers of those who separate religious beliefs from the rifle." With the steady decline of nationalist influences, the Muslim Brotherhood has become more vocal in its challenge of the PLO: "From now on, monopoly of Palestinian action by those movements, which proved their failures for the past 20 years, will not be tolerated. Nor will the exclusion of Islam from the Palestinian struggle be tolerated, because Islam, with its impact on life, is the sole element that is able, if given the opportunity to fight, to upset the balance and change realities. Islam can liberate the land and restore the usurped rights."

The Muslim Brotherhood condemns the PLO because "it is an organisation that does not serve God." The society is against the principles endorsed by the factions of the PLO. It sees the return of these factions to Islam as the beginning of the journey along the true path: " The Palestinian factions are founded on principles that are contradictory and controversial, and some of them are clearly based on leftist or rightist notions that are inimical to Islam. Some factions declare that they want a secular state in Palestine. This inconsistency has caused woes, disasters and tribulations. Therefore, we notice that the first step along the true path is to reject these destructive ideas, and bring these factions, leaders and ranks, back to God."

Since political activities under the Israeli occupation were legally banned, the various political tendencies, including the Muslim Brotherhood, have relied on student groups in the relatively autonomous Palestinian universities of the West Bank and the Gaza Strip as arenas for their political action. These factions have expressed the positions of the political trends they identified with through publications or statements or through other functions, whenever that was possible.

Another election statement gave the response of the Islamic Bloc to questions about the Muslim Brotherhood's absence of commitment to the PLO as the sole legitimate representative of the Palestinian people: " The Islamic Bloc supports all those who carry arms, who fight and become martyrs in order to liberate the land, help truth prevail, and triumph over the tyrants. However, the Islamic Bloc does not recognise as representatives (whoever they may be), those who attempt to reach an accord with the Jews at the expense of our usurped land, our displaced people, our plundered heritage, and our destroyed sacred places."

The Brotherhood opposes Palestinian links with progressive Jews or democratic forces in Israel on religious grounds. The question has been a matter of discord between the Brotherhood and PLO factions from the beginning. The Brotherhood also blamed PLO Chairman Yasser Arafat for his friendly and close ties with the now-defunct socialist regimes of Eastern Europe and the former USSR.

Ahmad Yasin Views

Ahmad Yasin, the head of the Islamic Centre in the Gaza Strip, summarises the Muslim Brotherhood's position toward the PLO as follows: " The PLO is secularist. It cannot be accepted as a representatives unless it becomes Islamic." However, in an interview during the *intifada*, Yasin said that the PLO did in fact represent the Palestinian masses, but he expressed certain reservations regarding its political line, which called for the establishment of a secular state on any part of Palestine. Yasin reiterated that Islam ought to be the state's religion and constitution.

Because of the Israeli occupation, and because of the massive support the PLO still enjoys among the Palestinians, the Muslim Brotherhood cannot boldly express its real intentions. Therefore, its statements are ambiguous and sometimes appear contradictory. The concept of *taqiyya* in Islam justifies concealing the true beliefs if expressing such beliefs would harm Muslims.

Yasin says that deep within his heart, he does not believe that there is a possibility of solving the Palestinian problem by political means. But from the tactical viewpoint, he should propose what the enemy repudiates. When the Israelis reject a proposal, their rejection gets him out of a critical situation.

There are other Islamic points of view that take essentially the same stand toward the PLO, but with more flexibility. Bassam Jarrar, one of the prominent intellectuals of the Islamic movement in the West Bank, asserts: "The Islamic movement does not base its considerations on the assumption that the decline of the PLO's influence means the rise of Islamic influence, or vice versa. On the contrary, the Islamisation of the PLO means the rise of Islam." Jarrar also believes that the PLO will form an affinity with the Islamic movement after it abandons its hopes for peaceful solutions. He adds that the Islamic movement cannot be an alternative to the PLO in negotiations with Israel. The role of the PLO is a political one and poses no threat to the ideological role of the Islamic movement. Jarrar says that there is no reason to reject alliances between the Islamic factions and the PLO if these alliances are established on clear and defined bases, and if they do not conflict with the principles of the Islamic movement.

In the context of clarifying this view, Jarrar asserts that the Islamic movement is as comprehensive as Islam itself and is only partly political. Therefore, it cannot limit itself and its work to a narrow, nationalist framework, as does the PLO. If the Islamic movement has focussed on political action at any particular state, it is because the nationalist movement has retreated. Jarrar says that when the PLO has restricted its activities to military actions only, the Islamic movement has not standed up to it. Other Muslim Brotherhood views are at variance with Jarrar's opinion. A Brotherhood alliance with a non-Islamic faction or movement, according to these views, is incompatible with Islam. The Brotherhood can not authorise the PLO to speak on its behalf or on behalf of the Muslims.

The Muslim Brotherhood has a particular concept regarding possible cooperation with the PLO. One Islamic publication in the Occupied Territories defined the terms of the kind of cooperation that is welcome to the Muslim Brotherhood: "The Islamists extend their hands to every sincere national group that is working for the liberation of the country and for ridding it of Zionist and imperialist dangers, provided that group has not condemned Islam and is not known to be an enemy of Islam or the Islamists." But, this publication further adds: "The Islamists look at the issue of cooperation and integration with secularist and heretical groups with utmost caution, because secularism and heresy are at war with Islam and are incompatible with its precepts." According to an Egyptian Islamic writer, Islam does not allow a Muslim to give up his "Islam" in the name of "national unity," no matter what the reasons are.

The PLO factions repudiate as pretexts the reasons that the Muslim Brotherhood offers to justify its reluctance to form an alliance with the PLO. In September 1987, the Birzeit student body reflecting the views of the PFLP distributed a statement entitled. "Why doesn't the Muslim Brotherhood recognise the PLO?" The statement pointed out that it was inconsistent for the Muslim Brotherhood to demand the Islamisation of the PLO as a must for cooperation, while the Brotherhood was already working with other organisations that did not have Islamic leadership. The statement said that Yusuf al'Azm, who is a Muslim Brotherhood leader in Jordan, "stands behind the rostrum of the Jordanian Parliament to praise the king and his constitution and his royal hereditary regime."

The statement added that the Muslim Brotherhood in Egypt was participating in a parliament that was certifying a peace treaty with Israel, and that the society allied itself with political parties, such as the Wafd party and the Socialist Labour party, which are not Islamic. The statement asked whether the Muslim Brotherhood perceived the regimes in Jordan and Egypt to be Islamic regimes and said it was unusual that the Muslim Brotherhood refused to recognise the PLO, while some Brotherhood members from the West Bank, such as Hafiz 'Abd-al-Nabi al-Natsha, were accepting membership in the Jordanian Parliament. The statement accused the Muslim Brotherhood of sedition: "Doesn't all this prove the depth of this group's capitulation to treacherous Arab regimes and this group's firm ties to the intelligence apparatus of those regimes and to imperialism?"

In a booklet published by a pro-Fatah student body, the Brotherhood in the Occupied Territories was compared to the Muslim Brotherhood in Egypt under the regime of President Anwar al-Sadat. The booklet asserted that Sadat had opened the door for the Brotherhood to operate unhesitatingly, because they were the only group capable of undermining the Egyptian nationalists who threatened the Sadat regime. The booklet also started that Sadat permitted the Brotherhood to dominate the universities to such an extent that the society's authority became stronger than the authority of the universities' presidents. This view corresponds to opinions expressed by frontline Egyptian writers. Dr. Hasan Hanafi wrote: "The political leadership decided to use the religious groups, which began to appear in the universities after the 1973 war and after the release [from jail] of the Muslim Brothers in 1971, to counter the Nasirite influence which was dominant in these universities. The Islamic groups were indebted to the government at that time for the release of many Brotherhood members from jail."

PLO and Israeli Authorities

PLO groups believe, and argue, that the Israeli authorities paved the way for the Palestinian Muslim Brotherhood in the same way the Egyptian authorities did to the society in Egypt, so that they could complete with, oppose, and undermine the PLO. Certain nationalist spheres go as far as to claim that Ahmad Yasin, the leader of the Islamic Centre in the Gaza Strip, swore on the Koran, before the Israeli investigators, that weapons seized in his possession in 1984 were meant to be used against leftist forces.

The Israeli authorities believed that the advent of the Islamic groups and the spread of their influence in the West Bank and the Gaza Strip was bound to destabilise the PLO in these two areas.

The PLO factions, for their part, arraign Israel of supporting the Islamic groups in order to weaken the PLO's influence and create rifts in the ranks of the Palestinian people. They usually point to courteous treatment and to the degree of tolerance the occupation authorities display towards Brotherhood activities. The PLO leaders abroad have urged their following in the Occupied Territories to avert open conflict with the Brotherhood and to continue to make conciliatory declarations, arguing that the Muslim Brotherhood's basic antagonism was with Israel. PLO leaders stress publicly their belief in pluralism. But as the influence of the Brotherhood grew and its opposition to the PLO became more expressive, the PLO leadership began to feel troubled by the potential threat.

Israeli security sources deny reports that Israel is giving support to the Islamic agitation, saying that the struggle between this movement and the PLO nationalists is an internal Palestinian affair in which Israel will not mediate, as long as Israeli security is not threatened. But while Israel hopes that the Islamic movement will undermine the strength of the PLO, Israel is also concerned that the growing Islamic influence may become a real problem that Israel will have to face in the longer term.

Failure of the Brotherhood to question the Israeli occupation, let alone cooperating with the occupation to weaken the PLO factions, would undermine the society's popular support. The Brotherhood would lose its following to other political groups if it is known that such cooperation does in fact exist. The fact of the matter is that the Israeli authorities deal with the various groups inside the Occupied Territories in ways that fulfil the interest of Israel. These authorities do not hesitate to strike at any individual or group. Events have shown, especially during the *intifada*, that Israeli measures against the Islamic factions are not less harsh than the stops taken against the PLO factions. Israeli's attempts to manipulate the various competing groups do not mean that these groups cooperate consciously or deliberately with the occupation authorities to subvert each other.

Friction and mutual accusations between the PLO and the

Muslim Brotherhood are embedded in political and ideological differences. The PLO supporters time and again refer to Brotherhood positions that are difficult to accept or to justify, at least from a nationalist vistas. The Muslim Brotherhood, the PLO nationalists argue, demands the liberation of all of Palestine from Jewish dominance and the establishment of an Islamic state in it, while the society practically refused to engage in armed resistance or in actual *Jihad* against the Israeli occupation, at least until the emergence of the *intifada* in 1987. The Brotherhood, for its part, bases its objection to armed revolt on two counts: that the Brotherhood has been preoccupied with preparing a Muslim generation capable of combating the enemy, and that mass support of armed struggle would simply give the Israeli authorities pretexts to strike at the Brotherhood prematurely.

Aware of consistent criticism by the nationalists, the Brotherhood's stance regarding resistance to the Israeli occupation began to reflect a gradual change even before the *intifada*. The Islamic student group in Birzeit University took part more than once in violent fends between Israeli troops and students in the university. Muslim Brotherhood students participated in subsequent demonstrations at the university. Supporters of the Islamic Bloc had previously justified the Muslim Brotherhood's reluctance to participate in armed resistance on the grounds of the society's convection that the intentions of the PLO nationalists were not sincere.

The gradual evolution of the Brotherhood's position toward a more militant role was manifested in the slogans the Islamic Bloc had raised during the student council elections at Birzeit university in January 1987. Only a few of these slogans contained the usual religious fervour and references.

In a liberal university, such as Birzeit, one could not find sympathy for the demand to isolate male and female students. Moreover, it would be difficult to ignore nationalist issues in a university considered to be a stronghold for the nationalists. Maximum focus on religion and the marginalisation of nationalist issues and politics was not the best formula to attract the student body. A blend of religion and nationalism was more appealing. Hence the evolution in the position of the Brotherhood.

In the continuing debate between the supporters of the PLO and the Brotherhood, the nationalists take issue with the Brotherhood's overstated claims of resisting the Israeli occupation. For example, the Brotherhood credits the Islamists for the continuing Islamic resistance against Israel in Lebanon, the assassination of Sadat by Islamic elements in Egypt, and the actions of the Islamic *Jihad* movement in Palestine. The nationalists argue that the Islamic factions that carried out these actions were different from the Muslim Brotherhood and do not even agree with the Brotherhood's stands on the PLO and resistance to the Israeli possession. The nationalists say that the Islamic resistance in Lebanon is carried out by the Hizbullah, which is loyal to Iran, which the Muslim Brotherhood views negatively for being a Shi'ite party. In additions, those who assassinated Sadat belonged to the *Jihad* Organisation in Egypt which split from the Muslim Brotherhood in protest. Finally, the supporters of the Islamic *Jihad* movement in Palestine, who carry out valiant attacks against Israeli targets in the Occupied Territories, also split away from the Brotherhood in protest.

In the same vein, the nationalists accuse the Muslim Brotherhood of constantly bragging about its role in Palestine in 1948, and they doubt the Brotherhood's role in the long years that followed 1948. They ask why the Brotherhood in Syria boasts of armed rebellion against the Syrian regime and at the same time does nothing of the sort against Israel. The PLO supporters also query how the Syrian Muslim Brotherhood can attack Syrian President Hafiz al-Asad because of his stance toward the PLO, and approve of an alliance between the Brotherhood and secularist parties in Syria to oppose him, while at the same time the Palestinian Brothers decline to make an alliance with the PLO in the Occupied Territories to oppose Israel. Reference is also made to alliances forged in Lebanon in the past between Fatah and Islamic factions, such as the Islamic Unification movement, led by Sheikha Sa'id Sha'ban, and also between Fatah and Hizbullah, headed by Sheikh Muhammad Hussein Fadlallah.

Muslim Brotherhood Condemned

The PLO nationalists condemn the Muslim Brotherhood of having abandoned the Palestinian resistance movement in Jordan in 1970 during the confrontation with King Hussein. But the Muslim Brotherhood questions that the Brotherhood could not work within the PLO framework "because the PLO had capitulated and conceded everything, and that the Society was then willing to coordinate with the PLO, but without having to accept it as a frame of reference." The Brotherhood points out that the leftist provocative steps in 1970 caused King Hussein to strike at the Palestinian resistance movement in Jordan. The Muslim Brotherhood's standpoint is that it would have been better for the PLO leaders, and especially Yasir Arafat, to have averted the trap that was set for them, saved their forces and weapons, spared the blood of their people, and gone to another place, where they could have saved their strength, weapons, and honour.

The Brotherhood in the Occupied Territories sees itself as part of a world movement. It also perceives itself as an organisation that is the oldest historically, the richest in heritage, and the most comprehensive in schemes. The society cannot subject its world ideology to a narrow nationalist programme championed by groups that endorse secular ideas. The Brotherhood believes that its ideas and strategy are the best for dealing with the various matters, including the Palestinian issue. Accordingly, the Muslim Brotherhood will not accept any alternative idea, strategy, or frame of reference.

Generally, the PLO nationalists express scepticism with regard to the Muslim Brotherhood's statements, positions, and actions. For example, the nationalists do not accept the Brotherhood's stance that they could not participate in the resistance against Israel because the society was educating and indoctrinating the Muslim generation. The nationalists also reject the Brotherhood's explanation that it stayed out of armed resistance so that it would not be prove to repression by Israel. After all, the nationalists argue, there is a price that must be paid in order to resist the occupation. The nationalists equally reject the Muslim Brotherhood's claims that the society was passing amidst an ordeal and harsh circumstances which deterred it from carrying out its obligations toward Palestine.

The Muslim Brotherhood is questioned by writers known to be sympathetic to the society about the reasons that prevented the

Brotherhood from involving in the *Jihad*. The well-known Egyptian Islamic writer Fahmi Huwaydi says: "Where was the Muslim Brotherhood throughout the 20 years that followed the 1967 defeat? Why did their *Jihad* stop during those years? Why did not their cadres defend Palestine, which is considered a *waqf* land, in order to fulfill the individual duty (*Jihad*), and embark on the armed struggle throughout that period?"

Reacting to Fahmi Huwaydi's questions, Ziad Abu-Ghanima, a Muslim Brotherhood spokesman in Jordan, says: " The Muslim Brotherhood was not absent from the field of *Jihad* by choice, but by force and compulsion. If you want evidence, ask the gallows of the revolutionaries who brought about the crime and shame of our defeat in 1967, and you will find out that the bodies of the Muslim Brothers were hung by the revolutionary ropes....Forget, if you wish, the prison cells of the revolutionary regimes in those lean years, but remember the thousands of youths and women of the Islamic movement who crouched in these cells unjustly, and the many thousands who still crouch in them until today...."

It is hardly known that some Muslim Brotherhood members had participated in Palestinian armed unrest in Jordan before 1970, but under the Fatah umbrella. Dr. Nawfal says: "We were completely independent, except in name. No one interfered in our decisions, operations, planning, or training. Fatah for us was only an umbrella." Muslim Brotherhood leaders cite in their writings the reasons why they were compelled to work under Fatah. Yusuf al-'Azm notes that after the refusal of some PLO leaders to allow the Brotherhood to engaged openly in armed retaliation under the Brotherhood's name, the society agreed to operate under Fatah. Al-'Azm says that the Muslim Brotherhood did not form a fighting organisation of its own because the society did not get support from anyone due to its position which demands the liberation of all of Palestine, while the other parties were looking for minimalist deals. Dr. Ahmad Nawfal points out that 'Abd-al-Nasir was putting pressure on Yasir Arafat to ward off the Muslim Brotherhood from forming its own armed organisation.

However, these reasons do not sufficiently justify the Muslim Brotherhood's acquiescence in submitting to the wishes or the will of others and not engaging in armed struggle as an independent movement. The Brotherhood was then one of the oldest and largest parties and had the resources as well as the experience to involve in this kind of resistance. The society even claims that it was the party which had inspired the Palestinian *fedayeen* movement to adopt armed means of resistance: "Despite the circumstances of the ordeal that surrounded the Muslim Brotherhood on all sides, no one could deny that the Islamic spirit, which prevailed in the Palestinian *fedayeen* movement from the outset, was one of the fruits of Muslim Brotherhood thought."

The nationalists find it difficult to accept Muslim Brotherhood castigation of PLO supporters for meeting with foreign and Israeli officials, when certain Brotherhood leaders in the Occupied Territories are themselves taking part in such meetings.

The PLO supporters say that the Muslim Brotherhood's rejectionist and confusing position with respect to the PLO's right to represent the Palestinian people and the Brotherhood's rejection of the notion of an international conference and a Palestinian state coincide objectively, indifferently what the motives or doctrinal justifications are, with positions of Israel and the United States regarding these issues.

Finally, the supporters of the PLO say that one cannot take seriously the Brotherhood's claims of its obligation to regain all of Palestine from the possession of the Jews while the Brotherhood is closely linked to regimes that do not believe in this goal and do nothing to achieve it, such as Jordan and Saudi Arabia. Jordan's public position favour the land for peace formula, and the establishment of a confederation between a Palestinian state in the West Bank and Gaza and Jordan. Regarding Saudi Arabia, it was the country which devised the "Fahd Plan" in August 1981, calling for the establishment of a Palestinian state, the acknowledgement of the existence of all states in the region, and the achievement of peace among those states. The PLO nationalists argue that the very verbal calls of the Brotherhood for the liberation of Palestine and the formation of an Islamic state in it, without matching such calls with deeds, is something that Israel can withstand hundreds of years.

Palestinian Leftist Publication

A Palestinian leftist publication depicted the Brotherhood during the *intifada* as an active, and even violent, opponent of the PLO. The publication signified that the Brotherhood acts with the direct support of reactionary Arab regimes, especially Saudi Arabia, Egypt, Jordan, and some of the Gulf states, in collusion with the Israeli occupation. This trend has carried out systematic and methodical sabotage operations which climaxed in direct attacks against nationalist institutions, such as the Red Crescent office in Gaza. The Islamic factions have continued to perpetuate crimes, even during the *intifada*, especially the so-called *al-Mujamma' al - 'Islami* in the Gaza Strip, which carried out attempts at the beginning of the *intifada* to turn it to its advantage. The *Mujamma'* tried to put the religious stamp on the *intifada,* banning pro-PLO slogans, spreading baseless rumours, and calling on the people to destroy the homes of communists. The risk of this trend, and the reactionary and conspiratorial role it plays, reached its zenith when certain demonstrations were organised against democratic, nationalist and communist strugglers in the al-Sabra quarter of Gaza. That was a serious move to serve the occupation authorities directly.

One of the worst manifestations of the worsening relationship between the PLO and the Muslim Brotherhood was the violent confrontations and clashes that took place between the two sides. These clashes broke out in more than one place in the West Bank and the Gaza Strip, and especially in the Palestinian universities. At the Islamic University in Gaza, disputes occurred over authority of the university, as well as over peripheral issues. The PLO supporters wanted the university in the Gaza Strip to be a secular nationalist educational institution for all social, political, and religious factions of the Palestinian masses. The Brotherhood wanted to maintain the university as an Islamic university. On June 4, 1983, a violent clash occurred between the Brotherhood and the nationalists on the campus of the university. More than two hundred students were injured in this clash. This incident coincided with another equally violent clash at Birziet University in which a number of students were injured. Both the PLO nationalists and the Brotherhood supporters alleged one another of triggering the clashes and held one another responsible about the fallout.

In a statement issued by the nationalists in the Occupied Territories, the pro-PLO elements held the Brotherhood of sending their followers to Birzeit University to fight the nationalists, who were making preparations to mark the first anniversary of the 1982, invasion of Lebanon. The statement narrated the Muslim Brotherhood as the "emergency reserve of Arab reactionaries in the midst of our masses, "and of being a constant and "willing weapon in the hands of these reactionaries, in order to achieve their targets and their capitulationist and liquidationist plots."

The pro-Brotherhood Islamic student bloc at Birzeit University issued a statement in which it clarified the events surrounding the clash that had occurred on the university campus. The bloc accused the nationalists of impeding an activity the youth were undertaking to "express their anger at everything that reminded them of the tragedy of our nation, upon which befell the 1967, war and the tragedy that struck Lebanon on June 6, 1982."

Birzeit University was founded by a Christian Palestinian family. In the aftermath of the Birzeit University episode, a committee was formed to investigate what had happened. In its report, the committee expressed regret that the university's administration had not interfered with the student council, which was dominated by the pro-PLO nationalists, to prevent the incident. The student council, on its part, issued a statement in response to the findings of the report. It said that those findings were nothing more than distortions by Muslim Brotherhood elements "who are well known for their connections with reactionary Arab intelligence organisations and with world imperialist intelligence agencies, especially the American."

Najah University in Nablus was the centre for other confrontations and clashes. In the last part of 1981, the university was the scene of violent clashes between Muslim Brotherhood and pro-PLO students. The conflict erupted following the nationalist students demand to restore four lecturers to their positions after the university administration had dismissed them.

It is worth mentioning that it was the Fatah supporters who in 1980-1981 confronted the supporters of the Muslim Brotherhood despite the historic relationship and general rapprochement between Fatah and the Brotherhood. The clashes that took place between 1982 and 1986 at the Islamic University in Gaza were also primarily between Fatah and the Brotherhood, except for a few cases in which confrontations took place between the Brotherhood and leftist groups, such as the PFLP or the Communists. Supporters of the Brotherhood were of the view that the only group capable of competing with them was the Fatah movement. It was easy for Brotherhood, for example, to undermine the leftist factions, which were easily discarded as Communists. However, the context was different with regard to Fatah, because the latter represented a nationalist mainstream, enjoyed strong influence inside and outside the Occupied Territories, and could not be arraigned of Communism.

Fatah and the Muslims

Later, the struggle between Fatah and the Muslim Brotherhood assumed greater proportions, when As'ad al-Saftawi, a Fatah leader in the Gaza Strip at that time, was attacked by the Muslim Brotherhood. The brotherhood, for its part, held Fatah responsible for the assassination of Dr. Isma'il al-Khatib, a Muslim Brotherhood lecturer in the Islamic University in Gaza. In January 1982, the Brotherhood expressed their discontent at Fatah's alliance with other nationalist groups in the Occupied Territories and its signing of a political statement condemning the Muslim Brotherhood.

Clashes were not confined to Islamic and nationalist outfits. Similar incidents broke out between the Islamic groups themselves, the Brotherhood, and the Islamic *Jihad*. Sheikh 'Abd-al-Majid Kallub, a Gaza cleric, wrote: "By God, tell us how you feel when you see Muslims using clubs, knives, and iron chains against other Muslims, under the roof of a holy place?...Everyone who is zealous of religion is embarrassed by these deeds." The reference here is to clashes that took place in Gaza between the ardent supporters of the Muslim Brotherhood and the Islamic *Jihad* movement.

The Muslim Brotherhood leaders in the Occupied Territories complained about what they believed to be a methodical media blackout campaign directed against them by the press which was dominated by the pro-PLO nationalists: "Every media outlet has been closed to us, especially in the Occupied Territories' newspapers and magazines, while they are wide open to communists to publish their lies and fabrications against the people. They agitate to strike blows at Islam and Muslims; but the communists are not content with that! On the contrary, they spread their insolent slogans everywhere, even on walls of houses. All of this is a well-conceived plot to destroy the facts, misguide the nation, and distort the reputation of sincere and respected people, who are prevented from responding to the lies, even if that was through a paid advertisement."

Despite the differences and the clashes between the PLO and the Muslim Brotherhood, some Fatah leaders at home and abroad maintained a healthy relationship with the Brotherhood leadership. Ideological affinity between the founders of Fatah and the Muslim Brotherhood Society underlies this attitude. Moreover, an alliance was formed between Fatah and the Islamic groups in Lebanon. Furthermore, the Fatah leaders needed the financial support of Saudi Arabia, also the Brotherhood's backer and supporter, and could not afford to alienate this valuable partner. In addition, the Fatah leaders were anxious to maintain friendly relations with the Muslim Brotherhood because the society could be a reserve strength for Fatah at home, if alliances shifted among the factions of the PLO. But a cordial relationship with the Brotherhood was not to be accepted by Fatah at any cost, as it became clear afterwards, when the Fatah dominated PLO leadership challenged the wishes and opposition of the Brotherhood and sanctioned Palestinian participation in peace negotiations with Israel in October 1991.

This Islamic assimilation of certain Fatah leaders became more apparent after 1982, and after the secession that occurred inside Fatah. For example, religious references in the words and speeches of Yasser Arafat, the leader of Fatah and chairman of the PLO, had become more frequent. Despite the fact that a part of these references could be a reflection of sincere convection and a religious background, it is plausible that some of these references have political aims and are intended to pacify the leaders and followers of the Islamic movement, not only in the Occupied

Territories, but also in other places, such as Lebanon, Syria, and Jordan. Moreover, these religious references were perhaps meant to alleviate the fears of conservative Arab states like Saudi Arabia and the gulf states with regard to leftist influence within the PLO ranks. The message that Yasser Arafat sent out to the Palestinian people in January 1987, on the 22nd anniversary of the formation of the Fatah movement, contained six Koranic verses, while the message he sent on the same occassion in 1988, contained five, and similar messages sent in earlier years contained about a similar number of verses.

The Fatah leaders were also keen to maintain cordial relations with the Muslim Brotherhood for practical purposes. Following one of the violent clashes that broke out between Fatah and Brotherhood supporters in Najah University in the summer of 1981, Fatah leaders abroad asked their followers not to burn their bridges with the Muslim Brotherhood because Fatah wanted the Brotherhood as a bargaining card in its relationship with Syria. The Syrian brothers were at the time engaged in a bloody conflict with the regime of President Hafiz al-Asad. In addition, the Fatah leaders abroad undertook certain decisions that were more favourable to the Muslim Brotherhood than to Fatah in the Occupied Territories in order to maintain a good relationship with the society. When rivalry between Dr. Riad al-Agha, a close aide of Fatah, and Dr. Muhammad Saqr, a Muslim Brotherhood sympathiser, over the position of president of the Islamic University in Gaza, the Fatah leadership supported Saqr. Saqr says that the decision to appoint him president came from the university's board of trustees and took place with the approval of Yasir Arafat and his deputy, Khalil al-Wazir.

The Fatah leaders made continuous attempts to co-opt the Islamic movement in the Occupied Territories through coordination and offers of support. Fatah appointed a frontline Islamic figure, Sheikh 'Abd-al-Hamid al-Sa'ih, to the presidency of the Palestine National Council (PNC), and in April 1987, it admitted three individuals, whom Fatah regarded to be Muslim Brotherhood representatives, into the membership of the council. Fatah also named Dr. Muhammad Siyam, the former acting president of the Islamic University in Gaza and one of the Muslim Brotherhood leaders, as a representative of the PLO to the Islamic World League. This appointment took place following Dr. Siyam's departure from the Gaza Strip at the end of July 1988.

Relations between Fatah and the Muslim Brotherhood in the Occupied Territories can generally be described as cooperative and coordinated at times, and affected with disputes and confrontations at other times. Evidence of this can be seen in the coordination between Fatah and the Muslim Brotherhood in designing the attack on the Red Crescent headquarters in Gaza on January 7, 1980. As stated by one of its leaders, Fatah had a hand in this incident. Nevertheless, Fatah publicity criticised it.

Following the secession that occurred within the Fatah movement in the spring of 1983, supporters of Fatah and the Brotherhood found themselves in the same camp. Both took a hostile stance toward Syria. The Brotherhood's sympathy with Fatah was evident in the society's condemnation of the secessionists, who were described as criminal. The Brotherhood held the Fatah secessionists of being tools manipulated by Syria and Libya to gain control over the Palestinian decision. The society also attributed the separation to the presence of Western ideologies inside the PLO and to a plot by Palestinian leftist forces, Arab Marxists, and the Soviet Union, in addition to Syria and Libya. The Muslim Brotherhood indicated that the goal of these forces was to tear down Fatah from within, liquidate the Palestinian issue, and nullify the military option. The Brotherhood flayed Arafat for allying himself with leftist forces, cooperating with the Soviet Union, and establishing relations with Syria and Libya. The society perceived the secession as "a first step in the process of finishing off the followers of Islam in the Occupied Territories and an attempt to abort the Fatah leaders' efforts to get closer to the Islamic movement. Therefore, the Brotherhood leadership urged Fatah to purge its ranks of Marxist elements, to be aware of the futility of secularism, and to cooperate closely with the Islamic groups."

The ouster of Arafat from Damascus on June 24, 1983, had incited the Islamists in the Occupied Territories. In mass rallies at al-Aqsa Mosque in Jerusalem, Sheikh Sa'd-al-Din al-'Alami, chairman of the Higher Islamic Council, lambasted the Syrian action and declared that the killing of President Hafiz al-Asad was a duty of every Muslim. It is not known whether this stance was motivated by the Islamic movement's hatred of the Syrian regime or was meant to show genuine solidarity with Arafat, or both. Sheikh al-'Alami is not a Muslim Brotherhood member, but only a prominent Islamic figure.

It is rumoured that in the 1986, elections of Birzeit University, supporters of the Fatah movement asked students of the Islamic Bloc to vote in favour of Fatah so that the latter could achieve victory over a leftist bloc which had faction like the PFLP, the DFLP, and the Palestine Communist Party (PCP), all of which formed an alliance to challenge Fatah. However, the Fatah Student Youth movement denied that the Islamic Bloc actually helped the movement win the elections and indicated that the Islamic Bloc had expected to win the election itself, in the absence of unity between the nationalist factions.

The Brotherhood is not inclined, even for tactical purposes, to surrender power or leadership to any other group. The society believes in undertaking responsibility and power, as expressed by a prominent Muslim intellectual: "The strategy of the Islamic movement must include the desire to assume the responsibility of achieving its programme of Islamic rule.... Undertaking, power is not something to escape or renounce, as some think ... The world and history do not know any movement whatsoever that gave the sap of its struggle to anyone other than those who believe in its targets and who join its paths to the battle and struggle."

Furthermore, both the Brotherhood and Hamas, which is a flank of the Brotherhood, are in essence political movements that embrace an Islamic ideology. As a political movement, the Brotherhood was compelled to respond to and interact with changing political realities. During the *intifada*, Hamas has engaged in discourse and conduct that reflects political realism and even pragmatism. In its charter, Hamas had pointed out that it "considers the PLO to be the closest to the Islamic Resistance Movement and regards it as a father, brother, relative or friend."

In addition, on more than one occasion, Hamas forged alliances with some PLO factions vis-à-vis others. Reference in this context can be made to statements issued and signed unitedly by Hamas, the Marxist Popular Front for the Liberation of Palestine (PFLP) and the Democratic Front for the Liberation of Palestine (DFLP) in protest against Palestinian involvement in the peace process that started with the Madrid Peace Conference in October 1991. This participation was supported by the mainstream Fatah movement.

Hamas's political pragmatism has become more evident as the movement's strength versus the PLO has grown. Five years after the eruption of the *intifada*, the Hamas leaders expressed preparedness to join the PLO if the organisation becomes more democratic and conducts elections inside and outside the Occupied Territories to elect a new Palestine National Council, the Palestinian parliament.

The Hamas leaders also indicated that Palestinian withdrawal from the peace negotiations is not a precondition for Hamas's joining of the PLO. According to Muhammad Nazzal, a prominent leader and the movement's representative in Jordan, Hamas will accept the formation of a Palestinian state on part of Palestine as a first step toward the liberation of the Occupied Territories from Israeli rule. But the Hamas leader also pointed out that while his movement accepted this interim solution, it would not recognise Israel. This position of Hamas reflects some accommodation to the PLO political programme, which calls for a two-state solution to the Palestinian-Israeli conflict.

Thirteen

Role of Political Terrorism

The period between the June 1967 and the October 1973 wars in the Middle East is often characterised as one in which the use of international terrorism as a political tactic considerably increased. Much of the recent attention devoted to the study of terrorism stems directly frcm the Middle East conflict and more particularly from the use of terror by sections of the Palestinian community. The emotional responses generated by acts of terrorism and the tendency to lump all acts of terrorism together have blemished many important distinctions. While the frequency of aerial hijackings, letter bombings, acts of sabotage, and isolated attacks on individuals, groups, and nations has increased, the targets, motivations, and attitudes toward the use of terrorism have not remained constant.

The focus of the world community and national governments on the prevention and control of terrorist act, while crucial and understandable, has often restricted and narrowed the discussion and understanding of the use of terror as a political strategy. The following discussion seeks to assess the role and describe the use of international terror and terrorism in the Middle East between the June 1967 war and thc October 1973 war. More specifically, attention is centred on terror as a political tactic, and its use by certain segments of the Palestinian movement and community. The resort to terror in the Middle East is quite an old story, nor is it limited to one of the contending parties. In the past, it had included not only individual and group actions, but also governmental actions—some sanctioned, others not. It has included widely contrasting types of attacks on widely differing victims and targets and has expressed widely differing goals and motivations.

By limiting the time frame and the participants involved, a more detailed analysis of the perspectives of the participants, their long-term and short-term goals, the relationship of terror to other tactics, and the response and counter-response of those most affected is possible. Although the crux is on an analysis of terror as a political tactic, it is argued that terror can best be understood within the wider context of the Arab-Israeli, Palestinian-Israeli conflict. It is also suggested that, in its broadest form, the use of terror as a political tactic differs with the changing goals and motivations and capabilities of the movement and participants involved, and with changing external political factors. Important, then, is the relationship over time between changing objectives and capabilities. A more inclusive study of terrorism in the Middle East would require more detailed event data, as well as a discussion of the interpretation of terrorism by all participants. An initial, descriptive survey, however, will allow the formulation of several generalisations based on initial empirical evidence concerning the nature and role of international terrorism as a political tactic in the Middle East.

In order to assess this role, several definitions and distinctions involving terrorism and terror are first raised. These definitions and distinctions are then generalised in a framework that is applied to the Palestinian case. Using this framework, various forms of terrorism that occurred from 1967 to 1973 are described. Included in this analysis are not only the different types of acts and their consequences, but also the objectives and motivations of those centrally involved. Finally, several assumptions are drawn concerning both the period under study and the use of terrorism as a political tactic.

Terror, Terrorism, and the Palestinian Case

Definitions of terror, terrorism, and the process of terror vary considerably. During crises, when terrorism appears to be on the increase, government's attention centres on prevention and control. For activists the prime concern is with the "effectiveness" of terror as a political tactic. Less frequently, the causes of terrorism are the pivotal concern. However, most broad generalisations about terror concur with Moss's statement that it is, in part, "the systematic use of intimidation for political ends," Crozier suggests that terrorism is "the threat or use of violence for political ends," whereas the Mallisons define terror as "the systematic use of extreme violence and threats of violence in order to achieve public or political objectives." These definitions have several points in common. All distinguish between actions and threats, all stress the notion of the systematic use of violence, and all stress the political nature of certain acts of terror and terrorism. There is also general agreement that terror introduces into the political process, in differing degrees, elements of fear, anxiety, disorientation, and disorganisation. Walter, for example, defines the process of terror — as different from terror itself — as "the acts or threat of violence; the emotional reaction; and the social effects."

In order to test the applicability of these generalisations to the Palestinian case, more strict distinctions are needed. Several are current: one of the most common is the distinction between governmental and nongovernmental terror. Hutchinson defines "revolutionary terrorism" (nongovernmental) as "a part of insurgency strategy in the context of internal warfare or revolution: the attempt to seize political power from the established regime of a state, if successful causing fundamental political and social change." Wilkinson distinguishes between forms of revolutionary terrorism, which are "the systematic tactics of terroristic violence with the objective of bringing about political revolution," subrevolutionary terrorism, which is 'employed for political motives other than revolution or governmental repression," and repressive terrorism, which is the "systematic use of terroristic acts of violence for purposes of suppressing, putting down, quelling or restraining certain groups, individuals or forms of behaviour deemed to be undesirable by the repressor." Evidently, most attention, at least recently, has focused on nongovernmental terror. Although interpretations may vary, the Palestinian case generally falls into the classification of either revolutionary terrorism or subrevolutionary terrorism.

An second distinction, and one central to the Palestinian case, is between internal (within nations) and international terror. Although this distinction is an important one, it is often difficult to determine boundaries. The problem of boundary definition is made even more difficult when there are not internationally or mutually accepted boundaries. Questions arise not only on border disputes (the status of the West Bank and Gaza, for example) but also on the relationship of host countries, sanctuaries, and the nature of responses to terrorist attacks. One of the central difficulties in the Palestinian case has been providing a mutually accepted definition of the character of the Palestinian community. Suggesting that at some time most states have given sanction to acts that may be largely defined as terrorist, Falk argues that "the politics of terror and the use of exile sanctuaries to disrupt `the enemy' society enjoys an ambiguous status in recent international experience." The primary concern in the following discussion is with what is broadly defined international terrorism rather than national terrorism. This excludes those acts that occurred throughout the 1967-1973 period within the borders of Israel or the Occupied Territory.

Just as perceptions of boundaries between the international and the national vary, so do perceptions of the legitimacy or illegitimacy of the use of terror as a strategy. Although the general conception that terror and the resort to terrorism are illegitimate political tools is commonly postulated, it is not universally accepted. Wilkinson points out that most of those who resort to terrorism defend or justify their actions in terms of what he refers to as "the morality of just vengeance," "the theory of the lesser evil," that no "other means were available to their movement or group," and that "terrorism has proved to be tactically 'successful' in identical conditions to one's own." The acceptance of terrorism as a "legitimate" political tactic to achieve political goals, then, depends in part not only on the acceptance of the goals of the movement engaged in terror, but also on an evaluation of terror tactics in relation to other potential tactics.

Most actions are justified either in terms of some long-term goal or short-term objective. This excludes those acts of terrorism that have no political content or purpose (for instance, the hijacking of an airplane for purposes of extorting money). A distinction may be drawn between the general acceptance of the goals of a movement and a rejection of specific tactics; this rejection may be based on moral valuation or on the effectiveness of the use of a particular tactic for achieving goals and objectives. If this is the case, attention focuses on the clear distinction between victim and target. Hutchinson recommends that one of the characteristics of terrorism is that "there is a consistent pattern of symbolic or representative selection of victims or objects of acts of terrorism." Thornton draws the distinction between "apparent indiscrimination" and "actual discrimination," asserting that the goal of the terrorist or the terroristic act is to appear indiscriminate but actually be discriminate. Terrorism, a fear - and anxiety—producing phenomenon, must create situations and acts that are directed toward a broader audience (specific or general), which is the target. This is done by selecting a victim that serves as a symbol to the target.

Weapons and Tactics

It appears that an individual or a group may have at its command a large arsenal of potential weapons and tactics, among which is terrorism, to achieve a political goal. The evaluation of terrorism as a tactic then requires answers to several crucial questions. The first, focuses on the nature of the terrorist. Those concerned primarily with the prevention of terrorism have concentrated part of their study on the "personality" of the potential terrorist. Walter states that a terror organisation requires a "directorate" that is responsible for planning and justifying acts and "agents of violence:' who actually carry out the attacks. Serge and Adler assert that "modern terrorists derive their high behavioural unpredictability largely from three factors: their multiple targets, their limited numbers and (above all) from the variety of their cultural roots. Although this suggests that terrorism may develop due to cultural and political conditions and depends on the specific characteristics and capabilities of the involved movements, studies that stress on personality or the development of personality profiles may tend to obscure the fact that terrorism rarely has a life of its own and is normally viewed as a tactic for achieving a goal.

A second question revolves around the acts themselves. What are the criteria of inclusion or exclusion? Airliner hijackings, the use of letter bombs, general bombings, the attacking of civilians are often cited as the most common forms of terrorism. Related to definitions of what is or is not a terroristic attack is the relationship between the type of act selected and the political goal or motive. Certain types of acts may be viewed as more effective or appropriate than others under specific circumstances.

A third concern, and one with much political significance, revolves around the choice of victims and intended targets. Walter identifies three actors in the course of terror, "a source of violence, a victim, and a target." As defined throughout the following discussion, victims are those individuals or groups at which a specific action is directed. The target, on the other hand, is the individual, group, or nation whom the action is intended to influence. The target is, in one sense, the recipient of the "message" of the "act" itself. Obviously, in specific cases, an individual or group may be both a victim and a target. Any analysis of the process of terrorism must include not only the identification of the victim but also the target of the said action.

The victim-target relationship raises the question of the goals and objectives of those considering the use of terror as a political tactic. If terrorist acts are not random, motiveless acts of violence, the target should, from the view of the terrorist, relate to both the victim and the goals and objectives of the movement. These objectives and goals fall into several rather broad categories. The first general category includes those acts that are particular to persuade the population, or perhaps more likely a government, to change its values and attitudes concerning a particular situation or issues, or to change a specific policy. Thornton refers to these acts as "negative" acts that are designed to induce "fright," "anxiety", or "despair." The goals of the terrorist may, for example, want to add a new variable into the political decision-making process by stressing the vulnerability of either a group or nation. Terror may also be used to create dissension among allies or potential allies. Distinctions on means of prevention and control of terrorism and differing responses to acts of terrorism may weaken the cohesion and unity not only of nations but of groups of nations. This is certainly the case, for instance, with differing attitudes toward the question of whether to negotiate with terrorists and meet their demands or to resist demands by force.

Terrorism directed at external targets and victims in general, then, seeks to create fear, stress, disorientation, and the appearance of disorganisation (the inability of the system to counteracts of terrorism), which in turn creates a climate for change.

However, terror may also be directed internally. Crozier for instance suggests that terror may be used to "eliminate traitors" within a movement (citing the Algerian example). A more "positive" role of terrorism within a movement would be the establishment of "enthusiasm among the adherents of the insurgent movement." Terrorism may provide the movement with a sense of "effectiveness" or the sense of an ability to influence or control a situation. It may serve to mobilise a targeted group to take a particular action, to create a solidarity and identity with the movement, or to ensure that a group will remain neutral or not actively hostile to a movement.

Role of International Terrorism

Any analysis of the role of international terrorism in the Palestinian case must then concentrate not only on the actors, victims, and targets, but also on the motivations, justifications, objectives, and goals of the participants. What is suggested here is that the acts of terrorism committed by certain fragments of the Palestinian community between the June 1967 war and the October 1973 war can be analysed in terms of (1) the participants involved, (2) the acts, (3) the victims of the acts, (4) the objectives of the acts, (5) the motivations, objectives, and goals of the participants, and (6) the consequences of the act. The key factor becomes the relationships between initiators, victims, targets, objectives, and goals. The pivotal question is not only the description of the differing types of actions, but whether trends emerged during this period. As indicated in Table 1, the key to an understanding of political terrorism as a political act rests with the linkages between the variables.

The history of the development of the Palestinian community and resistance is beyond the sphere of the present discussion.

However, it is important to isolate certain important events and trends that are crucial to an understanding of the role of terrorism. Included here, in addition to specific events, are the normal development of the Palestinian resistance, the relationship of the Palestinian movement to Israel and to other Arab states, the splits and divisions within the movement itself, and, finally, the relationship of the Palestinian movement and community to the larger international community. The prime concern is not with chronology, but with the relationship between the various participants, their differing objectives and goals, and the relationship of these goals to the use of terrorism as a political strategy.

Following the creation of Israel in 1948 the Palestinian population appeared dormant. Attention was focused primarily on the relationship between Israel and neighbouring Arab states. Discussions concerning the Palestinians focussed on the problems of refugees and on the collapse of Palestinian social, political, and economic institutions. Hudson describes this early stage, approximately 1948-1964, as a pre-stage to the development of the resistance. Although acts of resistance did occur, the organisation and the infrastructure generally considered indispensable for effective political action did not yet exist.

However, the conditions were generally favourable for the development of, if not a resistance movement, then a reassertion of a Palestinian sense of community. The period from 1964 to 1967 was essentially a period of gestation and formative growth. It was during this period that Al-Fatah, formed after the Suez war of 1956, first began military operations in Israel (January 1, 1965). It was also during this stage that the Arab states encouraged and supported the establishment of the Palestine Liberation Organisation (PLO) under the direction of Ahmed Shukairy. Although the PLO represented in many respects a bureaucratic, rather than an effective revolutionary organisation, and although it operated under the supervision of other Arab states, it did (as evidenced by the 1964 Arab summit conference) lend a particular legitimacy to the Palestinian movement and the conception of a Palestinian community.

TABLE 1
POSSIBLE FACTORS INFLUENCING THE RESORT TO TERRORISM BY THE PALESTINIAN RESISTANCE MOVEMENT, POTENTIAL TARGETS AND VICTIMS, AND POTENTIAL TERRORISTIC ACTS

	Movement characteristics			
Actors	*Capabilities and resources*	*Motivations*	*Potential victims and targets*	*Potential terroristic acts*
Leaders and planners	Size of movement	Long-term goals	Israel and Israelis	Airplane hijackings
Initiators and agents	Unity and cohesion of movement	Short-term objectives	Palestinians in occupied territories and Israeli Arabs	Attacks on air terminals
	Military capabilities of movement		Arab states perceived to be opposed to Israel	Letter bombings
	Freedom of movement; relationship with host nations		Arab states perceived to be positive or neutral to Israel	Attacks on governmental officials and embassies
			Great powers perceived to be opposed to Israeli	Attacks on nongovernmental individuals, groups, or concerns
			Great powers perceived to be positive or neutral to Israel	
			Other nations perceived to be positive or neutral to Israel	

[a]Great powers include the United States, the erstwhile Soviet Union, France, and Great Britain.

Increasing Conciousness and Organisation

Along with an increasing consciousness and organisation, however, came splits and divisions in the growing movement. The first, and during this period perhaps the most distinct, was between the PLO led by Shukairy and Fatah under the direction of Yasser Arafat. The questions focussed not only on the ultimate control of the movement but also on the tactics and the goals of the movement itself. Conflicts developed over whether conventional or guerrilla warfare was the more effective tactic, the length or duration of the conflict, and the long-run relationship between the Palestinians and their Arab sponsors and supporters. This last conflict became even conspicuous in the inter-war period following the occupation of the West Bank and Gaza. Thus, although there was general agreement on the broad outlines of long-term objectives, there was little agreement on (1) the best methods for achieving these goals and (2) short-term objectives. Splits occurred not only between the participant Arab states and the Palestinians but also within the Palestinian movement itself.

The defeat of the Arab states in the June 1967 war forced not only a military re-evaluation but also a political re-evaluation of the tactical realities of the area. The occupation of the West Bank and Gaza affected the organisation of the movement, at least temporarily, by limiting the scope of their action. At the same time, however, it released two potential new fronts. Low periods occurred in February and March 1966, in July and August 1966, and in November and December 1966 when internal power battle were occurring in Syria, when Syria attempted to limit and control the activities of Fatah, and when Egypt and Syria reached a mutual defence agreement. Following the 1967 war, attention shifted from attacks within the pre-1967 Israeli borders to attacks and actions in the occupied West Bank and Gaza.

As the strife began to escalate following the 1967 war, many of the distinctions that had begun to develop in the initial stages of the conflict began to sharpen. The distinction between short-term objectives and long-term goals became clearer. The Palestinian leadership, in diaspora, aimed at the utmost transformation of Israel. They remained, however, dependent on other Arab states not only for material supplies and training but also for bases of operation. As the "effectiveness" and "level" of activity enhanced, it provoked responses and counter-responses from Israel, which in turn forced Arab host states (primarily Jordan, Lebanon, and Syria) to re-evaluate their position vis-a-vis the Palestinians. This, in part, accounts for the almost cyclical nature of the resistance during this early stage. The situation was made more complex with occupation in 1967. The situation revolved around a stateless people (Palestinians), claiming a state (Israel), operating from sympathetic, but vulnerable neighbouring states (Lebanon, Syria, Jordan, and Egypt). The legitimacy or the illegitimacy of the claims from any of the participants did little to alter the understanding of the contestants or the realities of the conflict.

Just as the Arab states and Israel were forced to re-evaluate their positions following the 1967 defeat, so did the Palestinian movement. The defeat served to discredit both Ahmed Shukairy and the general organisation of the PLO. Questions were raised not only about the effectiveness of the PLO and its leadership, but also about who it actually served—the Palestinians or other Arab states. The debate within the Palestinian community focussed on the most effective and appropriate strategy and tactics in confronting Israel, given the new situation. In the broadest outlines of the debate there were two major schools. The first, generally argued by Fatah, was that the Palestinian case was most important. The overriding philosophy was Palestinian nationalism. Although there was intense and detailed discussion about the future of a Palestinian state and its features, most action, discussion, and policy formulation was directed toward the liberation of Israel. Because the ultimate goal was the "liberation" of Israel, most action should be directed specifically at Israel and the occupied territories rather than at other states. From approximately 1964 to 1969, Fatah argued for as little mediation in the internal politics of Arab states as possible. What Fatah wanted and needed were bases of operation and material support. This, from their consideration, was best achieved through accommodation rather than confrontation.

Countering this position, and emerging partly as a result of the defeat of the Arab states, was more "radical" ideological position that argued not only for the liberation of Palestine but at the same time, also for revolutionary change in what were termed the more "reactionary" Arab states. Again, although the general or long-term target remained fairly constant, this faction argued for the creation of a revolutionary struggle rather than a strictly nationalistic one. Only as a result of radical change in the Arab states could effective action against Israel be taken. Based on this position, involvement in the activities of other states became not only permissible but necessary. This position is most associated with the Popular Front for the Liberation of Palestine (PFLP) and George Habash.

From these two conflicting stances, attitudes toward tactics and specifically the use of terrorism emerge. For Fatah, from the

Palestinian perspective, action should be directed primarily at Israel, within Israel. For the PFLP, action should be directed not only at Israel but also at those Arab states that do not directly support the Palestinian movement and at other individuals, groups, or nations that actively support (or are neutral to) Israel. The inclusion of the latter group widens not only the level of the conflict but also its scope, moving the strife far beyond a Palestinian/Israeli one. The attitudes of Fatah and the PFLP on the use of terror as a legitimate tactic differ in part because of their differing perceptions of the situation.

If, as Crozier suggests, "terrorism is a weapon of the weak," and strong, well-organised resistance or revolutionary movements generally do not depend on terror as a tactic, then acts of terrorism should be expected in periods of weakness or crisis. These crises may be either internal or external to the movement. The resort to terrorism is thus at least in part determined by a realistic assessment of the capabilities of the organisation. What characterises the period between the 1967 and the 1973 wars, in addition to the resort to terrorism as a political tactic, is also a changing outlook among all of the Palestinian movements concerning its use, applicability, and effectiveness. Quite simply, as conditions changed, as the environment for political action changed, so did the objectives of the various movements. Because terror is only one tactic among many available, it is reasonable to expect that as the situation changed throughout the period so did attitudes toward terrorism and the relationship of terrorism to other tactics. While terrorism may appear, once begun, to be a never-ending, ever-increasing phenomenon, it is unusually complex and, in the Palestinian case, is directly related to the Palestinians' perception of the general and overriding causes of the conflict.

Emerging Palestinian Movement

The emerging Palestinian movement following the 1967 defeat faced several problems, each requiring a decision that in turn affected attitudes toward terrorism. First, the effective support of the Arab states was questioned. It was not clear precisely what role the Arab states might or would be able to play. Throughout the period, the changing relationship between the Arab states and

Israel and between the Arab states and the superpowers directly affected the Palestinian movement. The most explicit example of this influence was the discussion of the Rogers Peace Plan of 1970. The Palestinian movement during this period attempted to increase its independence as a political force in the Middle East and to ensure that, in any resolution or management of the confrontation, Palestinian interests would both be protected and represented, ideally by Palestinians.

A second problem was the introduction of a new boundary variable. The occupation of the West Bank and Gaza by Israel persuaded the Palestinian resistance to rely more heavily on states neighbouring Israel as bases of operation and host countries. In Jordan, the increasing tension between the Palestinian resistance movements and the monarchy consummated in the 1970-1971 Jordanian/Palestinian war. The trend throughout this period was that as the commando raids in both the occupied territories and Israel increased, the response and counter-response of the Israelis intensified. Many of these responses were directed not only at the Palestinians but at the host country held responsible. This, in turn, often led to an attempt by the host government to govern and restrict the operations and actions of the Palestinians.

Finally, throughout this period, the splits within the Palestinian movement continued and grew more acute. Much of this debate centred on tactics and strategy, on the effectiveness of various tactics, on the scope and nature of the conflict, and on the relationship between tactics and goals. Although the split between Fatah and the PFLP was one of the most distressing, there also emerged during this period a number of small, splinter groups. It is in this setting that the issue of terrorism moved centerstage.

Acts on Terrorism

In the following sections specific types of international terrorism are examined and described based on the criteria established earlier. It is admitted and realised that there is much controversy over what acts should be included as terroristic and which fall under the category of military actions and military situations. In the following discussion, acts between, for example, Palestinian commandos and Israeli military forces have been excluded. One of the broadest categories of actions throughout the period involved border infiltration into the occupied territories. Although many of these acts certainly involved aspects of terrorism (fear inducing, anxiety producing), it is argued here that they more precisely fall under classifications of guerrilla warfare. Also, because our discussion is concerned primarily with the Palestinian use of terror, we have excluded those acts by Israel that may be considered to be terroristic. A more elaborate analysis, involving a larger, more comprehensive and more comparative data set, is required to sort the complex nature of the response-counterresponse issue. Three major factions of international terroristic attacks are discussed. The first, and one of the most visible, includes air hijackings and attacks at air terminals. The second category includes letter and package bombs sent through the post. The third is attacks on individual and property, governmental as well as nongovernmental. Where appropriate, distinctions are drawn within these broad classification; acts of political assassination, political murder, sabotage (which does not involve the loss or wounding of human life) have been excluded. The prime factors used in determining inclusion or exclusion of specific acts are, first, the distinction between victims and targets and, second, whether the actions have been directed at people rather than simply at property. This has been done chiefly because terrorism, as discussed earlier, involves measuring not only the physical or material effects of an act, but also the psychological responses of both victims and targets.

Each of these three aforesaid is discussed in terms of a fivefold typology. First, each is discussed in terms of its duration and scope in the inter-war period. For example, was a particular act limited to a specific sub-period or did it span the entire period? Second, a determination of the initiators is made. This comprises both those who carry out the act and those who claim credit. The third category is an analysis of the victims and targets and, more specifically, whether particular victims and targets are more closely associated with specific types of terrorism than with others. Fourth, the motives and objectives of those committing the act are described. Are specific acts or types of terrorism more closely associated with certain targets and goals than with others? Finally, each of the acts is measured against the response it provokes. A distinction is drawn between intended and unintended responses; although based on available data, this difference remains at least partially speculative.

Air Hijackings and Attacks on Air Terminals

The general frequency of airplane hijackings has steadily increased. Figures indicate that in the period 1948-1958, for instance, there were approximately two hijackings per year. In the 1958-1963 period there were three per year; in the 1963-1968 period, seven per year; and in the 1969-1970 period, approximately fifty per year. Although airplane hijackings were not unprecedented to the Middle East in the 1967-1973 period, much of the international and national attention focused on several acts carried out mainly by the Popular Front for the Liberation of Palestine (PFLP). This section analyses and describes the general characteristics of these attacks during the interwar period.

There are three classifications of victims of aerial terrorism as practised by sections of the Palestinian resistance. The first includes Israeli citizens flying on Israeli aircraft (El Al). During the 1968-1969 period, the PFLP directed most of its attacks particularly at El Al planes (see Table 2). The justification for these attacks centred on the holding of hostages to secure the release of Palestinians held in Israeli detention and on the assertion that El Al was not a civilian airlines but an airlines serving a military purpose. The 1968 hijackers of an El Al plane in its way from Rome to Tel Aviv and the August 1969 hijackers of a TWA plane (with Israeli passengers) en route from Rome to Athens to Tel Aviv demanded the release of Palestinians and Arab prisoners then held in Israeli prisons. After the December 26, 1968, attack on an El Al plane in Athens, the PFLP stated that El Al was not "an airline undertaking innocent civilian transport" but was involved "in secret flights under supervision of the Israeli Defense Ministry" and that they were using "air force pilots trained in flying Phantom jets in preparation for a surprise attack and new aggression against the Arab states."

TABLE 2
AERIAL HIJACKINGS AND AIR TERMINAL ATTACKS, 1967-1973a, b

Date	*Group claiming credit*	*Victim-target relationship and location of attack*	*Vic-tims killed*	*Vic-tims wou-nded*	*Initi-ators killed*	*Initi-ators wou-nded*	*Destination of hijacked plane*
1	*2*	*3*	*4*	*5*	*6*	*7*	*8*
1967	-	-	-	-	-	-	-
7/23/68	PFLP	El Al-Israel in Rome	0	0	0	0	Algiers
12/28/68	PFLP	El Al-Israel in Athens	1	1	0	0	Ground attack
2/18/69	PFLP	El Al-Israel in Zurich	1	5	1	0	Ground attack
8/29/69	PFLP	TWA-Israel in Athens	0	4	0	0	Damascus
2/10/70	PFLP	Transit passengers in Munich-Israel	1	11	0	0	Ground attack
2/21/70	PFLP, Popular Com.	Explosion of Swiss plane, Zurich to London	47(all)	0	0	0	Explosion
7/22/70	Popular Struggle Front	Greek Olympic Air-Greek Government in Athens	0	0	0	0	Ground attack
9/6/70	PFLP	TWA, Pan Am, Swiss Air-Israel, Great Britain, Switzerland, West Germany from Frankfurt, Zurich, and Amsterdam	0	0	1	1	Jordan
11/9/70	Criminals expelled from Dubai	Iranian Air-Dubai in Dubai	0	0	0	0	Iran
11/10/70	Unidentified gunman	Saudi Arabian Air-unclear in Saudi Arabia	0	0	0	0	Damascus
1971	-	-	-	-	-	-	-
2/21/72	Organization for Victims of Zionist Occupation	Lufthansa-West Germany from New Delhi	0	0	0	0	South Yemen

1	*2*	*3*	*4*	*5*	*6*	*7*	*8*
5/8/72	Black Septem-ber	Sabena Belgian plane-Israel in Tel Aviv	1	4	2	1	Ground attack
5/30/72	Japanese Red Army	Attack on Lod Air Terminal-Israel in Tel Aviv	25	75	2	0	Ground attack
8/16/72	unclear	El Al plane-Israel, bomb found on plane	0	4	0	0	Bomb attempt
10/6/72	unclear	Royal Jordan Air-Jordan, bomb explodes in suitcase in Beirut	0	0	0	0	Bomb attempt
7/20/73	Japanese Red Army, several splinter groups	Japanese Air-Japan, Israel from Amsterdam to Tokyo	0	1	1	0	Dubai
8/5/73	Black Septem-ber	TWA-Israel, attack on Athens to New York plane	4	55	0	0	Ground attack
8/10/73	Israel air force	Iraqi-Palestinian, Beirut to Baghdad plane	0	0	0	0	Tel Aviv
8/16/73	Individual (Libyan)	Middle East Airline-unclear, Libya to Lebanon flight	0	0	0	0	Tel Aviv
12/17/73	PFLP (unclear)	Pan Am and Lufthansa-United States and Gre-ece, one attacked (U.S.), another hijacked (Lufthansa)	31	0	0	0	Kuwait

(a) All data are from Facts on File.

(b) Does not include unsuccessful attempts (those never carried out) or plots and reported plots.

A second form of aerial terrorism directed particularly at Israel and Israelis was attacked on air terminals. The most costly in terms of human life, and the most spectacular, was the May 30, 1972 attack on Lod Airport. This attack, which resulted in the death of twenty-five, has been attributed to both the PFLP and the Japanese "Army of the Red Star." Unlike airplane hijackings, this attack-according to its initiators —

was not designed to take hostages, but as a reprisal and a warning. The PFLP, claiming "complete responsibility," indicated that the attack was planned as a reprisal for the killing of two Arabs after an earlier attempted (but abortive) attack at Lod in May 1970. Clearly an additional motivation for both airplane hijackings and terminal attacks was to dissuade potential immigrants and tourists from either flying on Israeli-owned airliners or immigrating to or visiting Israel itself. By increasing the "cost" (psychological, material, and physical) to those willing flying Israeli carriers or going to Israel, the terrorists not only place an economic hardship on Israel but also call into question the ability of the government to safeguard both nationals and visitors. The August 1973 raid by Black September on the Athens airport, for example, was designed "to hit at emigrants to Israel because they kill our wives and children," while the PFLP, in claiming responsibility for the February 1969 hijacking of an El Al plane, stated that it was in retaliation for attacks on "unarmed and innocent civilians in occupied territory."

Another category of victim during this period was made up of European and American nationals flying on European or American carriers. In this case, the motivation again seems to be twofold—the taking of hostages and the issuance of a warning. The hijacking of a Greek Olympic airliner on July 22, 1970, a Lufthansa airliner on February 21, 1972, and a Pan Am and Lufthansa airliner on December 17, 1973, resulted in the demand for the release of Palestinians and Arabs held hostages in Athens, Rome, and Cologne prisons. Many of the Palestinians and Arabs held in European custody were, in fact, those convicted of earlier hijackings or hijack attempts. The cyclical nature of hijacking was such that an attempt during which the hijackers were captured often resulted in a subsequent hijacking designed to free those captured in the initial attempt. The hijacking of three planes by the PLFP in September 1970 (planes flown to Jordan) was carried out to secure the release of prisoners in Israel, Great Britain, Switzerland, and West Germany, to teach the Americans a lesson after they supported Israel all of these years, and as an indication of the Palestinian response to U.S. peace initiatives in the Middle East.

A third category of general victim was dissident or opposing factions within the movement itself or in other Arab states. Because most of the factions do not control or direct their own airlines, the use of air hijacking in such case becomes rather problematic. However, there were three reported hijackings of carriers belonging to other Arab states, and although it is unclear as to who the participants were or whether their motivations were political or apolitical, two merit mention. The first reported incident (November 1970) involved the hijacking of a Saudi Arabian plane to Damascus. The second was that of a bombing intended for a Royal Jordan airplane in Beirut. Although there have been relatively few attacks on carriers of Arab states, it is clear that, for example, the September 1970 hijacking to Jordan did have Jordan as a secondary target. As indicated earlier, by September 1970, the relationship between the Palestinians and the Jordanians had reached a low ebb. By the same token, the relationship between various commando organisation (Fatah and PFLP, Arafat and Habash, for example) was also highly strained.

In terms of the frequency of incidents reported, the years 1970 and 1972 show the greatest number of hijackings. Although five events were reported in 1973, one was the hijacking of an Iraqi plane by the Israeli air force (George Habash was thought to be on the plane) and the other apparently a nonpolitical act (August 16, 1973). The marked downturn in the number of hijackings in the latter part of 1970 and throughout 1971 is attributable to the shift in strategy within the Palestinian movement, to the internal struggles in the movement, and, perhaps most importantly, to the Jordanian/Palestinian war that had started in September 1970 and continued throughout 1971. From the perspective of the Palestinian movement, centerstage shifted from the external targets of Israel and her allies to the infightings facing the resistance movement.

The group most closely associated with the use of air hijacking as a tactic is the PFLP under the direction of George Habash. Also involved are various splinter groups and factions that had receded from the major Palestinian resistance groups. These include the Action Organisation for the Liberation of Palestine, the Popular Front for the Liberation of Palestine-Popular Command, the

Popular Struggle Front, the Organisation for Victims of Zionist Occupation (reportedly based in Gaza), and the Organisation of Sons of Occupied Territories. In addition, Black September, the splinter group from a Fatah nucleus following the Jordanian/ Palestinian war, claimed responsibility for two attacks during 1972-1973. Depending upon the source, Black September has been reported to be independent of Fatah or directly controlled by it. In general, however, those factions that have resorted to, and have advocated the use of, airplane hijackings and air terminal attacks are those groups that also support the expansion of the scope of the conflict beyond the Middle East. The nature of the victims and the targets, as well as the location of the attacks themselves, indicate that in addition to putting pressure on Israel, they are also designed to put pressure on those who either support Israel or are considering changing a particular policy (see below). Throughout that period, while air hijacking was almost universally condemned by the international community, it had served certain sectors of the Palestinian community as a tactic not only for securing short-term objectives (release of prisoners, discouraging international travel to Israel, and so on), but also for ensuring that the "Palestinian issue" remained articulated and in public view. It appears that although the PFLP and related groups were aware that acts such as those just described would not win general international support, they felt them necessary at a specific time and given specific situations and considered the "benefits" to outweigh the "costs."

Although there is a tendency to perceive the Palestinian movement as being monolithic, the use of this tactic was not universally approved or sanctioned. Sections of the Palestinian movement and various Arab governments expressed contrasting and often conflicting views throughout the period. In general, however, it appears that from the initial hijacking in the period (July 23, 1968) until the September 6, 1970 hijacking, reaction remained generally favourable. The exception to that was the explosion of a Swiss Air plane in February 1970, which resulted in the death of all forty-seven passengers and crew. In that case the General Command broadcast by Fatah had stated that "the Revolution strongly condemns such barbaric action," arguing that "no commando contingent would have carried out such an action."

Arafat had later stated that "the unified command of the commando organisations is now seriously reviewing the entire question of attacks on international airlines" and also that "the Palestine Revolution's policy is against endangering all civilians, wherever they are." The hijacking of three planes in September 1970, however, appears to signal a sharp break and shift in policy among both the Arab states and the more "moderate" sections of the Palestinian resistance. *Al Ahram* (September 8), reacting the use of the tactic, stated: "One of the main goals of the battle is to gain world public opinion on the side of the Palestinian struggle and not to lose it. It is evident that the attack on international civil aviation does not encourage world feeling of solidarity with the Palestinian cause." *Al Akhbar* (September 9) reacted in a similar manner stating that the international reaction "reflects the denunciation and disgust of people against those who carry out such acts."

As stated earlier, immediately following this action the Jordanian/Palestinian dispute reached an imbroglio (partly in response to the act itself), and the focus of the conflict changed. Following the resolution, or at least lessening, of the conflict between the two parties, the scope and the focus of acts of aerial terrorism appeared more blurred (see 1972-1973 in Table 2). With the exception of attacks such as those carried out had by the PFLP and the Japanese Red Army at Lod in May 1972 and the attack and hijacking of Pan Am and Lufthansa planes in December 1973, the victim-target relationship, as well as the motivations and objectives of the actors, is less precise and less explicitly stated. By the same token, the response of the Arab states and other factions of the Palestinian movement continued to be against the use of air hijacking as a political strategy. Speaking of the attack in December 1973 that resulted in the killing of thirty-one persons, Arafat asserted that it was "work of hands that do not belong to the Palestinian people" and that it was an act "of sabotage and crime aimed against the Palestinian revolution" rather than for it.

Throughout the inter-war period, the attitudes toward the legitimacy or illegitimacy of the use of aerial terrorism as well as the resort to aerial terrorism differed. These differences were due in part to the resource capabilities of those involved, to the internal splits and divisions within the movement itself, to the relationship between the Palestinian resistance movement and other states (specifically Jordan and Lebanon), and to the response of the badly-hit parties (mainly Israel, Western Europe, and the United States). Although aerial terrorism has never been generally accepted as a genuine political tool, the trend during this period suggests that following the September 1970 incident, the use of aerial terrorism became largely counterproductive for those who practised it. Increases in security precautions, among other factors, as well as changing attitudes and situations, appear to have lessened the effectiveness of the tactic. Initial evidence suggests that aerial terrorism was a strategy designed to meet a specific situation with limited goals. Mazrui speaking of the hijacking situation in 1970 states:

> But does aerial terrorism succeed only in alienating world opinion? Questions of this kind miss the whole point. In a propaganda campaign to win sympathy in the more influential parts of the world, the Arabs would be no match for the Jews ... The Palestinian purpose of aerial terrorism in 1970 was not, therefore, a quest for sympathetic publicity, but an attempt to arouse popular anxiety.

In addition, it highlighted public attention (whether that attention was favourable or unfavourable is beside the point) on the Palestinian issue and indicated to various targets, through attacks on a variety of victims, that the Palestinian resistance was cardinal, not peripheral, to the larger Middle East conflict. The goal was the creation of a specific situation (Palestinian recognition) by the use of a specific political tactic (aerial terrorism). When that tactic no longer proved effective or in most cases had started to be counterproductive, the strategy was changed and new political tactics evolved.

New Form of Terrorism: Letter Bombs and Packages

Several fundamental differences become readily apparent when aerial terrorism and terrorism by post are compared. The first is that acts of aerial terrorism are reported throughout most years of the inter-war period (with the exception of 1967 and

1971), whereas letter and package bombings are mostly restricted to 1972. As a tactic, it had a relatively short life. The intense focus on means of detection and defusing letter bombs and increased protection for potential victims led in the latter part of 1972 to a sharp decline in the number of bombs that were actually detonated. Although data are insufficient concerning letter bombs, several generalisations are possible.

Points of origin for letter and package bombs during this period were primarily European cities (Amsterdam, Athens, Vienna), Malaysia, or India. Most were addressed either to different areas in Israel or to Israeli embassies and businesses abroad. One of the most extensive of these mailings occurred on September 19, 1972, when letter or package bombs were sent to Israeli offices in at least nine cities. Among others letters and packages postmarked from Amsterdam were sent to Paris, New York, Montreal, Ottawa, Brussels, and Jerusalem. Another mailing two days later, September 21, again postmarked from Amsterdam, sent packages and letters to Israeli embassies in Kinshassa, Zaire, in Buenos Aires and to the Jerusalem post office. All of these were defused. During this same stage (on September 23) Jordan also reported that it had intercepted four letter bombs addressed to Jordanian officials (also with an Amsterdam postmark).

Other acts have included the sending of parcels directly to Israel, mailings to Jewish officials in different Zionist movements in the United States (October 14, 1972), a series of packages addressed to President Nixon, Secretary of State Rogers, and PLO officials in Lebanon, Libya, Algeria, and Egypt (many postmarked from Belgrade, Yugoslavia). Another series of packages included mailings from Malaysia and India to a rather disparate group in late October and early November 1972. Victims and potential victims included Jewish factions in London, Rome, and the United States, the Egyptian embassy in London, a British technical school with ties to Haifa University, and various Jewish individuals in London and Geneva. Finally, there were three reported cases of letter bombings in January 1973, including a letter bomb sent from Israel to Kiryat Gat in Israel, an intercepted letter from Turkey to Israel, and a letter sent from Athens to the honorary Israeli consul in Santiago, Chile.

As signified from this description of victims, they comprise a rather diverse group. Although there is some evidence to suggest that Black September was responsible for some of the mailings, it is difficult to assess responsibility. Unlike the case of aerial attacks, those responsible for the actions generally did not claim either credit or responsibility. Casualties from letter bombs remain relatively low throughout the period. In many cases, those most critically wounded were bomb-disposal experts injured as they attempted to defuse various letter bombs.

Whereas aerial hijacking and attacks on air terminals tended to have both multiple targets and varied goals, letter bombs appear to have a much more restricted focus. In some cases the letter and packages were addressed to particular individuals, while in other they were simply sent to a given address. In either case, as security and the ability to defuse these bombs increased, and at it became easier to predict when bombs would be sent and then intercept them, their use came down.

Commando Raids, Attacks, and Bombings

The final detailed category of acts of international terrorism includes a variety of different types of attacks against individuals and groups. This category includes not only those attacks on governmental officials and institutions (mainly embassies), but also attacks on non-governmental individuals, groups, and other concerns. The types of violence and terror used generally were either bombings or commando-style raids. Victims and targets comprised Israelis and Arabs, as well as Europeans and Americans.

The most severe attacks on governmental officials and institutions had taken place in 1972-1973. One of the earliest attacks reported, however, was the explosion of a bomb (one wounded) in the British consulate in Jerusalem in February 1969. Claiming responsibility, the PFLP stated that it was in response to a report that Britain planned to sell tanks to Israel. In December 1972 four members of Black September seized the Israeli embassy in Thailand and had demanded the release of thirty-six prisoners held in Israeli prisons. The six hostages had been held for 19 hours, after which the four commandos were flown to Cairo. Their demands were not met, and there were no reports of loss of life or serious injury. Al Icab, a relatively obscure and little known organisation, raided the Saudi Arabian embassy in Paris in September 1973; initially the five attackers took thirteen hostages (including nationals from Saudi Arabia, France, Tunisia, Egypt, Sudan and Yugoslavia) and demanded that Jordan release the Palestinian leader Abu Daoud, then being held in a Jordanian prison. Later the attackers released all but four Saudi Arabian hostages, dropped their demand for the release of Daoud, and requested safe passage. On September 8, having been criticised by the PLO and having had difficulty finding a safe haven, the five released their hostages and were arrested in Kuwait. Two of the victims were reported to have been injured.

The most spectacular and violent attack on an embassy had occurred in March 1973. Approximately ten members of Black September attacked the Saudi Arabian Embassy in Khartoum, Sudan, and held it for 3 days. The attack had taken place during a farewell reception for the US ambassador, and the hostages included a wide range of representatives from the diplomatic community. The demands comprised the release of prisoners held in Jordan (mainly Fatah prisoners and again including Abu Daoud), the release of women held in Israeli detention, the release of members of the Baader-Meinhof Group in West Germany, and reportedly the release of Sirhan Sirhan in the United States. The demands against Israel, West Germany, and the United States were later withdrawn.

This attack is indicative of several general trends. The first was that the attack was directed at the embassy of at least minimally sympathetic country (Saudi Arabia) within the borders of another nominally sympathetic country (Sudan). Second, the primary target was another Arab state, in this case Jordan.

The use of this strategy appears to be directly related to the Jordanian/Palestinian war of 1970-71. Although there were secondary targets, the primary goal appears to have been the release of prisoners taken during the 1970-1971 dispute. The execution of the attacks by members of Black September, which grew out of the Jordanian/Palestinian dispute, further supports this contention. Finally the tactic itself provoked a response that generally led to the disuse of the tactic. The killing of the diplomats, coupled with Sudan's refusal to negotiate, ultimately led to the collapse of the attack; and it has been reported that sections of the Palestinian movement aided in the negotiations that led to the eventual surrender when it became clear that there was no alternative.

A second analysis of commando-style attacks and bombings are those directed at non-governmental institutions and officials. These acts generally fall into broad types: The first includes bombings and general attacks of sabotage; the second includes attacks executed by commando units.

In November 1969 the PFLP carried out a series of coordinated attacks on Israeli staffed offices. These included the El Al office in Brussels and the Israeli embassies in Bonn as well as in the Netherlands. The stated reason for the attack was that the PFLP intended to attack Israeli interests that were involved in bringing people to Israel and the embassies that "are the centres of espionage and collection points for mercenaries and immigrants to our occupied Palestine."

It was reported that Bonn and the Netherlands were chosen because both countries were involved in the training of Israeli pilots. In November 1969 the Palestine Popular Struggle Front (based in Amman) claimed responsibility for a hand grenade attack on the EL Al office in Athens. No official reason was stated for the attack. A July 1973 attack, also at the El Al office, was foiled by a guard. There were no reported fatalities and the attackers (after holding seventeen hostages in a nearby hotel for 5 hours) were flown in Kuwait. A somewhat different kind of attack occurred in March 1970. Claiming credit, the PFLP launched rocket attacks on U.S. property in Beirut and southern Lebanon. In a statement the PFLP suggested that the attacks were in retaliation for "plans of the U.S. embassy in Beirut to incite religious strife and create civil massacres in Lebanon aimed at paralysing the Palestinian resistance movement." Little damage and no fatalities or injuries were reported.

Several other attacks during this period are significant. One incident involved an attack in Nicosia, Cyprus, on the apartment building in which the Israeli ambassador lived and was combined with a related attack on an El Al plane before takeoff. This double strike, carried out by an unnamed group in April 1973, resulted in the death of one victim and the wounding of two others. In September 1973, the Eagles of the Palestinian Revolution, reportedly a splinter faction from Al-Fatah, captured three Jewish hostages on a Moscow-Vienna train. The stated reason for the action was "because we feel that the immigration of Soviet Union Jews is a great danger to our cause." Part of ultimate goal of the action was the closing of the Austrian transit facilities for Soviet Jews immigrating to Israel. There were no reported fatalities.

Clearly, the most striking act of terrorism throughout the entire 1967-1973 period was the attack, in September 1972, on the Israeli Olympic team in Munich. The attack on the Olympic village and the subsequent battle at the airport resulted in the death of eleven Israeli athletes. This attack executed for the stated purpose of securing the release of Palestinians held in Israeli prisons, is significant, in part, because it illustrates the interrelatedness of terrorist activity during that period. For example, many subsequent incidents of terrorism and counter-terrorism were related directly to the Munich attack in 1972. The attack resulted not only in strong retaliatory action by Israel against guerrilla bases in Lebanon and Syria (on September 8, 1972, for example), but also in new acts by sections of the Palestinian movement that were thoroughly related to the Munich attack. The action/counteraction cycle for example resulted in the placing of curbs on guerrilla activity in Lebanon, which in turn led to a further straining of the Lebanese-Palestinian relationship. The Munich action also gave way to renewed activity within the United Nations on the question of terrorism and its control. The almost universal condemnation of the act forced on several sections of the Palestinian resistance a re-evaluation of the use of the strategy. The action in Germany also led to a restriction on both Palestinian and Arab individuals and organisations within the Germany and to an investigation of the relationship between the terrorists responsible for the attack and other radical outfits (the Baader-Meinhof group, for example). As suggested earlier, it was also during this period that a series of letter bombings and political murders occurred throughout Europe.

Conclusions

From the perspective of certain segments of the Palestinian resistance, the resort to international terrorism and the selection of particular acts of terrorism (aerial terrorism, letter bombs, commando attacks, and so forth) are based on an assessment of a set of specific criteria. These criteria include — in addition to the supposed "effectiveness" of specific acts — the objectives and targets of the movement, the victim-target relationship, the degree of cohesion or disunity within the movement, the definition of the scope of the conflict, and the resources and capabilities of the movement. In terms of the Palestinian movement, these factors and parameters were in a constant state of change in the period under study. As they changed, so did attitudes toward the use of international terrorism as a political tactic.

The nascent Palestinian resistance movement in this period was characterised by the need to achieve some degree of group cohesion and ideological consensus, to develop an effective institutional organisation, and to ensure that in any settlement reached concerning the Arab-Israeli impasse, Palestinian, interests would be safeguarded and represented. Factors that aided or hindered this growth were the general defeat of the Arab states in 1967, the occupation of the West Bank and Gaza, the fractionalisation of the movement itself, the Jordanian-Palestinian war of 1970-71, and the reaction of Israel to both acts of terrorism and guerrilla-style warfare. Any understanding of the role of terrorism has played in the development of the Palestinian consciousness and resistance is best understood from the interaction of these factors. For certain segments of the Palestinian resistance, the use of international terrorism was one strategy, among many, which was designed to secure the achievement of certain political goals.

A more complete and comprehensive treatment of the role of international terrorism in both the growth of the Palestinian movement and the general Middle East conflict requires a more detailed analysis of the relationship between terror as a political tactic and other tactics available to resistance movements.

This chapter suggests that acts of terrorism committed during this period are best understood within the wider context of both the development of the Palestinian movement and the larger Middle East strife. More empirically comprehensive and theoretically detailed studies should then concentrate not only on terror and terrorism but also on the relationship of terror and terrorism to both national and international violence. What is required is a larger body of empirical data on terror and terrorism that, while not condoning or accepting its use as a legitimate political tactic, can leads to an understanding of its causes, its extensive forms and its control.

The tendency in periods of crisis and stress is to predict and expect that terrorism and the use of terror will be with us and will continually increase. This, in fact, may be one of terrorism's objectives. Initial empirical evidence suggests otherwise, however. From 1967-1973 in the Middle East, the use of terrorism varied in terms of types of acts committed, their frequency, their intensity and their objectives. This suggests that terrorism will not either instinctively increase or decrease, but rather that it will vary according to the relationship between a series of complex, often contradictory, political, economic, and social variables.

Fourteen

Threat in Egypt

Islamic tradition runs deep in Egypt's age-old history and culture. Al-Azhar University mosque, which has graced the city of Cairo for a millennium, is eloquent testimony to the enduring strength of Islam. Since its founding in 972 and until the advent of the modern period in the nineteenth century, al-Azhar played a pivotal role in shaping the country's religious, educational, and cultural life, preserving its essentially Islamic mold. The focal religious institution for the study of law, theology, Qur'anic exegesis, and classical Arabic, it propagated religious conservatism and traditional values. It stood at the zenith of an educational system at the bottom of which were the *kuttab* (mosque, or Qur'anic school), the *madrasa* (religious school), and the Sufi (mystical) orders. The system was the only disseminator of education and culture to uncounted successive generations and remained dominant in Egyptian life until the introduction of modern European ways by the father of modern Egypt. Muhammad Ali Pasha (1805-1848).

However, the new secular educational system did not supplant, but existed alongside the old system, inculcating Western science and notions. Eventually, the two educational tracks, with their divergent orientations, created a dichotomized culture that has persisted to the present. The onset of nineteenth century modernism did not eclipse Islam, but rather precipitated an Islamic revivalist movement in the second half of the previous century.

Early Muslim Reformers

Early Muslim reformers, such as Jamal Al-Din Al-Afghani and Muhammad Abdu, called for a revitalisation of Islamic thought, institutions, and society through the adoption of modern science and education. These scholars were well versed in Islamic learning and, at the same time, had been equally exposed to European education and culture, some aspects of which they had come to appreciate and sought to incorporate into their own society. They argued that Muslims should be aware of overall development elsewhere in the world and adapt to the new circumstances it imposed. A synthesis of Islam and modernity could be the medium whereby their society could advance within the Islamic context. The objective was a renewal of Islam as the only means to recovery and power in the modern age.

The assumption of the reformers was that true Islam is not in conflict with modern life and can be reconciled with science and progress. They called for the revival of *ijtihad* (application of personal reasoning in the interpretation of Islamic doctrine) so that Islam could assimilate Western concepts and culture to the nearest equivalent of its principles. Thus, the reformers sought an awakening derived from religion. Indeed, they all consistently defended the very essence of Islam and its relevance to *al-nahda* (renaissance). Once Islam was purified of the accretions that had corrupted its essence and led to *al jumud* (stagnation), it would adapt to modernity. Further, it was deemed easier to institute reforms based upon religious restoration than upon European secular rationalism. Hence, change was given an Islamic justification, not an Occidental, empirical-utilitarian one. Attempts to develop an Islamic synthesis turned out to be fragile and inconclusive and had limited appeal for the conservative *ulema* (religious leaders) and the traditional masses. Neither faction was ready or willing to accept a liberalised Islam and all that it would entail. Not surprisingly, the Islamic reformation consequently failed to take root. In fact, it is even assailed by contemporary fundamentalists, who renounce the idea of a compromise between Islam and the modern West as tantamount to an abandonment of culture and identity. This is manifest in their anti-Western stance, which, contrary to that of the early revivalists, dismisses the Western example as an invalid and irrelevant to the Muslim context.

Despite the tenuous nature of early reforms, the fact remains that the initial voices for an Islamic renaissance clearly show that the very idea of Islamic revival is deeply entrenched in Egypt and has continued to express itself in one form or another under different Islamic movements until the present. Concomitant with the Islamic call, nineteenth-century Egypt developed a liberal tradition and culture that suffused its political life. The course of modernisation and an opening up to Europe, initiated by the modern Egyptian state under Muhammad Ali, proceeded steadily. The spread of Western cultural and educational influences promoted a semblance of modern liberal culture championed by a small, but growing Western-educated elite who wanted to incorporate Western notions and beliefs, values, and techniques into the predominantly traditional Islamic milieu in Egypt. Modernisers, such as Rifa'a al-Tahtawi, Qasim Amin, and Ahmad Lutfi al-Sayyid, looked to European thought, politics, and economics for *tajdid* (renewal).

Forerunners of a Liberal Movement

Forerunners of a liberal movement that sought an awakening not derived from religion, they never denounced religion or dismissed its vital role in society. They were simply more receptive to Western intellectual tradition than to earlier Islamic epistemology. By the turn of the century, a growing infatuation with the European model made the modernist message susceptible to European secular nationalist thought. The emergent liberal-nationalist faction, imbued with Western liberal principles, led the struggle for independence from Great Britain (1918-1922) and dominated the political and cultural landscape. As a result, Egypt's early encounter with modernity influenced its institutional and political development in accordance with the European example. Indeed, the modernisation of Egypt and its opening and exposure to the West made it the cultural and educational lighthouse of the larger Arab world, transmitting liberalism and modernism.

Islamic revivalism in Egypt, then, was counterbalanced and tempered from its inception by the ascendant forces of liberalism and nationalism, which guided the country on a modern path, starting with Muhammad Ali and continuing during the British rule (1882-1922) and after independence under the monarchy. The monarchic period (1922-1952) ushered in liberal constitutionalism and nationalism, led by a Western-oriented liberal elite. The stress was on building an integrated modern national community. Revolutionary nationalism and socialism followed in the post-1952 revolution under Gamal Abdul Nasser, with its emphasis on populism and Arab radicalism. Anwar Sadat (1970-1981) shifted toward a comparatively more open and liberalised economic and political direction, leading to free entrepreneurial activity and limited democratisation—which has continued, although slowly, under Hosni Mubarak. Throughout, all attempts by various Islamic groups to change the course of the Egyptian state proved to be unavailing.

Despite the ascendancy of the modernist-nationalists, the tradition of Islamic revivalism continued very much in the twentieth century with the establishment of Jama' at al-Ikhwan al-Muslimoun (the Society of the Muslim Brotherhood) in 1928 by Supreme Guide Hasan al-Banna. It became the major mainstream Islamic fundamentalist movement and has still remained so, with its adherents and branches in other Arab countries making it close to being a transnational pan-Islamic movement. Essentially, it is an indigenous Islamic protest movement against the forces of change and modernity, large-scale government corruption and social and economic injustice, and foreign influence. All these debilitating conditions were, in the words of its leader, plunging Egypt into a "pit of degradation" and defeat. Starting as a reform movement concerned largely with religious activities and individual and social morality, the Ikhwan—or Brotherhood—grew in the 1940s into a populist Islamic movement with an activist political bent, advocating an Islamic polity based on Islamic norms and laws (*Shari'a*). The movement quite surprisingly found its strongest support among the middle and lower-middle classes, who saw Islam as Egypt's salvation. Indeed, the Brotherhood spoke to the masses in their own language, the simple language of Islam, affirming the notion that "Islam provides thorough and sound solutions to all problems." This is in marked contradistinction to the elitist intellectual discourse of nineteenth-century Muslim reformers, which failed to penetrate the masses' sentiments and hence never moved them.

Moreover, the Brotherhood movement's popular appeal was greatly enhanced by the large-scale network of social, educational, religious, and charitable organisations it established in cities and towns across Egypt. Local volunteers and financial support from domestic and foreign (mainly Gulf area) pious wealthy Muslim philanthropists provided the backbone for these structures. They served as centres for dissemination of the Islamic message and recruitment of members. Equally, this network of service structures helped to institutionalise the movement in Egyptian life, giving it strength and durability to become practically an autonomous society—a society within the larger society. Another important feature of the Ikhwan that became a trademark of modern Islamic fundamentalism is that Hasan al-Banna and the successor leaders were intellectual laymen, products of modern Egyptian institutions and universities, not the traditional al-Azhar. And they sought to recruit young men of similar backgrounds.

Rise of Ikhwan

Indeed, with the rise of the Ikhwan, the Islamic movement came increasingly under the control of educated lay leaders, marking a shift away from the religious scholars' leadership of early Muslim revivalism. The shift reflects, too, the anticlerical attitude existing among modern fundamentalists. They accuse the official *ulema* of antiquated religious formalism and irrelevance and of political subservience as "the mouthpiece of the government." Actually, there was much current anxiety among the *ulema* about their diminishing role and authority in the society. Their position, which started to erode with the onset of modernisation, is now being chipped at further by the young fundamentalists. But the most important legacy of the Ikhwan is that it has politicised Islam and injected it with a new dynamism and activism, which thrust it to the fore-front of public affairs, a status that paved the way for the growth of Islamic militancy in Egypt. Indeed, today's militant fundamentalist groups are rooted in the Muslim Brotherhood. At centrestage during the 1940s—a period of increasing social and political turmoil and violence in Egypt—the Ikhwan saw the Egyptian state as a colony under British tutelage, despite official independence in the early 1920s, and ruled in conjunction with a privileged Westernised group.

It sought both to rid the country of undesirable forces and to establish an Islamic system in accord with *al-salaf al-salih* (the early pious ancestors in the seventh century). Also, it took up the cause of the Palestinian Arabs in the fight against the Zionists by sending volunteers to take part in the Palestine war of 1948. Its increasing power and popularity were viewed with considerable alarm by the Egyptian state, prompting the first government crackdown in 1948. This led to the gruesome assassination of Prime Minister Mahmoud Fahmi al-Nuqrashi by a member of the Ikhwan later the same year and the counter-assassination of the leader of the Ikhwan, Hasan al-Banna, shortly thereafter.

But the Brotherhood survived and continued to operate, though outside the law. In fact, during much of its history it was tolerated—but not legalised—as long as it neither undermined nor challenged the authority of the state. Historically, the centrality of the state in maintaining social and political order has always been vital in Egyptian life, and the state has always jealously guarded its prerogatives. Although the Brotherhood did not publicly espouse violence against the state, its clandestine paramilitary wing (*al-jihaz al-khas*, or special apparatus) occasionally committed destructive acts. Thus, on the few occasions the Ikhwan threatened the state, the latter moved forcefully to suppress it. Such was the case in the 1948 repression, in the 1954 banishment of the movement after the abortive attempt on Nasser's life, and in the 1965 arrest and repression of the younger leaders who had unremittingly castigated Nasser's "Godless" nationalist-socialist state. After a brief period of coexistence and maintenance of at least a pretense of cooperation with the new post-1952 revolutionary regime, the Ikhwan soon found itself in collision with the emergent nationalist state of Nasser, which it accused of deviating from Islamic tenets and deteriorating into military dictatorship. The military-state dictatorship was held responsible for the decline of Islam and the rise in the barbarity of *jahiliyya* (pre-Islamic paganism).

Over the next two decades, Nasser's stringent repressive measures incapacitated the Ikhwan politically, with fateful consequences for the future of the movement in Egypt. Thousands of members were jailed and tortured, and several top ideologists were executed such as Abdul Qader Odeh in 1955 and Sayyid

Qutb in 1966. The intensity of the crackdown, the inhuman prison experience, and the prolonged underground existence radicalised the movement and gave rise to militant splinter groups that split from the Ikhwan. Thus, a new breed of extremist Islamic outfit was created, incubated in Nasser's prison cells and hatched under Sadat's policies of *infitah* (openness) in the 1970s. Nearly two dozen radical groups emerged in the span of a decade, major among them the Islamic Liberation Party the Technical Military Academy Group), Jama'at al-Takfir wa al-Hijra (the Apostasy and Flight group), the Jihad Organisation, and al-Jama'a al-Islamiyya (the Islamic Jama'a or Group). They charted a path of confrontation and violence against the state and its symbols, while the revived main body of the Ikhwan eschewed violence in favour of a strategy of change by peaceful means.

The difference widened the division with the young zealots, who objected to the Ikhwan's moderation in seeking a modus vivendi with Sadat. But, despite the divergent strategies, they all remained deeply committed to the ultimate objective of bringing about an Islamic state system. Shortly after coming to power in 1970, Sadat unleashed the Islamic movement and even encouraged establishment of Islamic groups on university campuses and in various professional associations and trade unions with a view to stem the imminent threat to his regime posed by the leftist-Nasserist power centres. As well, he allowed the Ikhwan to operate publicly and to expand its social, educational, religious, and philanthropic service networks at a time of government retrenchment and retreat from state welfarism under the new economic policy of *infitah*. These moves paved the way for the Islamist forces to assume a significant role in Egypt's public life and for the emergence of the cluster groups of the Islamic Jama'a.

Role of Sadat

Sadat went beyond his accommodation of and cooperation with the movement to accept religious Islamic rhetoric and symbols in order to thereby gain respectability and buttress his position. His initiatives ranged from assuming the title *al-ra'is al-mou'min* (the believer-president) to using the first name Muhammad, invoking the name of God at the start of his public addresses, and wearing traditional dress (*jallabiyya*). More important, the 1971 constitution declared *Shari'a* "a principal source of legislation" in Egypt, thus tying the legal system of Islamic law. Sadat, then, helped to promote further the atmosphere of religiosity that had been in evidence since the 1967 war. Yet, the use of Islam by a national leader for political purposes has its price. It can set in motion inimical forces that will come back to haunt him. In fact, the more Sadat stressed the religious theme and the more he connected his state with religion, calling it "the state of science and faith," the more he became vulnerable to the Islamic opposition—which came to pass. His initial policies, aimed at containing the leftist-Nasserist threat, eventually gave rise to a far greater Islamic challenge with the blossoming of the radical fundamentalist organisations as they expanded recruitment and training. It was not long before the nascent Islamic formations of the early 1970s grew in strength and charisma, especially among the many disaffected young, the emerge later in the decade as the lading nay sayers to Sadat, rejecting his domestic and foreign policies and the legitimacy of his "un-Islamic" regime.

Meanwhile, the Ikhwan demonstrated its moderation by denouncing the militants' doctrine and tactics and keeping a working relationship with Sadat. It did so despite its opposition to his peace initiative with Israel and his general coalition with the United States as betraying the Islamic struggle and to some aspects of his economic and political liberalisation as leading to neither greater welfare of the society nor wider participation and freedoms. It continued to follow a peaceable course within the legal framework of the system, cooperating with other political forces.

In particular, it focussed on building wide-based networks of social-welfare, economic, educational, and medical services and on penetrating and controlling university bodies and professional associations. All were utilised to create a climate of Islamicity that was beneficial to mainstream Islamists. Under Mubarak, the Muslim Brotherhood was drawn further into the system, taking a pivotal part in the open social, economic, and political environment. In multiplying its economic and social welfare organisations, it gained a central role in public welfare eclipsing that of the dilapidated government agencies. It operated its own publishing houses and newspapers, propagating freely its Islamist message. Above all, it participated in free elections within unions and professional associations and won control of such frontline associations as those of lawyers, physicians, pharmacists, and engineers. And it ran candidates in parliamentary races in coalition with secular parties such as the New Wafd Party in 1984 and the Socialist Labor Party in 1987. It even repeatedly sought recognition as a political party itself, but was denied legitimacy because of the prohibition on religiously oriented parties.

Thus, despite a unsteady course that had taken the Ikhwan in and out of acceptability, coexistence has become a modus operandi. The Brotherhood by and large reconciled itself with the Egyptian state, using only legal means to move society and state in the desired Islamic direction. Although it remains "illegal," it had represented a viable substitute model of a just and orderly society juxtaposed to Nasser's and successor regimes. It acted as a real opposition intent on its role: opposing. Hence, Sadat was not willing, nor was Mubarak willing, to legitimise it. Mubarak, like Sadat, wants to temper its potential strength and keep it subject to government whims, while keeping whip in hand. Contrary to the mainstream Ikhwan movement, the new, younger fundamentalist factions pursued a course of violent confrontation with the state, a course that has been the centre of attention internally and externally since the mid-1970s. These groups represent the radical *jihadi* (invoking holy war) tendency in the Islamic movement: the holy warriors of Islam. Chief among them were the Technical Military Academy Group and the Apostasy and Flight Group in the 1970s and the two major cell groups that have proliferated since the 1980s: the *Jihad* Organisation and the Islamic Jama'a.

They have forsworn the Ikhwan because of its compromises and accommodation with the system; accused the state, or state and society, of being un-Islamic, living in a condition of *jahiliyya* (pre-Islamic unbelief, or apostasy); and declared *jihad* (armed struggle) as the mode to bring about an Islamic transformation in accord with their rigid religious interpretation. Thus, all the new groups are against the post-1952 nationalist state because it is inimical to Islam. Ironically, these neofundamentalists are themselves believed to be the product of the Nasserist policies of open, free education, egalitarianism, and high job expectations. The intellectual fountainhead and inspiration of the radical Islamic movement was Sayyid Qutb, the young chief ideologue of the Ikhwan in the 1960s. He elaborated an ideology of resistance (*jihad*) against authority based upon his doctrinal interpretation of the prevailing conditions of Muslim societies as vitiated by *jahiliyya* and their rulers as *kuffar* (un-Islamic, or apostates). And all those in the society who partake in this state of affairs are in the category of apostates. Qutb's conception of *takfir* (to apostatise, or to declare someone non-Muslim) and *jihad*, which sanctions the overthrow of corrupt rulers by force, established a dangerous precedent for future radical fundamentalists to follow.

In the same manner, the Jama'at al-Takfir wa al-Hijra (the Apostasy and Flight Group), led by veteran Ikhwan member Shukri Mustafa, declared that the Egyptian state and society were infested by *jahiliyya*, which required major moral overhauling to bring about a true Muslim society. To achieve that end, the group called for a retreat (*hijra*) by a nucleus of true believers to the desert and mountains to build a "model Islamic community" that could grow subsequently lead in a victorious struggle (*jihad*) against the *jahiliyya* society. The strategy of retreat and reconquest is analogous to the Prophet's flight in A.D. 622 from Mecca to Medina, where he founded the first Muslim community, and his recapture of Mecca eight years after. The group had a violent showdown with the authorities in July 1977 subsequent to the kidnapping and killing of a former minister of *al-awqaf* (religious endowments), Sheikh Muhammad Hussein Al-Dhahabi, a frontline member of the ulema. Many of the militants were either killed or imprisoned, and the top leaders, including Shukri Mustafa, were executed in 1978. One can surmise that the group's action shows its rejection of and brutality to the official *ulema*, whom they termed "*ulema' al-sulta*" (being slavish to the government). Al-Dhahabi had a record of vehemently characterising the militants as misguided, even deviant—a behaviour that, for the group, cast him in the role of a state agent echoing the government line.

Islamic Liberation Party

Similarly, the Islamic Liberation Party (the Technical Military Academy Group) and the successor groups of the Jihad Organisation and its ideological associate the Islamic Jama'a saw the prevalent corruption and decadence in the society as rooted in its ruling elite. To redeem the society, the elite would have to be transformed into an Islamic leadership that applied Shari'a. The transformation should be carried out not by the means of religious education and moral uplifting, but by direct action and open confrontation: an all-out *jihad*. In his ideological tract *Al-Farida al-Gha'iba* (The absent commandment), Muhammad Abdul Salam Farag, leader of the *Jihad* Organisation in 1979, pronounced the government to be apostate and an entity to be fought through a holy war by believers; a return to *jihad* was the only way to redemption.

The stridency and aggressive stance of these factions brought them into open conflict with the state, starting with the bloody attempted takeover of the Technical Military Academy in April 1974 by the Islamic Liberation Party as part of a coup. This was followed by the assassination of Sadat in October 1981 by members of the Jihad Organisation. The conflict has continued throughout much of the 1980s and into the 1990s. The assassination of Sadat and the abortive fundamentalist revolt that ensued in the city of Asyut in Upper Egypt (al-Sa'id) shook the Egyptian state to its foundation. Al-Sa'id, in southern Egypt—predominantly rural, traditional religious, and poor—is the hotbed of the militant Islamic Jama'a, which spearheaded the sanguinary rebellion. (In fact, the extremism of the Jama'a is heavily conditioned by its southern circumstances: economic impoverishment and deeply rooted traditions, such as *tha'r*, or vendetta, that supersede the power of the law). After a brief lull after Mubarak's accession and an initial attempt at a dialogue, the acts of violence were ongoing in the second half of the 1980s and escalated in the post-Gulf War period in the early 1990s. Led by the Islamic Jama'a and the Jihad Organisation, militants killed top government officials and security officers, members of the Coptic Christian minority, writers, and foreign tourists in a relentless murderous cycle.

Assasinations and Threats

Assassinations and threats of assassination of prominent state symbols, public figures, journalists, writers, and other leading personalities comprised the intimidating strategy of choice. It eventuated in the murder of Dr. Rif'at al-Mahgoub, former speaker of parliament, in 1990; abortive attempts on the lives of Minister of Interior Hasan al-Alfi and his two predecessors in the early 1990s; an abortive attempt at assassinating journalist Makram Muhammad Ahmad in the late 1980s; the assassination of secularist writer Farag Foda in 1992; and the attack on Nobel Prize laureate Naguib Mahfouz in 1994, among others. Violence against the Christian Copts in particular reached unprecedented proportions. Anti-Coptic riots and assaults were instigated between 1979 and 1981 by extremists and popular religious preachers such as Sheikh Abdul Hamid Kishk, whose fundamentalist sermons on cassettes were widely circulated inside Egypt and out. In al-Sa'id—where the Copts are the most numerous, constituting almost 20 per cent of the area population compared to less than 10 per cent of the overall population—the Islamic Jama'a vented its animus against the "Coptic danger." The militant fundamentalists waged a campaign of terror and intimidation against the Christian communities in various towns and villages in the south, sanctioning the robbing of businesses, attacks on churches, evictions, and even the murder of those who opposed Muslim dictates.

Muslim extremists saw the Coptic Christian minorities as alien subjects serving as agents of the West in the midst of Islam. In a nation that had traditionally prided itself on religious tolerance and social harmony, the actions of the extremists posed a tremendous threat to social order and stability an affront to government authority. Another target of high visibility and immense importance was tourism. Attacks on tourists were meant to damage the tourist industry, Egypt's main hard currency source of more than $3 billion annually; its loss or even diminution could aggravate the economic crisis in the country. It is estimated that the resultant fall in tourism cost between $700 million and $1 billion in 1992. The attacks, then, are not only a show of rejection of the West, Westerners, and their repugnant ways, but also a means to undercut a resource helpful to the regime and to stifle foreign investment—both vital for the regime's economic development schemes. The assumption of the fundamentalist militants is that the greater the economic hardships, the greater the prospects for popular revolt advantageous to their cause.

Equally important, the power of the Islamic militants flourished with the creation of "Islamised spaces" or zones, chipping away at the dominion of the state. The militants grew so strong that they were able to control whole poor neighbourhoods in Cairo, such as Ein Shams, Imbaba, Umraniyya, and eczawiya al-Hamra, and small towns and villages in Upper Egypt, such as el-Fayyum, Dayrut, al-Minya, and Sanbu. They had become virtually the principal domestic power in these geographic locations—imposing their own social and moral code; running their own mosques with their own preachers; providing rudimentary social welfare services; and settling disputes and applying Qur'anic *hudud*, or sanctions, completely outside government authority. The government presence was hardly to be noticed. These Islamised spaces not only were moral puritan enclaves representative of the ideal future society, but also provided competing networks of social and economic support services that rivalled and even supplanted the inefficient government system. These Islamic strongholds have witnessed repeated blood-baths with the security forces since 1987. As the Islamic opposition from below loomed large with its "frightening alternative," challenging openly and ferociously the power of the Egyptian state; the government launched an equally, fearsome and relentless counterattack. Its initial response was a combination of repression and accommodation. It sought to quell the militant opposition, while courting the moderate Ikhwan and orthodox Muslims generally.

Starting in the summer of 1992, great force and mass arrests were used to break up the power of the fundamentalists in their strongholds in the Cairo slums and in Upper Egypt—there to restore government hegemony. Entire neighbourhoods and villages were put under virtual siege, swamped by special police forces and kept under constant security watch. Further, a systematic campaign was instituted to "decapitate" the Jama'a and Jihad leaderships and deplete their ranks. In the clashes, more than six hundred people were killed. With the escalation of the government's campaign, military courts and the death penalty (introduced under emergency laws in effect since the early 1980s) were utilised to deal swiftly and severely with "terrorist crime". Mass executions of dozens of militants have occurred since, the largest number of Egyptian executions for political crimes in this century. Such a singularity was particularly shocking for a society that has been known for its traditional moderation and tolerance; it is tantamount to a loss of innocence.

Unprecedented Harshness

The unprecedented harshness and extent of the government blows evoked domestic criticism and international protestation from human rights organisations. But the government, impelled to greater authoritarianism by what it deemed threats to domestic security, dismissed such talk as injurious to Egypt's efforts to maintain stability and establish law and order. The High Constitutional Court supported the government over the legality of using military courts for trying civilians for acts of terrorism under the emergency laws. Also, the government refused to recognise the Egyptian Organisation for Human Rights. It accused the organisation of being foreign-supported and used by terrorist groups and dismissed it as a "voguish" enterprise run by a coalition of Nasserists and Islamists seeking publicity at home and abroad. Mubarak was emphatic. "I refuse to allow human rights to become a slogan to protect terrorists." At the end of the day, the Muslim extremists were no match for the strong arm of the state. The government's efforts to contain the radical fundamentalist threat extended to the foreign front. On one level, the Mubarak regime launched a global campaign to discredit and isolate Iran and Sudan as the two leading centres of Islamic radicalism, accusing them of supporting terrorism in Egypt and elsewhere in the region. Both countries have become favourite targets of governments facing intense internal fundamentalist opposition.

It is true that these two nations have furnished the fundamentalists some general support, but the fact is that Egyptian fundamentalism is a home-grown movement embedded in Egyptian circumstances. On another level, Mubarak moved to cut off the militants' foreign sources of support, appealing to the rich Gulf Arab states, where the bulk of contributions from pious affluent individuals and charitable foundations emanates, to control the outflow of money. He also sought to promote regional security cooperation with Tunisia, Algeria, Saudi Arabia, and Pakistan (some militant Egyptian radicals who had fought in the Afghan war maintained bases and training centres in Peshawar) in order to coordinate strategy in the fight against the radicals.

Role of Mubarak

Mubarak sought as well to place the issue of terrorism under the international attention following the bombing of the World Trade Centre in New York city in early 1993. Sheikh Omar Abdul Rahman, spiritual leader of the Islamic Jama'a in Egypt, and some of his followers were charged and convicted as the masterminds of that event. Mubarak called on the United States to play a "tough role" because terrorism is a source of problems not only for the Middle East, but also for other regions and countries. Additionally, at the International Conference on the Prevention of Crime and the Treatment of Offenders, held in Cairo in May 1995, Egypt pushed hard for adoption of a resolution equating terrorism with international organised crime and calling for a concerted international effort to combat it. Mubarak repeatedly emphasizes the theme of the international character and scope of today's terrorist acts. On this point, he seems to be in full agreement with the late Israeli Prime Minister Yitzhak Rabin, who viewed Islamic fundamentalism as a "global threat" that must be combated the way the West contained the communist threat.

Casting the problem into the international arena serves to raise the stakes in the fight against violent factions, gain acceptance of his heavy-handed tactics against the Muslim radicals, and deflect attention from the serious Islamic challenge at home. Equally skilful in the strategy of containment, the Egyptian government at the outset cloaked itself in the mantle of Islam to appease the general public's religious sentiments and to enlist the ulema's support. Indeed, because the grip of Islam at the popular level remain strong in Egypt, it has mostly been used by the state against opponents of the right and of the left—which has become a universal practice in the Muslim world, with governments of all manner of ideological persuasion resorting to it. Nasser invoked Islam to correspond socialism and nationalism with Muslim egalitarianism and strength. His twin policies had to be given Islamic garb to gain popularity and status among the masses. Sadat consistently promoted the image of the pious Muslim and used Islam to battle secular leftists and validate his peace schemes with Israel. Now, under Mubarak, the aim is to brandish state-supported Islam to combat the militant fundamentalists.

The Mubarak government and the official *ulema* question the authenticity of the extremists' "foreign-backed" doctrine of violence as something un-Egyptian and against the actual spirit of Islam. It is even suggested that the Egyptian fundamentalists acquired their increasingly violent tone during their long exile in Saudi Arabia in the 1960s. During that period, they were imbued with elements of Islamic Wahhabi revivalist thought, emphasising traditionalism, puritanism, and militancy, which is different from mainstream Egyptian Islam. The government branded all militant outfits as "deviant" and even "heretical," having no relationship Islam as a balanced "middle-course' religion with a noble, universal mission. The *ulema* rejected as contrary to the commonly accepted interpretations of early Muslim jurists and Sunni tradition the extremists' use of their own authoritative views and unorthodox interpretations of the Qur' an and prophetic traditions (*Sunna*) to justify violence against state and society. Muslim clerics have traditionally approached interpretation of Islamic doctrine with an eye toward consensus (*ijma'*). Consensus is always preferable to disagreement. The religious leaders accused the militant outfits of ignorance—stemming from either a lack of a systematic training in Islamic studies or, at best, a thin understanding of Islamic theology. They even branded the groups as *ghulat* (excessive)—outside mainstream Egyptian Islam; the groups were committing heterodoxy in the tradition of the Kharijites (the seceders) of the seventh century, who stood outside the consensus of the Muslim community under the fourth Caliph Ali (A.D. 656-661), revolting against him and killing him.

To add to its appearance of Islamicity, the government allowed circulation of a plethora of mainstream Islamist publications, promoted Islamic programming on radio and television, airing long hours of religious messages; and showed increasing deference to the *ulema*, soliciting opinions on a wide range of socioeconomic issues such as investment in government bonds, family planning, and even Salman Rushdie's request to visit Egypt to meet with Egyptian writers. Moreover, the Islamists, using the constitution stipulation that Islamic *Shari'a* is the foundation of Egyptian law, have in recent years pushed hard to extend the application of *Shari'a* to cover many aspects of the legal code and the drafting of new legislation. They introduced legislation in the People's Assembly seeking to incorporate the Islamic *hudud* (penal code) in cases of adultery, robbery, and the drinking of alcohol. They censured the Personal Status Law of 1979, which granted women more liberal rights in matters of divorce, child custody, and alimony. The 1985 amendment of this law restricted these rights, making it once again more difficult for women to initiate divorce or gain custody. The Islamists have also been able to freely penetrate the educational system, especially at the school levels, and influence the curriculum in an Islamic direction, turning schools into centres of indoctrination. This is in addition to controlling important public enclaves and bodies such as mosques, professional associations and unions, and local councils. Thus, with government acquiescence and even encouragement, the religious discourse has dominated public life and set the social and political agenda to foster even greater Islamisation.

The state-sponsored Islamisation to check Muslim extremists raised deep concerns among intellectuals about the future of secular liberalism in Egypt. Their apprehension was that it might turn "the average mind and discourse towards Islam" and even foster *tatarruf sha'bi* (popular extremism) that could backfire against the government. But, of more immediate concern, the dominant Islamic discourse gradually began to till the cultural balance against the tradition of liberalism that has been in place since the early nineteenth century. It could lead as well to further marginalisation and intimidation of the liberal secularists, threatening the dynamic cultural and intellectual life of modern Egypt. Indeed, intellectual freedom and expression, literature and scholarship, and the arts became less and less tolerated and increasingly imperilled. Suffice it to mention some of the important cases. The conservative *ulema* of al-Azhar banned some novels by the renowned Naguib Mahfouz, declaring them offensive to Islam. Mahfouz was later assailed for his outspoken stance against "intellectual terrorism." Similarly, Farag Fouda's books were nowhere to be seen at the Cairo book fair in 1993, a year after his assassination—they had been banned. (The annual book fair has become increasingly dominated by Islamic-oriented material). Other frontrank writers and artists, such as Said al-'Ashmawi, Fouad Zakariyya, Nawal Sa'dawi (a feminist author), Amina al-Said (a leading woman writer), and Adel Imam, were proclaimed "enemies of Islam" and even received death threats.

Dr. Nasr Hamid Abu Zeid, an academic at Cairo University, was denied promotion in 1993 because of his non-traditional writings on Islam, especially his *Naqd al-Khitab al-Dini* (Critique of religious discourse). Shortly thereafter, a court case was brought by a group of radical lawyers accusing him of apostasy and asking that his marriage therefore be annulled or that his wife be considered an adulteress subject to the death penalty. The mere fact that the case was allowed before the court reveals the flagrant invasion of religion into Egypt's secular life. Dr. Abu Zeid is currently on the death list of the Jihad Organisation following a higher court ruling that nullified his marriage based on the apostasy charge. Finally, a key argument in the defence of those accused of killing the writer Farag Fouda was that an ad hoc committee of al-Azhar had declared Fouda's writings anti-Islamic; therefore, he was an apostate who should be killed. Testifying for the defence, the late Sheikh Muhammad Al-Ghozali, a leading mainstream cleric, asserted that a secularist who opposes *Shari'a* is an apostate and hence must be killed by the state. If an individual carries out the punishment (extrajudicial killing) upon state failure to do so, that individual is a mere *mufta'it* (transgressor) upon the government authority, a violation for which there is no particular punishment in Islam. Surely the message is loud and abundantly clear, and it has dangerous implications for Egypt's Muslim liberals. Equally, this religiously charged atmosphere may further jeopardise the Coptic Christian community, already under attack by Muslim zealots.

All this is evidence enough that in manipulating Islam to defuse fundamentalism, the government is running the risk of incubating a zealotry that could lead to further the menace of extremism and ultimately undermine its authority. To prevent such a dangerous outcome, the government, having gained confidence in dealing with the Muslim extremists, has now expanded its authoritarian reach to the mainstream Islamist movement, the Ikhwan. The Mubarak regime has recently moved to clamp down on its various organised activities in order to contain the Ikhwan's growing influence in public life. New legislation changing counciliar election procedures in the unions and professional associations has brought the councils under the supervision of the judiciary. The purpose is to break the hold of the Islamists on these organisations and establish instead control by the ruling National Democratic Party. In a May 1995 Labour Day speech, Mubarak strongly denounced the Ikhwan's "power monopoly" over important unions and syndicates, accusing it of manipulating these organisations for its own political ends.

Further, the government acted to stem the proliferation of private mosques and associated charitable foundations and to end their extragovernmental autonomy. Indeed, recognising that private organisations could serve to enhance the potential for Islamic opposition, the government brought all civic organisations, already required by law to be registered and licensed by the authorities, under closer scrutiny and control. Additionally, the government made an attempt to rid the educational system of the Islamist influences that had crept into it over the past twenty years. It transferred hundreds of teachers to administrative posts, removed Islamist tracts from library shelves, and tried to prohibit the imposition of the *niqab* and the *hijab* (veiling) on young schoolgirls.

Equally, the Mubarak government continued to deny the Ikhwan legal party status, citing the constitutional prohibition of religion-based parties and national unity stipulation. In effect, it restrained the Brotherhood from participating in Egypt's limited multi-party politics, which remains circumscribed by lack of party institutional development and popular roots and by government controls of political life generally. In fact, Mubarak had no qualms about banishing the Ikhwan, as a leading opposition group, from Egypt's political life. Successive governments have always suspected its motives and hence have kept the outfit in a semi-political diaspora subject to the limits of government tolerance. Today, despite a semblance of moderation and cooperation within the framework of the system, the Brotherhood is still mistrusted for continuing to chip away at the present secular state institutions and to push for its Islamic agenda. In fact, since Sadat's initial attempt at co-optation of the Ikhwan in the 1970s, the relationship between it and the state has remained tenuous and uncertain. They Ikhwan never fully accepted the regimes of Sadat and Mubarak; despite its decision to adhere to the legal rules set by the state, it could not identify completely with either regime. Nor did Sadat or Mubarak feel comfortable enough to embrace the Ikhwan as a dependable ally, for their agendas are radically different. The Ikhwan remains committed to the goal of Islamisation of state, society, and culture, something it shares with the rebels, but pursues it with non-confrontational means.

The strong fear of Islamic political parties as a "grave error" and a danger has been intensified by the Algerian experience, about which Mubarak had warned the Algerian leaders. Accordingly, as the government became increasingly assertive and resolute in countering the Islamists, it launched a crackdown on the Brotherhood, arresting dozens of leading members and hounding many more, and ordered the closing of its headquarters in Cairo. Also, the outlawed Ikhwan was prevented from competing in the November 1995 national election in an effort to disenfranchise the group. The few members who ran as independents were subject to government restrictions, police harassment, and vote tampering that virtually eliminated them from the contest. Unable to win a single seat, the Ikhwan was totally excluded from taking part as an oppositional force in parliament. Mubarak seems determined to escalate the level of repression against what he characterised as "the forces that work in the dark" and remain deep-rooted in violence: the Ikhwan. Indeed, the government even suspects some association between the Ikhwan and the militants, for the Ikhwan is the father of all these breakaway factions. Thus, the Islamic movement as a whole is now under attack, with no distinction between moderate and radical tendencies. Surely the Ikhwan, cognizant of the overwhelming power of the state, which it had encountered more than once in the past, was in no position to challenge the state. It would be folly to try to contest the historical, millennia-old state in Egypt.

Growing State Authoritarianism

Meanwhile, the growing state authoritarianism under Mubarak, which increased proportionately with the longevity of the regime has raised fears among the liberals about the prospects of democratic reforms. But the regime remains unmoved by such liberal worries and was intent on staying the course under the pretext of maintaining "discipline and control," which is its view does not contradict democracy. Mubarak is determined to avoid repeating the experiences of the Soviet Union's Mikhail Gorbachev and Algeria's Chadli Benjedid. Both are believed to have moved too fast toward the path of democratisation and were seen overthrown. Algeria, in particular, provided a bitter lesson against full openness and participation lest it lead to a similar breakdown. Thus, democracy in Egypt remains limited, subject to preserving public order, stability, and regime continuity. And the government is believed to continue its policy of barring the Islamic movement from the political arena. Indeed, in the face of the mounting violence that has marred Egyptian life and threatened the cultural elite, the liberal intelligentsia have been hard-pressed to tone down its appeals for greater political liberalisation. And, despite the apparent retrogression in democratisation and the presence of rampant official corruption, the secularist liberals had no choice but to take cover under a disliked state apparatus to escape the menace of fundamentalism.

Likewise, the Coptic minority finds itself in desperate need to protection and order, even at the expense of having to submit to a repressive regime. Both factions have more to fear from the ascendancy of the Islamists than from the assertive power of the state. Surely all this has played into the hands of the regime in slowing the pace of political reforms and in playing off the liberals against the Islamists. To regain the cultural balance, the state decided to promote the dissemination of secularist discourse, which is currently witnessing a new rally. Today, as Mubarak wades through his third six-year tenure hardly anyone believes that the radical fundamentalists pose a fatal that to the regime. Their leadership has sustained grievous jolts and their ranks have been smashed. As to the mainstream Ikhwan movement, it is equally subject to government high handedness and is being discredited as a shadowy group with a violent past masquerading now as moderate.

Certainly the task of containment is greatly facilitated by the absence of an organised movement tying together the diverse Islamic forces. In fact, the multiplicity of the Islamic outfits, with their regional, social, and ideological divisions, rent the fundamentalists asunder and militated against an Islamic front in Egypt comparable to the Algerian Islamic Salvation Front. Yet, the fundamentalists are far from disappearing and will probably go on committing intermittent acts of violence, especially in the medium term, as socio-economic conditions remain intractable-probably only manageable, at best—and will continue to chip away at the regime's standing, which at the start of Mubarak's third term in October 1993 reached lows almost reminiscent of Sadat's last days. In the long-term, the only plausible way to stamp out the Islamic opposition is to remedy the painful economic conditions of the country. But, in the Egyptian context of overpopulation that is always pressing against limited resources and a mammoth inactive bureaucracy at the core of a centralised government that is lukewarm to reforms as too risky and explosive, the task is uphill.

Still, despite mounting disaffection, the regime is not in imminent danger of collapse, as the fundamentalists had thought or wanted the world to believe. The state remains strong and is supported by large segments of the elite, especially the armed forces. And Mubarak, despite lack of a towering personality and commanding leadership, will continue holding onto power by simply carrying on the business of managing public affairs in the usual Egyptian manner: by employing the power of the state. Ultimately, the durability of the Mubarak regime will probably depend on the loyalty of the military, the mainstay of the Egyptian state since 1952 and the traditional beneficiary of its favours. So far, the army has stood above the fray, as the regime has contained violence and even restricted it considerably. But should a calamity befall the government, and with no clear successor to Mubarak, the military is most likely to step in as the strongest power centre and the guardian of the state. The result would be a successor secular regime. The fundamentalists are not winning the day now, nor will they in the future; it seems highly unlikely that they can overwhelm the power of the state. The traditional mastery of the state in this ancient land will continue. So will the nagging socio-economic problems.

Fifteen

Tactics and Strategy

Although the Euro-Arab terrorist attack of 1977 proved again that a good deal of the urban terrorist's time is devoted to fund raising, it also demonstrated that the tactics are geared to ensure that the transnational factions should become self-perpetuating. Tactically, the terror club needed to secure the release of Germans, Japanese and Arabs who had been captured in previous raids. The Japanese Red Army in particular was short of trained operators and the hijacking of one airliner was all that they needed to put them back in business following a two-year respite in their activities. And it was with the co-operation of one powerful Arab group, and with support from the Germans, that they were able to carry it out successfully.

A gang of five notorious terrorists took over a Japanese Airlines DC8 carrying 156 passengers soon after it had taken off from Bombay. They obtained from the Tokyo government the release of six confined terrorists and were paid a ransom of $6 million for the lives of their hostages. It was a classic, successful terrorist operation. Just to complete the ritual scenario, the Japanese and their released comrades made their way to one of the traditional havens for hijackers — Algiers. Part of their wealth was paid into the funds of their backers, the PFLP. While that operation was taking place, the Red Army Faction the erstwhile West Germany, which had already killed a noted banker and the public prosecutor responsible for the trial of the Baader-Meinhof leaders, kidnapped Hans-Martin Schleyer, an industrialist and leader of the employers' federation.

Chancellor Schmidt's government refused to give in and played the long, hard bargaining game, demanding proof that the terrorists did hold their prisoner alive, while encouraging the terrorists by asking a number of Third World countries whether they would agree to the prisoners being delivered to their countries.

Then a dramatic turn of events took place, which demonstrated how the international terrorists improved their co-ordination and become more sophisticated in their tactics. They increased their pressure on the German government by mounting a new hijack from a totally different quarter. Four Palestinians, two men and two women of Wadi Hadad's PFLP-Special Operations, operating from Baghdad, hijacked a Lufthansa Boeing 737 homeward bound from Majorca packed with German tourists and a part of six beauty queens. Demanding the release of the same Baader-Meinhof leaders as the abductors of Herr Schleyer, together with two Palestinians held in Turkey (the same pair that the dutch girl Lidwina Jansen recognised at the Aden training school), they forced the aircraft to fly around the Middle East until ultimately it landed at Mogadishu in Somalia. There, while the bargaining still continued, the German government ordered a counter-raid, Entebbe style. This was conducted with great skill and spirit by twenty-eight men of the GSG9, the 180-strong anti-terrorist force which had been created and specifically trained for such an operation. This time it was the terrorists who died. But what was even more significant in the long-term was the fact that a British Major and an NCO from the Special Air Services Regiment went to Mogadishu carrying cardboard-bodied grenades which stunned their victims for a few seconds but did no permanent damage. These grenades were developed by the SAS specifically for dealing with hijacks. Here also, it was a fine example of co-operation between Western powers in fighting the common enemy.

It was a famous victory which heartened the anti-terrorist forces who had little success since Entebbe. Although the forces of terror had been beaten, they were still able to strike back by murdering Dr Schleyer, whose body was dumped in an abandoned car in Alsace. The hunted kidnap squad took refuge in the Middle East. The fact that the confined Baader-Meinhof leaders, Andreas Baader, Gudrun Ensslin and Jan-Carl Raspe, were able to commit suicide in their maximum security prison after learning that the attempt to free them had failed, produced an immediate counter-effect. As we have seen in earlier chapters describing the rise of the terrorist movements, it is an event of this kind which can influence the young generation and eventually provide more recruits for the infantry of terror.

While the long drama of the 1977 autumn offensive played itself out, it appeared that political life in Germany was at a standstill, paralysed by governmental concentration on this problem. The erstwhile Chancellor Helmut Schmidt was unable to receive James Challaghan, the then British Prime Minister, and he had to postpone his own official visit to Poland. Popular clamour for the death penalty and ever more strict security measures stimulated by the wave of terror played into the hands of the Red Army Faction and their international friends. For shooting in the streets and police revenge is what terrorism feeds upon.

A further heartening sign that the industrial democracies were strengthening their combined resolve to curb international terrorism was provided by the summit conference of leaders of Britain, West Germany, France, Italy, the United States, Canada and Japan in July 1978. Meeting in Bonn they unanimously resolved to take stern measures against countries which refused to extradite or prosecute terrorists and hijackers, or which refused to return hostages and aircraft. The issue was raised by Takeo Fukuda, the then Prime Minister of Japan, and the powers agreed to punish such offending nations by suspending their air traffic connections with the Seven.

Faced with a common international enemy, the countries of Western Europe consulted and secured general approval for a counter-action. The tragedy is that it had taken no less than five years for the powers of this sophisticated continent to unite against a global terrorist force, not strong in numbers — there are probably less than 1000 activist men and women — but which by its tactics had spread death and fear throughout the world.

The truth is that when the hijackers, killers and kidnappers first began to strike in Europe their tactics took the West by surprise. Their acts were unexpected in liberal nations where freedom of expression exists, in democracies whose one prime advantage is that governments can be changed by the simple process of voting, without men having to go out in the streets and kill in order to bring down an unwanted administration. It was known that in Latin American tyrannies guerrilla tactics might be justified to oust brutal regimes; it was accepted that the Palestinians, and even the Irish, might take up arms in the cause of national interest. But why should innocent men and women be slaughtered by gunmen in peaceful societies? The first response was that the terrorists must have some reasonable demands and that therefore their objectives should be studied, and attempts made to deal with their grievances. It is in the nature of Western societies to listen to argument and to try to discover what went wrong.

True Nature of Terrorism

If the young, and especially the university intellectuals, were worried enough to take up arms in the cause of changing and improving society they should be attended to. That was the attitude, and during the time it took for us to realise that the terrorism was in fact a destructive force, an aberration of reformist concept, rather than a worthy expression of disquiet, governments chose to give in to their tactical demands and to hope thereby to satisfy them. By the time realisation of the true nature of terrorism set in, and the West was prepared to recognise their strategic demands for the fraud they were, the tactics had toughened into a formal pattern, and their surprise value had been lost.

There is absolutely no mystery about the tactics. They shocked only by their unexpectedness and novelty, and by the fact that television coverage of violent events brought them into every home. The prime terrorist activities consist of:

1. Murder by spraying bullets at people in the streets.
2. Assassination of political leaders and other well-known personalities.
3. Bombing of public places or the residences of private individuals.
4. Kidnapping of prominent personalities for ransom or the release of prisoners.
5. Armed bank robbery and raids to get money, weapons, documents, etc., for smooth running of terrorist activities.

If there is no mystery about the methods it is equally true that there is in magic formula or secret weapon which will definitely counter them. It is obvious that in each case straight forward security measures involving more efficient police duty, security checks and personal precautions need to be taken for protection against terror. But even more important is better intelligence work, and more sincere effort to discover who the terrorists are and how they operate. The routines of security need to be improved, while freedom of movement and action for individuals is preserved.

Such procedures are unthinkable in the West, and what has to be contrived is a system of beefed up security which does not impose too much restriction on freedom. That said, it must be obvious that some freedom must be sacrificed in order to protect the masses from death and intimidation by terror and the very fabric of the state from disintegration. For instance, it may be tiresome and even humiliating to be body-searched, and have security men examine one's most personal possessions in a suitcase, but it is greatly preferable to being blown up in mid-air, or threatened with weapons by demented terrorists to whom you must cringe for permission to go to the toilet in a hijacked aircraft. The real battle of wits which calls for skill and courage takes place in terrorist acts involving the kidnap of individuals or the holding hostage of groups of people.

Let us take the early aircraft mass hijacks carried out by Arab terrorists. Two or three pirates boarded an aircraft with hidden arms and grenades; one moved forward to threaten the aircrew while the others held the passengers at bay. His tactic was to fly it to an airfield in a safe country, or one sympathetic to his cause, and there to utter increasingly frigthening threats until the government of the place from which the aircraft came agreed to his demands.

As the international terrorists increased the frequency of their attacks, Western governments began to make the necessary preparations for firmer stands. Slowly the means of communication between different police forces were improved.

In London there already existed a bomb squad accustomed to dealing with Provisional IRA outrages. It was expanded and its schemes improved as it was transformed in 1976 into an anti-terrorist squad which was kept busy by Provo activity, and was therefore sensitive to the possibility of global terrorism as well.

Because the British Army has long experience of subversive warfare in the colonial wars — it has been engaged worldwide since the end of the Second World War — a specialised military unit was already in being to combat the new techniques of terror. The Special Air Service, with 1000 carefully selected officers and men highly trained for delicate operations, was perfectly suited for use in so-called Phase II operations, that is to say when a situation has developed with which the police are no longer able to face. At this point they must call in superior firepower and essential military acumen.

Fallout of Munich Olympic Massacre

Following the massacre of the Israeli athletes at Munich in 1972 and the disastrous police counter-attack the then West German government set up its own specialised para-military unit known as GSG9 (Border Protection Group 9) under the command of a resilient professional officer named Ulrich Wegener.

The German force had received advice and training from Israel's General Intelligence and Reconnaissance Unit 269. This outfit descended from an anti-terror unit developed by General Arik Sharon, who led Israeli forces into Egypt in the Yom Kippur War. Among its battle honours were Entebbe, and the freeing of ninety hostages aboard a Sabena aircraft which had been seized by Palestinians and forced to land at Lod Airport in 1972. The United States was late to respond to the international terrorist threat but in March 1978 President Carter finally gave orders for the establishment and training of a specialised force 200 strong. This was somewhat a delayed response to the clear demonstration of the efficacy of GSG9 and the SAS. It was the lesson of the Mogadishu raid which belatedly convinced the President that new steps were urgently required to cure America's lack of means to cope with such incidents. Until then only small factions of US troops had received sporadic training in anti-terrorist operations. The new unit took several months to complete its course.

The French had a 40-strong special squad composed of men of the Gendarmerie National (which is the oldest regiment in the French army), known as Gigene. This unit had already proved its value in action abroad, for it rescued the children of French servicemen hijacked on their school bus by terrorists operating in Dijibouti in 1976. In addition there were special anti-terrorist brigades of police set up following the Munich massacre. Some of these men were on stand-by duty in Holland during the capture of the French embassy in the Hague by Japanese terrorists.

In Holland a special squad of marines attacked the train captured by South Moluccans. They too received help and advice from a detachment of the Special Air Service from Britain although they declined the offer of the 'stun grenades' preferring to use their own method of throwing the terrorists off balance — low-level flights by fighters whose pilots suddenly cut in their after-burners. Not until such forces as these were in existence and the political climate had been created for them to intervene in a crisis did governments feel able to take a tougher stand in the negotiation phase which precedes any attack on terrorists who have seized hostages.

After Mogadishu the erstwhile West Germany began a counter-offensive, despatching three-man *Zielfahndung* (target squads) to nab terrorists in foreign countries. This, of course, could only be done with the co-operation of authorities in the countries concerned. A significant success was scored through this new form of international co-operation when one such squad grabbed 28-year-old Angelika Loder, 27-year-old Gudrun Sturmer, and 28-year-old Gabriele Rollnik, at Bourgas, a prominent Bulgarian Black Sea resort. The was the first recorded case of co-operation being given by a Communist East European nation in the war against terrorism.

The obvious success of the Israeli assault at Entebbe and the then West German one at Mogadishu created a rather smug feeling that so long as Western states took a strong line against terrorists, and provided they had at their disposal a specially trained commando force everything would be well. This is a dangerous supposition, for as many things can go wrong in a counter-terror raid as in any form of warfare. Thorough training of the assault troops is important but even the most well-trained troops in the world are not always victorious unless they are lucky.

As if to point up this message there is the example of the Egyptian commandos at Larnaca Airport, Cyprus. They were good troops belonging to the Egyptian army, an army which succeeded only a few years ago in making a crossing of the Suez Canal against the opposition of the Israeli Army, also one of the most formidable in the world — yet their anti-terrorist raid ended in farce and disaster. In February 1978 two Palestinian gunmen entered the Hilton Hotel, Nicosia, and shot and killed Yusuf Sebai, an Egyptian editor and a personal friend of President Sadat. They then took hostages and subsequently forced the Cypriots to provide them with an Air Cyprus plane.

General Nabil Shukri personally commanded the 72-strong force aboard an Egyptian airforce Hercules and he had orders to nab the two terrorists and free the airliner they were holding. Insufficient diplomatic preparation had been made for this raid. Although President Sadat and President Kyprianou of Cyprus later accounts of the affair, it seems clear that the Egyptians did not have clear authorisation for their mission. The result was that when the Egyptian commandos attacked the plane, they were assaulted by strong forces of the Cypriot National Guard, lost fifteen dead, and were unable to get into the aircraft. The terrorists, terrified by the battle around the plane, eventually surrendered to the Cypriots, were tried and found guilty of murder.

But the confused battle of Larnaca demonstrates how easily things can go wrong if anti-terrorist assault forces are not adequately trained and are not given proper back-up from their own government. It may serve as a warning to any government planning such action. While in Western nations the police and the military developed their assault techniques, which are very much more delicate than those of the terrorists who do not care whether or not innocent people are killed, other methods were put forward. Psychiatrists started to probe the terrorist mind, and to suggest ways in which trained negotiators might exploit their shortcoming in the bargaining phase of a terror action.

One of the pioneers of the victory-through-talk technique of handling such situations is Dr Harvey Schlossberg, director of Psychological Services for the New York Police Department. It was he who framed the methods of talking out the hostage-holders which were put into practice by Lieutenant Frank Bolz, of the New York Negotiating Squad, whom we quoted in our first chapter as saying: 'We aim to bore them to death.' In practice it has been proved that the best person to conduct the negotiations is a police officer or some relatedly recognisable representative of authority with a psychiatrist giving advice but remaining in the background. What has been demonstrated by the use of such methods is that the advantage does not always lie with the terrorist. A display of steadfastness which breaks down the willpower of the terrorist can force him to surrender his hostages without bloodshed. In 1975 the Irish security authorities tried out this technique in the eighteen-day capture of the Provos Eddie Gallagher and Marian Coyle, who had kidnapped the Dutch businessman, Dr Tiede Herrema, and were demanding the release of many comrades — especially Gallagher's mistress, Rose Dugdale — in return for his life.

Troops and police surrounded the house in Country Kildare where Dr Herrema was being held and made use of modern surveillance apparatus, cameras and listening devices in order to discover every move and word of the kidnappers. Psychiatrists then advised the negotiator to choose times when the terrorists were relaxed but in low spirits to compel them to surrender. The authorities were particularly fortunate in this case in that the calm and towering personality of Dr Herrema himself made it possible for him to bring his own strength to bear in the developing relationship with his abductors. Eventually it was Eddie Gallagher and Marian Coyle, renowned for their wildness even among the Provos, who broke and surrendered. None of this would have been viable had not the Irish government made it clear that they would not capitulate under any circumstances and that they declined to make any deals or concessions. Such tactics demand a strong will and a realistic appreciation of what can happen.

During the Herrema incident the Irish authorities called upon the workforce of the Scotland Yard Technical Support Branch to take advantage of the latest surveillance and monitoring technology and for help with communications. The branch in Britain worked closely with the anti-terrorist squad which we have already discussed. Both units played a significant role in employing the 'wait-them-out' technique against the IRA in the famous siege of Balcombe Street in London in December 1975. Four of the Provo's

Active Service Unit were chased into an apartment in Balcombe Street where they held the occupants prisoners in their own flat. The SAS were alerted in this case and prepared a number of plans of attack but once again the terrorists, faced with the inevitability of death or imprisonment surrendered and released their hostages unharmed.

The Talk-out Technique

It must not be forgotten that the first step in such operations is to discover the locality where the terrorists are holding their victims. Until they can be pinned down and surrounded no fatal action can be taken at all. The kidnap in Rome early in 1978 of Aldo Moro revealed the power of the Red Brigades and the impotence of security and police forces, who for weeks on end were unable to track down the terrorist hideout where Signor Moro was being captived. The talk-out technique depends entirely on good detective work and it cannot be stressed too strongly how vital it is for the police either to infiltrate terror movements or to get informers among their members. Without detection nothing can be done. Hijackers, always in pursuit of publicity, perform part of the security task themselves by announcing where they are, but kidnapping, where the lair remains secret, is a stronger form of terrorist war. In order to succeed it is always essential that the talk-out specialists know that a well-armed force of police is in position to take action if it becomes necessary. Even in Britain where police and public alike have long stood against the notion of an armed police force, it is now recognised that in present-day conditions the forces of order must have specialist weapons available.

It is better from every point of view to employ policemen trained with the proper weapons than to use soldiers. For the police are trained in a different fashion and a soldier is in the nature of things disposed to be more aggressive than his civilian colleague in uniform.

This means that along with the psychological method of dealing with terrorists, attention must also be paid to providing the forces of order with the best available weapons for the job. Revolvers and pistols have the advantage of being light and easy to conceal in delicate situations but they are not always accurate. One of the sophisticated weapons now recommended for such work is the L39A1 sniper's rifle with the Rank image-intensifier night sight, particularly when it is remembered that most police raids requiring weapons take place by night.

At the Balcombe Street seizure, a police officer conducted the negotiations with a psychiatrist advising him. But when South Moluccan terrorists seized a train holding many hostages in Holland in the summer of 1977, it was the psychiatrist himself who negotiated with the terrorists. The seizure ended only when Dutch marines stormed the coaches after terrorists had been alarmed by Starfighter jets buzzing the train. Although the psychiatrist in question, Dr Dick Mulder considered a specialist in the talk-out technique, having dealt with previous sieges by Palestinians, Japanese Red Army and other South Moluccans in Holland, criticisms were afterwards expressed of the way the negotiations were conducted. Anti-terrorist experts and other psychiatrists claimed that he had not been sufficiently authoritative and had failed to exert enough pressure on the Moluccans.

He later explained his technique in detail. According to him, the first step is to build up a psychological picture of the terrorists, a difficult thing to do during phase one, which is the most dangerous period during which the terrorists act wildly, making extravagant threats and often shooting. After making it clear that there is no quick solution to it he even favoured allowing the terrorists to speak to the press and television on the grounds that this satisfies their inflated egos. At the same time Dr Mulder also prepared for phase two by arranging to have one direct telephone line to the terrorists for his own use. He asserted his own will by cutting off all other communication, then controlling what the terrorists shall eat and at what time. Eventually he claimed that he could tell them when to sleep by bidding them goodnight. In this way it is possible for the psychiatrist controller to know about the terrorists' activities.

In the view of the Dutch expert this leads ineluctably to phase three which starts when the terrorists begin to feel that they are losing their presence and their natural reaction is to want to go back to the shooting and adrenalin pumping time of phase one. At this point threats are made all over again and utmost care must be exercised by the control.

The situation was particularly delicate in this particular case because the Moluccans in the train were holding 56 hostages while another group held 105 children in school. Both factions demanded the release of imprisoned comrades and recognition of a non-existent independent state of South Molucca which it was not in the power of the Dutch government to grant. It is important also that the Moluccans were to some extent prepared for Dr Mulder's technique, for he had already employed it against their friends in an earlier capture. This is the first known case of terrorists themselves having undergone psychological training as a result of previous experience. At first they neither made contact with the outside world, nor asked for contact to be established with them and until there was some means of talking it was impossible for the negotiator to begin his work.

As discipline on the train broke down after twenty days, Dr Mulder had to admit that the talking-out technique was unlikely to prosper and he advised the government that the time had finally arrived for military action. Here again the psychiatrist thought fit to suggest the strategies to be adopted. The attack should be made at dawn when the terrorists were least alert and he could tell the military commander that most of the Moluccans slept in the front coach. Finally the marines went in to offensive, killing Max and five other Moluccans. Unfortunately two hostages were also killed, largely because they stood up although they had been asked to lie down when the assault started.

As in true warfare it is sometimes the defence and sometimes the attack which has the advantage. It would be unwise to forget that terrorists are intelligent and crafty people perfectly capable of learning operational lessons from experience. There is enough evidence that Provos in Ireland had been trained to resist the modern grilling techniques of the British Army. Their men were taught, for example, to avoid looking into the eyes of the questioner and how to evade his trickeries. Although these facts were unlikely to find their way into terror training manuals for some time there can hardly be any doubt but that in some Middle East camp terror controllers tried to buy the right kind of goggles and bulletproof vests for their teams. Events in Rome as early as in 1978 showed that members of the Red Brigades has learned tactical lessons about the psychological warfare aspects of their campaign. The Red Army Faction and other outfits had always insisted, once their victim was incarcerated in a 'people's prison', on the broadcast of communiques laying down the political objectives of their group. The Red Brigades employed different tactics.

There were plenty of Italians who took the letters at face value as though they had been written by a statesman in usual circumstances. But terror watchers and psychiatrists who had specialised in this field knew that after a man had been held even for a few days by threatening terrorists it was unlikely that any but the strongest willed was capable of writing letters anything like those he would normally compose. It was not torture, not even simply the fear of death, which brings aberrations of the mind. Just the circumstances of loss of freedom and loss of expectation can transform a person's way of thinking. The exploitation of such circumstances is a dangerous new phenomenon in terror techniques. It is ironic that if similar methods were used in liberal societies against captured terrorists there would have been cries of 'torture' and strong liberal protests and demonstrations. Although anti-terror squads have greater resources for invention and improving their equipment, the terrorists too take advantage of published material to reform their tactics and weapons.

Role of Security Forces

The security forces of Western nations are required remain constantly on the alert if they are not only to counter terrorist raids but also to stay ahead of the game. Whenever a particularly dramatic terrorist raid occurs the public at large begins suggesting what should be done. The tactics of public opinion, unlike the pragmatic ones of both terrorists and counter-terrorists, are always full of the formulae of wishful thinking and belief in magic weapons. During the autumn offensive of 1977 the old proposition was again put forward that gas should be pumped into hijacked airliners to put the pirates, and indeed the passengers to sleep.

Such hopes were effectively confounded by Professor D.R.

Lawrence of the Pharmacology and Therapeutics Department of the University College Hospital Medical School in a letter to *The Times* in late 1977. "When I consider the technology and skill required of my specialist colleagues in anaesthesia, caring for one unconscious person at a time, I tremble for the likely loss of life if a plane-load were simultaneously anaesthetised. Utopia might possibly develop such a gas, but Utopia would presumably have no need of it ...'

The second panacea of public opinion is the death sentence for terrorists. For would not that deprive the terrorists of further targets as they are constantly demanding the release of imprisoned colleagues? This too is a false argument. Death penalties would do no such thing, for it would be the renunciation of democracy for them to be shot on the spot after drumhead courts martial and would provide the terrorists with the support they so seriously need; if the sentences were not carried out immediately, the lengthy processes of appeal before sentence could reasonably be carried out would provide enough time for their comrades to launch raids to try to secure their release.

Sixteen

Various Militant Groups

Terrorist organisations emerge for a variety of reasons; they flourish like laboratory cultures of radical chic and international publicity, but each requires its own special cause to initiate its life-cycle. For some, like the Palestinians and the South Moluccans, it is nationalistic—they use terror as one of their weapons in an attempt to establish national right to an area of territory. For others, like the Baader-Meinhof gang and the Japanese Red Army, the cause is world revolution. Some, like the Spanish and Italian outfits, have internal political reasons for turning to terror and there are others still, such as the Islamic insurgents in the Philippines and the Warriors of Christ the King in Spain, who owe their existence to religion as much as to politics.

In each case the origin appears simple. The combination of a grievance and a vision can make a man hurl a bomb. But after the first clear burst of enthusiasm, rationalisation tends to blur. Some of the Palestinian groups, for instance, have developed a commitment to world revolution almost as total as their devotion to the recovery of their homeland. The failure of the German and Japanese outfits to plan a viable alternative society to the one they want to destroy points to anarchy. And the cynical support of the Soviet Union for almost any faction which could embarrass the West, whatever that group's political alignment, blurs the picture even more.

Nowhere could there be more confusion than in the welter of reasons the Provisional IRA gives for its promotion of terror. National, political, social and religious causes mixed together with a generous lump of historical mysticism provide the Provos with their rationalisation. The Provos are, of course, unique. But they do demonstrate the great range of justification that exists for blowing up cinemas, hijacking airliners and assassinating 'bourgeois pigs'. And even the Provos are bound by two fundamental laws of the terrorist experiment:

1. The use of violence is obligatory in order to induce fear and chaos.
2. It must be aimed at the people and the institutions of the established order.

This may appear a statement of the obvious. But these laws are the foundation of terrorism, for they provide the cement which surrounds each terrorist brick and binds together into a unity of purpose even those who are staunchly opposed to one another.

This unity is often disguised. Groups change their names—sometimes they split and amoeba-like spawn other groups or they may undergo a change in ideology, and abandon their old identities, while others give themselves new names in order to disguise their affiliations. Splinter groups with exotic names are sometimes set up with a view to carry out specific operations. For example, the combined PFLP and Baader-Meinhof group led by the Venezuelan Carlos which conducted the raid on the OPEC headquarters in Vienna, called itself 'The Arm of the Arab Revolution'. On a more permanent basis, Black September was formed as the terrorist arm of Al Fatah. Its origins were concealed in order to prevent political embarrassment of Fatah's leader, Yasser Arafat, and through him the whole of the Palestine Liberation Organisation.

We have prepared the following 'who's who' of the most active of the terrorist outfits in an attempt to clarify and codify. This section is planned to show how the groups came into being, who runs them, what their aims and objectives are. It also demonstrates their inter-group and international contacts, as well as their transpolitical and transnational capacity which is possibly the most dangerous weapon of modern terrorism.

PALESTINE

Black September

Origins

Formed by Yasser Arafat's Fatah organisation as a weapon of terror. It was based on Fatah's intelligence branch, Jihaz al-Razd, and took its name from the September of 1970, when King

Hussein crushed the Palestinian guerrilla movement in Jordan. Fatah has always denied its connection with Black September in order to keep Arafat stay away from charges of being involved in terrorism, thus enabling him to continue his political role, but evidence of the connection is now so damning that even Fatah tends not to protest too much.

Ideology and Aims

Nationalistic. The overthrow of Israel and its replacement by a Palestinian state governed by Fatah and led by Arafat.

Functions

Black September started its operations with bombing attacks on commercial installations in Europe which were connected with Israel. When these proved successful the name of Black September was announced to all corners of the world, and this was done in the most gruesome manner on November 28, 1971 with the murder of the Jordanian Prime Minister Wasfi Tell on the steps of the Sheraton Hotel in Cairo. The Palestinians had blamed Tell for their defeat in Jordan and, apart from King Hussein, he was their number-one target. There followed a series of outrages: the Munich Massacre, the carnage of the diplomats at Khartoum, the letter-bomb campaign of 1972, the hijacking of a Lufthansa jet to secure the release of the survivors of the Munich gang. Black September had also engaged in the war of kill and counter-kill which raged throughout Europe in the early 1970s. It ceased operations in 1974 when it became apparent that its terrorist outrages were harming the political image of Fatah and the PLO. At a time when Arafat was appearing before the United Nations, and introducing himself as the potential leader of a sovereign state, he could not afford to be linked with terrorism. It was, for example, Abu Iyad and his Black Septembrists who tried to kill King Hussein at the Arab summit meeting at Rabat in October 1974. There were also other rebel Black September groups, particularly that led by Abu Nidal, which still persevere with terrorism as a weapon of Palestinian nationalism.

International Connections

Because of its intimate but clandestine involvement with Fatah, Black September was able to use all of Fatah's associations with the Communist world. Arms, training and military allegiance had been provided by the erstwhile Soviet Union, Czechoslovakia and East Germany and they could legitimately claim that help was given to Fatah and not to Black September. Funds were channelled from the oil-rich Arab states through Fatah to the terrorists. There were links with the major European terrorist outfits and with supporters in France. Black September also used sympathisers among the many Arab students and workers in the erstwhile West Germany. This connection was important to them in setting up the Munich Olympic Games operation.

Achievements

Its activities have ensured that the whole world knows about the Palestinian cause. With the extensive TV coverage of the games, the Munich operation was transmitted into millions of homes around the world. In the will they left behind, the terrorists had written: 'Why should the whole world be having fun and entertainment while we suffer with all ears deaf to us?' What the rest of the world saw as a ghastly act of murder was considered a great triumph by the Arabs. However, Black September's later operations, especially the killing of the three diplomats at Khartoum — which may have been carried out by a splinter faction proved counterproductive. Khartoum was the last operation officially claimed by Black September.

Popular Front for the Liberation of Palestine (PFLP)

Origins

Formed in December 1967 following the disaster of the Six Day War by the merger of several small guerrilla outfits associated with the Arab nationalist movement. It was led by the founder of the ANM, Dr George Habash, and the operational commander until his death early in 1978 was Dr Wadi Hadad.

Ideology and Objectives

Nationalist and Marxist. Had been opposed to any settlement with Israel, leads the 'Rejection Front' and insisted on the complete liberation of Palestine. This, however, was only the first of its aims. Its targets were Israel, imperialism and capitalism.

Activities

Terrorism of the most ruthless nature. It fought the Israelis on the West Bank and especially in the Gaza Strip after the 1967 war but the Israelis annihilated the PFLP fighting cells and the group was forced to operate first from Jordan, then from Beirut and then from Aden and Baghdad. Since their defeat by the Israelis they had concentrated on international terrorism. Many acts of hijacking and murder caused from Wadi Hadad: the multiple hijacking to Dawson's Field; the Lod massacre by Japanese Red Army kamikaze killers; the attack on the OPEC headquarters in Vienna; the Entebbe hijack; the Mogadishu hijack. In 1975 it was announced that George Habash had expelled his friend Wadi Hadad because he stood against Hadad's obsession with terrorism, but there is evidence which shows that the expulsion was for propaganda reasons and that Hadad's 'Foreign Operations Group' enjoyed a relationship with PFLP similar to that of Black September with Fatah. Hadad concentrated on building up contacts with foreign terrorists and his operations almost invariably involved terrorists from other countries. He established training camps for transnational terrorists and built up a truly international gang. Following Hadad's death his organisation was taken over by his old friend Dr. George Habash, who by that time was moving into a more extreme position. With the assistance of the Iraqi government it began preparing for further action though there were signs from Baghdad that the new management had come to the conclusion that hijack exercises were no longer the most satisfactory ones.

International Links

The PFLP is supported by all the 'Rejectionist' countries, Libya, Iraqi, Algeria and the South Yemen, with its offices in all these countries. In addition, Habash established close ties with North Korea as well. He also maintained a love - hate relationship with both China and the erstwhile Soviet Union. It was Hadad however who established close operational links with European, Japanese and South American terrorists. Entebbe was undertaken by Germans and Palestinians, OPEC by Germans, Palestinians and Carlos, Mogadishu by Palestinians in support of the German kidnappers of Herr Schleyer, Lod by Japanese. Carlos was Hadad's number-one hit man. There were connections with outfits in Italy, Holland, France, Turkey, Iran and even the IRA. The PFLP can truly be described as the framework without which international terrorism could not work.

As-Sa'iqa (Thunderbolt)

Origin

Came into being in October 1968 as the military wing of the 'Vanguards of the Popular War for the Liberation of Palestine' which was formed before the Six Day War in 1967 from the Palestinian faction of the Syrian Ba'ath Party and the Palestine battalion of the Syrian Army. Is a Syrian creation and dependent on Syria.

Ideology and Aims

Nationalist, but obedient to Syria.

Functions

Has been involved in small-scale guerrilla warfare in Israel and in the internecine clashes in the Lebanon. Its leaders declare themselves opposed to international terrorism but it was members of this organisation, calling themselves 'Eagles of the Palestine Revolution', who attacked a train in Austria carrying Russian Jews on their way to Israel in September 1973. By holding hostages they forced chancellor Kreisky of Austria to promise to close Schonau transit camp for Jewish emigrants from Russia. In a similar discipline in September 1975 four Sa'iqa members were arrested in Amsterdam. They had planned to take train passengers hostage to force Holland to stop helping Jewish emigrants.

International Links

Delegates visited the former Soviet Union for talks on political co-operation but there was no evidence of terrorist links. It was suspected however that in the Schonau attack the terrorists were allowed to cross the border fully armed with the knowledge of the Czech authorities.

Achievements

The pressure they had put on Chancellor Kreisky and his capitulation produced an unprecedented result. The Israeli government, and in particular the then Prime Minister, Golda Meir, were so enraged that their attention had been diverted from the build-up by Egypt and Syria for the launching of the Yom Kippur War.

Democratic Front for the Liberation of Palestine (DFLP)

Origin

Formed in 1969 by the secession of extreme left-wingers from the PFLP. This secession led to bitter fighting in the streets of Beirut by adherents to both groups.

Ideology and Aims

Marxist-Leninist. The only Palestinian guerrilla group which undertreated armed struggle to political struggle. It was among the first to support the principle of Jewish national rights inside a liberated Palestine and had called on all 'progressive Israelis and Jews' to merge with it in one popular Palestinian front.

Functions

Opposed to the PFLP policy of international terrorism and had not been involved in any major operation outside Israel. It qualified as a terrorist organisation by its attacks on a school in the Israeli village of Ma'alot in May 1974 in which twenty-two children had been killed and on an apartment house in Beth Shean in November 1974.

International Links

Had no international terrorist connections but had enjoyed political links with left-wing students in Europe and America. Had been supported by the Soviet Union and had good relations with China where some of its members had been trained.

Achievements

Political rather than military. Attempts to woo Israeli leftists had more positive results than the raids on Ma'alot and Beth Shean which caused sheer outrage.

Popular Front for the Liberation of Palestine - General Command (PFLP-GC)

Origins

Stemmed from a small commando group called the Palestine Liberation Front formed in 1959 by the ex-Syrian Army captain, Ahmed Jibril. Its key aim was to wage a guerrilla war inside Israel. After 1967 it joined with other groups, some associated with the Arab Nationalist Movement to set up a branch of the PFLP. But a year later the Jibril faction broke away again, protesting that there was too much emphasis on ideological squabbling in the PFLP and too little fighting.

Ideology and Aims

Essentially a military organisation which, as a member of the Rejection Front, opposed a Middle East peace settlement except on Arab terms.

Activities

In keeping with its aim for waging a guerrilla war the group had made a number of forays across the border into Israel with fighting patrols of three to five men. In May 1970 an ambush party fired a rocket at a school-bus on a road running along the Lebanese border, killing eight children and four other passengers. In April 1974 a three member team attacked the Israeli village of Qiryat Shemona, mainly populated by refugees from North Africa, and killed eighteen people before it was wiped out. Ahmed Jibril later said that attack had been aimed at bringing into existence a 'new school of struggle based on the highest degree of revolutionary violence'. However there is no record of his outfit carrying out any attacks since that time. Between 1970 and 1972 the PFLP-GC also became involved in international terrorism. It specialised in letter bombs and the blowing up of airliners. Its aircraft technique became familiar. Agents persuaded naive girls to carry seemingly harmless parcels on board aircraft heading to Israel. The packages contained bombs which exploded when the aircraft reached a specific height. On 21 February 1970, one of the group's bombs destroyed a Swissair plane en-route from Zurich to Tel Aviv. Forty-seven people were killed.

International Connections

Supported by President Gaddafi of Libya as well as by Syria.

Achievements

None, apart from slaughter.

National Arab Youth for the Liberation of Palestine (NAYLP)

Origins

President Gaddafi formed this group in 1972 from a mixed bag of Black September and PFLP militants who wanted to conduct acts of terrorism so extreme that even their own organisations turned them down. Gaddafi chose as its leader Ahmed al-Ghaffour, a Lebanese who had been one of Arafat's closest adherents. Arafat had sent him to Libya to act as his ambassador to Gaddafi. But al-Ghaffour, disappointed by Arafat's adoption of political rather than military methods, deserted to Gaddafi and extremism.

Ideology and Objectives

The use of terror to bring about a total Arab victory and the destruction of Israel.

Activities

Some of the most vicious acts of terrorism were the handiwork of this group. One hit team carried out the Rome massacre, throwing two thermite bombs into a Pan American airliner, killing thirty-two people and wounding eighteen. When the killers eventually surrendered after hijacking a plane to Kuwait, they had told their interrogators that it was Gaddafi himself who had ordered them to carry out the attack.

International links

Libya.

Achievements

Blackmail-release of several members arrested for acts of terrorism.

Strength

No longer believed to exist as a terrorist group. It split up and its members drifted to other outfits, especially that of Abu Nidal, after al-Ghaffour had been arrested and executed by Fatah as a traitor. Fatah had tried him *in absentia,* but confident in his role as a major terrorist leader, and certain that Gaddafi would protect him, he did not take notice of this sentence. He went back to Beirut, where he was captured by Fatah's own internal security force - run by Abu Iyad, leader of Black September. The Libyans remembered him in a later operation by naming a hijack team 'The martyr Ahmed al-Ghaffour group'. But that was the last that was heard of him.

Black June (The Corrective Movement for Al Fatah)

Origins

Formed by Sabri al-Banna, code-named Abu Nidal, as a renegade Black September group to continue the fight against Israel by means of terror. Abu Nidal had taken a number of al-Ghaffour's men into his group and he was sentenced to death *in absentia* by Fatah just as al-Ghaffour was. His crime was to attempt to assassinate moderate Fatah leaders. He was described as the 'outstanding practitioner of pure unbridled terrorism'.

Ideology and aims

In late 1976 Abu Nidal told an interviewer that in his view inter-Arab terrorism, however regrettable, was the price that had to be paid for expediting the all-embracing Arab revolution that alone could lead to the liberation of Palestine.

Activities

Almost totally confined to inter-Arab terrorism. Black June was responsible for the murder of the moderate Said Hammami, Fatah's representative in London in January 1978. He was killed because he had established a dialogue with equally moderate

Israelis. The group was totally dependent on the Iraqis, with its headquarters in Baghdad and a training camp outside the city by the Euphrates. It undertook several terrorist missions on behalf of the Iraqi government, particularly against the Syrians. Three members of the outfit were publicly hanged in Damascus in 1977 after attacking a hotel and seizing hostages.

Achievements

Had terrified those Arabs who were seeking to bring about a peaceful settlement in the Middle East. He made common men frightened of being involved in peace talks and could so claim a measure of success in his aim of preventing any settlement which does not involve the destruction of Israel.

TURKEY

Turkish People's Liberation Army (TPLA)

Origin

Emerged in the early 1970s as one of a series of violent offshoots of Dev Genc — the Turkish Revolutionary Youth Federation which itself sprang from the student uprisings in France and Germany in 1968. It has since become the most aggressive. While most of Turkey's left-wing students engage in campus confrontation with right-wing students and the police, the TPLA uses terror as its weapon.

Activities

The usual mixture of murder, bombing and hijacking. On 27 July 1976, the TPLA plotted to kill opposition leader and former Prime Minister, Bulent Ecevit, during his visit to the United States. The most ruthless of their actions was the murder of the Israeli Consul General in Istanbul in 1971 and the kidnapping and subsequent murder of three radar technicians, two British and one Canadian. Ten TPLA terrorists were killed in the subsequent shoot-out.

International Links

Members of the TPLA had been trained by the Palestinians, they killed the Israeli Consul General in Istanbul at the request of the Palestinians, and the French police discovered a close allegiance between a foreign cell of the organisation and Carlos when they raided a villa at Villiers-sur-Marne, south of Paris. Also had links with Communist states, particularly the erstwhile East Germany and North Korea. Believed to receive financial aid and guidance from East Germany.

Achievements

On a broad scale, none. But inside Turkey has contributed to the instability of the political situation.

Seventeen

The Grey Areas

From Casablanca to Tashkent, the Islamists have moulded themselves into the framework of existing states, adopting their modes of exercising power, their strategic demands, and their nationalism. All the states that appeal to the Muslim *umma* nonetheless maintain the notion of nationality and passports; in terms of supranationality, they are far less advanced than the European Union. There is not as much dichotomy between the Algerian FIS and FLN as one might consider the same Third World, anti-Western discourse, the same single-party mould, the same patronage practices; if the FIS comes to power, the opposition to Tunisia and Morocco will merely be reinterpreted in ideological terms. On an economic level, future Islamist states will be faced with the same alternative that all governments already face; a fatigued state socialism offset by a black market, or a liberal neoconservatism constrained to follow the prescriptions of the International Monetary Fund, under the veil of "Islamic banks."

Islamism is above all a sociocultural movement exemplifying protest and frustration of a generation of youth that has not been integrated socially or politically.

Lack of an Islamist Alternative

Today's Islamist movements, like the Algerian FIS, do not offer a new model of society; far from venerating the return of a conquering, self-assured Islam, they reflect primarily the failure of the Western-style state model, which was imported and commandeered by single parties and patronage networks. They assemble the outcasts of a failed modernism, mobilising them around the myth of a return to an Islamic authenticity that never existed. In this sense, Islamism is indeed an agent of integration for the social sectors immediately produced by and excluded from the accelerated modernisation of Muslim societies (educated youth with no futures, recently urbanised masses). But this integration into politics has not brought into being a new model of society: those who placed their hopes in such a society may one day be amenable to new forms of protest.

There is no specific political, let alone economic, model inherent in Islamism. Islamism in power will systematise the policies of Islamisation " from the top" already evident in officially secular or moderate regimes. In terms of mores and personal status, the distance is not very great between many secular Muslim states and the neofundamentalist enterprise. Henceforth, the new motto will be "*sharia* and only *sharia*". This Islamisation will target personal law and penal law, leaving intact the traditional or reconstituted solidarity networks, as well as the existing economies, and adopting the political model inherited from the previous regimes — essentially that of the single party.

As we have seen, such a model in and of itself does not generate institutions capable of working on their own: the dream of justice and social redistribution can be based only on the virtue of those who implement it. But the transformation of Islamist parties into mass movements and the test of power will yield that is has with all other ideologies: the "pure" will be corrupted or will abandon politics to climbers, careerists, and dishonest businessmen.

Bleak Society

First of all, Islamisation will mean the destruction of the social charm between the state and the family. The Islamic society to which neofundamentalism refers never existed. The Islam that the FIS is proposing is (unfortunately) not a return to Muslim civilisation: this civilisation had its golden age long ago, before its internal decline and the advent of colonialism, but the FIS, like all neofundamentalist organisations, rejects the very concept of Muslim civilization, which had room for music, philosophy, poetry and, as we have seen...a certain secularity. What the Islamists preach is not the return to an incomparably rich classical age, but the establishment of an empty stage on which believer attempts to realise with each gesture the ethical model of the Prophet. The only place for conviviality here is the family, which is also, but only for men, the only place of pleasure. The resocialisation created by opposition Islamist movements cannot withstand the exercise of power.

What new urban space? We see it in Saudi Arabia. It is an empty space, with neither cinemas nor cafes, only teahouses and restaurants. The streets are guarded by a religious militia, responsible solely for enforcing good behaviour and imposing religious practice (prayer and fasting). The only space for retreat is the family. But these are no longer the families of the rural world, in which women get involved in the work and there is a popular, living culture. The modern family is mainly a place of consumption: television, videos, and so on. The Islamists will never be able to stop the flow of this consumption distinctly because the *sharia* protects family privacy. And what is circulating in the urban family is opposite the Islamic way of life: it is a product of the West. There are no "Islamic leisure activities." The new cultural models (videos) are blossoming into the very heart of the Islamic identity, even though the result is never a Westernisation of modes of behaviour, but a synthesis, or a juxtaposition, unable to be reduced to one system or another.

Although such a framework may be perfectly suitable to men involved in economic and social activities, in other words, to men of stature or celebrities, it is hard to imagine how the young generation who vote FIS can benefit from it — first, because establishing a family requires money and housing, and the economic miracle has not yet occurred and is not on the brink of doing so; second, because youth is not puritanical: today it is frustrated and will not tolerate the lassitude and boredom of "Islamic society."

The only model for sociability in Islamism is personal devotion within the structure of the mosque. Why create associations, leisure activities, opportunities for individuals to blossom, when the only model of behaviour is devotional? Between the sacred family space (the *haram*), the mosque, and the institution of the state, viewed as a simple tool of Islamisation, there is no structure for the social space, except through traditional or business solidarities, which are apparently not open to the young unemployed generation. In short, what prevents Islamic society from producing totalitarianism (its respect for the family and lack of interest in the social sphere) also defends it from producing any true social framework: it rejects any space for conviviality and sociability, if only by the strict implementation of the separation of the sexes and, specifically, of the confinement of women to the house (whereas in Iran, and this is the expectation, women have the right to work and access to the public sphere). This puritanism is extensively modern and urban , in the sense that the most rigorous Muslim peasant society (such as the Afghan *mujahidin*, who are as fundamentalist as can be) knows what it means to enjoy laughter, humour, song, and poetry.

The result is not alienation, but social conformity and boredom. A schizophrenia will arise, as it does in all puritan societies: the inexorable transgressions (drugs, alcohol, sex) will take place in hiding. But how long will youth accept being bored, especially when the other model is within arm's reach — on television or across the Mediterranean? The argument for virtue fails when one can enjoy the goods of this other society, through delinquency, money, emigration, or political power.

Islam of Resentment

In contrast to Egyptian or Afghan Islamism, contemporary neofundamentalism is not a response to colonial conquest or military confrontation, not a response to regimes that browbeat to take action against their own societies, but rather a response to acculturation. But the acculturation has already occurred, and the Islam being used to counter it is a reinvention, an imitation.

Neofundamentalist rhetoric exacerbates the cultural differences between the West and the Muslim world, but in a profoundly asymmetrical way: the Muslim world is in fact already Westernised, but thinks of this Westernisation only as alienation. Hence an apparent schizophrenia of behaviour in urban environments: the values of consumption, and thus of civilization, are Western; the values that are being trumpeted are those of a recently fabricated validity. Islamism is a discourse of protest and adaptation, thus of transition. Modernity is irreversible, but it has no language. A curious example is music: the first music against which the Islamists undertook war was the music of their own culture, classical or popular music (such as the Algerian *rai*); but when they produce music (the martial music of Radio Tehran, for example), it is composed based on the rules of Western music.

There is no Islamist "culture," and the *kulturkampf* of the Islamists against a culture that is an obstacle to pure devotion paves the way for the universal culture: that of Americanisation. Was it only by chance that Ali Belhadj, the leader of the FIS, proposed replacing French with English in Algerian schools? For him, there is indeed an international language, and therefore, whatever he may think of them, values and models with which one may identify and disseminated by the culture. In making this proposal, Belhadj is in touch with his electorate, which is enthusiastic about the Quran as well as about American series broadcast (in French) on French television and picked up by satellite antennas.

The renunciation of Western culture is thus on the order of a curse, a cry, an accusation; but it has an element of fascination. Neofundamentalist society does not represent hatred of the other, but rather hatred of oneself and of one's longings. The religion of the peasant, of the mullah, of the notable, who are tolerant because they are sure of their vision of the world, is being replaced by the Islam of resentment, which is defensive which demands acknowledgement.

Loss of Religion's Authenticity

Islamism is basically an agent in the secularisation of Muslim society because it brings the religious space into the political sphere through it claims to do the benefit of the former, its refusal to take the true functioning of politics and society into consideration causes it instead to carry out the unwritten rules of the traditional exercise of power and social segmentation. The autonomous functioning of the political and social arenas wins out, but only after the religious realm has been emptied of its value as a place of transcendence, refuge, and protest, since it is now identified with the new power.

A great deal is said about the return to Islam, but one must nuance this statement. There is a big difference, for instance between Islamist Iran, where one almost never sees a person praying in the street, and the new Islamised neighbourhoods of otherwise secular republics (Tunisia, Turkey), where certain streets are practically closed to cars by the crowd of men in prayer. Mosques are packed in places where they have become sites of mobilisation in opposition to a state perceived as particularist, client-oriented, and repressive; but they empty out when Islamism assumes power. They also fill when it is a matter of bringing immigrants together into a community group, with its own institutions and spokespeople, as in Great Britain. Ghettos are fertile soil for re-Islamisation. But in France, the *beur* (slang for "Arab") culture of proletarian, second-generation immigrants is a subculture of the dominant culture, and its values (music, consumption, the "look") are in discord with those of Islam. The protest against French society takes place in the name of the values of this society itself and not those of Islam.

Return of the Unconsidered

As we have seen, the myth of Islamic society presupposes a casting into sin or a plot of the part of anything that gives rise to social differentiation — whether ethnicity, tribalism, or clans and solidarity networks. Similarly, the corruption and injustice of leaders are attributed to a lack of virtue, and are thus susceptible to elimination through admonishment and counsel. The concept is that in an Islamic society the consensus, obtained in the "silence of passions," as Rousseau would say, must be the custom, the "silence of passions." Being the result of the efforts each one makes individually to emulate the Prophet.

Whatever is repressed naturally re-emerges, not as sin, but as a sociological or psychological fact. In most societies in which Islamists militate, the weakness of the state model means that politics, or, more frivolously, political games, end up ultimately being based on camaraderie groups or "clans," whether they are an expression of family, ethnic, or tribal ties that predate the emergence of a state authority, or the reinvention of communal solidarities in newly urbanised and devastated societies. If social segmentation, individual rivalries, patronage, the lure of profit, and so on are perceived as faults, sins, or plots, then there is no way to understand and defy their unthought-out and ruthless recurrence in the "new" society. This recurrence, as we have seen, is not simply the delaying effect of a tribal and peasant past, but the reformation in modern society of traditional modes of loyalty and exercise of power: matrimonial alliances, corporate camaraderie, patronage — that is, the exchange of material bribes for political loyalty.

It is true that tribalism *stricto sensu* remains strong in Saudi Arabia and in Yemen, where the fundamentalist party Islah is merely a political consequence of the Hashed tribe. But generally the appearance of political Islamism often masks a recomposition of *asabiyya*, solidarity groups, in a manner that is different from peasant tribalism Michel Seurat reveals, in his study of the Bab Tebbane section of Tripoli (Lebanon), how an urban faction functions as an *asabiyya* and translates politically into an Islamist party, the Movement of Islamic Unification, the particularist geographic and sociological base of which its leader, Sheikh Sha'ban, refuses to confess: "The movement is Islam. Does Islam have boundaries?"

Islamism has been unable to move beyond either nationalism or even ethnicity, and this inability has also been slammed on a Western plot. In Sudan, where a regime supported by the Muslim Brotherhood is in power, a former MB, Dawud Bulad, assumed leadership in 1991 of a black guerrilla faction in the Darfur that was against the "Arabs" of Khartoum; behind the politics of Islamisation, an age-old hostility between Arabs and blacks is also resurfacing. In Algeria, the Arabisation extolled by the FIS is to the detriment of the Kabyles. In Malaysia, Islamism is also the expression of ethnic tension with the Chinese. In Afghanistan, the old hostilities between Pakhtuns and non-Pakhtuns is dominating politics.

Finally, as we have seen, the Islamist movements fit into the moulds of the nation-states or become the tools of foreign policy of the large states. Islamo-nationalism wins out over pan-Islamism.

This phenomenon, which is the key to the functioning of politics in societies in which Islamists militate (tribalism, ethnicity, patronage, nationalism), is either rebuffed by them, attributed to lack of faith, or ascribed to a colonialist plot. The myth of unity prohibits thinking about conflict and differentiation, which thus reappear in often uncontrolled violence or in the commandeering of the economy and of state power by patronage networks. Indeed, the fact that one declines to admit that the sociological reality of differentiation exists does not mean one is unaware of it: on the contrary, it is perfectly mastered as a tactic, but ignored as a notion; hence the permanent cleavage between the subtlety of the tactical practices and the schizophrenia of the theory. The internal quarrels of the Islamist world — except, no doubt, in Iran — are constantly described as " misunderstandings" among Brothers. The real discords are masked behind the palinode of ruptures and reconciliations, such as those that have punctuated the history of the Afghan resistance. Personal ambition and ethnic segmentation will never recognised as genuine and will always be attributed to the West ... except that in private they are constant topics of conversation. Islamism furnishes no conceptual apparatus for thinking about one's own sociopolitical reality; hence it coast toward neofundamentalism.

Solidarity and patronage networks, whether Islamist or not, function and immortalise themselves because they are plugged into globalised circuits of distribution and circulation of goods; petrodollars, drugs, oil, arms, subsidies coming from other states and distributed to strategic ends, or simply global business (including taxes on freight and imports, the distribution of import licenses, and currency speculation). The globalisation of circulation networks is made possible by the weakness, but also by the stability, of the state.

The politics in which present day Islamist movements operate is thus a fallout of a new world-space and not of the return to a traditional culture arena. The triumphant neofundamentalism will be incapable of ensuring the insularity of Islamic societies: it depends economically on the world-space in the very exercise of its power: its society is too imbued with Western models, and no one can stop radio, television, cassettes, and travellers.

Islamists and the West

It is no doubt this awareness of the impossibility of insularity that causes Islamists to be obsessed with morality and sanctity and leads them to fight any Christian presence, even national ones that have always existed, such as the Copts in Egypt, despite the fact that conventional *ulemas* accept Christians and Jews.

Although the strategy of the neofundamentalists is not based on revolution, it is founded on a stated renunciation values, which wasn't always the case for the Islamists. It was in no small measure baffling, for those who have confused all these movements, to see Iran's minister of foreign affairs argue in favour of the right to vote for Afghan women in 1991. The political and even cultural models in operation in Iran's Islamic revolution are modern by comparison with regimes like the one in Saudi Arabia, or even comparison with dispute that animates the neofundamentalists on the virtues of the future "amir" of an Islamic state.

Sunni neofundamentalism applies an entirely religious reading to the North-South opposition: the theme of the new crusade reawakens that of imperialism, Israel is the bridgehead of the West (or vice versa in the most obsessive versions), Christian missionaries are everywhere. Western culture is judged to be a tainting influence, and its society is described in entirely negative terms (suicides, alcoholism, depravity, and so on). The neofundamentalist outlook of the world is defensive. One point that illustrates this evolution is the Afghan's vision of Jews: before the war in Afghanistan, the Pakhtun tribes boasted of being sprung from a lost tribe of Israel; during the war, many traditionalist mullahs could be heard extolling the virtues of the Torah (in opposition, of course, to the atheist communists), but today many Afghan neofundamentalists press the Zionist plot.

This cultural opposition to the West is unrelated to the strategic choices made by states. Anti-Christian attitudes and discourse reach their zenith among the Saudis, who, strategically, are in the Western camp, but who forbid the erection of churches on their soil, whereas Iran never had an anti-Christian political stance and has always accepted a certain christian visibility (to the point of authorising the Armenians to make wine).

The defensive stubbornness of neofundamentalism therefore demonstrates its inability to incorporate modernity. It has been a long time since Christianity was Islam's other. Even if there is a religious restoration among Christians and Jews, it is in no way parallel to that of the fundamentalists. The culture that threatens Muslim society is neither Jewish nor Christian; it is a composite culture of consumption and communication, a culture that is secular, atheist, and ultimately empty; it has no values or strategies, but it is already present, in the cassette and the transistor, present in the most remote village. This culture can withstand any reappropriation and rereading. It is a code and not a civilisation.

Neofundamentalism is seeking its devil in a different god, but does not see the desert within.

Index

H

I

J

K

L

N